classics Co omnibus

Daniel Defoe

2 Books in 1

Moll Flanders
&
Robinson Crusoe

A Wilco Book
Outstanding works of universal interest

This Omnibus edition printed in 2007

ISBN NO.: 81-8252-285-4

Daniel Defoe

Moll Flanders &
Robinson Crusoe

Complete and Unabridged

Published by
WILCO PUBLISHING HOUSE
33, Sri Saibaba Marg, Kalaghoda,
Mumbai - 400 023. INDIA
Tel: (91-22) 22041420 / 22842574
Fax: (91-22) 22041429
E mail: wilcos@vsnl.com

About The Author

Daniel Defoe

(1660-1731)

Daniel Defoe was born in 1660 to a Non-conformist and puritan father James Foe. He subsequently changed his name to Defoe in 1703. After enjoying a distinguished position in the court of William III, and later during the reign of Queen Anne of England, Defoe was imprisoned for writing a satirical piece *The Shortest Way with the Dissenters* that had annoyed the Establishment. Upon his release from the Newgate prison he founded a newspaper *The Review*. For his dexterous and energetic pursuit of fearless writings, which included over 200 works of non-fiction and over 1000 short essays, apart from his numerous political jottings, he came to be regarded as the founder of British journalism.

Daniel Defoe is however best remembered for his absorbing account of shipwrecked *Robinson Crusoe* (1720), published when he was 60, an age at which he began writing fiction. His absorbing novel *Moll Flanders* obviously drew heavily from his experiences as an inmate of the Newgate prison.

Even though the remainder of Defoe's life was overshadowed with heavy debts incurred in pursuit of failed businesses; in the literary world he gained immense popularity, often writing under assumed names: 'Eye witness' 'T.Tailor', and 'Heliostrapolis'. Defoe died in April 1731 at his home in Ropemaker's Alley, Moorlands, in the U.K.

MOLL FLANDERS

THE PREFACE

THE WORLD is so taken up of late with Novels and Romances, that it will be hard for a private History to be taken for Genuine, where the Names and other Circumstances of the Person are concealed, and on this Account we must be content to leave the Reader to pass his own Opinion upon the ensuing Sheets, and take it just as he pleases.

The Author is here suppos'd to be writing her own History, and in the very beginning of her Account, she gives the Reasons why she thinks fit to conceal her true Name, after which there is no Occasion to say any more about that.

It is true, that the original of this Story is put into new Words, and the Stile of the famous Lady we here speak of is a little alter'd, particularly she is made to tell her own Tale in modester Words than she told it at first; the Copy which came first to Hand, having been written in Language, more like one still in Newgate, than one grown Penitent and Humble, as she afterwards pretends to be.

The Pen employ'd in finishing her Story, and making it what you how see it to be, has had no little difficulty to put it into a Dress fit to be seen, and to make it speak Language fit to be read: When a Woman debauch'd from her Youth, nay, even being the Off-spring of Debauchery and Vice, comes to give an Account of all her vicious Practises, and even to descend to the particular Occasions and Circumstances, by which she first became wicked, and of all the progression of Crime which she run through in threescore Year, an Author must be hard put to it to wrap it up so clean, as not to give room, especially for vitious Readers to turn it to his Disadvantage.

All possible Care however has been taken to give no leud Ideas, no immodest Turns in the new dressing up this Story, no not to the worst parts of her Expressions; to this Purpose some of the vicious part of her Life, which cou'd not be modestly told, is quite left out, and several other Parts, are very much shortn'd; what is left 'tis hop'd will not offend the chastest Reader, or the modestest Hearer; and as the best use is made even of the worst Story, the Moral 'tis hop'd will keep the Reader serious, even where the Story might incline him to be otherwise: To give the History of a wicked Life repented of, necessarily requires that the wicked Part should be made as wicked, as the real History of it will bear; to illustrate and give a Beauty to the Penitent part, which is certainly the best and brightest, if related with equal Spirit and Life.

It is suggested there cannot be the same Life, the same Brightness and Beauty, in relating the penitent Part, as is in the criminal Part: if there is any Truth in that Suggestion, I must be allow'd to say, 'tis because there is not the same taste and relish in the Reading, and indeed it is too true, that the difference lyes not in the real worth of the Subject so much as in the Gust and Palate of the Reader.

But as this Work is chiefly recommended to those who know how to Read it, and how to make the good Uses of it, which the Story all along recommends to them; so it is to be hop'd that such Readers will be much more pleas'd with the End of the Writer, than with the Life of the Person written of.

There is in this Story abundance of delightful Incidents, and all of them usefully apply'd. There is an agreeable turn Artfully given them in the relating, that naturally Instructs the Reader, either one way, or other. The first part of her leud Life with the young Gentleman at *Colchester,* has so many happy

Turns given it to expose the Crime, and warn all whose Circumstances are adapted to it, of the ruinous End of such things, and the foolish Thoughtless and abhorr'd Conduct of both the Parties, that it abundantly attones for all the lively Discription she gives of her Folly and Wickedness.

The Repentance of her Lover at the *Bath,* and how brought by the just alarm of his fit of Sickness to abandon her; the just Caution given there against even the lawful Intimacies of the dearest Friends, and how unable they are to preserve the most solemn Resolutions of Vertue without divine Assistance; these are Parts, which to a just Discernment will appear to have more real Beauty in them, than all the amorous Chain of Story, which introduces it.

In a Word, as the whole Relation is carefully garbl'd of all the Levity, and Looseness that was in it: So it is all applied, and with the utmost care to vertuous and religious uses. None can without being guilty of manifest Injustice, cast any Reproach upon it, or upon our Design in publishing it.

The Advocates for the Stage, have in all Ages made this the great Argument to persuade People that their Plays are useful, and that they ought to be allow'd in the most civiliz'd, and in the most religious Government; Namely, That they are applyed to vertuous Purposes, and that by the most lively Representations; they fail not to recommend Vertue, and generous Principles, and to discourage and expose all sorts of Vice and Corruption of Manners; and were it true that they did so, and that they constantly adhered to that Rule, as the Test of their acting on the *Theatre,* much might be said in their Favour.

Throughout the infinite variety of this Book, this Fundamental is most strictly adhered to; there is not a wicked Action in any Part of it, but is first or last rendered Unhappy and Unfortunate: There is not a superlative Villain brought upon the Stage, but either he is brought to an unhappy End, or brought to be a

Penitent: There is not an ill thing mention'd, but it is condemn'd, even in the Relation, nor a vertuous just Thing, but it carries its Praise along with it: What can more exactly answer the Rule laid down, to recommend, even those Representations of things which have so many other just Objections lying against them? Namely, of Example, of bad Company, obscene Language, and the like.

Upon this Foundation this Book is recommended to the Reader, as a Work from every part of which something may be learned, and some just and religious Inference is drawn, by which the Reader will have something of Instruction, if he pleases to make use of it.

All the Exploits of this Lady of Fame, in her Depredations upon Mankind stand as so many warnings to honest People to beware of them, intimating to them by what Methods innocent People are drawn in, plunder'd and robb'd, and by Consequence how to avoid them. Her robbing a little innocent Child, dress'd fine by the vanity of the Mother, to go to the Dancing-School, is a good Memento to such People hereafter; as is likewise her picking the Gold-Watch from the young Ladies side in the *Park.*

Her getting a parcel from a hair-brained Wench at the Coaches in St *John-street;* her Booty made at the Fire, and again at *Harwich;* all give us excellent Warnings in such Cases to be more present to ourselves in sudden Surprizes of every Sort.

Her application to a sober Life, and industrious Management at last in *Virginia,* with her Transported Spouse, is a Story fruitful of Instruction, to all the unfortunate Creatures who are oblig'd to seek their Re-establishment abroad; whether by the Misery of Transportation, or other Disaster; letting them know, that Diligence and Application have their due Encouragement, even in the remotest Parts of the World, and that no Case can be so low, so despicable, or so empty of Prospect, but that an unwearied Industry will go a great way to deliver us from it, will in time raise the meanest Creature to appear again in the World, and give him a new Cast for his Life.

These are a few of the serious Inferences which we are led by the Hand to in this Book, and these are fully sufficient to Justifie any Man in recommending it to the World, and much more to Justifie the Publication of it.

There are two of the most beautiful Parts still behind, which this Story gives some idea of, and lets us into the Parts of them, but they are either of them too long to be brought into the same Volume; and indeed are, *as I may call them* whole Volumes of themselves, *(viz.)* I. The Life of her Governess, as she calls her, who had run thro', it seems in a few years all the eminent degrees of a Gentlewoman, a Whore, and a Bawd; a Midwife, and a Midwife-keeper, *as they are call'd,* a Pawn-broker, a Child-taker, a Receiver of Thieves, and of Thieves purchase, that is to say, of stolen Goods; and in a Word, her self a Thief, a Breeder up of Thieves, and the like, and yet at last a Penitent.

The second is the Life of her Transported Husband, a Highway-man; who it seems liv'd a twelve Years Life of successful Villany upon the Road, and even at last came off so well, as to be a Voluntier Transport, not a Convict; and in whose Life there is an incredible Variety.

But as I have said, these are things too long to bring in here, so neither can I make a Promise of their coming out by themselves.

We cannot say indeed, that this History is carried on quite to the End of the Life of this famous Moll Flanders, as she calls herself, for no Body can write their own Life to the full End of it, unless they can write it after they are dead; but her Husband's Life being written by a third Hand, gives a full Account of them both, how long they liv'd together in that country, and how they came both to *England* again, after about eight Year, in which time they were grown very Rich, and where she liv'd it seems, to be very old; but was not so extraordinary a Penitent, as she was at first; it seems only that indeed she always spoke with abhorence of her former Life, and of every Part of it.

In her last Scene at *Maryland,* and *Virginia,* many pleasant things happen'd, which makes that part of her Life very agreeable, but they are not told with the same Elegancy as those accounted for by herself; so it is still to the more Advantage that we break off here.

MY TRUE name is so well known in the Records, or Registers at *Newgate,* and in the Old-Baily, and there are some things of such Consequence still depending there, relating to my particular Conduct, that it is not to be expected I should set my Name, or the Account of my Family to this Work; perhaps, after my Death it may be better known; at present it would not be proper, no, not tho' a general Pardon should be issued, even without Exceptions and reserve of Persons or Crimes.

It is enough to tell you, that as some of my worst Comrades, who are out of the Way of doing me Harm, having gone out of the World by the Steps and the String, as I often expected to go, knew me by the Name of *Moll Flanders;* so you may give me leave to speak of myself under that Name till I dare own who I have been, as well as who I am.

I have been told, that in one of our Neighbour Nations, whether it be in *France,* or where else, I know not, they have on Order from the King, that when any Criminal is condemn'd, either to Die, or to the Gallies, or to be Transported, if they leave any Children, as such are generally unprovided for, by the Poverty or Forfeiture of their Parents, so they are immediately taken into the Care of the Government, and put into an Hospital call'd the *House of Orphans,* where they are Bred up, Cloath'd, Fed, Taught, and when fit to go out, are plac'd out to Trades, or to Services, so as to be well able to provide for themselves by an honest industrious Behaviour.

Had this been the Custom in our Country, I had not been left a poor desolate Girl without Friends, without Cloaths, without Help or Helper in the World, as was my Fate; and by which, I was not only expos'd to very great Distresses, even before I was capable either of Understanding my Case, or how to Amend it, nor brought into a Course of Life, which was not only scandalous in itself, but which in its ordinary Course, tended to the swift Destruction both of Soul and Body.

But the Case was otherwise here; my Mother was convicted of Felony for a certain petty Theft, scarce worth naming, (*viz.*) Having an opportunity of borrowing three Pieces of fine *Holland,* of a certain Draper in *Cheapside:* The Circumstances are too long to repeat, and I have heard them related so many Ways, that I can scarce be certain which is the right Account.

However it was, this they all agree in, that my Mother pleaded her Belly, and being found quick with Child, she was respited for about seven Months, in which time having brought me into the World, and being about again, she was call'd Down, as they term it, to her former Judgment, but obtain'd the Favour of being Transported to the Plantations, and left me about Half a Year old; and in bad Hands you may be sure.

This is too near the first Hours of my Life for me to relate any thing of myself, but by hear say; 'tis enough to mention, that as I was born in such an unhappy Place, I had no Parish to have Recourse to for my Nourishment in my Infancy, nor can I give the least Account how I was kept alive, other, than that as I have been told, some Relation of my Mothers took me away for a while as a Nurse, but at whose Expence or by whose Direction I know nothing at all of it.

The first account that I can Recollect, or could ever learn of myself, was, that I had wandred among a Crew of those People they call *Gypsies,* or *Egyptians;* but I believe it was but a very little while that I had been among them, for I had not had my Skin discolour'd, or blacken'd, as they do very young to all the Children they carry about with them, nor can I tell how I came among them, or how I got from them.

It was at *Colchester* in *Essex,* that those People left me; and I have a Notion in my Head, that I left them there, (that is, that I hid myself and wou'd not go any farther with them) but I am not able to be particular in that Account; only this I remember, that being taken up by some of the Parish Officers of *Colchester,* I gave an Account that I came into the Town with the *Gypsies,* but that I would not go any farther with them, and that so they had left me, but whither they were gone that I knew not, nor could they expect it of me; for tho' they sent round the Country to enquire after them, it seems they could not be found.

I was now in a Way to be provided for; for tho' I was not a Parish Charge upon this or that part of the Town by Law, yet as my Case came to be known, and that I was too young to do any Work, being not above three Years old, Compassion mov'd the Magistrates of the Town to order some Care to be taken of me, and I became one of their own, as much as if I had been born in the Place.

In the Provision they made for me, it was my good hap to be put to Nurse, as they call it, to a Woman who was indeed Poor, but had been in better Circumstances, and who got a little Livelihood by taking such as I was suppos'd to be, and keeping them with all Necessaries, till they were at a certain Age, in which it might be suppos'd they might go to Service, or get their own Bread.

This Woman had also a little School, which she kept to teach Children to Read and to Work; and having, as I have said, liv'd before that in good Fashion, she bred up the Children she took with a great deal of Art, as well as with a great deal of Care.

But that which was worth all the rest, she bred them up very Religiously, being herself a very sober pious Woman. (2.) Very Housewifly and Clean, and (3.) Very Mannerly, and with good Behaviour: So that in a Word, excepting a plain Diet, coarse Lodging, and mean Cloths, we were brought up as Mannerly and as Genteely as if we had been at the Dancing School.

I was continu'd here till I was eight years Old, when I was terrified with News that the Magistrates, as I think they call'd them, had order'd that I should go to Service; I was able to do but very little Service where ever I was to go, except it was to run of Errands, and be a Drudge to some Cook-Maid, and this they told me of often, which put me into a great Fright; for I had a thorough Aversion to going to Service, as they call'd it, that is to be a Servant, tho' I was so young; and I told my Nurse, as we call'd her, that I believ'd I could get my Living without going to Service if she pleas'd to let me; for she had Taught me to Work with my Needle and Spin Worsted, which is the chief Trade of that City, and I told her that if she wou'd keep me, I wou'd Work for her, and I would Work very hard.

I talk'd to her almost every Day of Working hard; And in short, I did nothing but Work and Cry all Day, which griev'd the good kind Woman so much, that at last she began to be concern'd for me, for she lov'd me very well.

One Day after this, as she came into the Room where all we poor Children were at Work, she sat down just over against me, not in her usual Place as Mistress, but as if she set herself on purpose to observe me, and see me Work: I was doing something she had set me to, as I remember, it was Marking some Shirts, which she had taken to Make, and after a while she began to Talk to me: Thou foolish Child, says she, thou art always Crying; (for I was Crying then) Prithee, What dost Cry for? because they will take me away, *says I,* and put me to Service, and I can't Work House-Work; well Child, says she, but tho' you can't Work House-Work, as you call it, you will learn it in time, and they won't put you to hard Things at first; yes they will, says I, and if I can't do it, they will Beat me, and the Maids will Beat me to make me do great Work, and I am but a little Girl, and I can't do it; and then I cry'd again, till I could not speak any more to her.

This mov'd my good Motherly Nurse, so that she from that time resolv'd I should not go to Service yet, so she bid me not Cry, and she wou'd speak to Mr *Mayor,* and I should not go to Service till I was bigger.

Well, this did not Satisfy me, for to think of going to Service was such a frightful Thing to me, that if she had assur'd me I should not have gone till I was twenty years old, it wou'd have been the same to me; I shou'd have cry'd, I believe all the time, with the very Apprehension of its being to be so at last.

When she saw that I was not pacify'd yet, she began to be angry with me; and what wou'd you have? *says she,* don't I tell you that you shall not go to Service till you are bigger? Ay, says I, but then I must go at last; why, what? said she, is the Girl mad? what, would you be a Gentlewoman? Yes *says I,* and cry'd heartily, till I roar'd out again.

This set the old Gentlewoman a Laughing at me, as you may be sure it would: Well, Madam, forsooth, says she, *Gibing at me,* you would be a Gentlewoman, and pray how will you come to be a Gentlewoman? what, will you do it by your Fingers Ends?

Yes, *says I again,* very innocently.

Why, what can you Earn, *says she,* what can you get at your Work?

Three-Pence, *said I,* when I Spin, and *4d.* when I Work plain Work.

Alas! poor Gentlewoman, *said she again,* Laughing, what will that do for thee?

It will keep me, *says I,* if you will let me live with you; and this *I said,* in such a poor petitioning Tone, that it made the poor Womans Heart yearn to me, as she told me afterwards.

But, *says she,* that will not keep you, and buy you Cloths too; and who must buy the little Gentlewoman Cloths, *says she,* and smil'd all the while at me.

I will Work Harder then, *says I,* and you shall have it all.

Poor Child! it won't keep you, *says she,* it will hardly keep you in Victuals.

Then I will have no Victuals, *says I,* again very Innocently, let me but live with you.

Why, can you live without Victuals? *says she;* yes, *again says I,* very much like a Child, you may be sure, and still I cry'd heartily.

I had no Policy in all this, you may easily see it was all Nature, but it was joyn'd with so much Innocence, and so much Passion, That in short, it set the good Motherly Creature a weeping too, and she cry'd at last as fast as I did, and then took me, and led me out of the teaching Room; come *says she,* you shan't go to Service, you shall live with me, and this pacify'd me for the present.

Sometime after this, she going to wait on the *Mayor,* and talking of such things as belong'd to her Business, at last my Story came up, and my good Nurse told Mr *Mayor* the whole Tale: He was so pleas'd with it, that he would call his Lady, and his two Daughters to hear it, and it made Mirth enough among them, you may be sure.

However, not a Week had pass'd over, but on a sudden comes Mrs *Mayoress* and her two Daughters to the House to see my old Nurse, and to see her School and the Children: When they had look'd about them a little: Well, Mrs – says the *Mayoress* to my Nurse, and pray which is the little Lass that intends to be a Gentlewoman? I heard her, and I was terrible frighted at first, tho' I did not know why neither; but Mrs *Mayoress* comes up to me, Well Miss says she, And what are you at Work upon? The Word Miss was a Language that had hardly been heard of in our School, and I wondred what sad Name it was she call'd me; However, I stood up, made a Curtsy, and she took my Work out of my Hand, look'd on it, and said it was very well; then she took up one of my Hands; nay, says she, the Child may come to be a Gentlewoman for ought any body knows; she has a Gentlewoman's Hand, says she; this pleas'd me mightily you may be sure, but Mrs *Mayoress* did not stop there, but giving me my Work again, she put her Hand in her Pocket, gave me a Shilling, and bid me mind my Work, and learn to Work well, and I might be a Gentlewoman for ought she knew.

Now all this while, my good old Nurse, Mrs *Mayoress,* and all the rest of them did not understand me at all, for they meant one Sort of thing, by the Word Gentlewoman, and I meant quite another; for alas, all I understood by being a Gentlewoman, was to be able to Work for myself, and get enough to keep me without that terrible Bug-bear *going to Service,* whereas they meant to live Great, Rich, and High, and I know not what.

Well, after Mrs *Mayoress* was gone, her two Daughters came in and they call'd for the Gentlewoman too, and they talk'd a long while to me, and I answer'd them in my Innocent way; but always if they ask'd me whether I resolv'd to be a Gentlewoman, I answer'd YES: At last one of them ask'd me, what a Gentlewoman was? that puzzel'd me much; but however, I explain'd myself negatively, that it was one that did not go to Service, to do House-Work; they were pleas'd to be familiar (with) me, and lik'd my little Prattle to them, which it seems was agreeable enough to them, and they gave me Money too.

As for my Money I gave it all to my Mistress Nurse, as I call'd her, and told her she should have all I got for myself when I was a Gentlewoman, as well as now; by this and some other of my talk, my old Tutoress began to understand me, about what I meant by being a Gentlewoman; and that I understood by it no more than to be able to get my Bread by my own Work; and at last, she ask'd me whether it was not so.

I told her *yes,* and insisted on it, that to do so, was to be a Gentlewoman; for says I, there is such a one, naming a Woman that mended Lace, and wash'd the Ladies Lac'dheads, she, *says I,* is a Gentlewoman, and they call her Madam.

Poor Child, says my good old Nurse, you may soon be such a Gentlewoman as that, for she is a Person of ill Fame, and has had two or three Bastards.

I did not understand any thing of that; but I answer'd, I am sure they call her Madam, and she does not go to Service nor do House-Work, and therefore I insisted that she was a Gentlewoman, and I would be such a Gentlewoman as that.

The Ladies were told all this again, to be sure, and they made themselves Merry with it, and every now and then the young

Ladies, Mr *Mayor's* Daughters would come and see me, and ask where the little Gentlewoman was, which made me not a little Proud of myself.

This held a great while, and I was often visited by these young Ladies, and sometimes they brought others with them; so that I was known by it, almost all over the Town.

I was now about ten Years old, and began to look a little Womanish, for I was mighty Grave and Humble; very Mannerly, and as I had often heard the Ladies say I was Pretty, and would be a very handsome Woman, so you may be sure, that hearing them say so, made me not a little Proud; however, that Pride had no ill effect upon me yet, only as they often gave me Money, and I gave it my old Nurse, she *honest* Woman, was so just to me, as to lay it all out again for me, and gave me Head-Dresses, and Linnen, and Gloves and Ribbons, and I went very Neat, and always Clean; for that I would do, and if I had Rags on, I would always be Clean, or else I would dabble them in Water myself; but *I say,* my good Nurse, when I had Money given me, very honestly laid it out for me, and would always tell the Ladies, this, or that, was bought with their Money; and this made them oftentimes give me more; Till at last, I was indeed call'd upon by the Magistrates as I understood it, to go out to Service; but then I was come to be so good a Workwoman myself, and the Ladies were so kind to me, that it was plain I could maintain myself, that is to say, I could Earn as much for my Nurse as she was able by it to keep me; so she told them, that if they would give her leave, she would keep the Gentlewoman as she call'd me, to be her Assistant, and teach the Children, which I was very well able to do; for I was very nimble at my Work, and had a good Hand with my Needle, though I was yet very young.

But the kindness of the Ladies of the Town did not End here, for when they came to understand that I was no more maintain'd by the publick Allowance, as before, they gave me Money oftner than formerly; and as I grew up, they brought me Work to do for them; such as Linnen to Make, and Laces to Mend, and Heads to

Dress up, and not only paid me for doing them, but even taught me how to do them; so that now I was a Gentlewoman indeed, as I understood that Word, and as I desir'd to be; for by that time, I was twelve Years old, I not only found myself Cloathes, and paid my Nurse for my keeping, but got Money in my Pocket too beforehand.

The Ladies also gave me Cloaths frequently of their own, or their Childrens, some Stockings, some Petticoats, some Gowns, some one thing, some another, and these my old Woman Managed for me like a meer Mother, and kept them for me, oblig'd me to Mend them, and turn them and twist them to the best Advantage, for she was a rare House-Wife.

At last one of the Ladies took so much Fancy to me that she would have me Home to her House for a Month she said, to be among her Daughters.

Now tho' this was exceeding kind in her, yet as my old good Woman said to her, unless she resolv'd to keep me for good and all, she would do the little Gentlewoman more harm than good: Well, says the Lady, that's true and therefore I'll only take her Home for a Week then, that I may see how my Daughters and she agree together, and how I like her Temper, and then I'll tell you more; and in the mean time, if any Body comes to see her as they us'd to do, you may only tell them, you have sent her out to my House.

This was prudently manag'd enough, and I went to the Ladies House, but I was so pleas'd there with the young Ladies, and they so pleas'd with me, that I had enough to do to come away, and they were as unwilling to part with me.

However, I did come away, and liv'd almost a Year more with my honest old Woman, and began now to be very helpful to her; for I was almost fourteen Years old, was tall of my Age, and look'd a little Womanish; but I had such a Taste of Genteel living at the Ladies House, that I was not so easie in my old Quarters as I us'd to be, and I thought it was fine to be a Gentlewoman indeed, for I had quite other Notions of a Gentlewoman now than I had before; and as I thought, I say, that it was fine to be a Gentlewoman, so I lov'd to be among Gentlewomen, and therefore I long'd to be there again.

About the Time that I was fourteen Years and a quarter Old, my good old Nurse, Mother I ought rather to call her, fell Sick and Dyed; I was then in a sad Condition indeed, for as there is no great Bustle in putting an end to a Poor bodies Family when once they are carried to the Grave, so the poor good Woman being Buried, the Parish Children she kept were immediately remov'd by the Church-Wardens; the School was at an End, and the Children of it had no more to do but just stay at Home till they were sent some where else, and as for what she left, her Daughter, a married Woman with six or seven Children, came and swept it all away at once, and removing the Goods, they had no more to say to me, than to Jest with me, and tell me that the little Gentlewoman might set up for her self if she pleas'd.

I was frighted out of my Wits almost, and knew not what to do, for I was, as it were, turn'd out of Doors to the wide World, and that which was still worse, the old honest Woman had two and twenty Shillings of mine in her Hand, which was all the Estate the little Gentlewoman had in the world; and when I ask'd the Daughter for it, she huft me and laught at me, and told me, she had nothing to do with it.

It was true the good poor Woman had told her Daughter of it, and that it lay in such a Place, that it was the Child's Money, and had call'd once or twice for me to give it me, but I was unhappily out of the way, some where or other; and when I came back she was past being in a Condition to speak of it: However, the Daughter was so Honest afterward as to give it me, tho' at first she us'd me Cruelly about it.

Now I was a poor Gentlewoman indeed, and I was just that very Night to be turn'd into the wide World; for the Daughter remov'd all the Goods, and I had not so much as a Lodging to go to, or a bit of Bread to Eat: But it seems some of the Neighbours who had known my Circumstances, took so much Compassion of me, as to acquaint the Lady in whose Family I had been a Week, as I mention'd above; and immediately she sent her Maid to fetch me away, and two of her Daughters came with the Maid tho' unsent; so I went with them Bag and Baggage, and with a glad Heart you may be sure: The fright of my Condition had made such an Impression upon me, that I did not want now to be a Gentlewoman, but was very willing to be a Servant, and that any kind of Servant they thought fit to have me be.

But my new generous Mistress had better thoughts for me; I call her generous for she exceeded the good Woman I was with before in every Thing, as well as in the matter of Estate; I say in every Thing except Honesty; and for that, tho' this was a Lady most exactly Just, yet I must not forget to say on all Occasions, that the First tho' Poor, was as uprightly Honest as it was possible for any One to be.

I was no sooner carried away as I have said by this good Gentlewoman, but the first Lady, *that is to say,* the *Mayoress* that was, sent her two Daughters to take Care of me; and another Family which had taken Notice of me when I was the little Gentlewoman, and had given me Work to do, sent for me after her, so that I was mightily made of, as we say; nay, and they were not a little Angry, especially, Madam the *Mayoress,* that her Friend had taken me away from her as she call'd it; for as she said, I was Hers by Right, she having been the first that took any Notice of me; but they that had me wou'd not part with me; and as for me, tho' I shou'd have been very well Treated with any of the others, yet I could not be better than where I was.

Here I continu'd till I was between seventeen and eighteen Years old, and here I had all the Advantages for my Education that could be imagin'd; the Lady had Masters home to the House to teach her Daughters to Dance, and to speak *French,* and to Write, and others to teach them Musick; and as I was always with them, I learn'd as fast as they; and tho' the Masters were not appointed to teach me, yet I learn'd by Imitation and enquiry, all that they learn'd by Instruction and Direction. So that in short, I learn'd to Dance and speak *French* as well as any of them, and to Sing much better, for I had a better Voice than any of them; I could not so readily come at playing on the Harpsicord or Spinnet, because I had no Instrument of my own to Practice on, and could only come at theirs in the intervals, when they left it, which was uncertain; but yet I learn'd tollerably well too, and the young Ladies at length got two Instruments, that is to say, a Harpsicord, and a Spinnet too, and then they Taught me themselves; But as to Dancing they could hardly help my learning Country Dances, because they always wanted me to make up even Number; and on the other Hand, they were as heartily willing to learn me every thing that they had been Taught themselves, as I could be to take the Learning.

By this Means I had, as I have said above, all the Advantages of Education that I could have had, if I had been as much a Gentlewoman as they were with whom I liv'd, and in some things, I had the Advantage of my Ladies, tho' they were my Superiors; but they were all the Gifts of Nature, and which all their Fortunes could not furnish. First, I was apparently Handsomer than any of them. Secondly, I was better shap'd, and Thirdly, I Sung better, by which I mean, I had a better Voice; in all which you will I hope allow me to say, I do not speak my own Conceit of myself, but the Opinion of all that knew the Family.

I had with all these the common Vanity of my Sex (*viz.*) That being really taken for very Handsome, or if you please for a great Beauty, I very well knew it, and had as good an Opinion of myself as any body else could have of me; and particularly I lov'd to hear any body speak of it, which could not but happen to me sometimes, and was a great Satisfaction to me.

Thus far I have had a smooth Story to tell of myself, and in all this Part of my Life, I not only had the Reputation of living in a very good Family, and a Family Noted and Respected every where, for Virtue and Sobriety, and for every valluable Thing; but

I had the Character too of a very sober, modest, and virtuous young Woman, and such I had always been; neither had I yet any occasion to think of any thing else, or to know what a Temptation to Wickedness meant.

But that which I was too vain of, was my Ruin, or rather my vanity was the Cause of it. The lady in the House where I was had two Sons, young Gentlemen of very promising Parts, and of extraordinary Behaviour; and it was my Misfortune to be very well with them both, but they manag'd themselves with me in a quite different Manner.

The eldest, a gay Gentleman that knew the Town as well as the Country, and tho' he had Levity enough to do an ill natur'd thing, yet had too much Judgment of things to pay too dear for his Pleasures, he began with that unhappy Snare to all Women, (*viz.*) taking Notice upon all Occasions how pretty I was, as he call'd it: how agreeable, how well Carriaged, and the like; and this he contriv'd so subtilly, as if he had known as well, how to catch a Woman in his Net as a Partridge when he went a Setting; for he wou'd contrive to be talking this to his Sisters when tho' I was not by, yet when he knew I was not so far off, but that I should be sure to hear him: His Sisters would return softly to him, Hush Brother, she will hear you, she is but in the next Room; then he would put it off, and Talk softlier, as if he had not known it, and begin to acknowledge he was Wrong; and then as if he had forgot himself, he would speak aloud again, and I that was so well pleas'd to hear it, was sure to Lissen for it upon all Occasions.

After he had thus baited his Hook, and found easily enough the Method how to lay it in my Way, he play'd an opener Game; and one Day going by his Sister's Chamber when I was there doing something about Dressing her, he comes in with an Air of gayty, O! Mrs Betty, said he to me, How do you do Mrs *Betty?* don't your Cheeks burn, Mrs *Betty? I* made a Curtsy and blush'd, but said nothing; what makes you talk so Brother, *says the Lady;* Why, says he, we have been talking of her below Stairs this half

Hour; *Well says his Sister,* you can say no Harm of her, that I am sure; so 'tis no matter what you have been talking about; nay, *says he,* 'tis so far from talking Harm of her, that we have been talking a great deal of good, and a great many fine Things have been said of Mrs *Betty,* I assure you; and particularly, that she is the Handsomest young Woman in *Colchester,* and, in short, they begin to Toast her Health in the Town.

I wonder at you Brother, *says the Sister; Betty* wants but one Thing, but she had as good want every Thing, for the Market is against our Sex just now; and if a young Woman have Beauty, Birth, Breeding, Wit, Sense, Manners, Modesty, and all these to an Extream; yet if she have not Money, she's no Body, she had as good want them all, for nothing but Money now recommends a Woman; the Men play the Game all into their own Hands.

Her younger Brother, who was by, cry'd *Hold Sister,* you run too fast, I am an Exception to your Rule; I assure you, if I find a Woman so Accomplish'd as you Talk of, I *say,* I assure you, I would not trouble myself about the Money.

O, *says the Sister,* but you will take Care not to Fancy one then, without the Money.

You don't know that neither, *says the Brother.*

But why Sister, (*says the elder Brother*) why do you exclaim so at the Men for aiming so much at the Fortune? you are none of them that want a Fortune, what ever else you want.

I understand you Brother, (*replies the Lady very smartly,*) you suppose I have the Money, and want the Beauty; but as Times go now, the first will do without the last, so I have the better of my Neighbours.

Well, *says the younger Brother,* but your Neighbours, as you call them may be even with you; for Beauty will steal a Husband sometimes in spite of Money; and when the Maid chances to be Handsomer than the Mistress, she oftentimes makes as good a Market, and rides in a Coach before her.

I thought it was time for me to withdraw and leave them, and I did so; but not so far but that I heard all their Discourse, in which I heard abundance of fine things said of myself, which serv'd to prompt my Vanity; but as I soon found, was not the way to encrease my Interest in the Family; for the Sister and the younger Brother fell grievously out about it; and as he said some very dissobliging things to her, upon my Account, so I could easily see that she Resented them by her future Conduct to me; which indeed was very unjust to me, for I have never had the least thought of what she suspected, as to her younger Brother: Indeed the elder Brother in his distant remote Way, had said a great many things, as in Jest, which I had the folly to believe were in earnest, or to flatter myself, with the hopes of what I ought to have suppos'd he never intended, and perhaps never thought of.

It happen'd one Day that he came running up Stairs, towards the Room where his Sisters us'd to sit and Work, as he often us'd to do; and calling to them before he came in, as was his way too, I bein g there alone, step'd to the Door, and said, Sir, the Ladies are not here, they are Walk'd down the Garden; as I step'd forward, to say this towards the Door, he was just got to the Door, and clasping me in his Arms, as if it had been by Chance, O! Mrs *Betty, says he,* are you here? that's better still; I want to speak with you, more than I do with them, and then having me in his Arms he Kiss'd me three or four times.

I struggl'd to get away, and yet did it but faintly neither, and he held me fast, and still Kiss'd me, till he was almost out of Breath, and then sitting down, says, *dear Betty* I am in Love with you.

His Words I must confess fir'd my Blood; all my Spirits flew about my Heart, and put me into Disorder enough, which he might easily have seen in my Face: He repeated it afterwards several times, that he was in Love with me, and my Heart spoke as plain as a Voice, that I lik'd it; nay, when ever he said, I am in Love with you, my Blushes plainly reply'd, *wou'd you were* Sir.

However nothing else pass'd at that time; it was but a Surprise, and when he was gone, I soon recover'd myself again. He had stay'd longer with me, but he happen'd to look out at the Window and see his Sisters coming up the Garden, so he took his leave, Kiss'd me again, told me he was very serious, and I should hear more of him very quickly, and away he went leaving me infinitely pleas'd tho' surpris'd; and had there not been one Misfortune in it, I had been in the Right, but the Mistake lay here, that Mrs *Betty* was in Earnest, and the Gentleman was not.

From this time my Head run upon strange Things, and I may truly say, I was not myself; to have such a Gentleman talk to me of being in Love with me, and of my being such a charming Creature, as he told me I was, these were things I knew not how to bear; my vanity was elevated to the last Degree: It is true, I had my Head full of Pride, but kn owing nothing of the Wickedness of the times, I had not one Thought of my own Safety or of my Virtue about me; and had my young Master offer'd it at first Sight, he might have taken any Liberty he thought fit with me; but he did not see his Advantage, which was my happiness for that time.

After this Attack, it was not long but he found an opportunity to catch me again, and almost in the same Posture, indeed it had more of Design in it on his Part, tho' not on my Part; *it was thus;* the young Ladies were all gone a Visiting with their Mother; his Brother was out of Town; and as for his Father, he had been at *London* for a Week before; he had so well watched me, that he knew where I was, tho' I did not so much as know that he was in the House; and he briskly comes up the Stairs, and seeing me at Work comes into the Room to me directly, and began just as he did before with taking me in his Arms, and Kissing me for almost a quarter of an Hour together.

It was his younger Sisters Chamber, that I was in, and as there was no Body in the House but the Maids below Stairs, he was it may be the ruder: In short, he began to be in Earnest with me indeed; perhaps he found me a little too easie, for God knows I made no Resistance to him while he only held me in his Arms and Kiss'd me; indeed I was too well pleas'd with it, to resist him much.

However as it were, tir'd with that kind of Work, we sat down, and there he talk'd with me a great while; *he said,* he was charm'd with me, and that he could not rest Night or Day till he had told me how he was in Love with me; and if I was able to Love him again, and would make him happy, I should be the saving of his Life; and many such fine things. I said little to him again, but easily discover'd that I was a Fool, and that I did not in the least perceive what he meant.

Then he walk'd about the Room, and taking me by the Hand, I walk'd with him; and by and by, taking his Advantage, he threw me down upon the Bed, and Kiss'd me there most violently; but to give him his Due, offer'd no manner of Rudeness to me, only Kiss'd me a great while; after this he thought he had heard some Body come up Stairs, so he got off from the Bed, lifted me up, professing a great deal of Love for me, but told me it was all an honest Affection, and that he meant no ill to me; and with that he put five Guineas into my Hand, and went away down Stairs.

I was more confounded with the Money than I was before with the Love, and began to be so elevated, that I scarce knew the Ground I stood on: I am the more particular in this part, that if my Story comes to be read by any innocent young Body, they may learn from it to Guard themselves against the Mischiefs which attend an early Knowledge of their own Beauty; if a young Woman once thinks herself Handsome, she never doubts the Truth of any Man that tells her he is in Love with her; for if she believes herself Charming enough to Captivate him, 'tis natural to expect the Effects of it.

This young Gentleman had fir'd his Inclinations as much as he had my vanity, and as if he had found that he had an opportunity and was sorry he did not take hold of it, he comes up again in half an Hour, or thereabouts, and falls to Work with me again as before, only with a little less Introduction.

And First, when he enter'd the Room, he turn'd about, and shut the' Door. Mrs *Betty,* said he, I fancy'd before, some Body was coming up Stairs, but it was not so; however, *adds he,* if they find me in the Room with you, they shan't catch me a Kissing of you; I told him I did not know who should be coming up Stairs, for I believ'd there was no Body in the House but the Cook and the other Maid, and they never came up those Stairs; well my Dear, *says he,* 'tis good to be sure however; and so he sits down and we began to Talk; and now, tho' I was still all on fire with his first visit, and said little, he did, as it were, put Words in my Mouth, telling me how passionately he lov'd me, and that tho' he could not mention such a thing till he came to his Estate, yet he was resolv'd to make me happy then, and himself too; *that is to say, to Marry me,* and abundance of such fine things, which I poor Fool did not understand the drift of; but acted as if there was no such thing as any kind of Love but that which tended to Matrimony; and if he had spoke of that, I had no Room, as well as no Power to have said No; but we were not come that length yet.

We had not sat long, but he got up, and stoping my very Breath with Kisses, threw me upon the Bed again; but then being both well warm'd, he went farther with me than Decency permits me to mention, nor had it been in my power to have deny'd him at that Moment, had he offer'd much more than he did.

However, tho' he took these Freedoms with me, it did not go to that, which they call the last Favour, which, to do him Justice, he did not attempt; and he made that Self-denial of his a Plea for all his Freedoms with me upon other Occasions after this: When this was over, he stay'd but a little while, but he put almost a Handful of Gold in my Hand, and left me; making a thousand Protestations of his Passion for me, and of his loving me above all the Women in the World.

It will not be strange if I now began to think, but alas! it was but with very little solid Reflection: I had a most un-bounded Stock of Vanity and Pride, and but a very little Stock of Virtue; I did indeed cast sometimes with myself what my young Master aim'd at, but thought of nothing but the fine Words, and the Gold; whether he intended to Marry me, or not to Marry me, seem'd a Matter of no great Consequence to me; nor did my Thoughts so much as suggest to me the Necessity of making any Capitulation for myself, till he came to make a kind of formal Proposal to me, as you shall hear presently.

Thus I gave up myself to a readiness of being ruined without the least concern, and am a fair *Memento* to all young Women, whose Vanity prevails over their Virtue: Nothing was ever so stupid on both Sides, had I acted as became me, and resisted as Virtue and Honour requir'd, this Gentleman had either Desisted his Attacks, finding no room to expect the Accomplishment of his Design, or had made fair, and honourable Proposals of Marriage; in which Case, whoever had blam'd him, no Body could have blam'd me. In short, if he had known me, and how easy the Trifle he aim'd at, was to be had, he would have troubled his Head no farther, but have given me four or five Guineas, and have lain with me the next time he had come at me; and if I had known his Thoughts, and how hard he thought I would be to be gain'd, I might have made my own Terms with him; and if I had not Capitulated for an immediate Marriage I might for a Maintenance till Marriage, and might have had what I would; for he was already Rich to Excess, besides what he had in Expectation; hut I seem'd wholly to have abandoned all such Thoughts as these, and was taken up Only with the Pride of my Beauty, and of being belov'd by such a Gentleman; as for the Gold, I spent whole Hours in looking upon it; I told the Guineas over and over a thousand times a Day: Never poor vain Creature was so wrapt up with every part of the Story, as I was, not Considering what was before me, and how near my Ruin was at the Door, indeed I think, I rather wish'd for that Ruin, than studyed to avoid it.

In the mean time however, I was cunning enough, not to give the least room to any in the Family to suspect me, or to imagine that I had the least Correspondence with this young Gentleman; I scarce ever look'd towards him in publick, or

Answer'd if he spoke to me, if any Body was near us; but for all that, we had every now and then a little Encounter, where we had room for a Word or two, and now and then a Kiss; but no fair opportunity for the Mischief intended; and especially considering that he made more Circumlocution than if he had known my Thoughts he had occasion for, and the Work appearing Difficult to him, he really made it so.

But as the Devil is an unwearied Tempter, so he never fails to find opportunity for that Wickedness he invites to: It was one Evening that I was in the Garden with his two younger Sisters and himself, and all very innocently Merry, when he found Means to convey a Note into my Hand, by which he Directed me to understand that he would to Morrow desire me publickly to go of an Errand for him into the Town, and that I should see him somewhere by the Way.

Accordingly after Dinner, he very gravely says to me, his Sisters being all by, Mrs *Betty,* I must ask a Favour of you: What's that? *Says his second Sister;* nay, Sister *says he,* very gravely, if you can't spare Mrs *Betty* to Day, any other time will do; *yes they said,* they could spare her well enough, and the Sister beg'd Pardon for asking; which she did but of meer Course, without any Meaning; Well, but Brother? says the eldest Sister, you must tell Mrs *Betty* what it is; if it be any private Business that we must not hear, you may call her out; there she is; Why Sister, says the Gentleman, very gravely, What do you mean? I only desire her to go into the *High-street,* (and then he pulls out a Turn-Over) to such a Shop, and then he tells them a long Story of two fine Neckcloths he had bid Money for, and he wanted to have me go and make an Errand to buy a Neck to the Turn-Over that he showed, to see if they would take my Money for the Neckcloths; to bid a Shilling more, and Haggle with them; and then he made more Errands, and so continued to have such petty Business to do, that *I* should be sure to stay a good while.

When he had given me my Errands, he told them a long Story

of a Visit he was going to make to a Family they all knew, and where was to be such and such Gentlemen, and how Merry they were to be; and very formally asks his Sisters to go with him, and they as formally excus'd themselves, because of Company that they had Notice was to come and Visit them that Afternoon, which by the Way he had contriv'd on purpose.

He had scarce done speaking to them, and giving me my Errand, but his Man came up to tell him that Sir W– H – s Coach stop'd at the Door; so he runs down, and comes up again immediately, alas! *says he,* aloud, there's all my Mirth spoil'd at once; Sir W– has sent his Coach for me, and desires to speak with me upon some earnest Business: It seems this Sir W– was a Gentleman, who liv'd about three Miles out of Town, to whom he had spoken on purpose the Day before, to lend him his Charriot for a particular occasion, and had appointed it to call for him, as it did about three a-Clock.

Immediately he calls for his best Wig, Hat and Sword, and ordering his Man to go to the other Place to make his Excuse, that was to say, he made an Excuse to send his Man away, he prepares to go into the Coach: As he was going, he stop'd a while, and speaks mighty earnestly to me about his Business, and finds an Opportunity to say very softly to me, *come away my Dear as soon as ever you can.* I said nothing, but made a Curtsy, as if I had done so to what he said in publick; in about a Quarter of an Hour I went out too; I had no Dress, other than before, except that I had a Hood, a Mask, a Fan and a pair of Gloves in my Pocket; so that there was not the least Suspicion in the House: He waited for me in the Coach in a back *Lane,* which he knew *I* must pass by; and had directed the Coachman whither to go, which as to a certain Place call'd Mile-End, where lived a Confident of his, where we went in, and where was all the Convenience in the World to be as Wicked as we pleas'd.

When we were together, he began to Talk very Gravely to me, and to tell me, he did not bring me there to betray me; that his

Passion for me would not suffer him to Abuse me; that he resolv'd to Marry me as soon as he came to his Estate; that in the mean time, if *I* would grant his Request, he would Maintain me very Honourably; and made me a thousand Protestations of his Sincerity and of his Affection to me; and That he would never abandon me, and as *I* may say, made a thousand more Preambles than he need to have done.

However as he press'd me to speak, I told him, I had no Reason to question the Sincerity of his Love to me, after so many Protestations, But – and there I stopp'd, as if I left him to Guess the rest; BUT WHAT my Dear? *says he,* I guess what you mean; what if you should be with Child, is not that it? Why then, *says he,* I'll take Care of you and Provide for you, and the Child too, and that you may see I am not in Jest, *says he,* here's an Earnest for you; and with that he pulls out a silk Purse, with an Hundred Guineas in it, and gave it me; and I'll give you such another, *says he,* every Year till I Marry you.

My Colour came and went, at the Sight of the Purse, and with the fire of his Proposal together; so that I could not say a Word, and he easily perceiv'd it; so putting the Purse into my Bosom, I made no more Resistance to him, but let him do just what he pleas'd; and as often as he pleas'd; and thus I finish'd my own Destruction at once, for from this Day, being forsaken of my Virtue, and my Modesty, I had nothing of Value left to recommend me, either to God's Blessing, or Man's Assistance.

But things did not End here; I went back to the Town, did the Business he publickly directed me to, and was at Home before any Body thought me long; as for my Gentleman, he staid out as he told me he would, till late at Night, and there was not the least Suspicion in the Family, either on his Account or on mine.

We had after this, frequent Opportunities to repeat our Crime; chiefly by his contrivance; especially at home, when his Mother and the young Ladies went Abroad a Visiting, which he watch'd so narrowly as never to miss; knowing always before-hand when they went out, and then fail'd not to catch me all alone, and securely enough; so that we took our fill of our wicked Pleasure for near half a Year; and yet, which was the most to my Satisfaction, I was not with Child.

But before this half Year was expir'd, his younger Brother, of whom I have made some mention in the beginning of the Story, falls to work with me; and he finding me alone in the Garden one Evening, begins a Story of the same Kind to me, made good honest Professions of being in Love with me, and in short, proposes fairly and Honourably to Marry me, and that before he made any other Offer to me at all.

I was now confounded and driven to such an Extremity as the like was never known; at least not to me; I resisted the Proposal with Obstinacy; and now I began to Arm myself with Arguments: I laid before him the inequality of the Match; the Treatment I should meet with in the Family; the Ingratitude it wou'd be to his good Father and Mother, who had taken me into their House upon such generous Principles, and when I was in such a low Condition; and in short, I said every thing to dissuade him from his Design that I could imagine, except telling him the Truth, which wou'd indeed have put an end to it all, but that I durst not think of mentioning.

But here happen'd a Circumstance that I did not expect indeed, which put me to my Shifts, for this young Gentleman as he was plain and Honest, so he pretended to nothing with me, but what was so too; and knowing his own Innocence, he was not so careful to make his having a Kindness for Mrs *Betty* a Secret in the House, as his Brother was; and tho' he did not let them know that he had talk'd to me about it, yet he said enough to let his Sisters perceive he Lov'd me, and his Mother saw it too which tho' they took no Notice of it to me, yet they did to him, and immediately I found their Carriage to me alter'd, more than ever before.

I saw the Cloud, tho' I did not foresee the Storm; it was easie, *I say,* to see that their Carriage to me was alter'd, and that it grew worse and worse every Day, till at last I got Information among the Servants, that I shou'd, in a very little while, be desir'd to remove.

I was not alarm'd at the News, having a full Satisfaction that I should be otherwise provided for; and especially, considering that I had Reason every Day to expect I should be with Child, and that then I should be oblig'd to remove without any Pretences for it.

After some time, the younger Gentleman took an Opportunity to tell me that the Kindness he had for me, had got vent in the Family; he did not Charge me with it, *he said,* for he knew well enough which way it came out; he told me his plain way of Talking had been the Occasion of it, for that he did not make his respect for me so much a Secret as he might have done, and the Reason was that he was at a Point; that if I would consent to have him, he would tell them all openly that he lov'd me, and that he intended to Marry me: That it was true his Father and Mother might Resent it, and be unkind, but that he was now in a Way to live, being bred to the Law, and he did not fear Maintaining me, agreeable to what I should expect; and that in short, as he believed I would not be asham'd of him, so he was resolv'd not to be asham'd of me, and that he scorn'd to be afraid to own me now, who he resolv'd to own after I was his Wife, and therefore I had nothing to do but to give him my Hand, and he would Answer for all the rest.

I was now in a dreadful Condition indeed, and now I repented heartily my easiness with the eldest Brother, not from any Reflection of Conscience, but from a View of the Happiness I might have enjoy'd, and had now made impossible; for tho' I had no great Scruples of Conscience *as I have said* to struggle with, yet I could not think of being a Whore to one Brother, and a Wife to the other; but then it came into my Thoughts, that the first Brother had promis'd to make me his Wife when he came to his Estate; but I presently remember'd what I had often thought of, that he had never spoken a Word of having me for a Wife after he had Conquer'd me for a Mistress; and indeed till now, tho' I said I thought of it often, yet it gave me no Disturbance at all, for as he did not seem in the least to lessen his Affection to me, so neither did he lessen his Bounty, tho' he had the Discretion himself to desire me not to layout a Penny of what he gave me in Cloaths, or to make the least show Extraordinary, because it would necessarily give Jealousie in the Family, since every Body knew I could come at such things no manner of ordinary Way, but by some private Friendship, which they would presently have suspected.

But I was now in a great strait, and really knew not what to do; the main Difficulty was this: the younger Brother not only laid close Siege to me, but suffered it to be seen; he would come into his Sisters Room, and his Mothers Room, and sit down, and Talk a Thousand kind things of me, and to me, even before their Faces, and when they were all there: This grew so Publick, that the whole House talk'd of it, and his Mother reprov'd him for it, and their Carriage to me appear'd quite Altered: In short, his Mother had let fall some Speeches, as if she intended to put me out of the Family; that is, in *English,* to turn me out of Doors. Now I was sure this could not be a Secret to his Brother, only that he might not think, as indeed no Body else yet did, that the youngest Brother had made any Proposal to me about it; But as I easily cou'd see that it would go farther, so I saw likewise there was an absolute Necessity to speak of it to him, or that he would speak of it to me, and which to do first I knew not; that is, whether I should break it to him, or let it alone till he should break it to me.

Upon serious Consideration, for indeed now I began to Consider things very seriously, and never till now: I say, upon serious Consideration, I resolv'd to tell him of it first, and it was not long before I had an Opportunity, for the very next Day his Brother went to *London* upon some Business, and the Family being out a Visiting, just as it had happen'd before, and as indeed was often the Case, he came according to his Custom to spend an Hour or Two with Mrs *Betty.*

When he came and had sat down a while, he easily perceiv'd there was an alteration in my Countenance, that I was not so free and pleasant with him as I us'd to be, and particularly, that I had been a Crying; he was not long before he took notice of it, and ask'd me in very kind Terms what was the Matter, and if any thing Troubl'd me: I wou'd have put it off if I could, but it was not to be Conceal'd; so after suffering many Importunities to draw that out of me, which I long'd as much as possible to Disclose; I told him that it was true, something did Trouble me, and something of such a Nature that I could not Conceal from him, and yet, that I could not tell how to tell him of it neither; that it was a thing that not only Surpriz'd me, but greatly perplex'd me, and that I knew not what Course to take, unless he would Direct me: He told me with great Tenderness, that let it be what it wou'd, I should not let it Trouble me, for he would Protect me from all the World.

I then begun at a Distance, and told him I was afraid the Ladies had got some secret Information of our Correspondence; for that it was easie to see that their Conduct was very much chang'd towards me for a great while, and that now it was come to that pass, that they frequently found Fault with me, and sometimes fell quite out with me, tho' I never gave them the least Occasion: That whereas I us'd always to lye with the Eldest Sister, I was lately put to lye by my self, or with one of the Maids; and that I had over-heard them several times talking very Unkindly about me; but that which confirm'd it all, was, that one of the Servants had told me, that she had heard I was to be Turn' d out, and that it was not safe for the Family that I should be any longer in the House.

He smil'd when he heard all this, and I ask'd him how he could make so light of it, when he must needs know that if there was any Discovery, I was Undone for ever? and that even it would hurt him, tho' not Ruin him, as it would me: I upbraided him, that he was like all the rest of the Sex, that when they had the Character and Honour of a Woman at their Mercy, often times made it their Jest, and at least look'd upon it as a Trifle, and counted the Ruin of those, they had had their Will of, as a thing of no value.

He saw me Warm and Serious, and he chang'd his Stile immediately; *he told me,* he was sorry I should have such a thought of him; that he had never given me the least Occasion for it, but had been as tender of my Reputation as he could be of his own; that he was sure our Correspondence had been manag'd with so much Address, that not one Creature in the Family had so much as a Suspicion of it; that if he smil'd when I told him my Thoughts, it was at the Assurance he lately receiv'd, that our understanding one another, was not so much as known or guess'd at; and that when he had told me, how much Reason he had to be Easie, I should Smile as he did, for he was very certain, it would give me a full Satisfaction.

This is a Mystery I cannot understand, *says I,* or how it should be to my Satisfaction that I am to be turn'd out of Doors; for if our Correspondence is not discover'd, I know not what else I have done to change the Countenances of the whole Family to me, or to have them Treat me as they do now, who formerly used me with so much Tenderness, as if I had been one of their own Children.

Why look you Child, *says he,* that they are Uneasie about you, that is true; but that they have the least Suspicion of the Case as it is, and as it respects you and I, is so far from being True, that they suspect my Brother *Robin;* and in short, they are fully persuaded he makes Love to you: Nay, the Fool has put it into their Heads too himself, for he is continually Bantring them about it, and making a Jest of himself; I confess, I think he is wrong to do so, because he can not but see it vexes them, and makes them Unkind to you; but 'tis a Satisfaction to me, because of the Assurance it gives me that they do not suspect me in the least, and I hope this will be to your Satisfaction too.

So it is, *says I,* one way, but this does not reach my Case at all, nor is this the chief Thing that Troubles me, tho' I have been concern'd about that too: What is it then, *says he?* With which, I fell into Tears, and could say nothing to him at all: He strove to pacifie me all he could, but began at last to be very pressing upon me to tell what it was; at last *I answer'd,* that I thought I ought to tell him too, and that he had some right to know it, besides, that I wanted his Direction in the Case, for I was in such Perplexity, that I knew not what Course to take, and then I related the whole Affair to him: *I told him* how imprudently his Brother had manag'd himself, in making himself so Publick; for that if he had kept it a Secret, as such a Thing ought to have been, I could but have Denied him Positively, without giving any Reason for it, and he would in Time have ceas'd his Solicitations; but that he had the Vanity, first, to depend upon it that I would not Deny him, and then had taken the Freedom to tell his Resolution of having me, to the whole House.

I told him how far I had resisted him, and *told him* how Sincere and Honourable his Offers were, but *says I,* my Case will be doubly hard; for as they carry it to me now, because he desires to have me, they'll carry it worse when they shall find I have Deny'd him; and they will presently say, there's something else in it, and then out it comes, that I am Marry'd already to somebody else, or else that I would never refuse a Match so much above me as this was.

This Discourse surpriz'd him indeed very much: He *told me,* that it was a critical Point indeed for me to Manage, and he did not see which way I should get out of it; but he would consider of it, and let me know next time we met, what Resolution he was come to about it; and in the mean time, desir'd I would not give my Consent to his Brother, nor yet give him a flat Denial, but that I would hold him in Suspence a while.

I seem'd to start at his saying I should not give him any Consent; I *told him,* he knew very well I had no Consent to give; that he had Engag'd himself to Marry me, and that my Consent was at the same time Engag'd to him; that he had all along told me I was his Wife, and I look'd upon my self as effectually so, as if the Ceremony had pass'd; and that it was from his own Mouth that I did so, he having all along persuaded me to call myself his Wife.

Well, my Dear *says he,* don't be Concern'd at that now, if I am not your Husband, I'll be as good as a Husband to you, and do not let those things Trouble you now, but let me look a little farther into this Affair, and I shall be able to say more next time we meet.

He pacify'd me as well as he could with this, but I found he was very Thoughtful, and that tho' he was very kind to me, and kiss'd me a thousand Times, and more I believe, and gave me Money too, yet he offer'd no more all the while we were together, which was above two Hours, and which I much wonder'd at, indeed at that Time, considering how it us'd to be, and what Opportunity we had.

His Brother did not come from *London* for five or six Days, and it was two Days more, before he got an Opportunity to talk with him; but then getting him by himself, he began to talk very Close to him about it; and the same Evening got an Opportunity, (for we had a long Conference together) to repeat all their Discourse to me, which as near as I can remember, was to the purpose following. He *told him* he heard strange News of him since he went, (*viz.*) that he made Love to Mrs *Betty:* Well, *says his* Brother, a little Angrily, and so *I do,* And what then? What has any body to do with that? Nay, *says his* Brother, don't be Angry *Robin,* I don't pretend to have any thing to do with it; nor do I pretend to be Angry with you about it: But I find they do concern themselves about it, and that they have used the poor Girl Ill about it, which I should take as done to my self; Who do you mean by THEY? *says* Robin, I mean my Mother, and the Girls, *says the* elder Brother.

But hark ye, *says his* Brother, are you in Earnest? do you really Love the Girl? you may be free with me you know. Why then *says* Robin, I will be free with you; I do Love her above all the Women in the World, and I will have Her; let *them say,* and do what they will, I believe the Girl will not Deny me.

It stuck me to the Heart when he *told me* this, for tho' it was most rational to think I would not Deny him, yet I knew in my own Conscience I must Deny him, and I saw my Ruin in my being oblig'd to do so; but I knew it was my business to Talk otherwise then, so I interrupted him in his Story thus.

Ay! *said I,* does he think I can not Deny him? but he shall find I can Deny him, for all that.

Well my dear *says he,* but let me give you the whole Story as it went on between us, and then say what you will.

Then he went on and *told me,* that he reply'd thus: But Brother, you know She has nothing, and you may have several Ladies with good Fortunes: 'Tis no matter for that, *said* Robin, I Love the Girl; and I will never please my Pocket in Marrying, and not please my Fancy; and so my Dear *adds he,* there is no Opposing him.

Yes, yes, *says I,* you shall see I can Oppose him; I have learnt to say No now, tho' I had not learnt it before; if the best Lord in the Land offer'd me Marriage now, I could very chearfully say No to him.

Well, but my Dear *says he,* what can you say to him? You know, as you said when we talk'd of it before, he will ask you many Questions about it, and all the House will wonder what the meaning of it should be.

Why *says I* smiling, I can stop all their Mouths at one Clap, by telling him and them too, that I am Married already to his elder Brother.

He smil'd a little too at the Word, but I could see it Startled him, and he could not hide the disorder it put him into; however, he return'd, Why tho' that may be true in some Sense, yet I suppose you are but in Jest when you talk of giving such an Answer as that, it may not be Convenient on many Accounts.

No, no, *says* I pleasantly, I am not so fond of letting that Secret come out without your Consent.

But what then can you say to him, or to them, *says he,* when they find you positive against a Match, which would be apparently so much to your Advantage?

Why, *says* I, should I be at a loss? First of all, I am not oblig'd to give them any Reason at all, on the other hand, I may tell them I am Married already, and stop there, and that will be a full Stop too to him, for he can have no Reason to ask one Question after it.

Ay, *says he,* but the whole House will tease you about that, even to Father and Mother, and if you deny them positively, they will be Disoblig'd at you, and Suspicious besides.

Why, *says* I, What can I do? What would you have me do? I was in strait enough before, and as I *told you,* I was in Perplexity before, and acquainted you with the Circumstances, that I might have your Advice.

My dear, *says he,* I have been considering very much upon it, you may be sure, and tho' it is a piece of Advice that has a great many Mortifications in it to me, and may at first seem Strange to you, yet all Things consider'd, I see no better way for you, than to let him go on; and if you find him hearty and in Earnest, Marry him.

I gave him a look full of Horror at those Words, and turning Pale as Death, was at the very point of sinking down out of the Chair I sat in: When giving a start, my Dear, *says he* aloud, What's the matter with you? Where are you a going? and a great many such things; and with jogging and calling to me, fetch'd me a little to my self, tho' it was a good while before I fully recover'd my Senses, and was not able to speak for several Minutes more.

When I was fully recover'd he began again; My dear *says he,* What made you so Surpriz'd at what I said? I would have you consider Seriously of it; you may see plainly how the Family stand in this Case, and they would be stark Mad if it was my Case, as it is my Brothers, and for ought I see, it would be my Ruin and yours too.

Ay! *says* I, still speaking angrily; are all your Protestations and Vows to be shaken by the dislike of the Family? Did I not always object that to you, and you made a light thing of it, as what you were above, and would not Value; and is it come to this now? *Said* I, is this your Faith and Honour, your Love, and the Solidity of your Promises?

He continued perfectly Calm, notwithstanding all my Reproaches, and I was not sparing of them at all; but *he reply'd* at last, My Dear, I have not broken one Promise with you yet; I did tell you I would Marry you when I was come to my Estate; but you see My Father is a hail healthy Man, and may live these thirty Years still, and not be Older than several are round us in the Town; and you never propos'd my Marrying you sooner, because you know it might be my Ruin; and as to all the rest, I have not fail'd you in any thing; you have wanted for nothing.

I could not deny a Word of this, and had nothing to say to it in general; but why then, *says* I, can you perswade me to such a horrid step, as leaving you, since you have not left me? Will you allow no Affection, no Love on my Side, where there has been so much on your Side? Have I made you no Returns? Have I given no Testimony of my Sincerity, and of my Passion? are the Sacrifices I have made of Honour and Modesty to you, no Proof of my being ty'd to you in Bonds too strong to be broken?

But here my Dear, *says he,* you may come into a safe Station, and appear with Honour and with splendor at once, and the Remembrance of what we have done may be wrapt up in an eternal Silence, as if it had never happen'd; you shall always have my Respect, and my sincere Affection, only then it shall be Honest, and perfectly Just to my Brother; you shall be, my Dear Sister, as now you are my Dear and there he stop'd.

Your Dear whore, *says* I, you would have said, if you had

gone on, and you might as well have said it; but I understand you: However, I desire you to remember the long Discourses you have had with me, and the many Hours pains you have taken to perswade me to believe myself an honest Woman; that I was your Wife intentionally, tho' not in the Eye of the World, and that it was as effectual a Marriage that had pass'd between us as if we had been publickly Wedded by the Parson of the Parish; you know and cannot but remember, that these have been your own Words to me.

I found this was a little too close upon him, but I made it up in what follows; he stood stock still for a while and said nothing, and I went on thus: you cannot, *says* I, without the highest injustice believe that I yielded upon all these Perswasions without a Love not to be questioned, not to be shaken again by any thing that could happen afterward: If you have such dishonourable Thoughts of me, I must ask you what Foundation in any of my Behaviour have I given for such a Suggestion.

If then I have yielded to the Importunities of my Affection, and if I have been perswaded to believe that I am really, and in the Essence of the Thing your Wife, shall I now give the Lye to all those Arguments, and call myself your Whore, or Mistress, which is the same thing? And will you Transfer me to your Brother?

Can you Transfer my Affection? Can you bid me cease loving you, and bid me love him? is it in my Power think you to make such a Change at Demand? No Sir, *said I,* depend upon it 'tis impossible, and whatever the Change of your Side may be, I will ever be True; and I had much rather, since it is come that unhappy Length, be your Whore than your Brothers Wife.

He appear'd pleas'd, and touch'd with the impression of this last Discourse, and told me that he stood where he did before; that he had not been Unfaithful to me in anyone Promise he had ever made yet, but that there were so many terrible things presented themselves to his View in the Affair before me, and that on my Account in particular, that he had thought of the other as a Remedy so effectual, as nothing could come up to it: That he thought this would not be an entire parting us, but we might love as Friends all our Days, and perhaps with more Satisfaction, than we should in the Station we were now in, as things might happen: That he durst say, I could not apprehend any thing from him, as to betraying a Secret, which could not but be the Destruction of us both, if it came out: That he had but one Question to ask of me, that could lye in the way of it, and if that Question was answer'd in the Negative, he could not but think still it was the only Step I could take.

I guess'd at his Question presently, namely, Whether I was sure I was not with Child? As to that, *I told him,* he need not be concern'd about it, for I was not with Child; why then my Dear, *says he,* we have no time to Talk farther now; consider of it, and think closely about it, I cannot but be of the Opinion still, that it will be the best Course you can take; and with this, he took his Leave, and the more hastily too, his Mother and Sisters Ringing at the Gate, just at the Moment that he had risen up to go.

He left me in the utmost Confusion of Thought; and he easily perceiv'd it the next Day, and all the rest of the Week, for it was but *Tuesday* Evening when we talked; but he had no Opportunity to come at me all that Week, till the *Sunday* after, when I being indispos'd did not go to Church, and he making some Excuse for the like, stay'd at Home.

And now he had me an Hour and a Half again by myself, and we fell into the same Arguments all over again, or at least so near the same, as it would be to no purpose to repeat them; at last, *I ask'd him* warmly what Opinion he must have of my Modesty, that he could suppose, I should so much as Entertain a thought of lying with two Brothers? And assur'd him it could never be: *I added* if he was to tell me that he would never see me more, than which nothing but Death could be more Terrible, yet I could never entertain a thought so Dishonourable to my self, and so Base to him; and therefore, I entreated him if he had one Grain of Respect or Affection left for me, that he would speak no more of it to me, or that he would pull his Sword out and Kill me. He appear'd surpriz'd at my Obstinancy as he call'd it, *told me* I was unkind to my self, and unkind to him in it; that it was a Crisis unlook'd for upon us both, and impossible for either of us to foresee; but that he did not see any other way to save us both from Ruin, and therefore he thought it the more Unkind; but that if he must say no more of it to me, he added with an unusual Coldness, that he did not know any thing else we had to talk of; and so he rose up to take his leave; I rose up too, as if with the same Indifference, but when he came to give me as it were a parting Kiss, I burst out into such a Passion of Crying, that tho' I would have spoke, I could not, and only pressing his Hand, seem'd to give him the Adieu, but cry'd vehemently.

He was sensibly mov'd with this; so he sat down again, and said a great many kind things to me to abate the excess of my Passion; but still urg'd the necessity of what he had proposed; all the while insisting, that if I did refuse, he would notwithstanding provide for me; but letting me plainly see that he would decline me in the main Point; nay, even as a Mistress; making it a point of Honour not to lye with the Woman, that for ought he knew, might come to be his Brothers Wife.

The bare loss of him as a Gallant was not so much my Affliction, as the loss of his Person, whom indeed I Lov'd to Distraction; and the loss of all the Expectations I had, and which I always had built my Hopes upon, of having him one Day for my Husband: These things oppress'd my Mind so much, that in short, I fell very ill; the agonies of my Mind, in a word, threw me into a high Feaver, and long it was that none in the Family expected my Life.

I was reduc'd very low indeed, and was often Delirious and light Headed; but nothing lay so near me, as the fear that when I was light Headed, I should say something or other to his Prejudice; I was distress'd in my Mind also to see him, and so he was to see me, for he really Lov'd me most passionately; but it could not be;

there was not the least Room to desire it, on one side, or other, or so much as to make it Decent.

It was near five Weeks that I kept my Bed, and tho' the violence of my Feaver abated in three Weeks, yet it several times Return'd; and the Physicians said two or three times, they could do no more for me, but that they must leave Nature and the Distemper to fight it Out, only strengthening the first with Cordials to maintain the Struggle: After the end of five Weeks I grew better, but was so Weak, so Alter'd, so Melancholly, and recover'd so Slowly, that the Physicians apprehended I should go into a Consumption; and which vex'd me most, they gave it as their Opinion, that my Mind was Oppress'd, that something Troubl'd me, and in short, that I was In Love; upon this, the whole House was set upon me to Examine me, and to press me to tell whether I was in Love or not, and with who? but as I well might, I deny'd my being in Love at all.

They had on this Occasion a Squable one Day about me at Table, that had like to have put the whole Family in an Uproar, and for sometime did so; they happen'd to be all at Table, but the Father; as for me I was Ill, and in my Chamber: At the beginning of the Talk, which was just as they had finish'd their Dinner, the old Gentlewoman who had sent me somewhat to Eat, call'd her Maid to go up, and ask me if I would have any more; but the Maid brought down Word I had not Eaten half what she had sent me already.

Alas, *says the* old Lady, that poor Girl; I am afraid she will never be well.

Well! *says the* elder Brother, How should Mrs *Betty* be well, *they say* she is in Love?

I believe nothing of it *says the* old Gentlewoman.

I don't know *says the* eldest Sister, what, to say to it, they have made such a rout about her being so Handsome, and so Charming, and I know not what, and that in her hearing too, that has turn'd the Creatures Head I believe, and who knows what possessions may follow such Doings? for my Part I don't know what to make of it.

Why Sister, you must acknowledge she is very *Handsome, says the* elder Brother.

Ay, and a great deal Handsomer than you Sister, *says* Robin, and that's your Mortification.

Well, well, that is not the Question, *says his* Sister, the Girl is well enough, and she knows it well enough; she need not be told of it to make her Vain.

We are not a talking of her being Vain, *says the* elder Brother, but of her being in Love; it may be she is in Love with herself, it seems my Sisters think so.

I would she was in Love with me, *says* Robin, I'd quickly put her out of her Pain.

What d' ye mean by that Son, *says the* old Lady, How can you talk so?

Why Madam, *says* Robin again, very honestly, Do you think I'd let the poor Girl Die for Love, and of one that is near at hand to be had too?

Fye Brother, *says the* second Sister, how can you talk so? would you take a Creature that has not a Groat in the World?

Prithee Child *says* Robin, Beauty's a Portion, and good Humour with it, is a double Portion; I wish thou hadst half her Stock of both for thy Portion: So there was her Mouth stopp'd.

I find, *says the* eldest Sister, if *Betty* is not in Love, my Brother is; I wonder he has not broke his Mind to *Betty,* I warrant she won't say No.

They that yield when they're ask'd *says* Robin, are one step before them that were never ask'd to yield, Sister, and two Steps before them that yield before they are ask'd: And that's an Answer to you Sister.

This fir'd the Sister, and she flew into a Passion, and said, things were come to that pass, that it was time the Wench, *meaning me,* was out of the Family; and but that she was not fit to be turn'd out, she hop'd her Father and Mother would consider of it as soon as she could be remov'd.

Robin reply'd, That was business for the Master and Mistress of the Family, who were not to be taught by One that had so little Judgment as his eldest Sister.

It run up a great deal farther; the Sister Scolded, *Robin* Rally'd and Banter'd, but poor *Betty* lost Ground by it extremely in the Family: I heard of it, and I cry'd heartily, and the old Lady came up to me, some body having told her that I was so much concern'd about it: I complain'd to her, that it was very hard the Doctors should pass such a Censure upon me, for which they had no Ground; and that it was still harder, considering the Circumstances I was under in the Family; that I hop'd I had done nothing to lessen her Esteem for me, or given any Occasion for the Bickering between her Sons and Daughters; and I had more need to think of a Coffin than of being in Love, and beg'd she would not let me suffer in her Opinion for any body's Mistakes, but my own.

She was sensible of the Justice of what I said, but *told me,* since there had been such a Clamour among them, and that her younger Son Talk'd after such a rattling way as he did, she desir'd I would be so Faithful to her as to Answer her but one Question sincerely; I told her I would with all my heart, and with the utmost plainess and Sincerity: Why then the Question was, Whether there was any thing between her Son *Robert* and me? I told her with all the Protestations of Sincerity that I was able to make, and as I might well do, that there was not, nor ever had been; I *told her* that Mr *Robert* had rattled and jested, as she knew it was his way, and that I took it always as I suppos'd he meant it, to be a wild airy way of Discourse that had no Signification in it: And again assured her that there was not the least tittle of what she understood by it between us; and that those who had Suggested it had done me a great deal of Wrong, and Mr *Robert* no Service at all.

The old Lady was fully satisfy'd, and kiss'd me, spoke chearfully to me, and bid me take care of my Health and want for nothing, and so took her leave: But when she came down, she found the Brother and all his Sisters together by the Ears; they were Angry even to Passion, at his upbraiding them with their being Homely, and having never had any Sweet hearts, never having been ask'd the Question, and their being so forward as almost to ask first: He rallied them upon the Subject of Mrs *Betty;* how Pretty, how good Humour'd, how she Sung better than they did, and Danc'd better, and how much Handsomer she was; and in doing this, he omitted no Ill-natur'd Thing that could vex them, and indeed, push'd too hard upon them: The old Lady came down in the height of it, and to put a stop to it, told them all the Discourse she had had with me, and how I answer'd, that there was nothing between Mr *Robert* and I.

She's wrong there, *says* Robin, for if there was not a great deal between us, we should be closer together than we are: I told her I Lov'd her hugely, *says he,* but I could never make the Jade believe I was in Earnest; I do not know how you should *says his* Mother, no body in their Senses could believe you were in Earnest, to Talk so to a poor Girl, whose Circumstances you know so well.

But prithee Son *adds she,* since you tell me that you could not make her believe you were in Earnest, what must we believe about it? for you ramble so in your Discourse, that no body knows whether you are in Earnest or in Jest: But as I find the Girl by your own Confession has answer'd truely, I wish you would do so too, and tell me seriously, so that I may depend upon it; Is there any thing in it or no? Are you in Earnest or no? Are you Distracted indeed, or are you not? 'Tis a weighty Question, and I wish you would make us easie about it.

By my Faith Madam, *says* Robin, 'tis in vain to mince the Matter, or tell any more Lyes about it; lam in Earnest, as much as a Man is that's going to be Hang'd. If Mrs *Betty* would say she Lov'd me, and that she would Marry me, I'd have her to morrow

Morning fasting, and say, *To have, and to hold,* instead of eating my Breakfast.

Well, *says the Mother,* then there's one Son lost; and she said it in a very mournful Tone, as one greatly concern'd at it.

I hope not Madam, *says* Robin, no Man is lost, when a good Wife has found him.

Why but Child, *says the* old Lady, she is a Beggar.

Why then Madam, she has the more need of Charity *says* Robin; I'll take her off of the hands of the Parish, and she and I'll Beg together.

Its bad Jesting with such things, *says the Mother.*

I don't Jest Madam, *says* Robin: We'll come and beg your Pardon Madam; and your Blessing Madam, and my Fathers.

This is all out of the way Son, *says the Mother,* if you are in Earnest you are Undone.

I am afraid not *says he,* for I am really afraid she won't have me, after all my Sisters huffing and blustring; I believe I shall never be able to persuade her to it.

That's a fine Tale indeed, she is not so far out of her Senses neither; Mrs *Betty is* no Fool, *says the youngest Sister,* Do you think she has learnt to say No, any more than other People?

No Mrs Mirth-Wit says Robin, Mrs *Betty's* no Fool; but Mrs *Betty* may be Engag'd some other way, And what then?

Nay, *says the eldest Sister,* we can say nothing to that, Who must it be to then? She is never out of the Doors, it must be between you.

I have nothing to say to that *says* Robin, I have been Examined enough; there's my Brother, if it must be *between* us, go to Work with him.

This stung *the elder Brother* to the Quick, and he concluded that *Robin* had discover'd something: However, he kept himself from appearing disturb'd; Prithee *says he,* don't go to sham your

Stories off upon me, I tell you, I deal in no such Ware; I have nothing to say to Mrs *Betty,* nor to any of the Miss *Betty's* in the Parish; and with that he rose up and brush'd off.

No, *says the eldest Sister,* I dare answer for my Brother, he knows the World better.

Thus the Discourse ended; but it left *the elder Brother* quite confounded: He concluded his Brother had made a full Discovery, and he began to doubt whether I had been concern'd in it or not; but with all his Management, he could not bring it about to get at me; at last, he was so perplex'd, that he was quite Desperate, and resolv'd he wou'd come into my Chamber and see me, whatever came of it: In order to this, he contriv'd it so, that one Day after Dinner, watching *his eldest Sister* till he could see her go up Stairs, he runs after her: *Hark ye Sister, says he,* Where is this sick Woman? may not a body see her? YES, *says the Sister,* I believe you may, but let me go first a little, an I'll tell you; so she run up to the Door and gave me notice; and presently call'd to him again: BROTHER, *says she,* you may come if you please; so in he came, just in the same kind of Rant: Well, *says he,* at the Door *as he came in,* Where is this sick Body that's in Love? How do ye do Mrs *Betty?* I would have got up out of my Chair, but was so Weak I could not for a good while; and he saw it and his Sister too, and she said, *Come do not strive to stand up,* my Brother desires no Ceremony, especially, now you are so Weak. No, No, *Mrs Betty,* pray sit still *says he,* and so sits himself down in a Chair over-against me, and appear'd as if he was mighty Merry.

He talk'd a deal of rambling Stuff to his Sister and to me; sometimes of one thing, sometimes of another, on purpose to Amuse his Sister; and every now and then, would turn it upon the old Story, directing it to me: Poor Mrs *Betty, says he,* it is a sad thing to be in Love, why it has reduced you sadly; at last I spoke a little; I am glad to see you so merry, Sir, *says I,* but I think the Doctor might have found some thing better to do than to make his Game at his Patients: if I had been Ill of no other

Distemper, I know the Proverb too well to have let him come to me: What Proverb *says he?* O! I remember it now: What;

Where Love is the Case,
The Doctor's *an Ass.*

Is not that it Mrs *Betty?* I smil'd, and said nothing: Nay, *says he,* I think the effect has prov'd it to be Love, for it seems the Doctor has been able to do you but little Service; you mend very slowly they say, I doubt there's somewhat in it Mrs *Betty,* I doubt you are sick of the Incureables, and that is Love; I smil'd and said, No, *indeed Sir,* that's none of my Distemper.

We had a deal of such Discourse, and sometimes others that signify'd as little; by and by He ask'd me to Sing them a Song; at which I smil'd, and said, my singing Days were over: At last he ask'd me, if he should Play upon his Flute to me; his Sister said she believ'd it wou'd hurt me, and that my Head could not bear it; I bow'd and said, No, it would not hurt me: And pray Madam, *says I,* do not hinder it, I love the Musick of the Flute very much; then his Sister said, well do then Brother; with that he pull'd out the Key of his Closet; Dear Sister, *says he,* I am very Lazy, do step to my Closet and fetch my Flute, it lies in *such a Drawer,* naming a Place where he was sure it was not, that she might be a little while a looking for it.

As soon as she was gone, he related the whole Story to me, of the Discourse his Brother had about me, and of his pushing it at him, and his concern about it, which was the Reason of his contriving this Visit to me: I assur'd him, I had never open'd my Mouth either to his Brother, or to any Body else: I told him the dreadful Exigence I was in; that my Love to him, and his offering to have me forget that Affection and remove it to another, had thrown me down; and that I had a thousand Times wish'd I might Die rather than Recover, and to have the same

Circumstances to struggle with as I had before; and that this backwardness to Life had been the great Reason of the slowness of my Recovering: I added that I foresaw, that as soon as I was well, I must quit the Family; and that as for Marrying his *Brother,* I abhor'd the thoughts of it, after what had been my Case with him, and that he might depend upon it, I would never see his Brother again upon that Subject: That if he would break all his Vows and Oaths, and Engagements with me, be that between his Conscience and his Honour, and himself: But he should never be able to say that I who he had persuaded to call my self his Wife, and who had given him the Liberty to use me as a Wife, was not as Faithful to him as a Wife ought to be, what ever he might be to me.

He was going to reply, and had said That he was sorry I could not be persuaded, and was a going to say more, but he heard his Sister a coming, and so did I; and yet I forc'd out these few Words as a reply, That I could never be persuaded to Love one Brother and Marry another: He shook his Head and said, *Then I am Ruin'd,* meaning himself; and that Moment his Sister enter'd the Room and told him she could not find the Flute; Well, *says he* merrily, this Laziness won't do, so he gets up, and goes himself to go to look for it, but comes back without it too; not but that he could have found it, but because his Mind was a little Disturb'd, and he had no mind to Play; and besides, the Errand he sent his Sister of, was answer'd another way; for he only wanted an Opportunity to speak to me, which he gain'd, tho' not much to his Satisfaction.

I had however, a great deal of Satisfaction in having spoken my Mind to him with Freedom, and with such an honest Plainess, as I have related; and tho' it did not at all Work the way, I desir'd, *that is to say,* to oblige the Person to me the more, yet it took from him all possibility of quitting me but by a down right breach of Honour, and giving up all the Faith of a Gentleman to me, which he had so often engaged by, never to abandon me, but to make me his Wife as soon as he came to his Estate.

It was not many Weeks after this before I was about the House again, and began to grow well; but I continu'd Melancholly, silent, dull, and retir'd, which amaz'd the whole Family, except he that knew the Reason of it; yet it was a great while before he took any Notice of it, and I *as backward to speak as he,* carried respectfully to him, but never offer'd to speak a Word to him, that was particular of any kind whatsoever; and this continu'd for sixteen or seventeen Weeks, so that as I expected every Day to be dismiss'd the Family, on Account of what Distaste they had taken another Way, in which I had no Guilt; so I expected to hear no more of this Gentleman, after all his solemn Vows, and Protestations, but to be ruin'd and abandon'd.

At last I broke the way myself in the Family for my Removing; for being talking seriously with the old Lady one Day, about my own Circumstances in the World, and how my Distemper had left a heaviness upon my Spirits, that I was not the same thing I was before: The old Lady said, I am afraid *Betty,* what I have said to you, about my Son has had some Influence upon you, and that you are Melancholly on his Account; Pray will you let me know how the Matter stands with you both? if it may not be improper, for as for *Robin,* he does nothing but Rally and Banter when I speak of it to him: Why truly Madam, *said I,* that Matter stands as I wish it did not, and I shall be very sincere with you in it, what ever befalls me for it; Mr *Robert* has several times propos'd Marriage to me, which is what I had no Reason to expect, my poor Circumstances consider'd; but I have always resisted him, and that perhaps in Terms more positive than became me, considering the Regard that I ought to have for every Branch of your Family: *But said I,* Madam, I could never so far forget my Obligations to you and all your House, to offer to Consent to a Thing, which I know must needs be Disobliging to you, and this I have made my Argument to him, and have possitively told him, that I would never entertain a Thought of that kind, unless I had your Consent, and his Fathers also, to whom I was bound by so many invincible Obligations.

And is this possible Mrs *Betty?* says the old Lady, then you have been much Juster to us, than we have been to you; for we have all look'd upon you as a kind of a Snare to my Son; and I had a Proposal to make to you for your Removing, for fear of it; but I had not yet mention'd it to you, because I thought you were not thorough Well, and I was afraid of grieving you too much, lest it should throw you down again, for we have all a Respect for you still, tho' not so much, as to have it be the Ruin of my Son; but if it be as you say, we have all wrong'd you very much.

As to the Truth of what I say, Madam, *said I,* I refer you to your Son himself; if he will do me any Justice, he must tell you the Story just as I have told it.

Away goes the old Lady to her Daughters, and tells them the whole Story, just as I had told it her, and they were surpris'd at it, you may be sure, as I believ'd they would be; one *said,* she could never have thought it; another said, *Robin* was a Fool, a *Third* said, she would not believe a Word of it, and she would warrant that *Robin* would tell the Story another way; but the old Gentlewoman, who was resolv'd to go to the bottom of it, before I could have the least Opportunity of Acquainting her Son, with what had pass'd, resolv'd too that she would Talk with her Son immediately, and to that purpose sent for him, for he was gone but to a Lawyers House in the Town, upon some petty Business of his own, and upon her sending, he return'd immediately.

Upon his coming up to them, for they were all still together: sit down *Robin, says the old Lady,* I must have some talk with you; with all my Heart, Madam, *says Robin, looking very Merry;* I hope it is about a good Wife, for I am at a great loss in that Affair: How can that be, *says his Mother,* did not you say, you resolved to have Mrs *Betty?* Ay Madam, says *Robin;* but there is one has *forbid the Banns:* Forbid the Banns! *says his Mother,* who can that be? Even Mrs *Betty* herself, says *Robin.* How so, *says his Mother,* Have you ask'd her the Question then? *Yes, indeed Madam, says* Robin; I have attack'd her in Form, five times since she was Sick, and am beaten off; the Jade is so stout, she won't Capitulate, nor yield upon any Terms, except such as I cannot effectually Grant: Explain your self, *says the Mother,* for I am surpris'd; I do not understand you, I hope you are not in Earnest.

Why, Madam, *says he,* the Case is plain enough upon me, it explains itself; she won't have me, *she says;* is not that plain enough? I think 'tis plain, and pretty rough too; well but *says the Mother,* you talk of Conditions, that you cannot Grant, what, does she want a Settlement? her Jointure ought to be according to her Portion; but what Fortune does she bring you? Nay, as to Fortune, *says* Robin, she is rich enough; I am satisfy'd in that Point; but *'tis I* that am not able to come up to her Terms, and she is positive she will not have me without.

Here the Sisters put in, Madam, *says the second Sister,* 'tis impossible to be serious with him; he will never give a direct Answer to anything; you had better let him alone, and talk no more of it to him; you know how to dispose of her out of his way if you thought there was any thing in it; *Robin* was a little warm'd with his Sisters rudeness, but he was even with her; and yet with good Manners too: There are two sorts of People, Madam, *says he, turning to his Mother,* that there is no contending with, that is a wise Body and a Fool, 'tis a little hard I should engage with both of them together.

The younger Sister then put in, we must be Fools indeed, *says she,* in my Brother's Opinion, that he should think we can believe he has seriously ask'd Mrs *Betty* to Marry him, and that she has refus'd him.

Answer, and *Answer not, says Solomon, replyed her Brother:* When your Brother had said to your Mother that he had ask'd her no less than five Times, and that it was so, that she positively Denied him, methinks a younger Sister need not question the Truth of it when her Mother did not: My Mother, you see, did not understand it, *says the second Sister:* There's some difference *says* Robin, between desiring me to Explain it, and telling me she did not believe it.

Well but Son, *says the old Lady,* if you are dispos'd to let us into the Mystery of it, What were these hard Conditions? Yes Madam *says* Robin, I had done it before now, if the *Teazers* here had not worried me by way of Interruption: The Conditions are that I bring my Father and you to Consent to it, and without that, she protests she will never see me more upon that Head; and these Conditions *as I said,* I suppose I shall never be able to Grant; I hope my warm Sisters will be Answer'd now, and Blush a little; if not, I have no more to say till I hear farther.

This Answer was surprizing to them all, tho' less to the Mother, because of what I had said to her; as to the Daughters they stood Mute a great while; but the Mother said with some Passion, WELL, I had heard this before, *but I cou'd not believe it;* but if it is so, then we have all done BETTY wrong, and she has behav'd better than I ever expected: Nay, *says the eldest Sister,* if it is so, she has acted Handsomely indeed: I confess *says the Mother,* it was none of her Fault, if he was Fool enough to take a Fancy to her; but to give such an Answer to him shews more Respect to your Father and me than I can tell how to Express; I shall value the Girl the better for it as long as I know her. But I shall not *says* Robin, unless you will give your Consent: I'll consider of that a while *says the Mother;* I assure *you,* if there were not some other Objections in the way, this Conduct of hers would go a great way to bring me to Consent: I wish it would go quite thro' with it, *says* Robin; if you had as much thought about making me Easie, as you have about making me Rich, you would soon Consent to it.

Why *Robin, says the Mother again,* Are you really in Earnest? Would you so fain have her as you pretend? Really Madam *says* Robin, I think 'tis hard you should Question me upon that Head after all I have said: I won't say that I will have her, how can I resolve that point when you see I cannot have her without your Consent? besides I am not bound to Marry at all: But this I will say, I am in Earnest in, that I will never have any body else if I can help it; so you may Determine for me; *Betty* or no Body is the Word; and the Question which of the Two shall be in your Breast to decide Madam; provided only, that *my good humour'd Sisters here, may have no Vote in it.*

All this was dreadful to me, for the Mother began to yield, and *Robin* press'd her Home in it: On the other hand, she advised with the eldest Son, and he used all the Arguments in the World to persuade her to Consent; alledging his Brothers passionate Love for me, and my generous Regard to the Family in refusing my own Advantages upon such a nice point of Honour, and a thousand such Things: And as to the Father, he was a Man in a hurry of publick Affairs and getting Money, seldom at Home, thoughtful of the main Chance; but left all those Things to his Wife.

You may easily believe, that when the Plot was thus, as *they thought* broke out, and that every one thought they knew how Things were carried: It was not so Difficult or so Dangerous for the elder Brother, who no body suspected of any thing, to have a freer Access to me than before: Nay the Mother, *which was just as he wish'd,* Propos'd it to him to Talk with Mrs *Betty;* for it may be Son *said she,* you may see farther into the Thing than I; and see if you think she has been so Positive as *Robin* says she has been, or no. This was as well as he could wish, and he as it were yielding to Talk with me at his Mother's Request, She brought me to him into her own Chamber, told me her Son had some Business with me at her Request, and desir'd me to be very Sincere with him; and then she left us together, and he went and shut the Door after her.

He came back to me, and took me in his Arms and kiss'd me very Tenderly; but told me, he had a long Discourse to hold with me, and it was now come to that Crisis, that I should make my self Happy or Miserable, as long as I Liv'd: That the Thing was now gone so far, that if I could not comply with his Desire, we should be both Ruin'd: Then he told me the whole Story between *Robin,* as he call'd him, and his Mother and Sisters and himself;

as it is above: And now dear Child, *says he,* consider what it will be to Marry a Gentleman of a good Family, in good Circumstances, and with the Consent of the whole House, and to enjoy all that the World can give you: And what on the other Hand, to be sunk into the dark Circumstances of a Woman that has lost her Reputation; and that tho' I shall be a private Friend to you while I live, yet as I shall be suspected always, so you will be afraid to see me, and I shall be afraid to own you.

He gave me no time to Reply, but went on with me thus: What has happen'd between us Child, so long as we both agree to do so, may be buried and forgotten: I shall always be your sincere Friend, without any Inclination to nearer Intimacy, when you *become* my Sister; and we shall have all the honest part of Conversation without any Reproaches between us of having done amiss: I beg of you to consider it, and do not stand in the way of your own Safety and Prosperity; and to satisfie you that I am Sincere, *added he,* I here offer you 500 *l.* in Money, *to* make you some Amends for the Freedoms I have taken with you, which we shall look upon as some of the Follies of our Lives, which 'tis hop'd we may Repent of.

He spoke this in so much more moving Terms than it is possible for me to Express, and with so much greater force of Argument than I can repeat, that I only recommend it to those who Read the Story, to suppose, that as he held me above an Hour and Half in that Discourse, so he answer'd all my Objections, and fortified his Discourse with all the Arguments, that human Wit and Art could Devise.

I cannot say however, that any thing he said, made Impression enough upon me, so as to give me any thought of the Matter, till he told me at last very plainly, that if I refus'd, he was sorry to add, that he could never go on with me in that Station as we stood before; that tho' he Lov'd me as well as ever, and that I was as agreeable to him, as ever; yet, Sense of Virtue had not so far forsaken him, as to suffer him to lye with a Woman, that his

Brother Courted to make his Wife; and if he took his leave of me, with a denial in this Affair, whatever he might do for me in the Point of support, grounded on his first Engagement of maintaining me, yet he would not have me be surpriz'd, that he was oblig'd to tell me, he could not allow himself to see me any more; and that indeed I could not expect it of him.

I receiv'd this last part with some tokens of Surprize and Disorder, and had much ado, to avoid sinking down, for indeed I lov'd him to an Extravagance not easie to imagine; but he perceiv'd my Disorder; he entreated me to consider seriously of it, assur'd me that it was the only way to Preserve our mutual Affection; that in this Station we might love as Friends, with the utmost Passion, and with a love of Relation untainted, free from our just Reproaches, and free from other Peoples Suspicions; that he should ever acknowledge his happiness owing to me; that he would be Debtor to me as long as he liv'd, and would be paying that Debt as long as he had Breath; Thus he wrought me up, in short, to a kind of Hesitation in the Matter; having the Dangers on one Side represented in lively Figures, and indeed heightn'd by my Imagination of being turn'd out to the wide World, a meer cast off Whore, *for it was no less,* and perhaps expos'd as such; with little to provide for myself; with no Friend, no Acquaintance in the whole World, out *of that Town,* and there I could not pretend to Stay; all this terrify'd me to the last Degree, and he took care upon all Occasions to lay it home to me, in the worst Colours that it could be possible to be drawn in; on the other Hand, he fail'd not to set forth the easy prosperous Life which I was going to live.

He answer'd all that I could object from Affection, and from former Engagements, with telling me the Necessity that, was before us of taking other Measures now; and as to his Promises of Marriage, the nature of things *he said,* had put an End to that, by the probability of my being his Brothers Wife, before the time to which his Promises all referr'd.

Thus in a Word, I may say, he Reason'd me out of my Reason;

he conquer'd all my Arguments, and I began to see a Danger that I was in, which I had not consider'd of before, and that was of being drop'd by both of them, and left alone in the World to shift for myself.

This, and his perswasion, at length Prevail'd with me to Consent, tho' with so much Reluctance, that it was easie to see I should go to Church, like a Bear to the Stake; I had some little Apprehensions about me too, lest my new Spouse, who by the way, I had not the least Affection for, should be skilful enough to Challenge me on another Account, upon our first coming to Bed together; but whether he did it with Design or not, I know not, but his elder Brother took care to make him very much Fuddled before he went to Bed, so that I had the Satisfaction of a drunken Bedfellow the first Night: How he did it I know not, but I concluded that he certainly contriv'd it that his Brother might be able to make no Judgment of the difference between a Maid and a married Woman; nor did he ever Entertain any Notions of it, or disturb his Thoughts about it.

I should go back a little here, to where I left off; the elder Brother having thus manag'd me, his next business was to Manage his Mother, and he never left till he had brought her to acquiesce, and be passive in the thing; Even without acquainting the Father, other than by Post Letters: So that she consented to our Marrying privately, and leaving her to manage the Father afterwards.

Then he Cajol'd with his Brother, and perswaded him what Service he had done him, and how he had brought his Mother to Consent, which *tho' True,* was not indeed done to serve him, but to serve himself; but thus diligently did he cheat him, and had the Thanks of a faithful Friend for shifting off his Whore into his Brothers Arms for a Wife. So certainly does Interest banish all manner of Affection, and so naturally do Men give up Honour and Justice, Humanity, and even Christianity, to secure themselves.

I must now come back to Brother *Robin,* as we always call'd him, who having got his Mother's Consent *as above,* came big with the News to me, and told me, the whole Story of it, with a Sincerity so visible, that I must confess it griev'd me that I must be the Instrument to abuse so honest a Gentleman; but there was no Remedy; he would have me, and I was not oblig'd to tell him, that I was his Brother's Whore, tho' I had no other way to put him off; so I came gradually into it, to his Satisfaction, and behold, we were Married.

Modesty forbids me to reveal the Secrets of the Marriage Bed, but nothing could have happen'd more suitable to my Circumstances than that, *as above,* my Husband was so Fuddled when he came to Bed, that he could not remember in the Morning, whether he had had any Conversation with me or no, and I was oblig'd to tell him *he had,* tho' in reality *he had not,* that I might be sure he could make no enquiry about any thing else.

It concerns the Story in hand very little to enter into the farther particulars of the Family, or of myself, for the five Years that I liv'd with this Husband; only to observe that I had two Children by him, and that at the end of five Year he Died: He had been really a very good Husband to me, and we liv'd very agreeably together; But as he had not receiv'd much from them, and had in the little time he liv'd acquir'd no great Matters, so my Circumstances were not great; nor was I much mended by the Match: Indeed I had preserv'd the elder Brother's Bonds to me, to pay me 500 *l.* which he offer'd me for my Consent to Marry his Brother; and this, with what I had saved of the Money he formerly gave me, and about as much more by my Husband, left me a Widow with about 1200 *l.* in my Pocket.

My two Children were indeed taken happily off of my Hands by my Husband's Father and Mother, and that by the way was all they got by Mrs *Betty.*

I confess I was not suitably affected with the loss of my Husband; nor indeed can I say that I ever Lov'd him as I ought to have done, or as was proportionable to the good Usage I had from him, for he was a tender, kind, good humour'd Man as any

Woman could desire; but his Brother being so always in my sight, *at least,* while we were in the Country, was a continual Snare to me; and I never was in Bed with my Husband, but I wish'd my self in the Arms of his Brother; and tho' his Brother never offer'd me the least Kindness that way, after our Marriage, but carried it just as a Brother ought to do; yet, it was impossible for me to do so to him: In short, I committed Adultery and Incest with him every Day in my Desires, which without doubt, was as effectually Criminal in the Nature of the Guilt, as if I had actually done it.

Before my Husband Died, his elder Brother was Married, and we being then remov'd to *London,* were written to by the old Lady to come and be at the Wedding; my Husband went, but I pretended Indisposition, and that I could not possibly Travel, so I staid behind; for in short, I could not bear the sight of his being given to another Woman, tho' I knew I was never to have him my self.

I was now *as above,* left loose to the World, and being still Young and Handsome, as every body said of me, *and I assure you I thought my self so,* and with a tollerable Fortune in my Pocket, I put no small value upon my self: I was Courted by several very considerable Tradesmen, and particularly, very warmly by one, a *Linnen-Draper,* at whose House after my Husband's Death I took a Lodging, his Sister being my Acquaintance; here I had all the Liberty and all the Opportunity to be Gay, and appear in Company that I could desire; my Landlord's Sister being one of the Maddest, Gayest things alive, and not so much Mistress of her Virtue, as I thought at first she had been: She brought me into a World of wild Company, and even brought home several Persons, *such as she lik'd well enough to Gratifie,* to see her pretty Widow, *so she was pleas'd to call me,* and that Name I got in a little time in Publick; now as Fame and Fools make an Assembly, I was here wonderfully Caress'd; had abundance of Admirers, and such as call'd themselves *Lovers;* but I found not one fair Proposal among them all; as for their common Design, that I understood too well to be drawn into any more Snares of that Kind: The Case was alter'd with me, I had Money in my Pocket, and had nothing to say to them: I had been trick'd once by *that Cheat call'd* LOVE, but the Game was over; I was resolv'd now to be Married or Nothing, and to be well Married or not at all.

I lov'd the Company indeed of Men of Mirth and Wit, Men of Gallantry and Figure, and was often entertain'd with such, as I was also with others; but I found by just Observation, that the brightest Men came upon the dullest Errand, *that is to say,* the Dullest as to what I aim'd at; on the other Hand, those who came with the best Proposals were the Dullest and most disagreeable Part of the World: I Was not averse to a Tradesman, but then I would have a Tradesman forsooth, that was something of a Gentleman too; that when my Husband had a mind to carry me to the Court, or to the Play, he ought become a Sword, and look as like a Gentleman, as another Man; and not be one that had the mark of his Apron strings upon his Coat, or the mark of his Hat upon his Perriwig; that should look as if he Was set on to his Sword, when his Sword was put on to him, and that carried his Trade in his Countenance.

Well, at last I found this amphibious Creature, this *Landwater-thing* call'd, *a Gentleman-Tradesman;* and as a just Plague upon my Folly, I was catch'd in the very Snare, which *as I might say,* I laid for my self; I *say laid for my self,* for I was not Trepan'd I confess, but I betray'd my self.

This was a *Draper* too, for tho' my Comrade would have brought me to a Bargain with her Brother, yet when it came to the Point, it was it seems for a Mistress, not a Wife, and I kept true to this Notion, that a Woman should never be kept for a Mistress, that had Money to keep her self.

Thus my Pride, not my Principle, my Money, not my Virtue, kept me Honest; tho' as it prov'd, I found I had much better have been Sold by my *She Comrade* to her Brother, than have Sold my self as I did to a Tradesman that was Rake, Gentleman, Shop keeper, and Beggar all together.

But I was hurried on (by my Fancy to a Gentleman) to Ruin my self in the grossest Manner that ever Woman did; for my new Husband coming to a lump of Money at once, fell into such a profusion of Expence, that all I had, and all he had before, if he had any thing worth mentioning, would not have held it out above one Year.

He was very fond of me for about a quarter of a Year, and what I got by that, was, that I had the pleasure of seeing a great deal of my Money spent upon my self, and as I may say, had some of the spending it too: Come, my dear, *says he to me one Day,* Shall we go and take a turn into the Country for about a Week? Ay, my Dear, *says I,* Whither would you go? I care not whither *says he,* but I have a mind to look like Quality for a Week; we'll go to OXFORD *says he:* How *says I,* shall we go, I am no Horse Woman, and 'tis too far for a Coach; too far *says he,* no Place is too far for a Coach and Six: If I carry you out, you shall Travel like a Dutchess; hum *says I,* my Dear 'tis a Frolick, but if you have a mind to it I don't care. Well the time was appointed, we had a rich Coach, very good Horses, a Coachman, Postilion, and two Footmen in very good Liveries; a Gentleman on Horseback, and a Page with a Feather in his Hat upon another Horse; The Servants all call'd him my Lord, and the Inn-Keepers you may be sure did the like, and I was *her Honour,* the Countess; and thus we Travel'd to OXFORD, and a very pleasant Journey we had; for, give him his due, not a Beggar alive knew better how to be a Lord than my Husband: We saw all the Rareties at OXFORD, talk'd with two or three Fellows of Colleges, about putting out a young Nephew, that was left to his Lordship's Care, to the University, and of their being his Tutors; we diverted our selves with bantering several other poor Scholars, with hopes of being at least his Lordship's Chaplains and putting on a Scarf; and thus having liv'd like Quality indeed, as to Expence, we went away for *Northampton,* and in a word, in about twelve Days ramble came Home again, to the Tune of about 93 *l* Expence.

Vanity is the perfection of a Fop; my Husband had this Excellence, that he valued nothing of Expence, and as his History you may be sure, has very little weight in it; 'tis enough to tell you, that in about two Years and a Quarter he Broke, and was not so happy to get over into the Mint, but got into a *Spunging-House,* being Arrested in an Action too heavy for him to give Bail to, so he sent for me to come to him.

It was no surprize to me, for I had foreseen *sometime* that all was going to Wreck, and had been taking care to reserve something if I could, *tho' it was not much* for myself: But when he sent for me, he behav'd much better than I expected, and told me plainly, he had played the Fool and suffer'd himself to be Surpriz'd which he might have prevented; that now he foresaw he could not stand it, and therefore he would have me go Home, and in the Night take away every thing I had in the House of any Value and secure it; and after that, he told me that if I could get away 100 *l.* or 200 *l.* in Goods out of the Shop, I should do it, only *says he,* let me know nothing of it, neither what you take, or whither you carry it; for as for me *says he,* I am resolv'd to get out of this House and be gone; and if you never hear of me more, my Dear, *says he,* I wish you well; I am only sorry for the Injury I have done you: He said some very handsome Things to me indeed at Parting; for *I told* you he was a *Gentleman,* and that was all the benefit I had of his being so; that he used, me very handsomely, and with good Manners upon all Occasions, even to the last, only spent all I had, and left me to Rob the Creditors for something to Subsist on.

However, I did as he bade me, *that you may be sure,* and having thus taken my leave of him, I never saw him more; for he found means to break out of the Bailiff's House that Night or the next, and got over into France, and for the rest, the Creditors scrambl'd for it as well as they could: How I knew not, for I could come at no Knowledge of any thing more than this, that he came Home about three a Clock in the Morning, caus'd the rest of his Goods to be remov'd into the *Mint,* and the Shop to be shut up; and having rais'd what Money he could get together, he got over as I said to *France,* from whence I had one or two Letters from him, and no more.

I did not see him when he came Home, for he having given me such Instructions as above, and I having made the best of my Time, I had no more Business back again at the House, not knowing but I might have been stop'd there by the Creditors; for a *Commission of Bankrupt,* being soon after Issued, they might have stop'd me by Orders from the *Commissioners:* But my Husband having so dextrously got out of the Bailiff's House by letting himself down in a most desperate Manner from almost the top of the House, to the top of another Building, and leaping from thence which was almost two Stories, and which was enough indeed to have broken his Neck: He came home and got away his Goods, before the Creditors could come to Seize, *that is to say,* before they could get out the Commission, and be ready to send their Officers to take Possession.

My Husband was so civil to me, *for still I say, he was much of a Gentleman,* that in the first Letter he wrote me from *France,* he let me know where he had Pawn'd 20 Pieces of fine *Holland* for 30 *l.* which were really worth above 90 *l.* and enclos'd me the Token, and an order for the taking them up, paying the Money, which I did, and made in time above 100 *l.* of them, having Leisure to cut them and sell them, some and some, to private Families, as opportunity offer'd.

However with all this, and all that I had secur'd before, I found upon casting things up, my Case was very much alter'd, and my Fortune much lessen'd, for including the Hollands, and a parcel of fine Muslins, which I carry'd off before, and some Plate, and other things; Hound I could hardly muster up 500 *l.* and my Condition was very odd, for tho' I had no Child, (I *had had one by my Gentleman* Draper, *but it was buried,*) yet I was a Widow bewitched, I had a Husband, and no Husband, and I could not pretend to Marry again, tho' I knew well enough my Husband would never see *England* any more, if he liv'd fifty Years: *Thus I say,* I was limitted from Marriage, what Offer soever might be made me: and I had not one Friend to advise with, in the Condition I was in, at least not one I durst Trust the Secret of my Circumstances to, for if the Commissioners were to have been inform'd where I was, I should have been fetch'd up and examin'd upon Oath, and all I had sav'd be taken away from me.

Upon these Apprehensions the first thing I did, was to go quite out of my Knowledge, and go by another Name: This I did effectually, for I went into the *Mint* too, took Lodgings in a very private Place, drest me up in the Habit of a Widow, and call'd myself *Mrs Flanders.*

Here, however I conceal'd myself, and tho' my new Acquaintances knew nothing of me, yet I soon got a great deal of Company about me; and whether it be that Women are scarce among the Sorts of People that generally are to be found there, or that some Consolation in the Miseries of the Place are more Requisite than on other Occasions, I soon found an agreeable Woman was exceedingly valuable among the Sons of Affliction there; and that those that wanted Money to pay Half a Crown in the Pound to their Creditors, and that run in Debt at the Sign of the *Bull* for their Dinners, would yet find Money for a Supper, if they lik'd the Woman.

However, I kept myself Safe yet, tho' I began like my Lord *Rochester's* Mistress, that lov'd his Company, but would not admit him farther, to have the Scandal of a Whore, without the Joy; and upon this score tir'd with the Place and indeed with the Company too, I began to think of Removing.

It was indeed a Subject of strange Reflection to me to see Men who were overwhelm'd in perplex'd Circumstances, who were reduc'd some Degrees below being Ruin'd; whose Families were Objects of their own Terror and other Peoples Charity; yet while a Penny lasted, nay, even beyond it, endeavouring to drown their Sorrow in their Wickedness; heaping up more Guilt upon themselves, labouring to forget former things, which now it was the proper time to remember, making more Work for Repentance, and Sinning on, as a Remedy for Sin past.

But it is none of my Talent to preach; these Men were too wicked, even for me; there was something horrid and absurd in their way of Sinning, for it was all a Force even upon themselves; they did not only act against Conscience, but against Nature; they put a Rape upon their Temper to drown the Reflections, which their Circumstances continually gave them; and nothing was more easie than to see how Sighs would interrupt their Songs, and paleness, and anguish sit upon their Brows, in spite of the forc'd Smiles they put on; nay, sometimes it would break out at their very Mouths when they had parted with their Money for a lewd Treat, or a wicked Embrace; I have heard them, turning about, fetch a deep Sigh, and cry *what a Dog am I!* Well *Betty,* my Dear, I'll drink thy Health tho', *meaning the Honest Wife,* that perhaps had not a Half a Crown for herself, and three or four Children: The next Morning they are at their Penitentials again, and perhaps the poor weeping Wife comes over to him, either brings him some Account of what his Creditors are doing, and how she and the Children are turn'd out of Doors, or some other dreadful News; and this adds to his self Reproaches; but when he has Thought and Por'd on it till he is almost Mad, having no principles to Support him, nothing within him or above him, to Comfort him; but finding it, all Darkness on every Side, he flyes to the same Relief again, (*viz.*) to Drink it away, Debauch it away, and a falling Into Company of Men in just the same Condition with himself, he repeats the Crime, and thus he goes every Day one Step onward of his way to Destruction.

I was not wicked enough for such Fellows as these *yet;* on the contrary, I began to consider here *very seriously* what I had to do, how things stood with me, and what Course I ought to take: I knew I had no Friends, no not one Friend or Relation in the World; and that little I had left apparently wasted, which when it was gone, I saw nothing but Misery and Starving was before me: Upon these Considerations, I say, and fill'd with Horror at the Place I was in, and the dreadful Objects, which I had always before me, *I resolv'd to be gone.*

I had made an Acquaintance with a very sober good sort of a Woman, who was a Widow too like me, but in better Circumstances; her Husband had been a Captain of a Merchant Ship, and havin'g had the Misfortune to be Cast away coming Home on a Voyage from the *West-Indies,* which would have been very profitable, if he had come safe, was so reduc'd by the Loss, that tho' he had saved his Life then, it broke his Heart, and kill'd him afterwards; and his Widow being persued by the Creditors was forc'd to take Shelter in the *Mint:* She soon made things up with the help of Friends, and was at Liberty again; and finding that I rather was there to be conceal'd, than by any particular Prosecutions, and finding also that I agreed with her, or *rather she with me* in a just Abhorrence of the Place and of the Company, she invited me to go Home with her, till I could put myself in some posture of settling in the World to my Mind; withal telling me that it was ten to one, but some good Captain of a Ship might take a Fancy to me, and Court me, in that part of the Town where she liv'd.

I accepted her Offer, and was with her Half a Year, and should have been longer, but in that interval what she propos'd to me happen'd to herself, and she marry'd very much to her Advantage; but whose Fortune soever was upon the Encrease, mine seem'd to be upon the Wane, and I found nothing present, except two or three Boatswains, or such Fellows, but as for the Commanders they were generally of two Sorts. I. Such as having good Business, *that is to say,* a good Ship, resolv'd not to Marry but with Advantage, that is, with a good Fortune. Such as being out of Employ, wanted a Wife to help them to a Ship, I mean. (1). A Wife, who having some Money could enable them to hold, as they call it, a good part of a Ship themselves, so to encourage Owners to come in; Or, (2.) A Wife who if she had not Money, had Friends who were concern'd in Shipping, and so could help to put the young Man into a good Ship, which to them is as good as a Portion, and neither of these was my Case; so I look'd like one that was to *lye on Hand.*

This Knowledge I soon learnt by Experience, (*viz.*) That the State of things was altered as to Matrimony, and that I was not to expect at *London,* what I had found in the Country; that Marriages were here the Consequences of politick Schemes for forming Interests, and, carrying on Business, and that LOVE had no Share, or but very little in the Matter.

That as my Sister in Law at *Colchester* had said, Beauty, Wit, Manners, Sence, good Humour, good Behaviour, Education, Virtue, Piety, or any other Qualification, whether of Body or Mind, had no power to recommend: That Money only made a Woman agreeable: That Men chose Mistresses indeed by the gust of their Affection, and it was requisite to a Whore to be Handsome, well shap'd, have a good Mien, and a graceful Behaviour; but that for a Wife, no Deformity would shock the Fancy, no ill Qualities, the Judgement; the Money was the thing; the Portion was neither crooked or Monstrous, but the Money was always agreeable, whatever the Wife was.

On the other Hand, as the Market run very Unhappily on the Mens side, I found the Women had lost the Privilege of saying No, that it was a Favour now for a Woman to have THE QUESTION ask'd, and if any young Lady had so much Arrogance as to Counterfeit a Negative, she never had the Opportunity given her of denying twice; much less of Recovering that false Step, and accepting what she had but seem'd to decline: The Men had such Choice every where, that the Case of the Women was very unhappy; for they seem'd to Ply at every Door; and if the Man was by great Chance refus'd at one House, he was sure to be receiv'd at the next.

Besides this, I observ'd that the Men made no scruple to set themselves out, and to go a Fortune Hunting, *as they call it,* when they had really no Fortune themselves to Demand it, or Merit to deserve it; and That they carry'd it so high, that a Woman was scarce allow'd to enquire after the Character or Estate of the Person that pretended to her. This I had an Example of in a young Lady at the next House to me, and with whom I had Contracted an intimacy; she was Courted by a young Captain, and though she had near 2000 *l.* to her Fortune, she did but enquire of some of his Neighbours about his Character, his Morals, or Substance; and he took Occasion at the next Visit to let her know, truly, that he took it very ill, and that he should not give her the Trouble of his Visits any more: I heard of it, and as I had begun my Acquaintance with her, I went to see her upon it: She enter'd into a close Conversation with me about it, and unbosom'd herself very freely; I perceiv'd presently that tho' she thought herself very ill us'd, yet she had no power to resent it, and was exceedingly Piqu'd that she had lost him, and particularly that another of less Fortune had gain'd him.

I fortify'd her Mind against such a Meanness, *as I call'd it;* I told her, that as low as I was in the World, I would have despis'd a Man that should think I ought to take him upon his own Recommendation only, without having the liberty to inform myself of his Fortune, and of his Character; also I *told her,* that as she had a good Fortune, she had no need to stoop to the Dissaster of the times; that it was enough that the Men could insult us that had but little Money to recommend us, but if she suffer'd such an Affront to pass upon her without Resenting it, she would be render'd low-priz'd upon all Occasions, and would be the Contempt of all the Women in that part of the Town; that a Woman can never want an Opportunity to be Reveng'd of a Man that has us'd her ill, and that there were ways enough to humble such a Fellow as that, or else certainly Women were the most unhappy Creatures in the World.

I found she was very well pleas'd With the Discourse, and she told me seriously that she would be very glad to make him sensible of her just Resentment, and either to bring him on again, or have the Satisfaction of her Revenge being as publick as possible.

I told her, that if she would take my Advice, I would tell her how she should obtain her Wishes in both those things; and that I would engage I would bring the Man to her Door again, and make him beg to be let in: *She smil'd at that,* and soon let me see that if he came to her Door, her Resentment was not so great as to give her leave to let him stand long there.

However, she lissened very willingly to my offer of Advice; so *I told her* that the first thing she ought to do, was a piece of Justice to herself; namely, that whereas she had been told by several People, that he had reported among the Ladies that he had left her, and pretended to give the Advantage of the Negative to himself; she should take care to have it well spread among the Women, which she could not fail of an Opportunity to do in a Neighbourhood, so addicted to Family News, as that she liv'd in was, that she had enquired into his Circumstances, and found he was not the Man as to Estate he pretended to be: Let them be told Madam, *said I,* that you had been well inform'd that he was not the Man that you expected, and that you thought it was not safe to meddle with him, that you heard he was of an ill Temper, and that he boasted how he had us'd the Women ill upon many Occasions, and that particularly he was Debauch'd in his Morals, etc. The last of which indeed had some Truth in it; but at the same time, I did not find that she seem'd to like him much the worst for that part.

As I had put this into her Head, she came most readily into it; immediately she went to Work to find Instruments, and she had very little difficulty in the Search, for telling her Story in general to a Couple of Gossips in the Neighbourhood, it was the Chat of the Tea Table all over that part of the Town, and I met with it where ever I visited: Also, as it was known that I was Acquainted with the young Lady herself, my Opinion was ask'd very often, and I confirm'd it with all the necessary Aggravations, and set out his Character in the blackest Colours; but then as a piece of secret Intelligence, I added, as what the other Gossips knew nothing of (*viz.*) That I had heard he was in very bad Circumstances; that he was under a Necessity of a Fortune to support his Interest with the Owners of the Ship he Commanded: That his own Part was not paid for, and if it was not paid quickly his Owners would put him out of the Ship, and his Chief Mate was likely to Command it, who offer'd to buy that Part which the Captain had promis'd to take.

I added, for I confess I was heartily piqu'd at the Rogue, as *I call'd him,* that I had heard a Rumour too, that he had a Wife alive at *Plymouth,* and another in the *West-Indies,* a thing which they all knew was not very uncommon for such kind of Gentlemen.

This work'd as we both desir'd it, for presently the young Lady at next Door, *who had a Father and Mother that Govern'd both her and her Fortune,* was shut up, and her Father forbid him the House: Also in one Place more where he went, the Woman had the Courage, *however strange it was,* to say No, and he could try no where but he was Reproached with his Pride, and that he pretended not to give the 'Women leave to enquire into his Character, *and the like.*

Well, by this time he began to be sensible of his mistake, and having allarm'd all the Women on that side the Water, he went over to *Ratcliff,* and got access to some of the Ladies there; but tho' the young Women there too, were according to the Fate of the Day, pretty willing to be ask'd, yet such was his ill luck, that his Character follow'd him over the Water, and his good Name was much the same there, as it was on our side; so that tho' he might have had Wives enough, yet it did not happen among the Women that had good Fortunes, which was what he wanted.

But this was not all; she very ingeniously manag'd another thing her self, for she got a young Gentleman, who was a Relation, and was indeed a marry'd Man, to come and visit her Two or Three times a Week in a very fine Chariot and good Liveries, and her Two Agents and I also, presently spread a Report all over, that this Gentleman came to Court her; that he was a Gentleman of a Thousand Pounds a Year, and that he was fallen in Love with her, and that she was going to her Aunt's in the City, because it was inconvenient for the Gentleman to come to her with his Coach in *Redriff,* the Streets being so narrow and difficult.

This took immediately; the Captain was laugh'd at in all Companies, and was ready to hang himself; he tryed all the ways possible to come at her again, and wrote the most passionate Letters to her in the World, excusing his former Rashness, and in short, by great Application, obtained leave to wait on her again, as *he said,* to clear his Reputation.

At this meeting she had her full Revenge of him; for *she told him* she wondred what he took her to be, that she should admit any Man to a Treaty of so much Consequence as that of Marriage, without enquiring very well into his Circumstances; that if he thought she was to be huff'd into Wedlock, and that she was in the same Circumstances which her Neighbours might be in, (*viz.*) to take up with the first good Christian that came, he was mistaken; that in a word his Character was really bad, or he was very ill beholding to his Neighbours; and that unless he could clear up some Points, in which she had justly been Prejudiced, she had no more to say to him, but to do herself Justice, and give him the Satisfaction of knowing that she was not afraid to say NO, either to him, or any Man else.

With that she told him what she had heard, or *rather rais'd herself by my means, of his Character;* his not having paid for the Part he pretended to Own of the Ship he Commanded; of the Resolution of his Owners to put him out of the Command, and to put his Mate in his stead; and of the Scandal rais'd on his Morals; his having been reproach'd with such and such Women; and his having a Wife at *Plymouth* and in the *West-Indies, and the like;* and she ask'd him, whether he could deny that she had good Reason, if these things were not clear'd up, to refuse him, and in the mean time to insist upon having Satisfaction in Points so significant as they were.

He was so confounded at her Discourse that he could not answer a word, and she almost began to believe that all was true, by his disorder, tho' at the same time she knew that she had been the raiser of all those Reports herself.

After some time he recover'd himself a little, and from that time became the most humble, the most modest, and the most importunate Man alive in his Courtship.

She carried her jest on a great way, she ask'd him, if he thought she was so at her last shift, that she could or ought to bear such Treatment, and if he did not see that she did not want those who thought it worth their while to come farther to her than he did, meaning the Gentleman who she had brought to visit her by way of sham.

She brought him by these tricks to submit to all possible measures to satisfie her, as well of his Circumstances, as of his Behaviour. He brought her undeniable Evidence of his having paid for his part of the Ship; he brought her Certificates from his Owners, that the Report of their intending to remove him from the Command of the Ship and put his chief Mate in, was false and groundless; in short, he was quite the reverse of what he was before.

Thus I convinc'd her, that if the Men made their Advantage of *our* Sex in the Affair of Marriage, upon the supposition of there being such Choice to be had, and of the Women being so easie, it was only owing to this, that the Women wanted Courage to maintain their Ground, and to play their Part; and that according to my Lord *Rochester,*

> A Woman's *ne'er so ruin'd but she can*
> Revenge herself on her undoer, Man.

After these things, this young Lady played her part so well, that tho' she resolved to have him, and that indeed having him was the main bent of her design, yet she made his obtaining her be TO HIM the most difficult thing in the World; and this she did, not by a haughty Reserv'd Carriage, but by a just Policy, turning the Tables upon him, and playing back upon him his own Game; for as he pretended by a kind of lofty Carriage, to place himself above the occasion of a Character, and to make enquiring into his Character a kind of an affront to him, she broke with him upon that Subject; and at the same time that she made him submit to all possible enquiry after his Affairs, she apparently shut the Door against his looking into her own.

It was enough to him to obtain her for a Wife, as to what she had, she told him plainly that as he knew her Circumstances, it was but just she should know his; and tho' at the same time he had only known her Circumstances by common Fame, yet he had made so many Protestations of his Passion for her, that he could ask no more but her Hand to his grand Request, *and the like ramble according to the Custom of Lovers:* In short, he left himself no room to ask any more questions about her Estate, and she took the advantage of it like a prudent Woman, for she plac'd part of her Fortune so in Trustees, without letting him know any thing of it, that it was quite out of his reach, and made him be very well content with the rest.

It is true she was pretty well besides, that is to say, she had about *1400 l.* in Money, which she gave him, and the other, after some time, she brought to light, as a perquisite to her self; which he was to accept as a mighty Favour, seeing though it was not to be his, it might ease him in the Article of her particular Expences; and I must add, that by this Conduct the Gentleman himself became not only the more humble in his Applications to her to obtain her, but also was much the more an obliging Husband to her when he had her: I cannot but remind the Ladies here how much they place themselves below the common Station of a Wife, which if I may be allow'd not to be Partial is low enough already; *I say* they place themselves below their common Station, and prepare their own Mortifications, by their submitting so to be insulted by the Men before-hand, which I confess I see no Necessity of.

This Relation may serve therefore to let the Ladies see that the Advantage is not so much on the other Side as the Men think it is; and tho' it may be true that the Men have but too much Choice among us, and that some Women may be found who will dishonour themselves, be Cheap, and Easy to come at, and will scarce wait to be ask'd; yet if they will have Women, *as I may say,* worth having, they may find them as uncomeatable as ever; and that those that are otherwise, are a Sort of People that have such Defficiencies, *when had,* as rather recommend the Ladies that are Difficult than encourage the Men to go on with their easie Courtship, and expect Wives equally valluable that will come at first call.

Nothing is more certain than that the Ladies always gain of the Men by keeping their Ground, and letting their pretended Lovers see they can Resent being slighted, and that they are not affraid of saying No. They, I observe insult us mightily with telling us of the Number of Women; that the Wars and the Sea, and Trade, and other Incidents have carried the Men so much away, that there is no Proportion between the Numbers of the Sexes, and therefore the Women have the Disadvantage; but I am far from Granting that the Number of the Women is so great, or the Number of the Men so small; but if they will have me tell the Truth, the Disadvantage of the Women is a terrible Scandal upon the Men, and it lyes here, and here only; *Namely,* that the Age is so Wicked, and the Sex so Debauch'd, that in short the Number of such Men, as an honest Woman ought to meddle with, is small indeed, and it is but here and there that a Man is to be found who is fit for a Woman to venture upon.

But the Consequence even of that too amounts to no more than this; that Women ought to be the more Nice, For how do we know the just Character of the Man that makes the offer? To say that the Woman should be the more easie on this Occasion, is to say we should be the forwarder to venture, because of the greatness of the Danger, which in my way of Reasoning is very absurd.

On the contrary, the Women have ten Thousand times the more Reason to be wary and backward, by how much the hazard of being betray'd is the greater; and would the Ladies consider this, and act the wary Part, they would discover every Cheat that offer'd; for, *in short,* the Lives of very few Men now a-Days will bear a Character; and if the Ladies do but make a little Enquiry, they will soon be able to distinguish the Men and deliver themselves: As for Women that do not think their own Safety worth their Thought, that impatient of their present State, resolve *as they call it* to take the first good Christian that comes, that run into Matrimony, as a Horse rushes into the Battle, I can say nothing to them, but this, that they are a Sort of Ladies that are to be pray'd for among the rest of distemper'd People, and to me they look like People that venture their whole Estates in a Lottery 'where there is a Hundred Thousand Blanks to one Prize.

No Man of common Sense will value a Woman the less for not giving up herself at the first Attack; or for not accepting his Proposal without enquiring into his Person or Character; on the contrary, he must think her the weakest of all Creatures in the World, as the Rate of Men now goes; In short, he must have a very contemptible Opinion of her Capacities, nay, even of her Understanding, that having but one Cast for her Life, shall cast that Life away at once, and make Matrimony like Death, be *a Leap in the Dark.*

I would fain have the Conduct of my Sex a little Regulated in this particular, which is the Thing, in which of all the parts of Life, I think at this Time we suffer most in: 'Tis nothing but lack of Courage, the fear of not being Marry'd at all, and of that frightful State of Life, call'd *an old Maid;* of which I have a Story to tell by itself: This I say, is the Woman's Snare; but would the Ladies once but get above that Fear and manage rightly, they would more certainly avoid it by standing their Ground, in a Case so absolutely Necessary to their Felicity, than by exposing themselves as they do; and if they did not Marry so soon as they may do otherwise, they would make themselves amends by Marrying safer; she is always Married too soon who gets a bad Husband, and she is never Married too late who gets a good one: In a word, there is no Woman, *Deformity, or lost Reputation excepted,* but if she manages well, may be Marry'd safely one time or other; but if she precipitates herself, it is ten Thousand to one but she is undone.

But I come now to my own Case, in which there was at this time no little Nicety. The Circumstances I was in, made the offer of a good Husband the most necessary Thing in the World to me; but I found soon that to be made Cheap and Easy was not the way: It soon began to be found that the Widow had no Fortune, and to say this, was to say all that was Ill of me, for I began to be dropt in all the Discourses of Matrimony: Being well Bred, Handsome, Witty, Modest and agreeable; all which I had allowed to my Character, whether justly or no, is not to the Purpose; I say, all these would not do without the Dross, which was now become more valuable than Virtue itself. In short, *the Widow,* they said, *had no Money.*

I resolv'd therefore, as to the State of my present Circumstances; that it was absolutely Necessary to change my Station, and make a new Appearance in some other Place where I was not known, and even to pass by another Name if I found Occasion.

I communicated my Thoughts to my intimate Friend the Captain's Lady, who I had so faithfully serv'd in her Case with the Captain; and who was as ready to serve me in the same kind as I could desire: I made no scruple to lay my Circumstances open to her; my Stock was but low, for I had made but about 540 *l.* at the Close of my last Affair, and I had wasted some of that; However, I had about 460 *l.* left, a great many very rich Cloaths, a gold Watch, and some Jewels, tho' of no extraordinary value, and about 30 or 40 *l.* left in Linnen not dispos'd of.

My Dear and faithful Friend, the Captain's Wife was so sensible of the Service I had done her in the Affair above, that she was not only a steddy Friend to me, but knowing my Circumstances, she frequently made me Presents as Money came into her Hands; such as fully amounted to a Maintenance, so that I spent none of my own; and at last she made this unhappy Proposal to me (*viz.*) that as we had observ'd, *as above,* how the Men made no scruple to set themselves out as Persons meriting a Woman of Fortune, when they had really no Fortune of their own; it was but just to deal with them in their own way, and if it was possible, to Deceive the Deceiver.

The Captain's Lady, in short, put this Project into my Head, and told me if I would be rul'd by her I should certainly get a Husband of Fortune, without leaving him any room to Reproach me with want of my own; I told her as I had Reason to do, That I would give up myself wholly to her Directions, and that I would have neither Tongue to speak, or Feet to step in that Affair, but as she should direct me, depending that she would Extricate one out of every Difficulty that she brought me into, which she said she would Answer for.

The first step she put me upon was to call her Cousin, and go to a Relations House of hers in the Country, where she directed me, and where she brought her Husband to visit me; and calling me Cousin, she work'd Matters so about, that her Husband and she together Invited me most passionately to come to Town and be with them, for they now liv'd in a quite different Place from where they were before. In the next Place she tells her Husband, that I had at least 1500 *l.* Fortune, and that after some of my Relations I was like to have a great deal more.

It was enough to tell her Husband this, there needed nothing on my Side; I was but to sit still and wait the Event, for it presently went all over the Neighbourhood that the young Widow at Captain – 's was a Fortune, that she had at least 1500 *l.* and perhaps a great deal more, and *that the Captain said so;* and if the Captain was ask'd at any time about me, he made no scruple to affirm it, tho' he knew not one Word of the Matter, other than that his Wife had told him so; and in this he thought no Harm, for he really believ'd it to be so, because he had it from his Wife; so slender a Foundation will those Fellows build upon, if they do but think there is a Fortune in the Game: With the Reputation of this Fortune, I presently found myself bless'd with admirers enough, and that I had my Choice of Men, as scarce as they said they were, *which by the way confirms what I was saying before:* This being my Case, I who had a subtile Game to play, had nothing now to do but to single out from them all, the properest Man that might be for my Purpose; *that is to say,* the Man who was most likely to depend upon the *hear say* of a Fortune, and not enquire too far into the particulars; and unless I did this, *I did nothing,* for my Case would not bear much Enquiry.

I Pick'd out my Man without much difficulty, by the judgment I made of his way of Courting me; I had let him run on with his Protestations and Oaths that he lov'd me above all the World; that if I would make him happy, that was enough; all which I knew was upon Supposition, nay, it was upon a full Satisfaction, that I was very Rich, tho' I never told him a Word of it myself.

This was my Man, but I was to try him to the bottom, and indeed in that consisted my Safety; for if he baulk'd, I knew I was undone, as surely as he was undone if he took me; and if I did not make some scruple about his Fortune, it was the way to lead him to raise some about mine; and first therefore, I pretended on all occasions to doubt his Sincerity, and told him, perhaps he only courted me for my Fortune; he stop'd my Mouth in that part, with the Thunder of his Protestations, *as above,* but still I pretended to doubt.

One morning he pulls off his Diamond Ring, and writes upon the Glass of the Sash in my Chamber this Line,

You I Love, and you alone.

I read it, and ask'd him to lend me his Ring, with which I wrote under it thus,

And so in Love says every one.

He takes his Ring again, and writes another Line thus,

Virtue alone is an Estate.

I borrow'd it again, and I wrote under it,

But Money's Virtue; Gold is Fate.

He colour'd as red as Fire to see me turn so quick upon him, and in a kind of a Rage told me he would Conquer me, and writes again *thus,*

I scorn your Gold, and yet I Love.

I ventur'd all upon the last cast of Poetry, as you'll see, for I wrote boldly under his last,

I'm Poor: Let's see how kind you'll prove.

This was a sad Truth to me, whether he believ'd me or no I cou'd not tell; I supposed then that he did not. However he flew to me, took me in his Arms, and kissing me very eagerly, and with the greatest Passion imaginable he held me fast till he call'd for a Pen and Ink, and then *told me* he could not wait the tedious writing on the Glass, but pulling out a piece of Paper, he began and wrote again,

Be mine, with all your Poverty.

I took his Pen and follow'd him immediately thus, Yet secretly you hope I lie.

He told me that was unkind, because it was not just, and that I put him upon contradicting me, which did not consist with good Manners, any more than with his Affection; and therefore since I had insensibly drawn him into this poetical scribble, he beg'd I would not oblige him to break it off, so he writes again,

Let Love alone be our Debate.

I wrote again,

She Loves enough, that does not hate.

This he took for a favour, and so laid down the Cudgels, that is to say the Pen; I say he took it for a favour, and a mighty one it was, if he had known all: However he took it as I meant it, that is, to let him think I was inclin'd to go on with him, as indeed I had all the Reason in the World to do, for he was the best humoured merry sort of a Fellow that I ever met with; and I often reflected on my self, how doubly criminal it was to deceive such a Man; but that Necessity, which press'd me to a Settlement suitable to my Condition, was my Authority for it; and certainly his Affection to me, and the Goodness of his Temper, however they might argue against using him ill, yet they strongly argued to me that he would better take the Disappointment than some fiery tempered Wretch, who might have nothing to recommend him but those Passions which would serve only to make a Woman miserable all her Days.

Besides, tho' I had jested with him, as he suppos'd it, so often about my Poverty, yet, when he found it to be true, he had foreclosed all manner of objection, seeing whether he was in jest or in earnest, he had declar'd he took me without any regard to my Portion, and whether I was in jest or in earnest, I had declar'd my self to be very Poor, so that *in a word,* I had him fast both ways; and tho' he might say afterwards he was cheated, yet he could never say that I had cheated him. .

He persued me close after this, and as I saw there was no need to fear losing him, I play'd the indifferent part with him longer than Prudence might otherwise have dictated to me: But I considered how much this caution and indifference would give me the advantage over him, when I should come to be under the Necessity of owning my own Circumstances to him; and I manag'd it the more warily, because I found he inferr'd from thence, as indeed he ought to do, that I either had the more Money, or the more Judgment, and would not venture at all.

I took the freedom one Day, after we had talk'd pretty close to the Subject, to tell him, that it was true I had receiv'd the

Compliment of a Lover from him; namely, that he would take me without enquiring into my Fortune, and I would make him a suitable return in this, (*viz.*) that I would make as little enquiry into his as consisted with Reason, but I hoped he would allow me to ask a few Questions, which he should answer or not as he thought fit; and that I would not be offended if he did not answer me at all; one of these Questions related to our manner of living, and the place where, because I had heard he had a great Plantation in *Virginia,* and that he had talk'd of going to live there, and I told him I did not care to be Transported.

He began from this Discourse to let me voluntarily into all his Affairs, and to tell me in a frank open way all his Circumstances, by which I found he was very well to pass in the World; but that great part of his Estate consisted of three Plantations, which he had in *Virginia,* which brought him in a very good Income, generally speaking, to the tune of 300 *l.* a Year; but that if he was to live upon them, would bring him in four times as much; very well thought I, you shall carry me thither as soon as you please, tho' I won't tell you so before-hand.

I jested with him extremely about the Figure he would make in *Virginia;* but I found he would do any thing I desired, tho' he did not seem glad to have me undervalue his Plantations, so I turn'd my Tale; I told him I had good reason not to desire to go there to live, because if his Plantations were worth so much there, I had not a Fortune suitable to a Gentleman of 1200 *l.* a Year, as he said his Estate would be.

He reply'd generously, he did not ask what my Fortune was, he had told me from the beginning he would not, and he would be as good as his word; But whatever it was, he assur'd me he would never desire me to go to *Virginia* with him, or go thither himself without me, unless I was perfectly willing, and made it my Choice.

All this, you may be sure, was as I wish'd, and indeed nothing could have happen'd more perfectly agreeable; I carried it on as far as this with a sort of indifferency that he often wondred at, more than at first, But which was the only support of his Courtship; and I mention it the rather to intimate again to the Ladies, that nothing but want of Courage for such an Indifferency, makes our Sex so cheap, and prepares them to be ill us'd as they are; would they venture the loss of a pretending Fop now and then, who carries it high upon the point of his own Merit, they would certainly be slighted less and courted more; had I discovered really and truly what my great Fortune was, and that in all I had not full 500 *l.* when he expected 1500 *l.* yet I had hook'd him so fast, and play'd him so long, that I was satisfied he would have had me in my worst Circumstances; and indeed it was less a surprize to him when he learnt the Truth than it would have been, because having not the least blame to lay on me, who had carried it with an air of indifference to the last, he could not say one word, except that indeed he thought it had been more, but that if it had been less he did not repent his bargain; only that he should not be able to maintain me so well as he intended.

In short, we were married, and very happily married on my side I assure you, as *to the Man;* for he was the best humour'd Man that ever Woman had, but his Circumstances were not so good as I imagined, as on the other hand he had not bettered himself by marrying so much as he expected.

When we were married I was shrewdly put to it to bring him that little Stock I had, and to let him see it was no more; but there was a necessity for it, so I took my opportunity one Day when we were alone, to enter into a short Dialogue with him about it; My Dear, *said I,* we have been married a Fortnight, is it not time to let you know whether you have got a Wife with something, or with nothing? Your own time for that, my Dear, *says he,* I am satisfied that I have got the Wife I love, I have not troubled you much, *says he,* with my enquiry after it.

That's true, *said I,* but I have a great difficulty upon me about it, which I scarce know how to manage.

What's that, my Dear, *says he?*

Why, *says I,* 'tis a little hard upon me, and 'tis harder upon you; I am told that Captain – (meaning my Friend's Husband) has told you I had a great deal more Money than I ever pretended to have, and I am sure I never employ'd him to do so.

Well, *says he,* Captain – may have told me so, but what then, if you have not so much that may lye at his Door, but you never told me what you had, so I have no reason to blame you if you have nothing at all.

That is so just, *said I,* and so generous, that it makes my having but a little a double Affliction to me.

The less you have, my *Dear, says he,* the worse for us both; but I hope your Affliction you speak of is not caus'd for fear I should be unkind to you, for want of a Portion, No no, if you have nothing tell me plainly, and at once; I may perhaps tell the Captain he has cheated me, but I can never say you have cheated me, for did you not give it under your Hand that you were Poor, and so I ought to expect you to be.

Well, said I, *my Dear,* I am glad I have not been concern'd in deceiving you before Marriage, if I deceive you since, 'tis ne'er the worse; *that I am Poor is* too true, but not so Poor as to have nothing neither; so I pull'd out some Bank Bills, and gave him about a Hundred and Sixty Pounds; there's something, my Dear, *says I,* and not quite all neither.

I had brought him so near to expecting nothing, by what I had said before, that the Money, tho' the Sum was small in it self, was doubly welcome to him; he own'd it was more than he look'd for, and that he did not question by my Discourse to him, but that my fine Cloths, Gold Watch, and a Diamond Ring or two had been all my Fortune.

I let him please himself with that 160 *l.* two or three Days, and then having been abroad that Day, and as if I had been to fetch it, I brought him a Hundred Pounds more home in Gold, and told him there was a little more Portion for him; and in short in about a Week more I brought him 180 *l.* more, and about 60 *l.* in Linnen, which I made him believe I had been oblig'd to take with the 100 *l.* which I gave him in Gold, as a Composition for a Debt of 600 *l.* being little more than Five Shilling in the Pound, and overvalued too.

And now, My DEAR, *says I to him,* I am very sorry to tell you, that there is all, and that I have given you my whole Fortune; I added, that if the Person who had my 600 *l.* had not abus'd me, I had been worth a Thousand Pound to him, but that as it was, I had been faithful to him, and reserv'd nothing to my self, but if it had been more he should have had it.

He was so oblig'd by the Manner, and so pleas'd with the Sum, for he had been in a terrible fright lest it had been nothing at all, that he accepted it very thankfully: And thus I got over the Fraud of *passing for a Fortune without Money,* and cheating a Man into Marrying me on pretence of a Fortune; which, by *the way,* I take to be one of the most dangerous Steps a Woman can take, and in which she runs the most hazard of being ill us'd afterwards.

My Husband, *to give him his due,* was a Man of infinite good Nature, but he was no Fool; and finding his Income not suited to the manner of Living which he had intended, if I had brought him what he expected, and being under a Disappointment in his return off his Plantations in *Virginia,* he discover'd many times his inclination of going over to Virginia to live upon his own; and often would be magnifying the way of living there, how cheap, how plentiful, how pleasant, *and the like.*

I began presently to understand his meaning, and I took him up very plainly one Morning, and told him that I did so; that I found his Estate turn'd to no account at this distance, compar'd to what it would do if he liv'd upon the spot, and that I found he had a mind to go and live there and I added, that I was sensible he had been disappointed in a Wife, and that finding his Expectations not answer'd that way, I could do no less to make him amends than tell him that I was very willing to go over to *Virginia* with him and live there.

He said a thousand kind things to me upon the subject of my making such a Proposal to him: He told me, that however he was disappointed in his Expectations of a Fortune, he was not disappointed in a Wife, and that I was all to him that a Wife could be, and he was more than satisfied in the whole when the particulars were put together; but that this offer was so kind, that it was more than he could express.

To bring the story short, we agreed to go; *he told me,* that he had a very good House there, that it was well Furnish'd, that his Mother was alive and liv'd in it, and one Sister, which was all the Relations he had; that as soon as he came there, his Mother would remove to another House which was her own for life, and his after her Decease; so that I should have all the House to my self; and I found all this to be exactly as he had said.

To make this part of the story short, we put on board the Ship, which *we went in,* a large quantity of good Furniture for our House, with stores of Linnen and other Necessaries, and a good Cargoe for Sale, and away we went.

To give an account of the manner of our Voyage, which was long and full of Dangers, is out of my way; I kept no Journal, neither did my Husband; all that I can say is, that after a terrible passage, frighted twice with dreadful Storms and once with what was still more terrible, I mean a Pyrate who came on board and took away almost all our Provisions; and which would have been beyond all to me, they had once taken my Husband to go along with them but by entreaties were prevail'd with to leave him: I say, after all these terrible things, we arriv'd in *York* River in *Virginia,* and coming to our Plantation, we were receiv'd with all the Demonstrations of Tenderness and Affection (by my Husband's Mother) that were possible to be express'd.

We liv'd here all together, my Mother-in-law, *at my entreaty* continuing in the House, for she was too kind a Mother to be parted with; my Husband likewise continued the same as at first, and I thought my self the happiest Creature alive; when an odd and surprizing Event put an end to all that Felicity in a moment, and rendred my Condition the most uncomfortable, if not the most miserable, in the World.

My Mother was a mighty chearful good humour'd old Woman, I may call her old Woman, for her Son was above Thirty; I say she was very pleasant, good Company, and us'd to entertain *me, in particular,* with abundance of Stories to divert me, as well of the Country we were in, as of the People.

Among the rest, she often told me how the greatest part of the Inhabitants of the Colony came thither in very indifferent Circumstances from *England;* that, generally speaking, they were of two sorts, either (1.) such as were brought over by Masters of Ships to be sold as Servants, *such as we call them,* my Dear, *says she,* but they are more properly call'd Slaves. Or, (2.) Such as are Transported from *Newgate* and other Prisons, after having been found guilty of Felony and other Crimes punishable with Death.

When they come here, *says she,* we make no difference; the Planters buy them, and they work together in the Field till their time is out; when 'tis expir'd, *said she,* they have Encouragement given them to Plant for themselves; for they have a certain number of Acres of Land allotted them by the Country, and they go to work to Clear and Cure the Land, and then to Plant it with Tobacco and Corn for their own use; and as the Tradesmen and Merchants will trust them with Tools, and Cloaths, and other Necessaries, upon the Credit of their Crop before it is grown, so they again Plant every Year a little more than the Year before, and so buy whatever they want with the Crop that is before them.

Hence Child, *says she,* many a Newgate Bird becomes a great Man, and we have, *continued she,* several Justices of the Peace, Officers of the Train Bands, and Magistrates of the Towns they live in, that have been burnt in the Hand.

She was going on with that part of the Story, when her own part in it interrupted her, and with a great deal of good-humour'd Confidence she told me' she was one of the second sort of Inhabitants herself; that she came away openly, having ventur'd too far in a particular Case, so that she was become a Criminal; and here's the Mark of it, CHILD, *says she,* pulling off her Glove, look ye here, *says she,* turning up the Palm of her Hand, and shewed me a very fine white Arm and Hand, but branded in the inside of the Hand, as in such cases it must be.

This Story was very moving to me, but my Mother (smiling) said, you need not think such a thing strange, *Daughter,* for as I told you, some of the best Men in this Country are burnt in the Hand, and they are not asham'd to own it; there's Major – *says she,* he was an Eminent Pickpocket; there's Justice Ba – r was a Shoplifter, and both of them were burnt in the Hand, and I could name you several, such as they are.

We had frequent Discourses of this kind, and abundance of instances she gave me of the like; after some time, as she was telling some Stories of one that was Transported but a few Weeks ago, I began in an intimate kind of way to ask her to tell me something of her own Story, which she did with the utmost plainness and Sincerity; how she had fallen into very ill Company in *London* in her young Days, occasion'd by her Mother sending her frequently to carry Victuals and other Relief to a Kinswoman of hers who was Prisoner in *Newgate,* and who lay in a miserable starving Condition, was afterwards Condemned to be Hang'd but having got Respite by pleading her Belly, dyed afterwards in the prison.

Here my Mother-in-Law ran out in a long account of the wicked practices in that dreadful Place, and how it ruin'd more young People than all the Town besides; and Child, *says my Mother,* perhaps you may know little of it, or it may be have heard nothing about it, but depend upon it, *says she,* we all know here, that there are more Thieves and Rogues made by that one Prison of

Newgate, than by all the Clubs and Societies of Villains in the Nation; 'tis that cursed Place, *says my Mother,* that half Peoples this Colony.

Here she went on with her own Story so long, and in so particular a manner, that I began to be very uneasy; but coming to one Particular that requir'd telling her Name, I thought I should have sunk down in the place; she perceived I was out of order, and asked me if I was not well, and what ail'd me? I told her I was so affected with the melancholy Story she had told, and the terrible things she had gone thro', that it had overcome me; and I beg'd of her to talk no more of it: Why, my Dear, *says she, very kindly,* what need these things trouble you? These Passages were long before your time, and they give me no trouble at all now; nay I look back on them with a particular Satisfaction, as they have been a means to bring me to this place. Then she went on to tell me how she very luckily fell into a good Family, where behaving herself well, and her Mistress dying, her Master married her, by whom she had my Husband and his Sister, and that by her Diligence and good Management after her Husband's Death, she had improv'd the Plantations to such a degree as they then were, so that most of the Estate was of her getting, not her Husband's, for she had been a Widow upwards of sixteen Year.

I heard this part of the Story with very little attention, because I wanted much to retire and give vent to my Passions, which I did soon after; and let anyone judge what must be the Anguish of my Mind, when I came to reflect that this was certainly no more or less *than my own Mother,* and I had now had two Children, and was big with another by my own Brother, and lay with him still every Night.

I was now the most unhappy of all Women in the World: O had the Story never been told me, all had been well; it had been no Crime to have lain with my Husband, since as to his being my Relation, I had known nothing of it.

I had now such a load on my Mind that it kept me perpetually waking; to reveal it, *which would have been some ease to me,* I cou'd not find wou'd be to any purpose, and yet to conceal it wou'd be next to impossible; nay, I did not doubt but I should talk of it in my sleep, and tell my Husband of it whether I would or no: If I discover'd it, the least thing I could expect was to lose my Husband, for he was too nice and too honest a Man to have continued my Husband after he had known I had been his Sister, so that I was perplex'd to the last degree.

I leave it any Man to judge what Difficulties presented to my view, I was away from my native Country at a distance prodigious, and the return to me unpassable; I liv'd very well, but in a Circumstance unsufferable in it self; if I had discover'd my self to my Mother, it might be difficult to convince her of the Particulars, and I had no way to prove them: *On the other hand,* if she had question'd or doubted me, I had been undone, for the bare Suggestion would have immediately separated me from my Husband, without gaining my Mother or him, who would have been neither a Husband or a Brother; so that between the surprise on one hand, and the uncertainty on the other, I had been sure to be undone.

In the mean time, as I was but too sure of the Fact, I liv'd therefore in open avowed Incest and "Whoredom, and all under the appearance of an honest Wife; and tho' I was not much touched with the Crime of it, yet the Action had something in it shocking to Nature, and made my Husband, *as he thought himself* even nauseous to me.

However, upon the most sedate Consideration, I resolv'd, that it was absolutely necessary to conceal it all, and not make the least Discovery of it either to Mother or Husband; and thus I liv'd with the greatest Pressure imaginable for three Year more, but had no more Children.

During this time my Mother used to be frequently telling me old Stories of her former Adventures, which however were no ways pleasant to me; for by it, tho' she did not tell it me in plain terms, yet I could easily understand, joyn'd with what I had heard my self of my first Tutors, that in her younger Days she had been both WHORE and THIEF; but I verily believe she had lived to repent sincerely of both, and that she was then a very Pious sober and religious Woman.

Well, let her Life have been what it would then, it was certain that my Life was very uneasie to me; for I liv'd, as I have said, but in the worst sort of "Whoredom, and as I cou'd expect no Good of it, so really no good Issue came of it, and all my seeming Prosperity wore off and ended in Misery and Destruction; it was some time indeed before it came to this, for, but I know not by what ill Fate guided, every thing went wrong with us afterwards, and that which was worse, my Husband grew strangely alter'd, froward, jealous, and unkind, and I was as impatient of bearing his Carriage, as the Carriage was unreasonable and unjust: These things proceeded so far, that we came at last to be in such ill Terms with one another, that I claim'd a promise of him which he entered willingly into with me, when I consented to come from *England* with him (*viz.*) that if I found the Country not to agree with me, or that I did not like to live there, I should come away to *England* again when I pleas'd, giving him a Year's warning to settle his Affairs.

I say *I now claim'd this promise of him,* and I must confess I did it not in the most obliging Terms that could be in the World neither; but I insisted that he treated me ill, that I was remote from my Friends, and could do my self no Justice, and that he was Jealous without cause, my Conversation having been unblameable, and he having no pretence for it, and that to remove to *England,* would take away all Occasion from him.

I insisted so peremptorily upon it, that he could not avoid coming to a point, either to keep his word with me or to break it; and this notwithstanding he used all the skill he was master of, and employ'd his Mother and other Agents to prevail with me to alter my Resolutions; indeed the bottom of the thing lay at my

Heart, and that made all his Endeavours fruitless, for my Heart was alienated from him, *as a Husband;* I loathed the Thoughts of Bedding with him, and used a thousand Pretences of Illness and Humour to prevent his touching me, fearing nothing more than to be with Child again by him, which to be sure would have prevented, or at least delay'd my going over to *England.*

However, at last I put him so out of Humour that he took up a rash and fatal Resolution. In short I should not go to *England;* and tho' he had promis'd me, yet it was an unreasonable thing for me to desire it, that it would be ruinous to his Affairs, would Unhinge his whole Family, and be next to an Undoing him in the World; That therefore I ought not to desire it of him, and that no Wife in the World that valu'd her Family and her Husbands prosperity would insist upon such a thing.

This plung'd me again, for when I considered the thing calmly, and took my Husband as he really was, a diligent careful Man in the main Work of laying up an Estate for his Children, and that he knew nothing of the dreadful Circumstances that he was in, I could not but confess to myself that my Proposal was very unreasonable; and what no Wife that had the good of her Family at Heart wou'd have desir'd.

But my Discontents were of another Nature; I look'd upon him no longer as a Husband, but as a near Relation, the Son of my own Mother, and I resolv'd some how or other to be clear of him, but which way I did not know, nor did it seem possible.

It is said *by the ill-natured World,* of our Sex, that if we are set on a thing, it is impossible to turn us from our Resolutions: *In short,* I never ceas'd poreing upon the Means to bring to pass my Voyage, and came that length with my Husband at last, as to propose going without him. This provok'd him to the last degree, and he call'd me not only an unkind Wife, but an unnatural Mother, and ask'd me how I could entertain such a Thought without horror as that of leaving my two Children (for one was dead) without a Mother, and to be brought up by Strangers, and never to see them more? *It was true,* had things been right, I should not have done it, but now, *it was* my real desire never to see them, or him either, any more; and as to the Charge of unnatural I could easily answer it to myself, while I knew that the whole Relation was Unnatural in the highest degree in the World.

However, it was plain there was no bringing my Husband to any thing; he would neither go with me, or let me go without him, and it was quite out of my Power to stir without his Consent, as anyone that knows the Constitution of the Country I was in, knows very well.

We had many Family quarrels about it, and they began (in time) to grow up to a dangerous Height, for as I was quite Estrang'd from my Husband (*as he was call'd*) in Affection, so I took no heed to my Words, but sometimes gave him Language that was provoking: And, *in short,* strove all I could to bring him to a parting with me, which was what above all things in the World I desir'd most.

He took my Carriage very ill, and indeed he might well do so, for at last I refus'd to Bed with him, and carrying on the Breach upon all occasions to extremity he told me once he thought I was Mad, and if I did not alter my Conduct, he would put me under Cure; *that is to say, into a Madhouse:* I told him he should find I was far enough from Mad, and that it was not in his power, or any other Villains to Murther me; I confess at the same time I was heartily frighted at his Thoughts of putting me into a Mad-House, which would at once have destroy'd all the possibility of breaking the Truth out, whatever the occasion might be; for that then, no one would have given Credit to a word of it.

This therefore brought me to a Resolution, *whatever came of it* to lay open my whole Case; but which way to do it, or to whom, was an inextricable Difficulty, and took me up many Months to Resolve; *in the mean time,* another Quarrel with my Husband happen'd, which came up to such a mad Extream as almost push'd me on to tell it him all to his Face; but tho' I kept it in so as not to come to the particulars, I spoke so much as put him into the utmost Confusion, and in the End brought out the whole Story.

He began with a calm Expostulation upon my being so resolute to go to *England;* I defended it, and one hard Word bringing on another as is usual in all Family strife, *he told me* I did not Treat him as if he was my Husband, or talk of my Children as if I was a Mother; and *in short,* that I did not deserve to be us'd as a Wife: That he had us'd all the fair Means possible with me; that he had Argu'd with all the kindness and calmness that a Husband or a Christian ought to do, and that I made him such a vile return, that I Treated him rather like a Dog than a Man, and rather like the most contemptible Stranger than a Husband: That he was very loth to use Violence with me, but that *in short,* he saw a Necessity of it now, and that for the future he should be oblig'd to take such Measures as should reduce me to my Duty.

My blood was now fir'd to the utmost, *tho' I knew what he had said was very true,* and nothing could appear more provok'd; I told him for his fair means and his foul they were equally contemn'd by me; that for my going to *England,* I was resolv'd on it, come what would; and that as to treating him not like a Husband, and not showing my self a Mother to my Children, there might be something more in it than he understood at present; but, for his farther consideration, I thought fit to tell him thus much, that he neither was my lawful Husband, nor they lawful Children, and that I had reason to regard neither of them more than I did.

I confess I was mov'd to pity him when I spoke it, for he turn'd pale as Death, and stood mute as one Thunder struck, and once or twice I thought he would have fainted; in *short,* it put him in a Fit something like an Apoplex; he trembl'd, a Sweat or Dew ran off his Face, and yet he was cold as a Clod, so that I was forced to run and fetch something for him to keep Life in him; when he recover'd of that, he grew sick and vomited, and in a little after was put to Bed, and in the next Morning was, as he had been indeed all Night, in a violent Fever.

However it went off again, and he recovered tho' but slowly, and when he came to be a little better, he told me, I had given him a mortal Wound with my Tongue, and he had only one thing to ask before he desir'd an Explanation; I interrupted him, and told him I was sorry I had gone so far, since I saw what disorder it put him into, but I desir'd him not to talk to me of Explanations, for that would but make things worse.

This heighten'd his impatience, and indeed perplex'd him beyond all bearing, for now he began to suspect that there was some Mystery yet unfolded, but could not make the least guess at the real Particulars of it; all that run in his Brain was, that I had another Husband alive, which I could not say in fact might not be true; but I assur'd him however, there was not the least of that in it; and indeed as to my other Husband he was effectually dead in Law to me, and had told me I should look on him as such, so I had not the least uneasiness on that score.

But now I found the thing too far gone to conceal it much longer, and my Husband himself gave me an opportunity to ease my self of the Secret much to my Satisfaction; he had laboured with me three or four Weeks, *but to no purpose,* only to tell him, whether I had spoken those words only as the effect of my Passion to put him in a Passion? Or whether there was anything of Truth in the bottom of them? But, I continued inflexible, and would explain nothing, unless he could first consent to my going to *England,* which he would never do, *he said,* while he liv'd; on the other hand I said it was in my power to make him willing when I pleas'd, NAY to make him entreat me to go; and this increased his Curiosity, and made him importunate to the highest degree, *but it was all to no purpose.*

At length he tells all this Story to his Mother, and sets her upon me to get the main Secret out of me, and she us'd her utmost Skill with me indeed; but I put her to a full stop at once, *by telling her* that the Reason and Mystery of the whole matter lay in herself; and that it was my Respect to her that had made me conceal it, and that in short I could go no farther, and therefore conjur'd her not to insist upon it.

She was struck dumb at this Suggestion, and could not tell what to say or to think; but laying aside the supposition as a Policy of mine, continued her importunity on account of her Son, and if possible to make up the breach between us two; as to that, *I told her,* that it was indeed a good design in her, but that it was impossible to be done; and that if I should reveal to her the Truth of what she desir'd, she would grant it to be impossible, and cease to desire it: At last I seem'd to be prevail'd on by her importunity, and told her I dar'd trust her with a Secret of the greatest Importance, and she would soon see that this was so, and that I would consent to lodge it in her Breast, if she would engage solemnly not to acquaint her Son with it without my consent.

She was long in promising this part, but rather than not come at the main Secret she agreed to that too, and after a great many other Preliminaries, I began and told her the whole Story: First I told her how much she was concern'd in all the unhappy breach which had happen'd between her Son and me, by telling me her own Story and her *London* Name; and that the surprize she see I was in was upon that Occasion: Then I told her my own Story and my Name, and assur'd her by such other Tokens as she could not deny that I was no other, nor more or less than her own Child, *her Daughter* born of her Body in *Newgate;* the same that had sav'd her from the Gallows by being in her Belly, and the same that she left in such and such Hands when she was Transported.

It is impossible to express the Astonishment she was in; she was not inclin'd to believe the Story, or to remember the Particulars, for she immediately foresaw the Confusions that must follow in the Family upon it; but every thing concurr'd so exactly with the Stories she had told me of her self, and which if she had not told me, she would perhaps have been content to have denied, that she had stop'd her own Mouth, and she had nothing to do but to take me about the Neck and kiss me, and cry most vehemently over me, without speaking one word for a long time together; at last she broke out, *Unhappy Child! says she,* what miserable chance could bring thee hither? And in the Arms of my own Son too! *Dreadful Girl!* says she, *why we are all undone!* Married to thy own Brother! Three Children, and two alive, all of the same Flesh and Blood! My Son and my Daughter lying together as Husband and Wife! All Confusion and Destraction for ever! *miserable Family!* what will become of us? what is to be said? what is to be done? and thus she run on for a great while, nor had I any power to speak, or if I had, did I know what to say, for every word wounded me to the Soul: With this kind of Amasement on our Thoughts we parted for the first time, tho' my Mother was more surpriz'd than I was, because it was more News to her than to me: However, she promis'd again to me at parting, that she would say nothing of it to her Son till we had talk'd of it again.

It was not long, you may be sure, before we had a second Conference upon the same Subject; when, as if she had been willing to forget the Story she had told me of herself, or to suppose that I had forgot some of the Particulars, she began to tell them with Alterations and Omissions; but I refresh'd her Memory, and set her to rights in many things which I supposed she had forgot, and then came in so opportunely with the whole History, that it was impossible for her to go from it; and then she fell into her Rhapsodies again, and Exclamations at the Severity of her Misfortunes: When these things were a little over with her we fell into a close Debate about what should be first done before we gave an account of the matter to my Husband, but to what purpose could be all our Consultations? we could neither of us see our way thro' it, nor see how it could be safe to open such a Scene to him; it was impossible to make any judgment, or give any guess at what Temper he would receive it in, or what Measures he would take upon it; and if he should have so little Government of himself as to make it publick, we easily foresaw that it would be the ruin of the whole Family, and expose my Mother and me to the last degree; and if at last he should take the Advantage the Law would give him, he might put me away with disdain, and leave me to Sue for the little Portion that I had, and perhaps waste it all in the Suit, and then be a Beggar; the Children would be ruin'd too, having no legal Claim to any of his Effects; and thus I should see him perhaps in the Arms of another Wife in a few Months, and be my self the most miserable Creature alive.

My Mother was as sensible of this as I; and upon the whole, we knew not what to do; after some time, we came to more sober Resolutions, but then it was with this Misfortune too, that my Mother's Opinion and mine were quite different from one another, and indeed inconsistent with one another; for my Mother's Opinion was that I should bury the whole thing entirely, and continue to live with him as my Husband, till some other Event should make the discovery of it more convenient; and that in the mean time she would endeavour to reconcile us together again, and restore our mutual Comfort and Family Peace; that we might lie as we us'd to do together, and so let the whole matter remain a secret as close as Death; for Child, *says she,* we are both undone if it comes out.

To encourage me to this, she promis'd to make me easy in my Circumstances as far as she was able, and to leave me what she could at her Death, secur'd for me separately from my Husband; so that if it should come out afterwards, I should not be left destitute, but be able to stand on my own Feet and procure Justice from him.

This Proposal did not agree at all with my Judgment of the thing, tho' it was very fair and kind in my Mother, but my Thoughts run quite another way.

As to keeping the thing in our own Breasts, and letting it all remain as it was, I told her it was impossible; and I ask'd her how she cou'd think I cou'd bear the thoughts of lying with my own Brother? In the next place I told her that her being alive was the only support of the Discovery, and that while she own'd me for her Child, and saw reason to be satisfyed that I was so, no body else would doubt it; but that if she should die before the Discovery, I should be taken for an impudent Creature that had forg'd such a thing to go away from my Husband, or should be counted Craz'd and Distracted: Then I told her how he had threaten'd already to put me into a Mad-house, and what concern I had been in about it, and how that was the thing that drove me to the necessity of discovering it to her as I had done.

From all which I told her, that I had on the most serious Reflections I was able to make in the Case, come to this Resolution, which I hop'd she would like, as a medium both, (*viz.*) that she should use her endeavours with her Son to give me leave to go for *England,* as I had desired, and to furnish me with a sufficient Sum of Money, either in Goods along with me, or in Bills for my Support there, all along suggesting, that he might one time or other think it proper to come over to me.

That when I was gone she should then in cold Blood, and after first obliging him in the solemnest manner possible to Secresie, discover the Case to him; doing it gradually, and as her own Discretion should guide her, so that he might not be surpriz'd with it, and fly out into any Passions and Excesses on my account, or on hers; and that she should concern herself to prevent his slighting the Children, or Marrying again, unless he had a certain account of my being Dead.

This was my Scheme, and my Reasons were good; I was really alienated from him in the Consequence of these things; indeed I mortally hated him as a Husband, and it was impossible to remove that riveted Aversion I had to him; *at the same time* it being an unlawful incestuous living added to that Aversion; and tho' I had not great concern about it in point of Conscience, yet every thing added to make Cohabiting with him the most nauseous thing to me in the World; and I think verily it was come to such a height, that I could almost as willingly have embrac'd a Dog, as have let him offer any thing of that kind to me, for which Reason I could not bear the thoughts of coming between the Sheets with him; I cannot say that I was right in point of Policy in carrying it such a length, while at the same time I did not resolve to discover the thing to him; but I am giving an account of what was, not of what ought or ought not to be.

In this directly opposite Opinion to one another my Mother and I continued a long time, and it was impossible to reconcile our Judgments; many Disputes we had about it, but we could never either of us yield our own, or bring over the other.

I insisted on my Aversion to lying with my own Brother, and she insisted upon its being impossible to bring him to consent to my going from him to *England;* and in this uncertainty we continued, not differing so as to quarrel, or any thing like it, but so as not to be able to resolve what we should do to make up that terrible breach that was before us.

At last I resolv'd on a desperate course, and *told my Mother* my Resolution, (*viz.*) that in short, I would tell him of it my self; my Mother was frighted to the last degree at the very thoughts of it; but I *bid her be easie,* told her I would do it gradually and softly, and with all the Art and good Humour I was Mistress of, and time it also as well as I could, taking him in good Humour too: *I told her* I did not question but if I cou'd be Hypocrite enough to feign more Affection to him than I really had, I should succeed in all my Design, and we might part by Consent, and with a good Agreement, for I might love him well enough for a Brother, tho' I could not for a Husband.

All this while he lay at my Mother to find out, if possible, what was the meaning of that dreadful Expression of mine, as he call'd it, which I mention'd before; namely, *That I was not his lawful wife, nor my Children his legal Children:* My Mother put him off, told him she could bring me to no Explanations, but found there was something that disturb'd me very much, and she hop'd she should get it out of me in time, and in the mean time recommended to him earnestly to use me more tenderly, and win me with his usual good Carriage; *told him* of his terrifying and affrighting me with his Threats of sending me to a Mad-house, and the like, and advis'd him not to make a Woman Desperate on any account whatever.

He promis'd her to soften his Behaviour, and bid her assure me that he lov'd me as well as ever, and that he had no such design as that of sending me to a Mad-house, whatever he might say in his Passion; also he desir'd my Mother to use the same 'Perswasions to me too, that our Affections might be renew'd, and we might live together in a good understanding as we us'd to do.

I found the Effects of this Treaty presently; my Husband's Conduct was immediately alter'd, and he was quite another Man to me; nothing could be kinder and more obliging than he was to me upon all Occasions; and I could do no less than make some return to it, *which I did as well as I cou'd;* but it was but in an awkward manner at best, for nothing was more frightful to me than his Caresses, and the Apprehensions of being with Child again by him was ready to throw me into Fits; and this made me see that there was an absolute necessity of breaking the Case to him without any more delay, which however I did with all the cauti'on and reserve imaginable.

He had continued his alter'd Carriage to me near a Month, and we began to live a new kind of Life with one another; and could I have satisfied my self to have gone on with it, I believe it might have continued as long as we had continued alive together. One Evening as we were sitting and talking very friendly together under a little Awning, which serv'd as an Arbour at the entrance from our House into the Garden, he was in a very pleasant agreeable Humour, and said abundance of kind things to me, relating to the Pleasure of our present good Agreement, and the Disorders of our past breach, and what a Satisfaction it was to him that we had room to hope we should never have any more of it.

I fetch' d a deep Sigh, and told him there was no Body in the World could be more delighted than I was in the good Agreement we had always kept up, or more afflicted with the Breach of it, and should, be so still; but I was sorry to tell him that there was an unhappy Circumstance in our Case, which lay too close to my Heart, and which I knew not how to break to him, that rendred my part of it very miserable, and took from me all the Comfort of the rest.

He importun'd me to tell him what it was; I told him I could not tell how to do it; that while it was conceal'd from him, I alone was unhappy; but if he knew it also, we should be both so, and that therefore to keep him in the dark about it was the kindest thing that I could do, and it was on that account alone that I kept a secret from him, the very keeping of which I thought would first or last be my Destruction.

It is impossible to express his Surprize at this Relation, and the double importunity which he used with me to discover it to him: He told me I could not be call'd kind to him, nay, I could not be faithful to him if I conceal'd it from him; I told him I thought so too, and yet I could not do it. He went back to what I had said before to him, and told me he hoped it did not relate to what I had said in my Passion, and that he had resolv'd to forget all that, as the Effect of a rash provok'd Spirit; I told him I wish'd I could forget it all too, but that it was not to be done, the Impression was too deep, and I cou'd not do it; it was impossible.

He then told me he was resolved not to differ with me in any thing, and that therefore he would importune me no more about it, resolving to acquiesce in whatever I did or said; only begg'd I would then agree, that whatever it was, it should no more interrupt our quiet and our mutual kindness.

This was the most provoking thing he could have said to me, for I really wanted his farther importunities, that I might be prevail'd with to bring out that which indeed it was like Death to me to conceal; so I answer'd him plainly, that I could not say I was glad not to be importuned, tho' I could not tell how to comply; but come, my *Dear, said I,* what Conditions will you make with me upon the opening this Affair to you?

Any Conditions in the World, *said he,* that you can in reason desire of me; well, *said I,* come, give it me under your Hand, that if you do not find I am in any fault, or that I am willingly concern'd in the Causes of the Misfortune that is to follow, you will not blame me, use me the worse, do me any Injury, or make me be the Sufferer for that which is not my fault.

That, *says he, is* the most reasonable demand in the World; not to blame you for that which is not your fault; give me a Pen and Ink, *says he,* so I ran in and fetch'd a Pen, Ink, and Paper, and he wrote the Condition down in the very words I had proposed it, and sign'd it with his Name; well, says he, *what is next,* my Dear?

Why, *says I,* the next is, that you will not blame me for not discovering the Secret of it to you before I knew it.

Very just again, *says he,* with all my Heart; so he wrote down that also and sign'd it.

Well, my *Dear,* says I, then I have but one Condition more to make with you, and that is, that as there is no body concern'd in it but you and I, you shall not discover it to any Person in the World, except your own Mother; and that in all the Measures you shall take upon the discovery, as I am equally concern'd in it with you, *tho' as innocent as your self,* you shall do nothing in a Passion, nothing to my Prejudice, or to your Mother's Prejudice, without my knowledge and consent.

This a little amaz'd him, and he wrote down the words distinctly, but read them over and over before he Sign'd them, hesitating at them several times, and repeating them; *my Mother's* Prejudice! *and your Prejudice!!* what mysterious thing can this be? however, at last he Sign'd it.

Well, *says I,* my Dear, I'll ask you no more under your Hand, but as you are to bear the most unexpected and surprizing thing that perhaps ever befel any Family in the World, I beg you to promise me you will receive it with Composure and a Presence of Mind suitable to a Man of Sense.

I'll do my utmost, *says he,* upon Condition you will keep me no longer in suspence, for you Terrify me with all these Preliminaries.

Well, then, *says I,* it is this; as I told you before in a Heat, that I was not your lawful Wife, and that our Children were not legal Children, so I must let you know now in calmness and in kindness, but with Affliction enough that I *am* your own Sister, *and you* my own Brother, and that we are both me Children of our Mother now alive, and in the House, who is convinc'd of the Truth of it, in a manner not to be denied or contradicted.

I saw him turn pale, and look wild, and I said, now remember your Promise, and receive it with Presence of mind; for who cou'd have said more to prepare you for it, than I have done? However I call'd a Servant, and got him a little Glass of Rum, which is the usual Dram of me Country, for he was just fainting away.

When he was a little recover'd, I *said to him,* this Story you may be sure requires a long Explanation, and therefore have patience and compose your Mind to hear it out, and I'll make it as short as I can; and with this, I told him what I thought was needful of me Fact, and particularly how my Mother came to discover it to me, as above; and now my Dear, *says I,* you will see Reason for my Capitulations, and that I neither have been the Cause of this Matter, nor could be so, and that I could know nothing of it before now.

I am fully satisfy'd of that, *says he,* but 'tis a dreadful Surprize to me; however, I know a Remedy for it all, and a Remedy that shall put an End to all your Difficulties, without your going to *England;* That would be strange, *said I,* as all the rest; No, No, *says he,* I'll make it easie, there's no Body in the way of it all, but myself: He look'd a little disorder'd, when he said this, but I did not apprehend any thing from it at that time, believing as it us'd to be said, that they who do those things never talk of them; or that they who talk of such things never do them.

But things were not come their height with him, and I observ'd he became Pensive and Melancholly; and in a Word, as I thought a little Distemper'd in his Head; I endeavour'd to talk him into Temper; and to Reason him into a kind of Scheme for our Government in the Affair, and sometimes he would be well, and talk with some Courage about it; but the Weight of it lay too heavy upon his Thoughts, and in short, it went so far that he made two attempts upon himself, and in one of them had actually strangled himself, and had not his Mother come into me Room in the very Moment, he had died; but with the help of a *Negro* Servant, she cut him down and recover'd him.

Things were now come to a lamentable height in the Family: My pity for him now began to revive that Affection which at first I really had for him, and I endeavour'd sincerely by all the kind Carriage I could to make up the Breach; but in short, it had gotten too great a Head, it prey'd upon his Spirits, and it threw him into a long lingering Consumption, tho' it happen'd not to be Mortal. In this Distress I did not know what to do, as his Life was apparently declining, and I might perhaps have Marry'd again there, very much to my Advantage, it had been certainly my Business to have staid in me Country, but my Mind was restless too, and uneasie; I hanker'd after coming to *England,* and nothing would satisfie me without it.

In short, by an unwearied importunity my Husband who was apparently decaying, as I observ'd, was at last prevail'd with; and so *my own Fate pushing me on,* me way was made clear for me, and my *Mother concurring,* I obtain'd a very good Cargo for my coming to *England.*

When I parted with my Brother, for such I am now to call him, we agreed that after I arriv'd he should pretend to have an Account that I was Dead in *England,* and so might Marry again when he would; he promis'd, and engag'd me to Correspond with me as a Sister, and to Assist and Support me as long as I liv'd; and that if he dy'd before me, he would leave sufficient to his Mother to take Care of me still, in the Name of a Sister, and he was in some respect Careful of me, when he heard of me; but it was so oddly manag'd that I felt the Disappointments very sensibly afterwards, as you shall hear in its time.

I came away for *England* in the Month of *August,* after I had been Eight Years in that Country, and now a new Scene of Misfortunes attended me, which perhaps few Women have gone thro' the like of.

We had an indifferent good Voyage till we came just upon the Coast of *England,* and where we arriv'd in two and thirty Days, but were then Ruffled with two or three Storms, one of which drove us away to the Coast of *Ireland,* and we put in at *Kinsale:* We remain'd there about thirteen Days, got some Refreshment on Shore, and put to Sea again, tho' we met with very bad Weather again in which the Ship sprung her Main-mast, *as they call'd it, for I knew not what they meant:* But we got at last into *Milford Haven* in *Wales,* where tho' it was remote from our Port, yet having my Foot safe upon the firm Ground of my Native Country the Isle of *Britain,* I resolv'd to venture it no more upon the Waters, which had been so terrible to me; so getting my Cloths and Money on Shore with my Bills of Loading and other Papers, I resolv'd to come for *London,* and leave the Ship to get to her Port as she could; the Port whither she was bound, was to *Bristol,* where my Brothers chief Correspondent liv'd.

I got to *London* in about three Weeks, where I heard a little while after that the Ship was arriv'd in *Bristol;* but at the same time had the Misfortune to know that by the violent Weather she had been in, and the breaking of her Mainmast; she had great damage on board, and that a great part of her Cargo was spoil'd.

I had now a new Scene of Life upon my Hands, and a dreadful Appearance it had; I was come away with a kind of final Farewel; what I brought with me was indeed considerable, had it come safe, and by the help of it I might have married again tollerably well; but as it was, I was reduc'd to between two or three Hundred Pounds in the whole, and this without any hope of Recruit: I was entirely without Friends, nay, even so much as without Acquaintance, for I found it was absolutely necessary not to revive former Acquaintances; and as for my subtle Friend that set me up formerly for a Fortune she was Dead, and her Husband also; as I was inform'd upon sending a Person unknown to enquire.

The looking after my Cargo of Goods soon after oblig'd me to take a Journey to *Bristol,* and during my attendance upon that Affair, I took the Diversion of going to the *Bath* for as I was still far from being old, so my Humour, which was always Gay, continu'd so to an Extream; and being now, *as it were,* a Woman of Fortune, tho' I was a Woman without a Fortune, I expected something or other might happen in my way, that might mend my Circumstances as had been my Case before. .

The *Bath is* a Place of Gallantry enough; Expensive, and full of Snares; I went thither indeed in the view of taking any thing that might offer, but I must do myself that Justice, as to protest I knew nothing amiss; I meant nothing but in an honest way; nor had I any Thoughts about me at first that look'd the way, which afterwards I suffered them to be guided.

Here I stay'd the whole latter Season, *as it is call'd there,* and Contracted some unhappy Acquaintance, which rather prompted the Follies, I fell afterwards into, than fortify'd me against them: I liv'd pleasantly enough, kept good Company, *that is to say,* gay fine Company; but had the Discouragement to find this way of Living sunk me exceedingly, and that as I had no settl'd Income, so spending upon the main Stock was but a certain kind of *bleeding to Death;* and this gave me many sad Reflections in the Intervals of my other Thoughts: However I shook them off, and still flatter'd myself that something or other might offer for my Advantage.

But I was in the wrong Place for it; I was not now at *Redriff,* where If I had set myself tollerably up, some honest Sea Captain or other might have ralk'd with me upon the honourable terms of

Matrimony; but I was at the *Bath* where Men find a Mistress sometimes, but very rarely look for a Wife; and Consequently all the particular Acquaintances a Woman can Expect to make there must have some Tendency that way.

I had spent the first Season well enough, for tho' I had Contracted some Acquaintance with a Gentleman who came to the *Bath* for his Diversion, yet I had enter'd into no *felonious Treaty,* as it might be call'd: I had resisted some Casual offers of Gallantry, and had manag'd that way well enough; I was not wicked enough to come into the Crime for the meer Vice of it, and I had no extraordinary Offers made me that tempted me with the main thing which I wanted.

However I went this length the first Season, (*viz.*) I contracted an Acquaintance with a Woman in whose House I Lodg'd, who tho' she did not keep an ill House, *as we call it,* yet had none of the best Principles in herself: I had on all Occasions behav'd myself so well as not to get the least Slur upon my Reputation on any Account whatever, and all the Men that I had Convers'd with, were of so good Reputation that I had not gotten the least Reflection by Conversing with them; nor did any of them seem to think there was room for a wicked Correspondence, if they had any of them offered it; yet there was one Gentleman, *as above,* who always singl'd me out for the Diversion of my Company, as he call'd it, which *as he was pleas'd to say* was very agreeable to him, but at that time there was no more in it.

I had many melancholly Hours at the *Bath* after all the Company was gone, for tho' I went to *Bristol* sometimes for the disposing my Effects and for Recruits of Money, yet I chose to come back to *Bath* for my Residence, because being on good Terms with the Woman in whose House I lodg'd in the Summer, I found that during the Winter I liv'd rather cheaper there than I could do any where else; here, *I say,* I pass'd the Winter as heavily as I had pass'd the Autumn chearfully; But having contracted a nearer intimacy with the said Woman, in whose House I Lodg'd, I could not avoid communicating to her something of what lay hardest upon my Mind, and particularly the narrowness of my Circumstances, and the loss of my Fortune by the Damage of my Goods by Sea: I told her also that I had a Mother and a Brother in *Virginia* in good Circumstances, and as I had really written back to my Mother in particular to represent my Condition, and the great Loss I had receiv'd, which indeed came to almost 500 *l.* so I did not fail to let my new Friend know that I expected a Supply from thence, and so indeed I did; and as the Ships went from *Bristol* to *York* River in *Virginia,* and back again generally in less time than from *London,* and that my Brother Corresponded chiefly at *Bristol,* I thought it was much better for me to wait here for my Returns than to go to *London,* where also I had not the least Acquaintance.

My new Friend appear'd sensibly affected with my Condition, and indeed was so very kind, as to reduce the Rate of my living with her to so low a Price during the Winter, that she convinced me she got nothing by me; and as for Lodging during the Winter, I paid nothing at all.

When the Spring Season came on, she continu'd to be as kind to me as she could, and I lodg'd with her for a time, till it was found necessary to do otherwise; she had some Persons of Character that frequently lodg'd in her House, and in particular the Gentleman who, as I said, singl'd me out for his Companion the Winter before; and he came down again with another Gentleman in his Company and two Servants, and lodg'd in the same House: I suspected that my Landlady had invited him thither, letting him know that I was still with her, but she deny'd it, and protested to me that she did not, and he said the same.

In a Word, this Gentleman came down and continu'd to single me out for his peculiar Confidence as well as Conversation; he was a compleat Gentleman, *that must be confess'd,* and his Company was very agreeable to me, as mine, *if I might believe him,* was to him; he made no Professions to me but of an extraordinary Respect, and he had such an Opinion of my Virtue, that as *he often profess'd,* he believ'd if he should offer any thing else, I should reject him with Contempt; he soon understood from me that I was a Widow; that I had arriv'd at *Bristol* from *Virginia* by the last ships; and that I waited at *Bath* till the next *Virginia Fleet* should arrive, by which I expected considerable Effects; I understood by him, and by others of him, that he had a Wife, but that the Lady was distemper'd in her Head, and was under the Conduct of her own Relations, which he consented to, to avoid any Reflections that might, *as was not unusual in such Cases,* be cast on him for mismanaging her Cure; and in the mean time he came to the *Bath* to divert his Thoughts from the Disturbance of such a melancholy Circumstance as that was.

My Landlady, who of her own accord encourag'd the Correspondence on all Occasions, gave me an advantageous Character of him, as a Man of Honour and of Virtue, as well as of a great Estate; and indeed I had a great deal of Reason to say so of him too; for tho' we lodg'd both on a Floor, and he had frequently come into my Chamber, even when I was in Bed; and I also into his when he was in Bed, yet he never offered any thing to me farther than a kiss, or so much as solicited me to any thing till long after, as you shall hear.

I frequently took notice to my Landlady of his exceeding Modesty, and she again used to tell me, she believ'd it was so from the beginning; however she used to tell me that she thought I ought to expect some Gratification from him for my Company, for indeed he did, as it were, engross me, and I was seldom from him; *I told her* I had not given him the least occasion to think I wanted it, or that I would accept of it from him; *she told me* she would take that part upon her, and she did so, and manag'd it so dextrously, that the first time we were together alone, after she had talk'd with him, he began to enquire a little into my Circumstances, as how I had subsisted my self since I came on shore? and whether I did not want Money? I stood off very boldly, I told him that tho' my Cargo of Tobacco was damag'd, yet that it was not quite lost; that the Merchant I had been consign'd to, had so honestly manag'd for me that I had not wanted, and that I hop'd, with frugal Management, I should make it hold out till more would come, which I expected by the next Fleet; that in the mean time I had retrench'd my Expences, and whereas I kept a Maid last Season, now I liv'd without; and whereas I had a Chamber and a Dining-room then on the first Floor, *as he knew,* I now had but one Room two pair of stairs, *and the like;* but I live *said I,* as well satisfy'd now as I did then; *adding,* that his Company had been a means to make me live much more chearfully than otherwise I should have done, for which I was much oblig'd to him; and so I put off all room for any offer for the present: However, it was not long before he attack'd me again, and told me he found that I was backward to trust him with the Secret of my Circumstances, *which he was sorry for,* assuring me that he enquir'd into it with no design to satisfie his own Curiosity, but meerly to assist me, if there was any occasion; but since I would not own my self to stand in need of any assistance, he had but one thing more to desire of me, and that was that I would promise him that when I was any way streighten'd, or like to be so, I would frankly tell him of it, and that I would make use of him with the same freedom that he made the offer, *adding,* that I should always find I had a true Friend, tho' perhaps I was afraid to trust him.

I omitted nothing *that was fit to be said by one infinitely oblig'd,* to let him know, that I had a due Sense of his Kindness; and indeed from that time, I did not appear so much reserv'd to him as I had done before, tho' still within the Bounds of the strictest Virtue on both sides; but how free soever our Conversation was, I cou'd not arrive to that sort of Freedom which he desir'd, (*viz.*) to tell him I wanted Money, tho' I was secretly glad of his offer.

Some Weeks pass'd after this, and still I never ask'd him for.

Money; when my Landlady, a cunning Creature, who had often press'd me to it, but found that I cou'd not do it, makes a Story of her own inventing, and comes in bluntly to me when we were together, O Widow, *says she,* I have bad News to tell you this Morning; What is that, said I, are the *Virginia* Ships taken by the *French? for that was my fear.* No, no, *says she,* but the Man you sent to *Bristol* Yesterday for Money is come back, and says he has brought none.

Now I could by no means like her Project; I thought it look'd too much like prompting him, which indeed he did not want, and I saw clearly that I should lose nothing by being backward to ask, so I took her up short; I can't imagine why he should say so to you, *said I,* for I assure you he brought me all the Money I sent him for, and here it is *said I,* (pulling out my Purse with about 12 Guineas in it) and added, I intend you shall have most of it by and by.

He seem'd distasted a little at her talking as she did at first, as well as I, taking it as I fancied he would as something forward of her; but when he saw me give such an Answer, he came immediately to himself again: The next Morning we talk'd of it again, when I found he was fully satisfy'd, and smiling said, he hop'd I would not want Money and not tell him of it, and that I had promis'd him otherwise: I told him I had been very much dissatisfy'd at my Landladies talking so publickly the Day before of what she had nothing to do with; but I suppos'd she wanted what I ow'd her, which was about Eight Guineas, which I had resolv'd to give her, and had accordingly given it her the same Night she talk'd so foolishly.

He was in a mighty good Humour, when he heard me say, *I had paid her,* and it went off into some other Discourse at that time; but the next Morning he having heard me up about my Room before him, he call'd to me, *and I answering,* he ask'd me to come into his Chamber; he was in bed when I came in, and he made me come and sit down on his Bed side, *for he said* he had something to say to me, which was of some Moment: After some very kind Expressions he ask'd me if I would be very honest to him, and give a sincere Answer to one thing he would desire of me? after some little Cavil with him at the word *Sincere,* and asking him if I had ever given him any Answers which were not

Sincere, I promis'd him I would; why then his Request was, *he said,* to let him see my Purse; I immediately put my Hand into my Pocket, *and Laughing at him,* pull'd it out, and there was in it three Guineas and a Half; *then he ask'd me,* if there was all the Money I had? I told him no, *Laughing again,* not by a great deal.

Well then, *he said,* he would have me promise to go and fetch him all the Money I had, every Farthing: *I told him I would,* and I went into my Chamber and fetch'd him a little private Drawer, where I had about six Guineas more, and some Silver, and threw it all down upon the Bed, and told him there was all my Wealth, honestly to a Shilling: He look'd a little at it, but did not tell it, and Huddled it all into the Drawer again, and reaching his Pocket, pull'd out a Key, and then bade me open a little Walnut-tree box, he had upon the Table, and bring him such a Drawer, which I did, in which Drawer there was a great deal of Money in Gold, I believe near 200 Guineas, but I knew not how much: He took the Drawer, and taking my Hand, made me put it in and take a whole handful; I was backward at that, but he held my Hand hard in his Hand, and put it into the Drawer, and made me take out as many Guineas almost as I could well take up at once.

When I had done so, he made me put them into my Lap, and took my little Drawer, and pour'd out all my own Money among his, and bade me get gone, and carry it all Home into my own Chamber.

I relate this Story the more particularly because of the good Humour there was in it, arid to show the temper with which we Convers'd: It was not long after this but he began every Day to find fault with my Cloths, with my Laces, and Head-dresses, and in a Word, press'd me to buy better which by the way I was willing enough to do, tho' I did not seem to be so; for I lov'd nothing in the World better than fine Clothes; I told him I must Housewife the Money he had lent me, or else I should not be able to pay him again. He then told me in a few Words, that as he had a sincere Respect for me, and knew my Circumstances, he had not Lent me that Money, but given it me, and that he thought I had merited it from him by giving him my Company so intirely as

I had done: After this, he made me take a Maid, and keep House, and his Friend that came with him to *Bath,* being gone, he oblig'd me to Dyet him, which I did very willingly, believing *as it appear'd,* that I should lose nothing by it, nor did the Woman of the House fail to find her Account in it too.

We had liv'd thus near three Months, when the Company beginning to wear away at the *Bath,* he talk'd of going away, and fain he would have me to go to *London* with him: I was not very easie in that Proposal not knowing what Posture I was to live in there, or how he might use me: But while this was in Debate he fell very Sick; he had gone out to a place in *Somersetshire* called *Shepton,* where he had some Business, and was there taken very ill, and so ill that he could not Travel; so he sent his Man back to *Bath* to beg me that I would hire a Coach and come over to him. Before he went, he had left all his Money and other things of Value with me, and what to do with them I did not know, but I secur'd them as well as I could, and Lock'd up the Lodgings and went to him, where I found him very ill indeed; however, I perswaded him to be carry'd in a Litter to the *Bath,* where there was more help and better advice to be had.

He consented, and I brought him to the *Bath,* which was about fifteen Miles, *as I remember;* here he continued very ill of a Fever, and kept his Bed five Weeks, all which time I nurs'd him and tended him my self, as much and as carefully as if I had been his Wife; indeed if I had been his Wife I could not have done more; I sat up with him so much and so often, that at last indeed he would not let me sit up any longer, and then I got a Pallate Bed into his Room, and lay in it just at his Bed's Feet.

I was indeed sensibly affected with his Condition, and with the Apprehension of losing such a Friend as he was, and was like to be to me, and I us'd to sit and Cry by him many Hours together: However, at last he grew Better, and gave hopes that he would recover, as indeed he did, tho' very slowly.

Were it otherwise than what I am going to say, I should not be backward to disclose it, as it is apparent I have done in other

Cases in this Account; but I affirm, that thro' all this Conversation, abating the freedom of coming into the Chamber when I or he was in Bed, and abating the necessary Offices of attending him Night and Day when he was Sick, there had not pass'd the least immodest Word or Action between us. O! that it had been so to the last.

After some time he gathered Strength and grew well apace, and I would have remov'd my Pallate Bed, but he would not let me till he was able to venture himself without any Body to sit up with him, and then I remov'd to my own Chamber.

He took many Occasions to express his Sense of my Tenderness and Concern for him; and when he grew quite well, he made me a Present of Fifty Guineas for my Care, and, as he call'd it, for hazarding my Life to save his.

And now he made deep Protestations of a sincere inviolable Affection for me, but all along attested it to be with the utmost reserve for my Virtue and his own: I told him I was fully satisfyed of it; he carried it that length that he protested to me, that if he was naked in Bed with me, he would as sacredly preserve my Virtue, as he would defend it if I was assaulted by a Ravisher; I believ'd him, and told him I did so; but this did not satisfie him; he would, *he said,* wait for some opportunity to give me an undoubted Testimony of it.

It was a great while after this that I had Occasion, on my own Business, to go to *Bristol,* upon which he hir'd me a Coach, and would go with me, and did so; and now indeed our intimacy increas'd: From *Bristol* he carry'd me to *Gloucester,* which was meerly a Journey of Pleasure to take the Air; and here it was our hap to have no Lodging in the Inn but in one large Chamber with two Beds in it: The Master of the House going up with us to show his Rooms, and coming into that Room, said very frankly to him, Sir, *It is none of my business to enquire whether the Lady be your Spouse or no,* but if not, you *may lie as honestly in these two Beds as if you were in two Chambers,* and with that he pulls a great Curtain which drew quite cross the Room, and effectually divided the Beds; well, *says my Friend,* very readily, these Beds will do, and as for the rest, we are too near a kin to lye together, tho' we may Lodge near one another; and this put an honest Face on the thing too. When we came to go to Bed he decently went out of the Room till I was in Bed, and then went to Bed in the Bed on his own side of the Room, but lay there talking to me a great while.

At last repeating his usual saying, that he could lye naked in the Bed with me and not offer me the least Injury, he starts out of his Bed, and now, my *Dear, says he,* you shall see how just I will be to you, and that I can keep my word, and away he comes to my Bed.

I resisted a little, but I must confess I should not have resisted him much if he had not made those Promises at all; so after a little struggle, *as* I *said,* I lay still and let him come to Bed; when he was there he took me in his Arms, and so I lay all Night with him, but he had no more to do with me, or offer'd any thing to me other than embracing me, as I say, in his Arms, no not the whole Night, but rose up and dress'd him in the Morning, and left me as innocent for him as I was the Day I was born.

This was a surprizing thing to me, and perhaps may be so to others who know how the Laws of Nature work; for he was a strong vigorous brisk Person; nor did he act thus on a principle of Religion at all, *but of meer Affection;* insisting on it, that tho' I was to him the most agreeable Woman in the World, yet because he lov'd me he cou'd not injure me.

I own it was a noble Principle, but as it was what! never understood before, so it was to me perfectly amazing. We Travel'd the rest of the Journey as we did before, and came back to the *Bath,* where, as he had opportunity to come to me when he would, he often repeated the Moderation, and I frequently lay with him, and he with me, and altho' all the familiarities between Man and Wife were common to us, yet he never once offered to go any farther, and he valued himself much upon it; I do not say that I was so wholly pleas'd with it as he thought I was: For I own I was much wickeder than he, *as you shall hear presently.*

We liv'd thus near two Year, only with this exception, that he went three times to *London* in that time, and once he continued there four Months; but, to do him Justice, he always supply'd me with Money to subsist me very handsomly.

Had we continued thus, I confess we had had much to boast of; but as wise Men say, it is ill venturing too near the brink of a Command, so we found it; and here again I must do him the Justice to own that the first Breach was not on his part: It was one Night that we were in Bed together warm and merry, and having drank, I think, a little more Wine that Night, both of us, than usual, tho' not in the least to disorder either of us, when after some other follies which I cannot name, and being clasp'd close in his Arms, I *told him,* (I *repeat it with shame and horror. of Soul*) that I cou'd find in my Heart to discharge him of his Engagement for one Night and no more.

He took me at my word immediately, and after that, there was no resisting him; neither indeed had I any mind to resist him any more, let what would come of it.

Thus the Government of our Virtue was broken, and I exchang'd the Place of Friend for that unmusical harsh-sounding Title of WHORE. In the Morning we were both at our Penitentials; I cried very heartily, he express'd himself very sorry; but that was all either of us could do at that time; and the way being thus clear'd, and the bars of Virtue and Conscience thus removed, we had the less difficulty afterwards to struggle with.

It was but a dull kind of Conversation that we had together for all the rest of that Week, I look'd on him with Blushes, and every now and then started that melancholy Objection, *what if I should be with Child now? What will become of me then?* He encourag'd me by telling me, that as long as I was true to him he would be so to me; and since it was gone such a length, (which indeed he never intended) yet if I was with Child, he would take care of that, and of me too: This harden'd us both; I assur'd him if I was with Child, I would die for want of a Midwife rather than Name him as the Father of it; and he assur'd me I should never want if I should be with Child: These mutual assurances harden'd us in the thing; and after this we repeated the crime as often as we pleas'd, till at length, as I had fear'd so it came to pass, and I was indeed with Child.

After I was sure it was so, and I had satisfied him of it too, we began to think of taking measures for the managing it, and I propos'd trusting the Secret to my Landlady, and asking her Advice, which he agreed to: My Landlady, a Woman (as I found) us'd to such things, made light of it; she said she knew it would come to that at last, and made us very merry about it: As I said above, we found her an Experienc'd old Lady at such Work; she undertook every thing, engag'd to procure a Midwife and a Nurse, to satisfie all Enquiries, and bring us off with Reputation, and she did so very dexterously indeed.

When I grew near my time, she desir'd my Gentleman to go away to *London,* or make as if he did so; when he was gone, she acquainted the Parish Officers that there was a Lady ready to lye in at her House, but that she knew her Husband very well, and gave them, as she pretended, an account of his Name, which she called Sir *Walter Cleave;* telling them, he was a very worthy Gentleman, and that she would answer for all Enquiries, and the like: This satisfied the Parish Officers presently and I lay INN with as much Credit as I could have done if I had really bee my Lady Cleave; and was assisted in my Travel by three or four of the best Citizens Wives of *Bath,* who liv'd in the Neighbourhood, which however made me a little the more expensive to him; I often expressed my concern to him about it, but he bid me not be concern'd at it.

As he had furnish'd me very sufficiently with Money for the extraordinary Expences of my Lying Inn, I had every thing very handsome about me; but did not affect to be Gay or Extravagant neither; besides, knowing my own Circumstances, and knowing the World as I had done, and that such kind of things do not often last long, I took care to lay up as much Money as I could for a wet Day, as I call'd it; making him believe it was all spent upon the extraordinary appearance of things in my Lying Inn.

By this means, and including what he had given me as above, I had at the end of my Lying Inn about 200 Guineas by me, including also what was left of my own.

I was brought to Bed of a fine Boy indeed, and a charming Child it was; and when he heard of it he wrote me a very kind obliging Letter about it, and then told me, he thought it would look better for me to come away for *London* as soon as I was up and well, that he had provided Appartrnents for me at *Hammersmith* as if I came thither only from *London,* and that after a little while I should go back to the *Bath,* and he would go with me.

I lik'd this offer very well, and accordingly hir'd a Coach on purpose, and taking my Child and a Wet-Nurse to Tend and Suckle it, and a Maid Servant with me, away I went for *London.*

He met me at *Reading* in his own Chariot, and taking me into that, left the Servant and the Child in the hir'd Coach, and so he brought me to my new Lodgings at *Hammersmith;* with which I had abundance of Reason to be very well pleas'd, for they were very handsome Rooms, and I was very well accommodated.

And now I was indeed in the height of what I might call my Prosperity, and I wanted nothing but to be a Wife, which however could not be in this Case, there was no room for it; and therefore on all Occasions I study'd to save what I could, as I have said above, against a time of scarcity; knowing well enough that such things as these do not always continue, that Men that keep Mistresses often change them, grow weary of them, or Jealous of them, or something or other happens to make them withdraw their Bounty; and sometimes the Ladies that are thus well us'd, are not careful by a prudent Conduct to preserve the Esteem of their Persons, or the nice Article of their Fidelity, and then they are justly cast off with Contempt.

But I was secur'd in this Point, for as I had no Inclination to change, so I had no manner of Acquaintance in the whole House, and so no Temptation to look any farther; I kept no Company but in the Family where I Lodg'd, and with a Clergyman's Lady at next Door; so that when he was absent I visited no Body, nor did he ever find me out of my Chamber or Parlor whenever he came down; if I went any where to take the Air it was always with him.

The living in this manner with him, and his with me, was certainly the most undesigned thing in the World; he often protested to me, that when he became first acquainted with me, and even to the very Night when we first broke in upon our Rules, he never had the least Design of lying with me; that he always had a sincere Affection for me, but not the least real inclination to do what he had done; I assur'd him I never suspected him, that if I had, I should not so easily have yielded to the freedoms which brought it on, but that it was all a surprize, and was owing to the Accident of our having yielded too far to our mutual Inclinations that Night; and indeed I have often observ'd since, and leave it as a caution to the Readers of this Story, that we ought to be cautious of gratifying our Inclinations in loose and lewd Freedoms, lest we find our Resolutions of Virtue fail us in the juncture when their Assistance should be most necessary.

It is true, *and I have confess'd it before,* that from the first hour I began to converse with him, I resolv'd to let him lye with me if he offer'd it; but it was because I wanted his help and assistance, and I knew no other way of securing him than that: But when we were that Night together, and, as I have said, had gone such a length, I found my Weakness, the Inclination was not to be resisted, but I was oblig'd to yield up all even before he ask'd it.

However he was so just to me that he never upbraided me with that; nor did he ever express the least dislike of my Conduct on any other Occasion, but always protested he was as much delighted with my Company as he was the first Hour we came together, I mean came together as Bedfellows.

It is true that he had no Wife, that is to say, she was as no Wife to him, and so I was in no Danger that way, but the just Reflections of Conscience oftentimes snatch a Man, especially a Man of Sense, from the Arms of a Mistress, as it did him at last, tho' on another Occasion.

On the other hand, tho' I was not without secret Reproaches of my own Conscience for: the Life I led, and that even in the greatest height of the Satisfaction I ever took, yet I had the terrible prospect of Poverty and Starving which lay on me as a frightful Spectre, so that there was no looking behind me: But as Poverty brought me into it, so fear of Poverty kept me in it, and I frequently resolv'd to leave it quite off, if I could but come to lay up Money enough to maintain me: But these were Thoughts of no weight, and whenever he came to me they vanish'd; for his Company was so delightful, that there was no being melancholly when he was there; the Reflections were all the Subject of those Hours when I was alone.

I liv'd six Year in this happy but unhappy Condition, in which time I brought him three Children, but only the first of them liv'd; and tho' I remov'd twice in those six Years, yet I came back the sixth Year to my first Lodgings at *Hammersmith:* Here it was that I was one Morning surpriz'd with a kind but melancholy Letter from my Gentleman; intimating, that he was very ill, and was afraid he should have another fit of Sickness, but that his Wife's Relations being in the House with him, it would not be practicable to have me with him, which however he express'd his great Dissatisfaction in, and that he wish'd I cou'd be allowed to Tend and Nurse him as I did before.

I was very much concern'd at this Account, and was very impatient to know how it was with him; I waited a Fortnight or thereabouts, and heard nothing, which surpriz'd me, and I began to be very uneasy indeed; I think I may say, that for the next Fortnight I was near to distracted: It was my particular difficulty, that I did not know directly where he was; for I understood at first he was in the Lodgings of his Wife's Mother; but having remov'd my self to *London,* I soon found by the help of the Direction I had for writing my Letters to him, how to enquire after him; and there I found that he was at a House in *Bloomsbury,* whither he had, a little before he fell Sick, remov'd his whole Family; and that his Wife and Wife's Mother were in the same House, tho' the Wife was not suffered to know that she was in the same House with her Husband.

Here, I also soon understood that he was at the last Extremity, which made me almost at the last Extremity too, to have a true account: One Night I had the Curiosity to disguise my self like a Servant Maid in a Round Cap and Straw Hat, and went to the Door, as sent by a Lady of his Neighbourhood, where he liv'd before, and giving Master and Mistresses Service, I said I was sent to know how Mr – did, and how he had rested that Night; in delivering this Message I got the opportunity I desir'd, for speaking with one of the Maids, I held a long Gossips Tale with her, and had all the Particulars of his Illness, which I found was a Pleurisie attended with a Cough and a Fever; she told me also who was in the House, and how his Wife was, who, by her Relation, they were in some hopes might Recover her Understanding; but as to the Gentleman himself, *in short* she told me the Doctors said there was very little hopes of him, that in the Morning they thought he had been dying, and that he was but little better then, for they did not expect that he could live over the next Night.

This was heavy News for me, and I began now to see an end of my Prosperity, and to see also that it was very well I had play'd the good Housewife, and secur'd or saved something while he was alive, for that now I had no view of my *own living* before me.

It lay very heavy upon my Mind too, that I had a Son, a fine lovely Boy, above five Years old, and no Provision made for it, at least that I knew of; with these Considerations, and a sad Heart, I went home that Evening, and began to cast with my self how I should live, and in what manner to bestow my self, for the residue of my Life.

You may be sure I could not rest without enquiring again very quickly what was become of him; and not venturing to go my self, I sent several sham Messengers, till after a Fortnights waiting longer, I found that there was hopes of his Life, tho' he was still very ill; then I abated my sending any more to the House, and in some time after I learnt in the Neighbourhood that he was about House, and then that he was Abroad again.

I made no doubt then but that I shou'd soon hear of him, and began to comfort my self with my Circumstances being, as I thought, recovered; I waited a Week, and two Weeks, and with much surprize and amazement I waited near two Months and heard nothing, but that being recover'd he was gone into the Country for the Air, and for the better Recovery after his Distemper; after this it was yet two Months more, and then I understood he was come to his City-House again, but still I heard nothing from him.

I had written several Letters for him, and Directed them as usual, and found two or three of them had been call'd for, *but not the rest:* I wrote again in a more pressing manner than ever, and in one of them let him know, that I must be forc'd to wait on him myself, Representing my Circumstances, the Rent of Lodgings to pay, and the Provision for the Child wanting, and my own deplorable Condition, destitute of Subsistence after his most solemn Engagement to take Care of and Provide for me; I took a Copy of this Letter, and finding it lay at the House near a Month and was not call'd for, I found means to have the Copy of it put into his own Hands at a Coffee-House, where I had by Enquiry found he us'd to go.

This Letter forc'd an Answer from him, by which, tho' I found I was to be abandon'd, yet I found he had sent a Letter to me sometime before, desiring me to go down *to the Bath again;* its Contents I shall come to presently.

It is True that Sick Beds are the times when such Correspondences, as this are look'd on with different

Countenance, and seen with other Eyes than we saw them with, or than they appear'd with before: My Lover had been at the Gates of Death, and at the very brink of Eternity; and it seems had been struck with a due remorse, and with sad Reflections upon his past Life of Gallantry and Levity; and among the rest, this criminal Correspondence with me, which was neither more or less than a long continu'd Life of Adultery had represented it self, as it really was, not as it had been formerly thought by him to be, and he look'd upon it now with a just, and a religious Abhorrence.

I cannot but observe also, and leave it for the Direction of my Sex in such Cases of Pleasure, that when ever sincere Repentance succeeds such a Crime as this, there never fails to attend a Hatred of the Object; and the more the Affection might seem to be before, the Hatred will be the more in Proportion: It will always be so, indeed it can be no otherwise; for there cannot be a true and sincere Abhorrence of the Offence, and the Love to the Cause of it remain, there will with an Abhorrence of the Sin be found a detestation of the fellow Sinner; you can expect no other.

I found it so here, tho' good Manners and Justice in this Gentleman kept him from carrying it on to any extream; but the short History of his Part in this Affair, was thus; he perceiv'd by my last Letter, and by all the rest, which he went for after, that I was not gone to the *Bath,* that his first Letter had not come to my Hand, upon which he writes me this;

> MADAM - I am surpriz'd that my Letter Dated the 8th of last Month did not come to your Hand; I give you my Word it was deliver'd at your Lodgings, and to the Hands of your Maid.
>
> *I need not acquaint you with what has been my condition for sometime past; and how having been at the Edge of the Grave, I am by the unexpected and undeserv'd Mercy of Heaven restor'd again: In the Condition I have been in, it cannot be strange to you that our unhappy Correspondence*

has not been the least of the Burthens which lay upon my Conscience; I need say no more, those things that must be repented of, must be also reform'd.

I wish you would think of going back to the Bath; I *enclose you here a Bill for* 50 *l. for clearing your self at your Lodgings, and carrying you down, and hope it will be no surprize to you to add, that on this account only, and not for any Offence given me on your side, I can* SEE YOU NO MORE; *I will take due care of the Child; leave him where he is, or take him with you, as you please; I wish you the like Reflections, and that they may be to your Advantage. I am,...etc.*

I was struck with his Letter as with a thousand Wounds, such as I cannot describe; the Reproaches of my own Conscience were such as I cannot express, for I was not blind to my own Crime: and I reflected that I might with less offence have continued with my Brother, and liv'd with him as a Wife, since there was no Crime in our Marriage on that score, neither of us knowing it.

But I never once reflected that I was all this while a marry'd Woman, a Wife to Mr – the Linnen Draper, who tho' he had left me by the Necessity of his Circumstances, had no power to Discharge me from the Marriage Contract which was between us, or to give me a legal liberty to marry again; so that I had been no less than a Whore and an Adultress all this while: I then reproach'd my self with the Liberties I had taken, and how I had been a Snare to this Gentleman, and that indeed I was principal, in the Crime; that now he was mercifully snatch'd out of the Gulph by a convincing Work upon his Mind, but that I was left as if I was forsaken of God's Grace, and abandon'd by Heaven to a continuing in my wickedness.

Under these Reflections I continu'd very pensive and sad for near a Month, and did not go down to the *Bath*, having no inclination to be with the Woman who I was with before; lest, as I thought, she should prompt me to some wicked course of Life again, as she had done; and besides, I was very loth she should know I was cast off as above.

And now I was greatly perplex'd about my little Boy; it was Death to me to part with the Child, and yet when I consider'd die Danger of being one time or other left with him to keep without a Maintenance to support him, I then resolv'd to leave him where he was; but then I concluded also to be near him my self too, that I might have the satisfaction of seeing him, without the Care of providing for him.

I sent my Gentleman a short Letter therefore, that I had obey'd his Orders in all things, but that of going back to the *Bath,* which I cou'd not think of for many Reasons; that however parting from him was a Wound to me that I could never recover, yet that I was fully satisfied his Reflections were just, and would be very far from desiring to obstruct his Reformation or Repentance.

Then I represented my own Circumstances to him in the most moving Terms that I was able: I told him that those unhappy Distresses which first mov'd him to a generous and an honest Friendship for me, would, I hope, move him to a little concern for me now; tho' the Criminal part of our Correspondence, which I believed neither of us intended to fall into at that time, was broken off, that I desir'd to Repent as sincerely as he had done, but entreated him to put me in some Condition that I might not be expos'd to the Temptations which the Devil never fails to excite us to from the frightful prospect of Poverty and Distress; and if he had the least Apprehensions of my being troublesome to him, I beg'd he would put me in a Posture to go back to my Mother in *Virginia,* from whence he knew I came, and that would put an end to all his Fears on that account; I concluded, that if he would send me 50 *l.* more to facilitate my going away, I would send him back a general Release, and would promise never to disturb him more with any Importunities; unless it was to hear of the well-doing of the Child, who if I found my Mother living, and my Circumstances able, I would send for to come over to me, and take him also effectually off of his Hands.

This was indeed all a Cheat thus far, *viz.* that I had no intention to go to *Virginia,* as the Account of my former Affairs there may convince any Body of; but the business was to get this last Fifty Pounds of him, if possible, knowing well enough it would be the last Penny I was ever to expect.

However, the Argument I us'd, namely, of giving him a general Release, and never troubling him any more, prevail'd effectually with him, and he sent me a Bill for the Money by a Person who brought with him a general Release for me to sign, and which I frankly sign'd, and receiv'd the Money; and thus, tho' full sore against my will, a final End was put to this Affair.

And here I cannot but reflect upon the unhappy Consequence of, too great Freedoms between Persons stated as we were, upon the pretence of innocent intentions, Love of Friendship, *and the like;* for the Flesh has generally so great a share in those Friendships, that it is great odds but inclination prevails at last over the most solemn Resolutions; and that Vice breaks in at the breaches of Decency, which really innocent Friendship ought to preserve with the greatest strictness; but I leave the Readers of these things to their own just Reflections, which they will be more able to make effectual than I, who so soon forgot my self, and am therefore but a very indifferent Monitor.

I was now a single Person again, *as I may call my self, I* was loos'd from all the Obligations either of Wedlock or Mistresship in the World; except my Husband the Linnen Draper, who I having not now heard from in almost Fifteen Year, no Body could blame me for thinking my self entirely freed from; seeing also he had at his going away 'told me, that if I did not hear frequently from him, I should conclude he was dead, and I might freely marry again to whom I pleas'd.

I now began to cast up my Accounts; I had by many Letters, and much Importunity, and with the Intercession of my Mother too, had a second return of some Goods from my Brother, *as I now call him,* in *Virginia,* to make up the Damage of the Cargo I brought away with me, and this too was upon the Condition of my sealing a general Release to him, and to send it him by his Correspondent at *Bristol,* which though I thought hard, but yet I was oblig'd to promise to do: However, I manag'd so well in this case, that I got my Goods away before the Release was sign'd, and then I always found something or other to say to evade the thing, and to put off the signing it at all; till *at length* I pretended I must write to my Brother, and have his Answer, before I could do it.

Including this Recruit, and before I got the last 50 *l.* I found my strength to amount, put all together, to about 450 *l.* so that with that I had above 450 *l.* I had sav'd above 100 *l.* more, but I met with a Disaster with that, which was this; that a Goldsmith in whose Hands I had trusted it, broke, so I lost 70 *l.* of my Money, the Man's Composition not making above 30 *l.* out of his 100 *l.* I had a little Plate, but not much, and was well enough stock'd with Cloaths and Linnen.

With this Stock I had the World to begin again; but you are to consider that I was not now the same Woman as when I liv'd at *Redriff,* for first of all I was near 20 Years older, and did not look the better for my Age, nor for my Rambles to *Virginia* and back again; and tho' I omitted nothing that might set me out to Advantage, except Painting, for that I never stoop'd to, and had Pride enough to think I did not want it, yet there would always be some difference seen between Five and Twenty, and Two and Forty.

I cast about innumerable ways for my future State of Life and began to consider very seriously what I should do, *but nothing offer'd;* I took care to make the World take me for something more than I was, and had it given out that I was a Fortune, and that my Estate was in my own Hands, the last of which was very true, the first of it was as above: I had no Acquaintance, which was one of my worst Misfortunes, and the Consequence of that was, I had no adviser, at least who cou'd advise and assist together; and above all, I had no Body to whom I could in confidence commit the Secret of my Circumstances to, and could depend upon for their Secresie and Fidelity; and I found by experience, that to be Friendless is the worst Condition, next to being in want, that a Woman can be reduc'd to: *I say a Woman,* because 'tis evident Men can be their own Advisers, and their own Directors, and know how to work themselves' out of Difficulties and into Business better than Women; but if a Woman has no Friend to Communicate her Affairs to, and to advise and assist her, 'tis ten to one but she is undone; nay, and the more Money she has, the more Danger she is in of being wrong'd and deceiv'd; and this was my Case in the Affair of the Hundred Pound which I left in the Hand of the Goldsmith, *as above,* whose Credit, it seems, was' upon the Ebb before but I that had no knowledge of things, and no Body to consult with, knew nothing of it, and so lost my Money.

In the next place, when a Woman is thus left desolate and void of Council, she is just like a Bag of Money, or a Jewel dropt on the Highway, which is a Prey to the next Comer; if a Man of Virtue and upright Principles happens to find it, he will have it cried, and the Owner may come to hear of it again; but how many times shall such a thing fall into Hands that will make no scruple of seizing it for their own, to once that it shall come into good Hands.

This was evidently my Case, for I was now a loose unguided Creature, and had no Help, no Assistance, no Guide for my Conduct: I knew what I aim'd at, and what I wanted, but knew nothing how to pursue the End by direct means; I wanted to be plac'd in a settled State of Living, and had I happen'd to meet with a sober good Husband, I should have been as faithful and true a Wife to him as Virtue it self could have form'd: If I had been otherwise, the Vice came in always at the Door of Necessity, not at the Door of Inclination; and I under stood too well, by the want of it, what the value of a settl'd Life was, to do any thing to forfeit the felicity of it; nay, I should have made the better Wife for all the Difficulties I had pass'd thro', by a great deal; nor did I in any of the Time that I had been a Wife, give my Husbands the least uneasiness on account of my Behaviour.

But all this was nothing; I found no encouraging Prospect; I waited, I liv'd regularly, and with as much frugality as became my Circumstances, but nothing offer'd; nothing presented, and the main Stock wasted apace; what to do I knew not, the Terror of approaching Poverty lay hard upon my Spirits: I had some Money, but where to place it I knew not, nor would the Interest of it maintain me, at least not in *London.*

At length a new Scene open'd: There was in the House where I Lodg'd, a North Country Woman that went for a Gentlewoman, and nothing was more frequent in her Discourse than her account of the cheapness of Provisions, and the easie way of living in her County; how plentiful and how cheap every thing was, what good Company they kept, and the like; till at last I told her she almost tempted me to go and live in her County; for I that was a Widow, tho' I had sufficient to live on, yet had no way of encreasing it; and that *London* was an expensive and extravagant Place; that I found I could not live here under a Hundred Pound a Year, unless I kept no Company, no Servant, made no Appearance, and buried my self in Privacy, as if I was oblig'd to it by Necessity.

I should have observ'd, that she was always made to believe, as every Body else was, that I was a great Fortune, or at least that I had Three or Four Thousand Pounds, if not more, and all in my own Hands; and she was mighty sweet upon me when she thought me inclin'd in the least to go into her Country; she said she had a Sister liv'd near *Liverpool,* that her Brother was a considerable Gentleman there, and had a great Estate also in *Ireland;* that she would go down there in about two Months, and if I would give her my Company thither, I should be as welcome as her self for a Month or more as I pleas'd, till I should see how I lik'd the Country; and if I thought fit to live there, she would undertake they would take care, tho' they did not entertain Lodgers themselves, they would recommend me to some agreeable Family, where I shou'd be plac'd to my content.

If this Woman had known my real Circumstances, she would

never have laid so, many Snares, and taken so many weary steps to catch a poor desolate Creature that was good for little when it was caught; and indeed I, whose case was almost desperate, and thought I cou'd not be much worse, was not very anxious about what might befall me, provided they did me no personal Injury; so I suffered my self, tho' not without a great deal of Invitation and great Professions of sincere Friendship and real Kindness, *I say* I suffer'd my self to be prevail'd upon to go with her, and accordingly I pack'd up my Baggage, and put my self in a Posture for a Journey, tho' I did not absolutely know whither I was to go.

And now I found my self in great Distress; what little I had in the World was all in Money, except as before, a little Plate, some Linnen, and my Cloaths; as for Household stuff I had little or none, for I had liv'd always in Lodgings; but I had not one Friend in the World with whom to trust that little I had, or to direct me how to dispose of it, and this perplex'd me Night and Day; I thought of the Bank, and of the other Companies in *London,* but I had no Friend to commit the Management of it to, and to keep and carry about with me Bank Bills, Talleys, Orders, and such things, I look'd upon it as unsafe; that if they were lost my Money was lost, and then I was undone; and on the other hand I might be robb'd, and perhaps murder'd in a strange place for them; this perplex'd me strangely, and what to do I knew not.

It came in my Thoughts one Morning that I would go to the *Bank* my self, where I had often been to receive the Interest of some Bills I had, which had Interest payable on them, and where I had found the Clark, to whom I applyed my self, very Honest and Just to me, and particularly so fair one time, that when I had misstold my Money, and taken less than my due, and was coming away, he set me to rights and gave me the rest, which he might have put into his own Pocket.

I went to him, and represented my Case very plainly, *and ask'd if he would trouble himself to be my Adviser, who was a poor friendless Widow, and knew not what to do: He told me,* if I desir'd his Opinion of any thing within the reach of his Business, he would do his Endeavour that I should not be wrong'd, but that he would also help me to a good sober Person who was a grave Man of his Acquaintance, who was a Clark in such business too, tho' not in their House, whose Judgment was good, and whose Honesty I might depend upon, for, added he, *I will answer for him, and for every step he takes: if he wrongs you,* Madam, *of one Farthing, it shall lye at my door, I will make it good;* and he delights to assist People in such Cases, he does it as an act of Charity.

I was a little at a stand at this Discourse, but after some pause I told him, I had rather have depended upon him because I had found him honest, but if that cou'd not be, I would take his Recommendation sooner than any ones else; *I dare say,* Madam, says he, *that you will be as well satisfied with my Friend as with me, and he is thoroughly able to assist you, which I am not;* it seems he had his Hands full of the Business of the Bank, and had engag'd to meddle with no other Business than that of his Office, which I heard afterwards, but did not understand then: He added, that his Friend should take nothing of me for his Advice or Assistance, and this indeed encourag'd me very much.

He appointed the same Evening after the Bank was shut and Business over, for me to meet him and his Friend; and indeed as soon as I saw his Friend, and he began but to talk of the Affair, I was fully satisfied that I had a very honest Man to deal with; his Countenance spoke it, and his Character, as I heard afterwards, was every where so good, that I had no room for any more doubts upon me.

After the first meeting, in which I only said what I had said before, we parted, and he appointed me to come the next Day to him, *telling me* I might in the mean time satisfie my self of him by enquiry, which I however I knew not how well to do, having no Acquaintance my self.

Accordingly I met him the next Day, when I entered more freely with him into my Case, *I told him my* Circumstances at large, that I was *a Widow* come over from *America,* perfectly desolate and friendless; that I had a little Money, and but a little, and was almost distracted for fear of losing it, having no Friend in the World to trust with the management of it; that I was going into the North of *England* to live cheap, that my stock might not waste; that I would willingly Lodge my Money in the Bank, but that I durst not carry the Bills about me, and the like as above; and how to Correspond about it, or with who, I knew not.

He told me I might lodge the Money in the Bank as an Account, and its being entred in the Books would entitle me to the Money at any time, and if I was in the North might draw Bills on the Cashire and receive it when I would; but that then it would be esteem'd as running Cash, and the Bank would give no Interest for it; that I might buy Stock with it, and so it would lye in store for me, but that then if I wanted to dispose of it, I must come up to Town on purpose to Transfer it, and even it would be with some difficulty I should receive the half yearly Dividend, unless I was here in Person, or had some Friend I could trust with having the Stock in his Name to do it for me, and that would have the same difficulty in it as before; and with that he look'd hard at me and *smil'd a little;* at last, *says he,* why do you not get a head Steward, Madam, that may take you and your Money together into keeping, and then you would have the trouble taken off of your Hands? Ay, Sir, and the Money too it may be, *said I,* for truly *I find the hazard that way is as much as 'tis t'other way;* but I remember, *I said,* secretly to my self, I wish you would ask me the Question fairly, I would consider very seriously on it before I said No.

He went on a good way with me, and I thought once or twice he was in earnest, but to my real Affliction, I found at last he had a Wife; but when he own'd he had a Wife he shook his Head, and said with some concern, that indeed he had a *Wife,* and *no Wife:* I began to think he had been in the Condition of my late Lover, and that his Wife had been Distemper'd or Lunatick, or some such thing: However, we had not much more Discourse at that time, but he told me he was in too much hurry of business then, but that if I would come home to his House after their Business was over, he would by that time consider what might be done for me, to put my affairs in a Posture of Security: I told him I would come, and desir'd to know where he liv'd: He gave me a Direction in Writing, and when he gave where he liv'd: He gave me a Direction in Writing, and when he gave it me he read it to me, and said, there 'tis, Madam, if you dare trust your self with me: Yes, Sir, *said I,* I believe I may venture to trust you with my self, for you have a Wife you say, and I don't want a Husband; besides, I dare trust you with my Money, which is all I have in the World, and if that were gone, I may trust my self any where.

He said some things in Jest that were very handsome and mannerly, and would have pleas'd me very well if they had been in earnest; *but that pass'd over,* I took the Directions, and appointed to attend him at his House at seven a Clock the same Evening.

When I came he made several Proposals for my placing my Money in the Bank, in order to my having Interest for it; but still some difficulty or other came in the way, which he objected as not safe; and I found such a sincere disinterested Honesty in him, that I began to muse with my self, that I had certainly found the honest Man I wanted; and that I could never put my self into better Hands; so I told him with a great deal of frankness that I had never met with Man or Woman yet that I could trust, or in whom I cou'd think my self safe, but that I saw he was so disinterestedly concern'd for my safety that *I said* I would freely trust him with the management of that little I had, if he would accept to be Steward for a poor Widow that could give him no Salary.

He smil'd, and standing up with great Respect saluted me; he told me he could not but take it very kindly that I had so good an Opinion of him; that he would not deceive me, that he would do any thing in his Power to serve me and expect no Sallary; but that he cou'd not by any means accept of a Trust, that it might bring him to be suspected of Self-interest, and that if I should die he might have Disputes with my Executors, which he should be very loth to encumber himself with.

I told him if those were all his Objections I would soon remove them, and convince him that there was not the least room for any difficulty; for that *first* as for suspecting him, if ever I should do it now was the time to suspect him, and not put the Trust into his Hands, and whenever I did suspect him, he could but throw it up then and refuse to go any farther; *Then* as to Executors, I assur'd him I had no Heirs, nor any Relations in England, and I would have neither Heirs or Executors but himself, unless I should alter my Condition before I died, and then his Trust and Trouble should cease together, which however I had no prospect of yet; but I told him if I died as I was, it should be all his own, and he would deserve it by being so faithful to me as I was satisfied he would be.

He chang'd his Countenance at this Discourse, and ask'd me how I came to have so much good will for him? and looking very much pleas'd, said, he might very lawfully wish he was a single Man for my sake; I smil'd and told him, that as he was not, my offer could have no design upon him in it, and to wish as he did was not to be allow'd, 'twas Criminal to his Wife.

He told me I was wrong; for, *says he,* Madam, as I said before, I have a Wife and no Wife, and 'twould be no Sin to me to wish her hang'd, if that were all; I know nothing of your Circumstances that way, Sir, *said I;* but it cannot be innocent to wish your Wife dead; I tell you, *says he again,* she is a Wife and no Wife; you don't know what I am, or what she is.

That's true, *said I,* Sir, I do not know what you are, but I believe you to be an honest Man, and that's the cause of all my Confidence in you.

Well, well, *says he,* and so I am, *I hope,* too; but I am something else too, Madam; for, *says he,* to be plain with you, I am a *Cuckold,* and she is a *Whore;* he spoke it in a kind of Jest, but it was with such an awkward smile, that I perceiv'd it was what stuck very close to him, and he look'd dismally when he said it.

That alters the case indeed, Sir, *said I,* as to that part you were speaking of; but a *Cuckold you* know may be an honest

Man, it does not alter that Case at all; besides I think, *said I,* since your Wife is so dishonest to you, you are too honest to her to own her for your Wife; but that, *said I,* is what I have nothing to do with.

Nay, *says he,* I do think to clear my Hands of her, for to be plain with you, Madam, *added he,* I am no contented Cuckold neither: *On the other hand,* I assure you it provokes me to the highest degree, but I can't help my self, she that will be *a Whore,* will be *a Whore.*

I wav'd the Discourse, and began to talk of my Business, but I found he could not have done with it, so I let him alone, and he went on to tell me all the Circumstances of his Case, too long to relate here; particularly, that having been out of *England* some time before he came to the Post he was in, she had had two Children in the mean time by an Officer of the Army; and that when he came to *England,* and, upon her Submission, took her again, and maintain'd her very well, yet she run away from him with a Linnen-Draper's Apprentice, robb'd him of what she could come at, and continued to live from him still; so that, Madam, *says he,* she is a Whore not by Necessity, which is the common Bait of your Sex, but by Inclination, and for the sake of the Vice.

Well, I pitied him and wish'd him well rid of her, and still would have talk'd of my Business, but it would not do; at last he looks steadily at me, *look you,* Madam, *says he,* you came to ask Advice of me, and I will serve you as faithfully as if you were my own Sister; but I must turn the Tables, since you oblige me to do it, and are so friendly to me, and I think I must ask advice of you; *tell me what must a poor abus'd Fellow do with a* Whore? *what can I do* to do my self Justice *upon her?*

Alas, *Sir, says I,* 'tis a Case too nice for me to advise in, but it seems she has run away from you, so you are rid of her fairly; what can you desire more? Ay, she is gone indeed, *said he,* but I am not clear of her for all that.

That's true, *says I,* she may indeed run you into Debt, but the

Law has furnish'd you with Methods to prevent that also, you may Cry her down, *as they call it.*

No, no, *says he,* that is not the Case neither, I have taken care of all that; 'tis not that part that I speak of, but I would be rid of her so that I might marry again.

Well, Sir, *says I,* then you must Divorce her; if you can prove what you say, you may certainly get that done, and then, I suppose, you are free.

That's very tedious and expensive, *says he.*

Why, *says I,* if you can get any Woman you like to take your word, I suppose your Wife would not dispute the Liberty with you that she takes herself.

Ay, *says he,* but 'twou'd be hard to bring an honest Woman to do that; and for the other sort, *says he,* I have had enough of her to meddle with any more Whores.

It occurr'd to me presently, I would have taken your word with all my Heart, if you had but ask'd me the Question; but that was to my self; *to him I reply'd,* why you shut the Door against any honest Woman accepting you, for you condemn all that should venture upon you at once, and conclude, that really a Woman that takes you now, can't be honest.

Why, *says he,* I wish you would satisfie me that an honest Woman would take me, I'd venture it; and then turns short upon me, *will you take me,* Madam?

That's not a fair Question, *says I,* after what you have said: however, lest you should think I wait only for a Recantation of it, I shall answer you plainly No *not I;* my Business is of another kind with you, and I did not expect you would have tunl'd my serious Application to you in my own distracted Case, into a Comedy.

Why, Madam, *says he,* my Case is as distracted as yours can be, and I stand in as much need of Advice as you do, for I think if I have not Relief some where, I shall be mad my self, and I know not what course to take, I protest to you.

Why, Sir, *says I,* 'tis easie to give Advice in your Case, much easier than it is in mine; speak then, *says he,* I beg of you, for now you encourage me.

Why, *says I,* if your Case is so plain as you say it is, you may be legally Divorc'd, and then you may find honest Women enough to ask the Question of fairly, the Sex is not so scarce that you can want a Wife.

Well then, *said he,* I am in earnest; I'll take your Advice, but shall I ask you one Question seriously before hand?

Any Question, *said I,* but that you did before.

No, that Answer will not do, *said he,* for, in short, that is the Question I shall ask.

You may ask what Questions you please, but you have my Answer to that already, *said I;* besides Sir, *said I,* can you think so Ill of me as that I would give any Answer to such a Question beforehand? Can any Woman alive believe you in earnest, or think you design any thing but to banter her?

Well, well, *says he,* I do not banter you, I am in earnest; consider of it.

But, Sir, *says I, a little gravely,* I came to you about my own Business; I beg of you let me know, what you will advise me to do?

I will be prepar'd, *says he,* against you come again.

Nay, *says I,* you have forbid my coming any more.

Why so, *said he,* and look'd a little surpriz'd?

Because, *said I,* you can't expect I should visit you on the account you talk of.

Well, *says he,* you shall promise me to come again however, and I will not say any more of it till I have gotten the Divorce, but I desire you will prepare to be better condition'd when that's done, for you shall be the Woman, or I will not be Divorc'd at all: Why I owe it to your unlooked for kindness, if it were to nothing else, but I have other Reasons too.

He could not have said any thing in the World that pleas'd me better; however, I knew that the way to secure him was to stand off while the thing was so remote, as it appear'd to be, and that it was time enough to accept of it when he was able to perform it; so I said very respectfully to him, it was time enough to consider of these things, when he was in a Condition to talk of them; in the mean time I told him, I was going a great way from him, and he would find Objects enough to please him better: We broke off here for the present, and he made me promise him to come again the next Day, for his Resolutions upon my own Business, which after some pressing I did; tho' had he seen farther into me, I wanted no pressing on that Account.

I came the next Evening accordingly, and brought my Maid with me, *to let him see* that I kept a Maid, but I sent her away, as soon as I was gone in: He would have had me let the Maid have staid, but I would not, but order'd her aloud to come for me again about Nine a-Clock, but he forbid that, and told me he would see me safe Home, which by the way I was not very well pleas'd with, supposing he might do that to know where I liv'd, and enquire into my Character and Circumstances: However, I ventur'd that, for all that the People there or thereabout knew of me, was to my Advantage; and all the Character he had of me, after he had enquir'd, was *that I was a Woman of Fortune,* and that I was a very modest sober Body; which whether true or not in the Main, yet you may see how necessary it is, for all Women who expect any thing in the World to preserve the Character of their Virtue, even when perhaps they may have sacrific'd the Thing itself.

I found, *and was not a little pleas'd with it,* that he had provided a Supper for me: I found also he lived very handsomely, and had a House very handsomely furnish'd, all which I was rejoyc'd at indeed, for I look'd upon it as all my own.

We had now a second Conference upon the Subject matter of the last Conference: He laid his business very Home indeed; he protested his Affection to me, and indeed I had no room to doubt it; he declar'd that it began from the first Moment I talk'd with him, and long before I had mention'd leaving my Effects with him; 'tis no matter when it begun, *thought I,* if it will not hold, 'twill be well enough: *He then told me,* how much the offer I had made of trusting him with my Effects, and leaving them to him, had engag'd him; so I intended it should, *thought I,* but then I thought you had been a single Man too: After we had Supp'd, I observ'd he press'd me very hard to drink two or three Glasses of Wine, which however I declined, but Drank one Glass or two: He then told he had a Proposal to make to me, which I should promise him I would not take ill, if I should not grant it: I told him I hop'd he would make no dishonourable Proposal to me, especially in his own House, and that if it was such, I desir'd he would not propose it, that I might not be oblig'd to offer any Resentment to him that did not become the respect I profess'd for him, and the Trust I had plac'd in him, in coming to his House; and beg'd of him he would give me leave to go away, and accordingly began to put on my Gloves and prepare to be gone, tho' at the same time I no more intended it than he intended to let me.

Well, he importun'd me not to talk of going; he assur'd me he had no dishonourable thing in his Thoughts about me, and was very far from offering any thing to me that was dishonourable and if I thought so, he would chuse to say no more of it.

That part I did not relish at all; I told him I was ready to hear any thing that he had to say, depending that he would say nothing unworthy of himself, or unfit for me to hear; upon this, he told me his Proposal was this, That I would Marry him, tho' he had not yet obtain'd the Divorce from the Whore his Wife; and to satisfie me that he meant honourably, he would promise not to desire me to live with him, or go to Bed to him till the Divorce was obtain'd: My Heart said yes to this offer at first Word, but it was necessary to Play the Hypocrite a little more with him; so I seem'd to decline the Motion with some warmth, and besides a little Condemning the thing as unfair, told him that such a Proposal could be of no Signification, but to entangle us both in great Difficulties; for if he should not at last obtain the Divorce, yet we could not dissolve the Marriage, neither could we proceed in it; so that if he was disappointed in the Divorce, I left him to consider what a Condition we should both be in.

In short, I carried on the Argument against this so far, that I convinc'd him, it was not a Proposal that had any Sense in it: WELL then he went from it to another, and that was, that I would Sign and Seal a Contract with him, Conditioning to Marry him as soon as the Divorce was obtain'd, and to be void if he could not obtain it.

I told him such a thing was more Rational than the other; but as this was the first time that ever I could imagine him weak enough to be in earnest in this Affair, I did not use to say YES at first asking, I would consider of it.

I play'd with this Lover as an Angler does with a Trout: I found I had him fast on the Hook, so I jested with his new Proposal and put him off: I told him he knew little of me, and bade him enquire about me; I let him also go Home with me to my Lodging, tho' I would not ask him to go in, for I told him it was not Decent.

In short, I ventur'd to avoid Signing a Contract of Marriage, and the Reason why I did it, was because the Lady that had invited me so earnestly to go with her into *Lancashire* insisted so possitively upon it, and promised me such great Fortunes, and such fine things there, that I was tempted to go and try; perhaps, *said I,* I may mend myself very much, and then I made no scruple in my Thoughts of quitting my honest Citizen, who I was not so much in Love with, as not to leave him for a Richer.

In a Word I avoided a Contract; but told him I would go into the *North,* that he should know where to write to me by the Consequence of the Business I had entrusted with him, that I would give him a sufficient Pledge of My Respect for him; for I would leave almost all I had in the World in his Hands; and I would thus far give him my Word, that as soon as he had sued out a Divorce from his first Wife, if he would send me an Account of it, I would come up to *London,* and that then we would talk seriously of the Matter.

It was a base Design I went with, *that I must confess,* tho' I was invited thither with a Design much worse than mine was, as the Sequel will discover; well I went with my Friend, *as I call'd her,* into *Lancashire;* all the way we went she Caressed me with the utmost appearance of a sincere undissembled Affection; treated me except my Coach hire all the way; and her Brother brought a Gentleman's Coach to *Warrington* to receive us, and we were carried from thence to *Liverpool* with as much Ceremony as I could desire: We were also entertain'd at a Merchant's House in *Liverpool* three or four Days very handsomely: I forbear to tell his Name, because of what follow'd; then she told me she would carry me to an Uncles House of hers, where we should be nobly entertain'd; she did so, her Uncle as she call'd him, sent a Coach and four Horses for us, and we were carried near forty Miles, I know not whither.

We came however to a Gentleman's Seat, where was a numerous Family, a large Park, extraordinary Company indeed, and where she was call'd Cousin; I told her if she had resolv'd to bring me into such Company as this, she should have let me have prepar'd my self, and have furnish'd my self with better Cloths; the Ladies took notice of that, and told me very genteely, they did not value People in their Country so much by their Cloths, as they did in *London;* that their Cousin had fully inform'd them of my Quality, and that I did not want Cloths to set me off; in short, they entertain'd me not like what I was, but like what they thought I had been, Namely, a Widow Lady of a great Fortune.

The first Discovery I made here was that the Family were all *Roman Catholicks,* and the Cousin too, who I call'd my Friend; however, *I must say,* that nothing in the World could behave better to me; and I had all the Civility shown me that I could have had if I had been of their Opinion: The Truth is, I had not so much

Principle of any kind, as to be Nice in Point of Religion; and I presently learn'd to speak favourably of the *Romish Church;* particularly I told them I saw little, but the prejudice of Education in all the Differences that were among Christians about Religion, and if it had so happen'd that my Father had been a *Roman Catholick,* I doubted not but I should have been as well pleas'd with their Religion as my own.

This oblig'd them in the highest Degree, and as I was besieg'd Day and Night with good Company and pleasant Discourse, so I had two or three old Ladies that lay at me upon the Subject of Religion too; I was so Complaisant that tho' I would not compleatly engage, yet I made no scruple to be present at their Mass, and to conform to all their Gestures as they shew'd me the 'Pattern, but I would not come too cheap; so that I only in the main encourag'd them to expect that I would turn *Roman Catholick,* if I was instructed in the *Catholick Doctrine* as they call'd it, and so the matter rested.

I stay'd here about six Weeks; and then my Conducter led me back to a Country Village about six Miles from *Liverpool,* where her Brother, (as she call'd him) came to Visit me in his own Chariot, and in a very good Figure, with two Footmen in a good Livery; and the next thing was to make Love to me: As it had happen'd to me, one would think I could not have been cheated, and indeed I thought so myself, having a safe Card at home, which I resolv'd not to quit, unless, I could mend myself very much: However in all appearance this Brother was a Match worth my lissening to, and the least his Estate was valued at was a 1000 *l.* a Year, but the Sister said it was worth 1500 *l.* a Year, and lay most of it in *Ireland.*

That was a great Fortune, and pass'd for such, I was above being ask'd how much my Estate was; and my false Friend taking it upon a foolish hearsay had rais'd it from 500 *l.* to 5000 *l.* and by the time she came into the Country she call'd it 15000 *l.* The *Irishman,* for such I understood him to be, was stark Mad at this

Bait: In short, he Courted me, made me Presents, and run in Debt like a mad Man for the Expences of his Equipage, and of his Courtship: He had, to give him his due, the Appearance of an extraordinary fine Gentleman; he was Tall, well Shap'd, and had an extraordinary Address; talk'd as' naturally of his Park and his Stables, of his Horses, his Game-Keepers, his Woods, his Tenants, and his Servants, as if we had been in the Mansion-House, and I had seen them all about me.

He never so much as ask'd me about my Fortune or Estate, but assur'd me that when we came to *Dublin* he would Joynture me in 600 *l.* a Year good Land; and that he would enter into a Deed of Settlement or Contract here, for the performance of it.

This was such Language indeed as I had not been us'd to, and I was here beaten out of all my Measures; I had a she Devil in my Bosom, every Hour telling me how great her Brother liv'd: One time she would come for my Orders, how I would have my Coaches painted, and how lin'd; and another time what Cloths my Page should wear: In short, my Eyes were dazl'd, I had now lost my Power of saying No, and to cut the Story short, I consented to be married, but to be the more private we were carried farther into the Country, and married by a Romish Clergyman, which I was assur'd would marry us as effectually as a Church of *England* Parson.

I cannot say, but I had some Reflections in this Affair, upon the dishonourable forsaking my faithful Citizen, who lov'd me sincerely, and who was endeavouring to quit himself of a scandalous Whore, by whom he had been indeed barbarously us'd, and promis'd himself infinite Happiness in his new choice; which choice was now giving up her self to another in a manner almost as scandalous as hers could be.

But the glittering show of a great Estate, and of fine Things, which the deceived Creature that was now my Deceiver represented every Hour to my Imagination, hurried me away, and gave me no time to think of *London,* or of any thing there, much less of the Obligation I had to a Person of infinitely more real Merit than what was now before me.

But the thing was done, I was now in the Arms of my new Spouse, who appear'd still the same as before; great even to Magnificence, and nothing less than a Thousand Pound a Year could support the ordinary Equipage he appear'd in.

After we had been marry'd about a Month, he began to talk of my going to *West-chester* in order to embark for *Ireland.* However, he did not hurry me, for we staid near three Weeks longer, and then he sent to *Chester* for a Coach to meet us at the *Black Rock,* as they call it, over-against *Liverpool:* Thither we went in a fine Boat they call a Pinnace with Six Oars, his Servants, and Horses, and Baggage going in the Ferry Boat. He made his excuse to me, that he had no Acquaintance at *Chester,* but he would go before and get some handsome Apartment for me at a private House; I ask'd him how long we should stay at *Chester?* he said not at all any longer than one Night or two, but he would immediately hire a Coach to go to *Holyhead;* then I told him he should by no means give himself the trouble to get private Lodgings for one Night or two, for that *Chester* being a great Place, I made no doubt but there would be very good Inns and Accommodation enough; so we lodg'd at an Inn in the West Street, not far from the Cathedral, I forget what Sign it was at.

Here my Spouse talking of my going to *Ireland,* ask'd me if I had no Affairs to settle at *London* before we went off; I told him no not of any great Consequence, but what might be done as well by Letter from *Dublin:* Madam, says he very respectfully, I suppose the greatest part of your Estate, which my Sister tells me is most of it in Money in the Bank of *England,* lies secure enough, but in case it requir'd Transferring, or any way altering its Property, it might be necessary to go up to *London* and settle those things before we went over.

I seemed to look strange at it, and told him I knew not what he meant; that I had no Effects in the Bank of *England* that I knew of; and I hoped he could not say that I had ever told him I had: No, he said, I had not told him so, but his Sister had said the greatest part of my Estate lay there; and *I only mention'd it my Dear,* said he, *that if there was any occasion to settle it, or order any thing about it, we might not be oblig'd to the hazard and trouble of another Voyage back again,* for he added, that he did not care to venture me too much upon the Sea.

I was surpriz'd at this talk, and began to consider very seriously, what the meaning of it must be? and it presently occurr'd to me that my Friend, who call'd him Brother, had represented me in Colours which were not my due; and I thought, since it was come to that pitch, that I would know the bottom of it before I went out of *England,* and before I should put my self into I knew not whose Hands, in a strange Country.

Upon this I call'd his Sister into my Chamber the next Morning, and letting her know the "Discourse her Brother and I had been upon the Evening before, I conjur'd her to tell me, what she had said to him, and upon what Foot it was that she had made this Marriage? She own'd that she had told him that I was a great Fortune, and said, that she was told so at *London: Told so,* says I warmly, *did I ever tell you so?* No, she said, it was true I did not tell her so, but I had said several times that what I had was in my own disposal: I did so, *return'd I very quickly and hastily,* but I never told you I had any thing call'd a Fortune; no not that I had one Hundred Pounds, or the value of an Hundred Pounds in the World; and how did it consist with my being a Fortune, *said I,* that I should come here into the North of *England* with you, only upon the account of living cheap? At these words which I spoke warm and high, my Husband, and her Brother, as she call'd him, came into the Room, and I desir'd him to come and sit down, for I had something of moment to say before them both, which it was absolutely necessary he should hear.

He look'd a little disturb'd at the assurance with which I seem'd to speak it, and came and sat down by me, having first shut the Door; upon which I began, for I was very much provok'd, and turning my self to him, I am afraid, says I, *my Dear,* for I spoke with kindness on his side, that you have a very great abuse put upon you, and an Injury done you never to be repair'd in your marrying me, which however as I have had no hand in it, I desire I may be fairly acquitted of it, and that the blame may lie where it ought to lie, and no where else, for I wash my Hands of every part of it.

What Injury can be done me, *my Dear,* says he, in marrying you? I hope it is to my Honour and Advantage every way; I will soon explain it to you, says I, and I fear you will have no reason to think your self well us'd, but I will convince you, *my Dear, says I again,* that I have had no hand in it, and there I stop'd a while.

He look'd now scar'd and wild, and began, I believ'd, to suspect what follow'd; however, looking towards me, and saying only *go on,* he sat silent, as if to hear what I had more to say; so I went on; I ask'd you last Night, said I, speaking to him, if ever I made any boast to you of my Estate, or ever told you I had any Estate in the Bank of *England,* or any where else, and you own'd I had not, as is most true; and I desire you will tell me here, before your Sister, if ever I gave you any Reason from me to think so, or that ever we had any Discourse about it; and he own'd again I had not, *but said,* I had appeared always as a Woman of Fortune, and he depended on it that I was so, and hoped he was not deceived. I am not enquiring yet whether you have been deceived or not, *said I,* I fear you have, *and I too;* but I am clearing my self from the unjust Charge of being concern'd in deceiving you.

I have been now asking your Sister if ever I told her of any Fortune or Estate I had, or gave her any: Particulars of it; and she owns I never did: And pray, Madam, *said I, turning my self to her,* be so just to me, before your Brother, to charge me, if you can, if ever I pretended, to you that I had an Estate; and why, if I had, should I come down into this Country with you on purpose to spare *that little I had,* and live cheap? She could not deny one word, but said she had been told in *London* that I had a very great Fortune, and that it lay in the Bank of *England.*

And now, *Dear Sir,* said I, *turning my self to my new Spouse again,* be so just to me as to tell me who has abus'd both you and me so much as to make you believe I was a Fortune, and prompt you to court me to this Marriage? He cou'd not speak a word, but pointed to her; and after some more pause, flew out in the most furious Passion that ever I saw a Man in my Life; cursing her, and calling her all the Whores and hard Names he could think of; and that she had ruin'd him, declaring that she had told him I had Fifteen Thousand Pounds, and that she was to have Five Hundred Pounds of him for procuring this Match for him: He then added, directing his Speech to me, that she was none of his Sister, but had been his Whore for two Years before, that she had had One Hundred Pound of him in part of this Bargain, and that he was utterly undone if things were as I said; and in his raving *he swore* he would let her Heart's Blood out immediately, which frighted her and me too; *she cried,* said she had been told so in the House where I Lodg'd; but this aggravated him more than before, that she should put so far upon him, and run things such a length upon no other Authority than a *hear-say;* and then turning to me again, said very honestly, he was afraid we were both undone; for to be plain, *my Dear,* I have no Estate, *says he,* what little I had, this Devil has made me run out in waiting on you, and putting me into this Equipage; she took the opportunity of his being earnest in talking with me, and got out of the Room, and I never saw her more.

I was confounded now as much as he, and knew not what to say: I thought many ways that I had the worst of it, but his saying he was undone, and that he had no Estate neither, put me into a meer distraction; why, *says I to him,* this has been a hellish Juggle, for we are married here upon the foot of a double Fraud; you are undone by the Disappointment it seems, and if I had had a Fortune I had been cheated too, for you say you have nothing.

You would indeed have been cheated, my Dear, *says he,* but you would not have been undone, for Fifteen Thousand Pound would have maintain'd us both very handsomly in this Country; and I assure you, *added he,* I had resolv'd to have dedicated every Groat of it to you; I would not have wrong'd you of a Shilling, and the rest I would have made up in my Affection to you, and Tenderness of you as long as I liv'd.

This was very honest indeed, and I really believe he spoke as he intended, and that he was a Man that was as well qualified to make me happy, as to his Temper and Behaviour, as any Man ever was; but his having no Estate, and being run into Debt on this ridiculous account in the Country, made all the Prospect dismal and dreadful, and I knew not what to say, or what to think of my self.

I told him it was very unhappy that so much Love, and so much Good-nature, as I discovered in him, should be thus precipitated into Misery; that I saw nothing before us but Ruin, for as to me, it was my unhappiness that what little I had was not able to relieve us a Week, and with that I pull'd out a Bank Bill of 20 *l.* and eleven Guineas, which I told him I had saved out of my little Income; and that by the account that Creature had given me of the way of living in that Country, I expected it would maintain me three or four Year; that if it was taken from me I was left destitute, and he knew what the Condition of a Woman among strangers must be, if she had no Money in her Pocket; however, I told him if he would take it, there it was.

He told me with a great concern, and I thought I saw Tears stand in his Eyes, that he would not touch it, that he abhorr'd the thoughts of stripping me, and making me miserable; that on the contrary, he had Fifty Guineas left, which was all he had in the World, and he pull'd it out and threw it down on the Table, bidding me take it, tho' he were to starve for want of it.

I return'd, with the same concern for him, that I could not bear to hear him talk so; that on the contrary, if he could propose any probable method of living, I would do any thing that became me on my part, and that I would live as close and as narrow as he cou'd desire.

He beg'd of me to talk no more at that rate, for it would make him Distracted; he said he was bred a Gentleman, tho' he was reduced to a low Fortune; and that there was but one way left which he cou'd think of, and that would not do, unless I cou'd answer him one Question, which however he said he would not press me to; I told him I would answer it honestly; whether it would be to his Satisfaction or no, that I could not tell.

Why then, my Dear, tell me plainly, *says he* will the little you have keep us together in any Figure, or in any Station or Place, or will it not?

It was my happiness hitherto that I had not discovered myself or my Circumstances at all; no not so much as my Name; and seeing there was nothing to be expected from him, however good Humoured and however honest he seem'd to be, but to live on what I knew would soon be wasted, I resolv'd to conceal everything but the *Bank Bill,* and the Eleven Guineas which I had own'd; and I would have been very glad to have lost that, and have been set down where he took me up; I had indeed another *Bank Bill* about me of 30 *l.* which was the whole of what I brought with me as well to Subsist on in the Country, as not knowing what might offer; because this Creature, the *go-between* that had thus betray'd us both, had made me believe strange things of my Marrying to my Advantage in the Country, and I was not willing to be without Money whatever might happen. This Bill I concealed, and that made me the freer of the rest, in Consideration of his Circumstances, for I really pittied him heartily.

But to return to his Question, I told him I never willingly Deceiv'd him, and I never would: I was very sorry to tell him that the little I had would not Subsist us; that it was not sufficient to Subsist me alone in the *South* Country; and that this was the Reason that made me put my self into the Hands of that Woman, who call'd him Brother, she having assur'd me that I might Board very handsomely at a Town call'd *Manchester,* where I had not yet been, for about six Pound a Year, and my whole Income not being above 15 *l.* a Year, I thought I might live easie upon it, and wait for better things.

He shook his Head, and remain'd Silent, and a very melancholly Evening we had; however we Supped together, and lay together that Night, and when we had almost Supp'd he look'd a little better and more chearful, and call'd for a Bottle of Wine; *come* my Dear, *says he,* tho' the Case is bad, it is to no purpose to be dejected, come be as easie as you can, I will endeavour, to find out some way or other to live; if you can but Subsist your self, that is better than nothing, I must try the World again; a Man ought to think like a Man: To be Discourag'd, is to yield to the Misfortune; with this he fill'd a Glass, and Drank to me, holding my Hand, and pressing it hard in his Hand all the while the Wine went down, and Protesting afterward his main concern was for me.

It was really a truly gallant Spirit he was of and it was the more Grevious to me: 'Tis something of Relief even to be undone by a Man of Honour, rather than by a Scoundrel; but here the greatest Disappointment was on his side, for he had really, spent a great deal of Money, deluded by this Madam the Procuress; and it was very remarkable on what poor Terms she proceeded; first the baseness of the Creature herself is to be observ'd, who for the getting One Hundred Pound herself, could be content to let him spend Three or Four more, tho' perhaps it was all he had in the World, and more than all; when she had not the least Ground, more than a little Tea-Table Chat, to say that I had any Estate, or was a Fortune, *or the like:* It is true the Design of deluding a Woman of a Fortune, if I had been so, was base enough; the putting the Face of great Things upon poor Circumstances was a Fraud, and bad enough; but the Case a little differ'd too, and that in his Favour, for he was not a Rake that made a Trade to delude Women, and as some have done get six or seven Fortunes after one another, and then rifle and run away from them; but he was really a Gentleman, unfortunate and low, but shad liv'd well; and tho' if I had had a Fortune I should have been enrag'd at the Slut for betraying me; yet really for the Man, a Fortune would not have been ill bestow'd on him, for he was a lovely Person indeed; of generous Principles, good Sense, and of abundance of good Humour.

We had a great deal of close Conversation that Night, for we neither of us Slept much; he was as Penitent for having put all those Cheats upon me as if it had been Felony, and that he was going to Execution; he offer'd me again every Shilling of the Money he had about him, and said, he would go into the Army and seek the World for more.

I ask'd him, why he would be so unkind to carry me into *Ireland,* when I might suppose he cou'd not have Subsisted me there? He took me in his Arms, my Dear, *said he,* depend upon it, I never design'd to go to *Ireland* at all, much less to have carried you thither, but came hither to be out of the Observation of the People who had heard what I pretended to, and withal, that No Body might ask me for Money before I was furnish'd to supply them.

But where then, *said I,* were we to have gone next?

Why my Dear, *said he,* I'll confess the whole Scheme to you as I had laid it; I purpos'd here to ask you something about your Estate, as you see I did, and when you, as I expected you would had enter'd into some Account with me of the particular, I would have made an excuse to you, to have put off our Voyage to *Ireland* for some time, and to have gone first towards *London.*

Then my Dear, *said he,* I resolv'd to have confess'd all the Circumstances of my own Affairs to you, and let you know I had indeed made use of these Artifices to obtain your Consent to marry me, but had now nothing to do but to ask you Pardon, and to tell you abundantly, *as I have said,* I would endeavour to make you forget what was past, by the felicity of the Days to come.

Truly, *said I to him,* I find you would soon have conquer'd me; and it is my Affliction now, that I am not in a Condition to let you see how easily I should have been reconcil'd to you; and have pass'd by all the Tricks you had put upon me, in Recompence of so much good Humour; but my Dear, *said* I, what can we do now? We are both undone, and what better are we for our being reconcil'd together, seeing we have nothing to live on.

We propos'd a great many things, but nothing could offer, where there was nothing to begin with: He beg'd me at last to talk no more of it, for *he said,* I would break his Heart; so we talk'd of other things a little, till at last he took a Husbands leave of me, and so we went to Sleep.

He rise before me in the Morning, and indeed having lain Awake almost all Night, I was very sleepy, and lay till near Eleven a-Clock, in this time he took his Horses and three Servants, and all his Linnen and Baggage, and away he went, leaving a short, but moving Letter for me on the Table, as follows:

> MY DEAR – *I am a Dog; I have abus'd you; but I have been drawn in to do it by a base Creature, contrary to my Principle and the general Practice of my Life: Forgive me,* my Dear! I *ask your Pardon with the greatest Sincerity; I am the most miserable of Men, in having deluded you: I have been so happy to Possess you, and am now so wretch'd as to be forc'd to fly from you: Forgive me,* my Dear; *once more I say forgive me! I am not able to see you Ruin'd by me, and myself unable to Support you: Our Marriage is nothing, I shall never be able to see you again: I here discharge you from it; if you can Marry to your Advantage do not decline it on my Account; I here swear to you on my Faith, and on the Word of a Man of Honour, I will never disturb your Repose if I should know of it, which however is not likely: On the other Hand, if you should not Marry, and if good Fortune should befall me, it shall be all yours where ever you are.*

I have put some of the Stock of Money I have left into your Pocket; take Places for your self and your Maid in the Stage Coach, and go for London; I hope it will bear your Charges thither, without breaking into your own: Again I sincerely ask your Pardon, and will do so, as often as I shall ever think of you.

Adieu my Dear for Ever,

I am yours most Affectionatly,

J. E.

Nothing that ever befel me in my Life sunk so deep into my Heart as this Farewel: I reproach'd him a Thousand times in my Thoughts for leaving me, for I would have gone with him thro' the World, if I had beg'd my Bread. I felt in my Pocket, and there I found ten Guineas, his Gold Watch, and two little Rings, one a small Diamond Ring worth only about six Pound, and the other a plain Gold Ring.

I sat me down and look'd upon these Things two Hours together, and scarce spoke a Word, till my Maid interrupted me by telling me my Dinner was ready: I eat but little, and after Dinner I fell into a vehement Fit of crying, every now and then, calling him by his Name, which was *James,* O *Jemy!* said I, *come back, come back,* I'll give you all I have; I'll beg, I'll starve with you, and thus I run Raving about the Room several times, and then sat down between whiles, and then walking about again, call'd upon him to *come back,* and then cry'd again; and thus I pass'd the Afternoon; till about seven a-Clock when it was near Dusk in the Evening, being *August,* when to my unspeakable Surprize he comes back into the Inn, but without a Servant, and comes directly up into my Chamber.

I was in the greatest Confusion imaginable, and so was he too: I could not imagine what should be the Occasion of it, and began to be at odds with myself whether to be glad or sorry; but my Affection byass'd all the rest, and it was impossible to conceal my Joy, which was too great for Smiles, for it burst out into Tears. He was no sooner entered the Room but he run to me and took me in his Arms, holding me fast and almost stopping my Breath with his Kisses, but spoke not a Word; at length I began: my Dear, *said* I, how could you go away from me? To which he gave no Answer, for it was impossible for him to speak.

When our Extasies were a little over, he told me he was gone about 15 Mile, but it was not in his Power to go any farther, without coming back to see me again, and to take his Leave of me once more.

I told him how I had pass'd my time, and how loud I had call'd him to *come back* again; he told me he heard me very plain upon *Delamere Forest,* at a Place about 12 Miles off: I *smil'd; Nay says he,* do not think I am in Jest, for if ever I heard your Voice in my Life, I heard you call me aloud, and sometimes I thought I saw you running after me; why said I, what did I say? for I had not nam'd the Words to him; you call'd aloud, says he, and said, O *Jemy* O *Jemy come back, come back.*

I Laught at him; *my Dear says he,* do not Laugh, for depend upon it, I heard your Voice as plain as you hear mine now; if you please, I'll go before a Magistrate and make Oath of it; I then began to be amaz'd and surpriz'd, and indeed frighted, and told him what I had really done, and how I had call'd after him, as above.

When we had amus'd ourselves a while about this, I said to him, well, you shall go away from me no more; I'll go all over the World with you rather: *He told me,* it would be a very difficult thing for him to leave me, but since it must be, he hoped I would make it as easie to me as I could; but as for him, it would be his Destruction, that he foresaw.

However he told me that he Consider'd he had left me to Travel to *London* alone, which was too long a Journey; and that as he might as well go that way, as any way else, he was resolv'd to see me safe thither, or near it; and if he did go away then without taking his leave, I should not take it ill of him, and this he made me promise.

He told me how he had dismiss'd his three Servants, sold their Horses, and sent the Fellows away to seek their Fortunes, and all in a little time, at a Town on the Road, I know not where; and *says he,* it cost me some Tears all alone by myself, to think how much happier they were than their Master, for they could go to the next Gentleman's House to see for a Service, whereas, *said he,* I knew not whither to go, or what to do with myself.

I told him, I was so compleatly miserable in parting with him, that I could not be worse; and that now he was come again, I would not go from him, if he would take me with him, let him go whither he would, or do what he would; and in the mean time I agreed that we would go together to *London;* but I could not be brought to Consent he should go away at last and not take his leave of me, as he propos'd to do; but told him Jesting, that if he did, I would call him back again as loud as I did before; Then I pull'd out his Watch and gave it him back, and his two Rings, and his Ten Guineas; but he would not take them, which made me very much suspect that he resolv'd to go off upon the Road, and leave me.

The truth is, the Circumstances he was in, the passionate Expressions of his Letter, the kind Gentlemanly Treatment I had from him, In all the Affair, with the Concern he show'd for me in it, his manner of Parting with that large Share which he gave me of his little Stock left, all these had joyn'd to make such Impressions on me, that I really lov'd him most tenderly, and could not bear the Thoughts of parting with him.

Two Days after this we quitted *Chester,* I in the Stage Coach, and he on Horseback; I dismiss'd my Maid at *Chester;* he was very much against my being without a Maid, but she being a Servant hired in the Country, and I resolving to keep no Servant at *London,* I told him it would have been barbarous to have taken the poor Wench, and have turn'd her away as soon as I came to

Town; and it would also have been a needless Charge on the Road, so I satisfy'd him, and he was easie enough on that Score.

He came with me as far as Dunstable, within 30 Miles of *London,* and then he told me Fate and his own Misfortunes oblig'd him to leave me, and that it was not Convenient for him to go to *London* for Reasons which it was of no value to me to know, and I saw him preparing to go. The Stage Coach we were in did not usually stop at *Dunstable,* but I desiring it but for a Quarter of an Hour, they were content to stand at an Inn-Door a while, and we went into the House.

Being in the Inn, I told him I had but one Favour more to ask of him, and that was, that since he could not go any farther, he would give me leave to stay a Week or two in the Town with him, that we might in that time think of something to prevent such a ruinous thing to us both, as a final Separation would be; and that I had something of Moment to offer to him, that I had never said yet, and which perhaps he might find Practicable to our mutual Advantage.

This was too reasonable a Proposal to be denied, so he call'd the Landlady of the House *and told her* his Wife was taken ill, and so ill that she cou'd not think of going any farther in the Stage Coach, which had tyr'd her almost to Death, and ask'd if she cou'd not get us a Lodging for two or three Days in a private House, where I might rest me a little, for the Journey had been too much for me. The Landlady, a good sort of Woman, well bred, and very obliging, came immediately to see me; *told me* she had two or three very good Rooms in a part of the House quite out of the noise, and if I saw them, she did not doubt but I would like them, and I should have one of her Maids, that should do nothing else but be appointed to wait on me; this was so very kind, that I could not but accept of it and thank her; so I went to look on the Rooms, and lik'd them very well, and indeed they were extraordinarily Furnish'd, and very pleasant Lodgings; so we paid the Stage Coach, took out our Baggage, and resolv'd to stay here a while.

Here *I told him* I would live with him now till all my Money was spent, but would not let him spend a Shilling of his own: We had some kind squabble about that, but *I told him* it was the last time I was like to enjoy his Company, and I desir'd he would let me be Master in that thing only, and he should govern in every thing else, so he acquiesc'd.

Here one Evening taking a Walk into the Fields, *I told him* I would now make the Proposal to him I had told him of; accordingly I related to him how I had liv'd in *Virginia,* that I had a Mother, I believ'd, was alive there still, tho' my husband was dead some Years; *I told him,* that had not my Effects miscarry'd, which by the way I magnify'd pretty much, I might have been Fortune good enough to him to have kept us from being parted in this manner: Then I entered into the manner of Peoples going over to those Countries to settle, how they had a quantity of Land given them by the Constitution of the Place; and if not, that it might be purchased at so easie a Rate that it was not worth naming.

I then gave him a full and distinct account of the nature of Planting, how with carrying over but two or three Hundred Pounds value in *English* Goods, with some Servants and Tools, a Man of Application would presently lay a Foundation for a Family, and in a very few Years be certain to raise an Estate.

I let him into the nature of the Product of the Earth, how the Ground was Cur'd and Prepared, and what the usual encrease of it was; and demonstrated to him, that in a very few Years, with such a beginning, we should be as certain of being Rich, as we were now certain of being Poor.

He was surpriz'd at my Discourse; for we made it the whole Subject of our Conversation for near a Week together, in which time I laid it down in black and white, *as we say,* that it was morally impossible, with a supposition of any reasonable good Conduct, but that we must thrive there and do very well.

Then I told him what measures I would take to raise such a Sum as 300 *l.* or thereabouts; and I argued with him how good a

Method it would be to put an end to our Misfortunes and restore our Circumstances in the World, to what we had both expected, and I added, that after seven Years, if we liv'd, we might be in a Posture to leave our Plantation in good Hands, and come over again and receive the Income of it, and live here and enjoy it; and I gave him Examples of some that had done so, and liv'd now in very good Circumstances in *London.*

In short, I press'd him so to it, that he almost agreed to it, but still something or other broke it off again; till at last he turn'd the Tables, and he began to talk almost to the same purpose of *Ireland.*

He told me that a Man that could confine himself to a Country Life, and that cou'd but find Stock to enter-upon any Land, should have Farms there for 50 *l.* a Year, as good as were here let for 200 *l.* a Year; that the Produce was such, and so Rich the Land, that if much was not laid up, we were sure to live as handsomely upon it as a Gentleman of 3000 *l.* a Year could do in *England;* and that he had laid a Scheme to leave me in *London,* and go over and try; and if he found he could lay a handsome Foundation of living suitable to the Respect he had for me, as he doubted not he should do, he would come over and fetch me.

I was dreadfully afraid that upon such a Proposal he would have taken me at my Word, (*viz.*) to sell my little Income, as I call'd it, and turn it into Money, and let him carry it over into *Ireland* and try his Experiment with it; but he was too just to desire it, or to have accepted it if I had offered it; and he anticipated me in that, for he added, that he would go and try his Fortune that way, and if he found he cou'd do any thing at it to live, then, by adding mine to it when I went over, we should live like our selves; but that he would not hazard a Shilling of mine till he had made the Experiment with a little, and he assur'd me that if he found nothing to be done in *Ireland,* he would then come to me and join in my Project for *Virginia.*

He was so earnest upon his Project being to be try'd first, that I cou'd not withstand him; however, he promis'd to let me hear from him in a very little time after his arriving there, to let me know whether his prospect answer'd his Design, that if there was not a probability of Success, I might take the Occasion to prepare for our other Voyage, and then, he assur'd me, he would go with me to *America* with all his Heart.

I could bring him to nothing farther than this: However, those Consultations entertain'd us near a Month, during which I enjoy'd his Company, which indeed was the most entertaining that ever I met with in my life before. In this time he let me into the whole Story of his own Life, which was indeed surprizing, and full of an infinite Variety sufficient to fill up a much brighter History for its Adventures and Incidents, than any I ever saw in Print: But I shall have occasion to say more of him hereafter.

We parted at last, tho' with the utmost reluctance on my side, and indeed he took his leave very unwillingly too, but Necessity oblig'd him, for his Reasons were very good why he would not come to *London,* as I understood more fully some time afterwards.

I gave him a Direction how to write to me, tho' still I reserv'd the grand Secret, and never broke my Resolution, which was not to let him ever know my true Name, who I was, or where to be found; he likewise let me know how to write a Letter to him, so that he said he wou'd be sure to receive it.

I came to *London* the next Day after we parted, but did not go directly to my old Lodgings; but for another name-less Reason took a private Lodging in St John's-street, or as it is vulgarly call'd St *Jones's* near *Clarkenwell;* and here being perfectly alone, I had leisure to sit down and reflect seriously upon the last seven Months Ramble I had made, for I had been abroad no less; the pleasant Hours I had with my last Husband I look'd back on with an infinite deal of Pleasure; but that Pleasure was very much lessen'd, when I found some time after that I was really with Child.

This was a perplexing thing because of the Difficulty which was before me, where I should get leave to Lye Inn; it being one of the nicest things in the World at that time of Day, for a Woman that was a Stranger, and had no Friends, to be entertain'd in that Circumstance without Security, which by the way I had not, neither could I procure any.

I had taken care all this while to preserve a Correspondence with my honest Friend at the Bank, or rather he took care to Correspond with me, for he wrote to me once a Week; and tho' I had not spent my Money so fast as to want any from him, yet I often wrote also to let him know I was alive; I had left Directions in *Lancashire, so* that I had these Letters, which he sent, convey'd to me; and during my Recess at *St Jones's* I receiv'd a very obliging Letter from him, assuring me that his Process for a Divorce from his Wife went on with Success, tho' he met with some Difficulties in it that he did not expect.

I was not displeas'd with the News that his Process was more tedious than he expected; for tho' I was in no condition to have had him yet, not being so foolish to marry him when I knew my self to be with Child by another Man, as some I know have ventur'd to do; yet I was not willing to lose him, and in a word, resolv'd to have him if he continu'd in the same mind, as soon as I was up again; for I saw apparently I should hear no more from my other Husband; and as he had all along press'd me to Marry, and had assur'd me he would not be at all disgusted at it, or ever offer to claim me again, so I made no scruple to resolve to do it if I could, and if my other Friend stood to his Bargain; and I had a great deal of Reason to be assur'd that he would stand to it, by the Letters he wrote to me, which were the kindest and most obliging that could be.

I now grew Big, and the People where I Lodg'd perceiv'd it, and began to take notice of it to me, and as far as Civility would allow, intimated that I must think of removing; this put me to extreme perplexity, and I grew very melancholy, for indeed I knew not what Course to take; I had Money, but no Friends, and was like now to have a Child upon my Hands to keep, which was a difficulty I had never had upon me yet, as the Particulars of my Story hitherto makes appear.

In the course of this Affair I fell very ill, and my Melancholy really encreas'd my Distemper; my illness prov'd at length to be only an Ague, but my Apprehensions were really that I should Miscarry; I should not say Apprehensions, for indeed I would have been glad to miscarry, but I cou'd never be brought to entertain so much as a thought of endeavouring to Miscarry, or of taking any thing to make me Miscarry; I abhorr'd, I say so much as the thought of it.

However, speaking of it in the House, the Gentlewoman who kept the House propos'd to me to send for a Midwife; I scrupled it at first, but after some time consented to it, but told her I had no particular Acquaintance with any Midwife, and so left it to her.

It seems the Mistress of the House was not so great a Stranger to such Cases as mine was, as I thought at first she had been, as will appear presently, and she sent for a Midwife of the right sort, that is to say, the right sort for me.

The Woman appear'd to be an experienc'd Woman in her Business, I mean as a Midwife, but she had another Calling too, in which she was as expert as most Women, if not more: My Landlady had told her I was very Melancholy, and that she believ'd that had done me harm; and once, *before me,* said to her, Mrs B – *meaning the Midwife,* I believe this Lady's Trouble is of a kind that is pretty much in your way, and therefore if you can do any thing for her, pray do, for she is a very civil Gentlewoman, and so she went out of the Room.

I really did not understand her, but my Mother Midnight began very seriously to explain what she meant, as soon as she was gone: Madam, *says she,* you seem not to understand what your Landlady means, and when you do understand it, you need not let her know at all that you do so.

She means that you are under some Circumstances that may render your Lying-Inn difficult to you, and that you are not willing to be expos'd; I need say no more, but to tell you, that if you think fit to communicate so much of your Case to me, *if it be* so, as is necessary; *for* I do not desire to pry into those things; I perhaps may be in a Condition to assist you, and to make you perfectly easie, and remove all your dull Thoughts upon that Subject.

Every word this Creature said was a Cordial to me, and put new Life and new Spirit into my very Heart; my Blood began to circulate immediately, and I was quite another Body; I eat my Victuals again, and grew better presently after it: She said a great deal more to the same purpose, and then having press'd me to be free with her, and promis'd in the solemnest manner to be secret, she stop'd a little, as if waiting to see what Impression it made on me, and what I would say.

I was too sensible of the want I was in of such a Woman, not to accept her offer; *I told her* my Case was partly as she guess'd, and partly not, *for* I was really married, and had a Husband, tho' he was in such Circumstances, and so remote at that time, as that he cou'd not appear publickly.

She took me short, *and told me,* that was none of her Business, all the Ladies that came under her Care were married Women to her; every Woman, *says she,* that is with Child has a Father *for* it, and whether that Father was a Husband or no Husband, was no Business of hers; her Business was to assist me in my present Circumstances, whether I had a Husband or no; *for, Madam, says she,* to have a Husband that cannot appear, is to have no Husband in the sense of the Case, and therefore whether you are a Wife or a Mistress is all one to me.

I found presently, that whether I was a Whore or a Wife, I was to pass *for* a Whore here, so I let that go; *I told her* it was true as she said, but that however, if I must tell her my Case, I must tell it her as it was: So I related it to her as short as I could, and I concluded it to her thus: *I trouble you with all this,* Madam, said I, *not that, as you said before, it is much to the purpose* in your Affair, but this is to the purpose, *namely, that I am not in any pain about being seen, or being publick or conceal'd, for 'tis perfectly indifferent to me; but my difficulty is, that I have no Acquaintance in this part of the Nation.*

I understand you, Madam, *says she,* you have no Security to bring to prevent the Parish Impertinences usual in such Cases; and perhaps, *says she,* do not know very well how to dispose of the Child when it comes; the last, *says I,* is not so much my concern as the first: Well, Madam, *answers the Midwife,* dare you put your self into my Hands, I live in such a place, tho' I do not enquire after you, you may enquire after me; my name is *B* – I live in such a Street, naming the Street, at the Sign of the Cradle; my Profession is a Midwife, and I have many Ladies that come to my House to Lye-Inn; I have given Security to the Parish in General Terms to secure them from any Charge from whatsoever shall come into the World under my Roof; I have but one Question to ask in the whole Affair, Madam, *says she,* and if that be answer'd, you shall be entirely easie for all the rest.

I presently understood what she meant, and told her, Madam, *I believe I understand you;* I thank God, *tho' I want Friends in this Part of the World, I do not want Money, so for as may be Necessary, tho' I do not abound in that neither:* This I added, because I would not make her expect great things; well Madam, *says she,* that is the thing indeed, without which nothing can be done in these Cases; and yet, *says she,* you shall see that I will not impose upon you, or offer any thing that is unkind to you, and if you desire it, you shall know every thing before hand, that may suit your self to the Occasion, and be either costly or sparing as you see fit.

I told her, she seem'd to be so perfectly sensible of my Condition, that I had nothing to ask of her but this, that as I had told her that I had Money sufficient, but not a great Quantity, she would order it so, that I might be at as little superfluous Charge as possible.

She replyed, that she would bring in an Account of the Expences of it, in two or three Shapes, and like a *Bill of Fare,* I should chuse as I pleas'd, and I desir'd her to do so.

The next Day she brought it, and the Copy of her three Bills was as follows:

	l.	*s.*	*d.*
1. For Three Months Lodging in her House, including my Dyet at 10*s*. a Week	6	0	0
2. For a Nurse for the Month, and *Use* of Child-bed Linnen	1	10	0
3. For a Minister to Christen the Child, and to the Godfathers and Clark	1	10	0
4. For a Supper at the Christening if I had five Friends at it	1	0	0
For her Fees as a Midwife, and the taking off the Trouble of the Parish	3	3	0
To her Maid-Servant attending		10	0
	13	13	0

This was the first Bill, the second was in the same Terms.

	l.	*s.*	*d.*
1. For Three Months Lodging and Dyet, *etc.* at 20s. *per* Week	13	0	0
2. For a Nurse for the Month, and the Use of Linnen and Lace	2	10	0
3. For the Minister to Christen the Child, *etc.* as above	2	0	0
4. For a Supper, and for Sweetmeats	3	3	0
For her Fees, as above	5	5	0
For a Servant-Maid	1	0	0
	26	18	0

This was the second rate Bill, the third, *she said,* was for a degree Higher, and when the Father, or Friends appeared.

	l.	*s.*	*d.*
1. For Three Months Lodging and Dyet, having two Rooms and a Garret for a Servant	30	0	0
2. For a Nurse for the Month, and the finest Suit of Child-bed Linnen	4	4	0
3. For the Minister to Christen the Child, *etc.*	2	10	0
4. For a Supper, the Gentlemen to send in the Wine	6	0	0
For my Fees, *etc.*	10	10	0
The Maid, besides their own Maid only		10	0
	53	14	0

I look'd upon all the three Bills, and smil'd, *and told her* did not see but that she was very reasonable in her Demands, all things Consider'd, and for that I did not doubt but her Accommodations were good.

She told me I should be Judge of that when I saw them: *I told her,* I was sorry to tell her that I fear'd I must be her lowest rated Customer; and *perhaps Madam,* said I, you will *make me the less Welcome upon that Account.* No not at all, *said she,* for where I have One of the third Sort, I have Two of the Second, and Four to One of the First, and I get as much by them in Proportion, as by any; but if you doubt my Care of you, I will allow any Friend you have to overlook, and see if you are well waited on, or no.

Then she explain'd the particulars of her Bill; in the first place, Madam, *said she,* I would have you Observe, that here is three Months Keeping; you are but a Week; I undertake to say you will not complain of my Table: I suppose, *says she, you* do not live

Cheaper where you are now; no indeed, *said I,* nor so Cheap, for I give six Shillings *per* Week for my Chamber, and find my own Diet as well as I can, which costs me a great deal more.

Then Madam, *says she,* if the Child should not live, or should be dead Born, as you know sometime happens, then there is the Minister's Article saved; and if you have no Friends to come to you, you may save the Expence of a Supper; so that take those Articles out Madam, *says she,* your Lying-In will not cost you above 5*l.* 3*s.* in all, more than your ordinary Charge of Living.

This was the most reasonable thing that I ever heard of; so I smil'd, and told her I would come and be her Customer; but *I told her also,* that as I had two Months, and more to go, I might perhaps be oblig'd to stay longer with her than three Months, and desir'd to know if she would not be oblig'd to remove me before it was proper; no, *she said,* her House was large, and besides, she never put any Body to remove that had lain Inn till they were willing to go; and if she had more Ladies offer'd, she was not so ill belov'd among her Neighbours but she could provide Accommodation for Twenty, if there was occasion.

I found she was an eminent Lady in her way, and *in short,* I agreed to put myself into her Hands, and promis'd her: She then talk'd of other things, look'd about into my Accommodations, where was found fault with my wanting Attendance, and Conveniences, and that I should not be us'd so at her House: *I told her,* I was shy of speaking, for the Woman of the House look'd stranger, or atleast I thought so since I had been Ill, because I was with Child; and I was afraid she would put some Affront or other upon me, supposing that I had been able to give but a slight Account of myself.

O Dear, *said she,* her Ladyship is no stranger to these things; she has try'd to entertain Ladies in your Condition several times, but could not secure the Parish; and besides, she is not such a nice Lady as you take her to be; however, since you are agoing you shall not meddle with her, but I'll see you are a little better look'd after while you are here, than I think you are, and it shall not cost you the more neither.

I did not understand her at all; however I thank'd her, and so we parted; the next Morning she sent me a Chicken roasted and hot, and a pint Bottle of Sherry, and order'd the Maid to tell me that she was to wait on me every Day as long as I stay'd there.

This was surprisingly good and kind, and I accepted it very Willingly: At Night she sent to me again, to know if I wanted any thing, and how I did, and to order the Maid to come to her in the morning for my Dinner; the Maid had order to make me so Chocolat in the Morning before she came away, and did so, and at Noon she brought me the Sweetbread of a Breast of Veal whole, and a Dish of Soup for my Dinner, and after this manner she Nurs'd me up at a distance, so that I was mightily well pleas'd, and quickly well, for indeed my Dejections before were the principal Part of my Illness.

I expected as usually is the Case among such People, that the Servant she sent me would have been some impudent brazen Wench of *Drury-Lane* Breeding and I was very uneasie at having her with me upon that Account, so I would not let her lie in that House, the first Night by any means, but had my Eyes about me as narrowly as if she had been a publick Thief.

My Gentlewoman guess'd presently what was the matter, and sent her back with a short Note, that I might depend, upon the honesty of her Maid; that she would be answerable for her upon all Accounts; and that she took no Servants into her House, without very good Security for their Fidelity: I was then perfectly easie, and indeed the Maids behaviour spoke for its self, for a modester, quieter, soberer Girl never came into any bodies Family, and I found her so afterwards.

As soon as I was well enough to go Abroad, I went with the Maid to see the House, and to see the Apartment I was to have; and every thing was so handsome and so clean and well, that in short, I had nothing to say, but was wonderfully pleas'd and satisfy'd with what I had met with, which considering the melancholy Circumstances I was in, was far beyond what I look'd for.

It might be expected that I should give some Account of the Nature of the wicked Practice of this Woman, in whose Hands I was now fallen; but it would be but too much Encouragement to the Vice, to let the World see what easie Measures were here taken to rid the Women's unwelcome Burthen of a Child clandestinely gotten: This grave Matron had several sorts of Practise, and this was one particular, that if a Child was born, tho' not in her House, for she had the occasion to be call'd to many private Labours, she had People at Hand, who for a Peice of Money would take the Child off their Hands, and off from the Hands of the Parish too; and those Children, as she said were honestly provided for, and taken care of: What should become of them all, Considering so many, as by her Account she was concern'd with, I cannot conceive.

I had many times Discourses upon the Subject with her; but she was full of this Argument, that she sav'd the Life of many an innocent Lamb, as she call'd them, which would otherwise perhaps have been Murder'd; and of many a Woman, who made Desperate by the Misfortune, would otherwise be tempted to Destroy their Children, and bring themselves to the Gallows: I granted her that this was true, and a very commendable thing, provided the poor Children fell into good Hands afterwards, and were not abus'd, starv'd, and neglected by the Nurses that bred them up; she answer'd, that she always took care of that, and had no Nurses in her Business, but what were very good honest People, and such as might be depended upon.

I cou'd say nothing to the contrary, and so was oblig'd to say, Madam I do not question you do your part honestly, but what those People do afterwards is the main Question, and she stop'd my Mouth again with saying, that she took the utmost Care about it.

The only thing I found in all her Conversation on these Subjects that gave me any distaste, was, that one time in Discoursing about my being so far gone with Child, and the time I expected to come, she said something that look'd as if she could help me off with my Burthen sooner, if I was willing; or in *English,* that she could give me something to make me Miscarry, if I had a desire to put an end to my Troubles that way; but I soon let her see that I abhorr'd the Thoughts of it, and to do her Justice, she put it off so cleverly, that I cou'd not say she really intended it, or whether she only mentioned the practise as a horrible thing; for she couch'd her words so well, and took my meaning so quickly, that she gave her Negative before I could explain my self.

To bring this part into as narrow a Compass as possible, I quitted my Lodging at *St Jones's* and went to my new Governess, for so they call'd her in the House, and there I was indeed treated with so much Courtesy, so carefully look'd to, so handsomely provided, and every thing so well, that I was surpris'd at it, and cou'd not at first see what Advantage my Governess made of it; but I found afterwards that she profess'd to make no Profit of the Lodgers Diet, nor indeed cou'd she get much by it, but that her Profit lay in the other Articles of her Management, and she made enough that way, I assure you; for 'tis scarce credible what Practice she had, as well Abroad as at Home, and yet all upon the private Account, or in plain *English,* the whoring Account.

While I was in her House, which was near Four Months, she had no less than Twelve Ladies of Pleasure brought to Bed within Doors, and I think she had Two and Thirty, or thereabouts, under her Conduct without Doors, whereof one, as nice as she was with me, was Lodg'd with my oid Landlady at *St Jones's.*

This was a strange Testimony of the growing Vice of the Age, and such a one, that as bad as I had been my self, it shock'd my very Senses, I began to nauceate the place I was in, and above all, the wicked Practice; and yet I must say that I never saw, or do I believe there was to be seen, the least indecency in the House the whole time I was there.

Not a Man was ever seen to come up Stairs, except to visit

the Lying-Inn Ladies within their Month, nor then without the old Lady with them, who made it a piece of the Honour of her Management, that no Man should touch a Woman, no not his own Wife, within the Month; nor would she permit any Man to lye in the House upon any pretence whatever, no not tho' she was sure it was with his own Wife, and her general saying for it was, that she car'd not how many Children was born in her house, but she would have none got there if she could help it.

It might perhaps be carried farther than was needful, but it was an Error of the right Hand if it was an Error, for by this she kept up the Reputation, such as it was, of her Business, and obtain'd this Character, that tho' she did take Care of the Women when they were Debauch'd, yet she was not Instrumental to their being Debauch'd at all; and yet it was a wicked Trade she drove too.

While I was here, and before I was brought to Bed, I receiv'd a Letter from my Trustee at the Bank full of kind obliging things, and earnestly pressing me to return to *London:* It was near a Fortnight old when it came to me, because it had been first sent into *Lancashire,* and then return'd to me; he concludes with telling me that he had obtain'd a Decree, I think he call'd it, against his Wife, and that he would be ready to make good his Engagement to me, if I would accept of him, adding a great many Protestations of Kindness and Affection, such as he would have been far from offering if he had known the Circumstances I had been in, and which as it was I had been very far from deserving.

I returned an Answer to this Letter, and dated it at *Leverpool,* but sent it by a Messenger, alledging that it came in Cover to a Friend in Town; I gave him Joy of his Deliverance, but rais'd some Scruples at the Lawfulness of his Marrying again, and told him I suppos'd he would consider very seriously upon that Point before he resolv'd on it, the Consequence being too great for a Man of his Judgment to venture rashly upon a thing of that Nature; so concluded, wishing him very well in whatever he resolv'd, without letting him into any thing of my own Mind, or giving any Answer to his Proposal of my coming to *London* to him, but mention'd at a distance my intention to return the latter end of the Year, this being dated in *April.*

I was brought to Bed about the middle of *May,* and had another brave Boy, and my self in as good Condition as usual on such Occasions: My Governess did her part as a Midwife with the greatest Art and Dexterity imaginable, and far beyond all that ever I had had any Experience of before.

Her Care of me in my Travail, and after in my Lying-Inn, was such, that if she had been my own Mother it cou'd not have been better; let none be encourag'd in their loose Practises from this Dexterous Lady's Management; for she is gone to her place, and I dare say has left nothing behind her that can or will come up to it.

I think I had been brought to Bed about twenty two Days when I receiv'd another Letter from my Friend at the Bank, with the surprizing News that he had obtain'd a final Sentence of Divorce against his Wife, and had serv'd her with it on such a Day, and that he had such an Answer to give to all my Scruples about his Marrying again, as I could not expect, and as he had no Desire of; for that his wife, who had been under some Remorse before for her usage of him, as soon as she had the account that he had gain'd his Point, had very unhappily destroy'd her self that same Evening.

He express'd himself very handsomely as to his being concern'd at her Disaster, but clear'd himself of having any hand in it, and that he had only done himself Justice in a Case in which he was notoriously Injur'd and Abus'd: However, he said that he was extremely afflicted at it, and had no view of any Satisfaction left in this World, but only in the hope that I wou'd come and relieve him by my Company; and then he press'd me violently indeed to give him some hopes that I would at least come up to Town and let him see me, when he would farther enter into Discourse about it.

I was exceedingly surpriz'd at the News, and began now seriously to reflect on my present Circumstances, and the inexpressible Misfortune it was to me to have a Child upon my Hands, and what to do in it I knew not; at last I open'd my Case at a distance to my Governess; I appear'd melancholy and uneasie for several Days, and she lay at me continually to know what troubl'd me; I could not for my life tell her that I had an offer of Marriage, after I had so often told her that I had a Husband, so that I really knew not what to say to her; I own'd I had something which very much troubl'd me, but at the same time told her I cou'd not speak of it to anyone alive.

She continued importuning me several Days, but it was impossible, *I told her,* for me to commit the Secret to any Body; this instead of being an Answer to her, encreas'd her Importunities; she urg'd her having been trusted with the greatest Secrets of this Nature, that it was her business to Conceal every thing, and that to Discover things of that Nature would be her Ruin; she ask'd me if ever I had found her Tatling of other People's Affairs, and how could I suspect her? *she told me to* unfold my self to her was telling it to no Body; that she was silent as Death; that it must be a very strange Case indeed, that she could not help me out of; but to conceal it, was to deprive myself of all possible Help, or means of Help, and to deprive her of the Opportunity of Serving me. *In short,* she had such a bewitching Eloquence, and so great a power of Perswasion, that there was no concealing any thing from her.

So I resolv'd to unbosome myself to her; I told her the History of my *Lancashire* Marriage, and how both of us had been Disappointed; how we came together, and how we parted: How he absolutely Discharg'd me, as far as lay in him, and gave me free Liberty to Marry again, protesting that if he knew it he would never Claim me, or Disturb, or Expose me; that I thought I was free, but was dreadfully afraid to venture, for the fear of Consequences that might follow in case of a Discovery.

Then I told her what a good Offer I had; show'd her my Friends two last Letters, inviting me to come to *London,* and let her see with what Affection and Earnestness they were written, but blotted out the Name, and also the Story about the Dissaster of his Wife, only that she was dead.

She fell a Laughing at my scruples about marrying, and told me the other was no Marriage, but a cheat on both Sides; and that as we were parted by mutual Consent, the nature of the Contract was destroy'd, and the Obligation was mutually discharg'd: She had Arguments for this at the tip of her Tongue; and *in short,* reason'd me out of my Reason; not but that it was too by the help of my own Inclination.

But then came the great and main Difficulty, and that was the Child; this she told me in so many Words must be remov'd, and that so, as that it should never be possible for anyone to discover it: I knew there was no Marrying without entirely concealing that I had had a Child, for he would soon have discover'd by the Age of it, that it was born, nay and gotten too, since my Parly with him, and that would have destroy'd all the Affair.

But it touch'd my Heart so forcibly to think of Parting entirely with the Child, and for ought I knew, of having it murther'd, or starv'd by Neglect and Ill-usage (which was much the same) that I could not think of it without Horror; I wish all those Women who consent to the disposing their Children out of the way, *as it is call'd* for Decency sake, would consider that 'tis only a contriv'd Method for Murther; that is to say, a killing their Children with safety.

It is manifest to all that understand any thing of Children, that we are born into the World helpless and uncapable either to supply our own Wants, or so much as make them known; and that without help we must Perish; and this help requires not only an assisting Hand, whether of the Mother or some Body else; but there are two Things necessary in that assisting Hand, that is, Care and Skill, without both which, half the Children that are born would die, nay, tho' they were not to be deny'd Food; and one half more of those that remain'd would be Cripples or Fools, lose their Limbs, and perhaps their Sense: I Question not, but that these are partly the Reasons why Affection was plac'd by Nature in the Hearts of Mothers to their Children; without which they would never be able to give themselves up, as 'tis necessary they should, to the Care and waking Pains needful to the Support of their Children.

Since this Care is needful to the Life of Children, to neglect them is to Murther them; again to give them up to be Manag'd by those People, who have none of that needful Affection, plac'd by Nature in them, is to Neglect them in the highest Degree; nay, in Some it goes farther, and is a Neglect in order to their being Lost; so that 'tis even an intentional Murther, whether the Child lives or dies.

All those things represented themselves to my View, and that in the blackest and most frightful Form; and as I was very free with my Governess, who I had now learn'd to call Mother, I represented to her all the dark Thoughts which I had upon me about it, and told her what distress I was in: She seem'd graver by much at this Part than at the other; but as she was harden'd in these things beyond all possibility of being touch'd with the Religious part, and the Scruples about the Murther, so she was equally impenetrable in that Part which related to Affection; She ask'd me if she had not been Careful and Tender of me in my Lying-Inn, as if I had been her own Child? I told her I own'd she had. Well my Dear, *says she,* and when you are gone, what are you to me? and what would it be to me if you were to be Hang'd? Do you think there are not Women, who as it is their Trade, and they get their Bread by it, value themselves upon their being as careful of Children as their own Mothers can be, and understand it rather better? Yes, yes, Child, *says she,* fear it not, How were we Nurs'd ourselves? Are you sure, you was Nurs'd up by your own Mother? and yet you look fat, and fair Child, says the old Beldam, and with that she stroak'd me over the Face; never be concern'd Child, *says she,* going on in her drolling way; I have no Murtherers about me; I employ the best, and the honestest Nurses that can be had, and have as few Children miscarry under their Hands as there would if they were all Nurs'd by Mothers; we want neither Care nor Skill.

She touch'd me to the Quick, when she ask'd if I was sure that I was Nurs'd by my own Mother; on the contrary I was sure I was not; and I trembled, and look'd pale at the very Expression; sure said I, to myself, this Creature cannot be a Witch, or have any Conversation with a Spirit that can inform her what was done with me before I was able to know it myself; and I look'd at her as if I had been frighted; but reflecting that it cou'd not be possible for her to know any thing about me, that Disorder went off, and I began to be easie, but it was not presently.

She perceiv'd the Disorder I was in, but did not know the meaning of it; so she run on in her wild Talk upon the weakness of my supposing that Children were murther'd, because they were not all Nurs'd by the Mother; and to perswade me that the Children she dispos'd of were as well us'd as if the Mothers had the Nursing of them themselves.

It may be true Mother, *says* I, for ought I know, but my Doubts are very strongly grounded, indeed; come then, *says she,* lets hear some of them: Why first, *says* I, you give a Piece of Money to these People to take the Child off the Parents Hands, and to take Care of it as long as it lives; now we know Mother, *said* I, that those are poor People and their Gain consists in being quit of the Charge as soon as they can; how can I doubt but that, as it is best for them to have the Child die, they are not over Solicitous about its Life?

This is all Vapours and Fancy, *says the old Woman,* I tell you their Credit depends upon the Child's Life, and they are as careful as any Mother of you all.

O Mother, *says* I, if I was but sure my little Baby would be carefully look'd to, and have Justice done it, I should be happy indeed; but it is impossible I can be satisfy'd in that Point unless I saw it, and to see it would be Ruin and Destruction to me, as now my Case stands, so what to do I know not.

A Fine Story! *says the Governess,* you would see the Child, and you would not see the Child; you would be Conceal'd and Discover'd both together; these are things impossible my Dear, so you must e'n do as other conscientious Mothers have done before you, and be contented with things as they must be, tho' they are not as you wish them to be.

I understood what she meant by conscientious Mothers; she would have said conscientious Whores, but she was not willing to disoblige me, for really in this Case I was not a Whore, because legally Married, the force of my former Marriage excepted.

However let me be what I would, I was not come up to that pitch of Hardness common to the Profession; I mean to be unnatural, and regardless of the Safety of my Child, and I preserv'd this honest Affection so long, that I was upon the Point of giving up my Friend at the *Bank,* who lay so hard at me to come to him and Marry him, that in *short,* there was hardly any room to deny him.

At last my old Governess came to me, with her usual Assurance. Come my Dear, *says she,* I have found out a way how you shall be at a certainty, that your Child shall be used well, and yet the People that take Care of it shall never know you, or who the Mother of the Child is.

O Mother, *says I,* If you can do so, you will engage me to you for ever: Well, *says she,* are you willing to be at some small Annual Expence, more than what we usually give to the People we Contract with? Ay, *says* I, with all my Heart, provided I may be conceal'd; as to that, says *the Governess,* you shall be Secure, for the Nurse shall never so much as dare to Enquire about you, and you shall once or twice a Year go with me and see your Child, and see how 'tis used, and be satisfy'd that it is in good Hands, no Body knowing who you are.

Why, *said* I, do you think Mother, that when I come to see

my Child, I shall be able to conceal my being the Mother of it, do you think that possible?

Well, well, *says my Governess,* if you discover it, the Nurse shall be never the wiser; for she shall be forbid to ask any Questions about you; or to take any Notice; if she offers it she shall lose the Money which you are to be suppos'd to give her, and the Child be taken from her too.

I was very well pleas'd with this; so the next Week a Country Woman was brought from *Hertford,* or thereabouts, who was to take the Child off our Hands entirely, for 10 *l.* in Money; but if I Would allow 5 *l.* a Year more to her, she would be obliged to bring the Child to my Governesses House as often as we desired, or we should come down and look at it, and see how well she us'd it.

The Woman was a very wholesome look'd likely Woman, a Cottager's Wife, but she had very good Cloaths and Linnen, and every thing well about her; and with a heavy Heart and many a Tear I let her have my Child: I had been down at *Hertford* and look'd at her and at her Dwelling, which I lik'd well enough; and I promis'd her great Things if she would be kind to the Child, so she knew at first word that I was the Child's Mother; but she seem'd to be so much out of the way, and to have no room to enquire after me, that I thought I was safe enough, so in short I consented to let her have the Child, and I gave her Ten Pound, that is to say I gave it to my Governess, who gave it the poor Woman before my Face, she agreeing never to return the Child back to me, or to claim any thing more for its keeping or bringing up; only that I promised, if she took a great deal of Care of it, I would give her something more as often as I came to see it; so that I was not bound to pay the Five Pound, only that I promised my Governess I would do it: And thus my great Care was over, after a manner, which tho' it did not at all satisfie my Mind, yet was the most convenient for me, as my Affairs then stood, of any that cou'd be thought of at that time.

I then began to write to my Friend at the Bank in a more kindly Style, and particularly about the beginning of *July* I sent him a Letter, that I purpos'd to be in Town sometime in *August;* he return'd me an Answer in the most Passionate Terms imaginable, and desir'd me to let him have timely Notice, and he would come and meet me two Days Journey. This puzzl'd me scurvily, and I did not know what Answer to make to it; once I was resolv'd to take the Stage Coach to *West-Chester* on purpose only to have the satisfaction of coming back, that he might see me really come in the same Coach; for I had a jealous thought, though I had no Ground for it at all, lest he should think I was not really in the Country, and it was no ill-grounded Thought, as you shall hear presently.

I endeavour'd to Reason my self out of it, but it was in vain, the Impression lay so strong on my Mind, that it was not to be resisted; at last it came as an Addition to my new Design of going in the Country, that it would be an excellent Blind to my old governess, and would cover entirely all my other Affairs, for she did not know in the least whether my new Lover liv'd in *London* or in *Lancashire;* and when I told her my Resolution, she was fully perswaded it was in *Lancashire.*

Having taken my Measures for this Journey, I let her know it, and sent the Maid that tended me from the beginning, to take a Place for me in the Coach; she would have had me let the Maid have waited on me down to the last Stage, and come up again in the Waggon, but I convinc'd her it wou'd not be convenient; when I went away she told me, she would enter into no Measures for Correspondence, for she saw evidently that my Affection to my Child would cause me to write to her, and to visit her too when I came to Town again; I assur'd her it would, and so took my leave, well satisfied to have been freed from such a House, however good my Accommodations there had been, as I have related above.

I took the Place in the Coach not to its full Extent, but to a place call'd *Stone* in *Cheshire,* I think it is, where I not only had no manner of Business, but not so much as the least Acquaintance with any Person in the Town or near it: But I knew that with Money in the Pocket one is at home any where, so I Lodg'd there two or three Days, till watching my opportunity, I found room in another Stage Coach, and took Passage back again for *London,* sending a Letter to my Gentleman, that I should be such a certain Day at *Stony-Stratford,* where the Coachman told me he was to Lodge.

It happen'd to be a Chance Coach that I had taken up, which having been hired on purpose to carry some Gentlemen to *Westchester* who were going for *Ireland,* was now returning, and did not tye it self up to exact Times or Places as the Stages did; so that having been oblig'd to lye still a *Sunday,* he had time to get himself ready to come out, which otherwise he cou'd not have done.

However, his warning was so short, that he could not reach to *Stony-Stratford* time enough to be with me at Night, but he met me at a Place call'd *Brickill* the next Morning, as we were just coming into the Town.

I confess I was very glad to see him, for I had thought my self a little disappointed over Night, seeing I had gone so far to contrive my coming on purpose: He pleas'd me doubly too by the Figure he came in, for he brought a very handsome (Gentleman's) Coach and four Horses with a Servant to attend him.

He took me out of the Stage Coach immediately, which stop'd at an Inn in *Brickill,* and putting in to the same Inn he set up his own Coach, and bespoke his Dinner; I ask'd him what he meant by that, for I was for going forward with the Journey; he said no, I had need of a little Rest upon the Road, and that was a very good sort of a House, tho' it was but a little Town; so we would go no farther that Night, whatever came of it.

I did not press him much, for since he had come so far to meet me, and put himself to so much Expence, it was but reasonable I should oblige him a little too, so I was easy as to that Point.

After Dinner we walk'd to see the Town, to see the Church, and to view the Fields, and the Country as is usual for Strangers to do, and our Landlord was our Guide in going to see the Church; I observ'd my Gentleman enquir'd pretty much about the Parson, and I took the hint immediately that he certainly would propose to be married; and tho' it was a sudden thought, it follow'd presently, that in short I would not refuse him; for to be plain with my Circumstances, I was in no condition now to say NO; I had no reason now to run any more such hazards.

But while these Thoughts run round in my Head, which was the work but of a few Moments, I observ'd my Landlord took him aside and whisper'd to him, tho' not very softly neither, for so much I over-heard, *Sir, if you shall have occasion* – the rest I cou'd not hear, but it seems it was to this purpose, *Sir, If you shall have occasion for a Minister, I have a Friend a little way off that will serve you, and be as private as you please*; my Gentleman answer'd loud enough for me to hear, *very well, I believe I shall.*

I was no sooner come back to the Inn, but he fell upon me with irresistable Words, that since he had, had the good Fortune to meet me, and every thing concurr'd, it wou'd be hastening his Felicity if I would put an end to the matter just there; what do you mean, *says I,* colouring a little, what in an Inn, and upon the Road! Bless us all, *said I,* as if I had been surpriz'd; how can you talk so! O I can talk so very well, *says he,* I came a purpose to talk so, and I'll show you that I did, and with that he pulls out a great Bundle of Papers; you fright me, *said I,* what are all these; don't be frighted, my Dear, *said he,* and kiss'd me; *this* was *the first time that he had been so free to call* me *my Dear;* then he repeated it, don't be frighted, you shall see what it is all; then he laid them all abroad; there was first the Deed or Sentence of Divorce from his Wife, and the full Evidence of her playing the Whore; then there was the Certificates of the Minister and Church-wardens of the Parish where she liv'd, proving that she was buried, and intimating the manner of her Death; the Copy of the

Coroner's Warrant for a *Jury* to sit upon her, and the Verdict of the *Jury,* who brought it in *Non Compos Mentis;* all this was indeed to the purpose, and to give I me Satisfaction, tho', by the way, I was not so scrupulous, had he known all, but that I might have taken him without it: However, I look'd them all over as well as I cou'd, and told him, that this was all very clear indeed, but that he need not have given himself the Trouble to have brought them out with him, for it was time enough: Well *he said,* it might be time enough for me, but no time but the present time was time enough for him.

There were other Papers roll'd up, and I ask'd 'him, what they were? Why, Ay, *says he,* that's the Question I wanted to have you ask me; so he unrolls them, and takes out a little Chagreen Case, and gives me out of it a very fine Diamond Ring; I could not refuse it, if I had a mind to do so, for he put it upon my Finger; so I made him a Curtsy, and accepted it; then he takes out another Ring, and this *says he,* is for another Occasion, so he puts that in his Pocket. Well, but let me see it tho', *says I,* and smil'd, I guess what it is, I think you are Mad: I should have been Mad if I had done less, *says he,* and still he did not show it me, and I had a great mind to see it; so I says, well but let me see it; hold, *sap he,* first look here, then he took up the Roll again, and read it, and behold! it was a License for us to be married: Why, *says I,* are you Distracted? why you were fully satisfy'd that I would comply and yield at first Word, or resolv'd to take no denial; the last is certainly the Case, *said he;* but you may be mistaken, *said I;* no, no, *says he,* how can you think so? I must not be denied, I can't be denied, and with that he fell to Kissing me so violently, I could not get rid of him.

There was a Bed in the Room, and we were walking to and again, eager in the Discourse, at last he takes me by surprize in his *Arms,* and threw me on the Bed and himself with me, and holding me fast in his Arms, but without the least offer of any Undecency, Courted me to Consent with such repeated Entreaties and Arguments; protesting his Affection and vowing he would not let me go, till I had promised him, that at last I said, why you resolve not to be deny'd indeed, I think: No, no, *says he,* I must not be denyed, I won't be deny'd, I can't be deny'd: Well, well, *said I,* and giving him a slight Kiss, then you shan't be deny'd, *said I,* let me get up.

He was so Transported with my Consent, and the kind manner of it, that I began to think Once, he took it for a Marriage, and would not stay for the Form, but I wrong'd him, for he gave over Kissing me, took me by the Hand, pull'd me up again, and then giving me two or three Kisses again, thank'd me for my kind yielding to him; and was so overcome with the Satisfaction and *Joy* of it, that I saw Tears stand in his Eyes.

I turn'd from him, for it fill'd my Eyes with Tears too; and I ask'd him leave to retire a little to my Chamber: If ever I had a Grain of true Repentance for a vicious and abominable Life for 24 Years past, it was then. O! what a felicity is it to Mankind, *said I,* to myself, that they cannot see into the Hearts of one another! How happy had it been for me, if I had been Wife to a Man of so much honesty, and so much Affection from the Beginning?

Then it occurr'd to me what an abominable Creature am I! and how is this innocent Gentleman going to be abus'd by me! How little does he think, that having Divorc'd a Whore, he is throwing himself into the *Arms* of another! that he is going to Marry one that has lain with two Brothers, and has had three Children by her own Brother! one that was born in *Newgate,* whose Mother was a Whore, and is now a transported Thief; one that has lain with thirteen Men, and has had a Child since he saw me! poor Gentleman! *said I,* What is he going to do? After this reproaching my self was over, it followed thus: Well; if I must be his Wife, if it please God to give me Grace, I'll be a true Wife to him, and love him suitably to the strange Excess of his Passion for me; I will make him amends, if possible, by what he shall see, for the Cheats and Abuses I put upon him, which he does not see.

He was impatient for my coming out of my Chamber, but finding me long, he went down Stairs and talk'd with my Landlord about the Parson.

My Landlord, an Officious tho' well-meaning Fellow, had sent away for the Neighbouring Clergy Man; and when my Gentleman began to speak of it to him, and talk of sending for him, Sir, says he to him, my Friend is in the House; so without any more words he brought them together: When he came to the Minister, he ask'd him if he would venture to marry a couple of Strangers that were both willing? The Parson said that Mr – had said something to him of it; that he hop'd it was no Clandestine Business; that he seem'd to be a grave Gentleman, and he suppos'd Madam was not a Girl, so that the consent of Friends should be wanted; to put you out of doubt of that, says my Gentleman, read this Paper, and out he pulls the License; I am satisfied, says the Minister, where is the Lady? you shall see her presently, says my Gentleman.

When he had said thus, he comes up Stairs, and I was by that time come out of my Room; so he tells me the Minister was below, and that he had talk'd with him, and that upon showing him the License, he was free to marry us with all his Heart, but he asks to see you; so he ask'd if I would let him come up.

'Tis time enough, *said I,* in the Morning, is it not? Why, *said he,* my Dear, he seem'd to scruple whether it was not some young Girl stolen from her Parents, and I assur'd him we were both of Age to command our own Consent; and that made him ask to see you; well, *said I,* do as you please; so up they brings the Parson, and a merry good sort of Gentleman he was; he had been told, it seems, that we had met there by accident, that I came in the *Chester* Coach, and my Gentleman in his own Coach to meet me; that we were to have met last Night at *Stony-Stratford,* but that he could not reach so far: Well, Sir, *says the Parson,* every ill turn has some good in it; the Disappointment, Sir, *says he to my Gentleman,* was yours, and the good Turn is mine, for if you had met at *Stony-Stratford* I had not had the Honour to Marry you: LANDLORD *have you a Common Prayer Book?*

I started as if I had been frighted; Lord, *says I,* what do you mean? what to marry in an Inn, and at Night too: Madam, *says the Minister,* if you will have it be in the Church you shall; but I assure you your Marriage will be as firm here as in the Church; we are not tyed by the Canons to Marry no where but in the Church; and if you will have it in the Church it will be as publick as a Country Fair; and as for the time of Day it does not at all weigh in this Case; our Princes are married in their Chambers, and at Eight or Ten a Clock at Night.

I was a great while before I could be perswaded, and pretended not to be willing at all to be married but in the Church; but it was all Grimace; so I seem'd at last to be prevail'd on, and my Landlord, and his Wife, and Daughter were call'd up: My Landlord was Father and Clark and all together, and we were married, and very Merry we were; tho' I confess the self-reproaches which I had upon me before lay close to me, and extorted every now and then a deep sigh from me, which my Bridegroom took notice of, and endeavour'd to encourage me, thinking, poor Man, that I had some little hesitations at the Step I had taken so hastily.

We enjoy'd our selves that Evening compleatly, and yet all was kept so private in the Inn, that not a Servant in the House knew of it, for my Landlady and her Daughter waited on me, and would not let any of the Maids come up Stairs, except while we were at Supper: My Landlady's Daughter I call'd my Bride-maid, and sending for a Shopkeeper the next Morning, I gave the young Woman a good Suit of Knots, as good as the Town would afford, and finding it was a Lace-making Town, I gave her Mother a piece of Bone-lace for a Head.

One Reason that my Landlord was so close was, that he was unwilling the Minister of the Parish should hear of it; but for all that somebody heard of it, so as that we had the Bells set a Ringing the next Morning early, and the Musick, such as the Town would afford, under our Window; but my Landlord brazen'd it out, that we were marry'd before we came thither, only that being his former Guests, we would have our Wedding Supper at his House.

We cou'd not find in our Hearts to stir the next Day; for in short having been disturb'd by the Bells in the Morning, and having perhaps not slept over much Before, we were so sleepy afterwards that we lay in Bed till almost Twelve a Clock.

I beg'd my Landlady that we might not have any more Musick in the Town, nor Ringing of Bells, and she manag'd it so well that we were very quiet: But an odd Passage interrupted all my Mirth for a good while; the great Room of the House look'd into the Street, and my new Spouse being below Stairs, I had walk'd to the end of the Room, and it being a pleasant warm Day, I had opened the Window, and was standing at it for some Air, when I saw three Gentlemen come by on Horseback and go into an Inn just against us.

It was not to be conceal'd, nor was it so doubtful as to leave me any room to question it, but the second of the three was my *Lancashire* Husband: I was frighted to Death, I never was in such a Consternation in my Life, I thought I should have sunk into the Ground, my Blood run Chill in my Veins, and I trembl'd as if I had been in a cold Fit of an Ague: I say there was no room to question the Truth of it, I knew his Cloaths, I knew his Horse, and I knew his Face.

The first sensible Reflection I made was, that my Husband was not to see my Disorder, and that I was very glad of: The Gentlemen had not been long in the House but they came to the Window of their Room, as is usual; but my Window was shut you may be sure: However, I cou'd not keep from peeping at them, and there I saw him again, heard him call out to one of the Servants of the House for something he wanted, and receiv'd all the terrifying Confirmations of its being the same Person that were possible to be had.

My next concern was to know, if possible, what was his Business there; but that was impossible; sometimes my Imagination form'd an Idea of one frightful thing, sometimes, of another; sometimes I thought he had discover'd me, and was come to upbraid me with Ingratitude and Breach of Honour; and every Moment I fancied he was coming up the Stairs to Insult me; and innumerable fancies came into my Head of what was never in his Head, nor ever could be, unless the Devil had reveal'd it to him.

I remain'd in this fright near two Hours, and scarce ever kept my Eye from the Window or Door of the Inn where they were: At last hearing a great clutter in the Passage of their Inn, I run to the Window, and, to my great Satisfaction, see them all three go out again and Travel on Westward; had they gone toward *London,* I should have been still in a fright, lest I should meet him on the Road again, and that he should know me; but he went the contrary way, and so I was eas'd of that Disorder.

We resolv'd to be going the next Day, but about six a Clock at Night we were alarm'd with a great uproar in the Street, and People riding as if they had been out of their Wits, and what was it but a Hue and Cry after three Highway Men, that had rob'd two Coaches, and some other Travellers near *Dunstable* Hill, and notice had, it seems, been given, that they had been seen at *Brickill* at such a House, meaning the House where those Gentlemen had been.

The House was immediately beset and search'd, but there were witnesses enough that the Gentlemen had been gone above three Hours; the Crowd having gathered about, we had the News presently; and I was heartily concern'd now another way: I presently told the People of the House, that I durst to say those were not the Persons, for that I knew one of the Gentlemen to be a very honest Person, and of a good Estate in *Lancashire.*

The Constable who came with the Hue and Cry was immediately inform'd of this, and came over tome to be satisfy'd from my own Mouth, and I assur'd him that I saw the three Gentlemen as I was at the Window; that I saw them afterwards at the Windows of the Room they din'd in; that I saw them afterwards take Horse, and I could assure him I knew one of them to be such a Man, that he was a Gentleman of very good Estate, and an undoubted Character in *Lancashire,* from whence I was just now upon my Journey.

The assurance with which I deliver'd this gave the Mob Gentry a Check, and gave the Constable such Satisfaction, that he immediately sounded a Retreat, told his People these were not the Men, but that he had an account they were very honest Gentlemen; and so they went all back again; what the Truth of the matter was I knew not, but certain it was that the Coaches were rob'd at *Dunstable* Hill, and 560 *l.* in Money taken, besides some of the Lace Merchants that always Travel that way had been visited too; as to the three Gentlemen, that remains to be explain'd hereafter.

Well, this Allarm stop'd us another Day, tho' my Spouse was for Travelling, and told me that it was always safest Travelling after a Robbery, for that the Thieves were sure to be gone far enough off when they had allarm'd the Country; but I was afraid and uneasy, and indeed principally lest my old Acquaintance should be upon the Road still, and should chance to see me.

I never liv'd four pleasanter Days together in my life; I was a meer Bride all this while, and my new Spouse strove to make me entirely easie in every thing; O could this State of Life have continued! how had all my past Troubles been forgot, and my future Sorrows been avoided! but I had a past life of a most wretched kind to account for, some of it in this World as well as in another.

We came away the fifth Day; and my Landlord, because he saw me uneasie, mounted himself, his Son, and three honest Country Fellows with good Fire-Arms, and, without telling us of it, follow'd the Coach, and would see us safe into *Dunstable;* we could do no less than treat them very handsomely at *Dunstable,* which Cost my Spouse about Ten or Twelve Shillings, and something he gave the Men for their Time too, but my Landlord would take nothing for himself.

This was the most happy Contrivance for me that could have fallen out, for had I come to *London* unmarried, I must either have come to him for the first Night's Entertainment, or have discovered to him that I had not one Acquaintance in the whole City of *London* that could receive a poor Bride for the first Night's Lodging with her Spouse: But now being an old married Woman, I made no scruple of going directly home with him, and there I took Possession at once of a House well Furnish'd, and a Husband in very good Circumstances, so that I had a prospect of a very happy Life, in knew how to manage it; and I had leisure to consider of the real Value of the Life I was likely to live; how different it was to be from the loose ungovern'd part I had acted before, and how much happier a Life of Virtue and Sobriety is, than that which we call a Life of Pleasure.

O had this particular Scene of Life lasted, or had I learnt from that time I enjoy'd it, to have tasted the true sweetness of it, and had I not fallen into the Poverty which is the sure Bane of Virtue, how happy had I been, not only here, but perhaps for ever? for while I liv'd thus, I was really a Penitent for all my Life pass'd, I look'd back on it with Abhorrence, and might truly be said to hate my self for it; I often reflected how my Lover at the *Bath,* strook by the Hand of God, repented and abandon'd me, and refus'd to see me any more, tho' he lov'd me to an extreme; but I, prompted by that worst of Devils, Poverty, return'd to the vile Practice, and made the Advantage of what they call a handsome Face, be the Relief to my Necessities, and Beauty be a Pimp to Vice.

Now I seem'd landed in a safe Harbour, after the Stormy Voyage of Life past was at an end; and I began to be thankful for my Deliverance; I sat many an Hour by my self, and wept over the Remembrance of past Follies, and the dreadful Extravagances of a wicked Life, and sometimes I flatter'd my self that I had sincerely repented.

But there are Temptations which it is not in the Power of Human Nature to resist, and few know what would be their Case, if driven to the same Exigences: As Covetousness is the Root of all Evil, so Poverty is, I believe, the worst of all Snares: But I wave that Discourse till I come to the Experiment.

I liv'd with this Husband in the utmost Tranquility; he was a Quiet, Sensible, Sober Man, Virtuous, Modest, Sincere, and in his Business Diligent and Just: His Business was in a narrow Compass, and his Income sufficient to a plentiful way of Living in the ordinary way; I do not say to keep an Equipage, and make a Figure as the World calls it, nor did I expect it, or desire it; for as I abhorr'd the Levity and Extravagance of my former Life, so I chose now to live retir'd, frugal, and within our selves; I kept no Company, made no Visits; minded my Family, and oblig'd my Husband; and this kind of Life became a Pleasure to me.

We liv'd in an uninterrupted course of Ease and Content for Five Years, when a sudden Blow from an almost invisible Hand, blasted all my Happiness, and turn'd me out into the World in a Condition the reverse of all that had been before it.

My Husband having trusted one of his Fellow Clarks with a Sum of Money too much for our Fortunes to bear the Loss of, the Clark fail'd, and the Loss fell very heavy on my Husband, yet it was not so great neither, but that if he had had Spirit and Courage to have look'd his Misfortunes in the Face, his Credit was so good, that as I told him, he would easily recover it; for to sink under Trouble is to double the Weight, and he that will Die in it shall Die in it.

It was in vain to speak comfortably to him, the Wound had sunk too deep, it was a Stab that touch'd the Vitals; he grew Melancholy and Disconsolate, and from thence Lethargick, and died; I foresaw the Blow, and was extremely oppress'd in my Mind, for I saw evidently that if he died I was undone.

I had had two Children by him and no more, for to tell the Truth, it began to be time for me to leave bearing Children, for I was now Eight and Forty, and I suppose if he had liv'd I should have had no more.

I was now left in a dismal and disconsolate Case indeed, and in several things worse than ever: First it was past the flourishing time with me when I might expect to be courted for a Mistress; that agreeable part had declin'd some time, and the Ruins only appear'd of what had been; and that which was worse than all was this, that I was the most dejected, disconsolate Creature alive; I that had encourag'd my Husband, and endeavour'd to support his Spirits under his Trouble, could not support my own; I wanted that Spirit in Trouble which I told him was so necessary to him for bearing the burthen.

But my Case was indeed Deplorable, for I was left perfectly Friendless and Helpless, and the Loss my Husband had sustain'd had reduc'd his Circumstances so low, that tho' indeed I was not in Debt, yet I could easily foresee that what was left would not support me long; that while it wasted daily for Subsistence, I had no way to encrease it one Shilling, so that it would be soon all spent, and then I saw nothing before me but the utmost Distress, and this represented it self so lively to my Thoughts, that it seem'd as if it was come, before it was really very near; also my very Apprehensions doubl'd the Misery, for I fancied every Sixpence that I paid but for a Loaf of Bread, was the last that I had in the World, and that Tomorrow I was to fast, and be starv'd to Death.

In this Distress I had no Assistant, no Friend to comfort or advise me, I sat and cried and tormented my self Night and Day; wringing my Hands, and sometimes raving like a distracted Woman; and indeed I have often wonder'd it had not affected my Reason, for I had the Vapours to such a degree, that my Understanding was sometimes quite lost in Fancies and Imaginations.

I liv'd Two Years in this dismal Condition wasting that little I had, weeping continually over my dismal Circumstances, and as it were only bleeding to Death, without the least hope or prospect of help from God or Man; and now I had cried so long, and so often, that Tears were, as I might say, exhausted, and I began to be Desperate, for I grew Poor apace.

For a little Relief I had put off my House and took Lodgings, and as I was reducing my Living so I sold off most of my Goods, which put a little Money in my Pocket, and I liv'd near a Year upon that, spending very sparingly, and eeking things out to the utmost; but still when I look'd before me, my very Heart would sink within me at the inevitable approach of Misery and Want: O let none read this part without seriously reflecting on the Circumstances of a desolate State, and how they would grapple with meer want of Friends and want of Bread; it will certainly make them think not of sparing what they have only, but of looking up to Heaven for support, and of the wise Man's Prayer, *Give me not Poverty lest I Steal.*

Let 'em remember that a time of Distress is a time of dreadful Temptation, and all the Strength to resist is taken away; Poverty presses, the Soul is made Desperate by Distress, and what can be done? It was one Evening, when being brought, as I may say, to the last Gasp, I think I may truly say I was Distracted and Raving, when prompted by I know not what Spirit, and as it were, doing I did not know what, or why, I dress'd me, for I had still pretty good Cloaths, and went out: I am very sure I had no manner of Design in my Head when I went out, I neither knew or considered where to go, or on what Business; but as the Devil carried me out and laid his Bait for me, so he brought me to be sure to the place, for I knew not whither I was going or what I did.

Wandring thus about I knew not whither, I pass'd by an Apothecary's Shop in *Leadenhall-street,* where I saw lye on a Stool just before the Counter a little Bundle wrapt in a white Cloth; beyond it, stood a Maid Servant with her Back to it, looking up towards the top of the Shop, where the Apothecary's Apprentice, as I suppose, was standing up on the Counter, with his Back also to the Door, and a Candle in his Hand, looking and reaching up to the upper Shelf for something he wanted, so that both were e'ngag'd mighty earnestly, and no Body else in the Shop.

This was the Bait; and the Devil who I said laid the Snare, as readily prompted me, as if he had spoke, for I remember, and shall never forget it, 'twas like a Voice spoken to me over my Shoulder, take the Bundle; be quick; do it this Moment; it was no sooner said but I step'd into the Shop, and with my Back to the Wench, as if I had stood up for a Cart that was going by, put my Hand behind me and took the Bundle, and went off with it, the Maid or the Fellow not perceiving me, or anyone else.

It is impossible to express the Horror of my Soul all the while I did it: When I went away I had no Heart to run, or scarce to mend my pace; I cross'd the Street indeed, and went down the first turning I came to, and I think it was a Street that went thro' into *Fenchurch-street,* from thence I cross'd and turn'd thro' so many ways and turnings that I could never tell which way it was, nor where I went, for I felt not the Ground, I stept on, and the farther I was out of Danger, the faster I went, till tyr'd and out of Breath, I was forc'd to sit down on a little Bench at a Door, and then I began to recover, and found I was got into *Thames-street* near *Billinsgate.* I rested me a little and went on, my Blood was all in a Fire, my Heart beat as if I was in a sudden Fright: In short, I was under such a Surprize that I still knew not whither I was a going, or what to do.

After I had tyr'd my self thus with walking a long way about, and so eagerly, I began to consider and make home to my Lodging, where I came about Nine a Clock at Night.

What the Bundle was made up for, or on what Occasion laid where I found it, I knew not, but when I came to open it I found there was a Suit of Child-bed Linnen in it, very good and almost new, the Lace very fme; there was a Silver Porringer of a Pint, a small Silver Mug and Six Spoons, some other Linnen, a good Smock, and Three Silk Handkerchiefs, and in the Mug wrap'd up in a Paper Eighteen Shillings and Six-pence in Money.

All the while I was opening these things I was under such

dreadful Impressions of Fear, and in such Terror of Mind, tho' I was perfectly safe, that I cannot express the manner of it; I sat me down and cried most vehemently; Lord, *said I,* what am I now? a Thief! why I shall be taken next time and be carry'd to *Newgate* and be Try'd for my Life! and with that I cry'd again a long time, and I am sure, as poor as I was, if I had durst *for* fear, I would certainly have carried the things back again, but that went off after a while: Well I went to Bed *for* that Night, but slept little, the Horror of the Fact was upon my Mind, and I knew not what I said or did all Night, and all the next Day: Then I was impatient to hear some News of the Loss; and would fain know how it was, whether they were a Poor Bodies Goods, or a Rich; perhaps, *said I,* it may be some poor Widow like me, that had pack'd up these Goods to go and sell them *for* a little Bread *for* herself and a poor Child, and are now starving and breaking their Hearts, *for* want of that little they would have fetch'd, and this Thought tormented me worse than all the rest, *for* three or *four* Days time.

But my own Distresses silenc'd all these Reflections, and the prospect of my own Starving, which grew every Day more frightful to me, harden'd my Heart by degrees; it was then particularly heavy upon my Mind, that I had been reform'd, and had, as I hop'd, repented of all my pass'd wickednesses; that I had liv'd a sober, grave, retir'd Life *for* several Years, but now I should be driven by the dreadful Necessity of my Circumstances to the Gates of Destruction, Soul and Body; and two or three times I fell upon my Knees, praying to God, as well as I could, *for* Deliverance; but I cannot but say my Prayers had no hope in them; I knew not what to do, it was all Fear without, and Dark within; and I reflected on my pass'd Life as not sincerely repented of, that Heaven was now beginning to punish me on this side the Grave, and would make me as miserable as I had been wicked.

Had I gone on here I had perhaps been a true Penitent; but I had an evil Counsellor within, and he was continually prompting me to relieve my self by the worst means; so one Evening he tempted me again by the same wicked Impulse that had said, *take that Bundle,* to go out again and seek *for* what might happen.

I went out now by Day-light, and wandred about I knew not whither, and in search of I knew not what, when the Devil put a Snare in my way of a dreadful Nature indeed, and such a one as I have never had before or since; going thro' *Aldersgate-street* there was a pretty little Child had been at a Dancing-School, and was going home, all alone, and my Prompter, like a true Devil, set me upon this innocent Creature; I talk'd to it, and it prattl'd to me again, and I took it by the Hand and led it a long till I came to a pav'd Alley that goes into *Bartholomew Close,* and I led it in there; the Child said that was not its way home; I said, yes, my Dear it is, I'll show you the way home; the Child had a little Necklace on of Gold Beads, and I had my Eye upon that, and in the dark of the Alley I stoop'd, pretending to mend the Child's Clog that was loose, and took off her Necklace and the Child never *felt* it, and so led the Child on again: Here, I say, the Devil put me upon killing the Child in the dark Alley, that it might not Cry; but the very thought frighted me so that I was ready to drop down, but I turn'd the Child about and bade it go back again, *for* that was not its way home; the Child said so she would, and I went thro' into *Bartholomew Close,* and then turn'd round to another Passage that goes into *Long-lane,* so away into *Charterhouse- Yard* and out into *St John's-street,* then crossing into *Smithfield,* went down *Chick-lane* and into *Field-lane* to *Holbourn-bridge,* when mixing with the Crowd of People usually passing there, it was not possible to have been found out; and thus I enterpriz'd my second Sally into the World.

The thoughts of this Booty put out all the thoughts of the first, and the Reflections I had made wore quickly off; Poverty, as I have said, harden'd my Heart, and my own Necessities made me regardless of any thing: The last Affair left no great Concern upon me, for as I did the poor Child no harm, I only said to my self, I had given the Parents a just Reproof *for* their Negligence in leaving the poor little Lamb to come home by it self, and it would teach them to take more Care of it another time.

This String of Beads was worth about Twelve or Fourteen Pounds; I suppose it might have been formerly the Mother's, for it was too big *for* the Child's wear, but that, perhaps, the Vanity of the Mother to have her Child look Fine at the Dancing School, had made her let the Child wear it; and no doubt the Child had a Maid sent to take care of it, but she, like a careless Jade, was taken up perhaps with some Fellow that had met her by the way, and so the poor Baby wandred till it fell into my Hands.

However, I did the Child no harm; I did not so much as fright it, for I had a great many tender Thoughts about me yet, and did nothing but what, as I may say, meer Necessity drove me to.

I had a great many Adventures after this, but I was young in the Business, and did not know how to manage, otherwise than as the Devil put things into my Head; and indeed he was seldom backward to me: One Adventure I had which was very lucky to me; I was going thro' *Lombard-street* in the dusk of the Evening, just by the end of *Three Kings Court,* when on a sudden comes a Fellow running by me as swift as Lightning, and throws a Bundle that was in his Hand just behind me, as I stood up against the corner of the House at the turning into the Alley; just as he threw it in he said, *God* bless you Mistress let it lie there a little, and away he runs swift as the Wind: After him comes two more, and immediately a young Fellow without his Hat crying stop Thief, and after him two or three more, they pursued the two last Fellows so close, that they were forced to drop what they had got, and one of them was taken into the bargain, the other got off free.

I stood stock still all this while till they came back, dragging the poor Fellow they had taken, and lugging the things they had found, extremely well satisfied that they had recovered the Booty and taken the Thief; and thus they pass'd by me, for I look'd only like one who stood up while the Crowd was gone.

Once or twice I ask'd what was the matter, but the People neglected answering me, and I was not very importunate; but after the Crowd was wholly pass'd, I took my opportunity to turn about and take up what was behind me and walk away: This indeed I did with less Disturbance than I had done formerly, for these things I did not steal, but they were stolen to my Hand: I got safe to my Lodgings with this Cargo, which was a Piece of fine black Lustring Silk, and a Peice of Velvet; the latter was but part of a Peice of about II Yards; the former was a whole Peice of near 50 Yards; it seems it was a *Mercer's* Shop that they had rifled, I say rifled, because the Goods were so considerable that they had Lost; for the Goods that they Recover'd were pretty many, and I believe came to about six or seven several Peices of Silk: How they came to get so many I could not tell; but as I had only robb'd the Thief I made no scruple at taking these Goods, and being very glad of them too.

I had pretty good Luck thus far, and I made several Adventures more, tho' with but small Purchase; yet with good Success, but I went in daily dread that some mischief would befal me, and that I should certainly come to be hang'd at last: The impression this made on me was too strong to be slighted, and it kept me from making attempts that for ought I know might have been very safely perform'd; but one thing I cannot omit, which was a Bait to me many a Day. I walk'd frequently out into the Villages round the Town to see if nothing would fall in my Way there; and going by a House near *Stepney,* I saw on the Window-board two Rings, one a small Diamond Ring, and the other a plain Gold Ring, to be sure laid there by some thoughtless Lady, that had more Money than Forecast, perhaps only till she wash'd her Hands.

I walk'd several times by the Window to observe if I could see whether there was any Body in the Room or no, and I could see no Body, but still I was not sure; it came presently into my Thoughts to rap at the Glass, as if I wanted to speak with some

Body, and if any Body was there they would be sure to come to the Window, and then I would tell them to remove those Rings, for that I had seen two suspicious Fellows take notice of them: This was a ready Thought, I rapt once or twice and no Body came, when seeing the Coast clear, I thrust hard against the Square of Glass, and broke it with very little Noise, and took out the two Rings, and walk'd away with them very safe; the Diamond Ring was worth about 3 *l.* and the other about *9s.*

I was now at a loss for a Market for my Goods, and especially for my two Peices of Silk, I was very loth to dispose of them for a Trifle; as the poor unhappy Thieves in general do, who after they have ventured their Lives for perhaps a thing of Value, are fain to sell it for a Song when they have done; but I was resolv'd I would not do thus whatever shift I made, unless I was driven to the last Extremity; however I did not well know what Course to take: At last I resolv'd to go to my old Governess, and acquaint myself with her again: I had punctually supply'd the 5 *l.* a Year to her for my little Boy as long as I ,was able; but at last was oblig'd to put a stop to it: However I had written a Letter to her, wherein I had told her that my Circumstances were reduc'd very low; that I had lost my Husband, and that I was not able to do it any longer, and so beg'd that the poor Child might not suffer too much for its Mother's Misfortunes.

I now made her a Visit, and I found that she drove something of the old Trade still, but that she was not in such flourishing Circumstances as before; for she had been Sued by a certain Gentleman who had had his Daughter stolen from him, and who it seems she had helped to convey away; and it was very narrowly that she escap'd the Gallows; the Expence also had ravag'd her, and she was become very poor; her House was but meanly Furnished, and she was not in such repute for her Practice as before; however she stood upon her Legs, as they say, and as she was a stirring bustling Woman, and had some Stock left, she was turn'd *Pawn Broker, and liv'd pretty well.*

She receiv'd me very civily, and with her usual obliging manner told me she would not have the less respect for me, for my being reduc'd; that she had taken Care my Boy was very well look'd after, tho' I could not pay for him, and that the Woman that had him was easie, so that I needed not to Trouble myself about him, till I might be better able to do it effectually.

I told her I had not much Money left, but that I had some things that were Monies worth, if she could tell me how I might turn them into Money; she ask'd me what it was I had, I pull'd out the string of gold Beads, and told her it was one of my Husbands Presents to me; then I show'd her the two Parcels of Silk which I told her I had from *Ireland,* and brought up to Town with me; and the little Diamond Ring; as to the small Parcel of Plate and Spoons, I had found means to dispose of them myself before; and as for the Childbed Linnen I had, she offer'd me to take it herself, believing it to have been my own; she told me that she was turn'd *Pawn-Broker,* and that she would sell those things for me as pawn'd to her; and so she sent presently for proper Agents that bought them, being in her Hands, without any scruple, and gave good Prizes too.

I now began to think this necessary Woman might help me a little in my low Condition to some Business, for I would gladly have turn'd my Hand to any honest Employment if I could have got it; but here she was defficient; honest Business did not come within her reach; if I had been younger, perhaps she might have helped me to Spark, but my Thoughts were off of that kind of Livelihood, as being quite out of the way after 50, which was my Case, and so I told her.

She invited me at last to come, and be at her House till I could find something to do, and it should cost me very little, and this I gladly accepted of, and now living a little easier, I enter'd into some Measures to have my little Son by my last Husband taken off; and this she made easie too, reserving a Payment only of 5 *l.* a Year, if I could pay it. This was such a help to me, that for a good while I left off the wicked Trade that I had so newly taken up; and gladly I would have got my Bread by the help of my Needle if I cou'd have got Work, but that was very hard to do for one that had no manner of Acquaintance in the World.

However at last I got some Quilting Work for Ladies Beds, Petticoats, and the like; and this I lik'd very well and work'd very hard, and with this I began to live; but the diligent Devil who resolv'd I should continue in his Service, continually prompted me to go out and take a Walk, that is to say, to see if any thing would offer in the old Way.

One Evening I blindly obeyed his *Summons,* and fetch'd a long Circuit thro' the Streets, but met with no purchase and came Home very weary, and empty; but not content with that, I went out the next Evening too, when going by an Alehouse I saw the Door of a little room open, next the very Street, and on the Table a silver Tankard, things much in use in publick Houses at that time; it seems some Company had been drinking there, and the careless Boys had forgot to take it away.

I went into the Box frankly, and setting the silver Tankard on the Corner of the Bench, I sat down before it, and knock'd with my Foot, a Boy came presently, and I. bade him fetch me a pint of warm Ale, for it was cold Weather; the Boy run, and I heard him go down the Cellar to draw the Ale; while the Boy was gone, another Boy come into the Room, and cried, *d' ye call?* I spoke with a melancholly Air, and said, no Child, the Boy is gone for a Pint of Ale for me.

While I sat here, I heard the Woman in the Bar say are they all gone in the Five? which was the Box I sat in, and the Boy said *yes;* who fetch'd the Tankard away? *says the Woman;* I did, *says another Boy,* that's it, pointing it seems to another Tankard, which he had fetch'd from another Box by Mistake; or else it must be, that the Rogue forgot that he had not brought it in, which certainly he had not.

I heard all this, much to my satisfaction, for I found plainly that the Tankard was not mist, and yet they concluded it was fetch'd away; so I drank my Ale, call'd to Pay, and as I went away, *I said,* take care of your Plate Child, meaning a silver pint Mug, which he brought me Drink in; the Boy said, *yes Madam, very welcome,* and away I came.

I came Home to my Governess, and now I thought it was a time to try her, that if I might be put to the Necessity of being expos'd, she might offer me some assistance; when I had been at Home some time, and had an opportunity of Talking to her, I told her I had a Secret of the greatest Consequence in the World to commit to her if she had respect enough for me to keep it a Secret: She told me she had kept one of my Secrets faithfully; why should I doubt her keeping another? I told her the strangest thing in the World had befallen me, and that it had made a Thief of me, even without any design; and so told her the whole Story of the Tankard: And have you brought it away with you my Dear? *says she,* to be sure I have, *says I,* and shew'd it her. But what shall I do now, *says I,* must not I carry it again?

Carry it again! *says she,* Ay, if you are minded to be sent to *Newgate* for stealing it; why, *says I,* they can't be so base to stop me, when I carry it to them again? You don't know those Sort of People Child, *says she,* they'll not only carry you to *Newgate,* but hang you too without any regard to the honesty of returning it; or bring in an Account of all the other Tankards they have lost for you to pay for: What must I do then? *says I;* Nay, *says she,* as you have played the cunning part and stole it, you must e'n keep it, there's no going back now; besides Child, *says she,* Don't you want it more than they do? I wish you cou'd light of such a Bargain once a Week.

This gave me a new Notion of my *Governess,* and that since she was turn'd *Pawn Broker,* she had a Sort of People about her, that were none of the honest ones that I had met with there before.

I had not been long there, but I discover'd it more plainly

than before, for every now and then I saw Hilts of Swords, Spoons, Forks, Tankards, and all such kind of Ware brought in, not to be Pawn'd, but to be sold down right; and she bought every thing that came without asking any Questions, but had very good Bargains as I found by her Discourse.

I found also that in the following this Trade, she always melted down the Plate she bought, that it might not be challeng'd; and she came to me and told me one Morning that she was going to Melt, and if I would, she would put my Tankard in, that it might not be seen by any Body; I told her with all my Heart; so she weigh'd it, and allow'd me the full value in Silver again; but I found she did not do the same to the rest of her Customers.

Sometime after this, as I was at Work, and very melancholly, she begins to ask me what the Matter was? as she was us'd to do; I told her my Heart was heavy, I had little Work, and nothing to live on, and knew not what Course to take; she Laugh'd and told me I must go out again and try my Fortune; it might be that I might meet with another Peice of Plate. O, Mother! *says I,* that is a Trade I have no skill in, and if I should be taken I am undone at once; *says she,* I cou'd help you to a School-Mistress, that shall make you as dexterous as her self: I trembled at that Proposal for hitherto I had had no Confederates, nor any Acquaintance among that Tribe; but she conquer'd all my Modesty, and all my Fears; and in a little time, by the help of this Confederate I grew as impudent a Thief, and as dexterous as ever *Moll Cut-Purse* was, tho' if Fame does not belie her, not half so Handsome.

The Comrade she helped me to dealt in three sorts of Craft, (*viz.*) Shop-lifting, stealing of Shop-Books and Pocket-Books, and taking off Gold Watches from the Ladies Sides, and this last she did so dexteriously that no Woman ever arriv'd to the Perfection of that Art, so as to do it like her: I lik'd the first and the last of these things very well, and I attended her some time in the Practise, just as a Deputy attends a Midwife without any Pay.

At length she put me to Practise; she had shewn me her Art,

and I had several times unhook'd a Watch from her own side with great dexterity; at last she show'd me a Prize, and this was a young Lady big with Child who had a charming Watch; the thing was to be done as she came out of Church; she goes on one side of the Lady, and pretends, just as she came to the Steps, to fall, and fell against the Lady with so much violence as put her into a great fright, and both cry'd out terribly; in the very moment that she jostl'd the Lady, I had hold of the Watch, and holding it the right way, the start she gave drew the Hook out and she never felt it; I made off immediately, and left my School mistress to come out of her pretended Fright gradually, and the Lady too; and presently the Watch was miss'd; ay, says my Comrade, then it was those Rogues that thrust me down, I warrant ye; I wonder the Gentlewoman did not miss her Watch before, then we might have taken them.

She humour'd the thing so well that no Body suspected her, and I was got home a full Hour before her: This was my first Adventure in Company; the Watch was indeed a very fine one, and had a great many Trinkets about it, and my Governess allow'd us 20 *l.* for it, of which I had half, and thus I was enter'd a compleat Thief, Harden'd to a Pitch above all the Reflections of Conscience or Modesty, and to a Degree which I must acknowledge I never thought possible in me.

Thus the Devil who began, by the help of an irresistable Poverty, to push me into this Wickedness, brought me on to a height beyond the common Rate, even when my Necessities were not so great, or the prospect of my Misery so terrifying; for I had now got into a little Vein of Work, and as I was not at a loss to handle my Needle, it was very probable, as Acquaintance came in, I might have got my Bread honestly enough.

I must say, that if such a prospect of Work had presented it self at first, when I began to feel the approach of my miserable Circumstances, I say, had such a prospect of getting my Bread by working presented it self then, I had never fallen into this wicked Trade, or into such a wicked Gang as I was now embark'd with; but practise had hardened me, and I grew audacious to the last degree; and the more so, because I had carried it on so long, and had never been taken; for in a word, my new Partner in Wickedness *and I* went on together so long, without being ever detected, that we not only grew Bold, but we grew Rich, and we had at one time One and Twenty Gold Watches in our Hands.

I remember that one Day being a little more serious than ordinary, and finding I had so good a Stock beforehand as I had, for I had near 200 *l.* in Money for my Share, it came strongly into my Mind, no doubt from some kind Spirit, if such there be, that as at first Poverty excited me, and my Distresses drove me to these dreadful Shifts; so seeing those Distresses were now relieved, and I could also get something towards a Maintenance by working, and had so good a Bank to support me, why should I not now leave off, as they say, while I was well; that I could not expect to go always free; and if I was once surpris'd, and miscarry'd, I was undone.

This was doubtless the happy Minute, when if I had hearken'd to the blessed hint from whatsoever hand it came, I had still a cast for an easie Life; but my Fate was otherwise determin'd; the busie Devil that so industriously drew me in, had too fast hold of me to let me go back; but as Poverty brought me into the Mire, so Avarice kept me in, till there was no going back; as to the Arguments which my Reason dictated for perswading me to lay down, Avarice stept in and said, go on, go on; you have had very good luck, go on till you have gotten Four or Five Hundred Pound, and then you shall leave off, and then you may live easie without working at all.

Thus I that was once in the Devil's Clutches, was held fast there as with a Charm, and had no Power to go without the Circle, till I was ingulph'd in Labyrinths of Trouble too great to get out at all.

However, these Thoughts left some Impression upon me, and made me act with some more caution than before, and more than my Directors us'd for themselves. My Comerade, as I call'd her, but rather she should have been called my Teacher, with another of her Scholars, was the first in the Misfortune, for happening to be upon the hunt for Purchase, they made an attempt upon a Linnen-Draper in Cheapside, but were snap'd by a Hawks-ey'd Journeyman, and seiz'd with two pieces of Cambrick, which were taken also upon them.

This was enough to Lodge them both in *Newgate,* where they had the Misfortune to have some of their former Sins brought to remembrance; two other Indictments being brought against them, and the Facts being prov'd upon them, they were both condemned to Die; they both pleaded their Bellies, and were both voted Quick with Child; tho' my Tutress was no more with Child than I was.

I went frequently to see them, and Condole with them, expecting that it would be my turn next; but the place gave me so much Horror, reflecting that it was the place of my unhappy Birth, and of my Mother's Misfortunes, that I could not bear it, so I was forc'd to leave off going to see them.

And O! cou'd I have but taken warning by their Disasters, I had been happy still, for I was yet free, and had nothing brought against me; but it could not be, my Measure was not yet fill'd up.

My Comerade having the Brand of an old Offender, was Executed; the young Offender was spar'd, having obtain'd a Reprieve; but lay starving a long while in Prison, till at last she got her Name into what they call a Circuit Pardon, and so came off.

This terrible Example of my Comerade frighted me heartily, and for a good while I made no Excursions; but one Night, in the Neighbourhood of my Governesses House, they cryed Fire; my Governess look'd out, for we were all up, and cryed immediately that such a Gentlewoman's House was all of a light Fire a top, and so indeed it was: Here she gives me a jog, now, Child, says she, there is a rare opportunity, the Fire being so near that you may go to it before the Street is block'd up with the Crowd; she presently gave me my Cue, go, Child, *says she,* to the House, and run in and tell the Lady, or any Body you see, that you come to help them, and that you came from such a Gentlewoman (that is one of her Acquaintance farther up the Street); she gave me the like Cue to the next House, naming another Name that was also an Acquaintance of the Gentlewoman of the House.

Away I went, and coming to the House I found them all in Confusion, you may be sure; I run in, and finding one of the Maids, Lord! Sweetheart, *said I,* how came this dismal Accident? Where is your Mistress? And how does she do? Is she safe? And where are the Children? I come from Madam – to help you; away runs the Maid; Madam, Madam, *says she,* screaming as loud as she cou'd yell, *here is a Gentlewoman come from Madam – to help us.* The poor Woman half out of her Wits, with a Bundle under her Arm, and two little Children, comes towards me, *Lord, Madam, says I,* let me carry the poor Children to Madam –, she desires you to send them; she'll take care of the poor Lambs, and immediately I takes one of them out of her Hand, and she lifts the tother up into my Arms; *ay, do, for God sake,* says she, *carry them to her;* O *thank her for her kindness: Have you any thing else to secure, Madam?* says *I, she will take care of it:* O *dear! ay,* says she, *God bless her, and thank her, take this bundle of Plate and carry it to her too;* O *she is a good Woman;* O *Lord, we are utterly ruin 'd, utterly undone;* and away she runs from me out of her Wits, and the Maids after her, and away comes I with the two Children and the Bundle.

I was no sooner got into the Street, but I saw another Woman come to me, O! *says she,* Mistress, in a piteous Tone, you will let fall the Child; come, this is a sad time, let me help you, and immediately lays hold of my Bundle to carry it for me; no, *says I,* if you will help me, take the Child by the Hand, and lead it for me but to the upper end of the Street, I'll go with you and satisfie you for your pains.

She cou'd not avoid going, after what I said, but the Creature, in short, was one of the Same Business with me, and wanted nothing but the Bundle; however, she went with me to the Door, for she cou'd not help it; when we were come there I whisper'd her, *go Child,* said I, I *understand your Trade,* you may meet with Purchase enough.

She understood me and walk'd off; I thundered at the Door with the Children, and as the People were rais'd before by the noise of the Fire, I was soon let in, and I said, *is Madam awake, pray tell her* Mrs – *desires the favour of her to take the two Children in;* poor Lady, *she will be undone, their House is all of a Flame;* they took the Children in very civily, pitied the Family in Distress, and away came I with my Bundle; one of the Maids ask'd me if I was not to leave the Bundle too? I said no, Sweetheart, 'tis to go to another place, it does not belong to them.

I was a great way out of the hurry now, and so I went on, clear of any Body's enquiry, and brought the bundle of Plate, which was very considerable, strait home, and gave it to my old Governess; she told me she would not look into it, but bade me go out again to look for more.

She gave me the like Cue to the Gentlewoman of the next House to that which was on Fire, and I did my endeavour to go, but by this time the allarm of Fire was so great, and so many Engines playing, and the Street so throng'd with People, that I cou'd not get near the House, whatever I cou'd do; so I came back again to my Governesses, and taking the Bundle up into my Chamber, I began to examine it: It is with Horror that I tell what a Treasure I found there; 'tis enough to say, that besides most of the Family Plate, which was considerable, I found a Gold Chain, an old fashion'd thing, the Locket of which was broken, so that I suppose it had not been us'd some Years, but the Gold was not the worse for that; also a little Box of burying Rings, the Lady's Wedding-Ring, and some broken bits of old Lockets of Gold, a Gold Watch, and a Purse with about value in old pieces of Gold Coin, and several other things of Value.

This was the greatest and the worst Prize that ever I was concern'd in, for indeed, tho' as I have said above, I was harden'd now beyond the Power of all Reflection in other Cases, yet it really touch'd me to the very Soul, when I look'd into this Treasure, to think of the poor disconsolate Gentlewoman who had lost so much by the Fire besides; and who would think to be sure that she had sav'd her Plate and best things; how she wou'd be surpriz'd and afflicted when she should find that she had been deceiv'd, and should find that the Person that took her Children and her Goods, had not come, as was pretended, from the Gentlewoman in the next Street, but that the Children had been put upon her without her own knowledge.

I say I confess the inhumanity of this Action mov'd me very much, and made me relent exceedingly, and Tears stood in my Eyes upon that Subject: But with all my Sense of its being cruel and Inhuman, I cou'd never find in my Heart to make any Restitution: The Reflection wore off, and I began quickly to forget the Circumstances that attended the taking them.

Nor was this all, for tho' by this jobb I was become considerably Richer than before, yet the Resolution I had formerly taken of leaving off this horrid Trade, when I had gotten a little more, did not return; but I must still get farther, and more; and the Avarice join'd so with the Success, that I had no more thoughts of coming to a timely Alteration of Life; tho' without it I cou'd cxpect no Safety, no Tranquility in the Possession of what I had so wickedly gain'd; but a little more, and a little more, was the Case still.

At length yielding to the Importunities of my Crime, I cast off all Remorse and Repentance; and all the Reflections on that Head, turn'd to no more than this, that I might perhaps come to have one Booty more than might compleat my Desires; but tho' I certainly had that one Booty, yet every hit look'd towards another, and was so encouraging to me to go on with the Trade, that I had no Gust to the Thought of laying it down.

In this Condition, harden'd by Success, and resolving to go on, I fell into the Snare in which I was appointed to meet with my last Reward for this kind of Life: But even this was not yet, for I met with several successful Adventures more in this way of being undone.

I remain'd still with my Governess, who was for a while really concern'd for the Misfortune of my Comerade that had been hang'd, and who it seems knew enough of my Governess to have sent her the same way, and which made her very uneasy; indeed she was in a very great fright.

It is true that when she was gone, and had not open'd her Mouth to tell what she knew, my Governess was easy as to that Point, and perhaps glad she was hang'd; for it was in her power to have obtain'd a Pardon at the Expence of her Friends; But on the other Hand, the loss of her, and the Sense of her Kindness in not making her Market of what she knew, mov'd my Governess to Mourn very sincerely for her: I comforted her as well as I cou'd, and she in return harden'd me to Merit more compleatly the same Fate.

However as I have said it made me the more wary, and particularly I was very shie of Shoplifting, especially among the *Mercers,* and *Drapers* who are a Set of Fellows that have their Eyes very much about them: I made a Venture or two among the Lace Folks, and the Milliners, and particularly at one Shop, where I got Notice of two young Women who were newly set up, and had not been bred to the Trade: There, I think I carried off a Peice of Bonelace, worth six or seven pound, and a Paper of Thread; but this was but once, it was a Trick that would not serve again.

It was always reckon'd a safe Job when we heard of a new Shop, especially when the People were such as were not bred to Shops; such may depend upon it, that they will be visited once or twice at their beginning, and they must be very Sharp indeed if they can prevent it.

I made another Adventure or two, but they were but Trifles too, tho' sufficient to live on; after this nothing considerable offering for a good while, I began to think that I must give over the Trade in Earnest; but my Governess, who was not willing to lose me, and expected great Things of me, brought me one Day into Company with a young Woman and a Fellow that went for her Husband, tho' as it appear'd afterwards she was not his Wife, but they were Partners it seems in the Trade they carried on, and Partners in something else too. In *short,* they robb'd together, lay together, were taken together, and at last were hang'd together.

I came into a kind of League with these two, by the help of my Governess, and they carried me out into three or four Adventures, where I rather saw them commit some Coarse and unhandy Robberies, in which nothing but a great Stock of impudence on their Side, and gross Negligence on the Peoples Side who were robb'd, could have made them Successful; so I resolv'd from that time forward to be very Cautious how I Adventur'd upon any thing with them; and indeed when two or three unlucky Projects were propos'd by them, I declin'd the offer, and perswaded them against it: One time they particularly propos'd Robbing a Watchmaker of 3 Gold Watches, which they had Ey'd in the Day time, and found the Place where he laid them; one of them had so many Keys of all kinds, that he made no Question to open the Place where the Watchmaker had laid them; and so we made a kind of an Appointment; but when I came to look narrowly into the Thing, I found they propos'd breaking open the House; and this as a thing out of my Way, I would not Embark in; so they went without me: They did get into the House by main Force, and broke up the lock'd Place where the Watches were, but found but one of the Gold Watches, and a Silver one, which they took and got out of the House again very clear, but the Family being alarm'd cried out, Thieves, and the Man was pursued and taken, the young Woman had got off too, but unhappily was stop'd at a Distance, and the Watches found upon her; and thus I had a second Escape, for they were convicted, and both hang'd, being old Offenders, tho' but young People; as *I said before,* that they robbed together, and lay together, so now they hang'd together, and there ended my new Partnership.

I began now to be very wary, having so narrowly escap'd a Scouring, and having such an Example before me; but I had a new Tempter, who prompted me every Day, I mean my Governess; and now a Prize presented, which as it came by her Management, so she expected a good Share of the Booty; there was a good Quantity of Flanders-Lace Lodg'd in a private House, where she had gotten Intelligence of it; and Flanders-Lace, being then Prohibited, it was a good Booty to any Custom-House Officer that could come at it: I had a full Account from my Governess, as well of the Quantity as of the very Place where it was-conceal'd, and I went to a Custom-House Officer, and told him I had such a Discovery to make to him, of such a Quantity of Lace, if he would assure me that I should have my due Share of the Reward: This was so just an offer, that nothing could be fairer; so he agreed, and taking a Constable and me with him, we beset the House; as I told him I could go directly to the Place, He left it to me, and the Hole being very dark, I squeez'd myself into it with a Candle in my Hand, and so reach'd the Peices out to him, taking care as I gave him some, so to secure as much about myself as I could conveniently Dispose of: There was near 300 *l.* worth of Lace in the whole, and I secur'd about 50 *l* worth of it to myself: The People of the House were not owners of the Lace, but a Merchant who had entrusted them with it; so that they were not so surpriz'd as I thought they would be.

I left the Officer overjoy'd with his Prize, and fully satisfy'd with what he had got, and appointed to meet him at a House of his own directing, where I came after I had dispos'd of the Cargo I had about me, of which he had not the least Suspicion; when I came to him, he began to Capitulate with me, believing I did not understand the right I had to a Share in the Prize, and would fain have put me off with Twenty Pound, but I let him know that I was not so ignorant as he suppos'd I was; and yet I was glad too, that he offer'd to bring me to a certainty; I ask'd 100 *l.* and he rise up to 30 *l.* I fell to 80 *l.* and he rise again to 40 *l.* in a Word, he offer'd 50 *l* and I consented, only demanding a Peice of Lace, which I thought came to about 8 or 9 Pound, as if it had been for my own Wear, and he agreed to it, so I got 50 *l.* in Money paid me that same Night, and made an End of the Bargain; nor did he ever know who I was, or where to enquire for me; so that if it had been discover'd, that part of the Goods were embezzl'd; he could have made no Challenge upon me for it.

I very punctually divided this Spoil with my Governess, and I pass'd with her from this time for a very dexterous Manager in the nicest Cases; I found that this last was the best, and easiest sort of Work that was in my way, and I made it my business to enquire out prohibited Goods; and after buying some usually betray'd them, but none of these Discoveries amounted to any thing Considerable, not like that I related just now; but I was willing to act safe, and was still Cautious of running the great Risques which I found others did, and in which they Miscarried every Day.

The next thing of Moment was an attempt at a Gentlewoman's gold Watch, it happen'd in a Crowd, at a Meeting-House, where I was in very great Danger of being taken; I had full hold of her Watch, but giving a great Jostle, as if some body had thrust me against her, and in the Juncture giving the Watch a fair pull, I found it would not come, so I let it go that Moment, and cried out as in had been kill'd, that some body had Trod upon my Foot, and that there was certainly *Pick-pockets* there; for some body or other had given a pull at my Watch; for you are to observe, that on these Adventures we always went very well Dress'd, and I had very good Cloaths on, and a Gold Watch by my Side, as like a Lady as other Folks.

I had no sooner said so, but the tother Gentlewoman cried out a *Pick-pocket* too, for some body, *she said,* had try d to pull her Watch away.

When I touch'd her Watch, I was close to her, but when I cry'd out, I stop'd as it were short, and the Crowd bearing her forward a little, she made a Noise too, but it was at some Distance from me, so that she did not in the least suspect me; but when she cried out *a Pickpocket* some body cried Ay, and here has been another, this Gentlewoman has been attempted too.

At that very instant, a little farther in the Crowd, and very Luckily too, they cried out *a Pick-pocket* again, and really seiz'd a young Fellow in the very Fact. This, tho' unhappy for the Wretch was very opportunely for my Case, tho' I had carried it off handsomely enough before, but now it was out of Doubt, and all the loose part of the Crowd run that way, and the poor Boy was deliver'd up to the Rage of the Street, which is a Cruelty I need not describe, and which however they are always glad of, rather than to be sent to *Newgate,* where they lie often a long time, till they are almost perish'd, and sometimes they are hang'd, and the best they can look for, if they are Convicted, is to be Transported.

This was a narrow Escape to me, and I was so frighted, that I ventur'd no more at Gold Watches a great while; there was indeed a great many concurring Circumstances in this Adventure, which assisted to my Escape; but the chief was, that the Woman whose Watch I had pull'd at was a Fool; that is to say, she was Ignorant of the nature of the Attempt, which one would have thought she should not have been, seeing she was wise enough to fasten her Watch, so, that it could not be slipt up; but she was in such a Fright, that she had no thought about her proper for the Discovery; for she, when she felt the pull scream'd out, and push'd herself forward, and put all the People about her into disorder, but said not a Word of her Watch, or of a *Pick-pocket,* for at least two Minutes time, which was time enough for me, and to spare; for as I had cried out behind her, *as I have said,* and bore myself back in the Crowd as she bore forward, there were several People, at least seven or eight, the Throng being Still moving on, that were got between me and her in that time, and then I crying out *a Pick-pocket,* rather sooner than she, or at least as soon, she might as well be the Person suspected as I, and the People were confus'd in their Enquiry; whereas, had she with a Presence of Mind needful on such an Occasion, as soon as she felt the pull, not scream'd out as she did, but turn'd immediately round, and seiz'd the next Body that was behind her, she had infallibly taken me.

This is a Direction not of the kindest Sort to the Fraternity; but 'tis certainly a Key to the Clue of a *Pick-pockets* Motions, and whoever can follow it, will as certainly catch the Thief as he will be sure to miss if he does not.

I had another Adventure, which puts this Matter out of doubt, and which may be an Instruction for Posterity in the Case of *a Pick-pocket;* my good old Governess to give a short touch at her History, tho' she had left off the Trade, was as I may say, born *a Pick-pocket,* and as I understood afterward had run thro' all the several Degrees of that Art, and yet had never been taken but once, when she was so grossly detected, that she was convicted and ordered to be Transported; but being a Woman of a rare Tongue, and withal having Money in her Pocket; she found Means, the Ship putting into *Ireland* for Provisions, to get on Shore there, where she liv'd and practis'd her old Trade for some Years; when falling into another sort of bad Company, she turn'd Midwife and Procuress, and play'd a Hundred Pranks there, which she gave me a little History of in Confidence between us as we grew more intimate; and it was to this wicked Creature that I ow'd all the Art and Dexterity I arriv'd to, in which there were few that ever went beyond me, or that practis'd so long without any Misfortune.

It was after those Adventures in *Ireland,* and when she was pretty well known in that Country, that she left *Dublin,* and came over to England, where the time of her Transportation being not expir'd, she left her former Trade, for fear of falling into bad Hands again, for then she was sure to have gone to

Wreck: Here she set up the same Trade she had followed in *Ireland,* in which she soon by her admirable Management, and a good Tongue, arriv'd to the Height, which I have already describ'd, and indeed began to be Rich tho' her Trade fell off again afterwards; as I have hinted before.

I mention thus much of the History of this Woman here, the better to account for the concern she had in the wicked Life I was now leading; into all the particulars of which she led me as it were by the Hand, and gave me such Directions, and I so well follow'd them, that I grew the greatest Artist of my time, and work'd myself out of every Danger with such Dexterity, that when several more of my Comrades run themselves into *Newgate* presently, and by that time they had been Half a Year at the Trade, I had now Practis'd upwards of five Year, and the People at *Newgate,* did not so much as know me; they had heard much of me indeed, and often expected me there, but I always got off, tho'many times in the extreamest Danger.

One of the greatest Dangers I was now in, was that I was too well known among the Trade, and some of them whose hatred was owing rather to Envy than any Injury I had done them began to be Angry that I should always Escape when they were always catch'd and hurried to *Newgate.* These were they that gave me the Name of *Moll Flanders:* For it was no more of Affinity with my real Name, or with any of the Names I had ever gone by, than black is of Kin to white, except that once, as before I call'd my self Mrs *Flanders,* when I sheltered myself in the *Mint;* but that these Rogues never knew, nor could I ever learn how they came to give me the Name, or what the Occasion of it was.

I was soon inform'd that some of these who were gotten fast into *Newgate,* had vowed to Impeach me; and as I knew that two or three of them were but too able to do it, I was under a great concern about it, and kept within Doors for a good while; but my Governess who I always made Partner in my Success, and who now played a sure Game with me, for that she had a Share of the Gain, and no Share in the hazard, *I say,* my

Governess was something impatient of my leading such a useless unprofitable Life, as she call'd it; and she laid a new Contrivance for my going Abroad, and this was to Dress me up in Mens Cloths, and so put me into a new kind of Practise.

I was Tall and Personable, but a little too smooth Fac'd for a Man; however as I seldom went Abroad but in the Night, it did well enough; but it was a long time before I could behave in my new Cloths: I mean, as to my Craft; it was impossible to be so Nimble, so Ready, so Dexterous at these things, in a Dress so contrary to Nature; and as I did every thing Clumsily, so I had neither the success, or the easiness of Escape that I had before, and I resolv'd to leave it off; but that Resolution was confirm'd soon after by the following Accident.

As my Governess had disguis'd me like a Man, so she joyn'd me with a Man, a young Fellow that was Nimble enough at his Business, and for about three Weeks we did very well together. Our principal Trade was watching Shop-Keepers Compters, and Slipping off any kind of Goods we could see carelesly laid any where, and we made several very good Bargains as we call'd them at this Work: And as we kept always together, so we grew very intimate, yet he never knew that I was not a Man; nay, tho' I several times went home with him to his Lodgings, according as our business directed, and four or five times lay with him all Night: But our Design lay another way, and it was absolutely necessary to me to conceal my Sex from him, as appear'd afterwards: The Circumstances of our Living, coming in late, and having such and such Business to do as requir'd that no Body should be trusted with coming into our Lodgings, were such as made it impossible to me to refuse lying with him, unless I would have own'd my Sex, and as it was I effectually conceal'd my self.

But his ill, and my good Fortune, soon put an end to this Life, which I must own I was sick of too, on several other Accounts: We had made several Prizes in this new way of Business, but the last would have been extraordinary; there was a Shop in a certain Street which had a Warehouse behind it that look'd into another Street, the House making the corner of the turning.

Through the Window of the Warehouse we saw lying on the Counter or Show-board which was just before it, Five pieces of Silks, besides other Stuffs; and tho' it was almost dark, yet the People being busie in the fore shop with Customers, had not had time to shut up those Windows, or else had forgot it.

This the young Fellow was so overjoy'd with, that he could not restrain himself; it lay all within his reach he said, and he swore violently to me that he would have it, if he broke down the House for it; I disswaded him a little, but saw there was no remedy, so he run rashly upon it, slipt out a Square out of the Sash Window dexterously enough, and without noise, and got out four pieces of the Silks, and came with them towards me; but was immediately pursued with a terrible Clutter and Noise; we were standing together indeed, but I had not taken any of the Goods out of his Hand, when I said to him hastily, you are undone, fly for God sake; he run like Lightning, and I too, but the pursuit was hotter after him because he had the Goods, than after me; he dropt two of the Pieces which stop'd them a little, but the Crowd encreas'd and pursued us both; they took him soon after with the other two pieces upon him, and then the rest followed me; I run for it and got into my Governesses House, whither some quick-eyed People follow'd me so warmly as to fix me there; they did not immediately knock at the Door, by which I got time to throw off my Disguise, and dress me in my own Cloths; besides, when they came there, my Governess, who had her Tale ready, kept her Door shut, and call'd out to them and told there was no Man came in there; the People affirm'd there did a Man come in there, and swore they would break open the Door.

My Governess, not at all surpriz'd, spoke calmly to them, told them they should very freely come and search her House, if they would bring a Constable, and let in none but such as the

Constable would admit, for it was unreasonable to let in a whole Crowd; this they could not refuse, tho' they were a Crowd; so a Constable was fetch'd immediately, and she very freely open'd the Door; and the Constable kept the Door, and the Men he appointed search'd the House, my Governess going with them from Room to Room; when she came to my Room she call'd to me, and said aloud; Cousin, pray open the Door, here's some Gentlemen that must come and look into your Room.

I had a little Girl with me, which was my Governesses Grandchild, as she call'd her; and I bade her open the Door, and there sat! at work with a great litter of things about me, as if I had been at Work all Day, being my self quite undress'd, with only Nightcloaths on my Head, and a loose Morning Gown wrapt about me: My Governess made a kind of excuse for their disturbing me, telling me partly the occasion of it, and that she had no Remedy but to open the Doors to them, and let them satisfie themselves, for all she could say to them would not satisfie them: I sat still, and bid them search the Room if they pleas'd, for if there was any Body in the House, I was sure they was not in my Room; and as for the rest of the House I had nothing to say to that, I did not understand what they look'd for.

Every thing look'd so innocent and so honest about me, that they treated me civiller than I expected, but it was not till they had search'd the Room to a nicety, even under the Bed, in the Bed, and every where else, where it was possible any thing cou'd be hid; when they had done this, and cou'd find nothing, they ask'd my Pardon for troubling me, and went down.

When they had thus searched the House from Bottom to Top, and then from Top to Bottom, and cou'd find nothing, they appeas'd the Mob pretty well; but they carried my Governess before the Justice: Two Men swore that they see the Man who they pursued go into her House: My Governess rattled and made a great noise that her House should be insulted, and that she should be used thus for nothing; that if a Man did come in, he might go out again presently for ought she knew, for she was ready to make Oath that no Man had been within her Doors all that Day as she knew of, and that was very true indeed; that it might be indeed that as she was above Stairs, any Fellow in a Fright might find the Door open, and run in for shelter when he was pursued, but that she knew nothing of it; and if it had been so, he certainly went out again, perhaps at the other Door, for she had another Door into an Alley, and so had made his escape and cheated them all.

This was indeed probable enough, and the Justice satisfied himself with giving her an Oath, that she had not receiv'd or admitted any Man into her House to conceal him, or protect or hide him from Justice: This Oath she might justly take, and did so, and so she was dismiss'd.

It is easie to judge what a fright I was in upon this occasion, and it was impossible for my Governess ever to bring me to Dress in that Disguise again; for, as I told her, I should certainly betray my self.

My poor Partner in this Mischief was now in a bad Case, for he was carried away before my Lord Mayor, and by his Worship committed to *Newgate,* and the People that took him were so willing, as well as able, to Prosecute him, that they offer'd themselves to enter into Recognisances to appear at the Sessions, and persue the Charge against him.

However, he got his Indictment deferr'd, upon promise to discover his Accomplices, and particularly, the Man that was concern'd with him in this Robbery, and he fail'd not to do his endeavour, for he gave in my Name who he call'd *Gabriel Spencer,* which was the Name I went by to him, and here appear'd the Wisdom of my concealing my Name and Sex from him, which if he had ever known, I had been undone.

He did all he cou'd to discover this *Gabriel Spencer;* he describ'd me, he discover'd the place where he said I Lodg'd, and in a word, all the Particulars that he cou'd of my Dwelling; but having conceal'd the main Circumstances of my Sex from him, I had a vast Advantage, and he never cou'd hear of me; he brought two or three Families into Trouble by his endeavouring to find me out, but they knew nothing of me, any more than that he had a Fellow with him that they had seen, but knew nothing of; and as for my Governess, tho' she was the means of his coming to me, yet it was done at second hand, and he knew nothing of her.

This turn'd to his Disadvantage, for having promis'd Discoveries, but not being able to make it good, it was look'd upon as a trifling with the Justice of the City, and he was the more fiercely persued by the Shopkeepers who took him.

I was however terribly uneasie all this while, and that I might be quite out of the way, I went away from my Governesses for a while; but not knowing whither to wander, I took a Maid Servant with me, and took the Stage Coach to *Dunstable* to my old Landlord and Landlady, where I had liv'd so handsomely with my *Lancashire* Husband: Here I told her a formal Story, that I expected my Husband every Day from *Ireland,* and that I had sent a Letter to him that I would meet him at *Dunstable* at her House, and that he would certainly Land, if the Wind was fair, in a few Days, so that I was come to spend a few Days with them till he should come, for he would either come Post, or in the *West-Chester* Coach, I knew not which, but which soever it was, he would be sure to come to that House to meet me.

My Landlady was mighty glad to see me, and My Landlord made such a stir with me that if I had been a Princess I cou'd not have been better used, and here I might have been welcome a Month or two if I had thought fit.

But my Business was of another Nature; I was very uneasie (tho' so well Disguis'd that it was scarce possible to Detect me) lest this Fellow should some how or other find me out; and tho' he cou'd not charge me with this Robbery, having perswaded him not to venture, and having also done nothing in it my self but run away, yet he might have charg'd me with other things, and have bought his own Life at the Expence of mine.

This fill'd me with horrible Apprehensions: I had no Recourse, no Friend, no Confident but my old Governess, and I knew no Remedy but to put my Life in her Hands, and so I did, for I let her know where to send to me, and had several Letters from her while I stayed here, some of them almost scar'd me out of my Wits; but at last she sent me the joyful News that he was hang'd, which was the best News to me that I had heard a great while.

I had stay'd here five Weeks, and liv'd very comfortably indeed, (the secret Anxiety of my Mind excepted) but when I receiv'd this Letter I look'd pleasantly again, and told my Landlady that I had receiv'd a Letter from my Spouse in *Ireland,* that I had the good News of his being very well, but had the bad News that his business would not permit him to come away so soon as he expected, and so I was like to go back again without him.

My Landlady complemented me upon the good News however, that I had heard he was well, for I have observ'd, Madam, *says she,* you han't been so pleasant as you us'd to be; you have been over Head and Ears in Care for him, I dare say, *says the good Woman;* 'tis easie to be seen there's an alteration in you for the better, *says she*: Well, I am sorry the Esquire can't come yet, *says my Landlord,* I should have been heartily glad to have seen him, but I hope, when you have certain News of his coming, you'll take a step hither again, Madam; *say he,* you shall be very welcome whenever you please to come.

With all these fine Complements we parted, and I came merry enough to *London,* and found my Governess as well pleas'd as I was; and now she told me she would never recommend any Partner to me again, for she always found, *she said,* that I had the best luck when I ventur'd by my self; and so indeed I had, for I was seldom in any Danger when I was by my self, or if I was, I got out of it with more Dexterity than when I was entangled with the, dull Measures of other People, who had perhaps less forecast, and were more rash and impatient than I; for tho' I had as much Courage to venture as any of them, yet I used more caution before I undertook a thing, and had more Presence of Mind when I was to bring my self off.

I have often wondered even at my own hardiness another way, that when all my Companions were surpriz'd, and fell so suddenly into the Hand of Justice, and that I so narrowly escap'd, yet I could not all that while enter into one serious Resolution to leave off this Trade; and especially Considering that I was now very far from being poor, that the Temptation of Necessity, which is generally the Introduction of all such Wickedness was now remov'd; for I had near *500 l.* by me in ready Money, on which I might have liv'd very well, if I had thought fit to have retir'd; but *I say,* I had not so much as the least inclination to leave off; no not so much as I had before when I had but 200 *l.* before-hand, and when I had no such frightful Examples before my Eyes as these were; From hence 'tis Evident to me, that when once we are harden'd in Crime, no Fear can affect us, no Example give us any warning.

I had indeed one Comrade whose Fate went very near me for a good while, tho' I wore it off too in time; that Case was indeed very unhappy; I had made a Prize of a Peice of very good Damask in a *Mercers* Shop, and went clear off myself; but had convey'd the Peice to this Companion of mine, when we went out of the Shop, and she went one way, and I went another: We had not been long out of the Shop, but the *Mercer* mist his Peice of Stuff, and sent his Messengers, one, one way, and one another, and they presently seiz'd her that had the Peice, with the Damask upon her; as for me, I had very Luckily step'd into a House where there was a Lace, Chamber, up one Pair of Stairs, and had the Satisfaction, or the Terror indeed of looking out of the Window upon the Noise they made, and seeing the poor Creature drag'd away in Triumph to the Justice, who immediately committed her to *Newgate.*

I was careful to attempt nothing in the Lace-Chamber, but tumbl'd their Goods pretty much to spend time; then bought a few Yards of Edging, and paid for it, and came away very sad Hearted indeed for the poor Woman who was in Tribulation for what I only had stolen.

Here again my old Caution stood me in good stead; Namely, that tho' I often robb'd with these People, yet I never let them know who I was, or where I Lodg'd; nor could they ever find out my Lodging, tho' they often endeavour'd to Watch me to it. They all knew me by the Name of *Moll Flanders,* tho' even some of them rather believ'd I was she, than knew me to be so; my Name was publick among them indeed; but how to find me out they knew not, nor so much as how to guess at my Quarters, whether they were at the East-End of the Town, or the West; and this wariness was my safety upon all these Occasions.

I kept close a great while upon the Occasion of this Womans disaster; I knew that if I should do any thing that should Miscarry, and should be carried to Prison she would be there, and ready to Witness against me, and perhaps save her Life at my Expence; I consider'd that I began to be very well known by Name at the *Old Baily,* tho' they did not know my Face; and that if I should fall into their Hands, I should be treated as an old Offender; and for this Reason, I was resolv'd to see what this poor Creatures Fate should be before I stirr'd Abroad, tho' several times in her Distress I convey'd Money to her for her Relief.

At length she came to her Tryal, she pleaded she did not steal the Things; but that one Mrs *Flanders,* as she heard her call'd, (for she did not know her) gave the Bundle to her after they came out of the Shop, and bade her carry it Home to her Lodging. They ask'd her where this Mrs *Flanders* was? but she could not produce her, neither could she give the least Account of me; and the *Mercers* Men swearing positively that she was in the Shop when the Goods were stolen; that they immediately miss'd them, and pursu'd her, and found them upon her; Thereupon the Jury brought her in Guilty; but the Court considering that she really was not the Person that stole the Goods, an inferiour Assistant, and that it was very possible she could not find out this Mrs *Flanders, meaning me,* tho' it would save her Life, which indeed was true, I say considering all this, they allow'd her to be Transported, which was the utmost Favour she could obtain, only that the Court told her, that if she could in the mean time produce the said Mrs *Flanders,* they would intercede for her Pardon; that is to say, if she could find me out, and hang me, she should not be Transported: This I took care to make impossible to her, and so she was Shipp'd off in pursuance of her Sentence a little while after.

I must repeat it again, that the Fate of this poor Woman troubl'd me exceedingly, and I began to be very pensive, knowing that I was really the Instrument of her disaster; but the Preservation of my own Life, which was so evidently in Danger, took off all my tenderness; and seeing she was not put to Death, I was very easie at her Transportation, because she was then out of the way of doing me any Mischief whatever should happen.

The Disaster of this Woman was some Months before that of the last recited Story, and was indeed partly the Occasion of my Governess proposing to Dress me up in Mens Cloths, that I might go about unobserv'd, as indeed I did; but I was soon tir'd of that Disguise, as *I have said,* for indeed it expos'd me to too many Difficuities.

I was now easie as to all Fear of Witnesses against me, for all those, that had either been concern'd with me, or that knew me by the Name of *Moll Flanders,* were either hang'd or Transported; and if I should have had the Misfortune to be taken, I might call myself any thing else, as well as *Moll Flanders,* and no old Sins could be plac'd to my Account; so I began to run a Tick again, with the more freedom, and several successful Adventures I made, tho' not such as I had made before.

We had at that time another Fire happen'd not a great way off from the Place where my Governess liv'd, and I made an attempt there, as before, but as I was not soon enough before the Crowd of People came in, and could not get to the House I aim'd at, instead of a Prize, I got a mischief, which had almost put a Period to my Life, and all my wicked doings together; for the Fire being very furious, and the People in a great Fright in removing their Goods, and throwing them out of Window; a Wench from out of a Window threw a Featherbed just upon me; it is true, the Bed being soft it broke no Bones; but as the weight was great, and made greater by the Fall, it beat me down, and laid me dead for a while; nor did the People concern themselves much to deliver me from it, or to recover me at all; but I lay like one Dead and neglected a good while, till some body going to remove the Bed out of the way, helped me up; it was indeed a wonder the People in the House had not thrown other Goods out after it, and which might have fallen upon it, and then I had been inevitably kill'd; but I was reserved for further Afflictions.

This Accident however spoil'd my Market for that time, and I came Home to my Governess very much hurt, and Bruised, and Frighted to the last degree, and it was a good while before she could set me upon my Feet again.

It was now a Merry time of the Year, and *Bartholomew* Fair was begun; I had never made any Walks that Way, nor was the common Part of the Fair of much Advantage to me; but I took a turn this Year into the Cloisters, and among the rest, I fell into one of the Raffling Shops: It was a thing of no great Consequence to me, nor did I expect to make much of it; but there came a Gentleman extreamly well Dress'd, and very Rich and as 'tis frequent to talk to every Body in those Shops he singl'd me out, and was very particular with me; first he told me he would put in for me to Raffle, and did so; and some small matter coming to his Lot, he presented it to me, I think it was a Feather Muff: Then he continu'd to keep talking to me with a more than common Appearance of Respect; but still very civil and much like a Gentleman.

He held me in talk so long till at last he drew me out of the Raffling Place to the Shop-Door, and then to take a walk in the Cloister, still talking of a Thousand things Cursorily without any thing to the purpose; at last he told me that without Complement he was charm'd with my Company, and ask'd me if I durst trust myself in a Coach with him; he told me he was a Man of Honour, and would not offer any thing to me unbecoming him as such: I seem'd to decline it a while, but suffer'd myself to be importun'd a little, and then yielded.

I was at a loss in my Thoughts to conclude at first what this Gentleman design'd; but I found afterward he had had some drink in his Head; and that he was not very unwilling to have some more: He carried me in the Coach to the *Spring-Garden,* at *Knight's-Bridge,* where we walk'd in the Gardens, and he Treated me very handsomely; but I found he drank very freely, he press'd me also to drink, but I declin'd it.

Hitherto he kept his Word with me, and offer'd me nothing amiss; we came away in the Coach again, and he brought me into the Streets and by this time it was near Ten a-Clock at Night, and he stop'd the Coach at a House, where it seems he was acquainted, and where they made no scruple to show us up Stairs into a Room with a Bed in it; at first I seem'd to be unwilling to go up, but after a few Words, I yielded to that too, being indeed willing to see the End of it, and in Hopes to make something of it at last; as for the Bed, *etc.* I was not much concern'd about that Part.

Here he began to be a little freer with me than he had promis'd; and I by little and little yielded to every thing, so that in a Word, he did what he pleas'd with me; I need say no more; all this while he drank freely too, and about One in the Morning we went into the Coach again; the Air, and the shaking of the Coach made the Drink he had get more up in his Head than it was before, and he grew uneasy in the Coach, and was for acting over again, what he had been doing before; but as I thought my

Game now secure, I resisted him, and brought him to be a little still, which had not lasted five Minutes, but he fell fast asleep.

I took this opportunity to search him to a Nicety; I took a gold Watch, with a silk Purse of Gold, his fine full bottom Perrewig, and silver fring'd Gloves, his Sword, and fine Snuff-box, and gently opening the Coach-door, stood ready to jump out while the Coach was going on; but the Coach stopping in the narrow Street beyond *Temple-Bar* to let another Coach pass, I got softly out, fasten'd the Door again, and gave my Gentleman and the Coach the slip both together.

This was an Adventure indeed unlook'd for, and perfectly undesign'd by me; tho' I was not so past the Merry part of Life, as to forget how to behave, when a Fop so blinded by his Appetite should not know an old Woman from a young: I did not indeed look so old as I was by ten or twelve Year; yet I was not a young Wench of Seventeen, and it was easie enough to be distinguish'd: There is nothing so absurd, so surfeiting, so ridiculous as a Man heated by Wine in his Head, and a wicked Gust in his Inclination together; he is in the possession of two Devils at once, and can no more govern himself by his Reason than a Mill can Grind without Water; His Vice tramples upon all that was in him that had any good in it, if any such thing there was; nay, his very Sense is blinded by its own Rage, and he acts Absurdities even in his View; such as Drinking more, when he is Drunk already; picking up a common Woman, without regard to what she is, or who she is; whether Sound or rotten, Clean or Unclean; whether Ugly or Handsome, whether Old or Young, and so blinded, as not really to distinguish; such a Man is worse than Lunatick; prompted by his vicious corrupted Head he no more knows what he is doing than this Wretch of mine knew when I pick'd his Pocket of his Watch and his Purse of Gold.

These are the Men of whom *Solomon says, they go like an Ox to the slaughter, till a Dart strikes through their Liver,* an admirable Description, *by the way,* of the foul Disease, which is a poisonous deadly Contagion mingling with the Blood, whose Center or Fountain is in the Liver; from whence, by the swift Circulation of the whole Mass, that dreadful nauceous Plague strikes immediately thro' his Liver, and his Spirits are infected, his Vitals stab'd thro' as with a Dart.

It is true this poor unguarded Wretch was in no Danger from me, tho' I was greatly apprehensive at first of what Danger I might be in from him; but he was really to be pityed in one respect, that he seem'd to be a good sort of a Man in himself; a Gentleman that had no harm in his Design; a Man of Sense, and of a fine Behaviour; a comely handsome Person, a sober solid Countenance, a charming beautiful Face, and everything that cou'd be agreeable; only had unhappily had some Drink the Night before, had not been in Bed, as he told me when we were together, was hot, and his Blood fir'd with Wine, and in that Condition his Reason *as it were* asleep, had given him up.

As for me, my Business was his Money, and what I could make of him, and after that if I could have found out any way to have done it, I would have sent him safe home to his House and to his Family, for 'twas ten to one but he had an honest virtuous Wife and innocent Children, that were anxious for his Safety, and would have been glad to have gotten him Home, and have taken care of him till he was restor'd to himself; and then with what Shame and Regret would he look back upon himself? how would he reproach himself with associating himself with a Whore? pick'd up in the worst of all Holes, the Cloister, among the Dirt and Filth of all the Town? how would he be trembling for fear he had got the Pox, for fear a Dart had struck through his Liver, and hate himself every time he look'd back upon the Madness and Brutality of his Debauch? how would he, if he had any Principles of Honour, as I verily believe he had, I say how would he abhor the Thought of giving any ill Distemper, if he had it, as for ought he knew he might, to his Modest and Virtuous Wife, and thereby sowing the Contagion in the Life-blood of his Posterity?

Would such Gentlemen but consider the contemptible Thoughts which the very Women they are concern'd with, in such Cases as these, have of them, it wou'd be a surfeit to them: As I said above, they value not the Pleasure, they are rais'd by no Inclination to the Man, the passive Jade thinks of no Pleasure but the Money; and when he is as it were drunk in the Extasies of his wicked Pleasure, her Hands are in his Pockets searching for what she can find there, and of which he can no more be sensible in the Moment of his Folly, than he can fore-think of it when he goes about it.

I knew a Woman that was so dexterous with a Fellow, who indeed deserv'd no better usage, that while he was busie with her another way, convey'd his Purse with twenty Guineas in it out of his Fob Pocket, where he had put it for fear of her, and put another Purse with guilded Counters in it into the room of it: After he had done, he says to her, now han't you pick'd my Pocket? she jested with him, and told him she suppos'd he had not much to lose; he put his Hand to his Fob, and with his Fingers felt that his Purse was there, which fully satisfy'd him, and so she brought off his Money; and this was a Trade with her, she kept a sham Gold Watch, that is a Watch of Silver Guilt, and a purse of Counters in her Pocket to be ready on all such Occasions; and I doubt not practis'd it with Success.

I came home with this last Booty to my Governess, and really when I told her the Story it so affected her that she was hardly able to forbear Tears, to think how such a Gentleman run a daily Risque of being undone, every time a Glass of Wine got into his Head.

But as to the Purchase I got, and how entirely I stript him, she told me it pleas'd her wonderfully; nay, Child, *says she,* the usage may, for ought I know, do more to reform him, than all the Sermons that ever he will hear in his Life, and if the remainder of the Story be true; so it did.

I found the next Day she was wonderful inquisitive about this Gentleman; the description I had given her of him, his Dress, ills Person, his Face, every thing concur'd to make her think of a Gentleman whose Character she knew, and Family too; she mus'd a while, and I going still on with the Particulars, she starts up, *says she,* I'll lay a Hundred Pound I know the Gentleman.

I am sorry you do, *says I,* for I would not have him expos'd on any account in the World; he has had Injury enough already by me, and I would not be instrumental to do him any more: No, no *says she,* I will do him no Injury, I assure you, but you may let me satisfie my Curiosity a little, for if it is he, I warrant you I find it out: I was a little startled at that, and told her with an apparent concern in my Face, that by the same Rule he might find me out, and then I was undone: *she return'd warmly,* why, do you think I will betray you, Child? No, no, *says she,* not for all he is worth in the World; I have kept your Counsel in worse things than these, sure you may trust me in this: So I said no more at that time.

She laid her Scheme another way, and without acquainting me of it, but she was resolv'd to find it out, if possible; so she goes to a certain Friend of hers who was acquainted in the Family, that she guess'd at, and told her Friend she had some extraordinary business with such a Gentleman (who by the way was no less than a Baronet, and of a very good Family) and that she knew not how to come at him without somebody to introduce her: Her Friend promis'd her very readily to do it, and accordingly goes to the House to see if the Gentleman was in Town.

The next Day she comes to my Governess and tells her that Sir was at Home, but that he had met with a Disaster and was very ill, and there was no speaking with him; what Disaster, *says my Governess hastily,* as if she was surpriz'd at it? Why, *says her Friend,* he had been at *Hompsteod* to Visit a Gentleman of his Acquaintance, and as he came back again he was set upon and

Robb'd, and having got a little Drink too, as they suppose; the Rogues abus'd him, and he is very ill: Robb'd, *says my Governess,* and what did they take from him? why, *says her Friend,* they took his Gold Watch, and his Gold Snuff-box, his fine Perriwig, and what Money he had in his Pocket, which was considerable to be sure, for Sir – never goes without a Purse of Guineas about him.

Pshaw! says my old Governess jeering, I warrant you he has got drunk now and got a Whore, and she has pick'd his Pocket, and so he comes home to his Wife and tells her he has been Robb'd; that's an old sham, a thousand such tricks are put upon the poor Women every Day.

Fye, *says her Friend,* I find you don't know Sir – , why he is as Civil a Gentleman, there is not a finer Man, nor a soberer grave modester Person in the whole City; he abhors such things, there's no Body that knows him will think such a thing of him: Well, well, *says my Governess,* that's none of my Business, if it was, I warrant I should find there was something of that kind in it; your Modest Men in common Opinion are sometimes no better than other People, only they keep a better Character, or if you please, are the better Hypocrites.

No, no, *says her Friend,* I can assure you Sir – is no Hypocrite; he is really an honest sober Gentleman, and he has certainly been Robb'd: Nay, *says my Governess,* it may be he has, it is no Business of mine I tell you; I only want to speak with him, my Business is of another Nature; but, *says her Friend,* let your Business be of what nature it will, you cannot see him yet, for he is not fit to be seen, for he is very ill, and bruis'd very much: Ay, *says my Governess,* nay then he has fallen into bad Hands to be sure; and then she ask'd gravely, pray where is he bruised? Why in his Head, *says her Friend,* and one of his Hands, and his Face, for they us'd him barbarously. Poor Gentleman, *says my Governess,* I must wait then till he recovers, and adds, I hope it will not be long, for I want very much to speak with him.

Away she comes to me and tells me this Story; I have found out your fine Gentleman, and a fine Gentleman he was, *says she,* but Mercy on him, he is in a sad pickle now; I wonder what the *D...l* you have done to him; why you have almost kill'd him: I look'd at her with disorder enough; I killed him! *says I,* you must mistake the Person, I am sure I did nothing to him, he was very well when I left him, *said I,* only drunk and fast asleep; I know nothing of that, *says she,* but he is in a sad pickle now, and so she told me all that her Friend had said to her: Well then, *says I,* he fell into bad Hands after I left him, for I am sure I left him safe enough.

About ten Days after, or a little more, my Governess goes again to her Friend, to introduce her to this Gentleman; she had enquir'd other ways in the mean time, and found that he was about again, if not abroad again, so she got leave to speak with him.

She was a Woman of an admirable Address, and wanted no Body to introduce her; she told her Tale much better than I shall be able to tell it for her, for she was a Mistress of her Tongue, as I have said already: She told him that she came, tho' a Stranger, with a single design of doing him a Service, and he should find she had no other End in it; that as she came purely on so Friendly an account, she beg'd a promise from him, that if he did not accept what she should officiously propose, he would not take it ill, that she meddl'd with what was not her Business; she assur'd him that as what she had to say was a Secret that belong'd to him only, so whether he accepted her offer or not, it should remain a Secret to all the World, unless he expos'd it himself; nor should his refusing her Service in it, make her so little show her Respect, as to do him the least Injury, so that he should be entirely at liberty to act as he thought fit.

He look'd very shy at first, and said he knew nothing that related to him that requir'd much secresie; that he had never done any Man any wrong, and car'd not what any Body might say of him; that it was no part of his Character to be unjust to any Body, nor could he imagine in what any Man cou'd render him any Service; but that if it was so disinterested a Service as she said, he could not take it ill from anyone that they should endeavour to serve him; and so, as it were, left her at liberty either to tell him, or not to tell him, as she thought fit.

She found him so perfectly indifferent, that she was almost afraid to enter into the point with him; but however, after some other Circumlocutions, she told him that by a strange and unaccountable Accident she came to have a particular knowledge of the late unhappy Adventure he had fallen into; and that in such a manner, that there was no Body in the World but herself and him that were acquainted with it, no not the very Person that was with him.

He look'd a little angrily at first; what Adventure? *said he;* why, Sir, *said she,* of your being Robb'd coming from *Knightsbr* – , *Hampstead,* Sir, I should say, *says she;* be not surpris'd, Sir, *says she,* that I am able to tell you every step you took that Day from the *Cloyster* in *Smithfield,* to the *Spring-Garden* at *Knightsbridge,* and thence to the – in the *Strand,* and how you were left asleep in the Coach afterwards; I say let not this surprize you, for Sir I do not come to make a Booty of you, I ask nothing of you, and I assure you the Woman that was with you knows nothing who you are, and never shall; and yet perhaps I may serve you farther still, for I did not come barely to let you know that I was inform'd of these things, as if I wanted a Bribe to conceal them; assure your self, Sir, *says she,* that whatever you think fit to do or say to me, it shall be all a secret as it is, as much as in were in my Grave.

He was astonish'd at her Discourse, and said gravely to her, Madam, you are a Stranger to me, but it is very unfortunate that you should be let into the Secret of the worst action of my Life, and a thing that I am so justly asham'd of, that the only satisfaction of it to me was that I thought it was known only to

God and my own Conscience: Pray, Sir, *says she,* do not reckon the Discovery of it to me, to be any part of your Misfortune; it was a thing, I believe, you were surprized into, and perhaps the Woman us'd some Art to prompt you to it; however, you will never find any just Cause, *said she,* to repent that I came to hear of it; nor can your own Mouth be more silent in it than I have been, and ever shall be.

Well, *says he,* but let me do some Justice to the Woman too, whoever she is, I do assure you she prompted me to nothing, she rather declin'd me; it was my own Folly and Madness that brought me into it all, ay and brought her into it too; I must give her her due so far; as to what she took from me, I cou'd expect no less from her in the condition I was in, and to this Hour I know not whether she Robb'd me or the Coachman; if she did it I forgive her, and I think all Gentlemen that do so, should be us'd in the same manner; but I am more concern'd for some other things than I am for all that she took from me.

My Governess now began to come into the whole matter, and he open'd himself freely to her; first, she said to him, in answer to what he had said about me, I am glad Sir you are so just to the Person that you were with; I assure you she is a Gentlewoman, and no Woman of the Town; and however you prevail'd with her so far as you did, I am sure 'tis not her Practise; you run a great venture indeed, Sir, but if that be any part of your Care, I am perswaded you may be perfectly easie, for I dare assure you no Man has touch'd her, before you, since her Husband, and he has been dead now almost eight Year.

It appear'd that this was his Grievance, and that he was in a very great fright about it; however, when my Governess said this to him he appeared very well pleased; and said, well, Madam, to be plain with you, if I was satisfy'd of that, I should not so much value what I lost; for as to that, the Temptation was great, and perhaps she was poor and wanted it: If she had not been poor Sir – , *says my Governess,* I assure you she would never have yielded to you; and as her Poverty first prevailed with her to let you do as you did, so the same Poverty prevail'd with her to pay her self at last, when she saw you was in such a Condition, that if she had not done it, perhaps the next Coachman or Chair-man might have done it.

Well, *says he,* much good may it do her; I say again, all the Gentlemen that do so, ought to be us'd in the same manner, and then they would be cautious of themselves; I have no more concern about it, but on the score which you hinted at before, Madam: Here he entered into some freedoms with her on the Subject of what pass'd between us, which are not so proper for a Woman to write, and the great Terror that was upon his Mind with relation to his Wife, for fear he should have receiv'd any Injury from me, and should communicate it farther; and ask'd her at last if she cou'd not procure him an opportunity to speak with me; my Governess gave him farther assurances of my being a Woman clear from any such thing, and that he was as entirely safe in that respect, as he was with his own Lady; but as for seeing me, she said it might be of dangerous consequence; but however, that she would talk with me, and let him know my Answer; using at the same time some Arguments to perswade him not to desire it, and that it cou'd be of no Service to him, seeing she hop'd he had no desire to renew a Correspondence with me, and that on my account it was a kind of putting my Life in his Hands.

He told her, he had a great desire to see me, that he would give her any assurances that were in his Power, not to take any Advantages of me, and that in the first place he would give me a general release from all Demands of any kind; she insisted how it might tend to a farther divulging the Secret, and might in the end be injurious to him, entreating him not to press for it, so at length he desisted.

They had some Discourse upon the Subject of the things he had lost, and he seem'd to be very desirous of his Gold Watch, and told her if she cou'd procure that for him, he would willingly give as much for it as it was worth, she told him she would endeavour to procure it for him and leave the valuing it to himself.

Accordingly the next Day she carried the Watch, and he gave her 30 Guineas for it, which was more than I should have been able to make of it, tho' it seems it cost much more; he spoke something of his Perriwig, which it seems cost him threescore Guineas, and his Snuffbox, and in a few Days more, she carried them too; which oblig'd him very much, and he gave her Thirty more, the next Day I sent him his fine Sword, and Cane *Gratis,* and demanded nothing of him, but I had no mind to see him, unless it had been so, that he might be satisfy'd I knew who he was, which he was not willing to.

Then he entered into a long Talk with her of the manner how she came to know all this matter; she form'd a long Tale of that part; how she had it from one that I had told the whole Story to, and that was to help me dispose of the Goods, and this Confident brought the Things to her, she being by Profession a *Pawn-Broker;* and she hearing of his Worship's dissaster, guess'd at the thing in general; that having gotten the Things into her Hands,; she had resolv'd to come and try as she had done: She then gave him repeated Assurances that it should never go out of her Mouth, and tho' she knew the Woman very well, yet she had not let her know, *meaning me,* any thing of it; *that is to say,* who the Person was, which by the way was false; but however it was not to his Damage, for I never open'd my Mouth of it to any Body.

I had a great many Thoughts in my Head about my seeing him again, and was often sorry that I had refus'd it; I was perswaded that if I had seen him, and let him know that I knew him, I should have made some Advantage of him, and perhaps have had some Maintenance from him; and tho' it was a Life wicked enough, yet it was not so full of Danger as this I was engag'd in. However those Thoughts wore off, and I declin'd seeing him again, for that time; but my Governess saw him often, and he was very kind to her, giving her something almost every time he saw her; one time in particular she found him very Merry, and as she thought he had some Wine in his Head, and he press'd her again very earnestly to let him see that Woman, that *as he said,* had Bewitch'd him so that Night; my Governess, who was from the beginning for my seeing him, told him, he was so desirous of it, that she could almost yield to it, if she cou'd prevail upon me; adding that if he would please to come to her House in the Evening she would endeavour it, upon his repeated Assurances of forgetting what was pass'd.

Accordingly she came to me and told me all the Discourse; *in short,* she soon byass'd me to consent, in a Case which I had some regret in my mind for declining before: so I prepar'd to see him: I dress'd me to all the Advantage possible I assure you, and for the first time us'd a little Art; I say for the first time, for I had never yielded to the baseness of Paint before, having always had vanity enough to believe I had no need of it.

At the Hour appointed he came; and as she observ'd before, so it was plain still, that he had been drinking, tho' very far from what we call being in drink: He appear'd exceeding pleas'd to see me, and enter'd into a long Discourse with me, upon the old Affair; I beg'd his pardon very often, for my share of it; protested I had not any such design when first I met him; that I had not gone out with him, but that I took him for a very civil Gentleman; and that he made me so many promises of offering no uncivility to me.

He alledg'd the Wine he drank, and that he scarce knew what he did, and that if it had not been so, I should never have let him take the freedom with me that he had done: He protested to me that he never touch'd any Woman but me since he was married to his Wife, and it was a surprise upon him; Complimented me upon being so particularly agreeable to him, and the like, and talk'd so much of that kind, till I found he, had talk'd himself almost into a temper to do the same thing over again: But I took him up short, I protested I had never suffer'd any Man to touch me since my Husband died, which was near eight Year; he said he believed it to be so truly; and added that Madam, had intimated as much to him, and that it was his Opinion of that part which made him desire to see me again; and that since he had once broke in upon his Virtue with me, and found no ill Consequences, he cou'd be safe in venturing there again; and so in short it went on to what I expected, and to what will not bear relating.

My old Governess had foreseen it, as well as I, and therefore led him into a Room which had not a Bed in it, and yet had a Chamber within it, which had a Bed, whither we withdrew for the rest of the Night, and in short, after some time being together, he went to Bed, and lay there all Night; I withdrew, but came again undress'd in the Morning before it was Day, and lay with him the rest of the time.

Thus you see having committed a Crime once, is a sad Handle to the committing of it again; whereas all the Regret, and Reflections wear off when the Temptation renews it self; had I not yielded to see him again, the Corrupt desire in him had worn off, and 'tis very probable he had never fallen into it, with any Body else, as I really believe he had not done before.

When he went away, I told him I hop'd he was satisfy'd he had not been robb'd again; he told me he was satisfy'd in that Point, and cou'd trust me again; and putting his Hand in his Pocket gave me five Guineas, which was the first Money I had gain'd that way for many Years.

I had several Visits of the like kind from him, but he never came into a settled way of Maintenance, which was what I would have been best pleas'd with: Once indeed he ask'd me how I did to live, I answer'd him pretty quick, that I assur'd him I had never taken that Course that I took with him; but that indeed I work'd at my Needle, and could just Maintain myself, that sometimes it was as much as I was able to do, and I shifted hard enough.

He seem'd to reflect upon himself that he should be the first Person to lead me into that, which he assur'd me he never intended to do himself; and it touch'd him a little, *he said,* that he should be the Cause of his own Sin, and mine too: He would often make just Reflections also upon the Crime itself, and upon the particular Circumstances of it, with respect to himself; how Wine introduc'd the Inclinations, how the Devilled him to the Place, and found out an Object to tempt him, and he made the Moral always himself.

When these thoughts were upon him he would go away, and perhaps not come again in a Months time or longer; but then as the serious part wore off, the lewd Part would wear in, and then he came prepar'd for the wick'd Part; thus we liv'd for some time; tho' he did not KEEP, as they call it, yet he never fail'd doing things that were Handsome, and sufficient to Maintain me without working, and which was better, without following my old Trade.

But this Affair had its End too; for after about a Year, I found that he did not come so often as usual, and at last he left it off altogether without any dislike, or bidding adieu; and so there was an End of that short Scene of Life, which added no great Store to me, only to make more Work for Repentance.

However during this interval, I confin'd my self pretty much at Home; at least being thus provided for, I made no Adventures, no not for a Quarter of a Year after he left me; but then finding the Fund fail, and being loth to spend upon the main Stock, I began to think of my old Trade, and to look Abroad into the Street again, and my first Step was lucky enough.

I had dress'd myself up in a very mean Habit, for as I had several Shapes to appear in I was now in an ordinary Stuff-Grown, a blue Apron and a Straw-Hat; and I plac'd myself at the Door of the three Cups-Inn in *St John Street:* There were several Carriers us'd the Inn, and the Stage Coaches for *Barnet,* for *Toteridge,* and other Towns that way, stood always in the Street in the Evening, when they prepar'd to set out, so that I was ready for any thing that offer'd for either one or other: The meaning was this, People come frequently with Bundles and small Parcels to those Inns, and call for such Carriers, or Coaches as they want, to carry them into the Country; and there generally attends Women, Porters Wives, or Daughters, ready to take in such things for their respective People that employ them.

It happen'd very odly that I was standing at the Inn-Gate, and a Woman that had stood there before, and which was the Porter's Wife belonging to the *Barnet* Stage Coach, having observ'd me, ask'd if I waited for any of the Coaches; I told her yes, I waited for my Mistress, that was coming to go to *Barnet;* she ask'd me who was my Mistress, and I told her any Madam's Name that came next me, but as it seem'd I happen'd upon a Name, a Family of which Name liv'd at *Hadly* just beyond *Barnet.*

I said no more to her, or she to me a good while, but by and by, some body calling her at a Door a little way off, she desir'd me that if any body call'd for the *Barnet* Coach, I would step and call her at the House, which it seems was an Ale-house; I said yes very readily, and away she went.

She was no sooner gone, but comes a Wench and a Child, puffing and sweating, and asks for the *Barnet* Coach; I answer'd presently, *here.* Do you belong to the *Barnet* Coach? *says she.* Yes, Sweetheart, *said I,* what do ye want? I want Room for two Passengers *says she;* Where are they Sweetheart? *said* I. Here's this Girl, pray let her go into the Coach, *says she,* and I'll go and fetch my Mistress; make haste then Sweetheart, *says I,* for we may be full else; the Maid had a great Bundle under Arm; so she put the Child into the Coach, and *I said,* you had best put your Bundle into the Coach too; No, *says she,* I am afraid some body should slip it away from the Child; give it me then, *said I,* and I'll take care of it; do then, *says she,* and be sure you take care of it; I'll answer for it, *said I,* if it were for Twenty Pound value. There take it then, *says she,* and away she goes.

As soon as I had got the Bundle, and the Maid was out of Sight, I goes on towards the Ale-house, where the Porter's Wife was, so that if I had met her, I had then only been going to give her the Bundle, and call her to her Business, as if I was going away, and cou'd stay no longer; but as I did not meet her I walk'd away, arid turning into *Charter-house-Lane,* made off thro' *Charter-house-Yard,* into *Long-Lane,* then cross'd into *Bartholomew-Close,* so into *Little Britain,* and thro' the *Blue-Coat-Hospital* into *Newgate-Street.*

To prevent my being known, I pull'd off my blue Apron, and wrapt the Bundle in it, which before was made up in a Piece of painted Callico, and very Remarkable; I also wrapt up my Straw-Hat in it, and so put the Bundle upon my Head; and it was very well, that I did thus, for coming thro' the *Blue-Coat Hospital,* who should I meet but the Wench, that had given me the Bundle to hold; it seems she was going with her Mistress, who she had been gone to fetch to the *Barnet* Coaches.

I saw she was in haste, and I had no Business to stop her: so away she went, and I brought my Bundle safe Home to my Governess; there was no Money, nor Plate, or Jewels in the Bundle, but a very good Suit of *Indian* Damask, a Gown and Petticoat, a lac'd Head and Ruffles of very good Flanders-Lace, and some Linnen, and other things, such as I knew very well the value of.

This was not indeed my own Invention, but was given me by one that had practis'd it with Success, and my Governess lik'd it extreamly; and indeed I try'd it again several times, tho' never twice near the same Place; for the next time I try'd it in *White-Chappel* just by the Corner of *Petty-Coat-Lane,* where the Coaches stand that go out to *Stratford* and *Bow,* and that Side of the Country, and another time at the *Flying-Horse,* without *Bishops-gate,* where the *Chester* Coaches then lay, and I had always the good Luck to come off with some Booty.

Another time I plac'd myself at a Warehouse by the Waterside, where the Coasting Vessels from the *North* come, such as from *Newcastle* upon *Tyne, Sunderland,* and other Places; here, the Warehouse being shut, comes a young Fellow with a Letter; and he wanted a Box, and a Hamper that was come from *New-Castle* upon *Tyne,* I ask'd him if he had the Marks of it, so he shows me the Letter, by Virtue of which he was to ask for it, and which gave an Account of the Contents, the Box being full of Linnen, and the Hamper full of Glass-Ware; I read the Letter, and took care to see the Name, and the Marks, the Name of the Person that sent the Goods, the Name of the Person that they were sent to, then I bade the Messenger come in the Morning for that the Warehouse Keeper, would not be there any more that Night.

Away went I, and getting Materials in a publick House, I wrote a Letter from Mr *John Richardson* of *New-Castle* to his Dear Cousin *Jemey Cole,* in *London,* with an Account that he had sent by such a Vessel, (for I remember'd all the Particulars to a tittle,) so many pieces of Huckaback Linnen, so many Ells of *Dutch* Holland and the like, in a Box, and a Hamper of Flint Glasses from Mr *Henzill's* Glass-house, and that the Box was mark'd I C. No1 and the Hamper was directed by a Label on the Cording.

About an Hour after, I came to the Warehouse, found the Ware house-keeper, and had the Goods deliver'd me without any scruple; the value of the Linnen being about 22 Pound.

I could fill up this whole Discourse with the variety of such Adventures which daily Invention directed to, and which I manag'd with the utmost Dexterity, and always with Success.

At length, as when does the Pitcher come safe home that goes so very often to the Well, I fell into some small Broils, which tho' they cou'd not affect me fatally, yet made me known, which was the worst thing next to being found Guilty, that cou'd befall me.

I had taken up the Disguise of a Widow's Dress; it was without any real design in view, but only waiting for any thing that might offer, as I often did: It happen'd that while I was going along the Street in *Covent Garden,* there was a great Cry of stop Thief, stop Thief; some Artists had it seems put a trick upon a Shop-keeper, and being pursued, some of them fled one way, and some another; and one of them was, they said, dress'd up in Widow's Weeds, upon which the Mob gathered about me, and some said I was the Person, others said no; immediately came the Mercer's Journey-man, and he swore aloud I was the Person, and so seiz'd on me; however, when I was brought back by the Mob to the Mercer's Shop, the Master of the House said freely that I was not the Woman that was in his Shop, and would have let me go immediately; but another Fellow said gravely, pray stay till Mr –, *meaning the Journeyman,* comes back for he knows her; so they kept me by force near half an Hour; they had call'd a Constable, and he stood in the Shop as my Jayler; and in talking with the Constable I enquir'd where he liv'd, and what Trade he was; the Man not apprehending in the least what happened afterwards, readily told me his Name, and Trade, and where he liv'd; and told me as a Jest, that I might be sure to hear of his Name when I came to the *Old Bayley.*

Some of the Servants likewise us'd me saucily, and had much ado to keep their Hands off of me, the Master indeed was civiler to me than they; but he would not yet let me go, tho' he owned he could not say I was in his Shop before.

I began to be a little surly with him, and told him I hop'd he would not take it ill, if I made my self amends upon him in a more legal way another time; and desir'd I might send for Friends to see me have right done me: No, *he said,* he could give no such liberty, I might ask it when I came before the Justice of Peace, and seeing I threaten'd him, he would take care of me in the mean time, and would lodge me safe in *Newgate:* I told him it was his time now, but it would be mine by and by, and govern'd my Passion as well as I was able; however, I spoke to the Constable to call me a Porter, which he did, and then I call'd for Pen, Ink, and Paper, but they would let me have none; I ask'd the Porter his Name, and where he liv'd, and the poor Man told it me very willingly; I bade him observe and remember how I was treated there; that he saw I was detain'd there by Force; I told him I should want his Evidence in another place, and it should not be the worse for him to speak; the Porter said he would serve me with all his Heart; but, Madam, *says he,* let me hear them refuse to let you go, then I may be able to speak the plainer.

With that I spoke aloud to the Master of the Shop, and said, Sir, you know in your own Conscience that I am not the Person you look for, and that I was not in your Shop before, therefore I demand that you detain me here no longer, or tell me the reason of your stopping me; the Fellow grew surlier upon this than before, and said he would do neither till he thought fit; very well, said I to the Constable and to the Porter, you will be pleas'd to remember this, Gentlemen, another time; the Porter said, *yes, Madam,* and the Constable began not to like it, and would have perswaded the Mercer to dismiss him, and let me go, since, as he said, he own'd I was not the Person; Good Sir, *says the Mercer to him Tauntingly,* are you a Justice of Peace, or a Constable? I charg'd you with her, pray do you do your Duty: The Constable told him a little mov'd, but very handsomely, *I know my Duty, and what I am, Sir, I doubt you hardly know what you are doing;* they had some other hard words, and in the mean time the Journey-men, impudent and unmanly to last degree, used me barbarously, and one of them, the same that first seized upon me, pretended he would search me, and began to lay Hands on me: I spit in his Face, call'd out to the Constable, and bade him take notice of my usage; and pray, Mr Constable, *said I,* ask that Villain's Name, pointing to the Man; the Constable reprov'd him decently, told him that he did not know what he did, for he knew that his Master acknowledg'd I was not the Person that was in his Shop; and, says the Constable, I am afraid your Master is bringing himself and me too into Trouble, if this Gentlewoman comes to prove who she is, and where she was, and it appears that she is not the Woman you pretend to; *Dam her, says the Fellow again,* with an impudent harden'd Face, she is the Lady, you may depend upon it, I'll swear she is the same Body that was in the Shop, and that I gave the pieces of Satin that is lost into her own hand, you shall hear more of it when Mr *William* and *Anthony, those were other*

Journeymen, come back, they will know her again as well as I.

Just as the insolent Rogue was talking thus to the Constable, comes back Mr *William* and Mr *Anthony,* as he call'd them, and a great Rabble with them, bringing along with them the true Widow that I was pretended to be; and they came sweating and blowing into the Shop, and with a great deal of Triumph dragging the poor Creature in a most butcherly manner up towards their Master, who was in the back Shop, and cried out aloud, here's the Widow, Sir, we have catch'd her at last; what do ye mean by that? *says the Master,* why we have her already, there she sits, *says he,* and *Mr – says he,* can swear this is she: The other Man who they call'd Mr *Anthony* replyed, Mr – may say what he will, and swear what he will, but this is the Woman, and there's the Remnant of Sattin she stole, I took it out of her Cloaths with my own Hand.

I sat still now, and began to take a better Heart, but smil'd and said nothing; the Master look'd Pale; the Constable turn'd about and look'd at me; *let 'em alone Mr Constable,* said I, *let 'em go* on; the Case was plain and could not be denied, so the Constable was charg'd with the right Thief; and the Mercer told me very civily he was sorry for the mistake, and hoped I would not take it ill; that they had so many things of this nature put upon them every Day, that they cou'd not be blam'd for being very sharp in doing themselves Justice; Not take it ill, Sir! *said I,* how can I take it well? if you had dismiss'd me when your insolent Fellow seiz'd on me in the Street, and brought me to you; and when you your self acknowledg'd I was not the Person, I would have put it by, and not taken it ill, because of the many ill things I believe you have put upon you daily; but your Treatment of me since has been unsufferable, and especially that of your Servant, I must and will have Reparation for that.

Then he began to party with me, said he would make me any reasonable Satisfaction, and would fain have had me told him what it was I expected; I told him I should not be my own Judge, the Law should decide it for me, and as I was to be carried before a Magistrate, I should let him hear there what I had to say he told me there was no occasion to go before the Justice now, I was at liberty to go where I pleased, and so calling to the Constable told him, he might let me go, for I was discharg'd; the Constable said calmly to him, Sir, you ask'd me just now, if I knew whether I was a Constable or a Justice, and bade me do my Duty, and charg'd me with this Gentlewoman as a Prisoner; now, Sir, I find you do not understand what is my Duty, for you would make me a Justice indeed; but I must tell you it is not in my Power: I may keep a Prisoner when I am charg'd with him, but 'tis the Law and the Magistrate alone that can discharge that Prisoner; therefore 'tis a mistake, Sir, I must carry her before a Justice now, whether you think well of it or not: The Mercer was very high with the Constable at first; but the Constable happening to be not a hir'd Officer, but a good Substantial kind of Man, I think he was a Com-chandler, and a Man of good Sense, stood to his Business, would not discharge me without going to a Justice of the Peace; and I insisted upon it too: When the Mercer see that, well, *says he to the Constable,* you may carry her where you please, I have nothing to say to her; but Sir, *says the Constable,* you will go with us, I hope, for 'tis you that charg'd me with her; no not I, *says the Mercer,* I tell you I have nothing to say to her: But pray Sir do, *says the Constable,* I desire it of you for your own sake, for the Justice can do nothing without you: Prithee Fellow, *says the Mercer,* go about your Business, I tell you I have nothing to say to the Gentlewoman, I charge you in the King's Name to dismiss her: Sir, *says the Constable,* I find you don't know what it is to be a Constable, I beg of you don't oblige me to be rude to you; I think I need not, you are rude enough already, *says the Mercer:* No, Sir, *says the Constable,* I am not rude, you have broken the Peace in bringing an honest Woman out of the Street, when she was about her lawful Occasion, confining her in your Shop, and ill using her here by your Servants; and now can you say I am rude to you? I think I am civil to you in not commanding or charging you in the King's Name to go with me, and charging every Man I see, that passes your Door, to aid and assist me in carrying you by Force, this you cannot but know I have power to do, and yet I forbear it, and once more entreat you to go with me: Well, he would not for all this, and gave the Constable ill Language: However, the Constable kept his Temper, and would not be provoked; and then I put in and said, come, Mr Constable, let him alone, I shall find ways enough to fetch him before a Magistrate, I don't fear that; but there's the Fellow, *says I,* he was the Man that seized on me, as I was innocently going along the Street, and you are a Witness of his Violence with me since; give me leave to charge you with him, and carry him before the Justice; yes, Madam, *says the. Constable;* and turning to the Fellow, come young Gentleman, *says he to the Journey-man,* you must go along with us, I hope you are not above the Constable's Power, tho' your Master is.

The Fellow look'd like a condemn'd Thief, and hung back, then look'd at his Master, as if he cou'd help him; and he, like a Fool, encourag'd the Fellow to be rude, and he truly resisted the Constable, and push'd him back with a good Force when he went to lay hold on him, at which the Constable knock'd him down, and call'd out for help; and immediately the Shop was fill'd with People, and the Constable seiz'd the Master and Man, and all his Servants.

The first ill Consequence of this Fray was, that the Woman they had taken, who was really the Thief, made off, and got clear away in the Crowd; and two others that they had stop'd also, whether they were really Guilty or not, that I can say nothing to.

By this time some of his Neighbours having come in, and, upon inquiry, seeing how things went, had endeavour'd to bring the hot brain'd Mercer to his Senses; and he began to be convinc'd that he was in the wrong; and so at length we went all very quietly before the Justice, with a Mob of about 500 People at our Heels; and all the way I went I could hear the People ask what was the matter? and others reply and say, a Mercer had stop'd a Gentlewoman instead of a Thief, and had afterwards taken the Thief, and now the Gentlewoman had taken the Mercer, and was carrying him before the Justice; this pleas'd the People strangely, and made the Crowd encrease, and they cry'd out as they went, which is the Rogue? which is the Mercer? and especially the Women; then when they saw him they cryed out, *that's he, that's he;* and every now and then came a good dab of Dirt at him; and thus we march'd a good while, till the Mercer thought fit to desire the Constable to call a Coach to protect himself from the Rabble; so we Rode the rest of the way, the Constable and I, and the Mercer and his Man.

When we came to the Justice, which was an ancient Gentleman in *Bloomsbury,* the Constable giving first a summary account of the Matter the Justice bade me speak, and tell what I had to say; and first he asked my Name, which I was very loath to give, but there was no remedy, so I told him my Name was *Mary Flanders,* that I was a Widow, my Husband being a Sea Captain, dyed on a Voyage to *Virginia;* and some other Circumstances I told, which he cou'd never contradict, and that I lodg'd at present in Town with such a Person, naming my Governess; but that I was preparing to go over to *America,* where my Husband's Effects lay, and that I was going that Day to buy some Cloaths to put my self into second Mourning, but had not yet been in any Shop, when that Fellow, pointing to the Mercer's Journeyman came rushing upon me with such fury, as very much frighted me, and carried me back to his Masters Shop; where tho' his Master acknowledg'd I was not the Person; yet he would not dismiss me, but charg'd a Constable with me.

Then I proceeded to tell how the Journeyman treated me; how they would not suffer me to send for any of my Friends; how afterwards they found the real Thief, and took the very Goods they had Lost upon her, and all the particulars as before.

Then the Constable related his Case; his Dialogue with the

Mercer about Discharging me, and at last his Servants refusing to go with him, when I had Charg'd him with him, and his Master encouraging him to do so; and at last his striking the Constable, and the like, all as I have told it already.

The Justice then heard, the *Mercer* and his Man; the *Mercer* indeed made a long Harangue of the great loss they have daily by Lifters and Thieves; that it was easy for them to Mistake, and that when he found it, he would have dismiss'd me, *etc.* as above; as to the Journeyman he had very little say, but that he pretended other of the Servants told him, that I was really the Person.

Upon the whole, the Justice first of all told me very courteously I was Discharg'd; that he was very sorry that the *Mercers* Man should in his eager pursuit have so little Discretion, as to take up an innocent Person for a guilty Person; that if he had not been so unjust as to detain me afterward, he believ'd I would have forgiven the first Affront; that however it was not in his Power to award me any Reparation for any thing, other than by openly reproving them, which he should do; but he suppos'd I would apply to such Methods as the Law directed; in the mean time he would bind him over.

But as to the Breach of the Peace committed by the Journeyman, he told me he should give me some satisfaction for that, for he should commit him to *Newgate* for Assaulting the Constable, and for Assaulting of me also.

Accordingly he sent the Fellow to *Newgate* for that Assault, and his Master gave Bail, and so we came away; but I had the satisfaction of seeing the Mob wait upon them both as they came out, Holooing, and throwing Stones and Dirt at the Coaches they rode in, and so I came Home to my Governess.

After this hustle, coming home and telling my Governess the Story, she falls a Laughing at me; Why are you merry, *says If* the Story has not so much Laughing room in it as you imagine; I am sure I have had a great deal of Hurry and Fright too, with a Pack of ugly Rogues. *Laugh,* says my Governess, I laugh Child to see what a lucky Creature you are; why this Jobb will be the best Bargain to you, that ever you made in your Life, if you manage it well: I warrant you, says she, you shall make the *Mercer* pay you 500 *l.* for Damages, besides what you shall get of the Journeyman.

I had other Thoughts of the Matter than she had; and especially, because I had given in my name to the Justice of Peace; and I knew that my Name was so well known among the People at *Hick's Hall,* the *Old Baily,* and such Places, that if this Cause came to be tryed openly, and my Name came to be enquir'd into, no Court would give much Damages, for the Reputation of a Person of such a Character; however, I was oblig'd to begin a Prosecution in Form, and accordingly my Governess found me out a very creditable sort of a Man to manage it, being an Attorney of very good Business, and of good Reputation, and she was certainly in the right of this; for had she employ'd a petty Fogging hedge Soliciter, or a Man not known, and not in good Reputation, I should have brought it to but little.

I met this Attorney, and gave him all the particulars at large, as they are recited above; and he assur'd me, it was a Case, *as he said,* that would very well support itself, and that he did not Question, but that a Jury would give very considerable Damages on such an Occasion; so taking his full Instructions, he began the Prosecution, and the *Mercer* being Arrested, gave Bail; a few Days after his giving Bail, he Comes with his Attorney to my Attorney, to let him know that he desir'd to Accommodate the matter; that it was all carried on in the Heat of an unhappy Passion; that his Client, *meaning me,* had a sharp provoking Tongue, that I us'd them ill, gibing at them, and jeering them, even while they believed me to be the very Person, and that I had provok'd them, and the like.

My Attorney manag'd as well on my Side; made them believe I was a Widow of Fortune, that I was able to do myself Justice, and had great Friends to stand by me too, who had all made me promise to Sue to the utmost, and that if it cost me a Thousand

Pound, I would be sure to have satisfaction, for that the Affronts I had receiv'd were unsufferable.

However they brought my Attorney to this, that he promis'd he would not blow the Coals, that if enclin'd to an Accommodation, he would not hinder me, and that he would rather perswade me to Peace than to War; for which they told him he should be no loser, all which he told me very honestly, and told me that if they offer'd him any Bribe, I should certainly know it; but upon the whole he told me very honestly that if I would take his Opinion, he would Advise me to make it up with them; for that as they were in a great Fright, and were desirous above all things to make it up, and knew that let it be what it would, they would be allotted to bear all the Costs of the Suit;' he believ'd they would give me freely more than any Jury or Court of Justice would give upon a Trial: I ask'd him what he thought they would be brought to; he told me he could not tell, as to that; but he would tell me more when I saw him again.

Some time after this, they came again to know if he had talk'd with me. He told them he had, that he found me not so Averse to an Accommodation as some of my Friends were, who resented the Disgrace offer'd me, and set me on; that they blow'd the Coals in secret, prompting me to Revenge, or to do myself Justice, as they call'd it; so that he could not tell what to say to it; he told them he would do his endeavour to persuade me, but he ought to be able to tell me what Proposal they made: They pretended they could not make any Proposal, because it might be made use of against them; and he told them, that by the same Rule he could not make any offers, for that might be pleaded in Abatement of what Damages a Jury might be inclin'd to give: However after some Discourse and mutual Promises that no Advantage should be taken on either Side, by what was transacted then, or at any other of those Meetings, they came to a kind of a Treaty; but so remote, and so wide from one another, that nothing could be expected from it; for my Attorney demanded 500 *l.* and

Charges, and they offer'd 50 *l.* without Charges; so they broke off, and the *Mercer* propos'd to have a Meeting with me myself; and my Attorney agreed to that very readily.

My Attorney gave me Notice to come to this Meeting in good Cloaths, and with some State, that the *Mercer* might see I was something more than I seem'd to be that time they had me: Accordingly I came in a new Suit of second Mourning, according to what I had said at the Justices; I set myself out too, as well as a Widows dress in second Mourning would admit; my Governess, also furnish'd me with a good Pearl Neck-lace, that shut in behind with a Locket of Diamonds, which she had in Pawn; and I had a very good gold Watch by my Side; so that in a Word, I made a very good Figure, and as I stay'd, till I was sure they were come, I came in a Coach to the Door with my Maid with me.

When I came into the Room, the *Mercer* was surpriz'd; he stood up and made his Bow, which I took a little Notice of, and but a little, and went and Sat down where my own Attorney had pointed to me to sit, for it was his House; after a little while, the *Mercer* said, he did not know me again, and began to make some Compliments his way, I told him, I believ'd he did not know me at first, and that if he had, I believ'd he would not have treated me as he did.

He told me he was very sorry for what had happen'd, and that it was to testifie the willingness he had to make all possible Reparation, that he had appointed this Meeting; that he hop'd I would not carry things to extremity, which might be not only too great a Loss to him, but might be the ruin of his Business and Shop, in which Case I might have the satisfaction of repaying an Injury with an Injury ten times greater; but that I would then get nothing, whereas he was willing to do me any Justice that was in his Power, without putting himself or me to the Trouble or Charge of a Suit at Law.

I told him I was glad to hear him talk so much more like a Man of Sense than he did before; that it was true, acknowledgement in most Cases of Affronts was counted Reparation sufficient; but this had gone too far to be made up so; that I was not Revengeful, nor did I seek his Ruin, or any Mans else, but that all my Friends were unanimous not to let me so far neglect my Character as to adjust a thing of this kind without a sufficient Reparation of Honour: That to be taken up for a Thief was such an Indignity as could not be put up, that my Character was above being treated so by any that knew me; but because in my Condition of a Widow, I had been for sometime Careless of myself, and Negligent of myself, I might be taken for such a Creature, but that for the particular usage I had from him afterward; and then I repeated all as before, it was so provoking I had scarce Patience to repeat it.

Well he acknowledg'd all, and was mighty humble indeed; he made Proposals very handsome; he came up to a Hundred Pounds, and to pay all the Law Charges, and added that he would make a Present of a very good Suit of Cloths; I came down to three Hundred Pounds, and I demanded that I should publish an Advertisement of the particulars in the common News Papers.

This was a Clause he never could comply with, however at last he came up by good Management of my Attorney to 150 *l.* and a Suit of black silk Cloaths, and there I agreed and as it were at my Attornies request complied with it; he paying my Attornies Bill and Charges, and gave us a good Supper into the Bargain.

When I came to receive the Money, I brought my Governess with me, dress'd like an old Dutchess, and a Gentleman very well dress'd, who we pretended Courted me, but I call'd him Cousin, and the Lawyer was only to hint privately to him, that this Gentleman Courted the Widow.

He treated us handsomely indeed, and paid the Money chearfully enough; so that it cost him 200 *l.* in all, or rather more: At our last Meeting when all was agreed, the Case of the Journeyman came up, and the *Mercer* beg'd very hard for him, told me he was a Man that had kept a Shop of his own, and been in good Business, had a Wife and several Children, and was very poor, that he had nothing to make satisfaction with, but he should come to beg my pardon on his Knees, if I desir'd it as openly as I pleas'd: I had no Spleen at the sawcy Rogue, nor were his Submissions any thing to me, since there was nothing to be got by him; so I thought it was as good to throw that in generously as not, so I told him I did not desire the Ruin of any Man, and therefore at his Request I would forgive the Wretch, it was below me to seek any Revenge.

When we were at Supper he brought the poor Fellow in to make acknowledgement, which he would have done with as much mean Humility, as his Offence was with insulting Haughtiness and Pride, in which he was an Instance of a compleat baseness of Spirit, imperious, cruel, and relentless when Uppermost, and in Prosperity; abject and low Spirited when Down in Affliction: However I abated his Cringes, told him I forgave him, and desir'd he might withdraw, as if I did not care for the sight of him, tho' I had forgiven him.

I was now in good Circumstances indeed, in could have known my time for leaving off, and my Governess often said I was the richest of the Trade in *England,* and so I believe I was; for I had 700 *l.* by me in Money, besides Cloaths, Rings, some Plate, and two gold Watches, and all of them stol'n, for I had innumerable Jobbs besides these I have mention'd; O! had I even now had the Grace of Repentance, I had still leisure to have look'd back upon my Follies, and have made some Reparation; but the satisfaction I was to make for the publick Mischiefs I had done, was yet left behind; and I could not forbear going Abroad again, *as I call'd it now,* any more than I could when my Extremity really drove me out for Bread.

It was not long after the Affair with the *Mercer* was made up, that I went out in an Equipage quite different from any I had ever appear'd in before; I dress'd myself like a Beggar Woman, in the coarsest and most despicable Rags I could get, and I walk'd about peering, and peeping into every Door and Window I came near; and indeed I was in such a Plight now, that I knew as ill how to behave in as ever I did in any; I naturally abhorr'd Dirt and Rags; I had been bred up Tite and Cleanly, and could be no other, what ever Condition I was in; so that this was the most uneasie Disguise to me that ever I put on. I said presently to myself that this would not do, for this was a Dress that every body was shy, and afraid of; and I thought every body look'd at me, as if they were afraid I should come near them, lest I should take something from them, or afraid to come near me, lest they should get something from me: I wandered about all the Evening the first time I went out, and made nothing of it, but came home again wet, draggl'd and tired; However I went out again, the next Night, and then I met with a little Adventure, which had like to have cost me dear; as I was standing near a Tavern Door, there comes a Gentleman on Horse back, and lights at the Door, and wanting to go into the Tavern, he calls one of the Drawers to hold his Horse; he stay'd pretty long in the Tavern, and the Drawer heard his Master call, and thought he would be angry with him; seeing me stand by him, he call'd to me, here Woman, *says he,* hold this Horse a while, till I go in, if the Gentleman comes, he'll give you something; *yes says I,* and takes the Horse and walks off with him very soberly, and carry'd him to my Governess.

This had been a Booty to those that had understood it; but never was poor Thief more at a loss to know what to do with any thing that was stolen; for when I came home, my Governess was quite confounded, and what to do with the Creature, we neither of us knew; to send him to a Stable was doing nothing, for it was certain that publick Notice would be given in the *Gazette,* and the Horse describ'd, so that we durst not go to fetch it again.

All the remedy we had for this unlucky Adventure was to go and set up the Horse at an Inn, and sent a Note by a Porter to the Tavern, that the Gentleman's Horse that was lost such a time, was left at such an Inn, and that he might be had there; that the poor Woman that held him, having led him about the' Street, not being able to lead him back again, had left him there; we might have waited till the owner had publish'd, and offer'd a Reward, but we did not care to venture the receiving the Reward.

So this was a Robbery and no Robbery, for little was lost by it, and nothing was got by it, and I was quite Sick of going out in a Beggar's dress, it did not answer at all, and besides I thought it was Ominous and Threatning.

While I was in this Disguise, I fell in with a parcel of Folks of a worse kind than any I ever sorted with, and I saw a little into their ways too, these were Coiners of Money, and they made some very good offers to me, as to profit; but the part they would have had me have embark'd in, was the most dangerous Part; I mean that of the very working the Dye, as they call it, which had I been taken, had been certain Death, and that at a Stake, *I say,* to be burnt to Death at a Stake, so that tho' I was to Appearance, but a Beggar; and they promis'd Mountains of Gold and Silver to me to engage; yet it would not do; it is True if I had been really a Beggar, or had been desperate as when I began, I might perhaps have dos'd with it; for what care they to Die, that can't tell how to Live? But at present this was not my Condition, at least I was for no such terrible Risques as those; besides the very Thoughts of being burnt at a Stake, struck terror into my very Soul, chill'd my Blood, and gave me the Vapours to such a degree as I could not think of it without trembling.

This put an End to my Disguise too, for as I did not like the Proposal, so I did not tell them so, but seem'd to relish it, and promis'd to meet again; but I durst see them no more, for in had seen them, and not complied, tho' I had declin'd it with the greatest assurances of Secresy in the World, they would have gone near to have murther'd me to make sure Work, and make themselves easy, *as they call it;* what kind of easiness that is, they may best Judge that understand how easy Men are that can Murther People to prevent Danger.

This and Horse stealing were things quite out of my way, and I might easily resolve I would have no more to say to them; my business seem'd to lye another way, and tho' it had hazard enough in it too, yet it was more suitable to me, and what had more of Art in it, more room to Escape, and more Chances for a coming off, if a Surprize should happen.

I had several Proposals made also to me about that time, to come into a Gang of House-Breakers; but that was a thing I had no mind to venture at neither, any more than I had at the Coining Trade; I offer'd to go along with two Men, and a Woman, that made it their Business to get into Houses by Stratagem, and with them I was willing enough to venture; but there was three of them already, and they did not care to part, nor I to have too many in a Gang, so I did not close with them, but declin'd them, and they paid dear for their next Attempt.

But at length I met with a Woman that had often told me what Adventures she had made, and with Success at the Water-side, and I clos'd with her, and we drove on our Business pretty well: One Day we came among some *Dutch* People at St *Catherines,* where we went on pretence to buy Goods that were privately got on Shore: I was two or three times in a House, where we saw a good Quantity of prohibited Goods, and my Companion once brought away three Peices of *Dutch* black Silk that turn'd to good Account, and I had my Share of it; but in all the Journeys I made by myself, I could not get an Opportunity to do any thing, so I laid it aside, for I had been so often, that they began to suspect something, and were so shy, that I saw nothing was to be done.

This baulk'd me a little, and I resolv'd to push at something or other, for I was not us'd to come back so often without Purchase; so the next Day I dress'd myself up fine, and took a Walk to the other End of the Town; I pass'd thro' the *Exchange* in the *Strand,* but had no Notion of finding any thing to do there, when on a sudden I saw a great Clutter in the Place, and all the People, Shop-keepers as well as others, standing up, and staring, and what should it be? but some great Dutchess come into the

Exchange; and they said the Queen was coming; I set myself close up to a Shop-side with my back to the Compter, as if to let the Crowd pass by, when keeping my Eye upon parcel of Lace, which the Shop-keeper was showing to some Ladies that stood by me; the Shop-keeper and her Maid were so taken up with looking to see who was a coming, and what Shop they would go to, that I found means to slip a Paper of Lace into my Pocket, and come clear off with it, so the Lady Millener paid dear enough for her gaping after the Queen.

I went off from the Shop, as if driven along by the Throng, and mingling myself with the Crowd, went out at the other Door of the *Exchange,* and so got away before they miss'd their Lace; and because I would not be follow'd,I call'd a Coach and shut myself up in it; I had scarse shut the Coach Doors up, but I saw the Milleners Maid, and five or six more come running out into the Street, and crying out as if they were frighted; they did not cry stop Thief, because no body ran away, but I cou'd hear the Word robb'd, and Lace, two or three times, and saw the Wench wringing her Hands, and run staring, to and again, like one scar'd; the Coachman that had taken me up was getting up into the Box, but was not quite up, so that the Horses had not begun to move, so that I was terrible uneasy; and I took the Packet of Lace and laid it ready to have dropt it out at the Flap of the Coach, which opens before, just behind the Coachman; but to my great satisfaction in less than a Minute, the Coach began to move, that is to say, as soon as the Coachman had got up and spoken to his Horses; so he drove away without any interruption, and I brought off my Purchase, which was worth near twenty Pound.

The next Day I dress'd me up again, but in quite different Cloths, and walk'd the same way again; but nothing offer'd till I came into *St James's Park,* where I saw abundance of fine Ladies in the *Park,* walking in the *Mall,* and among the rest, there was a little Miss, a young Lady of about twelve or thirteen Years old, and she had a Sister, as I suppose it was, with her, that might be about Nine Year old: I observ'd the biggest had a fine gold Watch on, and a good Necklace of Pearl, and they had a Footman in Livery with them; but as it is not usual for the Footmen to go behind the Ladies in the *Mall;* so I observ'd the Footman stop'd at their going into the *Mall,* and the biggest of the Sisters spoke to him, which I perceiv'd was to bid him be just there when they came back.

When I heard her dismiss the Footman, I step'd up to him, and ask'd him, what little Lady that was? and held a little Chat with him, about what a pretty Child it was with her, and how Genteel and well Carriag'd the Lady, the eldest would be, how Womanish, and how Grave; and the Fool of a Fellow told me presently who she was, that she was Sir *Thomas –'s* eldest Daughter of *Essex,* and that she was a great Fortune, that her Mother was not come to Town yet; but she was with Sir *William -'s* Lady of *Suffolk,* at her Lodgings in *Suffolk-Street,* and a great deal more; that they had a Maid and a Woman to wait on them, besides, Sir *Thomas's* Coach, the Coachman and himself, and that the young Lady was Governess to the whole Family as well here, as at Home too; and in short, told me abundance of things enough for my business.

I was very well dress'd, and had my gold Watch, as well as she; so I left the Footman, and I puts myself in a Rank with this young Lady, having stay'd till she had taken one double Turn in the *Mall,* and was going forward again, by and by, I saluted her by her Name, with the Title of Lady *Betty:* I ask'd her when she heard from her Father? when my Lady her Mother would be in Town and how she did?

I talk'd so familiarly to her of her whole Family that she cou'd not suspect but that I knew them all intimately: I ask'd her why she would come Abroad without Mrs *Chime* with her (that was the Name of her Woman) to take care of Mrs *Judith* that was her Sister. Then I enter'd into a long Chat with her about her Sister, what a fine little Lady she was, and ask'd her if she had learn'd *French,* and a Thousand such little things to entertain her, when on a sudden we see the Guards come, and the Crowd run to see the King go by to the Parliament-House.

The Ladies run all to the Side of the *Mall,* and I help'd my Lady to stand upon the edge of the Boards on the side of the *Mall,* that she might be high enough to see; and took the little one and lifted her quite up; during which, I took care to convey the gold Watch so clean away from the Lady *Betty,* that she never felt it, nor miss'd it, till all the Crowd was gone, and she was gotten into the middle of the *Mall* among the other Ladies.

I took my leave of her in the very Crowd, and said to her, as if in haste, dear Lady *Betty* take care of your little Sister, and so the Crowd did, as it were Thrust me away from her, and that I was oblig'd unwillingly to take my leave.

The hurry in such Cases is immediately over, and the Place clear as soon as the King is gone by; but as there is always a great running and clutter just as the King passes; so having drop'd the two little Ladies, and done my Business with them, without any Miscarriage, I kept hurrying on among the Crowd, as if I run to see the King, and so I got before the Crowd and kept so, till I came to the End of the *Mall,* when the King going on toward the Horse Guards; I went forward to the Passage, which went then thro' against the lower End of the *Hay-Market,* and there I bestow'd a coach upon myself, and made off; and I confess I have not yet been so good as my word (*viz.*) to go and visit my Lady *Betty.*

I was once of the mind to venture staying with Lady *Betty* till she mist the Watch, and so have made a great Out-cry about it with her, and have got her into her Coach, and put my self in the Coach with her, and have gone Home with her; for she appear'd so fond of me, and so perfectly deceiv'd by my so readily talking to her of all her Relations and Family, that I thought it was very easy to push the thing farther, and to have got atleast the Necklace of Pearl; but when I consider'd that tho' the Child would not perhaps have suspected me, other People might, and that if I was search'd I should be discover'd; I thought it was best to go off with what I had got, and be satisfy'd.

I came accidentally afterwards to hear, that when the young Lady miss'd her Watch, she made a great Out-cry in the *Park,* and sent her Footman up and down, to see if he could find me out, she having describ'd me so perfectly that he knew presently that it was the same Person that had stood and talked so long with him, and ask'd him so many Questions about them; but I was gone far enough out of their reach before she could come at her Footman to tell him the Story.

I made another Adventure after this, of a Nature different from all I had been concern'd in yet, and this was at a Gaming-House near *Covent-Garden.*

I saw several People go in and out; and I stood in the Passage a good while with another Woman with me, and seeing a Gentleman go up that seem'd to be of more than ordinary Fashion, I said to him, Sir, pray don't they give Women leave to go up? *yes Madam, says he,* and to play too if they please; I mean so Sir, *said I;* and with that, he said he would introduce me if I had a mind; so I followed him to the Door, and he looking in: there, Madam, *says he,* are the Gamesters, if you have a mind to venture; I look'd in and said to my Comrade, aloud, here's nothing but Men, I won't venture among them; at which one of the Gentlemen cry'd out, you need not be afraid Madam, here's none but fair Gamesters, you are very welcome to come and Set what you please; so I went a little nearer and look'd on, and some of them brought me a Chair, and I sat down and see the Box and Dice go round a pace; then I said to my Comrade, the Gentlemen play too high for us, come let us go.

The People were all very civil, and one Gentleman in particular encourag'd me, and said, come Madam, if you please to Venture, if you dare Trust me I'll answer for it; you shall have nothing put upon you here; no Sir, *said I,* smiling, I hope the Gentlemen wou'd not Cheat a Woman; but still I declin'd venturing, tho' I pull'd out a Purse with Money in it, that they might see I did not want Money.

After I had sat a while, one Gentleman said to me Jeering, come Madam, I see you are afraid to venture for yourself; I always had good luck with the Ladies, you shall Set for me, if you won't Set for yourself; I told him, Sir I should be very lath to lose your Money, tho' I added, I am pretty lucky too; but the Gentlemen play so high, that I dare not indeed venture my own.

Well, well, *says he,* there's ten Guineas Madam, Set them for me; so I took his Money and set, himself looking on; I run out Nine of the Guineas by One and Two at a Time, and then the Box coming to the next Man to me, my Gentleman gave me Ten Guineas more, and made me Set Five of them at once, and the Gentleman who had the Box threw out, so there was Five Guineas of his Money again; he was encourag'd at this, and made me take the Box, which was a bold Venture: However, I held the Box so long that I had gain'd him his whole Money, and had a good handful of Guineas in my Lap; and which was the better Luck, when I threw out, I threw but at One or Two of those that had Set me, and so went off easie.

When I was come this length, I offer'd the Gentleman all the Gold, for it was his own; and so would have had him play for himself, pretending I did not understand the Game well enough: He laugh'd, and said if I had but good Luck, it was no matter whether I understood the Game or no; but I should not leave off: However he took out the 15 Guineas that he had put in at first, and bade me play with the rest: I would have told them to see how much I had got, but he said, no, no, don't tell them, I believe you are very honest, and 'tis bad Luck to tell them, so I play'd on.

I understood the Game well enough, tho' I pretended I did not, and play'd cautiously; it was to keep a good Stock in my Lap, out of which I every now and then convey'd some into my Pocket, but in such a manner, and at such convenient times, as I was sure he cou'd not see it. I play'd a great while, and had a very good Luck for him, but the last time I held the Box, they Set me high, and I threw, boldly at all; I held the Box till I gain'd near Fourscore Guineas, but lost above half of it back at the last throw; so I got up, for I was afraid I should lose it all back again, and said to him, pray come Sir now and take it and play for your self, I think I have done pretty well for you; he would have had me play'd on, but it grew late, and I desir'd to be excus'd. When I gave it up to him, I told him I hop'd he would give me leave to tell it now, that I might see what I had gain'd, and how lucky I had been for him; when I told them, there was Threescore, and Three Guineas. Ay, *says I,* if it had not been for that unlucky Throw I had got you a Hundred Guineas; so I gave him all the Money, but he would not take it till I had put my Hand into it, and taken some for myself, and bid me please myself; I refus'd it, and was positive I would not take it myself, if he had a mind to any thing of that kind it should be all his own doings.

The rest of the Gentlemen seeing us striving, cry'd give it her all; but I absolutely refus'd that; then one of them said, D – n Jack, half it with her, don't you know you should be always upon even Terms with the Ladies; so in short, he divided it with me, and I brought away 30 Guineas, besides about 43, which I had stole privately, which I was sorry for afterwards, because he was so generous.

Thus I brought Home 73 Guineas, and let my old Governess see what good Luck I had at Play: However, it was her Advice that I should not venture again, and I took her Council, for I never went there any more; for I knew as well as she, if the Itch of Play came in, I might soon lose that, and all the rest of what I had got.

Fortune had smil'd upon me to that degree, and had Thriven so much, and my Governess too, for she always had a Share with me, that really the old Gentlewoman began to talk of leaving off while we were well, and being satisfy'd with what we had got; but, I know not what Fate guided me, I was as backward to it now as she was when I propos'd it to her before, and so in an ill Hour we gave over the Thoughts of it for the Present, and in a Word, I grew more hardn'd and audacious than ever, and the Success I had, made my Name as famous as any Thief of my sort ever had been at *Newgate,* and in the *Old-Bayly.*

I had sometimes taken the liberty to Play the same Game over again, which is not according to Practice, which however succeeded not amiss; but generally I took up new Figures, and contriv'd to appear in new Shapes every time I went abroad.

It was now a rambling time of the Year, and the Gentlemen being most of them gone out of Town, *Tunbridge,* and *Epsom,* and such Places were full of People, but the City was Thin, and I thought our Trade felt it a little, as well as others; so that at the latter End of the Year I joyn'd myself with a Gang, who usually go every Year to *Sturbridge* Fair, and from thence to *Bury Fair,* in *Suffolk:* We promis'd our selves great things here, but when I came to see how things were, I was weary of it presently; for except meer Picking of Pockets, there was little worth meddling with; neither if a Booty had been made, was it so easy carrying it off, nor was there such a variety of occasion for Business in our way, as in *London;* all that I made of the whole Joumey, was a gold Watch at *Bury* Fair, and a small parcel of Linnen at *Cambridge,* which gave me an occasion to take leave of the Place: It was an old Bite, and I thought might do with a Country Shop keeper, tho' in *London* it would not.

I bought at a Linnen Draper's shop, not in the Fair, but in the Town of *Cambridge,* as much fine Holland and other things as came to about seven Pound; when I had done, I bade them be sent to such an Inn, where I had purposely taken up my being the same Morning, as if I was to Lodge there that Night.

I order'd the Draper to send them Home to me, about such an Hour to the Inn where I lay, and I would pay him his Money; at the time appointed the Draper sends the Goods, when the

Innkeeper's Maid brought the Messenger to the Door, who was a young Fellow, an Apprentice, almost a Man, she tells him her Mistress was a sleep, but if he would leave the things, and call in about an Hour, I should be awake, and he might have the Money; he left the Parcel, very readily, and goes his way, and in about half an Hour my Maid and I walk'd off, and that very Evening I hired a Horse, and a Man to ride before me, and went to *Newmarket,* and from thence got my Passage in a Coach that was not quite full to St *Edmund's Bury;* Where as I told you I could make but little of my Trade, only at a little Country *Opera* House, made a shift to carry off a gold Watch from a Ladies side, who was not only intollerably Merry, but as I thought a little Fuddled, which made my Work much easier.

I made off with this little Booty to *Ipswich,* and from thence to *Harwich;* where I went into an Inn, as if I had newly arriv'd from *Holland,* not doubting but I should make some Purchase among the Foreigners that came on shore there; but I found them generally empty of things of value, except what was in their Portmanteaus, and *Dutch* Hampers, which were generally guarded by Footmen; however, I fairly got one of their Portmanteaus one Evening out of the Chamber where the Gentleman lay, the Footman being fast a sleep on the Bed, and I suppose very Drunk.

The room in which I lodg'd lay next to the *Dutchman's,* and having dragg'd the heavy thing with much a-do out of the Chamber into mine, I went out into the Street to see if I could find any possibility of carrying it off; I walk'd about a great while but could see no probability either of getting out the thing, or of conveying away the Goods that was in it if I had open'd it, the Town being so small, and I a perfect Stranger in it; so I returned with a resolution to carry it back again, and leave it where I found it: Just in that very Moment I heard a Man make a Noise to some People to make haste, for the Boat was going to put off, and the Tide would be spent; I call'd to the Fellow, What Boat is it Friend, *says I,* that you belong to? the *Ipswich* Wherry, Madam, *says he:* When do you go off, *says I?* this Moment Madam, *says he,* do you want to go thither? yes, *said I,* if you can stay till I fetch my things: Where are your things Madam, *says he?* At such an Inn, *said I:* Well I'll go with you Madam, *says he,* very civilly, and bring them for you; come away then, *says I,* and takes him with me.

The People of the Inn were in great hurry, the Packet-Boat from *Holland,* being just come in, and two Coaches just come also with Passengers from *London,* for another Packet-Boat that was going off for *Holland,* which Coaches were to go back next Day with the Passengers that were just Landed: In this hurry it was not much minded, that I come to the Bar, and paid my Reckoning, telling my Landlady I had gotten my Passage by Sea in a Wherry.

These Wherries are large Vessels, with good Accommodation for carrying Passengers from *Harwich* to *London;* and tho' they are call'd Wherries, which is a word us'd in the *Thames* for a small Boat, Row'd with one or two Men; yet these are Vessels able to carry twenty Passengers, and ten or fifteen Ton of Goods, and fitted to bear the Sea; all this I had found out by enquiring the Night before into the several ways of going to *London.*

My Landlady was very Courteous, took my Money for my Reckoning, but was call'd away, all the House being in a hurry; so I left her, took the Fellow up to my Chamber, gave him the Trunk, or Portmanteau, for it was like a Trunk, and wrapt it about with an old Apron, and he went directly to his Boat about it; as for the drunken *Dutch* Footman he was still a sleep, and his Master with other Foreign Gentlemen at Supper, and very Merry below; so I went clean off with it to *Ipswich,* and going in the Night, the People of the House knew nothing, but that I was gone to *London,* by the *Harwich* Wherry as I had told my Landlady.

I was plagu'd at *Ipswich* with the Custom-House Officers, who stopt my Trunk, *as I call'd it,* and would open, and search it; I was willing I told them, they should search it, but my Husband had the Key, and he was not yet come from *Harwich;* this I said, that if upon searching it, they should find all the things be such as properly belong'd to a Man rather than a Woman, it should not seem strange to them; however, they being possitive to open the Trunk, I consented to have it be broken open, that is to say, to have the Lock taken off, which was not difficult.

They found nothing for their turn, for the Trunk had been search'd before, but they discover'd several things very much to my satisfaction, as particularly a parcel of Money in *French* Pistoles, and some *Dutch* Ducatoons, or *Rix* Dollars, and the rest was chiefly two Perriwigs, wearing Linnen, and Razors, Wash-balls, Perfumes and other useful things, Necessaries for a Gentleman, which all pass'd for my Husband's, and so I was quit of them.

It was now very early in the Morning, and not Light, and I knew not well what Course to take; for I made no doubt but I should be pursued in the Morning, and perhaps be taken with the things about me; so I resolv'd upon taking new Measures; I went publickly to an Inn in the Town with my Trunk, *as I call'd it,* and having taken the Substance out, I did not think the Lumber of it worth my concern; however, I gave it the Landlady of the House with a Charge to take great Care of it, and lay it up safe till I should come again, and away I walk'd into the Street.

When I was got into the Town a great way from the Inn, I met with an antient Woman who had just open'd her Door, and I fell into Chat with her, and ask'd her a great many wild Questions of things all remote to my Purpose and Design, but in my Discourse I found by her how the Town was situated, that I was in a Street which went out towards *Hadly,* but that such a Street went towards the Water-side, such a Street went into the Heart of the Town, and at last such a Street went towards *Colchester,* and so the *London* Road lay there.

I had soon my Ends of this old Woman; for I only wanted to know which was *London* Road, and away I walk'd as fast as I could; not that I intended to go on Foot, either to *London* or to *Colchester,* but I wanted to get quietly away from *Ipswich.*

I walk'd about two or three Mile, and then I met a plain Countryman, who was busy about some Husbandry work I did not know what; and I ask'd him a great many Questions first, not much to the purpose, but at last told him I was going for *London,* and the Coach was full, and I cou'd not get a Passage, and ask'd him if he cou'd not tell me where to hire a Horse that would carry double, and an honest Man to ride before me to *Colchester, so* that I might get a Place there in the Coaches; the honest Clown, look'd earnestly at me, and said nothing for above half a Minute; when scratching his Pole, a Horse say you, and to *Colchester* to carry double; why yes Mistress, alack-a-day, you may have Horses enough for Money; well Friend, *says* I, that I take for granted, I don't expect it without Money: Why but Mistress, *says he,* how much are you willing to give; nay, says I again, Friend, I don't know what your Rates are in the Country here, for I am a Stranger; but if you can get one for me, get it as Cheap as you can, and I'll give you somewhat for your Pains.

Why that's honestly said too, says the Countryman; *not so honest neither,* said I, to myself, *if thou knewest all;* why Mistress, *says he,* I have a Horse that will carry Double, and I don't much care if I go my self with you; *and the like:* Will *you, says* I? well I believe you are an honest Man, if you will, I shall be glad of it, I'll pay you in Reason; why look ye Mistress, *says he,* I won't be out of Reason with you then, if I carry you to *Colechester,* it will be worth five Shillings for myself and my Horse, for I shall hardly come back to Night.

In short, I hir'd the honest Man and his Horse; but when we came to a Town upon the Road, I do not remember the Name of it, but it stands upon a River, I pretended myself very ill, and I could go no farther that Night, but if he would stay there with me, because I was a Stranger I would pay him for himself and his Horse with all my Heart.

This I did because I knew the *Dutch* Gentlemen and their Servants would be, upon the Road that Day, either in the Stage Coaches, or riding Post, and I did not know but the drunken Fellow, or somebody else that might have seen me at *Harwich,* might see me again, and so I thought that in one Days stop they would be all gone by.

We lay all that Night there, and the next Morning it was not very early when I set out, so that it was near Ten a-Clock by that time I got to *Colechester:* It was no little Pleasure that I saw the Town, where I had so many pleasant Days, and I made many Enquiries after the good old Friends I had once had there, but could make little out, they were all dead or remov'd: The young Ladies had been all married or gone to *London;* the old Gentleman, and the old Lady that had been my early Benefactress all dead; and which troubled me most the young Gentleman my first Lover, and afterwards my Brother-in-Law was dead; but two Sons Men grown, were left of him, but they too were Transplanted to *London.*

I dismiss'd my old Man here, and stay'd incognito for three or four Days in *Colechester,* and then took a Passage in a Waggon, because I would not venture being seen in the *Harwich* Coaches; but I needed not have used so much Caution, for there was no Body in *Harwich* but the Woman of the House could have known me; nor was it rational to think that she, considering the hurry she was in, and that she never saw me but once, and that by Candle light, should have ever discover'd me.

I was now return'd to *London,* and tho' by the Accident of the last Adventure, I got something considerable, yet I was not fond of any more Country rambles, nor should I have ventur'd Abroad again if I had carried the Trade on to the End of my Days; I gave my Governess a History of my Travels, she lik'd the *Harwich* Journey well enough, and in Discoursing of these things between ourselves she observ'd, that a Thief being a Creature that Watches the Advantages of other Peoples mistakes, 'tis impossible but that to one that is vigilant and industrious many

Opportunities must happen, and therefore she thought that one so exquisitely keen in the Trade as I was, would scarce fail of something extraordinary where ever I went.

On the other hand, every Branch of my Story, if duly consider'd, may be useful to honest People, and afford a due Caution to People of some sort or other to Guard against the like Surprizes, and to have their Eyes about them when they have to do with Strangers of any kind, for 'tis very seldom that some Snare or other is not in their way. The Moral indeed of all my History is left to be gather'd by the Senses and Judgment of the Reader; I am not Qualified to preach to them, let the Experience of one Creature compleatly Wicked, and completely Miserable be a Storehouse of useful warning to those that read.

I am drawing now towards a new Variety of the Scenes of Life: Upon my return, being hardened by a long Race of Crime, and Success unparalell'd, at least in the reach of my own Knowledge, I had, as I have said, no thoughts of laying down a Trade, which if I was to judge by the Example of others, must however End at last in Misery and Sorrow.

It was on the *Christmas-day* following in the Evening, that to finish a long Train of Wickedness, I went Abroad to see what might offer in my way; when going by a Working Silver-Smiths in *Foster-lane,* I saw a tempting Bait indeed, and not to be resisted by one of my Occupation; for the Shop had no Body in it, as I could see, and a great deal of loose Plate lay in the Window, and at the Seat of the Man, who usually as I suppose Work'd at one side of the Shop.

I went boldly in and was just going to lay my Hand upon a piece of Plate, and might have done it, and carried it clear off, for any care that the Men who belong'd to the Shop had taken of it; but an officious Fellow in a House, not a Shop, on the other side of the Way, seeing me go in, and observing that there was no Body in the Shop, comes running over the Street, and into the Shop, and without asking me what I was, or who, seizes upon me, and cries out for the People of the House.

I had not as I said above, touch'd any thing in the Shop, and seeing a glimpse of some Body running over to the Shop, I had so much presence of Mind, as to knock very hard with my Foot on the Floor of the House, and was just calling out too, when the Fellow laid Hands on me.

However as I had always most Courage when I was in most danger, so when the Fellow laid Hands on me, I stood very high upon it that I came in to buy half a Dozen of silver Spoons, and to my good Fortune, it was a Silversmith's that sold Plate, as well as work'd Plate, for other Shops: The Fellow laugh'd at that Part, and put such a value upon the Service that he had done his Neighbour, that he would have it be that I came not to buy, but to steal; and raising a great Crowd, I said to the Master of the Shop, who by this time was fetch'd Home from some Neighbouring Place, that it was in vain to make Noise, and enter into Talk there of the Case; the Fellow had insisted, that I came to steal, and he must prove it, and I desir'd we might go before a Magistrate without any more Words; for I began to see I should be too hard for the Man that had seiz'd me.

The Master and Mistress of the Shop were really not so violent as the Man from tother side of the Way, and the Man said, Mistress you might come into the Shop with a good Design for ought I know, but it seem'd a dangerous thing for you to come into such a shop as mine is, when you see no Body there, and I cannot do Justice to my Neighbour, who was so kind to me, as not to acknowledge he had reason on his Side; tho' upon the whole I do not find you attempt'd to take any thing, and I really know not what to do in it: I press'd him to go before a Magistrate with me, and if any thing cou'd be prov'd on me that was like a design of Robbery, I should willingly submit, but if not I expected reparation.

Just while we were in this Debate, and a Crowd of People gather'd about the Door, came by Sir *T. B.* an Alderman of the City, and Justice of the Peace, and the Goldsmith hearing of it goes out, and entreated his Worship to come in and decide the Case.

Give the Goldsmith his due, he told his Story with a great deal of Justice and Moderation, and the Fellow that had come over, and seiz'd upon me, told his with as much Heat and foolish Passion, which did me good still, rather than Harm: It came then to my turn to speak, and I told his Worship that I was a Stranger in *London,* being newly come out of the North, that I Lodg'd in such a Place, that I was passing this Street, and went into the Goldsmiths Shop to buy half a Dozen of Spoons; by great good Luck I had an old silver Spoon in my Pocket, which I pull'd out, and told him I had carried that Spoon to match it with half a Dozen of new ones, that it might match some I had in the Country.

That seeing no Body in the Shop, I knock'd with my Foot very hard to make the People hear, and had also call'd aloud with my Voice: Tis true, there was loose Plate in the Shop, but that no Body cou'd say I had touch'd any of it, or gone near it; that a Fellow came running into the Shop out of the Street, and laid Hands on me in a furious manner, in the very Moments while I was calling, for the People of the House; that if he had really had a mind to have done his Neighbour any Service, he should have stood at a distance, and silently watch' d to see whether I had touch'd any thing, or no, and then have clap'd in upon me, and taken me in the Fact: That is very true, *says Mr Alderman,* and turning to the Fellow that stopt me, he ask'd him if it was true that I knock'd with my Foot, he said yes I had knock'd, but that might be because of his coming; Nay, *says the Alderman,* taking him short, now you contradict yourself, for just now you said, she was in the Shop with her back to you, and did not see you till you came upon her; now it was true, that my back was partly to the Street, but yet as my Business was of a kind that requir'd me to have my Eyes every way, so I really had a glance of him running over, as I said before, tho' he did not perceive it.

After a full Hearing, the Alderman gave it as his Opinion, that his Neighbour was under a mistake, and that I was Innocent, and the Goldsmith acquiesc'd in it too, and his Wife, and so I was dismiss'd; but as I was going to depart, Mr *Alderman* said, but *hold Madam,* if you were designing to buy Spoons I hope you will not let my Friend here lose his Customer by the Mistake: I readily answer'd, no Sir, I'll buy the Spoons still if he can Match my odd Spoon, which I brought for a Pattern; and the Goldsmith shew'd me some of the very same Fashion; so he weigh'd the Spoons, and they came to five and thirty Shillings, so I pulls out my Purse to pay him, in which I had near 20 Guineas, for I never went without such a Sum about me, what ever might happen, and I found it of use at other times as well as now.

When Mr *Alderman* saw my Money, *he said,* well Madam, now I am satisfy'd you were wrong'd, and it was for this Reason that I mov'd you should buy the Spoons, and staid till you had bought them, for if you had not had Money to pay for them, I should have suspected that you did not come into the Shop with an intent to buy, for indeed the sort of People who come upon these Designs that you have been Charg'd with, are seldom traubl'd with much Gold in their Pockets, as I see you are.

I smil'd, and told his Worship, that then I ow'd something of his Favour to my Money, but I hop'd he saw reason also in the Justice he had done me before; he said, yes he had, but this had confirm'd his Opinion, and he was fully satisfy'd now of my having been injur'd; so I came off with flying Colours, tho' from an Affair, in which I was at the very brink of Destruction.

It was but three Days after this, that not at all made Cautious by my former Danger as I us'd to be, and still pursuing the Art which I had so long been employ'd in, I ventur'd into a House where I saw the Doors open, and furnish'd myself as I thought verily without being perceiv'd, with two Peices of flower'd Silks, such as they call Brocaded Silk, very rich; it was not a Mercers Shop, nor a Warehouse of a Mercer, but look'd like a private Dwelling-House, and was it seems Inhabited by a Man that sold

Goods for the Weavers to the Mercers, like a Broker or Factor.

That I may make short of this black Part of this Story, I was attack'd by two Wenches that came open Mouth'd at me just as I was going out at the Door, and one of them pull'd me back into the Room, while the other shut the Door upon me; I would have given them good Words, but there was no room for it; two fiery Dragons cou'd not have been more furious than they were; they tore my Cloths, bully'd and roar'd as if they would have murther'd me; the Mistress of the House came next, and then the Master, and all outrageous, for a while especially.

I gave the Master very good Words, told him the Door was open, and things were a Temptation to me, that I was poor, and distress'd, and Poverty was what many could not resist, and beg'd him with Tears to have pity on me; the Mistress of the House was mov'd with Compassion, and enclin'd to have let me go, and had almost perswaded her Husband to it also, but the sawcy Wenches were run even before they were sent, and had fetch'd a Constable, and then the Master said, he could not go back, I must go before a Justice, and answer'd his Wife that he might come into Trouble himself if he should let me go.

The sight of the Constable indeed struck me with terror, and I thought I should have sunk into the Ground; I fell into faintings, and indeed the People themselves thought I would have died, when the Woman argued again for me, and entreated her Husband, seeing they had lost nothing to let me go: I offer'd him to pay for the two Peices whatever the value was, tho' I had not got them, and argued that as he had his Goods, and had really lost nothing, it would be cruel to pursue me to Death, and have my Blood for the bare Attempt of taking them; I put the Constable in mind that I had broke no Doors, nor carried any thing away; and when I came to the justice, and pleaded there that I had neither broken any thing to get In, nor carried any thing out, the Justice was enclin'd to have releas'd me; but the first sawcy Jade that stop'd me, affirming that I was going out with the Goods, but that she stop'd me and pull'd me back as I was upon the Threshold, the Justice upon that point committed me, and I was carried to *Newgate;* that horrid Place! my very Blood chills at the mention of its Name; the Place, where so many of my Comrades had been lock'd up, and from whence they went to the fatal Tree, the Place where my Mother suffered so deeply, where I was brought into the World, and from whence I expected no Redemption, but by an infamous Death: To conclude, the Place that had so long expected me, and which with so much Art and Success I had so long avoided.

I was now fix'd indeed; 'tis impossible to describe the terror of my mind, when I was first brought in, and when I look'd round upon all the horrors of that dismal Place: I look'd on myself as lost, and that I had nothing to think of, but of going out of the World, and that with the utmost Infamy; the hellish Noise, the Roaring, Swearing and Clamour, the Stench and Nastiness, and all the dreadful croud of Afflicting things that I saw there; joyn'd together to make the Place seem an Emblem of Hell itself, and a kind of an Entrance into it.

Now I reproach'd myself with the many hints I had had, *as I have mentioned above,* from my own Reason, from the Sense of my good Circumstances, and of the many Dangers I had escap'd to leave off while I was well, and how I had withstood them all, and hardened my Thoughts against all Fear; it seem'd to me that I was hurried on by an inevitable and unseen Fate to this Day of Misery, and that now I was to Expiate all my Offences at the Gallows, that I was now to give satisfaction to Justice with my Blood, and that I was come to the last Hour of my Life, and of my Wickedness together: These things pour'd themselves in upon my Thoughts in a confus'd manner, and left me overwhelm'd with Melancholly and Despair.

Then I repented heartily of all my Life past, but that Repentance yielded me no Satisfaction, no Peace, no not in the least, because, *as I said to myself,* it was repenting after the

Power of farther Sinning was taken away: I seem'd not to Mourn that I had committed such Crimes, and for the Fact, as it was an Offence against God and my Neighbour; but I mourn'd that I was to be punish'd for it; I was a Penitent as I thought, not that I had sinn'd, but that I was to suffer, and this took away all the Comfort, and even the hope of my Repentance in my own Thoughts.

I got no sleep for several Nights or Days after I came into that wretch'd Place, and glad I wou'd have been for some time to have died there, tho' I did not consider dying as it ought to be consider'd neither; indeed nothing could be fill'd with more horror to my Imagination than the very Place, nothing was more odious to me than the Company that was there: O! if I had but been sent to any Place in the World, and not to *Newgate,* I should have thought myself happy.

In the next Place, how did the harden'd Wretches that were there before me Triumph over me? what! Mrs *Flanders* come to *Newgate* at last? what Mrs *Mary,* Mrs *Molly,* and after that plain *Moll Flanders?* They thought the Devil had help'd me they said, that I had reign'd so long, they expected me there many Years ago, and was I come at last? then they flouted me with my Dejections, welcom'd me to the Place, wish'd me Joy, bid me have a good Heart, not to be cast down, things might not be so bad as I fear'd, and the like; then call'd for Brandy, and drank to me; but put it all up to my Score, for they told me I was but just come to the College, *as they call'd it,* and sure I had Money in my Pocket, tho' they had none.

I ask'd one of this Crew how long she had been there? she said four Months; I ask'd her, how the Place look'd to her when she first came into it? just as it did now to me, *says she,* dreadful and frightful, that she thought she was in Hell, and I believe so still, *adds she, but it is natural to me now, I don't disturb myself about it:* I suppose says I, you are in no danger of what is to follow: Nay, *says she,* for you are mistaken there I assure you, for I am under Sentence, only I pleaded my Belly, but I am no more with Child than the Judge that try'dme, and I expect to be call'd down next Sessions; *this* CALLING DOWN, is calling down *to their former Judgement, when a Woman has been respited for her Belly, but proves not to be with Child, or if she has been with Child, and has been brought to Bed.* Well says I, and are you thus easy? ay, *says she,* I can't help myself, what signifyes being sad? If I am hang'd there's an End of me, *says she,* and away she turns Dancing, and Sings as she goes the following Peice of *Newgate* Wit,

If I swing by the String,
I shall hear the Bell ring. *
And then there's an End of poor *Jenny.*

I mention this, because it would be worth the Observation of any Prisoner, who shall hereafter fall into the same Misfortune and come to that dreadful Place of *Newgate;* how Time, Necessity, and Conversing with the Wretches that are there Familiarizes the Place to them; how at last they become reconcil'd to that which at first Was the greatest Dread upon their Spirits in the World, and are as impudently Chearful and Merry in their Misery, as they were when out of it.

I can not say, as some do, this Devil is not so black, as he is painted; for indeed no Colours can represent the Place to the Life, nor any Soul conceive aright of it, but those who have been Sufferers there: But how Hell should become by degrees so natural, and not only tollerable, but even agreeable, is a thing Unintelligible, but by those who have Experienc'd it, as I have.

The same Night that I was sent to *Newgate,* I sent the News of it to my old Governess, who was surpriz'd at it you may be sure, and spent the Night almost as ill out of *Newgate,* as I did in it.

The next Morning, she came to see me, she did what she cou'd to Comfort me, but she saw that was to no purpose; however, as she said, to sink under the Weight, was but to encrease

* (The Bell at St *Sepulcher's* which Tolls upon Execution Day.)

the Weight, she immediately applied her self to all the proper Methods to prevent the Effects of it, which we fear'd; and first she found out the two fiery Jades that had surpriz'd me; she tamper'd with them, persuad'd them, offer'd them Money, and in a Word, try'd all imaginable ways to prevent a Prosecution; she offer'd one of the Wenches 100 *l.* to go away from her Mistress, and not to appear against me; but she was so resolute, that tho' she was but a Servant-Maid, at 3 *l.* a Year Wages or thereabouts, she refus'd it, and would have refus'd it, as my Governess said she believ'd, if she had offer'd her 500 *l.* Then she attack'd the tother Maid, she was not so hard Hearted in appearance as the other; and sometimes seem'd inclin'd to be merciful; but the first Wench kept her up, and chang'd her Mind, and would not so much as let my Governess talk with her, but threaten'd to have her up for Tampering with the Evidence.

Then she apply'd to the Master, that is to say, the Man whose Goods had been stol'n, and particularly to his Wife, who as I told you was enclin'd at first to have some Compassion for me; she found the Woman the same still, but the Man alleg'd he was bound by the Justice that committed me, to Prosecute, and that he should forfeit his Recognizance.

My Governess offer'd to find Friends that should get his Recognizances off of the File, as they call it, and that he should not suffer; but it was not possible to Convince him, that could be done, or that he could be safe any way in the World, but by appearing against me; so I was to have three Witnesses of Fact against me, the Master and his two Maids; that is to say, I was as certain to be cast for my Life, as I was certain that I was alive, and I had nothing to do, but to think of dying, and prepare for it: I had but a sad foundation to build upon, as I said before, for all my Repentance appear'd to me to be only the Effect of my, fear of Death, not a sincere regret for the wicked Life that I had liv'd, and which had brought this Misery upon me, or for the offending my Creator, who was now suddenly to be my Judge. I liv'd many Days here under the utmost horror of Soul; I had Death as it were in view, and thought of nothing Night and Day, but of Gibbets and Halters, evil Spirits and Devils; it is not to be express'd by Words how I was harrass'd, between the dreadful Apprehensions of Death and the Terror of my Conscience reproaching me with my past horrible Life.

The Ordinary of *Newgate* came to me, and talk'd a little in his way, but all his Divinity run upon Confessing my Crime, as he call'd it, (tho' he knew not what I was in for) making a full Discovery, and the like, without which he told me God would never forgive me; and he said so little to the purpose, that I had no manner of Consolation from him; and then to observe the poor Creature preaching Confession and Repentance to me in the Morning, and find him drunk with Brandy and Spirits by Noon; this had something in it so shocking, that I began to Nauseate the Man more than his Work, and his Work too by degrees for the sake of the Man; so that I desir'd him to trouble me no more. I know not how it was, but by the indefatigable Application of my diligent Governess I had no Bill preferr'd against me the first Sessions, I mean to the Grand Jury, at *GuildHall;* so I had another Month, or five Weeks before me, and without doubt this ought to have been accepted by me, as so much time given me for Reflection upon what was past, and preparation for what was to come, or in a Word, I ought to have esteem'd it, as a space given me for Repentance, and have employ'd it as such, but it was not in me, I was sorry (*as before*) for being in *Newgate,* but had very few Signs of Repentance about me.

On the contrary, like the Waters in the Cavities, and Hollows of Mountains, which petrifies and turns into Stone whatever they are suffer'd to drop upon, so the continual Conversing with such a Crew of Hell-Hounds as I was, which had the same common Operation upon me as upon other People, I degenerated into Stone; I turn'd first Stupid and Senseless, then Brutish and thoughtless, and at last raving Mad as any of them were; and in short, I became as naturally pleas'd and easie with the Place, as if indeed I had been Born there.

It is scarce possible to imagine that our Natures should be capable of so much Degeneracy, as to make that pleasant and agreeable that in it self is the most compleat Misery. Here was a Circumstance, that I think it is scarce possible to mention a worse; I was as exquisitely miserable as speaking of common Cases, it was possible for anyone to be that had Life and Health, and Money to help them as I had.

I had a weight of Guilt upon me enough to sink any Creature who had the least power of Reflection left, and had any Sense upon them of the Happiness of this Life, or the Misery of another; then I had at first remorse indeed, but no Repentance; I had now neither Remorse or Repentance: I had a Crime charg'd on me, the Punishment of which was Death by our Law; the Proof so evident, that there was no room for me so much as to plead not Guilty; I had the Name of old Offender, so that I had nothing to expect but Death in a few Weeks time, neither had I myself any thoughts of Escaping, and yet a certain strange Lethargy of Soul possess'd me; I had no Trouble, no Apprehensions, no Sorrow about me, the first Surprize was gone; I was, I may well say I know not how, my Senses, my Reason, nay, my Conscience were all a sleep; my Course of Life for forty Years had been a horrid Complication of Wickedness, Whoredom, Adultery, Incest, Lying, Theft, and in a Word, every thing but Murther and Treason had been my Practice from the Age of Eighteen, or thereabouts to Threescore; and now I was ingulph'd in the misery of Punishment, and had an infamous Death just at the Door, and yet I had no Sense of my Condition, no Thought of Heaven or Hell at least, that went any farther than a bare flying Touch, like the Stitch or Pain that gives a Hint and goes off; I neither had a Heart to ask God's Mercy, or indeed to think of it, and in this I think I have given a brief Description of the compleatest Misery on Earth.

All my terrifying Thoughts were past, the Horrors of the

Place, were become Familiar, and I felt no more uneasinesses at the Noise and Clamours of the Prison, than they did who made that Noise; in a Word, I was become a meer *Newgate-Bird,* as Wicked and as Outragious as any of them; nay, I scarce retain'd the Habit and Custom of good Breeding and Manners, which all along till now run thro' my Conversation; so thoro' a Degeneracy had possess'd me, that I was no more the same thing that I had been, than if I had never been otherwise than what I was now.

In the middle of this harden'd Part of my Life, I had another sudden Surprize, which call'd me back a little to that thing call'd Sorrow, which indeed I began to be past the Sense of before: They told me one Night, that there was brought into the Prison late the Night before three Highway-Men, who had committed a Robbery somewhere on the Road to *Windsor, Hounslow-Heath,* I think it was, and were pursu'd to *Oxbridge* by the Country, and were taken there after a gallant Resistance, in which I know not how many of the Country People were wounded, and some kill'd.

It is not to be wonder'd that we Prisoners were all desirous enough to see these brave topping Gentlemen that were talk'd up to be such, as their Fellows had not been known, and especially because it was said they would in the Morning be remov'd into the Press-Yard, having given Money to the Head-Master of the Prison, to be allow'd the liberty of that better Part of the Prison: So we that were Women plac'd ourselves in the way that we would be sure to see them; but nothing cou'd express the Amazement and Surprize I was in, when the very first Man that came out I knew to be my *Lancashire* Husband, the same with whom I liv'd so well at *Dunstable,* and the same who I afterwards saw at *Brickill,* when I was married to my last Husband, as has been related.

I was struck Dumb at the Sight, and knew neither what to say, or what to do; he did not know me, and that was all the present Relief I had; I quitted my Company, and retir'd as much as that dreadful Place suffers any Body to retire, and I cry'd vehemently for a great while; dreadful Creature, that I am, *said I,* How many poor People have I made Miserable? How many desperate Wretches have I sent to the Devil; This Gentleman's Misfortunes I plac'd all to my own Account: He had told me at *Chester,* he was ruin'd by that Match, and that his Fortunes were made Desperate on my Account; for that thinking I had been a Fortune he was run into Debt more than he was able to pay, and that he knew not what Course to take; that he would go into the Army, and carry a Musquet, or buy a Horse and take a Tour, as he call'd it; and tho' I never told him that I was a Fortune, and so did not actually Deceive him myself, yet I did encourage the having it thought that I was so, and by that means I was the occasion originally of his Mischief.

The Surprize of this thing only, struck deeper into my Thoughts, and gave me stronger Reflections than all that had befallen me before; I griev'd Day and Night for him, and the more, for that they told me, he was the Captain of the Gang, and that he had committed so many Robberies, that *Hind,* or *Whitney,* or the *Golden Farmer* were Fools to him; that he would surely be hang'd if there were no more Men left in the Country he was born in; and that there would abundance of People come in against him.

I was overwhelm'd with grief for him; my own Case gave me no disturbance compar'd to this, and I loaded my self with Reproaches on his Account; I bewail'd his Misfortunes, and the ruin he was now come to, at such a Rate, that I relish'd nothing now, as I did before, and the first Reflections I made upon the horrid detestable Life I had liv'd, began to return upon me, and as these things return'd my abhorrance of the Place I was in, and of the way of living in it, return'd also; in a word, I was perfectly chang'd, and beco'me another Body.

While I was under these influences of sorrow for him, came Notice to me that the next Sessions approaching, there would be a Bill preferr'd to the Grand Jury against me, and that I should be certainly try'd for my Life at the *Old-Baily:* My Temper was touch'd before the harden'd wretch'd boldness of Spirit, which I had acquir'd in the Prison, abated and conscious Guilt began to flow in upon my Mind: In short, I began to think, and to think is one real Advance from Hell to Heaven; all that Hellish harden'd state and temper of Soul, which I have said so much of before, is but a deprivation of Thought; he that is restor'd to his Power of thinking, is restor'd to himself.

As soon as I began, I say to Think, the first thing that occurr'd to me broke out thus; Lord! what will become of me, I shall certainly die! I shall be cast to be sure, and there is nothing beyond that but Death! I have no Friends, what shall I do? I shall be certainly cast; Lord, have Mercy upon me, what will become of me? This was a sad Thought, you will say, to be the first after so long time that had started into my Soul of that kind, and yet even this was nothing but fright at what was to come; there was not a Word of sincere Repentance in it all: However, I was indeed dreadfully dejected, and disconsolate to the last degree; and as I had no Friend in the World to communicate my distress'd Thoughts to, it lay so heavy upon me, that it threw me into Fits, and Swoonings several times a-Day: I sent for my old Governess, and she, *give her her due,* acted the Part of a true Friend, she left me no Stone unturn'd to prevent the Grand Jury finding the Bill, she went to one or two of the Jury Men, talk'd with them, and endeavour'd to possess them with favourable Dispositions, on Account that nothing was taken away, and no House broken, *etc.* but all would not do, they were over-ruled by the rest, the two Wenches swore home to the Fact, and the Jury found the Bill against me for Robbery and Housebreaking, that is for Felony and Burglary.

I sunk down when they brought me News of it, and after I came to myself again, I thought I should have died with the weight of it: My Governess acted a true Mother to me, she pittied me, she cryed with me, and for me; but she cou'd not help me; and to add to the Terror of it, 'twas the Discourse all over the House, that I should die for it; I cou'd hear them talk it among themselves very often; and see them shake their Heads, and say they were sorry for it, and the like, as is usual in the Place; but still no Body came to tell me their Thoughts, till at last one of the Keepers came to me privately, and said with a Sigh, well Mrs *Flanders,* you will be tried a *Friday,* (this was but a *Wednesday,*) what do you intend to do? I turn'd as white as a Clout, and said, God knows what I shall do, for my part I know not what to do; why, *says he,* I won't flatter you, I would have you prepare for Death, for I doubt you will be Cast, and as they say, you are an old Offender, I doubt you will find but little Mercy; They say, *added he,* your Case is very plain, and that the Witnesses swear so home against you, there will be no standing it.

This was a stab into the very Vitals of one under such a Burthen as I was oppress'd with before, and I cou'd not speak to him a Word good or bad, for a great while, but at last I burst out into Tears, and said to him, Lord! Mr – What must I do? Do, *says he,* send for the Ordinary, send for a Minister, and talk with him, for indeed Mrs *Flanders,* unless you have very good Friends, you are no Woman for this World.

This was plain dealing indeed, but it was very harsh to me, at least I thought it so: He left me in the greatest Confusion imaginable, and all that Night I lay awake; and now I began to say my Prayers, which I had scarce done before since my last Husband's Death, or from a little while after; and truly I may well call it, saying my Prayers; for I was in such a Confusion, and had such horrour upon my Mind, that tho' I cry'd, and repeated several times the Ordinary Expression of, *Lord have Mercy upon me;* I never brought my self to any Sense of my being a miserable Sinner, as indeed I was, and of Confessing my Sins to God, and begging Pardon for the sake of Jesus Christ; I was overwhelm'd with the Sense of my Condition, being try'd for my Life, and being sure to be Condemn'd, and then I was as sure to be Executed, and on this Account, I cry'd out all Night, Lord! what will become of me?

Lord! what shall I do? Lord! I shall be hang'd, Lord have mercy upon me, and the like.

My poor afflicted Governess was now as much concern'd as I, and a great deal more truly Penitent; tho' she had no prospect of being brought to Tryal and Sentence, not but that she deserv'd it as much as I, and so she said herself; but she had not done any thing herself for many Years, other than receiving what I, and others stole, and encouraging us to steal it: But she cry'd and took on like a distracted Body, wringing her Hands, and crying out that she was undone, that she believ'd there was a Curse from Heaven upon her, that she should be damn'd, that she had been the Destruction of all her Friends, that she had brought such a one, and such a one, and such one to the Gallows; and there she reckon'd up ten or eleven People, some of which I have given an Account of that came to untimely Ends, and that now she was the occasion of my Ruin, for she had persuaded me to go on, when I would have left off: I interrupted her there; no Mother, no, *said I,* don't speak of that, for you would have had me left off when I got the Mercer's Money again, and when I came home from *Harwich,* and I would not hearken to you, therefore you have not been to blame, it is I only have ruin'd myself. I have brought myself to this Misery, and thus we spent many Hours together.

Well there was no Remedy, the Prosecution went on, and on the *Thursday* I was carried down to the Sessions-House, where I was arraign'd, as they call'd it, and the next Day I was appointed to be Try'd. At the Arraignment I pleaded not Guilty, and well I might, for I was indicted for Felony and Burglary; that is for feloniously stealing two Pieces of Brocaded Silk, value 46 *l.* the Goods of *Anthony Johnson,* and for breaking open his Doors; whereas I knew very well they could not pretend to prove I had broken up the Doors, or so much as lifted up a Latch.

On the *Friday* I was brought to my Tryal, I had exhausted my Spirits with Crying for two or three Days before, that I slept better the *Thursday* Night than I expected, and had more Courage for my Tryal, than indeed I thought possible for me to have.

When the Tryal began, and the Indictment was read, I would have spoke, but they told me the Witnesses must be heard first, and then I should have time to be heard. The Witnesses were the two Wenches, a Couple of hard Mouth'd Jades indeed, for tho' the thing was Truth in the main, yet they aggravated it to the utmost extremity, and swore I had the Goods wholly in my possession, that I had hid them among my Cloaths, that I was going off with them, that I had one Foot over the Threshold when they discovered themselves, and then I put tother over, so that I was quite out of the House in the Street with the Goods before they took hold of me, and then they seiz'd me, and brought me back again, and they took the Goods upon me: The Fact in general was all true, but I believe, and insisted upon it, that they stop'd me before I had set my Foot clear of the Threshold of the House; but that did not argue much, for certain it was, that I had taken the Goods, and that I was bringing them away, if I had not been taken.

But I pleaded that I had stole nothing, they had lost nothing, that the Door was open, and I went in seeing the Goods lye there, and with Design to buy, if seeing no Body in the House, I had taken any of them up in my Hand, it cou'd not be concluded that I intended to steal them, for that I never carried them farther than the Door to look on them with the better Light.

The Court would not allow that by any means, and make a kind of a Jest of my intending to buy the Goods, that being no Shop for the Selling of any thing, and as to carrying them to the Door to look at them, the Maids made their impudent Mocks upon that, and spent their Wit upon it very much; told the Court I had look'd at them sufficiently, and approv'd them very well, for I had pack'd them up under my Cloaths, and was a going with them.

In short, I was found Guilty of Felony, but acquited of the

Burglary, which was but small Comfort to me, the first bringing me to a Sentence of Death, and the last would have done no more: The next Day, I was carried down to receive the dreadful Sentence, and when they came to ask me what I had to say, why Sentence should not pass, I stood mute a while, but some Body that stood behind me, prompted me aloud to speak to the Judges, for that they cou'd represent things favourably for me: This encourag'd me to speak, and I told them I had nothing to say to stop the Sentence; but that I had much to say, to bespeak the Mercy of the Court, that I hop'd they would allow something in such a Case, for the Circumstances of it, that I had broken no Doors, and carried nothing off, that no Body had lost any thing; that the Person whose Goods they were was pleas'd to say, he desir'd Mercy might be shown, which indeed he very honesdy did, that at the worst it was the first Offence, and that I had never been before any Court of Justice before: And in a Word, I spoke with more Courage than I thought I cou'd have done, and in such a moving Tone, and tho' with Tears, yet not so many Tears as to obstruct my Speech, that I cou'd see it mov'd others to Tears that heard me.

The Judges sat Grave and Mute, gave me an easy Hearing, and time to say all that I would, but saying neither Yes or No to it, Pronounc'd the Sentence of Death upon me, a Sentence that was to me like Death itself, which after it was read confounded me; I had no more Spirit left in me, I had no Tongue to speak, or Eyes to look up either to God or Man.

My poor Governess was utterly Disconsolate, and she that was my Comforter before, wanted Comfort now herself, and sometimes Mourning, sometimes Raging, was as much out of herself (as to all outward Appearance) as any mad Woman in Bedlam. Nor was she only Disconsolate as to me, but she was struck with Horror at the Sense of her own wicked Life, and began to look back upon it with a Taste quite different from mine; for she was Penitent to the highest Degree for her Sins, as well as Sorrowful for the Misfortune: She sent for a Minister too, a serious pious good Man, and apply'd herself with such earnestness by his assistance to the Work of a sincere Repentance, that I believe, and so did the Minister too, that she was a true Penitent, and which is still more, she was not only so for the Occasion, and at that Juncture, but she continu'd so, as I was inform'd to the Day of her Death.

It is rather to be thought of than express'd what was now my Condition; I had nothing before me but present Death; and as I had no Friends to assist me, or to stir for me, I expected nothing but to find my Name in the Dead Warrant, which was to come down for the Execution the *Friday* afterward, of five more and myself.

In the mean time my poor distress'd Governess sent me a Minister, who at her request first, and at my own afterwards came to visit me: He exhorted me seriously to repent of all my Sins, and to dally no longer with my Soul; not flattering myself with hopes of Life, which he said, he was inform'd there was no room to expect, but unfeignedly to look up to God with my whole Soul, and to cry for Pardon in the Name of Jesus Christ. He back'd his Discourses with proper Quotations of Scripture, encouraging the greatest Sinner to Repent, and turn from their Evil way, and when he had done, he kneel'd down and pray'd with me.

It was now that for the first time I felt any real signs of Repentance; I now began to look back upon my past Life with abhorrence, and having a kind of view into the other Side of time, the things of Life, as I believe they do with every Body at such a time, began to look with a different Aspect, and quite another Shape, than they did before; the greatest and best things, die views of felicity, the joy, the griefs of Life were quite other things; and I had nothing in my Thoughts but what was so infinitely Superior to what I had known in Life, that it appear'd to me to be the greatest stupidity in Nature to lay any weight upon any thing tho' the most valuable in this World.

The word Eternity represented itself with all its

incomprehensible Additions, and I had such extended Notions of it, that I know not how to express them: Among the rest, how vile, how gross, how absurd did every pleasant thing look? I mean, that we had counted pleasant before; especially when I reflected that these sordid Trifles were the things for which we forfeited eternal Felicity.

With these Reflections came in, of meer Course, severe Reproaches of my own Mind for my wretched Behaviour in my past Life; that I had forfeited all hope of any Happiness in the Eternity that I was just going to enter into, and on the contrary was entitul'd to all that was miserable, or had been conceiv'd of Misery; and all this with the frightful Addition of its being also Eternal.

I am not capable of reading Lectures of Instruction to any Body, but I relate this in the very manner in which things then appear'd to me, as far as I am able; but infinitely short of the lively impressions which they made on my Soul at that time; indeed those Impressions are not to be explain'd by words, or if they are, I am not Mistress of Words enough to express them; It must be the Work of every sober Reader to make just Reflections on them, as their own Circumstances may direct; and without Question, this is what every one at sometime or other may feel something of; I mean a clearer Sight into things to come, than they had here,. and a dark view of their own Concern in them.

But I go back to my own Case; the Minister press'd me to tell him, as far as I thought convenient, in what State I found myself as to the Sight I had of things beyond Life; he told me he did not come as Ordinary of the Place, whose business it is to extort Confessions from Prisoners, for private Ends, or for the farther detecting of other Offenders; that his business was to move me to such freedom of Discourse as might serve to disburthen my own Mind, and furnish him to administer Comfort to me as far as was in his Power; and assur'd me, that whatever I said to him should remain with him, and be as much a Secret as if it was known only to God and myself; and that he desir'd to know nothing of me, but as above, to qualifie him to apply proper Advice and Assistance to me, and to pray to God for me.

This honest friendly way of treating me unlock'd all the Sluices of my Passions: He broke into my very Soul by it; and I unravell'd all the Wickedness of my Life to him: In a word, I gave him an Abridgement of this whole History; I gave him the Picture of my Conduct for 50 Years in Miniature.

I hid nothing from him, and he in return exhorted me to a sincere Repentance, explain'd to me what he meant by Repentance, and then drew out such a Scheme of infinite Mercy, proclaim'd from Heaven to Sinners of the greatest Magnitude, that he left me nothing to say, that look'd like despair or doubting of being accepted, and in this Condition he left me the first Night.

He visited me again the next Morning, and went on with his Method of explaining the Terms of Divine Mercy, which according to him consisted of nothing more, or more Difficult than that of being sincerely desirous of it, and willing to accept it; only a sincere Regret for, and hatred of those things I had done, which render'd me so just an Object of divine Vengeance: I am not able to repeat the excellent Discourses of this extraordinary Man; 'tis all that I am able to do to say, that he reviv'd *my* Heart, and brought me into such a Condition, that I never knew any thing of in my Life before: I was cover'd with Shame and Tears for things past, and yet had at the same time a secret surprizing Joy at the Prospect of being a true Penitent, and obtaining the Comfort of a Penitent, I mean the hope of being forgiven; and so swift did Thoughts circulate, and so high did the impressions they had made upon me run, that I thought I cou'd freely have gone out that Minute to Execution, without any uneasiness at all, casting *my* Soul entirely into the Arms of infinite Mercy as a Penitent.

The good Gentleman was so mov'd also in my behalf, with a view of the influence, which he saw these things had on me, that he blessed God he had come to visit me, and resolv'd not to leave me till the last Moment, that is not to leave visiting me.

It was no less than 12 Days after our receiving Sentence, before any were order'd for Execution, and then upon a *Wednesday* the Dead Warrant, *as they call it,* came down, and I found my Name was among them; a terrible blow this was to my new Resolutions; indeed my Heart sunk within me, and I swoon'd away twice, one after another, but spoke not a word: The good Minister was sorely Afflicted for me, and did what he could to comfort me with the same Arguments, and the same moving Eloquence that he did before, and left me not that Evening so long as the Prison-keepers would suffer him to stay in the Prison, unless he wou'd be lock'd up with me all Night, which he was not willing to be.

I wonder'd much that I did not see him all the next Day, *it being but the Day before the time appointed for Execution;* and I was greatly discouraged, and dejected in my Mind, and indeed almost sunk for want of that Comfort, which he had so often, and with such Success yeilded me on his former Visits; I waited with great impatience, and under the greatest oppressions of Spirits imaginable; till about four a-Clock he came to my Apartment, for I had obtain'd the Favour by the help of Money, nothing being to be done in that Place without it, not to be kept in the Condemn'd Hole, as they call it, among the rest of the Prisoners, who were to die, but to have a little dirty Chamber to my self.

My heart leap'd within me for Joy, when I heard his Voice at the Door even before I saw him; but let anyone Judge what kind of Motion I found in my Soul, when after having made a short excuse for his not coming, he shew'd me that his time had been employ'd on my Account; that he had obtain'd a favourable Report from the Recorder to the Secretary of State in my particular Case, and in short that he had brought me a Reprieve.

He us'd all the Caution that he was able in letting me know a thing which it would have been a double Cruelty to have conceal'd;

and yet it was too much for me; for as Grief had overset me before, so did Joy overset now, and I fell into a much more dangerous Swooning than I did at first, and it was not without a great Difficulty that I was recover'd at all.

The good Man having made a very Christian Exhortation to me, not to let the Joy of my Reprieve put the Remembrance of my past Sorrow out of my Mind, and having told me that he must leave me to go and enter the Reprieve in the Books, and show it to the Sheriffs, stood up just before his going away, and in a very earnest manner pray'd to God for me that my Repentance might be made Unfeign'd and Sincere; and that my coming back as it were into Life again, might not be a returning to the Follies of Life which I had made such solemn Resolutions to forsake, and to repent of them; I joyn'd heartily in the Petition, and must needs say I had deeper Impressions upon my Mind all that Night, of the Mercy of God in sparing my Life; and a greater Detestation Of my past Sins, from a Sense of the goodness which I had tasted in this Case, than I had in all my Sorrow before.

This may be thought inconsistent in it self, and wide from the Business of this Book; Particularly, I reflect that many of those who may be pleas'd and diverted with the Relation of the wild and wicked part of my Story, may not relish this, which is really the best part of my Life, the most Advantageous to myself, and the most instructive to others; such however will I hope allow me the liberty to make my Story compleat: It would be a severe Satyr on such, to say they do not relish the Repentance as much as they do the Crime; and that, they had rather the History were a compleat Tragedy, as it was very likely to have been.

But I go on with my Relation; the next Morning there was a sad Scene indeed in the Prison; the first thing I was saluted with in the Morning was the Tolling of the great Bell at St *Sepulchres,* as they call it, which usher'd in the Day: As soon as it began to Toll, a dismal groaning and crying was heard from the Condemn'd Hole, where there lay six poor Souls, who were to be Executed that Day, some for one Crime, some for another, and two of them for Murther.

This was follow'd by a confus'd Clamour in the House among the several sorts of Prisoners, expressing their awkward Sorrows for the poor Creatures that were to die, but in a manner extreamly differing one from another; some cried for them; some huzza'd, and wish'd them a good Journey; some damn'd and curst those that had brought them to it, that is meaning the Evidence, or Prosecutors; many pittying them; and some few, but very few praying for them.

There was hardly room for so much Composure of Mind, as was requir'd for me to bless the merciful Providence that had as it were snatch'd me out of the Jaws of this Destruction: I remained as it were Dumb and Silent, overcome with the Sense of it, and not able to express what I had in my Heart; for the Passions on such Occasions as these, are certainly so agitated as not to be able presently to regulate their own Motions.

All the while the poor condemn'd Creatures were preparing to their Death, and the Ordinary *as they call him,* was busy with them, disposing them to submit to their Sentence: I say all this while I was seiz'd with a fit of trembling, as much as I cou'd have been if I had been in the same Condition, as to be sure the Day before I expected to be; I was so violently agitated by this Surprising Fit, that I shook as if it had been in the cold Fit of an Ague; so that I could not speak or look but like one Distracted: As soon as they were all put into the Carts and gone, which however I had not Courage enough to see, *I say,* as soon as they were gone, I fell into a fit of crying involuntarily, and without Design, but as a meer Distemper, and yet so violent, and it held me so long, that I knew not what Course to take, nor could I stop, or put a Checque to it, no not with all the Strength and Courage I had.

This fit of crying held me near two Hours and as I believe held me till they were all out of the World, and then a most humble

Penitent serious kind of Joy succeeded; a real transport it was, or Passion of Joy, and Thankfulness, but [I was] still unable to give vent to it by Words, and in this I continued most part of the Day.

In the Evening the Good Minister visited me again, and then fell to his usual good Discourses; he Congratulated my having a space yet allow'd me for Repentance, whereas the state of those six poor Creatures was determin'd, and they were now pass'd the offers of Salvation; he earnestly press'd me to retain the same Sentiments of the things of Life, that I had when I had a view of Eternity; and at the End of all, told me I should not conclude that all was over, that a Reprieve was not a Pardon, that he could not yet answer for the Effects of it; however, I had this Mercy, that I had more time given me, and that it was my business to improve that time.

This Discoarse, tho' very seasonable, left a kind of sadness on my Heart, as if I might expect the Affair would have a tragical Issue still, which however he had no certainty of, and I did not indeed at that time question him about it, he having said that he would do his utmost to bring it to a good End, and that he hoped he might, but he would not have me secure, and the Consequence prov'd that he had Reason for what he said.

It was about a Fortnight after this, that I had some just Apprehensions that I should be included in the next dead Warrant at the ensuing Sessions; and it was not without great difficulty, and at last an humble Petition for Transportation that I avoided it, so ill was I beholding to Fame, and so prevailing was the fatal Report of being an old Offender, tho' in that they did not do me strict Justice, for I was not in the Sense of the Law an old Offender, whatever I was in the Eye of the Judge; for I had never been before them in a judicial way before, so the Judges could not Charge me with being an old Offender, but the Recorder was pleas'd to represent my Case as he thought fit.

I had now a certainty of Life indeed, but with the hard Conditions of being order'd for Transportation, which indeed was a hard Condition in it self, but not when comparatively considered; and therefore I shall make no Comments upon the Sentence, nor upon the Choice I was put to; we shall all choose any thing rather than Death, especially when 'tis attended with an uncomfortable prospect beyond it, which was my Case.

The good Minister whose interest, tho' *a Stranger to me,* had obtain'd me the Reprieve, mourn'd sincerely for this part; he was in hopes, *he said,* that I should have ended my Days under the Influence of good Instruction, that I might not have forgot my former Distresses, and that I should not have been turned loose again among such a wretched a Crew as they generally are, who are thus sent Abroad where, *as he said,* I must have more than ordinary secret Assistance from the Grace of God, if I did not turn as wicked again as ever.

I have not for a good while mentioned my Governess, who had during most, if not all of this part been dangerously Sick, and being in as near a view of Death by her Disease, as I was by my Sentence, was a very great Penitent; I say, I have not mention'd her, nor indeed did I see her in all this time, but being now recovering, and just able to come Abroad, she came to see me.

I told her my Condition, and what a different flux and reflux of Fears and Hopes I had been agitated with; I told her what I had escap'd, and upon what Terms; and she was present, when the Minister express'd his fears of my relapsing into wickedness upon my falling into the wretch'd Companies that are generally Transported: Indeed I had a melancholly Reflection upon it in my own Mind, *for* I knew what a dreadful Gang was always sent away together, and I said to my Governess that the good Minister's fears were not without Cause: Well, well, *says she,* but I hope you will not be tempted with such a horrid Example as that; and as soon as the Minister was gone, she told me, she would not have me discourag'd, *for* perhaps ways and means might be found out to dispose of me in a particular way, by my self, of which she would talk farther to me afterward.

I look'd earnestly at her, and I thought she look'd more chearful than she usually had done, and I entertain'd immediately a Thousand Notions of being deliver'd, but could not *for* my Life imagine the Methods, or think of one that was in the least feasible; but I was too much concerned in it, to let her go from me without explaining herself, which tho' she was very loth to do, yet my importunity prevail'd, and while I was still pressing, she answer'd me in a few Words, thus, Why, *you have Money, have you not?* did you ever know one in your Life that was Transported and had a Hundred Pound in his Pocket, I'll warrant you [have not] Child, *says she.*

I understood her presently, but told her I would leave all that to her, but I saw no room to hope *for* any thing but a strict Execution of the order, and as it was a severity that was esteem'd a Mercy, there was no doubt but it would be strictly observ'd; she said no more, but this, we *will try what can be done,* and so we parted *for* that Night.

I lay in the Prison near fifteen Weeks after this order *for* Transportation was sign'd; what the Reason of it was, I know not, but at the end of this time I was put on Board of a Ship in the *Thames,* and with me a Gang of Thirteen, as harden'd vile Creatures as ever *Newgate* produc'd in my time; and it would really well take up a History longer than mine to describe the degrees of Impudence, and audacious Villany that those Thirteen were arriv'd to; and the manner of their behaviour in the Voyage; of which I have a very diverting Account by me, which the Captain of the Ship, who carried them over gave me the Minutes of, and which he caus'd his Mate to write down at large.

It may perhaps be thought Trifling to enter here into a Relation of all the little incidents which attended me in this interval of my Circumstances; I mean between the final order *for* my Transportation and the time of my going on board the Ship, and I am too near the End of my Story, to allow room *for* it, but something relating to me, *and my Lancashire Husband,* I must not omit.

He had, *as I have observ'd already* been carried from the Master's side of the ordinary Prison into the Press-Yard, with three of his Comrades, *for* they found another to add to them after some time; here *for* what Reason I knew not, they were kept in Custody without being brought to Tryal almost three Months; it seems they found means to Bribe or buy off some of those who were expected to come in against them, and they wanted Evidence some time to Convict them: After some puzzle on this Account at first, they made a shift to get proof enough against two of them, to carry them off; but the other two, of which my *Lancashire* Husband was one, lay still in Suspence: They had I think one positive Evidence against each of them; but the Law strictly obliging them to have two Witnesses, they cou'd make nothing of it; yet it seems they were resolv'd not to part with the Men neither, not doubting but a farther Evidence would at last come in; and in order to this, I think Publication was made, that such Prisoners being taken, anyone that had been robb'd by them might come to the Prison and see them.

I took this opportunity to satisfy my Curiosity, pretending that I had been robb'd in the *Dunstable* Coach, and that I would go to see the two Highway-Men; but when I came into the Press-Yard, I so disguis'd myself, and muffled my Face up so, that he cou'd see little of me, and consequently knew nothing of who I was; and when I came back, I said publickly that I knew them very well.

Immediately it was Rumour'd all over the Prison that *Moll Flanders* would turn Evidence against one of the Highway Men, and that I was to come off by it from the Sentence of Transportation.

They heard of it, and immediately my Husband desir'd to see this Mrs *Flanders* that knew him so well, and was to be an Evidence against him, and accordingly, I had leave given to go to him. I dress'd myself up as well as the best Cloths that I suffer'd myself ever to appear in there would allow me, and went to the Press-

Yard, but had *for* some time a Hood over my Face; he said little to me at first, but ask'd me if I knew him; I told him, yes, very well; but as I conceal'd my Face, so I Counterfeited my Voice, that he had not the least guess at who I was: He ask'd me where I had seen him; I told him between *Dunstable* and *Brickhill,* but turning to the Keeper that stood by, I ask'd if I might not be admitted to talk with him alone, he said, yes, yes, as much as I pleas'd, and so very civilly withdrew.

As soon as he was gone, and I had shut the Door, I threw off my Hood, and bursting out into Tears, *my Dear,* says *I, do you not know* me? He turn'd pale and stood Speechless, like one Thunder struck, and not able to conquer the Surprize, said no more but this, *let* me *sit down;* and sitting down by a Table, he laid his Elbow upon the Table, and leaning his Head on his Hand, fix'd his Eyes on the Ground as one stupid: I cry'd so vehemently, on the other Hand, that it was a good while e'er I could speak any more; but after I had given some vent to my Passion by Tears, I repeated the same Words: My DEAR, *do you not know me?* at which he answer'd YES, and said no more a good while.

After some time continuing in the Surprize, *as above,* he cast up his Eyes towards me and said, *How could you be so cruel?* I did not readily understand what he meant; and I answer'd, How can you call me Cruel? What have I been Cruel to you in? *To come to me,* says he, *in such a Place as this, is it not to insult me? I have not robb'd you, at least not on* the *Highway?*

I perceiv'd by this that he knew nothing of the miserable Circumstances I was in, and thought that having got some Intelligence of his being there, I had come to upbraid him with his leaving me; but I had too much to say to him to be affronted, and told him in few Words that I was far from coming to Insult him, but at best I came to Condole mutually; that he would be easily satisfy'd that I had no such View, when I should tell him that *my Condition was worse than his, and that many ways:* He look'd a little concern'd at the general Expression of my Condition being worse than his; but with a kind of a smile, look'd a little wildly, and said, How can that be? when you see me Fetter'd, and in *Newgate,* and two of my Companions Executed already; can you say your Condition is worse than Mine?

Come my Dear, *says I,* we have a long piece of Work to do, if I should be to relate, or you to hear my unfortunate History; but if you are dispos'd to hear it, you will soon conclude with me that my Condition is worse than yours: How is that possible, *says he again,* when I expect to be cast for my Life the very next Sessions? Yes *says I,* 'tis very possible when I shall tell you that I have been cast for my Life three Sessions ago, and am under Sentence of Death, is not my Case worse than yours?

Then indeed he stood silent again, like one struck Dumb, and after a little while he starts up; unhappy Couple! *says he,* How can this be possible? I took him by the Hand; come My DEAR, *said I,* sit down, and let us compare our Sorrows: I am a Prisoner in this very House, and in a much worse Circumstance than you, and you will be satisfy'd I do not come to Insult you, when I tell you the particulars; and with this we sat down together, and told him so much of my Story as I thought was convenient, bringing it at last to my being reduc'd to great Poverty, and representing myself as fallen into some Company that led me to relieve my Distresses by a way that I had been utterly unacquainted with, and that they making an attempt at a Tradesman's House I was seiz'd upon, for having been but just at the Door, the Maid-Servant pulling me in; that I neither had broke any Lock, or taken any thing away, and that notwithstanding that I was brought in Guilty, and Sentenc'd to Die; but that the Judges having been made sensible of the Hardship of my Circumstances, had obtain'd leave to remit the Sentence upon my consenting to be transported.

I told him I far'd the worse for being taken in the Prison for one *Moll Flanders,* who was a famous successful Thief, that all of them had heard of, but none of them had ever seen, but that *as he knew well* was none of my Name; but I plac'd all to the account of my ill Fortune, and that under this Name I was dealt with as an old Offender, tho' this was the first thing they had ever known of me. I gave him a long particular of things that had befallen me, since I saw him; but I told him [that] I had seen him since he might think I had, and then gave him an Account how I had seen him at *Brickhill;* how furiously he was pursued, and how by giving an Account that I knew him, and that he was a very honest Gentleman, one Mr – the *Hue and Cry* was stopp'd, and the High Constable went back again.

He listen'd most attentively to all my Story, and smil'd at most of the particulars, being all of them petty Matters, and infinitely below what he had been at the Head of; but when I came to the Story of little *Brickill,* he was surpriz'd; *and was it you my Dear,* says he, *that gave the Check to the Mob that was at our Heels there at Brickill:* Yes *said I,* it was I indeed, and then I told him the particulars which I had observ'd of him there. *Why then,* said he, *it was you that sav'd my Life at that time,* and I am glad I owe my Life to you, for I will pay the Debt to you now, and I'll deliver you from the present Condition you are in, or I will die in the attempt.

I told him by no means; it was a Risque too great, not worth his running the hazard of, and for a Life not worth his saving; 'twas no matter for that he said, it was a Life worth all the World to him; a Life that had given him a new Life; for *says he,* I was never in real Danger of being taken, but that time; till the last Minute when I was taken: Indeed *he told* me his Danger then lay in his believing he had not been pursued that way; for they had gone off from *Hockly* quite another way, and had come over the enclos'd Country into *Brickill,* not by the Road and were sure they had not been seen by any Body.

Here he gave a long History of his Life, which indeed would make a very strange History, and be infinitely diverting. He told me he took to the Road about twelve Year before he marry'd me; that the Woman which call'd him Brother, was not really his

Sister, or any Kin to him; but one that belong'd to their Gang, and who keeping Correspondence with them, liv'd always in Town, having good store of Acquaintance, that she gave them a perfect Intelligence of Persons going out of Town, and that they had made several good Booties by her Correspondence; that she thought she had fix'd a Fortune for him, when she brought me to him, but happen'd to be Disappointed, which he really could not blame her for: That, if it had been his good Luck, that I had had the Estate, which she was inform'd I had, he had resolv'd to leave off the Road, and live a retired sober Life, but never to appear in publick till some general Pardon had been pass'd, or till he could, for Money have got his Name into some particular Pardon, that so he might have been perfectly easy, but that as it had proved otherwise he was oblig'd to put off his Equipage, and take up the old Trade again.

He gave me a long Account of some of his Adventures, and particularly one, when he robb'd the *West Chester* Coaches, near *Lichfield,* when he got a very great Booty; and after that, how he robb'd five Grasiers, in the *West,* going to *Burford* Fair in *Wiltshire* to buy Sheep; he told me he got so much Money on those two Occasions, that if he had known where to have found me, he would certainly have embrac'd my Proposal of going with me to *Virginia,* or to have settled in a Plantation on some other Parts of the English Colonies in *America.*

He told me he wrote two or three Letters to me, directed according to my Order, but heard nothing from me: This I indeed knew to be true, but the Letters coming to my Hand in the time of my latter Husband, I could do nothing in it, and therefore chose to give no answer, that so he might rather believe they had miscarried.

Being thus Disappointed, *he said,* he carried on the old Trade ever since, tho' when he had gotten so much Money, *he said,* he did not run such desperate Risques as he did before, then he gave me some Account of several hard and desperate Encounters which he had with Gentlemen on the Road, who parted too hardly with their Money; and shew'd me some Wounds he had receiv'd, and he had one or two very terrible Wounds indeed, as particularly one by a Pistol Bullet which broke his Arm; and another with a Sword, which ran him quite thro' the Body, but that missing his Vitals he was cur'd again; one of his Comrades having kept with him so faithfully, and so Friendly, as that he assisted him in riding near 80 Miles before his Arm was Set, and then got a Surgeon in a considerable City, remote from that Place where it was done, pretending they were Gentlemen Traveling towards *Carlisle,* and that they had been attack'd on the Road by Highway-Men, and that one of them had shot him into the Arm, and broke the Bone.

This *he said,* his Friend manag'd so well, that they were not suspected at all, but lay still till he was perfectly cur'd: He gave me so many distinct Accounts of his Adventures, that it is with great reluctance, that I decline the relating them; but I consider that this is my own Story, not his.

I then enquir'd into the Circumstances of his present Case at that time, and what it was he expected when he came to be try'd; he told me that they had no Evidence against him, or but very little; for that of three Robberies, which they were all Charg'd with, it was his good Fortune, that he was but in one of them, and that there was but one Witness to be had for that Fact, which was not sufficient; but that it was expected some others would come in against him; that he thought indeed, when he first see me, that I had been one that came of that Errand; but that if no Body came in against him, he hop'd he should be clear'd; that he had had some intimation, that if he would submit to Transport himself, he might be admitted to it without a Tryal, but that he could not think of it with any Temper, and thought he could much easier submit to be Hang'd.

I blam'd him for that, and told him I blam'd him on two Accounts; first because if he was Transported, there might be an Hundred ways for him that was a Gentleman, and a bold enterprizing Man to find his way back again, and perhaps some Ways and Means to come back before he went. He smil'd at that Part, and said he should like the last the best of the two, for he had a kind of Horror upon his Mind at his being sent over to the Plantations as *Romans* sent condemn'd Slaves to Work in the Mines; that he thought the Passage into another State, let it be what it would, much more tolerable at the Gallows, and that this was the general Notion of all the Gentlemen who were driven by the Exigence of their Fortunes to take the Road; that at the Place of Execution there was at least an End of all the Miseries of the present State, and as for what was to follow, a Man was in his Opinion, as likely to Repent sincerely in the last Fortnight of his Life under the Pressures and Agonies of a Jayl, and the condemn'd Hole, as he would ever be in the Woods and Wildernesses of *America;* that Servitude and hard Labour were things Gentlemen could never stoop to, that it was but the way to force them to be their own Executioners afterwards, which was much worse; and that therefore he could not have any Patience when he did but think of being Transported.

I used the utmost of my endeavour to perswade him, and joyn'd that known Womans Rhetorick to it, I mean that of Tears: I told him the Infamy of a publick Execution was certainly a greater pressure upon the Spirits of a Gentleman, than any of the Mortifications that he could meet with Abroad could be; that he had at least in the other a Chance for his Life, whereas here he had none at all; that it was the easiest thing in the World for him to manage the Captain of the Ship, who were generally speaking, Men of good Humour and some Gallantry; and a small matter of Conduct, especially if there was any Money to be had, would make way for him to buy himself off, when he came to *Virginia.*

He look'd wishfully at me, and I thought I guess'd at what he meant, *that is to say,* that he had no Money, but I was mistaken, his meaning was another way; you *hinted just now,* my Dear said he, that there might be a way of coming back before I went, by which I understand you, that it might *be possible to buy it off here; I had rather give 200 l. to prevent going, than 100 l. to be set at Liberty when I came there.* That is my Dear, said *I, because you do not know the Place so well as I do:* that may be, said he, *and yet I believe as well as you know it, you would do the same unless it is because,* as you told me, you *have a Mother there.*

I told him, as to my Mother, it was next to impossible, but that she must be dead many Years before; and as for any other Relations that I might have there, I knew them not now: That since the Misfortunes I had been under, had reduc'd me to the Condition I had been in for some Years, I had not kept up any Correspondence with them, and that he would easily believe, I should find but a cold Reception from them, if I should be put to make my first visit in the Condition of a Transported Felon; that therefore if I went thither, I resolv'd not to see them; But that I had many Views in going there, if it should be my Fate, which took off all the uneasy Part of it; and if he found himself oblig'd to go also, I should easily Instruct him how to manage himself, so as never to go a Servant at all, especially since I found he was not destitute of Money, which was the only Friend in such a Condition.

He smil'd, and said, he did not tell me he had Money; I took him up short, and told him I hop'd he did not understand by my speaking, that I should expect any supply from him if he had Money; that on the other Hand, tho' I had not a great deal, yet I did not want, and while I had any I would rather add to him than weaken him in that Article, seeing what ever he had, I knew in the Case of Transportation he would have Occasion of it all.

He express'd himself in a most tender manner upon that Head: he told me what Money he had was not a great deal, but that he would never hide any of it from me if I wanted it; and that he assur'd me he did not speak with any such Apprehensions; that he was only intent upon what I had hinted to him before he went; that here he knew what to do with himself, but there he should be the most ignorant helpless Wretch alive.

I told him he frighted and terrify'd himself with that which had no Terror in it; that if he had Money, as I was glad to hear he had, he might not only avoid the Servitude suppos'd to be the Consequence of Transportation; but begin the World upon a new Foundation, and that such a one as he cou'd not fail of Success in, with but the common Application usual in such Cases; that he could not but call to Mind, that it was what I had recommended to him many Years before, and had propos'd it for our mutual Subsistence, and restoring our Fortunes in the World; and I would tell him now, that to convince him both of the certainty of it, and of my being fully acquainted with the Method, and also fully satisfy'd in the probability of Success, he should first see me deliver myself from the Necessity of going over at all, and then that I would go with him freely, and of my own Choice, and perhaps carry enough with me to satisfy him that I did not offer it for want of being able to live without Assistance from him; but that I thought our mutual Misfortunes had been such, as were sufficient to Reconcile us both to quitting this part of the World, and living where no Body could upbraid us with what was past, or we be in any dread of a Prison, and without the Agonies of a condemn'd Hole to drive us to it, where we should look back on all our past Disasters with infinite Satisfaction, when we should consider that our Enemies should entirely forget us, and that we should live as new People in a new World, no Body having any thing to say to us, or we to them.

I press'd this Home to him with so many Arguments, and answer'd all his own passionate Objections so effectually, that he embrac'd me, and told me I treated him with such a Sincerity, and Affection as overcame him; that he would take my Advice, and would strive to submit to his Fate, in hope of having the comfort of my Assistance, and of so faithful a Counsellor and such a Companion in his Misery; but still he put me in mind of what I had mention'd before, Namely, that there might be some way to get off before he went, and that it might be possible to avoid going at all, which he said would be much better. I told him he should see, and be fully satisfy'd that I would do my utmost in that Part too, and if it did not succeed, yet that I would make good the rest.

We parted after this long Conference with such Testimonies of Kindness and Affection as I thought were Equal if not Superior to that at our parting at *Dunstable;* and now I saw more plainly than before, the Reason why he declin'd coming at that time any farther with me toward *London* than *Dunstable;* and why when we parted there, he told me it was not convenient for him to come part of the way to *London* to bring me going, as he would otherwise have done: I have observ'd that the Account of his Life, would have made a much more pleasing History, than this of mine; and indeed nothing in it, was more strange than this Part, (*viz.*) that he had carried on that desperate Trade full five and Twenty Year, and had never been taken, the Success he had met with, had been so very uncommon, and such, that sometimes he had liv'd handsomely and retir'd, in one Place for a Year or two at a time, keeping himself and a Man-Servant to wait on him, and has often sat in the Coffee-Houses, and heard the very People who he had robb'd give Accounts of their being robb'd, and of the Places and Circumstances, so that he cou'd easily remember that it was the same.

In this manner it seems he liv'd near *Leverpool* at the time, he unluckily married me for a Fortune: Had I been the Fortune he expected, I verily believe, as he said, that he would have taken up and liv'd honestly all his Days.

He had with the rest of his Misfortunes the good luck not to be actually upon the spot when the Robbery was done which he was committed for; and so none of the Persons robb'd cou'd swear to him, or had any thing to Charge upon him; but it seems as he was taken, with the Gang, one hard-mouth'd Countryman swore home to him; and they were like to have others come in according to the

Publication they had made, so that they expected more Evidence against him, and for that Reason he was kept in hold.

However, the offer which was made to him of admitting him to Transportation was made; as I understand upon the intercession of some great Person who press'd him hard to accept of it before a Tryal; and indeed as he knew there were several that might come in against him, I thought his Friend was in the Right, and I lay at him Night and Day to delay no longer.

At last, with much difficulty he gave his consent, and as he was not therefore admitted to Transportation in Court, and on his Petition as I was, so he found himself under a difficulty to avoid embarking himself as I had said he might have done; his great Friend, who was his Intercessor for the Favour of that Grant, having given Security for him that he should Transport himself, and not return within the Term.

This hardship broke all my Measures, for the steps I took afterwards for my own deliverance, were hereby render'd wholly ineffectual, unless I would abandon him, and leave him to go to *America* by himself; than which he protested he would much rather venture, altho' he were certain to go directly to the Gallows.

I must return to my own Case; the time of my being Transported according to my Sentence was near at Hand; my Governess who continu'd my fast Friend, had try'd to obtain a Pardon, but it could not be done unless with an Expence too heavy for my Purse, considering that to be left naked and empty, unless I had resolv'd to return to my old Trade again, had been worse than my Transportation, because there I knew I could live, here I could not. The good Minister stood very hard on another Account to prevent my being Transported also; but he was answer'd, that indeed my Life had been given me at his first Solicitations, and therefore he ought to ask no more; he was sensibly griev'd at my going, because, *as he said,* he fear'd I should lose the good impressions, which a prospect of Death had at first made on me, and which were since encreas'd by his

Instructions, and the pious Gentleman was exceedingly concern'd about me on that Account.

On the other Hand, I really was not so sollicitous about it as I was before, but I industriously conceal'd my Reasons for it from the Minister, and to the last he did not know, but that I went with the utmost reluctance and affliction.

It was in the Month of February that I was with seven other Convicts, *as they call'd us,* deliver'd to a Merchant that Traded to *Virginia,* on board a Ship, riding, as they call'd it, in *Deptford* Reach: The Officer of the Prison deliver'd us on board, and the Master of the Vessel gave a Discharge for us.

We were for that Night clapt under Hatches, and kept so close, that I thought I should have been suffocated for want of Air, and the next Morning the Ship weigh'd, and fell down the River to a Place they call *Bugby's Hole,* which was done, as they told us by the agreement of the Merchant, that all opportunity of Escape should be taken from us: However when the Ship came thither, and cast Anchor, we were allow'd more Liberty, and particularly were permitted to come upon the Deck, but not upon the Quarter-Deck, that being kept particularly for the Captain, and for Passengers.

When by the Noise of the Men over my Head, and the Motion of the Ship, I perceiv'd that they were under Sail, I was at first greatly surpriz'd, fearing we should go away directly, and that our Friends would not be admitted to see us any more; but I was easy soon after when I found they had come to an Anchor again, and soon after that we had Notice given by some of the Men where we were, that the next Morning we should have the Liberty to come upon Deck, and to have our Friends come and see us if we had any.

All that Night I lay upon the hard Boards of the Deck, as the other Prisoners did, but we had afterwards the Liberty of little Cabins for such of us as had any Bedding to lay in them; and room to stow any Box or Trunk for Cloths, and Linnen, if we had it, (which might well be put in) for some of them had neither Shirt or Shift, or a Rag of Linnen or Woollen, but what was on their Backs, or a Farthing of Money to help themselves; and yet I did not find but they far'd well enough in the Ship, especially the Women, who got Money of the Seamen for washing their Cloths sufficient to purchase any common things that they wanted.

When the next Morning we had the liberty to come upon the Deck, I ask'd one of the Officers of the Ship, whether I might not have the liberty to send a Letter on Shore to let my Friends know where the Ship lay, and to get some necessary things sent to me. This was it seems the Boatswain, a very civil courteous sort of Man, who told me I should have that, or any other liberty that I desir'd, that he could allow me with Safety; I told him I desir'd no other; and he answer'd that the Ships Boat would go up to *London* the next Tide, and he would order my Letter to be carried.

Accordingly when the Boat went off, the Boatswain came to me, and told me the Boat was going off, and that he went in it himself, and ask'd me if my Letter was ready, he would take care of it; I had prepared myself you may be sure, Pen, Ink and Paper beforehand, and I had gotten a Letter ready directed to my Governess, and enclos'd another for my fellow Prisoner, which however I did not let her know was my Husband, not to the last; in that to my Governess, I let her know where the Ship lay, and press'd her earnestly to send me what things I knew she had got ready for me, for my Voyage.

When I gave the Boatswain the Letter, I gave him a Shilling with it, which I told him was for the Charge of a Messenger or Porter, which I entreated him to send with the Letter, as soon as he came on Shore, that if possible I might have an Answer brought back by the same Hand, that I might know what was become of my things, for SIR, *says I,* if the Ship should go away before I have them on Board I am undone.

I took care when I gave him the Shilling to let him see that I had a little better Furniture about me, than the ordinary Prisoners, for he saw that I had a Purse, and in it a pretty deal of Money, and I found that the very sight of it, immediately furnish'd me with very different Treatment from what I should otherwise have met with in the Ship; for tho' he was very Courteous indeed before, in a kind of natural Compassion to me, as a Woman in distress; yet he was more than ordinarily so, afterwards, and procur'd me to be better treated in the Ship, than, *I say,* I might otherwise have been; as shall appear in its Place.

He very honestly had my Letter deliver'd to my Governess own Hands, and brought me back an Answer from her in writing; and when he gave me the Answer, gave me the Shilling again; *there,* says he, there's your Shilling again too, for I deliver'd the Letter my self; I could not tell what to say, I was so surpris'd at the thing; but after some Pause, *I said,* Sir you are too kind, it had been but Reasonable that you had paid yourself Coach hire then.

No, no, *says he,* I am overpaid: What is the Gentlewoman, your Sister?

No, Sir, *says I,* she is no Relation to me, but she is a dear Friend, and all the Friends I have in the World: well, *says he,* there are few such Friends in the World: why she cryes after you like a Child, Ay, *says I again,* she would give a Hundred Pound, I believe, to deliver me from this dreadful Condition I am in.

Would she so? *says he,* for half the Money I believe, I cou'd put you in a way how to deliver yourself, but this he spoke softly that no Body cou'd hear.

Alas! Sir, *said I,* but then that must be such a Deliverance as if I should be taken again, would cost me my Life; Nay, *said he,* if you were once out of the Ship you must look to yourself afterwards, that I can say nothing to; so we drop'd the Discourse for that time.

In the mean time my Governess faithful to the last Moment, convey'd my Letter to the Prison to my Husband, and got an Answer to it, and the next Day came down herself to the Ship, bringing me in the first Place a *Sea-Bed* as they call it, and all its

Furniture, such as was convenient, but not to let the People think it was extraordinary; she brought with her a *Sea-Chest,* that is a Chest such as are made for Seamen with all the Conveniences in it, and fill'd with every thing almost that I could want; and in one of the corners of the Chest, where there was a Private Drawer was my Bank of Money, *that is to say, so* much of it as I had resolv'd to carry with me; for I order'd a part of my Stock to be left behind me, to be sent afterwards in such Goods as I should want when I came to settle; for Money in that Country is not of much use where all things are bought for Tobacco, much more is it a great loss to carry it from Hence.

But my Case was particular; it was by no Means proper to me to go thither without Money or Goods, and for a poor Convict that was to be sold as soon as I came on Shore, to carry with me a Cargo of Goods would be to have Notice taken of it, and perhaps to have them seiz'd by the Publick; so I took part of my Stock with me thus, and left the other part with my Governess.

My Governess brought me a great many other things, but it was not proper for me to look too well provided in the Ship, at least, till I knew what kind of a Captain we should have. When she came into the Ship, I thought she would have died indeed; her Heart sunk at the sight of me, and at the thoughts of parting with me in that Condition, and she cry'd so intolerably, I cou'd not for a long time have any talk with her.

I took that time to read my fellow Prisoners Letter, which however greatly perplex'd me; he told me he was determin'd to go, but found it would be impossible for him to be Discharg'd time enough for going in the same Ship, and which was more than all, he began to question whether they would give him leave to go in what Ship he pleas'd, tho' he did voluntarily Transport himself; but that they would see him put on Board such a Ship as they should direct, and that he would be charg'd upon the Captain as other convict Prisoners were; so that he began to be in dispair of seeing me till he came to *Virginia,* which made him almost desperate; seeing that on the other Hand, if I should not be there, if any Accident of the Sea, or of Mortality should take me away, he should be the most undone Creature there in the World.

This was very perplexing, and I knew not what Course to take; I told my Governess the Story of the Boatswain, and she was mighty eager with me to treat with him; but I had no mind to it, till I heard whether my Husband, or fellow Prisoner, *so she call'd him,* cou'd be at liberty to go with me or no; at last I was forc'd to let her into the whole matter, except only, that of his being my Husband; I told her I had made a positive Bargain or Agreement with him to go, if he could get the liberty of going in the same Ship, and that I found he had Money.

Then I read a long Lecture to her of what I propos'd to do when we came there, how we could Plant, Settle, and in short, grow Rich without any more Adventures, and as a great Secret, I told her that we were to Marry as soon as he came on Board.

She soon agreed chearfully to my going, when she heard this, and she made it her business from that time to get him out of the Prison in time, so that he might go in the same Ship with me, which at last was brought to pass tho' with great difficulty, and not without all the Forms of a Transported Prisoner *Convict,* which he really was not yet, for he had not been try'd, and which was a great Mortification to him. As our Fate was not determin'd, and we were both on Board, actually bound to *Virginia,* in the despicable Quality of Transported Convicts destin'd to be sold for Slaves, I for five Year, and he under Bonds and Security not to return to *England* any more, as long as he liv'd; he was very much dejected and cast down; the Mortification of being brought on Board as he was, like a Prisoner, piqu'd him very much, since it was first told him he should Transport himself, and so that he might go as a Gentleman at liberty; it is true he was not order'd to be sold when he came there, as we were, and for that Reason he was oblig'd to pay for his Passage to the Captain, which we were not; as to the rest, he was as much at a loss as a Child what to do with himself, or with what he had, but by Directions.

Our first business was to compare our Stock: He was very honest to me, and told me his Stock was pretty good when he came into the Prison, but the living there as he did in a Figure like a Gentleman, *and which was ten times as much,* the making of Friends, and soliciting his Case, had been very Expensive; and in a Word, all his Stock that he had left was an Hundred and Eight Pounds, which he had about him all in Gold.

I gave him an Account of my Stock as faithfully, that is to say of what I had taken to carry with me, for I was resolv'd what ever should happen, to keep what I had left with my Governess, in Reserve; that in case I should die, what I had with me was enough to give him, and that which was left in my Governess Hands would be her own, which she had well deserv'd of me indeed.

My Stock which I had with me was two Hundred forty six Pounds, some odd Shillings; so that we had three Hundred and fifty four Pound between us, but a worse gotten Estate was scarce ever put together to begin the World with.

Our greatest Misfortune as to our Stock was that it was all in Money, which every one knows is an unprofitable Cargoe to be carryed to the Plantations; I believe his was really all he had left in the World, as he told me it was; but I who had between seven and eight Hundred Pounds in Bank when this Disaster befel me, and who had one of the faithfulest Friends in the World to manage it for me, considering she was a Woman of no manner of Religious Principles, had still Three Hundred Pounds left in her Hand, which I reserv'd, as above; besides some very valuable things, as particularly two gold Watches, some small Peices of Plate, and some Rings; all stolen Goods; the Plate, Rings and Watches were put up in my Chest with the Money, and with this Fortune, and in the Sixty first Year of my Age, I launch'd out into a new World, as I may call it, in the Condition (as to what appear'd) only of a poor nak'd Convict, order'd to be Transported in respite from the Gallows; my Cloaths were poor and mean, but not ragged or dirty, and none knew in the whole Ship that I had any thing of value about me.

However, as I had a great many very good Cloaths, and Linnen in abundance, which I had order'd to be pack'd up in two great Boxes, I had them Shipp'd on Board, not as my Goods, but as consign'd to my real Name in *Virginia;* and had the Bills of Loading sign'd by a Captain in my Pocket; and in these Boxes was my Plate and Watches, and every thing of value except my Money, which I kept by itself in a private Drawer in my Chest, which cou'd not be found, or open'd if found, without splitting the Chest to pieces.

In this Condition I lay for three Weeks in the Ship, not knowing whether I should have my Husband with me or no; and therefore not resolving how, or in what manner to receive the honest Boatswain's proposal, which indeed he thought a little strange at first.

At the End of this time, behold my Husband came on Board; he look'd with a dejected angry Countenance, his great Heart was swell'd with Rage and Disdain; to be drag'd along with three Keepers of *Newgate,* and put on Board like a Convict, when he had not so much as been brought to a Tryal; he made loud complaints of it by his Friends, for it seems he had some interest; but his Friends got some Checque in their Application, and were told he had had *Favour enough,* and that they had receiv'd such an Account of him since the last Grant of his Transportation, that he ought to think himself very well treated that he was not prosecuted a new. This answer quieted him at once, for he knew too much what might have happen'd, and what he had room to expect; and now he saw the goodness of the Advice to him, which prevail'd with him to accept of the offer of a voluntary Transportation, and after his chagrin at these Hell Hounds, *as he call'd them,* was a little over, he look'd a little compos'd, began to be chearful, and as I was telling him how glad I was to have him once more out of their Hands, took me in his Arms, and acknowledg'd with great Tenderness, that I had given him the best Advice possible, *My Dear,* says he, *Thou hast twice sav'd my Life; from hence forward it shall be all employ'd for you, and I'll always take your Advice.*

The Ship began now to fill, several Passengers came on Board who were embark'd on no Criminal account, and these had Accommodations assign'd them in the great Cabin, and other Parts of the Ship, whereas we *as Convicts* were thrust down below, I know not where; but when my Husband came on Board, I spoke to the Boatswain, who had so early given me Hints of his Friendship in carrying my Letter; I told him he had befriended me in many things, and I had not made any suitable Return to him, and with that I put a Guinea into his Hands; I told him that my Husband was now come on Board, that tho' we were both under the present Misfortunes, yet we had been Persons of a differing Character from the wretched Crew that we came with, and desir'd to know of him, whether the Captain might not be mov'd, to admit us to some Conveniences in the Ship, for which we would make him what Satisfaction he pleas'd, and that we would gratifie him for his Pains in procuring this for us. He took the Guinea as I cou'd see with great Satisfaction, and assur'd me of his Assistance. Then he told us, he did not doubt but that the Captain, who was one of the best humour'd Gentlemen in the World, would be easily brought to Accommodate us, as well as we cou'd desire, and to make me easie, told me he would go up the next Tide on purpose to speak to the Captain about it. The next Morning happening to sleep a little longer than ordinary, when I got up, and began to look Abroad, I saw the Boatswain among the Men in his ordinary Business; I was a little melancholly at seeing him there, and going forwards to speak to him, he saw me, and came towards me, but not giving him time to speak first, I said smiling, *I doubt, Sir, you have forgot us,* for I see you are very busy; he return'd presently, come along with me, and you shall see, so he took me into the great Cabbin, and there sat a good sort of a Gentlemanly Man for a Seaman writing, and with a great many Papers before him.

Here says the Boatswain to him that was a writing, is the Gentlewoman that the Captain spoke to you of, and turning to me, he said, I have been so far from forgetting your Business, that I have been up at the Captain's House, and have represented faithfully to the Captain what you said, relating to your being furnished with better Conveniences for your self, and your Husband; and the Captain has sent this Gentleman, who is Mate of the Ship down with me, on purpose to show you every thing, and to Accommodate you fully to your Content, and bid me assure you that you shall not be treated like what you were at first expected to be, but with the same respect as other Passengers are treated.

The Mate then spoke to me, and not giving me time to thank the Boatswain for his kindness confirm'd what the Boatswain had said, and added that it was the Captain's delight to show himself Kind and Charitable, specially, to those that were under any Misfortunes, and with that he shew'd me several Cabbins built up, some in the Great Cabbin, and some partition'd off, out of the Steerage, but opening into the great Cabbin on purpose for the Accommodation of Passengers, and gave me leave to choose where I would; however I chose a Cabbin, which open'd into the Steerage, in which was very good Conveniences to set our Chest, and Boxes, and a Table to eat on.

The Mate then told me that the Boatswain had given so good a Character of me, and of my Husband, as to our civil Behaviour, that he had orders to tell me, we should eat with him, if we thought fit, during the whole Voyage on the common Terms of Passengers; that we might lay in some fresh Provisions, if we pleas'd; or if not, he should lay in his usual Store, and we should have Share with him: This was very reviving News to me, after so many Hardships, and Afflictions as I had gone thro' of late; I thank'd him, and told him, the Captain should make his own Terms with us, and ask'd him leave to go and tell my Husband of it who was not very well, and was not yet out of his Cabbin: Accordingly I went, and my Husband whose Spirits were still so much sunk with the Indignity (as he understood it) offered him, that he was scarce yet himself, was so reviv'd with the Account I gave him of the Reception we were like to have in the Ship, that he was quite another Man, and new vigour and Courage appear'd in his very Countenance; so true is it, that the greatest of Spirits, when overwhelm'd by their Afflictions, are subject to the greatest Dejections, and are the most apt to Despair and give themselves up.

After some little Pause to recover himself, my Husband come up with me, and gave the Mate thanks for the kindness, which he express'd to us, and sent suitable acknowledgement by him to the Captain, offering to pay him by Advance, what ever he demanded for our Passage, and for the Conveniences he had help'd us to; the Mate told him that the Captain would be on Board in the Aftemoon, and that he would leave all that till he came; accordingly, in the Afternoon the Captain came, and we found him the same courteous obliging Man, that the Boatswain had represented him to be; and he was so well pleas'd with my Husband's Conversation, that in short, he would not let us keep the Cabbin we had chosen, but gave us one, that as I said before, open'd into the great Cabbin.

Nor were his Conditions exorbitant, or the Man craving and eager to make a Prey of us, but for fifteen Guineas we had our whole Passage and Provisions, and Cabbin, eat at the Captain's Table, and were very handsomely Entertain'd.

The Captain lay himself in the other part of the Great Cabbin, having let his round House, *as they call it,* to a rich Planter, who went over with his Wife and three Children, who eat by themselves; he had some other ordinary Passengers, who Quarter'd in the Steerage, and as for our old Fraternity, they were kept under the Hatches while the Ship lay there, and came very little on the Deck.

I could not refrain acquainting my Governess with what had happen'd, it was but just that she, who was so really concern'd for me, should have part in my good Fortune; besides I wanted her Assistance to supply me with several Necessaries, which before I was shy of letting any Body see me have, that it might not be publick; but now I had a Cabbin and room to set things in, I order'd abundance of good things for our Comfort in the Voyage, as Brandy, Sugar, Lemons, *etc.* to make Punch, and Treat our Benefactor, the Captain; and abundance of things for eating and drinking in the Voyage; also a larger Bed, and Bedding proportion'd to it; so that in a Word, we resolv'd to want for nothing in the Voyage.

All this while I had provided nothing for our Assistance when we should come to the Place and begin to call ourselves Planters; and I was far from being ignorant of what was needful on that Occasion; particularly all sorts of Tools for the Planters Work, and for building; and all kinds of Furniture for our Dwelling, which if to be bought in the Country, must necessarily cost double the Price.

So I discours'd that Point with my Governess and she went and waited upon the Captain, and told him, that she hop'd ways might be found out, for her two unfortunate Cousins, *as she call'd us,* to obtain our Freedom when we came into the Country, and so enter'd into a Discourse with him about the Means and Terms also, of which I shall say more in its Place; and after thus sounding the Captain, she let him know, tho' we were unhappy in the Circumstance that occasion'd our going, yet that we were not unfurnish'd to set our selves to Work in the Country; and were resolv'd to settle, and live there as Planters, if we might be put in a way how to do it: The Captain readily offer'd his Assistance, told her the Method of entering upon such Business, and how easy, nay, how certain it was for industrious People to recover their Fortunes in such a manner: Madam, *says he,* 'tis no Reproach to any Man in that Country to have been sent over in worse Circumstances than I perceive your Cousins are in, provided they do but apply with diligence and good Judgment to the Business of that Place when they come there.

She then enquir'd of him what things it was Necessary we should carry over with us, and he like a very honest as well as knowing Man, told her thus: Madam, your Cousins in the first Place must procure some Body to buy them as Servants, in Conformity to the Conditions of their Transportation, and then in the Name of that Person, they may go about what they will; they may either Purchase some Plantations already begun, or they may purchase Land of the Government of the Country, and begin where they please, and both will be done reasonably; she bespoke his Favour in the first Article, which he promis'd to her to take upon himself, and indeed faithfull perform'd it; and as to the rest, he promis'd to recommend us to such as should give us the best Advice, and not to impose upon us, which was as much as could be desir'd.

She then ask'd him if it would not be Necessary to furnish us with a Stock of Tools and Materials for the Business of Planting, and he said, yes, by all means, and then she begg'd his Assistance in it; she told him she would furnish us with every thing that was Convenient whatever it cost her; he accordingly gave her a long particular of things Necessary for a Planter, which by his Account came to about fourscore, or an Hundred Pounds; and in short, she went about as dexterously to buy them, as if she had been an old *Virginia* Merchant; only that she bought by my Direction above twice as much of every thing as he had given her a List of.

These she put on Board in her own Name, took his Bills of Loading for them, and Endorst those Bills of Loading to my Husband, Ensuring the Cargo afterwards in her own Name, by our order; so that we were provided for all Events, and for all Disasters.

I should have told you that my Husband gave her all his whole Stock of 100 *l.* which as I have said, he had about him in Gold, to lay out thus, and I gave her a good Sum besides; so that I did not break into the Stock, which I had left in her Hands at all, but after we had sorted out our whole Cargo, we had yet near 200 *l.* in Money, which was more than enough for our purpose.

In this Condition, very chearful, and indeed joyful at being so happily Accommodated as we were, we set Sail from *Bugby's-Hole* to *Gravesend,* where the Ship lay about ten Days more, and where the Captain came on Board for good and all. Here the Captain offer'd us a civility, which indeed we had no Reason to expect. Namely, to let us go on Shore, and refresh ourselves, upon giving our Words in a solemn manner, that we would not go from him, and that we would return peaceably on Board again: This was such an Evidence of his Confidence in us, that it overcome my Husband, who in a meer Principle of Gratitude, told him as he could not be in any Capacity to make a suitable return for such a Favour; so he could not think of accepting of it, nor could he be easy that the Captain should run such a Risque: After some mutual Civilities, I gave my Husband a Purse, in which was 80 Guineas, and he puts it into the Captain's hand: There Captain, *says he,* there's part of a Pledge for our Fidelity, if we deal dishonestly with you on any Account, 'tis your own, and on this we went on Shore.

Indeed the Captain had assurance enough of our Resolutions to go, for that having made such Provision to Settle there, it did not seem Rational that we would chuse to remain here at the Expence and Peril of Life, for such it must have been, if we had been taken again. In a Word, we went all on Shore with the Captain, and Supp'd together in *Gravesend;* where we were very Merry, staid all Night, lay at the House where we Supp'd, and came all very honestly on Board again with him in the Morning. Here we bought ten dozen Bottles of good Beer, some Wine, some Fowls, and such things as we thought might be acceptable on Board.

My Governess was with us all this while, and went with us Round into the *Downs,* as did also the Captain's Wife with whom she went back; I was never so sorrowful at parting with my own Mother as I was at parting with her, and I never saw her more: We had a fair Easterly Wind sprung up the third Day after we came to the *Downs,* and we sail'd from thence the 10th of *April;* nor did we touch any more at any Place; till being driven on the Coast of *Ireland* by a very hard Gale of Wind, the Ship came to an Anchor in a little *Bay,* near the Mouth of a River, whose Name I remember not, but they said the River came down from *Limerick,* and that it was the largest River in *Ireland.*

Here being detain'd by bad Weather for some time, the Captain who continu'd the same kind good humour'd Man as at first, took us two on Shore with him again: He did it now in kindness to my Husband indeed, who bore the Sea very ill, and was very Sick, especially when it blew so hard: Here we bought in again, store of fresh Provisions, especially Beef, Pork, Mutton and Fowls, and the Captain stay'd to Pickle up five or six Barrels of Beef to lengthen out the Ships Store. We were here not above five Days, when the Weather turning mild, and a fair Wind; we set Sail again and in two and Forty Days came safe to the Coast of *Virginia.*

When we drew near to the Shore, the Captain call'd me to him, and told me that he found by my Discourse, I had some Relations in the Place, and that I had been there before, and so he suppos'd I understood the Custom, in their disposing the convict Prisoners when they arriv'd; I told him I did not, and that as to what Relations I had in the Place, he might be sure I would make my self known to none of them while I was in the Circumstances of a Prisoner, and that as to the rest, we left ourselves entirely to him to Assist us, as he was pleas'd to promise us he wou'd do. He told me I must get some Body in the Place to come and buy us as Servants, and who must answer for us to the Governor of the Country, if he demanded us; I told him we should do as he should direct; so he brought a Planter to treat with him, as it were for the Purchase of these two Servants, my Husband and me, and there we were formally sold to him, and went a Shore with him: The

Captain went with us, and carried us to a certain House whether it was to be call'd a Tavern or not, I know not, but we had a Bowl of Punch there made of Rum, *etc.* and were very Merry. After some time the Planter gave us a Certificate of Discharge, and an Acknowledgement of having serv'd him faithfully, and we were free from him the next Morning, to go whither we would.

For this Peice of Service the Captain demanded of us 6000 weight of Tobacco, which he said he was Accountable for to his Freighter, and which we immediately bought for him, and made him a present of 20 Guineas, besides, with which he was abundantly satisfy'd.

It is not proper to Enter here into the particulars of what Part of the Colony of *Virginia* we Settled in, for divers Reasons; it may suffice to mention that we went into the great River of *Potomack,* the Ship being bound thither; and there we intended to have Settled at first, tho' afterwards we altered our Minds.

The first thing I did of Moment after having gotten all our Goods on Shore, and plac'd them in a Storehouse, or Warehouse, which with a Lodging we hir'd at the small Place or Village where we Landed; I say the first thing was to enquire after my Mother, and after my Brother, (that fatal Person who I married as a Husband, as I have related at large;) a little enquiry furnish'd me with Information that Mrs – , that is my Mother, was Dead; that my Brother (or Husband) was alive, which I confess I was not very glad to hear; but which was worse, I found he was remov'd from the Plantation where he liv'd formerly, and where I liv'd with him, and liv'd with one of his Sons in a Plantation just by the Place where we Landed, and where we had hir'd a Warehouse.

I was a little surpriz'd at first, but as I ventured to satisfy my self that he could not know me, I was not only perfectly easy, but had a great mind to see him, if it was possible to do so without his seeing me; in order to that I found out by enquiry the Plantation where he liv'd, and with a Woman of that Place who I got to help me, like what we call a *Chairwoman,* I rambl'd about towards the Place, as if I had only a mind to see the Country, and look about me; at last I came so near that I saw the Dwelling-house: *I ask'd the Woman* whose Plantation that was, *she said,* it belong'd to such a Man, and looking out a little to our right Hands, there says she, is the Gentleman that owns the Plantation, and his Father with him: What are their Christian Names? said I, I know not, *said she,* what the old Gentlemans Name is, but his Sons Name is *Humphry,* and I believe, *says she,* the Fathers is so too; you may guess, if you can, what a confus'd mixture of Joy and Fright possest my Thoughts upon this Occasion, for I immediately knew that this was no Body else but my own Son, by that Father she shewed me, who was my own Brother: I had no Mask, but I ruffled my Hoods so about my Face, that I depended upon it that after above 20 Years absence, and withal not expecting any thing of me in that part of the World, he would not be able to know any thing of me; but I need not have us'd all that Caution, for the old Gentleman was grown dim Sighted by some Distemper which had fallen upon his Eyes, and could but just see well enough to walk about, and not run against a Tree or into a Ditch. The Woman that was with me had told me that by a meer Accident, knowing nothing of what importance it was to me: As they drew near to us, *I said,* does he know you Mrs *Owen?* so they call'd the Woman, yes, *said she,* if he hears me speak, he will know me; but he can't see well enough to know me, or any Body else; and so she told me the Story of his Sight, as I have related: This made me secure, and so I threw open my Hoods again, and let them pass by me: It was a wretched thing for a Mother thus to see her own Son, a handsome comely young Gentleman in flourishing Circumstances, and durst not make herself known to him; and durst not take any notice of him; let any Mother of Children that reads this consider it, and but think with what anguish of Mind I restrain'd myself; what yearnings of Soul I had in me to embrace him, and weep over him; and how I thought all my Entrails turn'd within me, that my very Bowels mov'd, and I knew not what to do; as I now know not how to express those Agonies: When he went from me I stood gazing and trembling, and, looking after him as long as I could see him; then sitting down on the Grass, just at a Place I had mark'd, I made as in lay down to rest me, but turn'd from her, and lying on my Face wept, and kiss'd the Ground that he had set his Foot on.

I cou'd not conceal my Disorder so much from the Woman, but that she perceiv'd it, and thought I was not well, which I was oblig'd to pretend was true; upon which she press'd me to rise, the Ground being damp and dangerous, which I did accordingly, and walk'd away.

As I was going back again, and still Talking of this Gentleman and his Son, a new Occasion of melancholy offer'd itself *thus:* The Woman began, as if she would tell me a Story to divert me; there goes, *says she,* a very odd Tale among the Neighbours where this Gentleman formerly liv'd: What was that, *said* I? why, says she, that old Gentleman going to *England,* when he was a young Man, fell in Love with a young Lady there, one of the finest Women that ever was seen, and Married her, and brought her over hither to his Mother, who was then living. He liv'd here several Years with her, *continu'd she,* and had several Children by her, of which the young Gentleman that was with him now, was one, but after some time, the old Gentlewoman his Mother talking to her of something relating to herself when she was in *England,* and of her Circumstances in *England,* which were bad enough, the Daughter-in-Law, began to be very much surpriz'd and uneasy; and in short, examining further into things it appear'd past all Contradiction, that she (the old Gentlewoman) was her own Mother, and that consequently that Son was his Wives own Brother, which struck the whole Family with Horror, and put them into such Confusion, that it had almost ruin'd them all; the young Woman would not live with him, the Son, her Brother and Husband, for a time went Distracted, and at last, the young Woman went away for *England,* and has never been heard of since.

It is easy to believe that I was strangely affected with this

Story, but 'tis impossible to describe the Nature of my Disturbance: I seem'd astonish'd at the Story, and ask'd her a Thousand Questions about the particulars, which I found she was thoroughly acquainted with; at last I began to enquire into the Circumstances of the Family, how the old Gentlewoman, I *mean, my Mother* died, and how she left what she had; for my Mother had promis'd me very solemnly, that when she died, she would do something for me, and leave it so, as that, if I was Living, I should one way or other come at it, without its being in the Power of her Son, *my Brother and Husband* to prevent it: She told me she did not know exactly how it was order'd; but she had been told that my Mother had left a Sum of Money, and had tyed her Plantation for the Payment of it, to be made good to the Daughter, if ever she could be heard of, either in *England,* or else where; and that the Trust was left with this Son, who was the Person that we saw with his Father.

This was News too good for me to make light of, and you may be sure fill'd my Heart with a Thousand Thoughts, what Course I should take, how, and when, and in what manner I should make myself known, or whether I should ever make myself known, or no.

Here was a Perplexity that I had not indeed skill to manage myself in, neither knew I what Course to take: It lay heavy upon my mind Night, and Day, I could neither Sleep or Converse, so that my Husband perceiv'd it, and wonder'd what ail'd me, strove to divert me, but it was all to no purpose; he press'd me to tell him what it was troubled me, but I put it off, till at last importuning me continually, I was forc'd to form a Story, which yet had a plain Truth to lay it upon too; I told him I was troubled because I found we must shift our Quarters and alter our Scheme of Settling, for that I found I should be known, in stay'd in that part of the Country, for that my Mother being dead, several of my Relations were come into that Part where we then was, and that I must either discover myself to them, which in our present Circumstances was not proper on many Accounts, or remove;

and which to do I knew not, and that this it was that made me so Melancholly, and so Thoughtful.

He joyn'd with me in this, that it was by no means proper for me to make myself known to any Body in the Circumstances in which we then were; and therefore he told me he would be willing to remove to any other part of the Country, or even to any other Country if I thought fit; but now I had another Difficulty, which was, that if I remov'd to any other Colony, I put myself out of the way of ever making a due Search after those Effects which my Mother had left: Again, I could never so much as think of breaking the Secret of my former Marriage to my new Husband; It was not a Story, as I thought that would bear telling, nor could I tell what might be the Consequences of it; and it was impossible to search into the bottom of the thing without making it Publick all over the Country, as well who I was, as what I now was also.

In this perplexity I continu'd a great while, and this made my Spouse very uneasy; for he found me perplex'd, and yet thought I was not open with him, and did not let him into every part of my Grievance; and he would often say, he wondred what he had done, that I would not Trust him with what ever it was, especially if it was Grievous and Afflicting; the Truth is, he ought to have been trusted with every thing, for no Man in the World could deserve better of a Wife; but this was a thing I knew not how to open to him, and yet having no Body to disclose any part of it to, the Burthen was too heavy for my mind; for let them say what they please of our Sex not being able to keep a Secret, my Life is a plain Conviction to me of the contrary; but be it our Sex, or the Man's Sex, a Secret of Moment should always have a Confident, a bosom Friend, to whom we may Communicate the Joy of it, or the Grief of it, be it which it will, or it will be a double weight upon the Spirits, and perhaps become even insupportable in itself; and this I appeal to all human Testimony for the Truth of.

And this is the Cause why many times Men as well as Women, and Men of the greatest, and best Qualities other ways, yet have found themselves weak in this part, and have not been able to bear the weight of a secret Joy, or of a secret sorrow; but have been oblig'd to disclose it, even for the meer giving vent to themselves, and to unbend the Mind, opprest with the Load and Weights which attended it; nor was this any Token of Folly or Thoughtlessness at all, but a natural Consequence of the thing; and such People had they struggl'd longer with the Oppression, would certainly have told it in their Sleep, and disclos'd the Secret, let it have been of what fatal Nature soever, without regard to the Person to whom it might be expos'd: This Necessity of Nature, is a thing which Works sometimes with such yehemence in the Minds of those who are guilty of any atrocious Villany; such as secret Murther in particular, that they have been oblig'd to Discover it, tho' the Consequence would necessarily be their own Destruction: Now tho' it may be true that the divine Justice ought to have the Glory of all those Discoveries and Confessions, yet 'tis as certain that Providence which ordinarily Works by the Hands of Nature, makes use here of the same natural Causes to produce those extraordinary Effects.

I could give several remarkable Instances of this in my long Conversation with Crime and with Criminals; I knew one Fellow, that while I was a Prisoner in *Newgate,* was one of those they called the *Night-Flyers,* I know not what other Word they may have understood it by since; but he was one, who by Connivance was admitted to go Abroad every Evening, when he play'd his Pranks, and furnish'd those honest People they call Thief-Catchers with business to find out next Day, and restore *for a Reward,* what they had stolen the Evening before: This Fellow was as sure to tell in his sleep all that he had done, and every Step he had taken, what he had stole, and where, as sure as if he had engag'd to tell it waking, and that there was no Harm or Danger in it; and therefore he was oblig'd after he had been out to lock himself up, or be lock'd up by some of the Keepers that had him in Fee, that no Body should hear him; but on the other Hand, if he had told all the Particulars, and given a full account of his Rambles and *Success* to any Comrade, any Brother Thief, or to his Employers, *as I may justly call them,* then all was well with him, and he slept as quietly as other People.

As the publishing this Account of my Life is for the sake of the just Moral of every part of it, and for Instruction, Caution, Warning and Improvement to every Reader, so this will not pass I hope for an unnecessary Digression concerning some People being oblig'd to disclose the greatest Secrets either of their own or other Peoples Affairs.

Under the certain Oppression of this weight upon my Mind, I labour'd in the Case I have been Naming; and the only relief I found for it was to let my Husband into so much of it as I thought would convince him of the Necessity there was for us to think of Settling in some other Part of the World; and the next Consideration before us, was, which part of the *English* settlements we should go to; my Husband was a perfect Stranger to the Country, and had not yet so much as a Geographical knowledge of the Situation of the several Places; and I, that till I wrote this, did not know what the word Geographical signify'd, had only a general Knowledge from long Conversation with People that came from, or went to several Places; but this I knew, that *Maryland, Pensilvania,* East and West *Jersy, New York,* and *New England,* lay all North of *Virginia,* and that they were consequently all colder Climates, to which, for that very Reason, I had an Aversion; for that as I naturally lov'd warm Weather, so now I grew into Years, I had a stronger Inclination to shun a cold Climate; I therefore consider'd of going to *Carolina,* which is the most Southern Colony of the *English,* on the Continent of *America,* and hither I propos'd to go; and the rather, because I might with great ease come from thence at any time, when it might be proper to enquire after my Mothers effects, and to make myself known enough to demand them.

With this Resolution, I propos'd to my Husband our going

away from where we was, and carrying all our Effects with us to *Carolina,* where we resolv'd to Settle, for my Husband readily agreed to the first Part (*viz.*) that it was not at all proper to stay where we was, since I had assur'd him we should be known there, and the rest I effectually conceal'd from him.

But now I found a new Difficulty upon me: The main Affair grew heavy upon my Mind still, and I could not think of going out of the Country without *some how or other* making enquiry into the grand Affair of what my Mother had done for me; nor cou'd I with any patience bear the thought of going away, and not make myself known to my old Husband, (*Brother*) or to my Child, his Son, only I would fain have had this done without my new Husband having any knowledge of it, or they having any knowledge of him, or that I had such a thing as a Husband.

I cast about innumerable ways in my Thoughts how this might be done: I would gladly have sent my Husband away to *Carolina,* with all our Goods, and have come after myself; but this was impracticable, he would never stir without me, being himself perfectly unacquainted with the Country, and with the Methods of settling there, or any where else: Then I thought we would both go first with part of our Goods, and that when we were Settled I should come back to *Virginia* and fetch the remainder; but even then I knew he would never part with me, and be left there to go on alone; the Case was plain; he was bred a Gentleman, and by Consequence was not only unacquainted, but indolent, and when we did Settle, would much rather go out into the Woods with his Gun, which they call there Hunting, and which is the ordinary Work of the *Indians,* and which they do as Servants; I say he would much rather do that, than attend the natural Business of his Plantation.

These were therefore difficulties unsurmountable, and such as I knew not what to do in; I had such strong impressions on my Mind about discovering myself to my *Brother,* formerly my *Husband,* that I could not withstand them; and the rather, because it run constantly in my Thoughts, that if I did not do it while he liv'd, I might in vain endeavour to convince my Son afterward that I was really the same Person, and that I was his Mother, and so might both lose the assistance and comfort of the Relation, and the benefit of whatever it was my Mother had left me; and yet on the other Hand, I cou'd never think it proper to discover myself to them in the Circumstances I was in; as well relating to the having a Husband with me, as to my being brought over by a legal Transportation as a Criminal; on both which Accounts it was absolutely necessary for me to remove from the Place where I was, and come again to him, as from another Place, and in another Figure.

Upon those Considerations; I went on with telling my Husband the absolute necessity there was of our not Settling in *Potomack* River, at least that we should be presently made publick there, whereas if we went to any other Place in the World, we should come in with as much Reputation as any Family that came to Plant: That as it was always agreeable to the Inhabitants to have Families come among them to Plant, who brought Substance with them, either to purchase Plantations, or begin New ones, so we should be sure of a kind agreeable Reception, and that without any possibility of a Discovery of our Circumstances.

I told him in general too, that as I had several Relations in the Place where we was, and that I durst not now let myself be known to them, because they would soon come into a knowledge of the Occasion and Reason of my coming over, which would be to expose myself to the last degree; so I had Reason to believe that my Mother who died here had left me something, and perhaps considerable, which it might be very well worth my while to enquire after; but that this too could not be done without exposing us publickly, unless we went from hence; and then, where ever we Settled, I might come as it were to visit and to see my Brother and Nephews, make myself known to them, claim and enquire after what was my Due, be receiv'd with Respect, and at the same time have justice done me with chearfulness and good will; whereas if I did it now, I could expect nothing but with trouble, such as exacting it by force, receiving it with Curses and Reluctance, and with all kinds of Affronts, which he would not perhaps bear to see; that in Case of being oblig'd to legal Proofs of being really her Daughter, I might be at loss, be oblig'd to have recourse to *England,* and it may be to fail at last, and so lose it, whatever it might be: With these Arguments, and having thus acquainted my Husband with the whole Secret so far as was needful to him, we resolv'd to go and seek a Settlement in some other Colony, and at first Thoughts, *Carolina* was the Place we pitch'd upon.

In' order to this we began to make enquiry for Vessels going to *Carolina,* and in a very little while got information, that on the other side the *Bay, as they call it,* namely, in *Maryland* there was a Ship, which came from *Carolina,* loaden with Rice, and other Goods, and was going back again thither, and from thence to Jamaica, with Provisions: On this News we hir'd a Sloop to take in our Goods, and taking as it were a final farewel of *Potowmack* River, we went with all our Cargo over to *Maryland.*

This was a long and unpleasant Voyage, and my Spouse said it was worse to him than all the Voyage from *England,* because the Weather was but indifferent, the Water rough, and the Vessel small and inconvenient; in the next Place we were full a hundred Miles up *Potowmack* River, in a part which they call *Westmorland* County, and as that River is by far the greatest in *Virginia,* and I have heard say, it is the greatest River in the World that falls into another River, and not directly into the Sea; so we had base Weather in it, and were frequently in great Danger; for tho' they call it but a River, 'tis frequently so broad, that when we were in the middle, we could not see Land on either Side for many Leagues together: Then we had the great River, or Bay of *Chesapeake* to cross, which is where the River *Potowmack* falls into it, near thirty Miles broad, and we entered more great vast Waters, whose

Names I know not, so that our Voyage was full two hundred Mile, in a poor sorry Sloop with all our Treasure, and if any Accident had happened to us, we might at last have been very miserable; supposing we had lost our Goods and saved our Lives only, and had then been left naked and destitute, and in a wild strange Place, not having one Friend or Acquaintance in all that part of the World? The very thoughts of it gives me some horror, even since the Danger is past.

Well, we came to the Place in five Days sailing, I think they call it *Phillips's Point,* and behold when we came thither, the Ship bound to *Carolina,* was loaded and gone away but three Days before. This was a Disappointment, but however, I that was to be discourag'd with nothing, told my Husband that since we could not get Passage to *Carolina,* and that the Country we was in was very fertile and good; we would if he lik'd of it, see if we could find out any thing for our Turn where we was, and that if he lik'd things we would Settle here.

We immediately went on Shore, but found no Conveniences just at that Place, either for our being on Shore, or preserving our Goods on Shore, but was directed by a very honest Quaker, who we found there to go to a Place, about sixty Miles East; that is to say, nearer the Mouth of the *Bay,* where he said he liv'd, and where we should be Accommodated, either to Plant, or to wait for any other Place to Plant in, that might be more Convenient, and he invited us with so much kindness and simple Honesty that we agreed to go, and the Quaker himself went with us.

Here we bought us two Servants, (*viz.*) an *English* Woman-Servant just come on Shore from a Ship of *Leverpool,* and a *Negro* Man-Servant; things absolutely necessary for all People that pretended to Settle in that Country: This honest Quaker was very helpful to us, and when we came to the Place that he propos'd to us, found us out a convenient Storehouse for our Goods, and Lodging for ourselves and our Servants; and about two Months, or thereabout afterwards, by his Direction we took up a large peice of Land from the Governor of that Country, in order to form our Plantation, and so we laid the thoughts of going to *Carolina* wholly aside, having been very well receiv'd here, and Accommodated with a convenient Lodging, till we could prepare things, and have Land enough cur'd, and Timber and Materials provid'd for building us a House, all which we manag'd by the Direction of the Quaker; so that in one Years time, we had near fifty Acres of Land clear'd, part of it enclos'd, and some of it Planted with Tobacco, tho' not much; besides, we had Garden ground, and Corn sufficient to help supply our Servants with Roots, and Herbs, and Bread.

And now I perswaded my Husband to let me go over the *Bay* again, and enquire after my Friends; he was the willinger to consent to it now, because he had business upon his Hands sufficient to employ him, besides his Gun to divert him, which they call Hunting there, and which he gready delighted in; and indeed we us'd to look at one another, sometimes with a great deal of Pleasure, reflecting how much better that was, not than *Newgate* only, but than the most prosperous of our Circumstances in the wicked Trade that we had been both carrying on.

Our Affair was in a very good posture; we purchased of the Proprietors of the Colony, as much Land for 35 Pound, paid in ready Money, as would make a sufficient Plantation to employ between fifty and sixty Servants, and which being well improv'd, would be sufficient to us as long as we could either of us live; and as for Children I was past the prospect of any thing of that kind.

But our good Fortune did not End here; I went, *as I have said,* over the *Bay,* to the Place where my Brother, once a Husband liv'd; but I did not go to the same Village where I was before, but went up another great River, on the East side of the River *Potowmack,* call'd *Rapahannock* River, and by this means came on the back of his Plantation, which was large, and by the help of a Navigable Creek, or little River, that run into the *Rapahannock,* I came very near it.

I was now fully resolv'd to go up *Point-blank,* to my Brother (Husband) and to tell him who I was; but not knowing what Temper I might find him in, or how much out of Temper rather, I might make him by such a rash visit, I resolv'd to write a Letter to him first to let him know who I was, and that I was come not to give him any trouble upon the old Relation, which I hop'd was entirely forgot; but that I apply'd to him as a Sister to a Brother, desiring his Assistance in the Case of that Provision, which our Mother at her decease had left for my Support, and which I did not doubt but he would do me Justice in, especially considering that I was come thus far to look after it.

I said some very tender kind things in the Letter about his Son, which I told him he knew to be my own Child, and that as I was guilty of nothing in Marrying him any more than he was in Marrying me, neither of us having then known our being at all related to one another, so I hop'd he would allow me the most Passionate desire of once seeing my one, and only Child, and of showing something of the Infirmities of a Mother in preserving a violent Affection for him, who had never been able to retain any thought of me one way or other.

I did believe that having receiv'd this Letter he would immediately give it to his Son to Read, I having understood his Eyes being so dim, that he cou'd not see to read it; but it fell out better than so, for as his Sight was dim, so he had allow'd his Son to open all Letters that came to his Hand for him, and the old Gentleman being from Home, or out of the way when my Messenger came, my Letter came directly to my Sons Hand, and he open'd and read it.

He call'd the Messenger in, after some little stay, and ask'd him where the Person was who gave him the Letter, the Messenger told him the Place, which was about seven Miles off, so he bid him stay, and ordering a Horse to be got ready, and two Servants, away he came to me with the Messenger: Let anyone judge the Consternation I was in when my Messenger came back, and told me the old Gentleman was not at Home, but his Son was come along with him, and was just coming up to me: I was perfectly confounded, for I knew not whether it was Peace or War, not cou'd I tell how to behave: However, I had but a very few Moments to think, for my Son was at the Heels of the Messenger, and coming up into my Lodgings, ask'd the Fellow at the Door something, I suppose it was, *for I did not hear it so as to understand it,* which was the Gentlewoman that sent him, for the Messenger said, *there she is* Sir, at which he comes directly up to me, kisses me, took me in his Arms, and embrac'd me with so much Passion, that he could not speak, but I could feel his Breast heave and throb like a Child that Cries, but Sobs, and cannot cry it out.

I can neither express or describe the Joy that touch'd my very Soul when I found, *for it was easy to discover that Part,* that he came not as a Stranger, but as a Son to a Mother, and indeed as a Son, who had never before known what a Mother of his own was; in short, we cryed over one another a considerable while, when at last he broke out first, My Dear Mother, says he, *are you still alive! I never expected to have seen your Face;* as for me, I cou'd say nothing a great while.

After we had both recover'd ourselves a little, and were able to talk, he told me how things stood; as to what I had written to his Father, he told me he had not shewed my Letter to his Father, or told him any thing about it; that what his Grandmother left me, was in his Hands, and that he would do me Justice to my full Satisfaction; that as to his Father, he was old and infirm both in Body and Mind, that he was very Fretful, and Passionate, almost Blind, and capable of nothing; and he question'd whether he would know how to act in an Affair which was of so nice a Nature as this, and that therefore he had come himself, as well to satisfy himself in seeing me, which he could not restrain himself from, as also to put it into my Power, to make a Judgement after I had seen how things were, whether I would discover myself to his Father, or no.

This was really so prudently and wisely manag'd, that I found my Son was a Man of Sense, and needed no Direction from me; I told him, I did not wonder that his Father was, as he had describ'd him, for that his Head was a little touch'd before I went away; and principally his Disturbance was because I could not be perswaded to conceal our Relation and to live with him as my Husband, after I knew that he was my Brother: That as he knew better than I, what his Fathers present Condition was, I should readily joyn with him in such Measures as he would direct: That I was indifferent as to seeing his Father, since I had seen him first, and he cou'd not have told me better News, than to tell me that what his Grandmother had left me, was entrusted in his Hands, who I doubted not now he knew who I was, would *as he said,* do me Justice: I enquir'd then how long my Mother had been dead, and where she died, and told so many particulars of the Family, that I left him no room to doubt the Truth of my being really and truly his Mother.

My Son then enquir'd where I was, and how I had dispos'd myself; I told him I was on the *Maryland* side of the *Bay,* at the Plantation of a particular Friend, who came from *England* in the same Ship with me, that as for that side of the *Bay* where he was, I had no Habitation; he told me I should go Home with him, and live with him, if I pleas'd, as long as I liv'd: That as to his Father he knew no Body, and would never so much as guess at me; I consider'd of that a little and told him, that tho' it was really no little concern to me to live at a distance from him; yet I could not say it would be the most comfortable thing in the World to me to live in the House with him, and to have that unhappy Object always before me, which had been such a blow to my Peace before; that tho' I should be glad to have his Company (my Son) or to be as near him as possible while I stay'd, yet I could not think of being in the House where I should be also under constant Restraint for fear of betraying myself in my Discourse, nor should I be able to refrain some Expressions in my Conversing with him as my Son, that might discover the whole Affair, which would by no means be Convenient.

He acknowleged that I was right in all this, but then DEAR MOTHER, says he, you *shall be as near me as you can;* so he took me with him on Horseback to a Plantation, next to his own, and where I was as well entertain'd as I cou'd have been in his own; having left me there he went away home, telling me we would talk of the main Business the next Day; and having first called me his Aunt, and given a Charge to the People, who it seems were his Tenants, to treat me with all possible Respect; about two Hours after he was gone, he sent me a Maid-Servant, and a *Negro* Boy to wait on me, and Provisions ready dress'd for my Supper; and thus I was as if I had been in a new World, and began secretly now to wish that I had not brought my *Lancashire* Husband from *England* at all.

However, that wish was not hearty neither, for I lov'd my *Lancashire* Husband entirely, as indeed I had ever done from the beginning; and he merited from me as much as it was possible for a Man to do, but that by the way.

The next Morning my Son came to visit me again almost as soon as I was up; after a little Discourse, he first of all pull'd out a Deer skin Bag, and gave it me, with five and fifty *Spanish* Pistoles in it, and told me that was to supply my Expences from *England,* for tho' it was not his Business to enquire, yet he ought to think I did not bring a great deal of Money out with me; it not being usual to bring much Money into that Country: Then he pull'd out his Grandmother's Will, and read it over to me, whereby it appear'd, that she had left a small Plantation, *as he call'd it,* on *York* River, that is, where my Mother liv'd, to me, with the Stock of Servants and Cattle upon it, and given it in Trust to this Son of mine for my Use, when ever he should hear of my being alive, and to my Heirs, in had any Children, and in default of Heirs, to whomsoever I should by Will dispose of it; but gave the Income of it, till I should be heard of, or found, to my said Son; and if I should not be living, then it was to him and his Heirs.

This Plantation, tho' remote from him, he said he did not let out; but manag'd it by a head Clerk, Steward, as he did another that was his Fathers, that lay hard by it, and went over himself three or four times a Year to look after it; I ask'd him what he thought the Plantation might be worth; *he said,* if I would let it out, he would give me about sixty Pounds a Year for it; but if I would live on it, then it would be worth much more, and he believ'd would bring me in about 150 *l.* a Year; but seeing I was likely either to Settle on the other side the *Bay,* or might perhaps have a mind to go back to *England* again, if I would let him be my Steward he would manage it for me, as he had done for himself, and that he believ'd he should be able to send me as much Tobacco to *England* from it, as would yeild me about 100 *l.* a Year, sometimes more.

This was all strange News to me, and things I had not been us'd to; and really my Heart began to look up more seriously, than I think it ever did before, and to look with great Thankfulness to the Hand of Providence, which had done such wonders for me, who had been myself the greatest wonder of Wickedness, perhaps that had been suffered to live in the World; and I must again observe, that not on this Occasion only, but even on all other Occasions of Thankfulness, my past wicked and abominable Life never look'd so Monstruous to me, and I never so compleatly abhorr'd it, and reproach'd myself with it, as when I had a Sense upon me of Providence doing good to me, while I had been making those vile Returns on my part.

But I leave the Reader to improve these Thoughts, as no doubt they will see Cause, and I go on to the Fact; my Sons tender Carriage, and kind Offers fetch'd Tears from me, almost all the while he talk'd with me; indeed I could scarce Discourse with him, but in the intervals of my Passion; however, at length I began, and expressing myself with wonder at my being so happy to have the Trust of what I had left put into the Hands of my own

Child, I told him, that as to the Inheritance of it, I had no Child but him in the World and now was past having any, in should Marry, and therefore would desire him to get a Writing Drawn, which I was ready to execute, by which I would after me give it wholly to him and to his Heirs; and in the mean time smiling, I ask'd him, what made him continue a Batchelor so long; his answer was kind, and ready, that *Virginia* did not yield any great plenty of Wives, and since I talk'd of going back to *England,* I should send him a Wife from *London.*

This was the Substance of our first days Conversation, the pleasantest Day that ever past over my Head in my Life, and which gave me the truest Satisfaction: He came every Day after this, and spent great part of his time with me, and carried me about to several of his Friends Houses, here I was entertain'd with great Respect; also I Dined several times at his own House, when he took care always to see his half dead Father so out of the way, that I never saw him, or he me: I made him one Present, and it was all I had of value, and that was one of the gold Watches, of which I mention'd above, that I had two in my Chest, and this I happen'd to have with me, and I gave it him at his third Visit: I told him, I had nothing of any value to bestow but that, and I desir'd he would now and then kiss it for my sake; *I did not indeed tell him* that I had stole it from a Gentlewomans side, at a Meeting-House in *London,* that's by the way.

He stood a little while Hesitating, as if doubtful whether to take it or no; but I press'd it on him, and made him accept it, and it was not much less worth than his Leatherpouch full of *Spanish* Gold; no, tho' it were to be reckon'd, as if at *London,* whereas it was worth twice as much there, where I gave it him; at length he took it, kiss'd it, told me the Watch should be a Debt upon him, that he would be paying, as long as I liv'd.

A few Days after he brought the Writings of Gift, and the Scrivener with them, and I sign'd them very freely, and deliver'd them to him with a hundr'd Kisses; for sure nothing ever pass'd between a Mother and a tender dutiful Child, with more Affection: The next Day he brings me an Obligation under his Hand and Seal, whereby he engag'd himself to Manage and Improve the Plantation for my account, and with his utmost Skill, and to remit the Produce to my order where-ever I should be, and withal, to be oblig'd himself to make up the Produce a hundred Pound a year to me: When he had done so, he told me, that as I came to demand it before the Crop was off, I had a right to the Produce of the current Year, and so he paid me an hundred Pound in *Spanish* Peices of Eight, and desir'd me to give him a Receipt for it as in full for that Year, ending at *Christmas* following; this being about the latter End of *August.*

I stay'd here above five Weeks, and indeed had much a do to get away then. Nay, he would have come over the *Bay* with me, but I would by no means allow him to it; however, he would send me over in a Sloop of his own, which was built like a Yatch, and serv'd him as well for Pleasure as Business: This I accepted of, and so after the utmost Expressions both of Duty and Affection, he let me come away, and I arriv'd safe in two Days at my Friends the Quakers.

I brought over with me for the use of our Plantation, three Horses with Harness, and Saddles; some Hogs, two Cows, and a thousand other things, the Gift of the kindest and tenderest Child that ever Woman had: I related to my Husband all the particulars of this Voyage, except that I called my Son my Cousin; and first I told him, that I had lost my Watch, which he seem'd to take as a Misfortune; but then I told him how kind my Cousin had been, that my Mother had left me such a Plantation, and that he had preserv'd it for me, in hopes some time or other he should hear from me; then I told him that I had left it to his Management, that he would render me a faithful Account of its Produce; and then I pull'd him out the hundred Pound in Silver, as the first Years produce, and then pulling out the Deer skin Purse with the Pistoles, and here my Dear, *says I,* is the gold Watch. My Husband, *so is*

Heavens goodness sure to work the same Effects, in all sensible Minds, where Mercies touch the Heart, lifted up both his Hands, and with an extasy *of Joy, What is God a doing* says he, *for such an ungrateful Dog as I am!* Then I let him know what I had brought over in the Sloop, besides all this; I mean the Horses, Hogs and Cows, and other Stores for our Plantation; all which added to his surprize, and fill'd his Heart with thankfulness; and from this time forward I believe he was as sincere a Penitent, and as thoroughly a reform'd Man, as ever God's goodness brought back from a Profligate, a Highwayman, and a Robber. I could fill a larger History than this, with the Evidence of this Truth, and but that I doubt that part of the Story will not be equally diverting as the wicked Part, I have had thoughts of making a Volume of it by itself.

As for myself, as this is to be my own Story, not my Husbands, I return to that Part which relates to myself; we went on with our Plantation, and manag'd it with the help and Direction of such Friends as we got there by our obliging Behaviour, and especially the honest Quaker, who prov'd a faithful generous and steady Friend to us; and we had very good Success; for having a flourishing Stock to begin with, as *I have said;* and this being now encreas'd, by the Addition of a Hundred and fifty Pound *Sterling* in Money, we enlarg'd our Number of Servants, built us a very good House, and cur'd every Year a great deal of Land. The second Year I wrote to my old Governess, giving her part with us of the Joy of our Success, and order'd her how to layout the Money l had left with her, which was 250 *l.* as above, and to send it to us in Goods, which she perform'd, with her usual Kindness and Fidelity, and all this arriv'd safe to us.

Here we had a supply of all sorts of Cloaths, as well for my Husband as for myself; and I took especial care to buy for him all those things that I knew he delighted to have; as two good long Wigs, two silver hilted Swords, three or four fine Fowling peices, a fine Saddle with Holsters and Pistoles very handsome, with a

Scarlet Cloak; and in a Word, every thing I could think: of to oblige him; and to make him appear, as he really was, a very fine Gentleman: I order'd a good Quantity of such Household-Stuff, as we yet wanted, with Linnen of all sorts for us both; as for my self, I wanted very little of Cloths or Linnen, being very well furnished before: The rest of my Cargo consisted in Iron-Work of all sorts, Harness for Horses, Tools, Cloaths for Servants, and Woollen-Cloth, stuffs, Serges, Stockings, Shoes, Hats and the like, such as Servants wear, and whole Peices also, to make up for Servants, all by direction of the Quaker; and all this Cargo arriv'd safe, and in good Condition, with three Women Servants, lusty Wenches, which my old Governess had pick'd up for me, suitable enough to the Place, and to the Work we had for them to do; one of which happen'd to come double, having been got with Child by one of the Seamen in the Ship, as she own'd afterwards, before the Ship got so far as *Gravesend;* so she brought us a stout Boy, about 7 Months after her Landing.

My Husband you may suppose was a little surpriz'd at the arriving of all this Cargo from *England,* and talking with me after he saw the Account of the particular; my Dear, *says he,* what is the meaning of all this? I fear you will run us too deep in Debt: When shall we be able to make Return for it all? I smil'd, and told him that it was all paid for; and then I told him, that not knowing what might befal us in the Voyage, and considering what our Circumstances might expose us to; I had not taken my whole Stock with me, that I had reserv'd so much in my Friends Hands, which now we were come over safe, and was Settled in a way to live, I had sent for as he might see.

He was amaz'd, and stood a while telling upon his Fingers, but said nothing, at last he began thus: Hold, lets see, *says he, telling upon his Fingers still;* and first on his Thumb, there's *246 l.* in Money at first, then two gold Watches, Diamond Rings, and Plate, *says he,* upon the fore Finger, then upon the next Finger, here's a Plantation on *York* River, a 100 *l.* a Year, then in Money;

then a Sloop load of Horses, Cows, Hogs and Stores, and so on to the Thumb again; and now, *says he,* a Cargo cost 250 *l.* in *England,* and worth here twice the Money; well, *says I,* What do you make of all that? make of it, *says he,* why who says I was deceiv'd, when I married a Wife in *Lancashire?* I think I have married a Fortune, and a very good Fortune too, *says he.*

In a Word, we were now in very considerable Circumstances, and every Year encreasing, for our new Plantation grew upon our Hands insensibly, and in eight Year which we lived upon it, we brought it to such a pitch, that the Produce was, at least, 300 *l.* Sterling a Year; I mean, worth so much in *England.*

After I had been a Year at Home again, I went over the Bay to see my Son, and to receive another Year's Income of my Plantation; and I was surpriz'd to hear, just at my Landing there, that my old Husband was dead, and had not been bury'd above a Fortnight. This, I confess, was not disagreeable News, because now I could appear as I was in a marry'd Condition; so I told my Son before I came from him, that I believed I should marry a Gentleman who had a Plantation near mine; and tho' I was legally free to marry, as to any Obligation that was on me before, yet that I was shye of it, lest the Blot should some time or other be reviv'd, and it might make a Husband uneasy; my Son the same kind dutiful and obliging Creature as ever, treated me now at his own House, paid me my hundred Pound, and sent me Home again loaded with Presents.

Some time after this, I let my Son know I was marry'd, and invited him over to see us; and my Husband wrote a very obliging Letter to him also, inviting him to come and see him; and he came accordingly some Months after, and happen'd to be there just when my Cargo from *England* came in, which I let him believe belong'd all to my Husband's Estate, not to me.

It must be observ'd, that when the old Wretch, my Brother (Husband) was dead, I then freely gave my Husband an Account of all that Affair, and of this Cousin, as I had call'd him before, being my own Son by that mistaken unhappy Match: He was perfectly easy in the Account, and told me he should have been as easy if the old Man, as we call'd him, had been alive; for, *said he,* it was no Fault of yours, nor of his; it was a Mistake impossible to be prevented; he only reproach'd him with desiring me to conceal it, and to live with him as a Wife, after I knew that he was my Brother, that, he said, was a vile part: Thus all these little Difficulties were made easy, and we liv'd together with the greatest Kindness and Comfort imaginable; we are now grown Old: I am come back to *England,* being almost seventy Years of Age, my Husband sixty eight, having perform'd much more than the limited Terms of my Transportation: And now notwithstanding all the Fatigues, and all the Miseries we have both gone thro', we are both in good Heart and Health; my Husband remain'd there sometime after me to settle our Affairs, and at first I had intended to go back to him, but at his desire I alter'd that Resolution, and he is come over to *England* also, where we resolve to spend the Remainder of our Years in sincere Penitence, for the wicked Lives we have lived.

Written in the Year 1683

THE END

ROBINSON CRUSOE

I WAS born in the year 1632, in the city of York, of a good family, though not of that country, my father being a foreigner of Bremen, who settled first at Hull. He got a good estate by merchandise, and leaving off his trade lived afterward at York, from whence he had married my mother, whose relations were named Robinson, a very good family in that country, and from whom I was called Robinson Kreutznaer; but by the usual corruption of words in England we are now called, nay, we call ourselves, and write our name, Crusoe, and so my companions always called me.

I had two elder brothers, one of which was lieutenant colonel to an English regiment of foot in Flanders, formerly commanded by the famous Colonel Lockhart, and was killed at the battle near Dunkirk against the Spaniards; what became of my second brother I never knew, any more than my father and mother did know what was become of me.

Being the third son of the family, and not bred to any trade, my head began to be filled very early with rambling thoughts. My father, who was very ancient, had given me a competent share of learning, as far as house-education and a country free school generally goes, and designed me for the law; but I would be satisfied with nothing but going to sea; and my inclination to this led me so strongly against the will, nay, the commands, of my father, and against all the entreaties and persuasions of my mother and other friends, that there seemed to be something fatal in that propension of nature tending directly to the life of misery which was to befall me.

My father, a wise and grave man, gave me serious and excellent counsel against what he foresaw was my design. He called me one morning into his chamber, where he was confined by the gout, and expostulated very warmly with me upon this subject. He asked me what reasons more than a mere wandering inclination I had for leaving my father's house and my native country, where I might be well introduced, and had a prospect of raising my fortunes by application and industry, with a life of ease and pleasure. He told me it was for men of desperate fortunes on one hand, or of aspiring, superior fortunes on the other, who went abroad upon adventures, to rise by enterprise, and make themselves famous in undertakings of a nature out of the common road; that these things were all either too far above me, or too far below me; that mine was the middle state, or what might be called the upper station of low life, which he had found by long experience was the best state in the world, the most suited to human happiness, not exposed to the miseries and hardships, the labour and sufferings, of the mechanic part of mankind, and not embarrassed with the pride, luxury, ambition, and envy of the upper part of mankind. He told me I might judge of the happiness of this state by this one thing, viz., that this was the state of life which all other people envied; that kings have frequently lamented the miserable consequences of being born to great things, and wished they had been placed in the middle of the two extremes, between the mean and the great; that the wise man gave his testimony to this as the just standard of true felicity, when he prayed to have neither poverty nor riches.

He bid me observe it, and I should always find that the calamities of life were shared among the upper and lower part of mankind, but that the middle station had the fewest disasters, and was not exposed to so many vicissitudes as the higher or lower part of mankind. Nay, they were not subjected to so many distempers and uneasiness either of body or mind as those were who, by vicious living, luxury, and extravagances on one hand, or by hard labour, want of necessaries, and mean or insufficient diet on the other hand, bring distempers upon themselves by the natural consequences of their way of living; that the middle station of life was calculated for all kind of virtues and all kind of enjoyments; that peace and plenty were the handmaids of a middle fortune; that temperance, moderation, quietness, health, society, all agreeable diversions, and all desirable pleasures, were the blessings attending the middle station of life; that this way men went silently and smoothly through the world, and comfortably out of it, not embarrassed with the labours of the hands or of the head, not sold to the life of slavery for daily bread, or harassed with perplexed circumstances, which rob the soul of peace, and the body of rest; not enraged with the passion of envy, or secret burning lust of ambition for great things; but in easy circumstances sliding gently through the world, and sensibly tasting the sweets of living, without the bitter, feeling that they are happy, and learning by every day's experience to know it more sensibly.

After this, he pressed me earnestly, and in the most affectionate manner, not to play the young man, not to precipitate myself into miseries which Nature and the station of life I was born in seemed to have provided against; that I was under no necessity of seeking my bread; that he would do well for me, and endeavour to enter me fairly into the station of life which he had been just recommending to me; and that if I was not very easy and happy in the world it must be my mere fate or fault that must hinder it, and that he should have nothing to answer for, having thus discharged his duty in warning me against measures which he knew would be to my hurt; in a word, that as he would do very kind things for me if I would stay and settle at home as he directed, so he would not have so much hand in my misfortunes, as to give me any encouragement to go away. And to close all, he told me I had my elder brother for an example, to whom he had used the same earnest persuasions to keep him from going into the Low Country wars, but could not prevail, his young desires prompting him to run into the army, where he was killed; and though he said he would not cease to pray for me, yet he would venture to say to me, that if I did take this foolish step, God would not bless me, and I would have leisure hereafter to reflect upon having neglected his counsel when there might be none to assist in my recovery.

I observed in this last part of his discourse, which was truly prophetic, though I suppose my father did not know it to be so himself – I say, I observed the tears run down his face very plentifully, and especially when he spoke of my brother who was killed; and that when he spoke of my having leisure to repent, and none to assist me, he was so moved, that he broke off the discourse, and told me, his heart was so full he could say no more to me.

I was sincerely affected with this discourse, as indeed who could be otherwise? and I resolved not to think of going abroad any more, but to settle at home according to my father's desire. But alas! a few days wore it all off; and, in short, to prevent any of my father's farther importunities, in a few weeks after I resolved to run quite away from him. However, I did not act so hastily neither as my first heat of resolution prompted, but I took my mother, at a time when I thought her a little pleasanter than ordinary, and told her that my thoughts were so entirely bent upon seeing the world that I should never settle to anything with resolution enough to go through with it, and my father had better give me his consent than force me to go without it; that I was now eighteen years old, which was too late to go apprentice to a trade, or clerk to an attorney; that I was sure if I did, I should never serve out my time, and I should certainly run away from my master before my time was out, and go to sea; and if she would speak to my father to let me go but one voyage abroad, if I came home again and did not like it, I would go no more, and I would promise by a double diligence to recover that time I had lost.

This put my mother into a great passion. She told me, she knew it would be to no purpose to speak to my father upon any such subject; that he knew too well what was my interest to give his consent to anything so much for my hurt, and that she wondered how I could think of any such thing after such a discourse as I had had with my father, and such kind and tender expressions as she knew my father had used to me; and that, in short, if I would ruin myself there was no help for me; but I might depend I should never have their consent to it; that for her part, she would not have so much hand in my destruction, and I should never have it to say, that my mother was willing when my father was not.

Though my mother refused to move it to my father, yet, as I have heard afterwards, she reported all the discourse to him, and that my father, after showing a great concern at it, said to her with a sigh, "That boy might be happy if he would stay at home, but if he goes abroad he will be the miserablest wretch that was ever born: I can give no consent to it."

It was not till almost a year after this that I broke loose, though in the meantime I continued obstinately deaf to all proposals of settling to business, and frequently expostulating with my father and mother about their being so positively determined against what they knew my inclinations prompted me to. But being one day at Hull, where I went casually, and without any purpose of making an elopement that time; but I say, being there, and one of my companions being going by sea to London, in his father's ship, and prompting me to go with them, with the common allurement of seafaring men, viz., that it should cost me nothing for my passage, I consulted neither father nor mother any more, nor so much as sent them word of it; but leaving them to hear of it as they might, without asking God's blessing, or my father's, without any consideration of circumstances or consequences, and in an ill hour, God knows, on the first of September, 1651, I went on board a ship bound for London. Never any young adventurer's misfortunes, I believe, began sooner, or continued longer than mine. The ship was no sooner gotten out of the Humber, but the wind began to blow, and the waves to rise in a most frightful manner; and as I had never been at sea before, I was most inexpressibly sick in body, and terrified in my mind. I began now seriously to reflect upon what I had done, and how justly I was overtaken by the judgment of heaven for my wicked leaving my father's house, and abandoning my duty; all the good counsel of my parents, my father's tears and my mother's entreaties, came now fresh into my mind, and my conscience, which was not yet come to the pitch of hardness which it has been since, reproached me with the contempt of advice, and the breach of my duty to God and my father.

All this while the storm increased, and the sea, which I had never been upon before, went very high, though nothing like what I have seen many times since; no, nor like what I saw a few days after. But it was enough to affect me then, who was but a young sailor, and had never known anything of the matter. I expected every wave would have swallowed us up, and that every time the ship fell down, as I thought, in the trough or hollow of the sea, we should never rise more; and in this agony of mind I made many vows and resolutions, that if it would please God here to spare my life this one voyage, if ever I got once my foot upon dry land again, I would go directly home to my father, and never set it into a ship again while I lived; that I would take his advice, and never run myself into such miseries as these any more. Now I saw plainly the goodness of his observations about the middle station of life, how easy, how comfortably he had lived all his days, and never had been exposed to tempests at sea, or troubles on shore; and I resolved that I woul d, like a true repenting prodigal, go home to my father.

These wise and sober thoughts continued all the while the storm continued, and indeed some time after; but the next day the wind was abated and the sea calmer, and I began to be a little inured to it. However, I was very grave for all that day, being also a little sea-sick still; but towards night the weather cleared up, the wind was quite over, and a charming fine evening followed; the sun went down perfectly clear, and rose so the next morning; and having little or no wind, and a smooth sea, the sun shining upon it, the sight was, as I thought, the most delightful that ever I saw.

I had slept well in the night, and was now no more sea-sick but very cheerful, looking with wonder upon the sea that was so rough and terrible the day before, and could be so calm and so pleasant in so little time after. And now lest my good resolutions should continue, my companion, who had indeed enticed me away, comes to me: "Well, Bob," says he, clapping me on the shoulder, "how do you do after it? I warrant you were frighted, wa'n't you, last night, when it blew but a capful of wind?"

"A capful, d'you call it?" said I; 'twas a terrible storm."

"A storm, you fool you," replies he; "do you call that a storm? Why, it was nothing at all; give us but a good ship and sea-room, and we think nothing at all; give us but a good ship and sea-room, and we think nothing of such a squall of wind as that; but you're but a fresh-water sailor, Bob. Come, let us make a bowl of punch, and we'll forget all that; d'ye see what charming weather 'tis now?"

To make short this sad part of my story we went the old way of all sailors; the punch was made, and I was made drunk with it, and in that one night's wickedness I drowned all my repentance, all my reflections upon my past conduct, and all my resolutions for my future. In a word, as the sea was returned to its smoothness of surface and settled calmness by the abatement of that storm, so the hurry of my thoughts being over, my fears and apprehensions of being swallowed up by the sea being forgotten, and the current of my former desires returned, I entirely forgot the vows and promises that I made in my distress. I found indeed some intervals of reflection, and the serious thoughts did, as it were, endeavour to return again sometimes; but I shook them off, and roused myself from them as it were from a distemper, and applying myself to drink and company, soon mastered the return of those fits, for so I called them, and I had in five or six days got as complete a victory over conscience as any young fellow that resolved not to be troubled with it could desire. But I was to have another trial for it still; and Providence, as in such cases generally it does, resolved to leave me entirely without excuse. For if I would not take this for a deliverance, the next was to be such a one as the worst and most hardened wretch among us would confess both the danger and the mercy.

The sixth day of our being at sea we came into Yarmouth roads; the wind having been contrary and the weather calm, we had made but little way since the storm. Here we were obliged to come to an anchor, and here we lay, the wind continuing contrary, viz., at south-west, for seven or eight days, during which time a great many ships from Newcastle came into the same roads, as the common harbour where the ships might wait for a wind for the river.

We had not, however, rid here so long, but should have tided it up the river, but that the wind blew too fresh; and after we had lain four or five days, blew very hard. However, the roads being reckoned as good as a harbour, the anchorage good, and our ground-tackle very strong, our men were unconcerned, and not in the least apprehensive of danger, but spent the time in rest and mirth, after the manner of the sea; but the eighth day in the morning the wind increased, and we had all hands at work to strike our topmasts, and make everything snug and close, that the ship might ride as easy as possible. By noon the sea went very high indeed, and our ship rid forecastle in, shipped several seas, and we thought once or twice our anchor had come home; upon which our master ordered out the sheet-anchor, so that we rode with two anchors ahead, and the cables veered out to the bitter end.

By this time it blew a terrible storm indeed, and now I began to see terror and amazement in the faces even of the seamen themselves. The master, though vigilant to the business of perserving the ship, yet as he went in and out of his cabin by me,

I could hear him softly to himself say several times, "Lord be merciful to us, we shall be all lost, we shall be all undone"; and the like. During these first hurries I was stupid, lying still in my cabin, which was in the steerage, and cannot describe my temper; I could ill reassume the first penitence, which I had so apparently trampled upon, and hardened myself against; I thought the bitterness of death had been past, and that this would be nothing too, like the first. But when the master himself came by me, as I said just now, and said we should be all lost, I was dreadfully frighted; I got up out of my cabin, and looked out. But such a dismal sight I never saw; the sea went mountains high, and broke upon us every three or four minutes; when I could look about, I could see nothing but distress round us. Two ships that rid near us we found had cut their masts by the board, being deep loaden; and our men cried out, that a ship which rid about a mile ahead of us was foundered. Two more ships being driven from their anchors, were run out of the roads to sea at all adventures, and that with not a mast standing. The light ships fared the best, as not so much labouring in the sea; but two or three of them drove, and came close by us, running away with only their sprit-sail out before the wind.

Towards evening the mate and boatswain begged the master of our ship to let them cut away the foremast, which he was very unwilling to. But the boatswain protesting to him that if he did not the ship would founder, he consented; and when they had cut away the foremast, the mainmast stood so loose, and shook the ship so much, they were obliged to cut her away also, and make a clear deck.

Anyone may judge what a condition I must be at in all this, who was but a young sailor, and who had been in such a fright before at but a little. But if I can express at this distance the thoughts I had about me at that time, I was in tenfold more horror of mind upon account of my former convictions, and then having returned from them to the resolutions I had wickedly taken at first, than I was at death itself; and these, added to the terror of the storm, put me into such a condition, that I can by no words describe it. But the worst was not come yet; the storm continued with such fury, that the seamen themselves acknowledged they had never known a worse. We had a good ship, but she was deep loaden, and wallowed in the sea, that the seamen every now and then cried out she would founder. It was my advantage in one respect, that I did not know what they meant by founder till I inquired. However, the storm was so violent, that I saw what is not often seen, the master, the boatswain, and some others more sensible than the rest, at their prayers, and expecting every moment when the ship would go to the bottom. In the middle of the night, and under all the rest of our distresses, one of the men that had been down on purpose to see, cried out we had sprung a leak; another said there was four foot water in the hold. Then all hands were called to the pump. At that very word my heart, as I thought, died within me, and I fell backwards upon the side of my bed where I sat, into the cabin. However, the men roused me, and told me that I, that was able to do nothing before, was as well able to pump as another; at which I stirred up and went to the pump and worked very heartily. While this was doing, the master seeing some light colliers, who, not able to ride out the storm, were obliged to slip and run away to sea, and would come near us, ordered to fire a gun as a signal of distress. I, who knew nothing what that meant, was so surprised that I thought the ship had broke, or some dreadful thing had happened. In a word, I was so surprised that I fell down in a swoon. As this was a time when everybody had his own life to think of, nobody minded me, or what was become of me; but another man stepped up to the pump, and thrusting me aside with his foot, let me lie, thinking I had been dead; and it was a great while before I came to myself.

We worked on, but with the water increasing in the hold, it was apparent that the ship would founder, and though the storm began to abate a little, as yet it was not possible she could swim till we might run into a port, so the master continued firing guns for help; and a light ship, who had rid it out just ahead of us, ventured a boat out to help us. It was with the utmost hazard the boat came near us, but it was impossible for us to get on board, or for the boat to lie near the ship's side, till at last the men rowing very heartily, and venturing their lives to save ours, our men cast them a rope over the stern with a buoy to it, and then veered it out a great length, which they, after great labour and hazard, took hold of, and we hauled them close under our stern, and got all into their boat. It was to no purpose for them or us after we were in the boat to think of reaching to their own ship, so all agreed to let her drive, and only to pull her in towards shore as much as we could, and our master promised them that if the boat was staved upon shore he would make it good to their master; so partly rowing and partly driving, our boat went away to the norward, sloping towards the shore almost as far as Winterton Ness.

We were not much more than a quarter of an hour out of our ship but we saw her sink, and then I understood for the first time what was meant by a ship foundering in the sea. I must acknowledge I had hardly eyes to look up when the seamen told me she was sinking; for from that moment they rather put me into the boat than that I might be said to go in; my heart was as it were dead within me, partly with fright, partly with horror of mind and the thoughts of what was yet before me.

While we were in this condition, the men yet labouring at the oar to bring the boat near the shore, we could see, when, our boat mounting the waves, we were able to see the shore, great many people running along the shore to assist us when we should come near. But we made but slow way towards the shore, nor were we able to reach the shore, till being past the lighthouse at Winterton, the shore falls off to the westward towards Cromer, and so the land broke off a little the violence of the wind. Here we got in, and though not without much difficulty got all safe on shore, and walked afterwards on foot to Yarmouth, where, as unfortunate men, we were used with great humanity as well by the magistrates of the town, who assigned us good quarters, as by particular merchants and owners of ships, and had money given to us sufficient to carry us either to London or back to Hull, as we thought fit.

Had I now had the sense to have gone back to Hull, and have gone home, I had been happy, and my father, an emblem of our blessed Saviour's parable, had even killed the fatted calf for me; for hearing the ship I went away in was cast away in Yarmouth road, it was a great while before he had any assurance that I was not drowned.

But my ill fate pushed me on now with an obstinacy that nothing could resist; and though I had several times loud calls from my reason and my more composed judgment to go home, yet I had no power to do it. I knew not what to call this, nor will I urge that it is a secret overruling decree that hurries us on to be the instruments of our own destruction, even though it be before us, and that we rush upon it with our eyes open. Certainly nothing but some such decreed unavoidable misery attending, and which it was impossible for me to escape, could have pushed me forward against the calm reasonings and persuasions of my most retired thoughts, and against two such visible instructions as I had met with in my first attempt.

My comrade, who had helped to harden me before, and who was the master's son, was now less forward than I. The first time he spoke to me after we were at Yarmouth, which was not till two or three days, for we were separated in the town to several quarters – I say, the first time he saw me, it appeared his tone was altered, and looking very melancholy and shaking his head, asked me how I did, and telling his father who I was, and how I came this voyage only for a trial in order to go farther abroad, his father turning to me with a very grave and concerned tone, "Young man," says he, "you ought never to go to sea any more, you ought to take this for a plain and visible token, that you are not to be a seafaring man." "Why, sir," said I, "will you go to sea no more?" "That is another case," said he; "it is my calling, and therefore my duty; but as you made this voyage for a trial, you see what a taste Heaven has given you of what you are to expect if you persist; perhaps this is all befallen us on your account, like Jonah in the ship of Tarshish. Pray," continues he, "what are you? and on what account did you go to sea?" Upon that I told him some of my story, at the end of which he burst out with a strange kind of passion. "What had I done," says he, "that such an unhappy wretch should come into my ship? I would not set my foot in the same ship with thee again for a thousand pounds." This indeed, was, as I said, an excursion of his spirits, which were got agitated by the sense of his loss, and was farther than he could have authority to go. However, he afterwards talked very gravely to me, exhorted me to go back to my father, and not tempt Providence to my ruin; told me I might see a visible hand of Heaven against me. "And, young man," said he, "depend upon it, if you do not go back, wherever you go you will meet with nothing but disasters and disappointments, till your father's words are fulfilled upon you."

We parted soon after; for I made him little answer, and I saw him no more; which way he went, I know not. As for me, having some money in my pocket, I travelled to London by land; and there, as well as on the road, had many struggles with myself what course of life I should take, and whether I should go home or go to sea.

As to going home, shame opposed the best motions that offered to my thoughts; and it immediately occurred to me how I should be laughed at among the neighbours, and should be ashamed to see, not my father and mother only, but even everybody else; from whence I have since often observed how incongruous and irrational the common temper of mankind is, especially of youth, to the reason which ought to guide them in such cases, viz., that they are not ashamed to sin, and yet are ashamed to repent; not ashamed of the action for which they ought justly to be esteemed fools, but are ashamed of the returning, which only can make them be esteemed wise men.

In this state of life, however, I remained some time, uncertain what measures to take, and what course of life to lead. An irresistible reluctance continued to going home; and as I stayed a while, the remembrance of the distress I had been in wore off; and as that abated, the little motion I had in my desires to a return wore off with it, till at last I quite laid aside the thoughts of it, and looked out for a voyage.

That evil influence which carried me first away from my father's house, that hurried me into the wild and indigested notion of raising my fortune, and that impressed those conceits so forcibly upon me as to make me deaf to all good advice, and to the entreaties and even command of my father – I say, the same influence, whatever it was, presented the most unfortunate of all enterprises to my view; and I went on board a vessel bound to the coast of Africa, or as our sailors vulgarly call it, a voyage to Guinea.

It was my great misfortune that in all these adventures I did not ship myself as a sailor, whereby, though I might indeed have worked a little harder than ordinary, yet at the same time I had learned the duty and office of a foremast man, and in time might have qualified myself for a mate or lieutenant, if not for a master. But as it was always my fate to choose for the worse, so I did here; for having money in my pocket, and good clothes upon my back, I would always go on board in the habit of a gentleman; and so I neither had any business in the ship, or learned to do any.

It was my lot first of all to fall into pretty good company in London, which does not always happen to such loose and misguided young fellows as I then was; the devil generally not omitting to lay some snare for them very early; but it was not so with me. I first fell acquainted with the master of a ship who had been on the coast of Guinea, and who, having had very good success there, was resolved to go again; and who, taking a fancy to my conversation, which was not at all disagreeable at that time, hearing me say I had a mind to see the world, told me if I would go the voyage with him I should be at no expense; I should be his messmate and his companion; and if I could carry anything with me, I should have all the advantage of it that the trade would admit, and perhaps I might meet with some encouragement.

I embraced the offer; and, entering into a strict friendship with this captain, who was an honest and plain-dealing man, I went the voyage with him, and carried a small adventure with me, which by the disinterested honesty of my friend the captain, I increased very considerably, for I carried about £40 in such toys and trifles as the captain directed me to buy. This £40 I had mustered together by the assistance of some of my relations whom I corresponded with, and who, I believe, got my father, or at least my mother, to contribute so much as that to my first adventure.

This was the only voyage which I may say was successful in all my adventures, and which I owe to the integrity and honesty of my friend the captain; under whom also I got a competent knowledge of the mathematics and the rules of navigation, learned how to keep an account of the ship's course, to take an observation, and, in short, to understand some things that were needful to be understood by a sailor. For, as he took delight to introduce me, I took delight to learn; and, in a word, this voyage made me both a sailor and a merchant; for I brought home five pounds nine ounces of gold dust for my adventure, which yielded me in London at my return almost £300, and this filled me with those aspiring thoughts which have since so completed my ruin.

Yet even in this voyage I had my misfortunes too; particularly, that I was continually sick, being thrown into a violent calenture by the excessive heat of the climate; our principal trading being upon the coast, from the latitude of 15 degrees north even to the line itself.

I was now set up for a Guinea trader; and my friend, to my great misfortune, dying soon after his arrival, I resolved to go the same voyage again, and I embarked in the same vessel with one who was his mate in the former voyage, and had now got the command of the ship. This was the unhappiest voyage that ever man made; for though I did not carry quite £100 of my new-gained wealth, so that I had £200 left, and which I lodged with my friend's widow, who was very just to me, yet I fell into terrible misfortunes in this voyage; and from the first was this, viz., our ship making her course towards the Canary Islands, or rather between those islands and the African shore, was surprised in the grey of the morning by a Turkish rover of Sallee, who gave chase to us with all the sail she could make. We crowded also as much canvas as our yards would spread, or our masts carry, to have got clear; but finding the pirate gained upon us, and would certainly come up with us in a few hours, we prepared to fight, our ship having twelve guns, and the rogue eighteen. About three in the afternoon he came up with us, and bringing to, by mistake, just athwart our quarter, instead of athwart our stern, as he intended, we brought eight of our guns to bear on that side, and poured in a broadside upon him, which made him sheer off again, after returning our fire and pouring in also his small-shot from near 200 men which he had on board. However, we had not a man touched, all our men keeping close. He prepared to attack us again, and we to defend ourselves; but laying us on board the next time upon our other quarter, he entered sixty men upon our decks, who immediately fell to cutting and hacking the decks and rigging. We plied them with small shot, half-pikes, powder-chests, and such like, and cleared our deck of them twice. However, to cut short this melancholy part of our story, our ship being disabled, and three of our men killed and eight wounded, we were obliged to yield, and were carried all prisoners into Sallee, a port belonging to the Moors.

The usage I had there was not so dreadful as at first I had apprehended, nor was I carried up the country to the emperor's court, as the rest of our men were, but was kept by the captain of the rover as his proper prize, and made his slave, being young and nimble, and fit for his business. At this surprising change of my circumstances from a merchant to a miserable slave, I was perfectly overwhelmed; and now I looked back upon my father's prophetic discourse to me, that I should be miserable, and have none to relieve me, which I thought was now so effectually brought to pass, that it could not be worse; that now the hand of Heaven had overtaken me, and I was undone without redemption. But alas! this was but a taste of the misery I was to go through, as will appear in the sequel of this story.

As my new patron, or master, had taken me home to his house, so I was in hopes that he would take me with him when he went to sea again, believing that it would some time or other be his fate to be taken by a Spanish or Portugal man-of-war; and that then I should be set at liberty. But this hope of mine was soon taken away; for when he went to sea, he left me on shore to look after his little garden, and do the common drudgery of slaves about his house; and when he came home again from his cruise, he ordered me to lie in the cabin to look after the ship.

Here I meditated nothing but my escape, and what method I might take to effect it, but found no way that had the least probability in it. Nothing presented to make the supposition of it rational; for I had nobody to communicate it to that would embark with me, no fellow-slave, no Englishman, Irishman, or Scotsman there but myself; so that for two years, though I often pleased myself with the imagination, yet I never had the least encouraging prospect of putting it in practice.

After about two years an odd circumstance presented itself, which put the old thought of making some attempt for my liberty again in my head. My patron lying at home longer than usual without fitting out his ship, which, as I heard, was for want of money, he used constantly, once or twice a week, sometimes oftener, if the weather was fair, to take the ship's pinnace, and go out into the road a-fishing; and as he always took me and a young Maresco with him to row the boat, we made him very merry, and I proved very dexterous in catching fish; insomuch, that sometimes he would send me with a Moor, one of his kinsmen, and the youth the Maresco, as they called him, to catch a dish of fish for him.

It happened one time that, going a-fishing in a stark calm morning, a fog rose so thick, that though we were not half a league from the shore we lost sight of it; and rowing we knew not whither or which way, we laboured all day, and all the next night, and when the morning came we found we were pulled off to sea instead of pulling in for the shore; and that we were at least two leagues from the shore. However, we got well in again, though with a great deal of labour, and some danger, for the wind began to blow pretty fresh in the morning; but particularly we were all very hungry.

But our patron, warned by this disaster, resolved to take more care of himself for the future; and having lying by him the long-boat of our English ship which he had taken, he resolved he would not go a-fishing any more without a compass and some provision; so he ordered the carpenter of his ship, who was also an English slave, to build a little state-room, or cabin, in the middle of the long-boat, like that of a barge, with a place to stand behind it to steer and haul home the main-sheet, and room before for a hand or two to stand and work the sails. She sailed with what we call a shoulder-of-mutton sail; and the boom jibbed over the top of the cabin, which lay very snug and low, and had in it room for him to lie, with a slave or two, and a table to eat on, with some small lockers to put in some bottles of such liquor as he thought fit to drink; particularly his bread, rice, and coffee.

We went frequently out with this boat a-fishing, and as I was most dexterous to catch fish for him, he never went without me. It happened that he had appointed to go out in this boat, either for pleasure or for fish, with two or three Moors of some distinction in that place, and for whom he had provided extraordinarily; and had therefore sent on board the boat overnight a larger store of provisions than ordinary; and had ordered me to get ready three fuzees with powder and shot, which were on board his ship, for that they designed some sport of fowling as well as fishing.

I got all things ready as he had directed, and waited the next morning with the boat, washed clean, her ancient and pendants out, and everything to accommodate his guests; when by and by my patron came on board alone, and told me his guests had put off going, upon some business that fell out, and ordered me with the man and boy, as usual, to go out with the boat and catch them some fish, for that his friends were to sup at his house; and commanded that as soon as I had got some fish I should bring it home to his house; all which I prepared to do.

This moment my former notions of deliverance darted into my thoughts, for now I found I was to like have a little ship at my command; and my master being gone, I prepared to furnish myself, not for a fishing business, but for a voyage; though I knew not, neither did I so much as consider, whither I should steer; for anywhere, to get out of that place, was my way.

My first contrivance was to make a pretence to speak to this Moor, to get something for our subsistence on board; for I told him we must not presume to eat of our patron's bread. He said that was true; so he brought a large basket of rusk or biscuit of their kind, and three jars with fresh water, into the boat. I knew where my patron's case of bottles stood, which it was evident by the make were taken out of some English prize; and I conveyed them into the boat while the Moor was on shore, as if they had been there before for our master. I conveyed also a great lump of beeswax into the boat, which weighed above half a hundredweight, with a parcel of twine or thread, a hatchet, a saw, and a hammer, all of which were great use to us afterwards, especially the wax to make candles. Another trick I tried upon him, which he innocently came into also. His name was Ishmael, who they call Muly, or Moely; so I called to him, "Moely," said I, "our patron's guns are on board the boat; can you not get a little powder and shot? it may be we may kill some alcamies (a fowl like our curlews) for ourselves, for I know he keeps the gunner's stores in the ship." "Yes," says he, "I'll bring some"; and accordingly he brought a great leather pouch which held about a pound an a half of powder, or rather more; and another with shot, that had five or six pounds, with some bullets, and put all into the boat. At the same time I had found some powder of my master's in the great cabin, with which I filled one of the large bottles in the case, which was almost empty, pouring what was in it into another; and thus furnished with everything needful, we sailed out of the port to fish. The castle, which is at the entrance of the port, knew who we were, and took no notice of us; and we were not above a mile out of the port before we hauled in our sail, and set us down to fish. The wind blew from the N.N.E., which was contrary to my desire; for had it blown southerly I had been sure to have made the coast of Spain, and at least reached to the bay of Cadiz; but my resolutions were, blow which way it would, I would be gone from the horrid place where I was, and leave the rest to Fate.

After we had fished some time and catched nothing, for when I had fish on my hook I would not pull them up, that he might not see them, I said to the Moor, "This will not do; our master will not be thus served; we must stand farther off." He, thinking no harm, agreed, and being in the head of the boat set the sails; and as I had the helm I run the boat out near a league farther, and then brought her to as if I would fish; when giving the boy the helm, I stepped forward to where the Moor was, and making as if I stooped for something behind him, I took him by surprise with my arm under his twist, and tossed him clear overboard into the sea. He rose immediately, for he swam like a cork, and called to me, begged to be taken in, told me he would go all the world over with me. He swam so strong after the boat, that he would have reached me very quickly, there being but little wind; upon which I stepped into the cabin, and fetching one of the fowling-pieces, I presented it at him, and told him I had done him no hurt, and if he would be quiet I would do him none. "But," said I, "you swim well enough to reach to the shore, and the sea is calm; make the best of your way to shore, and I will do you no harm; but if you come near the boat I'll shoot you through the head, for I am resolved to have my liberty." So he turned himself about, and swam for the shore, and I make no doubt but he reached it with ease, for he was an excellent swimmer.

I could have been content to have taken this Moor with me, and have drowned the boy, but there was no venturing to trust him. When he was gone I turned to the boy, whom they called Xury, and said to him, "Xury, if you will be faithful to me I'll make you a great man; but if you will not stroke your face to be true to me," that is, swear by Mahomet and his father's beard, "I must throw you into the sea too." The boy smiled in my face, and spoke so innocently, that I could not mistrust him, and swore to be faithful to me, and go all over the world with me.

While I was in view of the Moor that was swimming, I stood out directly to sea with the boat, rather stretching to windward, that they might think me gone towards the straits' mouth (as indeed anyone that had been in their wits must have been supposed to do); for who would have supposed we were sailed on to the southward to the truly barbarian coast, where whole nations of negroes were sure to surround us with their canoes, and destroy us; where we could ne'er once go on shore but we should be devoured by savage beasts, or more merciless savages of human kind?

But as soon as it grew dusk in the evening, I changed my course, and steered directly south and by east, bending my course a little toward the east, that I might keep in with the shore; and having a fair, fresh gale of wind, and a smooth, quiet sea, I made such sail that I believe by the next day, at three o'clock in the afternoon, when I first made the land, I could not be less than 150 miles south of Sallee; quite beyond the Emperor of Morocco's dominions, or indeed of any other king thereabouts, for we saw no people.

Yet such was the fright I had taken at the Moors, and the dreadful apprehensions I had of falling into their hands, that I would not stop, or go on shore, or come to an anchor, the wind continuing fair, till I had sailed in that manner five days; and then the wind shifting to the southward, I concluded also that if any of our vessels were in chase of me, they also would now give over; so I ventured to make to the coast, and came to an anchor in the mouth of a little river, I knew not what, or where; neither what latitude, what country, what nations, or what river. I neither saw, nor desired to see, any people; the principal thing I wanted was fresh water. We came into this creek in the evening, resolving to swim on shore as soon as it was dark, and discover the country; but as soon as it was quite dark we heard such dreadful noises of the barking, roaring, and howling of wild creatures, of we knew not what kinds, that the poor boy was ready to die with fear, and begged me not to go on shore till day. "Well, Xury," said I, "then I won't; but it may be we may see men by day, who will be as bad to us as these lions."

"Then we give them the shoot gun," says Xury, laughing; "make them run away."

Such English Xury spoke by conversing among us slaves. However, I was glad to see the boy so cheerful, and I gave him a dram (out of our patron's case of bottles) to cheer him up. After all, Xury's advice was good, and I took it; we dropped our little anchor and lay still all night. I say still, for we slept none; for in two or three hours we saw vast great creatures (we knew not what to call them) of many sorts come down to the sea shore and run into the water, wallowing and washing themselves for the pleasure of cooling themselves; and they made such hideous howlings and yellings, that I never indeed heard the like.

Xury was dreadfully frighted, and indeed so was I too; but we were both more frighted when we heard one of these mighty creatures come swimming towards our boat; we could not see him, but we might hear him by his blowing to be a monstrous huge and furious beast. Xury said it was a lion, and it might be so for aught I know; but poor Xury cried to me to weigh the anchor and row away. "No," says I, "Xury; we can slip our cable with the buoy to it, and go off to sea; they cannot follow us far." I had no sooner said so, but I perceived the creature (whatever it was) within two oars' length, which something surprised me; however, I immediately stepped to the cabin door, and taking up my gun, fired at him, upon which he immediately turned about and swam towards the shore again.

But is is impossible to describe the horrible noises, and hideous cries and howlings, that were raised, as well upon the edge of the shore as higher within the country, upon the noise or report of the gun, a thing I have some reason to believe those creatures had never heard before. This convinced me that there was no going on shore for us in the night upon that coast; and how to venture on shore in the day was another question too; for to have fallen into the hands of any of the savages, had been as bad as to have fallen into the hands of lions and tigers; at least we were equally apprehensive of the danger of it.

Be that as it would, we were obliged to go on shore somewhere or other for water, for we had not a pint left in the boat; when or where to get to it, was the point. Xury said if I would let him go on shore with one of the jars, he would find if there was any water and bring some to me. I asked him why he would go? why I should not go and he stay in the boat? The boy answered with so much affection, that made me love him ever after. Says he, "If wild mans come, they eat me, you go way."

"Well, Xury," said I, "we will both go; and if the wild mans come, we will kill them, they shall eat neither of us." So I gave Xury a piece of rusk bread to eat, and a dram out of our patron's case of bottles which I mentioned before; and we hauled in the boat as near the shore as we thought was proper, and so waded on shore, carrying nothing but our arms and two jars for water.

I did not care to go out of sight of the boat, fearing the coming of canoes with savages down the river; but the boy seeing a low place about a mile up the country, rambled to it; and by and by I saw him come running towards me. I thought he was pursued by some savage, or frighted with some wild beast, and I ran forward towards him to help him; but when I came nearer to him, I saw something hanging over his shoulders, which was a creature that he had shot, like a hare, but different in colour, and longer legs. However, we were very glad of it, and it was very good meat; but the great joy that poor Xury came with was to tell me he had found good water, and seen no wild men.

But we found afterwards that we need not take such pains for water, for a little higher up the creek where we were we found the water fresh when the tide was out, which flowed but a little way up; so we filled our jars, and feasted on the hare we had killed, and prepared to go on our way, having seen no footsteps of any human creature in that part of the country.

As I had been one voyage to this coast before, I knew very well that the islands of the Canaries, and the Cape de Verde Islands also, lay not far off from the coast. But as I had no instruments to take an observation to know what latitude we were in, and did not exactly know, or at least remember, what latitude they were in, I knew not where to look for them, or when to stand off to sea towards them; otherwise I might now easily have found some of these islands. But my hope was, that if I stood along this coast till I came to that part where the English traded, I should find some of their vessels upon their usual design of trade, that would relieve and take us in.

By the best of my calculation, that place where I now was must be that country which, lying between the Emperor of Morocco's dominions and the negroes, lies waste and uninhabited, except by wild beasts; the negroes having abandoned it and gone farther south for fear of the Moors, and the Moors not thinking it worth inhabiting, by reason of its barrenness; and indeed both forsaking it because of the prodigious numbers of tigers, lions, leopards, and other furious creatures which harbour there; so that the Moors use it for their hunting only, where they go like an army, two or three thousand men at a time; and indeed for near a hundred miles together upon this coast we saw nothing but a waste uninhabited country by day, and heard nothing but howlings and roarings of wild beasts by night.

Once or twice in the daytime I thought I saw the Pico of Teneriffe being the high top of the Mountain Teneriffe in the Canaries, and had a great mind to venture out in hopes of reaching thither; but having tried twice, I was forced in again by contrary winds, the sea also going too high for my little vessel; so I resolved to pursue my first design, and keep along the shore.

Several times I was obliged to land for fresh water after we had left this place; and once in particular, being early in the morning, we came to an anchor under a little point of land which was pretty high; and the tide beginning to flow, we lay still to go farther in. Xury, whose eyes were more about him than it seems mine were, calls softly to me, and tells me that we had best go farther off the shore; "For," says he, "look, yonder lies a dreadful monster on the side of that hillock fast asleep." I looked where he pointed, and saw a dreadful monster indeed, for it was a terrible great lion that lay on the side of the shore, under the shade of a piece of the hill that hung as it were a little over him. "Xury," says I, "you shall go on shore and kill him." Xury looked frighted, and said, "Me kill! he eat me at one mouth"; one mouthfull he meant. However, I said no more to the boy, but bade him lie still, and I took our biggest gun, which was almost musket-bore, and loaded it with a good charge of powder, and with two slugs, and laid it down; then I loaded another gun with two bullets; and the third (for we had three pieces) I loaded with five smaller bullets. I took the best aim I could with the first piece to have him shot into the head, but he lay so with his leg raised a little above his nose, that the slugs hit his leg about the knee, and broke the bone. He started up growling at first, but finding his leg broke, fell down again, and then got up upon three legs and gave the most hideous roar that ever I heard. I was a little surprised that I had not hit him on the head. However, I took up the second piece immediately, and, though he began to move off, fired again, and shot him into the head, and had the pleasure to him drop, and make but little noise, but lay struggling for life. Then Xury took heart, and would have me let him go on shore. "Well, go," said I; so the boy jumped into the water, and taking a little gun in one hand, swam to shore with the other hand, and coming close to the creature, put the muzzle of the piece to his ear, and shot him into the head again, which despatched him quite.

This was game indeed to us, but this was no food; and I was very sorry to lose three charges of powder and shot upon a creature that was good for nothing to us. However, Xury said he would have some of him; so he comes on board, and asked me to give him the hatchet. "For what, Xury?" said I. "Me cut off his head," said he. However, Xury could not cut off his head, but he cut off a foot, and brought it with him, and it was a monstrous great one.

I bethought myself, however, that perhaps the skin of him might one way or other be of some value to us; and I resolved to take off his skin if I could. So Xury and I went to work with him; but Xury was much the better workman at it, for I knew very ill how to do it. Indeed, it took us up both the whole day, but at last we got off the hide of him, and spreading it on the top of our cabin, the sun effectually dried it in two days' time, and it afterwards served me to lie upon.

After this stop we made on to the southward continually for ten or twelve days, living very sparing on our provisions, which began to abate very much, and going no oftener into the shore than we were obliged to for fresh water. My design in this was to make the river Gambia or Senegal – that is to say, anywhere about the Cape de Verde – where I was in hopes to meet with some European ship; and if I did not, I knew not what course I had to take, but to seek out for the lands, or perish there among the negroes. I knew that all the ships from Europe, which sailed either to the coast of Guinea or to Brazil, or to the East Indies, made this cape, or those islands; and in a word, I put the whole of my fortune upon this single point, either that I must meet with some ship, or must perish.

When I had pursued this resolution about ten days longer, as I have said, I began to see that the land was inhabited; and in two or three places, as we sailed by, we saw people stand upon the shore to look at us; we could also perceive they were quite black, and stark naked. I was once inclined to have gone on shore to them; but Xury was my better counsellor, and said to me, "No go, no go." However, I hauled in nearer the shore that I might talk to them, and I found they ran along the shore by me a good way. I observed they had no weapons in their hands, except one, who had a long slender stick, which Xury said was a lance, and that they would throw them a great way with good aim. So I kept a distance, but talked with them by signs as well as I could, and particularly made signs for something to eat; they beckoned to me to stop my boat, and that they would fetch me some meat. Upon this I lowered the top of my sail, and lay by, and two of them ran up into the country, and in less than half an hour came back, and brought with them two pieces of dried flesh and some corn, such as is the produce of their country; but we neither knew what the one or the other was. However, we were willing to accept it, but how to come at it was our next dispute, for I was not for venturing on shore to them, and they were as much afraid of us; but they took a safe way for us all, for they brought it to the shore and laid it down, and went and stood a great way off till we fetched it on board, and then came close to us again.

We made signs of thanks to them, for we had nothing to make them amends. But an opportunity offered that very instant to oblige them wonderfully; for while we were lying by the shore came two mighty creatures, one pursuing the other (as we took it) with great fury from the mountains towards the sea; whether it was the male pursuing the female, or whether they were in sport or in rage, we could not tell, any more than we could tell whether it was usual or strange, but I believe it was the latter; because, in the first place, those ravenous creatures seldom appear but in the night; and in the second place, we found the people terribly frighted, especially the women. The man that had the lance or dart did not fly from them, but the rest did; however, as the two creatures ran directly into the water, they did not seem to offer to fall upon any of the negroes, but plunged themselves into the sea, and swam about, as if they had come for their diversion. At last, one of them began to come nearer our boat than at first I expected; but I lay ready for him, for I had loaded my gun with all possible expedition, and bade Xury load both the others. As soon as he came fairly within my reach, I fired, and shot him directly into the head; immediately he sunk down into the water, but rose instantly, and plunged up and down, as if he was struggling for life, and so indeed he was. He immediately made to the shore; but between the wound, which was his mortal hurt, and the strangling of the water, he died just before he reached the shore.

It is impossible to express the astonishment of these poor creatures, at the noise and the fire of my gun; some of them were even ready to die for fear, and fell down as dead with the very terror. But when they saw the creature dead, and sunk in the water, and that I made signs to them to come to the shore, they took heart and came to the shore, and began to search for the creature. I found him by his blood staining the water: and by the help of a rope, which I slung round him, and gave the negroes to haul, they dragged him on the shore, and found that it was a most curious leopard, spotted, and fine to an admirable degree; and the negroes held up their hands with admiration, to think what it was I had killed him with.

The other creature, frighted with the flash of fire and the noise of the gun, swam on shore, and ran directly to the mountains from whence they came; nor could I, at that distance, know what it was. I found quickly the negroes were for eating the flesh of this creature, so I was willing to have them take it as a favour from me; which, when I made signs to them that they might take him, they were very thankful for. Immediately they fell to work with him; and though they had no knife yet, with a sharpened piece of wood, they took off his skin as readily, and much more readily, than we could have done it with a knife. They offered me some of the flesh, which I declined, making as if I would give it to them, but made signs for the skin, which they gave me very freely, and brought me a great deal more of their provision, which, though I did not understand, yet I accepted. Then I made signs to them for some water and held out one of my jars to them, turning it bottom upward, to show that it was empty, and that I wanted to have it filled. They called immediately to some of their friends, and there came two women, and brought a great vessel made of earth, and burnt, as I suppose, in the sun; this they set down for me, as before, and I sent Xury on shore with my jars, and filled them all three. There women were as stark naked as the men.

I was now furnished with roots and corn, such as it was, and water; and leaving my friendly negroes, I made forward for about eleven days more, without offering to go near the shore, till I saw the land run out a great length into the sea, at about the distance of four or five leagues before me; and the sea being very calm, I kept a large offing, to make this point. At length, doubling the point, at about two leagues from the land, I saw plainly land on the other side, to seaward; then I concluded, as it was most certain indeed, that this was the Cape de Verde, and those the islands, called from thence Cape de Verde Islands. However, they were at a great distance, and I could not well tell what I had best to do; for if I should be taken with a fresh of wind, I might neither reach one or other.

In this dilemma, as I was very pensive, I stepped into the cabin, and sat me down, Xury having the helm; when, on a sudden, the boy cried out, "Master, master, a ship with a sail!" and the foolish boy was frighted out of his wits, thinking it must be some of his master's ships sent to pursue us, when I knew we were gotten far enough out of their reach. I jumped out of the cabin, and immediately saw, not only the ship, but what she was, viz., that it was a Portuguese ship, and, as I thought, was bound to the coast of Guinea, for negroes. But when I observed the course she steered, I was soon convinced they were bound some other way, and did not design to come any nearer to the shore; upon which I stretched out to sea as much as I could, resolving to speak with them, if possible.

With all the sail I could make, I found I should not be able to come in their way, but they would be gone by before I could make any signal to them; but after I had crowded to the utmost, and began to despair, they, it seems, saw me by the help of their perspective-glasses, and that it was some European boat, which, as they supposed, must belong to some ship that was lost, so they shortened sail to let me come up. I was encouraged with this; and as I had my patron's ancient on board, I made a waft of it to them for a signal of distress, and fired a gun, both of which they saw; for they told me they saw the smoke, though they did not hear the gun. Upon these signals they very kindly brought to, and lay by for me; and in about three hours' time I came up with them.

They asked me what I was, in Portuguese, and in Spanish, and in French, but I understood none of them; but at last a Scots sailor, who was on board, called to me, and I answered him, and told him I was an Englishman, that I had made my escape out of slavery from the Moors, at Sallee. Then they bade me come on board, and very kindly took me in, and all my goods.

It was an inexpressible joy to me, that anyone will believe, that I was thus delivered, as I esteemed it, from such a miserable, and almost hopeless, condition as I was in; and I immediately offered all I had to the captain of the ship, as a return for my deliverance. But he generously told me he would take nothing from me, but that all I had should be delivered safe to me when I came to the Brazils. "For," says he, "I have saved your life on no other terms than I would be glad to be saved myself; and it may, one time or other, be my lot to be taken up in the same condition. Besides," says he, "when I carry you to the Brazils, so great a way from your own country, if I should take from you what you have, you will be starved there, and then I only take away that life I have given. No, no, Seignior Inglese," says he, "Mr. Englishman, I will carry you thither in charity, and those things will help you to buy your subsistence there, and your passage home again."

As he was charitable in his proposal, so he was just in the performance to a tittle; for he ordered the seamen that none should offer to touch anything I had; then he took everything into his own possession, and gave me back an exact inventory of them, that I might have them, even so much as my three earthen jars.

As to my boat, it was a very good one, and that he saw, and told me he would buy it of me for the ship's use, and asked me what I would have for it? I told him he had been so generous to me in everything, that I could not offer to make any price of the boat, but left it entirely to him; upon which he told me he would give me a note of his hand to pay me eighty pieces of eight for it at Brazil, and when it came there, if anyone offered to give more, he would make it up. He offered me also sixty pieces of eight for my boy Xury, which I was loth to take; not that I was not willing to let the captain have him, but I was very loth to sell the poor boy's liberty, who had assisted me so faithfully in procuring my own. However, when I let him know my reason, he owned it to be just, and offered me this medium, that he would give the boy an obligation to set him free in ten years if he turned Christian. Upon this, and Xury saying he was willing to go to him, I let the captain have him.

We had a very good voyage to the Brazils, and arrived in the Bay de Todos los Santos, or All Saints' Bay, in about twenty-two days after. And now I was once more delivered from the most miserable of all conditions of life; and what to do next with myself, I was now to consider.

The generous treatment the captain gave me, I can never enough remember. He would take nothing of me for my passage, gave me twenty ducats for the leopard's skin, and forty for the lion's skin, which I had in my boat, and caused everything I had in the ship to be punctually delivered to me; and what I was willing to sell he bought, such as the case of bottles, two of my guns, and a piece of the lump of beeswax – for I had made candles of the rest; in a word, I made about 220 pieces of eight of all my cargo, and with this stock I went on shore in the Brazils.

I had not been long here, but being recommended to the house of a good honest man like himself, who had an *ingenio* as they call it, that is, a plantation and a sugar-house, I lived with him some time, and acquainted myself by that means with the manner of their planting and making of sugar; and seeing how well the planters lived, and how they grew rich suddenly, I resolved, if I could get license to settle there, I would turn planter among them, resolving in the meantime to find out some way to get my money which I had left in London remitted to me. To this purpose, getting a kind of a letter of naturalisation, I purchased as much land that was uncured as my money would reach, and formed a plan for my planation and settlement, and such a one as might be suitable to the stock which I proposed to myself to receive from England.

I had a neighbour, a Portuguese of Lisbon, but born of English parents, whose name was Wells, and in much such circumstances as I was. I called him my neighbour, because his plantation lay next to mine, and we went on very sociably together. My stock was but low, as well as his; and we rather planted for food than anything else, for about two years. However, we began to increase, and our land began to come into order; so that the third year we planted some tobacco, and made each of us a large piece of ground ready for planting canes in the year to come. But we both wanted help; and now I found, more than before, I had done wrong in parting with my boy Xury.

But alas! for me to do wrong that never did right was no great wonder. I had no remedy but to go on. I had gotten into an employment quite remote to my genius, and directly contrary to the life I delighted in, and for which I forsook my father's house, and broke through all his good advice; nay, I was coming into the very middle station, or upper degree of low life, which my father advised me to before; and which, if I resolved to go on with, I might as well have stayed at home, and never have fatigued myself in the world as I had done. And I used often to say to myself, I could have done this as well in England among my friends, as have gone 5000 miles off to do it among strangers and savages, in a wilderness, and at such a distance as never to hear from any part of the world that had the least knowledge of me.

In this manner I used to look upon my condition with the utmost regret. I had nobody to converse with, but now and then this neighbour; no work to be done, but by the labour of my hands; and I used to say, I lived just like a man cast away upon some desolate island, that had nobody there but himself. But how just has it been! and how should all men reflect, that when they compare their present conditions with others that are worse, Heaven may oblige them to make the exchange, and be convinced of their former felicity by their experience; – I say, how just has it been, that the truly solitary life I reflected on in an island of mere desolation should be my lot, who had so often unjustly compared it with the life which I then led, in which, had I continued, I had in all probability been exceedingly prosperous and rich.

I was in some degree settled in my measures for carrying on the plantation before my kind friend, the captain of the ship that took me up at sea, went back; for the ship remained there in providing his loading, and preparing for his voyage, nearly three months; when, telling him what little stock I had left behind me in London, he gave me this friendly and sincere advice: "Seignior Inglese," says he, for so he always called me, "if you will give me letters, and a procuration here in form to me, with orders to the person who has your money in London to send your effects to Lisbon, to such persons as I shall direct, and in such goods as are proper for this country, I will bring you the produce of them, God willing, at my return. But since human affairs are all subject to changes and disasters, I would have you give orders but for one hundred pounds sterling, which, you say, is half your stock, and let the hazard be run for the first; so that if it come safe, you may order the rest the same way; and if it miscarry, you may have the other half to have recourse to for your supply."

This was so wholesome advice, and looked so friendly, that I could not but be convinced it was the best course I could take; so I accordingly prepared letters to the gentlewoman with whom I had left my money, and a procuration to the Portuguese captain, as he desired.

I wrote the English captain's widow a full account of all my adventures; my slavery, escape, and how I had met with the Portugal captain at sea, the humanity of his behaviour, and in what condition I was now in, with all necessary directions for my supply. And when this honest captain came to Lisbon, he found means, by some of the English merchants there, to send over not the order only, but a full account of my story to a merchant at London, who represented it effectually to her; whereupon, she not only delivered the money, but out of her own pocket sent the

Portugal captain a very handsome present for his humanity and charity to me.

The merchant in London vesting this hundred pounds in English goods, such as the captain had writ for, sent them directly to him at Lisbon, and he brought them all safe to me to the Brazils; among which, without my direction (for I was too young in my business to think of them), he had taken care to have all sorts of tools, iron-work, and utensils necessary for my plantation, and which were of great use to me.

When this cargo arrived, I thought my fortune made, for I was surprised with joy of it; and my good steward, the captain, had laid out the five pounds, which my friend had sent him for a present for himself, to purchase and bring me over a servant under bond for six years' service, and would not accept of any consideration, except a little tobacco, which I would have him accept, being of my own produce.

Neither was this all; but my goods being all English manufactures, such as cloth, stuffs, baize, and things particularly valuable and desirable in the country, I found means to sell them to a very great advantage; so that I may say I had more than four times the value of my first cargo, and was now infinitely beyond my poor neighbour, I mean in the advancement of my plantation; for the first thing I did, I bought me a negro slave, and a European servant also; I mean another besides that which the captain brought me from Lisbon.

But as abused prosperity is oftentimes made the very means of our greatest adversity, so was it with me. I went on the next year with great success in my plantation. I raised fifty great rolls of tobacco on my own ground, more than I had disposed of for necessaries among my neighbours; and these fifty rolls, being each of above a hundredweight, were well cured, and laid by against the return of the fleet from Lisbon. And now, increasing in business and in wealth, my head began to be full of projects and undertakings beyond my reach, such as are, indeed, often the ruin of the best heads in business.

Had I continued in the station I was now in, I had room for all the happy things to have yet befallen me for which my father so earnestly recommended a quiet, retired life, and of which he had so sensibly described the middle station of life to be full of. But other things attended me, and I was still to be the willful agent of all my own miseries; and particularly, to increase my fault and double the reflections upon myself, which in my future sorrows I should have leisure to make. All these miscarriages were procured by my apparent obstinate adhering to my foolish inclination of wandering abroad, and pursuing that inclination in contradiction to the clearest views of doing myself good in a fair and plain pursuit of those prospects, and those measures of life, which Nature and Providence concurred to present me with, and to make my duty.

As I had once done thus in my breaking away from my parents, so I could not be content now, but I must go and leave the happy view I had of being a rich and thriving man in my new plantation, only to pursue a rash and immoderate desire of rising faster than the nature of the thing admitted; and thus I cast myself down again into the deepest gulf of human misery that ever man fell into, or perhaps could be consistent with life and a state of health in the world.

To come, then, by the just degrees to the particulars of this part of my story. You may suppose, that having now lived almost four years in the Brazils, and beginning to thrive and prosper very well upon my plantation, I had not only learned the language, but had contracted acquaintance and friendship among my fellow-planters, as well as among the merchants at St. Salvador, which was our port, and that in my discourses among them I had frequently given them an account of my two voyages to the coast of Guinea, the manner of trading with the negroes there, and how easy it was to purchase upon the coast for trifles – such as beads, toys, knives, scissors, hatchets, bits of glass, and the like

– not only gold-dust, Guinea grains, elephants' teeth, etc, – but negroes, for the service of the Brazils, in great numbers.

They listened always very attentively to my discourses on these heads, but especially to that part which related to the buying negroes; which was a trade, at that time, not only not far entered into, but, as far as it was, had been carried on by the *assiento,* or permission, of the Kings of Spain and Portugal, and engrossed in the publick, so that few negroes were brought, and those excessive dear.

It happened, being in company with some merchants and planters of my acquaintance, and talking of those things very earnestly, three of them came to me the next morning, and told me they had been musing very much upon what I had discoursed with them of, the last night, and they came to make a secret proposal to me. And after enjoining me secrecy, they told me that they had a mind to fit out a ship to go to Guinea; that they had all plantations as well as I, and were straitened for nothing so much as servants; that as it was a trade that could not be carried on because they could not publicly sell the negroes when they came home, so they desired to make but one voyage, to bring the negroes on shore privately, and divide them among their own plantations; and, in a word, the question was, whether I would go their supercargo in the ship, to manage the trading part upon the coast of Guinea; and they offered me that I should have my equal share of the negroes without providing any part of the stock.

This was a fair proposal, it must be confessed, had it been made to anyone that had not a settlement and plantation of his own to look after, which was in a fair way of coming to be very considerable, and with a good stock upon it. But for me, that was thus entered and established, and had nothing to do but go on as I had begun, for three or four years more, and to have sent for the other hundred pounds from England; and who, in that time, and with that little addition, could scarce have failed of being worth three or four thousand pounds sterling, and that increasing too – for me to think of such a voyage, was the most preposterous thing that ever man, in such circumstances, could be guilty of.

But I, that was born to be my own destroyer, could no more resist the offer than I could restrain my first rambling designs, when my father's good counsel was lost upon me. In a word, I told them I would go with all my heart, if they would undertake to look after my plantation in my absence, and would dispose of it to such as I should direct if I miscarried. This they all engaged to do, and entered into writings or covenants to do so; and I made a formal will disposing of my plantation and effects, in case of my death; making the captain of the ship that had saved my life, as before, my universal heir, but obliging him to dispose of my effects as I had directed in my will; one-half of the produce being to himself, and the other to be shipped to England.

In short, I took all possible caution to preserve my effects and keep up my plantation. Had I used half as much prudence to have looked into my own interest, and have made a judgment of what I ought to have done and not to have done, I had certainly never gone away from so prosperous an undertaking, leaving all the probable views of a thriving circumstance, and gone upon a voyage to sea, attended with all its common hazards, to say nothing of the reasons I had to expect particular misfortunes to myself.

But I was hurried on, and obeyed blindly the dictates of my fancy rather than my reason. And accordingly, the ship being fitted out, and the cargo furnished, and all things done as by agreement by my partners in the voyage, I went on board in an evil hour, the [first] of [September 1659], being the same day, eight year that I went from my father and mother at Hull, in order to act the rebel to their authority, and the fool to my own interest.

Our ship was about 120 tons burthen, carried six guns and fourteen men, besides the master, his boy, and myself. We had on board no large cargo of goods, except of such toys as were fit for our trade with the negroes – such as beads, bits of glass, shells, and odd trifles, especially little looking-glasses, knives, scissors, hatchets, and the like.

The same day I went on board we set sail, standing away to the northward upon our own coast, with design to stretch over for the African coast, when they came about 10 or 12 degrees of northern latitude, which, it seems, was the manner of their course in those days. We had very good weather, only excessivelyely hot, all the way upon our own coast, till we came to the height of Cape St. Augustino, from whence, keeping farther off at sea, we lost sight of land, and steered as if we were bound for the Isle Fernando de Noronha, holding our course N.E. by N., and leaving those isles on the east. In this course we passed the line in about twelve days' time, and were, by our last observation, in 7 degrees 22 minutes northern latitude, when a violent tornado, or hurricane, took us quite out of our knowledge. It began from the south-east, came about to the north-west, and then settled into the north-east, from whence it blew in such a terrible manner, that for twelve days together we could do nothing but drive, and, scudding away before it, let it carry us wherever fate and the fury of the winds directed; and during these twelve days, I need not say that I expected every day to be swallowed up, nor, indeed, did any in the ship expect to save their lives.

In this distress we had, besides the terror of the storm, one of our men died of the calenture, and one man and the boy washed overboard. About the twelfth day, the weather abating a little, the master made an observation as well as he could, and found that he was in about 11 degrees north latitude, but that he was 22 degrees of longitude difference west from Cape St. Augustino; so that he found he had gotten upon the coast of Guiana, or the north part of Brazil, beyond the river Amazon, toward that of the River Orinoco, commonly called the Great River, and began to consult with me what course he should take, for the ship was leaky and very much disabled, and he was going directly back to the coast of Brazil.

I was positively against that; and looking over the charts of the sea-coast of America with him, we concluded there was no inhabited country for us to have recourse to till we came within the circle of the Carribbee Islands, and, therefore resolved to stand away for Barbadoes, which by keeping off at sea, to avoid the in-draft of the Bay or Gulf of Mexico, we might easily perform, as we hoped, in about fifteen days' sail; whereas we could not possibly make our voyage to the coast of Africa without some assistance, both to our ship and to ourselves.

With this design we changed our course, and steered away N.W. by W. in order to reach some of our English islands, where I hoped for relief; but our voyage was otherwise determined; for being in the latitude of 12 degrees 18 minutes, a second storm came upon us, which carried us away with the same impetuosity westward, and drove us so out of the very way of all human commerce, that had all our lives been saved, as to the sea, we were rather in danger of being devoured by savages than ever returning to our own country.

In this distress, the wind still blowing very hard, one of our men early in the morning cried out, "Land!" and we had no sooner ran out of the cabin to look out, in the hopes of seeing whereabouts in the world we were, but the ship struck upon a sand, and in a moment, her motion being so stopped, the sea broke over her in such a manner, that we expected we should all have perished immediately; and we were immediately driven into our close quarters, to shelter us from the very foam and spray of the sea.

It is not easy for anyone, who has not been in the like condition, to describe or conceive the consternation of men in such circumstances. We knew nothing where we were, or upon what land it was we were driven, whether an island or the main, whether inhabited or not inhabited; and as the rage of the wind was still great, though rather less than at first, we could not so much as hope to have the ship hold many minutes without breaking in pieces, unless the winds, by a kind of miracle, should turn immediately about. In a word, we sat looking one upon another, and expecting death every moment, and every man acting accordingly, as preparing for another world; for there was little or nothing more for us to do in this. That which was our present comfort, and all the comfort we had, was that, contrary to our expectation, the ship did not break yet, and that the master said the wind began to abate.

Now, though we thought that the wind did a little abate, yet the ship having thus struck upon the sand, and sticking too fast for us to expect her getting off, we were in a dreadful condition indeed, and had nothing to do but to think of saving our lives as well as we could. We had a boat at our stern just before the storm, but she was first staved by dashing against the ship's rudder, and in the next place, she broke away, and either sunk, or was driven off to sea, so there was no hope from her; we had another boat on board, but how to get her off into the sea, was a doubtful thing. However, there was no room to debate, for we fancied the ship would break in pieces every minute, and some told us she was actually broken already.

In this distress, the mate of our vessel lays hold of the boat, and with the help of the rest of the men they got her slung over the ship's side; and getting all into her, let go, and committed ourselves, being eleven in number, to God's mercy, and the wild sea; for though the storm was abated considerably, yet the sea went dreadful high upon the shore, and might well be called *den wild zee,* as the Dutch call the sea in a storm.

And now our case was very dismal indeed, for we all saw plainly that the sea went so high, that the boat could not live, and that we should be inevitably drowned. As to making sail, we had none; nor, if we had, we could have done anything with it; so we worked at the oar towards the land, though with heavy hearts, like men going to execution, for we all knew that when the boat came nearer the shore, she would be dashed in a thousand pieces by the breach of the sea. However, we committed our souls to God in the most earnest manner; and the wind driving us towards the shore, we hastened our destruction with our own hands, pulling as well as we could towards land.

What the shore was, whether rock or sand, whether steep or shoal, we knew not; the only hope that could rationally give us the least shadow of expectation was, if we might happen into some bay or gulf, or the mouth of some river, where by great chance we might have run our boat in, or got under the lee of the land, and perhaps made smooth water. But nothing of this appeared; but as we made nearer and nearer the shore, the land looked more frightful than the sea.

After we had rowed, or rather driven, about a league and a half, as we reckoned it, a raging wave, mountainlike, came rolling astern of us, and plainly bade us expect the *coup de grace.* In a word, it took us with such a fury, that it overset the boat at once; and separating us, as well from the boat as from one another, gave us not time hardly to say, "O God!" for we were all swallowed up in a moment.

Nothing can describe the confusion of thought which I felt when I sunk into the water; for though I swam very well, yet I could not deliver myself from the waves so as to draw breath, till that wave having driven me, or rather carried me, a vast way on towards the shore, and having spent itself, went back, and left me upon the land almost dry, but half dead with the water I took in. I had so much presence of mind, as well as breath left, that seeing myself nearer the mainland than I expected, I got upon my feet, and endeavoured to make on towards the land as fast as I could, before another wave should return and take me up again. But I soon found it was impossible to avoid it; for I saw the sea come after me as high as a great hill, and as furious as an enemy, which I had no means or strength to contend with. My business was to hold my breath, and raise myself upon the water, if I could; and so, by swimming, to preserve my breathing, and pilot myself towards the shore, if possible; my greatest concern now being, that the sea, as it would carry me a great way towards the shore when it came on, might not carry me back again with it when it gave back towards the sea.

The wave that came upon me again, buried me at once 20 or 30 feet deep in its own body, and I could feel myself carried with a mighty force and swiftness towards the shore a very great way; but I held my breath, and assisted myself to swim still forward with all my might. I was ready to burst with holding my breath, when, as I felt myself rising up, so, to my immediate relief, I found my head and hands shoot out above the surface of the water; and though it was not two seconds of time that I could keep myself so, yet it relieved me greatly, gave me breath and new courage. I was covered again with water a good while, but not so long but I held it out; and finding the water had spent itself, and began to return, I struck forward against the return of the waves, and felt ground again with my feet. I stood still a few moments to recover breath, and till the water went from me, and then took to my heels and ran with what strength I had farther towards the shore. But neither would this deliver me from the fury of the sea, which came pouring in after me again, and twice more I was lifted up by the waves and carried forwards as before, the shore being very flat.

The last time of these two had well near been fatal to me; for the sea, having hurried me along as before, landed me, or rather dashed me, against a piece of a rock, and that with such force, as it left me senseless, and indeed helpless, as to my own deliverance; for the blow taking my side and breast, beat the breath as it were quite out of my body; and had it returned again immediately, I must have been strangled in the water. But I recovered a little before the return of the waves, and seeing I should be covered again with the water, I resolved to hold fast by a piece of the rock, and so to hold my breath, if possible, till the wave went back. Now as the waves were not so high as at first, being near land, I held my hold till the wave abated, and then fetched another run, which brought me so near the shore, that the next wave, though it went over me, yet did not so swallow me up as to carry me away, and the next run I took I got to the mainland, where, to my great comfort, I clambered up the cliffs of the shore, and sat down upon the grass, free from danger, and quite out of the reach of the water.

I was now landed, and safe on shore, and began to look up and thank God that my life was saved in a case wherein there was some minutes before scarce any room to hope. I believe it is impossible to express to the life what the ecstacies and transports of the soul are when it is so saved, as I may say, out of the very grave; and I do not wonder now at the custom, viz., that when a malefactor, who has the halter about his neck, is tied up, and just going to be turned off, and has a reprieve brought to him – I say, I do not wonder that they bring a surgeon with it, to let him blood that very moment they tell him of it, that the surprise may not drive the animal spirits from the heart, and overwhelm him:

For sudden joys, like griefs, confound at first.

I walked about on the shore, lifting up my hands, and my whole being, as I may say, wrapt up in the contemplation of my deliverance, making a thousand gestures and motions which I cannot describe, reflecting upon all my comrades that were drowned, and that there should not be one soul saved by myself; for, as for them, I never saw them afterwards, or any sign of them except three of their hats, one cap, and two shoes that were not fellows.

I cast my eyes to the stranded vessel, when the breach and froth of the sea being so big, I could hardly see it, it lay so far off, and considered, Lord! how was it possible I could get on shore?

After I had solaced my mind with the comfortable part of my condition, I began to look round me to see what kind of place I was in, and what was next to be done, and I soon found my comforts abate, and that, in a word, I had a dreadful deliverance;

for I was wet, had no clothes to shift me, nor anything either to eat or drink to comfort me, neither did I see any prospect before me but that of perishing with hunger, of being devoured by wild beasts; and that which was particularly afflicting to me was, that I had no weapon either to hunt and kill any creature for my sustenance, or to defend myself against any other creature that might desire to kill me for theirs. In a word, I had nothing about me but a knife, a tobacco-pipe, and a little tobacco in a box. This was all my provision; and this threw me into terrible agonies of mind, that for a while I ran about like a madman. Night coming upon me, I began, with a heavy heart, to consider what would be my lot if there were any ravenous beasts in that country, seeing at night they always come abroad for their prey.

All the remedy that offered to my thoughts at that time was to get up into a thick bushy tree like a fir, but thorny, which grew near me, and where I resolved to sit all night, and consider the next day what death I should die, for as yet I saw no prospect of life. I walked about a furlong from the shore, to see if I could find any fresh water to drink, which I did, to my great joy; and having drank, and put a little tobacco in my mouth to prevent hunger, I went to the tree, and getting up into it, endeavoured to place myself so, as that if I should sleep I might not fall; and having cut me a short stick, like a truncheon, for my defence, I took up my lodging, and having been excessively fatigued, I fell fast asleep, and slept as comfortably as, I believe, few could have done in my condition, and found myself the most refreshed with it that I think I ever was on such an occasion.

When I waked it was broad day, the weather clear, and the storm abated, so that the sea did not rage and swell as before. But that which surprised me most was, that the ship was lifted off in the night from the sand where she lay, by the swelling of the tide, and was driven up almost as far as the rock which I first mentioned, where I had been so bruised by the dashing me against it. This being within about a mile from the shore where I was, and the ship seeming to stand upright still, I wished myself on board, that, at least, I might have some necessary things for my use.

When I came down from my apartment in the tree I looked about me again, and the first thing I found was the boat, which lay as the wind and the sea had tossed her up upon the land, about two miles on my right hand. I walked as far as I could upon the shore to have got to her, but found a neck or inlet of water between me and the boat, which was about half a mile broad; so I came back for the present, being more intent upon getting at the ship, where I hoped to find something for my present subsistence.

A little after noon I found the sea very calm, and the tide ebbed so far out, that I could come within a quarter of a mile of the ship; and here I found a fresh renewing of my grief, for I saw evidently, that if we had kept on board we had been all safe, that is to say, we had all got safe on shore, and I had not been so miserable as to be left entirely destitute of all comfort and company, as I now was. This forced tears from my eyes again; but as there was little relief in that, I resolved, if possible, to get to the ship; so I pulled off my clothes, for the weather was hot to extremity, and took the water. But when I came to the ship, my difficulty was still greater to know how to get on board; for as she lay aground, and high out of the water, there was nothing within my reach to lay hold of. I swam around her twice, and the second time I spied a small piece of rope, which I wondered I did not see at first, hang down by the fore-chains so low, as that with great difficulty I got hold of it, and by the help of that rope got up into the forecastle of the ship. Here I found that the ship was bulged, and had a great deal of water in her hold, but that she lay so on the side of a bank of hard sand, or rather earth, that her stern lay lifted up upon the bank, and her head low almost to the water. By this means all her quarter was free, and all that was in that part was dry; for you may be sure my first work was to search and to see what was spoiled and what was free. And first I found that all the ship's provisions were dry and untouched by the water; and being very well disposed to eat, I went to the bread-room and filled my pockets with biscuit, and eat it as I went about other things, for I had no time to lose. I also found some rum in the great cabin, of which I took a large dram, and which I had indeed need enough of to spirit me for what was before me. Now I wanted nothing but a boat, to furnish myself with many things which I foresaw would be very necessary for me.

It was in vain to sit still and wish for what was not to be had, and this extremity roused my application. We had several spare yards, and two or three large spars of wood, and a spare top-mast or two in the ship. I resolved to fall to work with these, and flung as many of them overboard as I could manage for their weight, tying every one with a rope, that they might not drive away. When this was done I went down the ship's side, and, pulling them to me, I tied four of them fast together at both ends as well as I could, in the form of a raft; and laying two or three short pieces of plank upon them, crossways, I found I could walk upon it very well, but that it was not able to bear any great weight, the pieces being too light. So I went to work, and with the carpenter's saw I cut up a spare topmast into three lengths, and added them to my raft, with a great deal of labour and pains; but hope of furnishing myself with necessaries encouraged me to go beyond what I should have been able to have done upon another occasion.

My raft was now strong enough to bear any reasonable weight. My next care was what to load it with, and how to preserve what I laid upon it from the surf of the sea; but I was not long considering this. I first laid all the planks or boards upon it that I could get, and having considered well what I most wanted, I first got three of the seamen's chests, which I had broken open and emptied, and lowered them down upon my raft. The first of these I filled with provisions, viz., bread, rice, three Dutch cheeses, five pieces of dried goat's flesh, which we lived much upon, and a little remainder of European corn, which had been laid by for some fowls which we brought to sea with us, but the fowls were killed. There had been some barley and wheat together, but, to my great disappointment, I found afterwards that the rats had eaten or spoiled it all. As for liquors, I found several cases of bottles belonging to our skipper, in which were some cordial waters, and, in all, about five or six gallons of rack. These I stowed by themselves, there being no need to put them into the chest, nor no room for them. While I was doing this, I found the tide began to flow, though very calm, and I had the mortification to see my coat, shirt, and waistcoat, which I had left on shore upon the sand, swim away; as for my breeches, which were only linen, and open-kneed, I swam on board in them, and my stockings. However, this put me upon rummaging for clothes, of which I found enough, but took no more than I wanted for present use; for I had other things which my eye was more upon, as first tools to work with on shore; and it was after long searching that I found out the carpenter's chest, which was indeed a very useful prize to me, and much more valuable than a ship-loading of gold would have been at that time. I got it down to my raft, even whole as it was, without losing time to look into it, for I knew in general what it contained.

My next care was for some ammunition and arms; there were two very good fowling-pieces in the great cabin, and two pistols; these I secured first, with some powder-horns, and a small bag of shot, and two old rusty swords. I knew there were three barrels of powder in the ship, but knew not where our gunner had stowed them; but with much search I found them, two of them dry and good, the third had taken water; those two I got to my raft with the arms. And now I thought myself pretty well freighted, and began to think how I should get to shore with them, having neither sail, oar, nor rudder; and the least capful of wind would have overset all my navigation.

I had three encouragements.

1. A smooth, calm sea.
2. The tide rising and setting in to the shore.
3. What little wind there was blew me towards the land.

And thus, having found two or three broken oars belonging to the boat, and besides the tools which were in the chest, I found two saws, an axe, and a hammer, and with this cargo I put to sea. For a mile or thereabouts my raft went very well, only that I found it drive a little distant from the place where I had landed before, by which I perceived that there was some in-draft of the water, and consequently I hoped to find some creek or river there, which I might make use of as a port to get to land with my cargo.

As I imagined, so it was; there appeared before me a little opening of the land, and I found a strong current of the tide set into it, so I guided my raft as well as I could to keep in the middle of the stream. But here I had like to have suffered a second shipwreck, which, if I had, I think verily would have broke my heart; for knowing nothing of the coast, my raft ran aground at one end of it upon a shoal, and not being aground at the other end, it wanted but a little that all my cargo had slipped off towards that end that was afloat, and so fallen into the water. I did my utmost by setting my back against the chests to keep them in their places, but could not thrust off the raft with all my strength, neither could I stir from the posture I was in, but holding up the chests with all my might, stood in that manner nearly half an hour in which time the rising of the water brought me a little more upon a level; and a little after, the water still rising, my raft floated again, and I thrust her off with the oar I had into the channel, and then driving up higher, I at length found myself in the mouth of a little river, with land on both sides, and a strong current or tide running up. I looked on both sides for a proper place to get to shore, for I was not willing to be driven too high up the river, hoping in time to see some ship at sea, and therefore resolved to place myself as near to the coast as I could.

At length I spied a little cove on the right shore of the creek, to which, with great pain and difficulty, I guided my raft, and at last got so near, as that, reaching ground with my oar, I could thrust her directly in; but here I had like to have dipped all my cargo in the sea again; for that shore lying pretty steep, that is to say, sloping, there was no place to land but where one end of my float, if it run on shore, would lie so high and the other sink lower, as before, that it would endanger my cargo again. All that I could do was to wait till the tide was at the highest, keeping the raft with my oar like an anchor to hold the side of it fast to the shore, near a flat piece of ground, which I expected the water would flow over; and so it did. As soon as I found water enough, for my raft drew about a foot of water, I thrust her on upon that flat piece of ground, and there fastened or moored her by sticking my two broken oars into the ground; one on one side near the end, and one on the other side near the other end; and thus I lay till the water ebbed away, and left my raft and all my cargo safe on shore.

My next work was to view the country and seek a proper place for my habitation, and where to stow my goods to secure them from whatever might happen. Where I was, I yet knew not; whether on the continent, or on an island; whether inhabited, or not inhabited; whether in danger of wild beasts, or not. There was a hill, not above a mile from me, which rose up very steep and high, and which seemed to over-top some other hills, which lay as in a ridge from it, northward. I took out one of the fowling-pieces and one of the pistols, and a horn of powder; and thus armed, I travelled for discovery up to the top of that hill, where, after I had with great labour and difficulty got to the top, I saw my fate to my great affliction, viz., that I was in an island environed every way with the sea, no land to be seen, except some rocks which lay a great way off, and two small islands less than this, which lay about three leagues to the west.

I found also that the island I was in was barren, and, as I saw good reason to believe, uninhabited, except by wild beasts, of whom, however, I saw none; yet I saw abundance of fowls, but knew not their kind; neither when I killed them, could I tell what was fit for food, and what not. At my coming back, I shot at a great bird which I saw sitting upon a tree on the side of a great wood. I believe it was the first gun that had been fired there since the creation of the world. I had no sooner fired, but from all the parts of the wood there arose an innumerable number of fowls of many sorts, making a confused screaming, and crying, every one according to his usual note; but not one of them of any kind that I knew. As for the creature I killed I took it to be a kind of a hawk, its colour and beak resembling it, but had no talons or claws more than common; its flesh was carrion, and fit for nothing.

Contented with this discovery, I came back to my raft, and fell to work to bring my cargo on shore, which took me up the rest of that day; and what to do with myself at night, I knew not, or, indeed where to rest; for I was afraid to lie down on the ground, not knowing but some wild beast might devour me, though, as I afterwards found, there was really no need for those fears. However, as well as I could, I barricaded myself round with the chests and boards that I had brought on shore, and made a kind of a hut for that night's lodging; as for food, I yet saw not which way to supply myself, except that I had seen two or three creatures like hares run out of the wood where I shot the fowl.

I now began to consider that I might yet get a great many things out of the ship, which would be useful to me, and particularly some of the rigging and sails, and such other things as might come to land; and I resolved to make another voyage on board the vessel, if possible. And as I knew that the first storm that blew must necessarily break her all in pieces, I resolved to set all other things apart till I got everything out of the ship that I could get. Then I called a council, that is to say, in my thoughts, whether I should take back the raft, but this appeared impracticable; so I resolved to go as before, when the tide was down: and I did so, only that I stripped before I went from my hut, having nothing on but a chequered shirt and a pair of linen drawers, and a pair of pumps on my feet.

I got on board the ship as before, and prepared a second raft, and having had experience of the first, I neither made this so unwieldy, nor loaded it so hard; but yet I brought away several things very useful to me; as, at first, in the carpenter's stores I found two or three bags full of nails and spikes, a great screw-jack, a dozen or two of hatchets, and above all, that most useful thing called a grindstone. All these I secured, together with several things belonging to the gunner, particularly two or three iron crows, and two barrels of musket bullets, seven muskets, and another fowling-piece, with some small quantity of powder more; a large bag full of small-shot, and a great roll of sheet lead; but this last was so heavy, I could not hoist it up to get it over the ship's side. Besides these things, I took all the men's clothes that I could find, and a spare fore-top sail, a hammock, and some bedding; and with this I loaded my second raft, and brought them all safe on shore, to my very great comfort.

I was under some apprehensions during my absence from the land, that at least my provisions might be devoured on shore; but when I came back, I found no sign of any visitor, only there sat a creature like a wild cat upon one of the chests, which, when I came towards it, ran away a little distance, and then stood still. She sat very composed and unconcerned, and looked full in my face, as if she had a mind to be acquainted with me. I presented my gun at her; but as she did not understand it, she was perfectly unconcerned at it, nor did she offer to stir away; upon which I tossed her a bit of biscuit, though, by the way, I was not very free of it, for my store was not great. However, I spared her a bit, I say, and she went to it, smelled of it, and ate it, and looked (as pleased) for more; but I thanked her, and could spare no more, so she marched off.

Having got my second cargo on shore, though I was fain to open the barrels of powder and bring them by parcels, for they were too heavy, being large casks, I went to work to make me a little tent with the sail and some poles which I cut for that purpose; and into this tent I brought everything that I knew would spoil either with rain or sun; and I piled all the empty chests and casks up in a circle round the tent, to fortify it from any sudden attempt, either from man or beast.

When I had done this, I blocked up the door of the tent with some boards within, and an empty chest set up on end without; and spreading one of the beds upon the ground, laying my two pistols just at my head, and my gun at length by me, I went to bed for the first time, and slept very quietly all night, for I was very weary and heavy; for the night before I had slept little, and had laboured very hard all day, as well to fetch all those things from the ship, as to get them on shore.

I had the biggest magazine of all kinds now that ever was laid up, I believe, for one man; but I was not satisfied still, for while the ship sat upright in that posture, I thought I ought to get everything out of her that I could. So every day at low water I went on board, and brought away something or other; but, particularly the third time I went I brought away as much of the rigging as I could, as also all the small ropes and rope-twine I could get, with a piece of spare canvas, which was to mend the sails upon occasion, the barrel of wet gunpowder; in a word, I brought away all the sails first and last, only that I was fain to cut them in pieces, and bring as much at a time as I could; for they were no more useful to be sails, but as mere canvas only.

But that which comforted me more still was, that at last of all, after I had made five or six such voyages as these, and thought I had nothing more to expect from the ship that was worth my meddling with; I say, after all this, I found a great hogshead of bread, and three large runlets of rum or spirits, and a box of sugar, and a barrel of fine flour; this was surprising to me, because I had given over expecting any more provisions, except what was spoilt by the water. I soon emptied the hogshead of that bread, and wrapped it up parcel by parcel in pieces of the sails, which I cut out; and, in a word, I got all this safe on shore also.

The next day I made another voyage. And now, having plundered the ship of what was portable and fit to hand out, I began with the cables; and cutting the great cable into pieces, such as I could move, I got two cables and a hawser on shore, with all the iron-work I could get; and having cut down the sprit-sail yard, and the mizzen-yard, and everything I could to make a large raft, I loaded it with all those heavy goods, and came away. But my good luck began now to leave me; for this raft was so unwieldy, and so overladen, that after I was entered the little cove where I had landed the rest of my goods, not being able to guide it so handily as I did the other, it overset, and threw me and all my cargo into the water. As for myself, it was no great harm, for I was near the shore; but as to my cargo, it was great part of it lost, especially the iron, which I expected would have been great use to me. However, when the tide was out I got most of the pieces of cable ashore, and some of the iron, though with infinite labour; for I was fain to dip for it into the water, a work which fatigued me very much. After this I went every day on board, and brought away what I could get.

I had been now thirteen days on shore, and had been eleven times on board the ship; in which time I had brought away all that one pair of hands could well be supposed capable to bring, though I believe verily, had the calm weather held, I should have brought away the whole ship piece by piece. But preparing the twelfth time to go on board, I found the wind begin to rise. However, at low water I went on board, and though I thought I had rummaged the cabin so effectually as that nothing more could be found, yet I discovered a locker with drawers in it, in one of which I found two or three razors, and one pair of large scissors, with some ten or a dozen of good knives and forks; in another, I found about thirty-six pounds value in money, some European coin, some Brazil, some pieces of eight, some gold, some silver.

I smiled to myself at the sight of this money. "O drug!" said I aloud, "what art thou good for? Thou art not worth to me, no, not the taking off of the ground; one of those knives is worth all this heap. I have no manner of use for thee; even remain where thou art, and go to the bottom as a creature whose life is not worth saving." However, upon second thoughts, I took it away; and wrapping all this in a piece of canvas, I began to think of making another raft; but while I was preparing this, I found the sky overcast, and the wind began to rise, and in a quarter of an hour it blew a fresh gale from the shore. It presently occurred to me that it was in vain to pretend to make a raft with the wind off shore, and that it was my business to be gone before the tide of flood began, otherwise I might not be able to reach the shore at all. Accordingly I let myself down into the water, and swam across the channel, which lay between the ship and the sands, and even that with difficulty enough, partly with the weight of the things I had about me, and partly the roughness of the water; for the wind rose very hastily, and before it was quite high water it blew a storm.

But I was gotten home to my little tent, where I lay with all my wealth about me very secure. It blew very hard all that night, and in the morning, when I looked out, behold, no more ship was to be seen. I was a little surprised, but recovered myself with this satisfactory reflection, viz., that I had lost no time, nor abated no diligence, to get everything out of her that could be useful to me, and that indeed there was little left in her that I was able to bring away if I had had more time.

I now gave over any more thoughts of the ship, or of anything out of her, except what might drive on shore from her wreck, as indeed divers pieces of her afterwards did; but those things were of small use to me.

My thoughts were now wholly employed about securing myself against either savages, if any should appear, or wild beasts, if any were in the island; and I had many thoughts of the method how to do this, and what kind of dwelling to make, whether I should make me a cave in the earth, or a tent upon the earth; and, in short, I resolved upon both, the manner and description of which it may not be improper to give an account of.

I soon found the place I was in was not for my settlement, particularly because it was upon a low moorish ground near the sea, and I believed would not be wholesome; and more particularly because there was no fresh water near it. So I resolved to find a more healthy and more convenient spot of ground.

I consulted several things in my situation, which I found would be proper for me. First, health and fresh water, I just now mentioned. Secondly, shelter from the heat of the sun. Thirdly, security from ravenous creatures, whether men or beasts. Fourthly, a view to the sea, that if God sent any ship in sight I might not lose any advantage for my deliverance, of which I was not willing to banish all my expectation yet.

In search of a place proper for this, I found a little plain on the side of a rising hill, whose front towards this little plain was steep as a houseside, so that nothing could come down upon me from the top; on the side of this rock there was a hollow place, worn a little way in, like the entrance or door of a cave; but there was not really any cave, or way into the rock at all.

On the flat of the green, just before this hollow place, I resolved to pitch my tent. This plain was not above a hundred yards broad, and about twice as long, and lay like a green before my door, and at the end of it descended irregularly every way down into the low grounds by the seaside. It was on the N.N.W. side of the hill, so that I was sheltered from the heat every day, till it came to a W. and by S. sun, or thereabouts, which in those countries is near setting.

Before I set up my tent, I drew a half circle before the hollow place, which took in about ten yards in its semi-diameter from the rock, and twenty yards in its diameter from its beginning and ending. In this half-circle I pitched two rows of strong stakes, driving them into the ground till they stood very firm like piles, the biggest end being out of the ground about five feet and a half, and sharpened on the top. The two rows did not stand above six inches from one another.

Then I took the pieces of cable which I had cut in the ship, and laid them in rows one upon another, within the circle, between these two rows of stakes, up to the top, placing other stakes in the inside leaning against them, about two feet and a half high, like a spur to a post; and this fence was so strong, that neither man or beast could get into it, or over it. This cost me a great deal of time and labour, especially to cut the piles in the woods, bring them to the place, and drive them into the earth.

The entrance into this place I made to be not by a door, but by a short ladder to go over the top; which ladder, when I was in, I lifted over after me, and so I was completely fenced in, and fortified, as I thought, from all the world, and consequently slept secure in the night, which otherwise I could not have done; though as it appeared afterwards, there was no need of all this caution from the enemies that I apprehended danger from.

Into this fence or fortress, with infinite labour, I carried all my riches, all my provisions, ammunition, and stores, of which you have the account above; and I made me a large tent, which, to preserve me from the rains that in one part of the year are very violent there, I made double, viz., one smaller tent within, and one larger tent above it, and covered the uppermost with a large tarpaulin, which I had saved among the sails. And now I lay no more for a while in the bed which I had brought on shore, but in a hammock, which was indeed a very good one, and belonged to the mate of the ship.

Into this tent I brought all my provisions, and everything that would spoil by the wet; and having thus enclosed all my goods I made up the entrance, which, till now, I had left open, and so passed and repassed, as I said, by a short ladder.

When I had done this, I began to work my way into the rock; and bringing all the earth and stones that I dug down out through my tent, I laid them up within my fence in the nature of a terrace, so that it raised the ground within about a foot and a half; and thus I made me a cave just behind my tent, which served me like a cellar to my house.

It cost me much labour, and many days, before all these things were brought to perfection, and therefore I must go back to some other things which took up some of my thoughts. At the same time it happened, after I had laid my scheme for the setting up of my tent, and making the cave, that a storm of rain falling from a thick dark cloud, a sudden flash of lightning happened, and after that a great clap of thunder, as is naturally the effect of it. I was not so much surprised with the lightning, as I was with a thought which darted into my mind as swift as the lightning itself. O my powder! My very heart sunk within me when I thought that at one blast all my powder might be destroyed, on which, not my defence only, but the providing me food, as I thought, entirely depended. I was nothing near so anxious about my own danger; though had the powder took fire, I had never known who had hurt me.

Such impression did this make upon me, that after the storm was over I laid aside all my works, my building, and fortifying, and applied myself to make bags and boxes to separate the powder, and keep it a little and a little in a parcel, in hope that whatever might come it might not all take fire at once, and to keep it so apart that it should not be possible to make one part fire another.

I finished this work in about a fortnight; and I think my powder, which in all was about 240 pounds weight, was divided in not less than a hundred parcels. As to the barrel that had been wet, I did not apprehend any danger from that, so I placed it in my new cave, which in my fancy I called my kitchen, and the rest I hid up and down and in holes among the rocks, so that no wet might come to it, marking very carefully where I laid it.

In the interval of time while this was doing, I went out once, at least, every day with my gun, as well to divert myself, as to see if I could kill anything fit for food, and as near as I could to acquaint myself with what the island produced. The first time I went out, I presently discovered that there were goats in the island, which was a great satisfaction to me; but then it was attended with this misfortune to me, viz., that they were so shy, so subtle, and so swift of foot, that it was the difficultest thing in the world to come near them. But I was not discouraged at this, not doubting but I might now and then shoot one, as it soon happened; for after I had found their haunts a little, I laid wait in this manner for them. I observed if they saw me in the valleys, though they were upon the rocks, they would run away as in a terrible fright; but if they were feeding in the valleys, and I was upon the rocks, they took no notice of me, from whence I concluded that, by the position of their optics, their sight was so directed downward, that they did not readily see objects that were above them. So afterward I took this method: I always climbed the rocks first to get above them, and then had frequently a fair mark. The first shot I made among these creatures I killed a she-goat, which had a little kid by her, which she gave suck to, which grieved me heartily; but when the old one fell, the kid stood stock still by her till I came and took her up; and not only so, but when I carried the old one with me upon my shoulders, the kid followed me quite to my enclosure; upon which I laid down the dam, and took the kid in my arms, and carried it over my pale, in hopes to have breed it up tame; but it would not eat, so I was forced to kill it, and eat it myself. These two supplied me with flesh a great while, for I eat sparingly, and saved my provisions, my bread especially, as much as possibly I could.

Having now fixed my habitation, I found it absolutely necessary to provide a place to make a fire in, and fuel to burn; and what I did for that, as also how I enlarged my cave, and what conveniences I made, I shall give a full account of in its place. But I must first give some little account of myself, and of my thoughts about living, which it may well be supposed were not a few.

I had a dismal prospect of my condition; for as I was not cast away upon that island without being driven, as is said, by a violent storm, quite out of the course of our intended voyage, and a great way, viz., some hundreds of leagues out of the ordinary course of the trade of mankind, I had great reason to consider it as a determination of Heaven, that in this desolate place, and in this desolate manner, I should end my life. The tears would run plentifully down my face when I made these reflections, and sometimes I would expostulate with myself, why Providence should thus completely ruin its creatures, and render them so absolutely miserable, so without help abandoned, so entirely depressed, that it could hardly be rational to be thankful for such a life.

But something always returned swift upon me to check these thoughts, and to reprove me; and particularly one day, walking with my gun in my hand by the seaside, I was very pensive upon the subject of my present condition, when Reason, as it were, expostulated with me t'other way, thus: "Well, you are in a desolate condition it is true, but pray remember, where are the rest of you? Did not you come eleven of you in the boat? Where are the ten? Why were not they saved, and you lost? Why were you singled out? Is it better to be here, or there?" And then I pointed to the sea. All evils are to be considered with the good that is in them, and with what worse attends them.

Then it occurred to me again, how well I was furnished for my subsistence, and what would have been my case if it had not happened, which was an hundred thousand to one, that the ship had floated from the place where she first struck and was driven so near to the shore that I had time to get all these things out of her; what would have been my case, if I had been to have lived in the condition in which I at first came on shore, without necessaries of life, or necessaries to supply and procure them? "Particularly," said I aloud (though to myself), "what should I have done without a gun, without ammunition, without any tools to make anything or to work with, without clothes, bedding, a tent, or any manner of covering?" and that now I had all these to a sufficient quantity, and was in a fair way to provide myself in such a manner, as to live without my gun when my ammunition was spent; so that I had a tolerable view of subsisting without any want as long as I lived. For I considered from the beginning how I would provide for the accidents that might happen, and for the time that was to come, even not only after my ammunition should be spent, but even after my health or strength should decay.

I confess I had not entertained any notion of my ammunition being destroyed at one blast – I mean, my powder being blown up by lightning; and this made the thoughts of it so surprising to me when it lightened and thundered, as I observed just now.

And now being to enter into a melancholy relation of a scene of silent life, such, perhaps, as was never heard of in the world before, I shall take it from its beginning and continue it in its order. It was by my account, the 30th of September when, in the manner as above said, I first set foot upon this horrid island, when the sun being to us in its autumnal equinox, was almost just over my head, for I reckoned myself, by observation, to be in the latitude of 9 degrees 22 minutes north of the line.

After I had been there about ten or twelve days it came into my thoughts that I should lose my reckoning of time for want of books and pen and ink, and should even forget the Sabbath days from the working days; but to prevent this, I cut it with my knife upon a large post, in capital letters; and making it into a great cross, I set it up on the shore where I first landed, viz., "I came on shore here the 30th of September 1659." Upon the sides of this square post I cut every day a notch with my knife, and every seventh notch was as long again as the rest, and every first day of the month as long again as that long one; and thus I kept my calendar, or weekly, monthly, and yearly reckoning of time.

In the next place we are to observe that among the many things which I brought out of the ship in the several voyages, which, as above mentioned, I made to it, I got several things of less value, but not all less useful to me, which I omitted setting down before; as in particular, pens, ink, and paper, several parcels in the captain's, mate's, gunner's, and carpenter's keeping, three or four compasses, some mathematical instruments, dials, perspectives, charts, and books of navigation, all of which I huddled together, whether I might want them or no. Also I found three very good Bibles, which came to me in my cargo from England and which I had packed up among my things; some Portuguese books, also, and among them two or three Popish prayer-books, and several other books, all of which I carefully secured. And I must not forget, that we had in the ship a dog and two cats, of whose eminent history I may have occasion to say something in its place; for I carried both the cats with me; and as for the dog he jumped out of the ship himself, and swam on shore to me the day after I went on shore with my first cargo, and was a trusty servant to me many years. I wanted nothing that he could fetch me, nor any company that he could make up to me; I only wanted to have him talk to me, but that would not do. As I observed before, I found pen, ink, and paper, and I husbanded them to the utmost; and I shall show that while my ink lasted, I kept things very exact; but after that was gone, I could not, for I could not make any ink by any means that I could devise.

And this put me in mind that I wanted many things, notwithstanding all that I had amassed together; and of these, this of ink was one, as also spade, pick-axe, and shovel, to dig or remove the earth, needles, pins, and thread; as for linen, I soon learned to want that without much difficulty.

This want of tools made every work I did go on heavily; and it was near a whole year before I had entirely finished my little pale or surrounded habitation. The piles or stakes, which were as heavy as I could well lift, were a long time in cutting and preparing in the woods, and more by far in bringing home; so that I spent sometimes two days in cutting and bringing home one of those posts, and a third day in driving it into the ground; for which purpose I got a heavy piece of wood at first, but at last bethought myself of one of the iron crows, which, however, though I found it, yet it made driving those posts or piles very laborious and tedious work.

But what need I have been concerned at the tediousness of anything I had to do, seeing I had time enough to do it in? nor had I any other employment, if that had been over, at least, that I could foresee, except the ranging the island to seek for food, which I did more or less every day.

I now began to consider seriously my condition, and the circumstance I was reduced to; and I drew up the state of my affairs in writing; not so much to leave them to any that were to come after me, for I was likely to have but few heirs, as to deliver my thoughts from daily poring upon them, and afflicting my mind. And as my reason began now to master my despondency, I began to comfort myself as well as I could, and to set the good against the evil, that I might have something to distinguish my case from worse; and I stated it very impartially, like a debtor and creditor, the comforts I enjoyed against the miseries I suffered, thus:

Evil	*Good*
I am cast upon a horrible desolate island, void of all hope of recovery.	But I am alive, and not drowned, as all my ship's company was.
I am singled out and separated, as it were, from all the world, to be miserable.	But I am singled out, too, from all the ship's crew to be spared from death; and He that miraculously saved me from death, can deliver me from this condition.
I am divided from mankind, a solitaire, one banished from human society.	But I am not starved and perishing on a barren place, affording no sustenance.
I have no clothes to cover me.	But I am in a hot climate, where if I had clothes I could hardly wear them.
I am without any defence or means to resist any violence of man or beast.	But I am cast on an island, where I see no wild beasts to hurt me, as I saw on the coast of Africa; and what if I had been shipwrecked there?
I have no soul to speak to, or relieve me.	But God wonderfully sent the ship in near enough to the shore, that I have gotten out so many necessary things as will either supply my wants, or enable me to supply myself even as long as I live.

Upon the whole, here was an undoubted testimony, that there was scarce any condition in the world so miserable, but there was something negative or something positive to be thankful for in it; and let this stand as a direction from the experience of the most miserable of all conditions in this world, that we may always find in it something to comfort ourselves from, and to set in the description of good and evil on the credit side of the account.

Having now brought my mind a little to relish my condition, and given overlooking out to sea, to see if I could spy a ship; I say, giving over these things, I began to apply myself to accomodate my way of living, and to make things as easy to me as I could.

I have already described my habitation, which was a tent under the side of a rock, surrounded with a strong pale of posts and cables; but I might now rather call it a wall, for I raised a kind of wall up against it of turfs, about two feet thick on the outside, and after some time – I think it was a year and a half – I raised rafters from it leading to the rock, and thatched or covered it with boughs of trees and such things as I could get to keep out the rain, which I found at some times of the year very violent.

I have already observed how I brought all my goods into this pale, and into the cave which I had made behind me. But I must observe, too, that at first this was a confused heap of goods, which as they lay in no order, so they took up all my place; I had no room to turn myself. So I set myself to enlarge my cave and works farther into the earth; for it was a loose sandy rock which yielded easily to the labour I bestowed on it. And so, when I found I was pretty safe as to beasts of prey, I worked sideways to the right hand into the rock; and then, turning to the right again, working quite out, and made me a door to come out on the outside of my pale or fortification. This gave me not only egress and regress, as it were a back-way to my tent and to my storehouse, but gave me room to stow my goods.

And now I began to apply myself to make such necessary

things as I found I most wanted, as particularly a chair and a table; for without these I was not able to enjoy the few comforts I had in the world. I could not write or eat, or do several things with so much pleasure without a table.

So I went to work: and here I must observe, that as reason is the substance and original of the mathematics, so by stating and squaring everything by reason, and by making the most rational judgment of things, every man may be in time master of every mechanic art. I had never handled a tool in my life; and yet in time, by labour, application, and contrivance, I found at last that I wanted nothing but I could have made it, especially if I had had more tools. However, I made abundance of things even without tools, and some with no more tools than an adze and a hatchet, which, perhaps, were never made that way before, and that with infinite labour. For example, if I wanted a board, I had no other way but to cut down a tree, set it on an edge before me, and hew it flat on either side with my axe, till I had brought it to be thick as a plank, and then dub it smooth with my adze. It is true, by this method I could make but one board out of a whole tree; but this I had no remedy for but patience, any more than I had for the prodigious deal of time and labour which it took me up to make a plank or board. But my time or labour was little worth, and so it was as well employed one way as another.

However, I made me a table and a chair, as I observed above, in the first place, and this I did out of the short pieces of boards that I brought on my raft from the ship. But when I had wrought out some boards, as above, I made large shelves of the breadth of a foot and a half one over another, all along one side of my cave, to lay all my tools, nails, and iron-work; and, in a word, to separate everything at large in their places, that I might come easily at them. I knocked pieces into the wall of the rock to hang my guns and all things that would hang up; so that had my cave been to be seen, it looked like a general magazine of all necessary things; and I had everything so ready at my hand, that it was a great pleasure to me to see all my goods in such order, and especially to find my stock of all necessaries so great.

And now it was when I began to keep a journal of every day's employment; for, indeed, at first, I was in too much hurry, and not only hurry as to labour, but in too much discomposure of mind; and my journal would have been full of many dull things. For example, I must have said thus: *Sept. the 30th.*– After I got to shore, and had escaped drowning, instead of being thankful to God for my deliverance, having first vomited with the great quantity of salt water which had gotten into my stomach, and recovering myself a little, I ran about the shore, wringing my hands, and beating my head and face, exclaiming at my misery, and crying out, I was undone, undone, till, tired and faint, I was forced to lie down on the ground to repose; but durst not sleep, for fear of being devoured.

Some days after this, and after I had been on board the ship, and got all that I could out of her, yet I could not forbear getting up to the top of a little mountain, and looking out to sea, in hopes of seeing a ship; then fancy at a vast distance I spied a sail, please myself with the hopes of it, and then, after looking steadily till I was almost blind, lose it quite, and sit down and weep like a child, and thus increase my misery by my folly.

But having gotten over these things in some measure, and having settled my household stuff and habitation, made me a table and a chair, and all as handsome about me as I could, I began to keep my journal, of which I shall here give you the copy (though in it will be told all these particulars over again) as long as it lasted; for, having no more ink, I was forced to leave it off.

The Journal

SEPTEMBER 30, 1659. – I, poor miserable Robinson Crusoe, being shipwrecked, during a dreadful storm, in the offing, came on shore in this dismal unfortunate island, which I called the Island of Despair, all the rest of the ship's company being drowned, and myself almost dead.

All the rest of that day I spent in afflicting myself at the dismal circumstances I was brought to, viz., I had neither food, house, clothes, weapon, or place to fly to; and in despair of any relief, saw nothing but death before me; either that I should be devoured by wild beasts, murdered by savages, or starved to death for want of food. At the approach of night, I slept in a tree for fear of wild creatures, but slept soundly, though it rained all night.

October 1. – In the morning I saw, to my great surprise, the ship had floated with the high tide, and was driven on shore again 0much nearer the island; which, as it was some comfort on one hand, for seeing her sit upright, and not broken to pieces, I hoped, if the wind abated, I might get on board, and get some food and necessaries out of her for my relief; so, on the other hand, it renewed my grief at the loss of my comrades, who, I imagined, if we had all stayed on board, might have saved the ship, or at least that they would not have been all drowned as they were; and that had the men been saved, we might perhaps have built us a boat out of the ruins of the ship, to have carried us to some other part of the world. I spent great part of this day in perplexing myself on these things; but at length seeing the ship almost dry, I went upon the sand as near as I could, and then swam on board; this day also it continued raining, though with no wind at all.

From the 1st of October to the 24th. – All these days entirely spent in many several voyages to get all I could out of the ship, which I brought on shore, every tide of flood, upon rafts. Much rain also in these days, though with some intervals of fair weather; but, it seems, this was the rainy season.

October 20. – I overset my raft, and all the goods I had got upon it; but being in shoal water, and the things being chiefly heavy, I recovered many of them when the tide was out.

October 25. – It rained all night and all day, with some gusts of wind, during which time the ship broke in pieces, the wind blowing a little harder than before, and was no more to be seen, except the wreck of her, and that only at low water. I spent this day in covering and securing the goods which I had saved, that the rain might not spoil them.

October 26. – I walked about the shore almost all day to find out a place to fix my habitation, greatly concerned to secure myself from an attack in the night, either from wild beasts or men. Towards night I fixed upon a proper place under a rock, and marked out a semicircle for my encampment, which I resolved to strengthen with a work, wall, or fortification made of double piles, lined within with cables, and without with turf.

From the 26th to the 30th I worked very hard in carrying all my goods to my new habitation, though some part of the time it rained exceeding hard.

The 31st, in the morning, I went out into the island with my gun to see for some food, and discover the country; when I killed a she-goat, and her kid followed me home, which I afterwards killed also, because it would not feed.

November 1. – I set up my tent under a rock, and lay there for the first night, making it as large as I could, with stakes driven in to swing my hammock upon.

November 2. – I set up all my chests and boards, and the pieces of timber which made my rafts, and with them formed a fence round me, a little within the place I had marked out for my fortification.

November 3. – I went out with my gun, and killed two fowls

like ducks, which were very good food. In the afternoon went to work to make me a table.

November 4. – This morning I began to order my times of work, of going out with my gun, time of sleep, and time of diversion, viz., every morning I walked out with my gun for two or three hours, if it did not rain; then employed myself to work till about eleven o'clock; then eat what I had to live on; and from twelve to two I lay down to sleep, the weather being excessive hot; and then in the evening to work again. The working part of this day and of the next were wholly employed in making my table; for I was yet but a very sorry workman, though time and necessity made me a complete natural mechanic soon after, as I believe it would do any one else.

November 5. – This day went abroad with my gun and my dog, and killed a wild cat; her skin pretty soft, but her flesh good for nothing. Every creature I killed, I took off the skins and preserved them. Coming back by the sea-shore, I saw many sorts of sea-fowls, which I did not understand; but was surprised, and almost frighted, with two or three seals, which, while I was gazing at, not well knowing what they were, got into the sea, and escaped me for that time.

November 6. – After my morning walk I went to work with my table again, and finished it, though not to my liking; nor was it long before I learned to mend it.

November 7. – Now it began to be settled fair weather. The 7th, 8th, 9th, 10th, and part of the 12th (for the 11th was Sunday) I took wholly up to make me a chair, and with much ado, brought it to a tolerable shape, but never to please me; and even in the making, I pulled it to pieces several times. Note, I soon neglected my keeping Sundays; for, omitting my mark for them on my post, I forgot which was which.

November 13. – This day it rained, which refreshed me exceedingly, and cooled the earth; but it was accompanied with terrible thunder and lightning, which frighted me dreadfully, for fear of my powder. As soon as it was over, I resolved to separate my stock of powder into as many little parcels as possible, that it might not be in danger.

November 14, 15, 16. – These three days I spent in making little square chests or boxes, which might hold about a pound, or two pound at most, of powder; and so putting the powder in, I stowed it in places as secure and remote from one another as possible. On one of these three days I killed a large bird that was good to eat, but I know not what to call it.

November 17. – This day I began to dig behind my tent into the rock, to make room for my farther conveniency. Note, three things I wanted exceedingly for this work, viz., a pick-axe, a shovel, and a wheelbarrow or basket; so I desisted from my work, and began to consider how to supply that want, and make me some tools. As for a pick-axe, I made use of the iron crows, which were proper enough, though heavy; but the next thing was a shovel or spade. This was so absolutely necessary, that indeed I could do nothing effectually without it; but what kind of one to make, I knew not.

November 18. – The next day, in searching the woods, I found a tree of that wood, or like it, which in the Brazils they call the iron tree, for its exceeding hardness; of this, with great labour, and almost spoiling my axe, I cut a piece, and brought it home, too, was difficulty enough, for it was exceedingly heavy.

The excessive hardness of the wood, and having no other way, made me a long while upon this machine, for I worked it effectually, by little and little, into the form of a shovel or spade, the handle exactly shaped like ours in England, only that the broad part having no iron shod upon it at bottom, it would not last me so long. However, it served well enough for the uses which I had occasion to put it to; but never was a shovel, I believe, made after that fashion, or so long a-making.

I was still deficient, for I wanted a basket or a wheelbarrow. A basket I could not make by any means, having no such things as twigs that would bend to make wicker ware, at least none yet found out. And as to a wheelbarrow, I fancied I could make all but the wheel, but that I had no notion of, neither did I know how to go about it; besides, I had no possible way to make the iron gudgeons for the spindle or axis of the wheel to run in, so I gave it over; and so for carrying away the earth which I dug out of the cave, I made me a thing like a hod which the labourers carry mortar in, when they serve the bricklayers.

This was not so difficult to me as making the shovel; and yet this, and the shovel, and the attempt which I made in vain to make a wheelbarrow, took me up no less than four days; I mean always, excepting my morning walk with my gun, which I seldom failed, and very seldom failed also bringing home something fit to eat.

November 23. – My other work having now stood still because of my making these tools, when they were finished I went on, and working every day, as my strength and time allowed, I spent eighteen days entirely in widening and deepening my cave, that it might hold my goods commodiously.

Note. – During all this time I worked to make this room or cave spacious enough to accomodate me as a warehouse or magazine, a kitchen, a dining-room, and a cellar; as for my lodging, I kept to the tent, except that sometimes in the wet season of the year it rained so hard, that I could not keep myself dry, which caused me afterwards to cover all my place within my pale with long poles, in the form of rafters, leaning against the rock, and load them with flags and large leaves of trees, like a thatch.

December 10. – I began now to think my cave or vault finished, when on a sudden (it seems I had made it too large) a great quantity of earth fell down from the top and one side, so much, that, in short, it frighted me, and not without reason too; for if I had been under it, I had never wanted a grave-digger. Upon this disaster I had a great deal of work to do over again; for I had the loose earth to carry out; and, which was of more importance, I had the ceiling to prop up, so that I might be sure no more would come down.

December 11. – This day I went to work with it accordingly, and got two shores or posts pitched upright to the top, with two pieces of boards across over each post. This I finished the next day; and setting more posts up with boards, in about a week more I had the roof secured; and the posts standing in rows, served me for partitions to part of my house.

December 17. – From this day to the twentieth I placed shelves, and knocked up nails on the posts to hang everything up that could be hung up; and now I began to be in some order within doors.

December 20. – Now I carried everything into the cave, and began to furnish my house, and set up some pieces of boards, like a dresser, to order my victuals upon; but boards began to be very scarce with me; also I made me another table.

December 24. – Much rain all night and all day; no stirring out.

December 25. – Rain all day.

December 26. – No rain, and the earth much cooler than before, and pleasanter.

December 27. – Killed a young goat, and lamed another, so that I catched it, and led it home in a string. When I had it home, I bound and splintered up its leg, which was broke.

N.B. – I took such care of it, that it lived; and the leg grew well and as strong as ever; but by my nursing it so long it grew tame, and fed upon the little green at my door, and would not go away. This was the first time that I entertained a thought of breeding up some tame creatures, that I might have food when my powder and shot was all spent.

December 28, 29, 30. – Great heats and no breeze, so that there was no stirring abroad, except in the evening, for food. This time I spent in putting all my things in order within doors.

January 1. – Very hot still, but I went abroad early and late with my gun, and lay still in the middle of the day. This evening, going farther into the valleys which lay towards the centre of the island, I found there was plenty of goats, though exceedingly shy, and hard to come at. However, I resolved to try if I could not bring my dog to hunt them down.

January 2. – Accordingly, the next day, I went out with my dog, and set him upon the goats; but I was mistaken, for they all faced about upon the dog; and he knew his danger too well, for he would not come near them.

January 3. – I began my fence or wall; which being still jealous of my being attacked by somebody, I resolved to make very thick and strong.

N.B. – This wall being described before, I purposely omit what was said in the journal. It is sufficient to observe that I was not in less time than from the 3rd of January to the 14th of April working, finishing, and perfecting this wall, though it was no more than about twenty four yards in length, being a half circle from one place in the rock to another place about eight yards from it, the door of the cave being in the centre behind it.

All this time I worked very hard, the rains hindering me many days, nay, sometimes weeks together; but I thought I should never be perfectly secure till this wall was finished. And it is scarcely credible what inexpressible labour everything was done with, especially the bringing piles out of the woods, and driving them into the ground; for I made them much bigger than I need to have done.

When this wall was finished, and the outside double-fenced with a turf-wall raised up close to it, I persuaded myself that if any people were to come on shore there, they would not perceive anything like a habitation; and it was very well I did so, as may be observed hereafter upon a very remarkable occasion.

During this time, I made my rounds in the woods for game

every day, when the rain permitted me, and made frequent discoveries in these walks of something or other to my advantage; particularly I found a kind of wild pigeons, who built, not as wood pigeons in a tree, but rather as house pigeons, in the holes of the rocks. And taking some young ones, I endeavoured to breed them up tame, and did so; but when they grew older they all flew away, which, perhaps, was at first for want of feeding them, for I had nothing to give them. However, I frequently found their nests, and got their young ones, which were very good meat.

And now in managing my household affairs I found myself wanting in many things, which I thought at first it was impossible for me to make, as indeed, as to some of them, it was. For instance, I could never make a cask to be hooped; I had a small runlet or two, as I observed before, but I could never arrive to the capacity of making one of them, though I spent many weeks about it. I could neither put in the heads, nor joint the staves so true to one another as to make them hold water; so I gave that also over.

In the next place, I was at a great loss for candle; so that as soon as ever it was dark, which was generally by seven o'clock, I was obliged to go to bed. I remembered the lump of beeswax with which I made candles in my African adventure, but I had none of that now. The only remedy I had was, that when I had killed a goat I saved the tallow, and with a little dish made of clay, which I baked in the sun, to which I added a wick of some oakum, I made me a lamp; and this gave me light, though not a clear steady light like a candle.

In the middle of all my labours it happened, that rummaging my things, I found a little bag, which, as I hinted before, had been filled with corn for the feeding of poultry, not for this voyage, but before, as I suppose, when the ship came from Lisbon. What little remainder of corn had been in the bag was all devoured with the rats, and I saw nothing in the bag but husks and dust; and being willing to have the bag for some other use, I think it was to put powder in, when I divided it for fear of the lightning, or some such use, I shook the husks of corn out of it on one side of my fortification, under the rock. It was a little before the great rains, just now mentioned, that I threw this stuff away, taking no notice of anything there; when, about a month after, or thereabout, I saw some few stalks of something green shooting out of the ground, which I fancied might be some plant I had not seen; but I was surprised, and perfectly astonished, when, after a little longer time, I saw about ten or twelve ears come out, which were perfect green barley of the same kind as or European, nay, as our English barley.

It is impossible to express the astonishment and confusion of my thoughts on this occasion. I had hitherto acted upon no religious foundation at all; indeed, I had very few notions of religion in my head, or had entertained any sense of anything that had befallen me otherwise than as a chance, or, as we lightly say, what pleases God; without so much as inquiring into the end of Providence in these things, or His order in governing events in the world. But after I saw barley grow there in a climate which I knew was not proper for corn, and especially that I knew not how it came there, it startled me strangely, and I began to suggest that God had miraculously caused this grain to grow without any help of seed sown, and it was so directed purely for my sustenance on that wild miserable place.

This touched my heart a little, and brought tears out of my eyes; and I began to bless myself, that such a prodigy of Nature should happen upon my account; and this was more strange to me, because I saw near it still, all along by the side of the rock, some other straggling stalks, which proved to be stalks of rice, and which I knew, because I had seen it grow in Africa, when I was ashore there.

I not only thought these the pure productions of Providence for my support, but, not doubting but that there was more in the place, I went all over that part of the island where I had been before, peering in every corner, and under every rock, to see for more of it; but I could not find any. At last it occurred to my thoughts that I had shook a bag of chickens' meat out in that place, and then the wonder began to cease; and I must confess, my religious thankfulness to God's providence began to abate too, upon the discovering that all this was nothing but what was common; though I ought to have been as thankful for so strange and unforseen providence, as if it had been miraculous; for it was really the work of Providence as to me, that should order or appoint, that ten or twelve grains of corn should remain unspoiled (when the rats had destroyed all the rest), as if it had been dropped from heaven; as also that I should throw it out in that particular place, where, it being in the shade of a high rock, it sprang up immediately; whereas, if I had thrown it anywhere else at that time, it had been burnt up and destroyed.

I carefully saved the ears of this corn, you may be sure, in their season, which was about the end of June; and laying up every corn, I resolved to sow them all again, hoping in time to have some quantity sufficient to supply me with bread. But it was not till the fourth year that I could allow myself the least grain of this corn to eat, and even then but sparingly, as I shall say afterwards in its order; for I lost all that I sowed the first season, by not observing the proper time; for I sowed it just before the dry season, so that it never came up at all, at least not as it would have done; of which in its place.

Besides this barley, there was, as above, twenty or thirty stalks of rice, which I preserved with the same care, and whose use was of the same kind, or to the same purpose, viz., to make me bread, or rather food; for I found ways to cook it up without baking, though I did that also after some time. But to return to my journal.

I worked excessive hard these three or four months to get my wall done; and the 14th of April I closed it up, contriving to go into it, not by a door, but over the wall by a ladder, that there might be no sign in the outside of my habitation.

April 16. – I finished the ladder, so I went up with the ladder to the top, and then pulled it up after me, and let it down on the inside. This was a complete enclosure to me; for within I had room enough, and nothing could come at me from without, unless it could first mount my wall.

The very next day after this wall was finished, I had almost had all my labour overthrown at once, and myself killed. The case was thus: As I was busy in the inside of it, behind my tent, just in the entrance into my cave, I was terribly frightened with a most dreadful surprising thing indeed; for all on a sudden I found the earth come crumbling down from the roof of my cave, and from the edge of the hill over my head, and two of the posts I had set up in the cave cracked in a frightful manner. I was heartily scared, but thought nothing of what was really the cause, only thinking that the top of my cave was falling in, as some of it had done before; and for fear I should be buried in it, I ran forward to my ladder; and not thinking myself safe there neither, I got over my wall for fear of the pieces of the hill which I expected might roll down upon me. I had no sooner stepped down upon the firm ground, but I plainly saw it was a terrible earthquake; for the ground I stood on shook three times at about eight minutes' distance, with three such shocks, as would have overturned the strongest building that could be supposed to have stood on the earth; and a great piece of the top of a rock which stood about half a mile from me next the sea, fell down with such a terrible noise, as I never heard in all my life. I perceived also the very sea was put into violent motion by it; and I believe the shocks were stronger under the water than on the island.

I was so amazed with the thing itself, having never felt the like, or discoursed with any one that had, that I was like one dead or stupefied; and the motion of the earth made my stomach sick, like one that was tossed at sea. But the noise of the falling of the rock awaked me, as it were, and rousing me from the stupefied condition I was in, filled me with horror, and I thought of nothing then but the hill falling upon my tent and all my household goods, and burying all at once; and this sunk my very soul within me a second time.

After the third shock was over, and I felt no more for some time, I began to take courage; and yet I had not heart enough to go over my wall again, for fear of being buried alive, but sat still upon the ground, greatly cast down and disconsolate, not knowing what to do. All this while I had not the least serious religious thought, nothing but the common, "Lord, have mercy upon me!" and when it was over, that went away too.

While I sat thus, I found the air overcast, and grow cloudy, as if it would rain. Soon after that the wind rose by little and little, so that in less than half an hour it blew a most dreadful hurricane. The sea was all of a sudden covered over with foam and froth; the shore was covered with the breach of the water; the trees were torn up by the roots; and a terrible storm it was: and this held about three hours, and then began to abate; and in two hours more it was stark calm, and began to rain very hard.

All this while I sat upon the ground, very much terrified and dejected; when on a sudden it came into my thoughts, that these winds and rain being the consequences of the earthquake, the earthquake itself was spent and over, and I might venture into my cave again. With this thought my spirits began to revive; and the rain also helping to persuade me, I went in and sat down in my tent. But the rain was so violent that my tent was ready to be beaten down with it, and I was forced to go into my cave, though very much afraid and uneasy, for fear it should fall on my head.

This violent rain forced me to a new work, viz., to cut a hole through my new fortification, like a sink, to let the water go out, which would else have drowned my cave. After I had been in my cave some time, and found still no more shocks of the earthquake follow, I began to be more composed. And now to support my spirits, which indeed wanted it very much, I went to my little store, and took a small sup of rum, which, however, I did then, and always, very sparingly, knowing I could have no more when that was gone.

It continued raining all that night and a great part of the next day, so that I could not stir abroad; but my mind being more composed, I began to think of what I had best do, concluding that if the island was subject to these earthquakes, there would be no living for me in a cave, but I must consider of building me some little hut in an open place, which I might surround with a wall, as I had done here, and so make myself secure from wild beasts or men; but concluded, if I stayed where I was, I should certainly, one time or another be buried alive.

With these thoughts I resolved to remove my tent from the place where it stood, which was just under the hanging precipice of the hill, and which, if it should be shaken again, would certainly fall upon my tent; and I spent the two next days, being the 19th and 20th of April, in contriving where and how to remove my habitation.

The fear of being swallowed up alive made me that I never slept in quiet; and yet the apprehension of lying abroad without any fence was almost equal to it. But still, when I looked about and saw how everything was put in order, how pleasantly concealed I was, and how safe from danger, it made me very loth to remove.

In the meantime it occurred to me that it would require a vast deal of time for me to do this, and that I must be contented to run the venture where I was, till I had formed a camp for myself, and had secured it so as to remove to it. So with this resolution I composed myself for a time, and resolved that I would go to work with all speed to build me a wall with piles and cables, etc., in a circle as before, and set my tent up in it when it was finished, but that I would venture to stay where I was till it was finished, and fit to remove to. This was the 21st.

April 22. – The next morning I began to consider of means to put this resolve in execution; but I was at a great loss about my tools. I had three large axes, and abundance of hatchets (for we carried the hatchets for traffic with the Indians), but with much chopping and cutting knotty hard wood, they were all full of notches and dull; and though I had a grindstone, I could not turn it and grind my tools too. This cost me as much thought as a statesman would have bestowed upon a grand point of politics, or a judge upon the life and death of a man. At length I contrived a wheel with a string, to turn it with my foot, that I might have both my hands at liberty. Note, I had never seen any such thing in England, or at least not to take notice how it was done, though since I have observed it is very common there; besides that, my grindstone was very large and heavy.

This machine cost me a full week's work to bring it to perfection.

April 28, 29. – These two whole days I took up in grinding my tools, my machine for turning my grindstone performing very well.

April 30. – Having perceived my bread had been low a great while, now I took a survey of it, and reduced myself to one biscuit-cake a day, which made my heart very heavy.

May 1. – In the morning, looking towards the seaside, the tide being low, I saw something lie on the shore bigger than ordinary, and it looked like a cask. When I came to it, I found a small barrel, and two or three pieces of the wreck of the ship, which were driven on shore by the late hurricane; and looking towards the wreck itself, I thought it seemed to lie higher out of the water than it used to do. I examined the barrel which was driven on shore, and soon found it was a barrel of gunpowder; but it had taken water, and the powder was caked as hard as a stone. However, I rolled it farther on shore for the present, and went on upon the sands as near as I could to the wreck of the ship to look for more.

When I came down to the ship I found it strangely removed. The forecastle, which lay before buried in sand, was heaved up at least six feet; and the stern, which was broken to pieces, and parted from the rest by the force of the sea soon after I had left rummaging her, was tossed, as it were, up, and cast on one side, and the sand was thrown so high on that side next to her stern, that whereas there was a great place of water before, so that I could not come within a quarter of a mile of the wreck without swimming, I could now walk quite up to her when the tide was out. I was surprised with this at first, but soon concluded it must be done by the earthquake. And as by this violence the ship was more broken open than formerly, so many things came daily on shore, which the sea had loosened, and which the winds and water rolled by degrees to the land.

This wholly diverted my thoughts from the design of removing my habitation; and I busied myself mightily, that day especially, in searching whether I could make any way into the ship. But I found nothing was to be expected of that kind, for that all inside of the ship was choked up with sand. However, as I had learned not to despair of anything, I resolved to pull everything to pieces that I could of the ship, concluding that everything I could get from her would be of some use or other to me.

May 3. – I began with my saw, and cut a piece of a beam through, which I thought held some of the upper part or quarter-deck together; and when I had cut it through, I cleared away the sand as well as I could from the side which lay highest; but the tide coming in, I was obliged to give over for that time.

May 4. – I went a-fishing, but caught not one fish that I could eat of, till I was weary of my sport; when, just going to leave off I caught a young dolphin. I had made me a long line of some rope-yarn, but I had no hooks; yet I frequently caught fish enough, as much as I cared to eat; all which I dried in the sun, and eat them dry.

May 5. – Worked on the wreck, cut another beam asunder, and brought three great fir planks off from the decks, which I tied together, and made swim on shore, when the tide of flood came on.

May 6. – Worked on the wreck, got several iron bolts out of her, and other pieces of iron-work; worked very hard, and came home very much tired, and had thoughts of giving it over.

May 7. – Went to the wreck again, but with an intent not to work, but found the weight of the wreck had broke itself down, the beams being cut; that several pieces of the ship seemed to lie loose, and the inside of the hold lay so open, that I could see into it, but almost full of water and sand.

May 8. – Went to the wreck, and carried an iron crow to wrench up the deck, which lay now quite clear of the water or sand. I wrenched open two planks, and brought them on shore also with the tide. I left the iron crow in the wreck for next day.

May 9. – Went to the wreck, and with the crow made way into the body of the wreck, and felt several casks, and loosened them with the crow, but could not break them up. I felt also the roll of English lead, and could stir it, but it was too heavy to remove.

May 10, 11, 12, 13, 14. – Went every day to the wreck, and got a great deal of pieces of timber, and boards, or plank, and two or three hundredweight of iron.

May 15. – I carried two hatchets to try if I could not cut a piece off of the roll of lead, by placing the edge of one hatchet, and driving it with the other; but as it lay about a foot and a half in the water, I could not make any blow to drive the hatchet.

May 16. – It had blown hard in the night, and the wreck appeared more broken by the force of the water; but I stayed so long in the woods to get pigeons for food, that the tide prevented me going to the wreck that day.

May 17. – I saw some pieces of the wreck blown on shore,

at a great distance, near two miles off me, but resolved to see what they were, and found it was a piece of lead, but too heavy for me to bring away.

May 24. – Every day to this day I worked on the wreck, and with hard labour I loosened some things so much with the crow that the first blowing tide several casks floated out, and two of the seamen's chests. But the wind blowing from the shore, nothing came to land that day but pieces of timber, and a hogshead, which had some brazil pork in it, but the salt water and the sand had spoiled it.

I continued this work every day to the 15th of June, except the time necessary to get food, which I always appointed, during this part of my employment, to be when the tide was up, that I might be ready when it was ebbed out. And by this time I had gotten timber, and plank, and iron work enough to have built a good boat, if I had known how; and also, I got at several times, and in several pieces, near one hundredweight of the sheet lead.

June 16. – Going down to the seaside, I found a large tortoise, or turtle. This was the first I had seen, which it seems was only my misfortune, not any defect of the place, or scarcity; for had I happened to be on the other side of the island, I might have had hundreds of them every day, as I found afterwards; but, perhaps, had paid dear enough for them.

June 17. – I spent in cooking the turtle. I found in her threescore eggs; and her flesh was to me, at that time, the most savory and pleasant that ever I tasted in my life, having had no flesh, but of goats and fowls, since I landed in this horrid place.

June 18. – Rained all day, and I stayed within. I thought at this time the rain felt cold, and I was something chilly, which I knew was not usual in that latitude.

June 19. – Very ill, and shivering, as if the weather had been cold.

June 20. – No rest all night; violent pains in my head, and

feverish.

June 21. – Very ill, frighted almost to death with the apprehensions of my sad condition, to be sick, and no help. Prayed to God for the first time since the storm off of Hull, but scarce knew what I said, or why; my thoughts being all confused.

June 22. – A little better, but under dreadful apprehensions of sickness.

June 23. – Very bad again; cold and shivering, and then a violent headache.

June 24. – Much better.

June 25. – An ague very violent; the fit held me seven hours; cold fit, and hot, with faint sweats after it.

June 26. – Better; and having no victuals to eat, took my gun, but found myself very weak. However, I killed a she-goat, and with much difficulty got it home, and broiled some of it, and eat. I would fain have stewed it, and made some broth, but had no pot.

June 27. – The ague again so violent that I lay abed all day, and neither eat nor drank. I was ready to perish for thirst; but so weak, I had not strength to stand up, or to get myself any water to drink. Prayed to God again, but was light-headed; and when I was not, I was so ignorant that I knew not what to say; only I lay and cried, "Lord, look upon me! Lord, pity me! Lord, have mercy upon me!" I suppose I did nothing else for two or three hours, till the fit wearing off, I fell asleep, and did not wake till far in the night. When I awaked, I found myself much refreshed, but weak, and exceedingly thirsty. However, as I had no water in my whole habitation, I was forced to lie till morning, and went to sleep again. In this second sleep I had this terrible dream.

I thought that I was sitting on the ground, on the outside of my wall, where I sat when the storm blew after the earthquake, and that I saw a man descend from a great black cloud, in a bright flame of fire, and light upon the ground. He was all over as bright as a flame, so that I could but just bear to look towards him. His countenance was most inexpressibly dreadful, impossible for words to describe. When he stepped upon the ground with his feet, I thought the earth trembled, just as it had done before in the earthquake, and all the air looked, to my apprehension, as if it had been filled with flashes of fire.

He was no sooner landed upon the earth, but he moved forward towards me, with a long spear or weapon in his hand, to kill me; and when he came to a rising ground, at some distance, he spoke to me, or I heard a voice so terrible, that it is impossible to express the terror of it. All that I can say I understood was this: "Seeing all these things have not brought thee to repentance, now thou shalt die"; at which words I thought he lifted up the spear that was in his hand to kill me.

No one that shall ever read this account, will expect that I should be able to describe the horrors of my soul at this terrible vision; I mean, that even while it was a dream, I even dreamed of those horrors; nor is it any more possible to describe the impression that remained upon my mind when I awaked, and found it was but a dream.

I had, alas! no divine knowledge; what I had received by the good instruction of my father was then worn out, by an uninterrupted series, for eight years, of seafaring wickedness, and a constant conversation with nothing but such as were, like myself, wicked and profane to the last degree. I do not remember that I had, in all that time, one thought that so much as tended either to looking upwards toward God, or inwards towards a reflection upon my ways; but a certain stupidity of soul, without desire of good, or conscience of evil, had entirely overwhelmed me; and I was all that the most hardened, unthinking, wicked creature among our common sailors can be supposed to be; not having the least sense, either of the fear of God, in danger, or of thankfulness to God, in deliverances.

In the relating what is already past of my story, this will be the more easily believed, when I shall add, that through all the variety of miseries that had to this day befallen me, I never had so much as one thought of it being the hand of God, or that it was a just punishment for my sin; my rebellious behaviour against my father, or my present sins, which were great; or so much as a punishment for the general course of my wicked life. When I was on the desperate expedition on the desert shores of Africa, I never had so much as one thought of what would become of me; or one wish to God to direct me whither I should go, or to keep me from the danger which apparently surrounded me, as well from voracious creatures as cruel savages. But I was merely thoughtless of a God or a Providence; acted like a mere brute from the principles of Nature, and by the dictates of common sense only, and indeed hardly that.

When I was delivered and taken up at sea by the Portugal captain, well used, and dealt justly and honourably with, as well as charitably, I had not the least thankfulness in my thoughts. When again I was shipwrecked, ruined, and in danger of drowning on this island, I was as far from remorse, or looking on it as a judgment; I only said to myself often, that I was an unfortunate dog, and born to be always miserable.

It is true, when I got on shore first here, and found all my ship's crew drowned, and myself spared, I was surprised with a kind of ecstasy, and some transports of soul, which, had the grace of God assisted, might have come up to true thankfulness; but it ended where it begun, in a mere common flight of joy, or, as I may say, being glad I was alive, without the least reflection upon the distinguishing goodness of the hand which had preserved me, and had singled me out to be preserved, when all the rest were destroyed; or an inquiry why Providence had been thus merciful to me; even just the same common sort of joy which seamen generally have after they are got safe ashore from a shipwreck, which they drown all in the next bowl of punch, and forget almost as soon as it is over, and all the rest of my life was like it.

Even when I was afterwards, on due consideration, made sensible of my condition, how I was cast on this dreadful place, out of the reach of human kind, out of all hope of relief, or prospect of redemption, as soon as I saw but a prospect of living, and that I should not starve and perish for hunger, all the sense of my affliction wore off, and I began to be very easy, applied myself to the works proper for my preservation and supply, and was far enough from being afflicted at my condition, as a judgment from heaven, or as the hand of God against me; these were thoughts which very seldom entered my head.

The growing up of the corn, as is hinted in my journal, had at first some little influence upon me, and began to affect me with seriousness, as long as I thought it had something miraculous in it; but as soon as ever that part of the thought was removed, all the impression which was raised from it wore off also, as I have noted already.

Even the earthquake, though nothing could be more terrible in its nature, or more immediately directing to the invisible Power, which alone directs such things, yet no sooner was the first fright over, but the impression it had made went off also. I had no more sense of God or His judgments, much less of the present affliction of my circumstances being from His hand, than if I had been in the most prosperous condition of life.

But now, when I began to be sick, and a leisurely view of the miseries of death came to place itself before me; when my spirits began to sink under the burthen of a strong distemper, and Nature was exhausted with the violence of the fever; conscience, that had slept so long, began to awake, and I began to reproach myself with my past life, in which I had so evidently, by uncommon wickedness, provoked the justice of God to lay me under uncommon strokes, and to deal with me in so vindictive a manner.

These reflections oppressed me for the second or third day of my distemper; and in the violence, as well of the fever as of the dreadful reproaches of my conscience, extorted some words from me, like praying to God, though I cannot say they were either a prayer attended with desires or with hopes; it was rather the voice of mere fright and distress. My thoughts were confused, the convictions great upon my mind, and the horror of dying in such a miserable condition, raised vapours into my head with the mere apprehensions; and in these hurries of my soul, I know not what my tongue might express; but it was rather exclamation, such as, "Lord! what a miserable creature am I! If I should be sick, I shall certainly die for want of help; and what will become of me?" Then the tears burst out of my eyes, and I could say no more for a good while.

In this interval, the good advice of my father came to my mind, and presently his prediction which I mentioned at the beginning of this story, viz., that if I did take this foolish step, God would not bless me, and I would have leisure hereafter to reflect upon having neglected his counsel, when there might be none to assist in my recovery. "Now," said I aloud, "my dear father's words are come to pass; God's justice has overtaken me, and I have none to help or hear me. I rejected the voice of Providence, which had mercifully put me in a posture or station of life wherein I might have been happy and easy; but I would neither see it myself, or learn to know the blessing of it from my parents. I left them to mourn over my folly, and now I am left to mourn under the consequences of it. I refused their help and assistance, who would have lifted me into the world, and would have made everything easy to me; and now I have difficulties to struggle with, too great for even Nature itself to support, and no assistance, no help, no comfort, no advice." Then I cried out, "Lord, be my help, for I am in great distress."

This was the first prayer, if I may call it so, that I had made for many years. But I return to my journal.

June 28. – Having been somewhat refreshed with the sleep I had had, and the fit being entirely off, I got up; and though the fright and terror of my dream was very great, yet I considered that the fit of the ague would return again the next day, and now was my time to get something to refresh and support myself when I should be ill. And the first thing I did I filled a large square case-bottle with water, and set it upon my table, in reach of my bed; and to take off the chill or aguish disposition of the water, I put about a quarter of a pint of rum into it, and mixed them together. Then I got me a piece of the goat's flesh, and broiled it on the coals, but could eat very little. I walked about, but was very weak, and withal very sad and heavy hearted in the sense of my miserable condition, dreading the return of my distemper the next day. At night I made my supper of three of the turtle's eggs, which I roasted in the ashes, and eat, as we call it, in the shell; and this was the first bit of meat I had ever asked God's blessing to, even as I could remember, in my whole life.

After I had eaten, I tried to walk, but found myself so weak, that I could hardly carry the gun (for I never went out without that); so I went but a little way, and sat down upon the ground, looking out upon the sea, which was just before me, and very calm and smooth. As I sat here, some such thoughts as these occurred to me.

What is this earth and sea, of which I have seen so much? whence is it produced? And what am I, and all the other creatures, wild and tame, human and brutal, whence are we? Sure we are all made by some secret Power, who formed the earth and sea, the air and sky. And who is that?

Then it followed most naturally, It is God that has made it all. Well, but then it came on strangely, if God has made all these things, He guides and governs them all, and all things that concern them; for the Power that could make all things, must certainly have power to guide and direct them.

If so, nothing can happen in the great circuit of His works, either without His knowledge or appointment. And if nothing happens without His knowledge, He knows that I am here, and am in this dreadful condition. And if nothing happens without His appointment, He has appointed all this to befall me.

Nothing occurred to my thoughts to contradict any of these conclusions; and therefore it rested upon me with the greater force, that it must needs be that God has appointed all this to befall me; that I was brought to this miserable circumstance by His direction, He having the sole power, not of me only, but of everything that happened in the world. Immediately it followed, Why has God done this to me? What have I done to be thus used?

My conscience presently checked me in that inquiry, as if I had blasphemed, and methought it spoke to me like a voice: "Wretch! dost thou ask what thou hast done? Look back upon a dreadful misspent life, and ask thyself what thou hast not done? Ask, why is it that thou wert not long ago destroyed? Why wert thou not drowned in Yarmouth Roads; killed in the fight when the ship was taken by the Sallee man of war; devoured by the wild beasts on the coast of Africa; or drowned here, when all the crew perished but thyself. Dost thou ask, What have I done?"

I was struck dumb with these reflections, as one astonished, and had not a word to say, no, not to answer to myself, but rose up pensive and sad, walked back to my retreat, and went up over my wall, as if I had been going to bed. But my thoughts were sadly disturbed, and I had no inclination to sleep; so I sat down in my chair, and lighted my lamp, for it began to be dark. Now, as the apprehension of the return of my distemper terrified me very much, it occurred to my thought that the Brazilians take no physic but their tobacco for almost all distempers; and I had a piece of a roll of tobacco in one of the chests, which was quite cured, and some also that was green, and not quite cured.

I went, directed by Heaven no doubt; for in this chest I found a cure both for soul and body. I opened the chest, and found what I looked for, viz., the tobacco; and as the few books I had saved lay there too, I took out one of the Bibles which I mentioned before, and which to this time I had not found leisure, or so much as inclination, to look into. I say, I took it out, and brought both that and the tobacco with me to the table.

What use to make of the tobacco I knew not, as to my distemper, or whether it was good for it or no; but I tried several experiments with it, as if I was resolved it should hit one way or other. I first took a piece of a leaf, and chewed it in my mouth, which indeed at first almost stupefied my brain, the tobacco being green and strong, and that I had not been much used to it. Then I took some and steeped it an hour or two in some rum, and resolved to take dose of it when I lay down. And lastly, I burnt some upon a pan of coals, and held my nose close over the smoke of it, as long as I could bear it, as well for the heat, as almost for suffocation.

In the interval of this operation, I took up the Bible, and began to read, but my head was too much disturbed with the tobacco to bear reading, at least that time; only having opened the book casually, the first words that occurred to me were these, "Call on Me in the day of trouble, and I will deliver, and thou shalt glorify Me."

The words were very apt to my case, and made some impression upon my thoughts at the time of reading them, though not so much as they did afterwards; for as for being delivered, the word had no sound, as I may say, to me, the thing was so remote, so impossible in my apprehension of things, that I began to say, as the children of Israel did when they were promised flesh to eat, "Can God spread a table in the wilderness?" so I began to say, Can God Himself deliver me from this place? And as it was not for many years that any hope appeared, this prevailed very often upon my thoughts. But, however, the words made a great impression upon me, and I mused upon them very often.

It grew now late, and the tobacco had, as I said, dozed my head so much, that I inclined to sleep; so I left my lamp burning in the cave, lest I should want anything in the night, and went to bed. But before I lay down, I did what I never had done in all my life; I kneeled down, and prayed to God to fulfill the promise to me, that if I called upon Him in the day of trouble, He would deliver me. After my broken and imperfect prayer was over, I drank the rum in which I had steeped the tobacco; which was so strong and rank of the tobacco, that indeed I could scarcely get it down. Immediately upon this I went to bed. I found presently it flew up in my head violently; but I fell into a sound sleep, and waked no more till, by the sun, it must necessarily be near three o'clock in the afternoon the next day. Nay, to this hour I am partly of the opinion that I slept all the next day and night, and till almost three that day after; for otherwise I knew not how I should lose a day out of my reckoning in the days of the week, as it appeared some years after I had done. For if I had lost it by crossing and re-crossing the line, I should have lost more than one day. But certainly I lost a day in my account, and never knew which way.

Be that, however, one way or the other, when I awaked I found myself exceedingly refreshed, and my spirits lively and cheerful. When I got up, I was stronger than I was the day before, and my stomach better, for I was hungry; and, in short, I had no fit the next day, but continued much altered for the better. This was the 29th.

The 30th was my well day, of course, and I went abroad with my gun, but did not care to travel too far. I killed a sea-fowl or two, something like a brand goose, and brought them home, but was not very forward to eat them; so I eat some more of the turtle's eggs, which were very good. This evening I renewed the medicine, which I had supposed did me good the day before, viz., the tobacco steeped in rum; only I did not take so much as before, nor did I chew any of the leaf, or hold my head over the smoke. However, I was not so well the next day, which was the first of July, as I hoped I should have been; for I had a little of the cold fit, but it was not much.

July 2. – I renewed the medicine all the three ways; and dosed myself with it as at first, and doubled the quantity which I drank.

July 3. – I missed the fit for good and all, though I did not recover my full strength for some weeks after. While I was thus gathering strength, my thoughts ran exceedingly upon this Scripture, "I will deliver thee"; and the impossibility of my deliverance lay much upon my mind, in bar of my ever expecting it. But as I was discouraging myself with such thoughts, it occurred to my mind that I pored so much upon my deliverance from the main affliction, that I disregarded the deliverance I had received; and I was, as it were, made to ask myself such questions as these, viz., Have I not been delivered, and wonderfully too, from sickness? from the most distressed condition that could be, and that was so frightful to me? and what notice I had taken of it? Had I done my part? God had delivered me, but I had not glorified Him; that is to say, I had not owned and been thankful for that as a deliverance; and how could I expect greater deliverance?

This touched my heart very much; and immediately I kneeled down, and gave God thanks aloud for my recovery from my sickness.

July 4. – In the morning I took the Bible; and beginning at the new Testament, I began seriously to read it, and imposed upon myself to read awhile every morning and every night, not tying myself to the number of chapters, but as long as my thoughts should engage me. It was not long after I set seriously to this work, but I found my heart more deeply and sincerely affected with the wickedness of my past life. The impression of my dream revived, and the words, "All these things have not brought thee to repentance," ran seriously in my thought. I was earnestly begging of God to give me repentance, when it happened providentially, the very day, that, while reading the Scripture, I came to these words, "He is exalted a Prince and a Saviour, to give repentance, and to give remission." I threw down the book; and with my heart as well as my hands lifted up to heaven, in a kind of ecstasy of joy, I cried out aloud, "Jesus, Thou son of David! Jesus, Thou exalted Prince and Saviour, give me repentance!"

This was the first time that I could say, in the true sense of the words, that I prayed in all my life; for now I prayed with a sense of my condition, and with a true Scripture view of hope founded on the encouragement of the Word of God; and from this time, I may say, I began to have hope that God would hear me.

Now I began to construe the words mentioned above, "Call on Me, and I will deliver you," in a different sense from what I had ever done before; for then I had no notion of anything being called deliverance but my being delivered from the captivity I was in; for though I was indeed at large in the place, yet the island was certainly a prison to me, and that in the worst sense in the world. But now I learned to take it in another sense; now I looked back upon my past life with such horror, and my sins appeared so dreadful, that my soul sought nothing of God but deliverance from the load of guilt that bore down all my comfort. As for my solitary life, it was nothing; I did not so much as pray to be delivered from it, or think of it; it was all of no consideration, in comparison to this. And I add this part here, to hint to whoever shall read it, that whenever they come to a true sense of things, they will find deliverance from a sin a much greater blessing than deliverance from affliction.

But leaving this part, I return to my journal.

My condition began now to be, though not less miserable as to my way of living, yet much easier to my mind; and my thoughts being directed, by a constant reading the Scripture, and praying to God, to things of a higher nature, I had a great deal of comfort within, which, till now, I knew nothing of. Also, as my health and strength returned, I bestirred myself to furnish myself with everything that I wanted, and make my way of living as regular as I could.

From the 4th of July to the 14th, I was chiefly employed in walking about with my gun in my hand, a little and a little at a time, as a man that was gathering up his strength after a fit of sickness; for it is hardly to be imagined how low I was, and to what weakness I was reduced. The application which I made use of was perfectly new, and perhaps what had never cured an ague before; neither can I recommend it to anyone to practise, by this experiment; and though it did carry off the fit, yet it rather contributed to weakening me; for I had frequent convulsions in my nerves and limbs for some time.

I learnt from it also this, in particular, that being abroad in the rainy season was the most pernicious thing to my health that could be, especially in those rains which came attended with storms and hurricanes of wind; for as the rain which came in the dry season was always most accompanied with such storms, so I found that rain was much more dangerous than the rain which fell in September and October.

I had been now on this unhappy island above ten months; all possibility of deliverance from this condition seemed to be entirely taken from me; and I firmly believed that no human shape had ever set foot upon that place. Having now secured my habitation, as I thought, fully to my mind, I had a great desire to make a more perfect discovery of the island, and to see what other productions I might find, which I yet knew nothing of.

It was the 15th of July that I began to take a more particular survey of the island itself. I went up the creek first, where, as I hinted, I brought my rafts on shore. I found, after I came about two miles up, that the tide did not flow any higher, and that it was no more than a little brook of running water, and very fresh and good; but this being the dry season, there was hardly any water in some parts of it, at least, not enough to run in any stream, so as it could be perceived.

On the bank of this brook I found many pleasant savannas or meadows, plain, smooth, and covered with grass; and on the rising parts of them, next to the higher grounds, where the water, as might be supposed, never overflowed, I found a great deal of tobacco, green, and growing to a great and very strong stalk. There were divers, other plants, which I had no notion of, or understanding about, and might, perhaps, have virtues of their own, which I could not find out.

I searched for the cassava root, which the Indians, in all that climate, make their bread of, but I could find none. I saw large plants of aloes, but did not then understand them. I saw several sugar-canes, but wild, and, for want of cultivation, imperfect. I contented myself with these discoveries for this time, and came back, musing with myself what course I might take to know the virtue and goodness of any of the fruits or plants which I should discover; but could bring it to no conclusion; for, in short, I had made so little observation while I was in the Brazils, that I knew little of the plants in the field, at least very little that might serve me to any purpose now in my distress.

The next day, the 16th, I went up the same way again; and after going something farther than I had gone the day before, I found the brook and the savannas began to cease, and the country became more woody than before. In this part I found different fruits, and particularly I found melons upon the ground in great abundance, and grapes upon the trees. The vines had spread indeed over the trees, and the clusters of grapes were just now in their prime, very ripe and rich. This was a surprising discovery, and I was exceedingly glad of them; but I was warned by my experience to eat sparingly of them, remembering that when I was ashore in Barbary the eating of grapes killed several of our Englishmen, who were slaves there, by throwing them into fluxes and fevers. But I found an excellent use of these grapes and that was, to cure or dry them in the sun, and keep them as dried grapes or raisins are kept, which I thought would be, as indeed they were, as wholesome as agreeable to eat, when no grapes might be to be had.

I spent all that evening there, and went not back to my habitation; which, by the way, was the first night, as I might say, I had lain from home. In the night, I took my first contrivance, and got up into a tree, where I slept well; and the next morning proceeded upon my discovery, travelling near four miles, as I might judge by the length of the valley, keeping still due north, with a ridge of hills on the south and north side of me.

At the end of this march I came to an opening, where the country seemed to descend to the west; and a little spring of fresh water, which issued out of the side of the hill by me, ran the other way, that is, due east; and the country appeared so fresh, so green, so flourishing, everything being in a constant verdure or flourish of spring, that it looked like a planted garden.

I descended a little on the side of that delicious vale, surveying it with a secret kind of pleasure, though mixed with my other afflicting thoughts, to think that this was all my own; and I was king and lord of all this country indefeasibly, and had a right of possession; and, if I could convey it, I might have it in inheritance as completely as any lord of a manor in England. I saw here abundance of cocoa trees, orange, and lemon, and citron trees; but all wild, and very few bearing any fruit, at least not then. However, the green limes that I gathered were not only pleasant to eat, but very wholesome; and I mixed their juice afterwards with water, which made it very wholesome, and very cool and refreshing.

I found now I had business enough to gather and carry home; and I resolved to lay up a store, as well of grapes as limes and lemons to furnish myself for the wet season, which I knew was approaching.

In order to this, I gathered a great heap of grapes in one place, and a lesser heap in another place, and a great parcel of limes and lemons in another place; and taking a few of each with me, I travelled homeward; and resolved to come again, and bring a bag or sack, or what I could make, to carry the rest home.

Accordingly, having spent three days in this journey, I came home (so I must now call my tent and my cave); but before I got thither, the grapes were spoiled; the richness of the fruits, and the weight of the juice, having broken them and bruised them, they were good for little or nothing: as to the limes, they were good, but I could bring but a few.

The next day, being the 19th, I went back, having made me two small bags to bring home my harvest; but I was surprised, when, coming to my heap of grapes, which were so rich and fine when I gathered them, I found them all spread about, trod to pieces, and dragged about, some here, some there, and abundance eaten and devoured. By this I concluded there were some wild creatures thereabouts, which had done this; but what they were, I knew not.

However, as I found that there was no laying them up on heaps, and no carrying them away in a sack, but that one way they would be destroyed, and the other way they would be crushed with their own weight, I took another course; for I gathered a large quantity of the grapes, and hung them up upon the out-branches of the trees, that they might cure and dry in the sun; and as for the limes and lemons, I carried as many back as I could well stand under.

When I came home from this journey, I contemplated with great pleasure the fruitfulness of that valley, and the pleasantness of the situation; the security from storms on that side the water and the wood; and concluded that I had pitched upon a place to fix my abode, which was by far the worst part of the country. Upon the whole, I began to consider of removing my habitation, and to look out for a place equally safe as where I now was situate, if possible, in that pleasant fruitful part of the island.

This thought ran long in my head, and I was exceeding fond of it for some time, the pleasantness of the place tempting me;

but when I came to a nearer view of it, and to consider that I was now by the seaside, where it was at least possible that something might happen to my advantage and, by the same ill fate that brought me hither, might bring some other unhappy wretches to the same place; and though it was scarce probable that any such thing should ever happen, yet to enclose myself among the hills and woods in the centre of the island, was to anticipate my bondage, and to render such an affair not only improbable, but impossible; and that therefore I ought not by any means to remove.

However, I was so enamoured of this place that I spent much of my time there for the whole remaining part of the month of July; and though, upon second thoughts, I resolved, as above, not to remove, yet I built me a little kind of bower, and surrounded it at a distance with a strong fence, being a double hedge as high as I could reach, well staked, and filled between with brushwood. And here I lay very secure, sometimes two or three nights together, always going over it with a ladder, as before; so that I fancied now I had my country house and my sea-coast house; and this work took me up to the beginning of August.

I had but newly finished my fence, and began to enjoy my labour, but the rains came on, and made me stick close to my first habitation; for though I had made me a tent like the other, with a piece of a sail, and spread it very well, yet I had not the shelter of a hill to keep me from storms, nor a cave behind me to retreat into when the rains were extraordinary.

About the beginning of August, as I said, I had finished my bower, and began to enjoy myself. The 3rd of August, I found the grapes I had hung up were perfectly dried, and indeed were excellent good raisins of the sun; so I began to take them down from the trees. And it was very happy that I did so, for the rains which followed would have spoiled them, and I had lost the best part of my winter food; for I had above two hundred large bunches of them. No sooner had I taken them all down, and carried most of them home to my cave, but it began to rain; and from hence, which was the 14th of August, it rained, more or less, every day till the middle of October, and sometimes so violently, that I could not stir out of my cave for several days.

In this season, I was much surprised with the increase of my family. I had been much concerned for the loss of one of my cats, who run away from me, or, as I thought, had been dead, and I heard no more tale or tidings of her, till, to my astonishment, she came home about the end of August with three kittens. This was more strange to me, because, though I had killed a wildcat, as I called it, with my gun, yet I thought it was a quite different kind from our European cats; yet the young cats were the same kind of house-breed like the old one; and both my cats being females, I thought it very strange. But from these three cats I afterwards came to be so pestered with cats, that I was forced to kill them like vermin, or wild beasts, and to drive them from my house as much as possible.

From the 14th of August to the 26th, incessant rain, so that I could not stir, and was now very careful not to be much wet. In this confinement, I began to be straitened for food; but venturing out twice, I one day killed a goat, and the last day, which was the 26th, found a very large tortoise, which was a treat to me, and my food was regulated thus: I eat a bunch of raisins for my breakfast, a piece of the goat's flesh, or of the turtle, for my dinner, broiled; for, to my great misfortune, I had no vessel to boil or stew anything; and two or three of the turtle's eggs for my supper.

During this confinement in my cover by the rain, I worked daily two or three hours at enlarging my cave, and by degrees worked it on towards one side, till I came to the outside of the hill, and made a door, or way out, which came beyond my fence or wall; and so I came in and out this way. But I was not perfectly easy at lying so open; for as I had managed myself before, I was in a perfect enclosure; whereas now, I thought I lay exposed, and open for anything to come in upon me; and yet I could not perceive that there was any living thing to fear, the biggest creature that I had yet seen upon the island being a goat.

September 30. – I was now come to the unhappy anniversary of my landing. I cast up the notches on my post, and found I had been on shore three hundred and sixty-five days. I kept this day as a solemn fast, setting it apart to religious exercise, prostrating myself on the ground with the most serious humiliation, confessing my sins to God, acknowledging His righteous judgments upon me, and praying to Him to have mercy on me through Jesus Christ; and having not tasted the least refreshment for twelve hours, even till the going down of the sun, I then ate a biscuit-cake and a bunch of grapes, and went to bed, finishing the day as I began it.

I had all this time observed no Sabbath day, for as at first I had no sense of religion upon my mind, I had, after some time, omitted to distinguish the weeks, by making a longer notch than ordinary for the Sabbath day, and so did not really know what any of the days were. But now, having cast up the days, as above, I found I had been there a year, so I divided it into weeks, and set apart every seventh day for a Sabbath; though I found at the end of my account, I had lost a day or two in my reckoning.

A little after this my ink began to fail me, and so I contented myself to use it more sparingly, and to write down only the most remarkable events of my life, without continuing a daily memorandum of other things.

The rainy season and the dry season began now to appear regular to me, and I learned to divide them so as to provide for them accordingly; but I bought all my experience before I had it, and this I am going to relate was one of the most discouraging experiments that I made at all. I have mentioned that I had saved the few ears of barley and rice, which I had so surprisingly found spring up, as I thought, of themselves, and believe there were about thirty stalks of rice, and about twenty of barley; and now I thought it a proper time to sow it after the rains, the sun being in its southern position, going from me.

Accordingly I dug up a piece of ground as well as I could with my wooden spade, and dividing it into two parts, I sowed my grain; but as I was sowing it, it casually occurred to my thoughts that I would not sow it all at first, because I did not know when was the proper time for it, so I sowed about two-thirds of the seed, leaving about a handful of each.

It was a great comfort to me afterwards that I did so, for not one grain of that I sowed this time came to anything, for the dry months following, the earth having had no rain after the seed was sown, it had no moisture to assist its growth, and never came up at all till the wet season had come again, and then it grew as if it had been but newly sown.

Finding my first seed did not grow, which I easily imagined was by the drought, I sought for a moister piece of ground to make another trial in, and I dug up a piece of ground near my new bower, and sowed the rest of my seed in February, a little before the vernal equinox. And this having the rainy months of March and April to water it, sprung up very pleasantly, and yielded a very good crop; but having part of the seed left only, and not daring to sow all that I had, I had but a small quantity at last, my whole crop not amounting to above half a peck of each kind. But by this experiment I was made master of my business, and knew exactly when the proper season was to sow, and that I might expect two seed-times and two harvests every year.

While this corn was growing, I made a little discovery, which was of use to me afterwards. As soon as the rains were over, and the weather began to settle, which was about the month of November, I made a visit up the country to my bower, where, though I had not been some months, yet I found all things just as I left them. The circle or double hedge that I had made was not only firm and entire, but the stakes which I had cut out of some trees that grew thereabouts were all shot out, and grown with long branches, as much as a willow-tree usually shoots the first year after lopping its head. I could not tell what tree to call it that these stakes were cut from. I was surprised, and yet very well pleased to see the young trees grow, and I pruned them, and led them up to grow as much alike as I could. And it is scarce credible how beautiful a figure they grew into in three years; so that though the hedge made a circle of about twenty-five yards in diameter, yet the trees, for such I might now call them, soon covered it, and it was a complete shade, sufficient to lodge under all the dry season.

This made me resolve to cut some more stakes, and make me a hedge like this, in a semicircle round my wall (I mean that of my first dwelling), which I did; and placing the trees or stakes in a double row, at about eight yards distance from my first fence, they grew presently, and were at first a fine cover to my habitation, and afterward served for defence also, as I shall observe in its order.

I found now that the seasons of the year might generally be divided, not into summer and winter, as in Europe, but into the rainy seasons and the dry seasons; which were generally thus:

Half February, March, *Half* April:	Rainy, the sun being then on, or near, the equinox.
Half April, May, June, July, *Half* August:	Dry, the sun being then to the north of the line.

Half August, September, *Half* October:	Rainy, the sun being then come back.
Half October, November, December, January, *Half* February:	Dry, the sun being then to the south of the line.

The rainy season sometimes held longer or shorter as the winds happened to blow, but this was the general observation I made. After I had found by experience the ill consequence of being abroad in the rain, I took care to furnish myself with provisions beforehand, that I might not be obliged to go out; and I sat within doors, as much as possible during the wet months.

In this time I found much employment, and very suitable also to the time, for I found great occasion of many things which I had no way to furnish myself with but by hard labour and constant application; particularly, I tried many ways to make myself a basket; but all the twigs I could get for the purpose proved so brittle, that they would do nothing. It proved of excellent advantage to me now, that when I was a boy I used to take great delight in standing at a basket-maker's in the town where my father lived, to see them make their wicker-ware; and being, as boys usually are, very officious to help, and a great observer of the manner how they work those things, and sometimes lending a hand, I had by this means full knowledge of the methods of it, that I wanted nothing but the materials; when it came into my mind that the twigs of that tree from whence I cut my stakes that grew might possibly be as tough as the sallows, and willows, and osiers in England, and I resolved to try.

Accordingly, the next day, I went to my country house, as I called it; and cutting some of the smaller twigs, I found them to my purpose as much as I could desire; whereupon I came the next time prepared with a hatchet to cut down a quantity, which I soon found, for there was great plenty of them. These I set up to dry within my circle or hedge, and when they were fit for use, I carried them to my cave; and here during the next season I employed myself in making, as well as I could, a great many baskets, both to carry earth, or to carry or lay up anything as I had occasion. And though I did not finish them very handsomely, yet I made them sufficiently serviceable for my purpose. And thus, afterwards, I took care never to be without them; and as my wicker-ware decayed, I made more, especially I made strong deep baskets to place my corn in, instead of sacks, when I should come to have any quantity of it.

Having mastered this difficulty, and employed a world of time about it, I bestirred myself to see, if possible, how to supply two wants. I had no vessels to hold anything that was liquid, except two runlets, which were almost full of rum, and some glass bottles, some of the common size, and others which were case-bottles square, for the holding of waters, spirits, etc. I had not so much as a pot to boil anything except a great kettle, which I saved out of the ship, and which was too big for such use as I desired it, viz., to make broth, and stew a bit of meat by itself. The second thing I would fain have had was a tobacco-pipe; but it was impossible to me to make one. However, I found contrivance for that, too, at last.

I employed myself in planting my second rows of stakes or piles, and in this wicker-working all the summer or dry season, when another business took me up more time that it could be imagined I could spare.

I mentioned before that I had a great mind to see the whole island, and that I had travelled up the brook, and so on to where

I built my bower, and where I had an opening quite to the sea, on the other side of the island. I now resolved to travel quite across to the seashore on that side; so taking my gun, a hatchet, and my dog, and a larger quantity of powder and shot than usual, with two biscuit-cakes and a great bunch of raisins in my pouch for my store, I began my journey. When I had passed the vale where my bower stood, as above, I came within view of the sea to the west; and it being a very clear day, I fairly descried land, whether an island or a continent I could not tell; but it lay very high, extending from the west to the W.S.W. at a very great distance; by my guess, it could not be less than fifteen or twenty leagues off.

I could not tell what part of the world this might be, otherwise than that I know it must be part of America, and, as I concluded, by all my observations, must be near the Spanish dominions, and perhaps was all inhabited by savages, where, if I should have landed, I had been in a worse condition than I was now; and therefore I acquiesced in the dispositions of Providence, which I began now to own and to believe ordered everything for the best. I say, I quieted my mind with this, and left afflicting myself with fruitless wishes of being there.

Besides, after some pause upon this affair, I considered that if this land was the Spanish coast I should certainly, one time or other, see some vessel pass or repass one way or other; but if not, then it was the savage coast between the Spanish country and Brazils, which are indeed the worst of savages; for they are cannibals or men-eaters, and fail not to murder and devour all the human bodies that fall into their hands.

With these considerations I walked very leisurely forward. I found that side of the island, where I now was, much pleasanter than mine, the open or savanna fields sweet, adorned with flowers and grass, and full of very fine woods.

I saw abundance of parrots, and fain would have caught one, if possible, to have kept it to be tame, and taught it to speak to me. I did, after some painstaking, catch a young parrot, for I knocked it down with a stick, and having recovered it, I brought it home; but it was some years before I could make him speak. However, at last I taught him to call me by my name very familiarly. But the accident that followed, though it be a trifle, will be very diverting in its place.

I was exceedingly diverted with this journey. I found in the low grounds hares, as I thought them to be, and foxes; but they differed greatly from all the other kinds I had met with, nor could I satisfy myself to eat them, though I killed several. But I had no need to be venturous, for I had no want of food, and of that which was very good too; especially these three sorts, viz., goats, pigeons, and turtle, or tortoise; which, added to my grapes, Leadenhall Market could not have furnished a table better than I, in proportion to the company. And though my case was deplorable enough, yet I had great cause for thankfulness, and that I was not driven to any extremities for food, rather plenty, even to dainties.

I never travelled in this journey above two miles outright in a day, or thereabouts; but I took so many turns and returns, to see what discoveries I could make, that I came weary enough to the place where I resolved to sit down for all night; and then I either reposed myself in a tree, or surrounded myself with a row of stakes, set upright in the ground, either from one tree to another, or so as no wild creature could come at me without waking me.

As soon as I came to the seashore, I was surprised to see that I had taken up my lot on the worst side of the island, for here indeed the shore was covered with innumerable turtles; whereas, on the other side, I had found but three in a year and a half. Here was also an infinite number of fowls of many kinds, some which I had seen, and some which I had not see of before, and many of them were very good meat, but such as I knew not the names of, except those called penguins.

I could have shot as many as I pleased, but was very sparing of my powder and shot, and therefore had more mind to kill a she-goat, if I could, which I could better feed on; and though there were many goats here, more than on my side the island, yet it was with much more difficulty that I could come near them, the country being flat and even, and they saw me much sooner then when I was on the hill.

I confess this side of the country was much pleasanter than mine; but yet I had not the least inclination to remove, for as I was fixed in my habitation, it became natural to me, and I seemed all the while I was here to be as it were upon a journey, and from home. However, I travelled along the shore of the sea towards the east, I suppose about twelve miles, and then setting up a great pole upon the shore for a mark, I concluded I would go home again; and that the next journey I took should be on the other side of the island, east from my dwelling, and so round till I came to my post again; of which in its place.

I took another way to come back than that I went, thinking I could easily keep all the island so much in my view that I could not miss finding my first dwelling by viewing the country. But I found myself mistaken; for being come about two or three miles, I found myself de-descended into a very large valley, but so surrounded with hills, and those hill covered with wood, that I could not see which was my way by any direction but that of the sun, nor even then, unless I knew very well the position of the sun at that time of the day.

It happened to my farther misfortune that the weather proved hazy for three or four days while I was in this valley; and not being able to see the sun, I wandered about very uncomfortably, and at last was obliged to find out the seaside, look for my post, and come back the same way I went; and then by easy journeys I turned homeward, the weather being exceeding hot, and my gun, ammunition, hatchet, and other things very heavy.

In this journey my dog surprised a young kid, and seized upon it, and I running in to take hold of it, caught it, and saved it alive from the dog. I had a great mind to bring it home if I could, for I had often been musing whether it might not be possible to get a kid or two, and so raise a breed of tame goats, which might supply me when my powder and shot should be all spent.

I made a collar to this little creature, and with a string, which I made of some rope-yarn, which I always carried about me, I led him along, though with some difficulty, till I came to my bower, and there I enclosed him and left him, for I was very impatient to be at home, from whence I had been absent above a month.

I cannot express what a satisfaction it was to me to come into my old hutch, and lie down in my hammock-bed. This little wandering journey, without settled place of abode, had been so unpleasant to me, that my own house, as I called it to myself, was a perfect settlement to me compared to that; and it rendered everything about me so comfortable, that I resolved I would never go a great way from it again, while it should be my lot to stay on the island.

I reposed myself here a week, to rest and regale myself after my long journey; during which most of the time was taken up in the weighty affair of making a cage for my Poll, who began now to be a mere domestic, and to be mighty well acquainted with me. Then I began to think of the poor kid which I had penned in within my little circle, and resolved to go and fetch it home, or give it some food. Accordingly I went, and found it where I left it, for indeed it could not get out, but almost starved for want of food. I went out and cut boughs of trees, and branches of such shrubs as I could find, and threw it over, and having fed it, I tied it as I did before, to lead it away; but it was so tame with being hungry, that I had no need to have tied it, for it followed me like a dog. And as I continually fed it, the creature became so loving, so gentle, and so fond, that it became from that time one of my domestics also, and would never leave me afterwards.

The rainy season of the autumnal equinox was now come,

and I kept the 30th of September in the same solemn manner as before, being the anniversary of my landing on the island, having now been there two years, and no more prospect of being delivered than the first day I came there. I spent the whole day in humble and thankful acknowledgments of the many wonderful mercies which my solitary condition was attended with, and without which it might have been infinitely more miserable. I gave humble and hearty thanks that God had been pleased to discover to me even that it was possible I might be more happy in this solitary condition, than I should have been in a liberty of society, and in all the pleasures of the world; that He could fully make up to me the deficiences of my solitary state, and the want of human society, by His presence, and the communication of His grace to my soul, supporting, comforting, and encouraging me to depend upon His providence here, and hope for His eternal presence hereafter.

It was now that I began sensibly to feel how much more happy this life I now led was, with all its miserable circumstances, than the wicked, cursed, abominable life I led all the past part of my days. And now I changed both my sorrows and my joys; my very desires altered, my affections changed their gusts, and my delights were perfectly new from what they were at my first coming, or indeed for the two years past.

Before, as I walked about, either on my hunting, or for viewing the country, the anguish of my soul at my condition would break out upon me on a sudden, and my very heart would die within me, to think of the woods, the mountains, the deserts I was in, and how I was a prisoner, locked up with the eternal bars and bolts of the ocean, in an uninhibited wilderness, without redemption. In the midst of the greatest composures of my mind, this would break out upon me like a storm, and make me wring my hands and weep like a child. Sometimes it would take me in the middle of my work, and I would immediately sit down and sigh, and look upon the ground for an hour or two together; and this was still worse to me, for if I could burst out into tears, or vent myself by words, it would go off, and the grief, having exhausted itself, would abate.

But now I began to exercise myself with new thoughts. I daily read the Word of God, and applied all the comforts of it to my present state. One morning, being very sad, I opened the Bible upon these words, "I will never, never leave thee, nor forsake thee." Immediately it occurred that these words were for me; why else should they be directed in such a manner, just at the moment when I was mourning over my condition, as one forsaken of God and man? "Well then," said I, "if God does not forsake me, of what ill consequence can it be, or what matters it, though the world should all forsake me, seeing on the other hand if I had all the world, and should lose the favour and blessing of God, there would be no comparison in the loss?"

From this moment I began to conclude in my mind that it was possible for me to be more happy in this forsaken solitary condition, that it was probable I should ever have been in any other particular state in the world, and with this thought I was going to give thanks to God for bringing me to this place.

I know not what it was, but something shocked my mind at that thought, and I durst not speak the words. "How canst thou be such a hypocrite," said I, even audibly, "to pretend to be thankful for a condition which, however thou mayest endeavour to be contented with, thou wouldest rather pray heartily to be delivered from?" So I stopped there; but though I could not say I thanked God for being there, yet I sincerely gave thanks to God for opening my eyes, by whatever afflicting providences, to see the former condition of my life, and to mourn for my wickedness, and repent. I never opened the Bible, or shut it, but my very soul within me blessed God for directing my friend in England, without any order of mine, to pack it up among my goods, and for assisting me afterwards to save it out of the wreck of the ship.

Thus, and in this disposition of mind, I began my third year; and though I have not given the reader the trouble of so particular account of my works this year as the first, yet in general it may be observed, that I was very seldom idle, but having regularly divided my time, according to the several daily employments that were before me, such as, first, my duty to God, and the reading of the Scriptures, which I constantly set apart some time for, thrice every day; secondly, the going abroad with my gun for food, which generally took me up three hours in every morning, when it did not rain; thirdly, the ordering, curing, preserving, and cooking what I had killed or catched for my supply; these took up great part of the day; also it is to be considered that the middle of the day, when the sun was in the zenith, the violence of the heat was too great to stir out; so that about four hours in the evening was all the time I could be supposed to work in, with this exception, that sometimes I changed my hours of hunting and working, and went to work in the morning, and abroad with my gun in the afternoon.

To this short time allowed for labour I desire, may be added the exceeding laboriousness of my work; the many hours which, for want of tools, want of help, and want of skill, everything I did took up out of my time. For example, I was full two and forty days making me a board for a long shelf, which I wanted in my cave; whereas two sawyers, with their tools and a saw-pit, would have cut six of them out of the same tree in half a day.

My case was this: it was to be a large tree which was to be cut down, because my board was to be a broad one. This tree I took three days a-cutting down, and two more cutting off the boughs, and reducing it to a log, or piece of timber. With inexpressible hacking and hewing, I reduced both sides of it into chips till it began to be light enough to move; then I turned it, and made one side of it smooth and flat as a board from end to end; then turning that side downward, cut the other side, till I brought the plank to be about three inches thick, and smooth on both sides. Anyone may judge the labour of my hands in such a piece of work; but labour and patience carried me through that, and many other things. I only observe this in particular, to show the reason why so much of my time went away with so little work, viz., that what might be a little to be done with help and tools, was a vast labour, and required a prodigious time to do alone, and by hand. But not withstanding this, with patience and labour, I went through many things, and, indeed, everything that my circumstances made necessary for me to do, as will appear by what follows.

I was now, in the months of November and December, expecting my crop of barley and rice. The ground I had manured or dug up for them was not great; for as I observed, my seed of each was not above the quantity of half a peck; for I had lost one whole crop by sowing in the dry season. But now my crop promised very well, when on a sudden I found I was in danger of losing it all again by enemies of several sorts, which it was scarcely possible to keep from it; as, first the goats and wild creatures which I called hares, who, tasting the sweetness of the blade, lay in it night and day, as soon as it came up, and eat it so close, that it could get no time to shoot up into stalk.

This I saw no remedy for but by making an enclosure about it with a hedge, which I did with a great deal of toil, and the more, because it required speed. However, as my arable land was small, suited to my crop, I got it totally well fenced in about three weeks' time, and shooting some of the creatures in the daytime, I set my dog to guard it in the night, tying him up to a stake at the gate, where he would stand and bark all night long; so in a little time the enemies forsook the place, and the corn grew very strong and well, and began to ripen apace.

But as the beasts ruined me before while my corn was in the blade, so the birds were as likely to ruin me now when it was in the ear; for going along by the place to see how it throve, I saw my little crop surrounded with fowls, of I know not how many sorts, who stood, as it were, watching till I should be gone. I immediately let fly among them, for I always had my gun with me. I had no sooner shot, but there rose up a little cloud of fowls, which I had not seen at all, from among the corn itself.

This touched me sensibly, for I foresaw that in a few days they would devour all my hopes, that I should be starved, and never be able to raise a crop at all, and what to do I could not tell. However, I resolved not to lose my corn, if possible, though I should watch it night and day. In the first place, I went among it to see what damage was already done, and found they had spoiled a good deal of it; but that as it was yet too green for them, the loss was not so great but that the remainder was likely to be a good crop if it could be saved.

I stayed by it to load my gun, and then coming away, I could easily see the thieves sitting upon all the trees about me, as if they only waited till I was gone away. And the event proved it to be so; for as I walked off, as if I was gone, I was no sooner out of their sight but they dropped down, one by one, into the corn again. I was so provoked, that I could not have patience to stay till more came on, knowing that every grain that they eat now was, as it might be said, a peck-loaf to me in the consequence; but coming up to the hedge, I fired again, and killed three of them. This was what I wished for; so I took them up, and served them as we serve notorious thieves in England, viz., hanged them in chains, for a terror to others. It is impossible to imagine almost that this should have such an effect as it had, for the fowls would not only not come at the corn, but, in short, they forsook all that part of the island, and I could never see a bird near the place as long as my scare-crows hung there.

This I was very glad of, you may be sure; and about the latter end of December, which was our second harvest of the year, I reaped my crop.

I was sadly put to it for a scythe or a sickle to cut it down, and all I could do was to make one as well as I could out of one of the broadswords, or cutlasses, which I saved among the arms out of the ship. However, as my first crop of corn was but small,

I had no great difficulty to cut it down; in short, I reaped it my way, for I cut nothing off but the ears, and carried it away in a great basket which I had made, and so rubbed it out with my hands; and at the end of all my harvesting, I found that out of my half peck of seed I had near two bushels of rice, and above two bushels and a half of barley, that is to say, by my guess, for I had no measure at that time.

However, this was a great encouragement to me, and I foresaw that, in time, it would please God to supply me with bread. And yet here I was perplexed again, for I neither knew how to grind or make meal of my corn, or indeed how to clean it and part it; nor, if made into meal, how to make bread of it, and if to make it, yet I knew not how to bake it. These things being added to my desire of having a good quantity for store, and to secure a constant supply, I resolved not to taste any of this crop, but to preserve it all for seed against the next season, and, in the meantime, to employ all my study and hours of working to accomplish this great work of providing myself with corn and bread.

It might be truly said, that now I worked for my bread. 'Tis a little wonderful, and what I believe few people have thought upon, viz., the strange multitude of little things necessary in the providing, producing, curing, dressing, making, and finishing this one article of bread.

I, that was reduced to a mere state of nature, found this to my daily discouragement, and was made more and more sensible of it every hour, even after I had got the first handful of seed-corn, which, as I have said, came up unexpectedly, and indeed, to a surprise.

First, I had no plough to turn up the earth, no spade or shovel to dig it. Well, this I conquered by making a wooden spade, as I observed before, but this did my work in but a wooden manner; and though it cost me a great many days to make it, yet, for want of iron, it not only wore out the sooner, but made my work the harder, and made it to be performed much worse.

However, this I bore with, and was content to work it out with patience, and bear with the badness of the performance. When the corn was sowed, I had no harrow, but was forced to go over it myself, and drag a great heavy bough of a tree over it, to scratch it, as it may be called, rather than rake or harrow it.

When it was growing and grown, I have observed already how many things I wanted to fence it, secure it, mow or reap it, cure and carry it home, thrash, part it from the chaff, and save it. Then I wanted a mill to grind it, sieves to dress it, yeast and salt to make it into bread, and an oven to bake it, and yet all these things I did without, as shall be observed; and yet the corn was an inestimable comfort and advantage to me too. All this, as I said, made everything laborious and tedious to me, but that there was no help for; neither was my time so much loss to me, because, as I had divided it, a certain part of it was every day appointed to these works, and as I resolved to use none of the corn for bread till I had a greater quantity by me, I had the next six months to apply myself wholly, by labour and invention, to furnish myself with utensils proper for performing all the operations necessary for the making the corn, when I had it, fit for my use.

But first I was to prepare more land, for I had now seed enough to sow above an acre of ground. Before I did this, I had a week's work at least to make me a spade, which, when it was done, was but a sorry one indeed, and very heavy, and required double labour to work with it. However, I went through that, and sowed my seed in two large flat pieces of ground, as near my house as I could find them to my mind, and fenced them in with a good hedge, the stakes of which were all cut of that wood which I had set before, and knew it would grow; so that in one year's time I knew I should have a quick or living hedge, that would want but little repair. This work was not so little as to take me up less than three months, because great part of that time was of the wet season, when I could not go abroad.

Within doors, that is, when it rained, and I could not go out, I found employment on the following occasions; always observing, that all the while I was at work, I diverted myself with talking to my parrot, and teaching him to speak, and I quickly learned him to know his own name, and at last to speak it out pretty loud, "Poll," which was the first word I ever heard spoken in the island by any mouth but my own. This, therefore, was not my work, but an assistant to my work; for now, as I said, I had a great employment upon my hands, as follows, viz., I had long studied, by some means or other, to make myself some earthern vessels, which indeed I wanted sorely, but knew not where to come at them. However, considering the heat of the climate, I did not doubt but if I could find out any such clay, I might botch up some such a pot as might, being dried in the sun, be hard enough and strong enough to bear handling, and to hold anything that was dry, and required to be kept so; and as this was necessary in the preparing corn, meal, etc., which was the thing I was upon, I resolved to make some as large as I could, and fit only to stand like jars, to hold what should be put into them.

It would make the reader pity me, or rather laugh at me, to tell how many awkward ways I took to raise this paste; what odd, misshapen, ugly things I made; how many of them fell in, and how many fell out, the clay not being stiff enough to bear its own weight; how many cracked by the over-violent heat of the sun, being set out too hastily; and how many fell in pieces with only removing, as well before as after they were dried; and, in a word, how, after having laboured hard to find the clay, to dig it, to temper it, to bring it home, and work it, I could not make above two large earthen ugly things (I cannot call them jars) in about two months labour.

However, as the sun baked these two very dry and hard, I lifted them very gently up, and set them down again in two great wicker baskets, which I had made on purpose for them, that they might not break; and as between the pot and the basket there was a little room to spare, I stuffed it full of the rice and barley straw, and these two pots being to stand always dry, I thought would hold my dry corn, and perhaps the meal, when the corn was bruised.

Though I miscarried so much in my design for large pots, yet I made several smaller things with better success; such as little round pots, flat dishes, pitchers, and pipkins, and any things my hand turned to; and the heat of the sun baked them strangely hard. But all this would not answer my end, which was to get an earthen pot to hold what was liquid, and bear the fire, which none of these could do. It happened after some time, making a pretty large fire for cooking my meat, when I went to put it out after I had done with it, I found a broken piece of one of my earthenware vessels in the fire, burnt as hard as a stone, and red as a tile. I was agreeably surprised to see it, and said to myself, that certainly they might be made to burn whole, if they would burn broken.

This set me to studying how to order my fire, so as to make it burn me some pots. I had no notion of a kiln, such as the potters burn in, or of glazing them with lead, though I had some lead to do it with; but I placed three large pigskins, and two or three pots in a pile, one upon another, and placed my firewood all round it, with a great heap of embers under them. I plied the fire with fresh fuel round the outside, and upon the top, till I saw the pots in the inside hot quite through, and observed that they did not crack at all. When I saw them clear red, I let them stand in that heat about five or six hours, till I found one of them, though it did not crack, did melt or run, for the sand which was mixed with the clay melted by the violence of the heat, and would have run into glass, if I had gone on; so I slacked my fire gradually till the pots began to abate of the red colour; and watching them all night, that I might not let the fire abate too fast, in the morning I had three very good, I will not say handsome, pipkins, and two other earthen pots, as hard burnt as could be desired, and one of them perfectly glazed with the running of the sand.

After this experiment, I need not say that I wanted no sort of earthenware for my use; but I must needs say, as to the shapes of them, they were very indifferent, as any one may suppose, when I had no way of making them but as the children make dirt pies, or as a woman would make pies that had never learned to raise paste.

No joy at a thing of so mean a nature was ever equal to mine, when I found I had made an earthen pot that would bear the fire; and I had hardly patience to stay till they were cold, before I set one upon the fire again, with some water in it, to boil me some meat, which it did admirably well; and with a piece of a kid I made some very good broth, though I wanted oatmeal and several other ingredients requisite to make it so good as I would have had it been.

My next concern was to get me a stone mortar to stamp or beat some corn in; for as to the mill, there was no thought at arriving to that perfection of art with one pair of hands. To supply this want I was at a great loss; for, of all trades in the world, I was as perfectly unqualified for a stone-cutter as for any whatever; neither had I any tools to go about it with. I spent many a day to find out a great stone big enough to cut hollow, and make fit for a mortar, and could find none at all, except what was in the solid rock, and which I had no way to dig or cut out; nor indeed were the rocks in the island of hardness sufficient, but were all of a sandy crumbling stone, which neither would bear the weight of a heavy pestle, or would break the corn without filling it with sand. So, after a great deal of time lost in searching for a stone, I gave it over, and resolved to look out for a great block of hard wood, which I found indeed much easier; and getting one as big as I had strength to stir, I rounded it, and formed it in the outside with my axe and hatchet, and then, with the help of fire, and infinite labour, made a hollow place in it, as the Indians in Brazil make their canoes. After this, I made a great heavy pestle, or beater, of the wood called the iron-wood; and this I prepared and laid by against I had my next crop of corn, when I proposed to myself to grind, or rather pound, my corn into meal, to make my bread.

My next difficulty was to make a sieve, or search, to dress my meal, and to part it from the bran and the husk, without which I did not see it possible I could have any bread. This was a most difficult thing, so much as but to think on, for to be sure I had nothing like the necessary thing to make it; I mean fine thin canvas or stuff, to search the meal through. And here I was at a full stop for many months, nor did I really know what to do; linen I had none left, but what was mere rags; I had goats'-hair, but neither knew I how to weave it or spin it; and had I known how, here was no tools to work it with. All the remedy that I found for this was, that at last I did remember I had, among the seamen's clothes which were saved out of the ship, some neckcloths of calico or muslin; and with some pieces of these I made three small sieves, but proper enough for the work; and thus I made shift for some years. How I did afterwards, I shall show in its place.

The baking part was the next thing to be considered, and how I should make bread when I came to have corn; for, first, I had no yeast. As to that part, as there was no supplying the want, so I did not concern myself much about it; but for an oven I was indeed in great pain. At length I found out an experiment for that also, which was this: I made some earthen vessels very broad, but not deep, that is to say, about two feet diameter, and not above nine inches deep; these I burned in the fire, as I had done the other, and laid them by; and when I wanted to bake, I made a great fire upon my hearth, which I had paved with some square tiles, of my own making and burning also; but I should not call them square.

When the firewood was burned pretty much into embers, or live coals, I drew them forward upon this hearth, so as to cover it all over, and there I let them lie till the hearth was very hot, then sweeping away all the embers, I set down my loaf, or loaves, and whelming down the earthen pot upon them, drew the embers all round the outside of the pot, to keep in and add to the heat. And thus, as well as in the best oven in the world, I baked my barley-loaves, and became, in a little time, a mere pastry-cook into the bargain; for I made myself several cakes of the rice, and puddings; indeed I made no pies, neither had I anything to put into them, supposing I had, except the flesh either of fowls or goats.

It need not be wondered at, if all these things took me up most part of the third year of my abode here; for it is to be observed, that in the intervals of these things I had my new harvest and husbandry to manage; for I reaped my corn in its season, and carried it home as well as I could, and laid it up in the ear, in my large baskets, till I had time to rub it out, for I had no floor to thrash it on, or instrument to thrash it with.

And now, indeed, my stock of corn increasing, I really wanted to build my barns bigger. I wanted a place to lay it up in, for the increase of the corn now yielded me so much, that I had of the barley about twenty bushels, and of the rice as much, or more, insomuch that now I resolved to begin to use it freely; for my bread had been quite gone a great while; also, I resolved to see what quantity would be sufficient for me a whole year, and to sow but once a year.

Upon the whole, I found that the forty bushels of barley and rice was much more than I could consume in a year; so I resolved to sow just the same quantity every year that I sowed the last, in hopes that such a quantity would fully provide me with bread, etc.

All the while these things were doing, you may be sure my thoughts ran many times upon the prospect of land which I had seen from the other side of the island, and I was not without secret wishes that I were on shore there, fancying the seeing the mainland, and in an inhabited country, I might find some way or other to convey myself farther, and perhaps at last find some means of escape.

But all this while I made no allowance for the dangers of such a condition, and how I might fall into the hands of savages, and perhaps such as I might have reason to think far worse than the lions and tigers of Africa; that if I once came into their power, I should run a hazard more than a thousand to one of being killed, and perhaps of being eaten; for I had heard that the people of the Caribbean coasts were cannibals, or man-eaters, and I knew by the latitude that I could not be far off from that shore. That suppose they were not cannibals, yet that they might kill me, as many Europeans who had fallen into their hands had been served, even when they had been often or twenty together, much more I, that was but one, and could make little or no defence; all these things, I say, which I ought to have considered well of, and did cast up in my thoughts afterwards, yet took up none of my apprehensions at first, but my head ran mightily upon the thought of getting over to the shore.

Now I wished for my boy Xury, and the longboat with the shoulder-of-mutton sail, with which I sailed above a thousand miles on the coast of Africa; but this was in vain. Then I thought I would go and look at our ship's boat, which, as I have said, was blown up upon the shore a great way, in the storm, when we were first cast away. She lay almost where she did at first, but not quite; and was turned, by the force of the waves and the winds, almost bottom upward, against a high ridge of beachy rough sand, but no water about her, as before.

If I had had hands to have refitted her, and to have launched her into the water, the boat would have done well enough, and I might have gone back into the Brazils with her easily enough; but I might have foreseen that I could no more turn her and set her upright upon her bottom, that I could remove the island. However, I went to the woods, and cut levers and rollers, and brought them to the boat, resolved to try what I could do; suggesting to myself that if I could but turn her down, I might easily repair the damage she had received, and she would be a very good boat, and I might go to sea in her very easily.

I spared no pains, indeed, in this piece of fruitless toil, and spent, I think, three or four weeks about it. At last finding it impossible to heave it up with my little strength, I fell to digging away the sand, to undermine it, and so make it fall down, setting pieces of wood to thrust and guide it right in the fall. But when I had done this, I was unable to stir it up again, or to get under it, much less to move it forward towards the water; so I was forced to give it over. And yet, though I gave over the hopes of the boat, my desire to venture over for the main increased, rather than decreased, as the means for it seemed impossible.

This at length put me upon thinking whether it was not possible to make myself a canoe, or *periegua,* such as the natives of those climates make, even without tools, or, as I might say, without hands, viz., of the trunk of a great tree. This I not only thought possible, but easy, and pleased myself extremely with the thoughts of making it, and with my having much more convenience for it than any of the negroes or Indians; but not at all considering the particular inconveniences which I lay under more than the Indians did, viz., want of hands to move it, when it was made, into the water, a difficulty much harder for me to surmount than all the consequences of want of tools could be to them. For what was it to me, that when I had chosen a vast tree in the woods, I might with much trouble cut it down, if, after I might be able with my tools to hew and dub the outside into the proper shape of a boat, and burn or cut out the inside to make it hollow, so to make a boat of it; if, after this, I must leave it just there where I found it, and was not able to launch it into the water?

One would have thought I could not have had the least reflection upon my mind of my circumstance while I was making this boat, but I should have immediately thought how I should get it into the sea; but my thoughts were so intent upon my voyage over the sea in it, that I never once considered how I should get it off the land; and it was really, in its own nature, more easy for me to guide it over forty-five miles of sea, than about forty-five fathoms of land, where it lay, to set it afloat in the water.

I went to work upon this boat the most like a fool that ever man did who had any of his senses awake. I pleased myself with the design, without determining whether I was ever able to undertake it. Not but that the difficulty of launching my boat came often into my head; but I put a stop to my own inquiries into it, by this foolish answer which I gave myself, "Let's first make it; I'll warrant I'll find some way or other to get it along when 'tis done."

This was a most preposterous method; but the eagerness of my fancy prevailed, and to work I went. I felled a cedar tree: I questioned much whether Solomon ever had such a one for the building of the Temple at Jerusalem. It was five feet ten inches diameter at the lower part next to the stump, and four feet eleven inches diameter at the end of twenty-two feet, after which it lessened for awhile, and then parted into branches. It was not without infinite labour that I felled this tree. I was twenty days hacking and hewing at it at the bottom; it took fourteen more days getting the branches and limbs, and the vast spreading head of it cut off, which I hacked and hewed through with axe and hatchet, and inexpressible labour. After this, it cost me a month to shape it and dub it to a proportion, and to something like the bottom of a boat, that it might swim upright as it ought to do. It cost me near three months more to clear the inside, and work it so as to make an exact boat of it. This I did, indeed, without fire, by mere mallet and chisel, and by the dint of hard labour, till I had brought it to be a very handsome *periegua,* and big enough to have carried six and twenty men, and consequently big enough to have carried me and my cargo.

When I had gone through this work, I was extremely delighted with it. The boat was really much bigger than I ever saw a canoe or *periegua,* that was made of one tree, in my life. Many a weary stroke it had cost, you may be sure; and there remained nothing but to get it into the water; and had I gotten it into the water, I make no question but I should have begun the maddest voyage, and the most unlikely to be performed, that ever was undertaken.

But all my devices to get it into the water failed me, they cost me infinite labour too. It lay about one hundred yards from the water, and not more; but the first inconvenience was, it was uphill towards the creek. Well, to take away this discouragement, I resolved to dig into the surface of the earth, and so make a declivity. This I began, and it cost me a prodigious deal of pains; but who grudges pains, that have their deliverance in view? But when this was worked through, and this difficulty managed, it was still much at one, for I could no more stir the canoe than I could the other boat.

Then measured the distance of ground, and resolved to cut a dock or canal, to bring the water up to the canoe, seeing I could not bring the canoe down to the water. Well, I began this work; and when I began to enter into it, and calculate how deep it was to be dug, how broad, how the stuff to be thrown out, I found that by the number of hands I had, being none but my own, it must have been ten or twelve years before I should have gone through with it; for the shore lay high, so that at the upper end it must have been at least twenty feet deep; so at length, though with great reluctancy, I gave this attempt over also.

This grieved me heartily; and now I saw, though too late, the folly of beginning a work before we count the cost, and before we judge rightly of our own strength to go through with it.

In the middle of this work I finished my fourth year in this place, and kept my anniversary with the same devotion, and with as much comfort as ever before; for, by a constant study and serious application of the Word of God, and by the assistance of His grace, I gained a different knowledge from what I had before.

I entertained different notions of things. I looked now upon the world as a thing remote, which I had nothing to do with, no expectation from, and, indeed, no desires about. In a word, I had nothing indeed to do with it, nor was ever like to have; so I thought it looked, as we may perhaps look upon it hereafter, viz., as a place I had lived in, but was come out of it; and well might I say, as father Abraham to Dives, "Between me and thee is a great gulf fixed."

In the first place, I was removed from all the wickedness of the world here. I had neither the lust of the flesh, the lust of the eye, or the pride of life. I had nothing to covet, for I had all that I was now capable of enjoying. I was lord of the whole manor; or, if I pleased, I might call myself king or emperor over the whole country which I had possession of. There were no rivals: I had no competitor, none to dispute sovereignty or command with me. I might have raised ship loadings of corn, but I had no use for it; so I let as little grow as I thought enough for my occasion. I had tortoise or turtles enough, but now and then one was as much as I could put to any use. I had timber enough to have built a fleet of ships. I had grapes enough to have made wine, or to have cured into raisins, to have loaded that fleet when they had been built.

But all I could make use of was all that was valuable. I had enough to eat and to supply my wants, and what was all the rest to me? If I killed more flesh than I could eat, the dog must eat it, or the vermin. If I sowed more corn than I could eat, it must be spoiled. The trees that I cut down were lying to rot on the ground; I could make no more use of them than for fuel, and that I had no occasion for but to dress my food.

In a word, the nature and experience of things dictated to me, upon just reflection, that all the good things of this world are no farther good to us than they are for our use; and that whatever we may heap up indeed to give others, we enjoy just as much as we can use, and no more. The most covetous, griping miser in the world would have been cured of the vice of covetousness, if he had been in my case; for I possessed infinitely more than I knew what to do with. I had no room for desire, except it was of things which I had not, and they were but trifles, though indeed of great use to me. I had, as I hinted before, a parcel of money, as well gold as silver, about thirty-six pounds sterling. Alas! There the nasty, sorry, useless stuff lay; I had no manner of business for it; and I often thought with myself, that I would have given a handful of it for a gross of tobacco-pipes, or for a hand mill to grind my corn; nay, I would have given it all for sixpennyworth of turnip and carrot seed out of England, or for a handful of peas and beans, and a bottle of ink. As it was, I had not the least advantage by it, or benefit from it; but there it lay in a drawer, and grew mouldy with the damp of the cave in the wet season; and if I had had the drawer full of diamonds, it had been the same case, and they had been of no manner of value to me because of no use.

I had now brought my state of life to be much easier in itself than it was at first, and much easier to my mind, as well as to my body. I frequently sat down to my meat with thankfulness, and admired the hand of God's providence, which had thus spread my table in the wilderness. I learned to look more upon the bright side of my condition, and less upon the dark side, and to consider what I enjoyed, rather than what I wanted; and this gave me sometimes such secret comforts, that I cannot express them; and which I take notice of here, to put those discontented people in mind of it, who cannot enjoy comfortably what God has given them, because they see and covet something that He has not given them. All our discontents about what we want, appeared to me to spring from the want of thankfulness for what we have.

Another reflection was of great use to me, and doubtless would be so to any that should fall into such distress as mine was; and this was, to compare my present condition with what I at first expected it should be; nay, with what it would certainly have been, if the good providence of God had not wonderfully ordered the ship to be cast up nearer to the shore, where I not only could come at her, but could bring what I got out of her to the shore, for my relief and comfort; without which I had wanted for tools to work, weapons for defence, or gunpowder and shot for getting my food.

I spent whole hours, I may say whole days, in representing to myself, in the most lively colours, how I must have acted if I had got nothing out of the ship. How I could not have so much as got any food, except fish and turtles; and that as it was long before I found any of them, I must have perished first; that I should have lived, if I had not perished, like a mere savage; that if I had killed a goat or a fowl, by any contrivance, I had no way to flay or open them, or part the flesh from the skin and the bowels, or to cut it up; but must gnaw it with my teeth, and pull it with my claws, like a beast.

These reflections made me very sensible of the goodness of Providence to me, and very thankful for my present condition, with all its hardships and misfortunes; and this part also I cannot but recommend to the reflection of those who are apt, in their misery, to say, Is any affliction like mine? Let them consider how much worse the cases of some people are, and their case might have been, if Providence had thought fit.

I had another reflection, which assisted me also to comfort my mind with hopes; and this was, comparing my present condition with what I had deserved, and had therefore reason to expect from the hand of Providence. I had lived a dreadful life, perfectly destitute of the knowledge and fear of God. I had been well instructed by father and mother; neither had they been wanting to me in their early endeavours to infuse a religious awe of God into my mind, a sense of my duty, and of what the nature and end of my being required of me. But, alas! falling early into the seafaring life, which, of all the lives, is the most destitute of the fear of God, though His terrors are always before them; I say, falling early into the seafaring life, and into seafaring company, all that little sense of religion which I had entertained was laughed out of me by my messmates; by a hardened despising of dangers, and the views of death, which grew habitual to me; by my long absence from all manner of opportunities to converse with anything but what was like myself, or to hear anything that was good, or tended towards it.

So void was I of everything that was good, or of the least sense of what I was, or was to be, that in the greatest deliverances I enjoyed, such as my escape from Sallee; my being taken up by the Portuguese master of the ship; my being planted so well in the Brazils; my receiving the cargo from England, and the like; I never had once the words, "Thank God," so much as on my mind, or in my mouth; nor in the greatest distress had I so much as thought to pray to Him, or so much as to say, "Lord, have mercy upon me!" no, nor to mention the name of God, unless it was to swear by and blaspheme it.

I had terrible reflections upon my mind for many months, as I have already observed, on the account of my wicked and hardened life past; and when I looked about me, and considered what particular providences had attended me since my coming into this place, and how God had dealt bountifully with me, had not only punished me less than my iniquity had deserved, but had so plentifully provided for me; this gave me great hopes that my repentance was accepted, and that God had yet mercy in store for me.

With these reflections, I worked my mind up, not only to resignation to the will of God in the present disposition of my circumstances, but even to a sincere thankfulness for my condition; and that I, who was yet a living man, ought not to complain, seeing I had not the due punishment of my sins; that I enjoyed so many mercies, which I had no reason to have expected in that place; that I ought nevermore to repine at my condition, but to rejoice, and to give daily thanks for that daily bread, which nothing but a crowd of wonders could have brought; that I ought to consider I had been fed even by miracle, even as great as that of feeding Elijah by ravens; nay, by a long series of miracles; and that I could hardly have named a place in the unhabitable part of the world where I could have been cast more to my advantage; a place where, as I had no society, which was my affliction on one hand, so I found no ravenous beasts, no furious wolves or tigers, to threaten my life; no venomous creatures, or poisonous, which I might feed on to my hurt; no savages to murder and devour me.

In a word, as my life was a life of sorrow one way, so it was a life of mercy another; and I wanted nothing to make it a life of comfort; but to be able to make my sense of God's goodness to me, and care over me in this condition, be my daily consolation; and after I did make a just improvement of these things, I went away, and was no more sad.

I had now been here so long, that many things which I brought on shore for my help were either quite gone, or very much wasted, and near spent. My ink, as I observed, had been gone for some time, all but a very little, which I eked out with water, a little and a little, till it was so pale it scarce left any appearance of black upon the paper. As long as it lasted, I made use of it to minute down the days of the month on which any remarkable thing happened to me. And, first, by casting up times past, I remember that there was a strange concurrence of days in the various providences which befell me, and which, if I had been superstitiously inclined to observe days as fatal or fortunate, I might have had reason to have looked upon with a great deal of curiosity.

First, I had observed that the same day that I broke away from my father and my friends, and run away to Hull, in order to go to sea, the same day afterwards I was taken by the Sallee man-of-war, and made a slave.

The same day of the year that I escaped out of the wreck of that ship in Yarmouth Roads, that same day-year afterwards I made my escape from Sallee in the boat.

The same day of the year I was born on viz., the 30th of September, that same day I had my life so miraculously saved twenty-six years after, when I was cast on the shore in this island; so that my wicked life and my solitary life began both on a day.

The next thing to my ink's being wasted, was that of my bread; I mean the biscuit, which I brought out of the ship. This I had husbanded to the last degree, allowing myself but one cake of read a day for above a year; and yet I was quite without bread or near a year before I got any corn of my own; and great reason I had to be thankful that I had any at all, the getting it being, as has been already observed, next to miraculous.

My clothes began to decay, too, mightily. As to linen, I had none a good while, except some chequered shirts which I found in the chests of the other seamen, and which I carefully preserved, because many times I could bear no other clothes on but a shirt; and it was a very great help to me that I had, among all the men's clothes of the ship, almost three dozen of shirts. There were also several thick watch-coats of the seamen's which were left indeed, but they were too hot to wear; and though it is true that the weather was so violent hot that there was no need of clothes, yet I could not go quite naked, no, though I had been inclined to it, which I was not, nor could abide the thoughts of it, though I was all alone.

The reason why I could not go quite naked was, I could not bear the heat of the sun so well when quite naked as with some clothes on; nay, the very heat frequently blistered my skin; whereas, with a shirt on, the air itself made some motion, and whistling under that shirt, was twofold cooler than without it. No more could I ever bring myself to go out in the heat of the sun without a cap or a hat. The heat of the sun beating with such violence, as it does in that place, would give me the headache presently, by darting so directly on my head, without a cap or hat on, so that I could not bear it; whereas, if I put on my hat, it would presently go away.

Upon those views, I began to consider about putting the few rags I had, which I called clothes, into some order. I had worn out all the waistcoats I had, and my business was now to try if I could not make jackets out of the great watch-coats which I had by me, and with such other materials as I had; so I set to work a-tailoring, or rather, indeed, a-botching, for I made most piteous work of it. However, I made shift to make two or three new waistcoats, which I hoped would serve me a great while. As for breeches or drawers, I made but a very sorry shift indeed till afterward.

I have mentioned that I saved the skins of all the creatures that I killed, I mean four-footed ones, and I had hung them up stretched out with sticks in the sun, by which means some of them were so dry and hard that they were fit for little, but others it seems were very useful. The first thing I made of these was a great cap for my head, with the hair on the outside, to shoot off the rain; and this I performed so well, that after this I made me a suit of clothes wholly of these skins, that is to say, a waistcoat, and breeches open at knees, and both loose, for they were rather wanting to keep me cool than to keep me warm. I must not omit to acknowledge that they were wretchedly made; for if I was a bad carpenter, I was a worse tailor. However, they were such as I made very good shift with; and when I was abroad, if it happened to rain, the hair of my waistcoat and cap being outermost, I was kept very dry.

After this I spent a great deal of time and pains to make me an umbrella. I was indeed in great want of one, and had a great mind to make one. I had seen them made in the Brazils, where they are very useful in the great heats which are there; and I felt the heats every jot as great here, and greater too, being nearer the equinox. Besides, as I was obliged to be much abroad, it was a most useful thing to me, as well for the rains as the heats. I took a world of pains at it, and was a great while before I could make anything likely to hold; nay, after I thought I had hit the way, I spoiled two or three before I made one to my mind; but at last I made one that answered indifferently well. The main difficulty I found was to make it to let down. I could make it to spread; but if it did not let it down too, and draw in, it was not portable for me any way but just over my head, which would not do. However, at last, as I said, I made one to answer, and covered with skins, the hair upwards, so that it cast off the rains like a penthouse, and kept off the sun so effectually that I could walk out in the hottest of the weather with greater advantage than I could before in the coolest; and when I had no need of it, could close it, and carry it under my arm.

Thus I lived mighty comfortably, my mind being entirely composed by resigning to the will of God, and throwing myself wholly upon the disposal of His providence. This made my life better than sociable; for when I began to regret the want of conversation, I would ask myself whether thus conversing mutually with my own thoughts and, as I hope I may say, with even God Himself, by ejaculations, was not better than the utmost enjoyment of human society in the world?

I cannot say that after this, for five years, any extraordinary thing happened to me; but I lived on in the same course, in the same posture and place, just as before. The chief things I was employed in, besides my yearly labour of planting my barley and rice, and curing my raisins, of both which I always kept up just enough to have sufficient stock of one year's provisions beforehand I say, besides this yearly labour, and my daily labour of going out with my gun, I had one labour, to make me a canoe, which at last I finished; so that by digging a canal to it of six feet wide, and four feet deep, I brought it into the creek, almost half a mile. As for the first, which was so vastly big, as I made it without considering beforehand, as I ought to do, how I should be able to launch it; so, never being able to bring it to the water, or bring the water to it, I was obliged to let it lie where it was, as a memorandum to teach me to be wiser next time. Indeed, the next time, though I could not get a tree proper for it, and in a place where I could not get the water to it at any less distance than, as I have said, near half a mile, yet as I saw it was at last, I never gave it over; and though I was near two years about it, yet I never grudged my labour, in hopes of having a boat to go off to sea at last.

However, though my little *periegua* was finished, yet the size of it was not at all answerable to the design which I had in view when I made the first; I mean, of venturing over to the *terra firma,* where it was above forty miles broad. Accordingly, the smallness of my boat assisted to put an end to that design, and now I thought no more of it. But as I had a boat, my next design was to make a tour round the island; for as I had been on the other side in one place, crossing, as I have already described it, over the land, so the discoveries I made in that little journey made me very eager to see other parts of the coast; and now I had a boat, I thought of nothing but sailing round the island.

For this purpose, that I might do everything with discretion and consideration, I fitted up a little mast to my boat, and made a sail to it out of some of the pieces of the ship's sail, which lay in store, and of which I had a great stock by me.

Having fitted my mast and sail, and tried the boat, I found she would sail very well. Then I made little lockers, or boxes, at either end of my boat, to put provisions, necessaries, and ammunition, etc., into, to be kept dry, either from rain or the spray of the sea; and a little long hollow place I cut in the inside of the boat, where I could lay my gun, making a flap to hang down over it to keep it dry.

I fixed my umbrella also in a step at the stern, like a mast, to stand over my head, and keep the heat of the sun off of me, like an awning; and thus I every now and then took a little voyage upon the sea, but never went far out, nor far from the little creek. But at last, being eager to view the circumference of my little kingdom, I resolved upon my tour; and accordingly I victualled my ship for the voyage, putting in two dozen of my loaves (cakes I should rather call them) of barley bread, an earthen pot full of parched rice, a food I eat a great deal of, a little bottle of rum, half a goat, and powder and shot for killing more, and two large watch-coats, of those which, as I mentioned before, I had saved out of the seamen's chests; these I took, one to lie upon, and the other to cover me in the night.

It was the 6th of November, in the sixth year of my reign, or my captivity, which you please, that I set out on this voyage, and I found it much longer than I expected; for though the island itself was not very large, yet when I came to the east side of it I found a great ledge of rocks lie out above two leagues into the sea, some above water, some under it, and beyond that a shoal of sand, lying dry half a league more; so that I was obliged to go a great way out to sea to double the point.

When first I discovered them, I was going to give over my enterprise, and come back again, not knowing how far it might oblige me to go out to sea, and, above all, doubting how I should get back again, so I came to an anchor; for I had made me a kind of an anchor with a piece of broken grappling which I got out of the ship.

Having secured my boat, I took my gun and went on shore, climbing up upon a hill, which seemed to overlook that point, where I saw the full extent of it, and resolved to venture.

In my viewing the sea from that hill, where I stood, I perceived a strong, and indeed a most furious current, which run to the east, and even came close to the point; and I took more notice of because I saw there might be some danger that when I came into it I might be carried out to sea by the strength of it, and not be able to make the island again. And indeed, had I not gotten first up upon this hill, I believe it would have been so; for there was the same current on the other side of the island, only that it set off at a farther distance; and I saw there was a strong eddy under the shore; so I had nothing to do but to get in out of the first current, and I should presently be in an eddy.

I lay here, however, two days; because the wind, blowing pretty fresh at E.S.E., and that being just contrary to the said current, made a great breach of the sea upon the point; so that it was not safe for me to keep too close to the shore for the breach, nor to go too far off because of the stream.

The third day, in the morning, the wind having abated overnight, the sea was calm, and I ventured. But I am a warning piece again to all rash and ignorant pilots; for no sooner was I come to the point, when even I was not my boat's length from the shore, but I found myself in a great depth of water, and a current like the sluice of a mill. It carried my boat along with it with such violence, that all I could do could not keep her so much as on the edge of it, but I found it hurried me farther and farther out from the eddy, which was on my left hand. There was no wind stirring to help me, and all I could do with my paddlers signified nothing. And now I began to give myself over for lost; for, as the current was on both sides of the island, I knew in a few leagues distance they must join again, and then I was irrecoverably gone. Nor did I see any possibility of avoiding it; so that I had no prospect before me but of perishing; not by the sea, for that was calm enough, but of starving for hunger. I had indeed found a tortoise on the shore, as big almost as I could lift, and had tossed it into the boat; and I had a great jar of fresh water, that is to say, one of my earthen pots; but what was all this to being driven into the vast ocean, where, to be sure, there was no shore, no mainland or island, for a thousand leagues at least.

And now I saw how easy it was for the providence of God to make the most miserable condition mankind could be in worse. Now I looked back upon my desolate solitary island as the most pleasant place in the world, and all the happiness my heart could wish for was to be but there again. I stretched out my hands to it, with eager wishes. "O happy desert!" said I, "I shall never see thee more. O miserable creature," said I, "whither am I going?"

Then I reproached myself with my unthankful temper, and how I had repined at my solitary condition; and now what would I give to be on shore there again. Thus we never see the true state of our condition till it is illustrated to us by its contraries; nor know how to value what we enjoy, but by the want of it. It is scarce possible to imagine the consternation I was now in, being driven from my beloved island (for so it appeared to me now to be) into the wide ocean, almost two leagues, and in the utmost despair of ever recovering it again. However, I worked hard, till indeed my strength was almost exhausted, and kept my boat ass much to the northward, that is, towards the side of the current which the eddy lay on, as possibly I could; when about noon, as the sun passed the meridian, I thought I felt a little breeze of wind in my face, springing up from the S.S.E. This cheered my heart a little, and especially when, in about an hour more, it blew a pretty small gentle gale. By this time I was gotten at a frightful distance from the island; and had the least cloud or hazy weather intervened, I had been undone another way too; for I had no compass on board, and should never have known how to have steered towards the island if I had but once lost sight of it. But the weather continuing clear, I applied myself to get up my mast again, and spread my sail, standing away to the north as much as possible, to get out of the current.

Just as I had set my mast and sail, and the boat began to stretch away, I saw even by clearness of the water some alteration of the current was near; for where the current was so strong, the water was foul. But perceiving the water clear, I found the current abate, and presently I found to the east, at about half a mile, a breach of the sea upon some rocks. These rocks I found caused the current to part again; and as the main stress of it ran away more southerly, leaving the rocks to the north-east, so the other returned by the repulse of the rocks, and made a strong eddy, which ran back again to the north-west with a very sharp stream.

They who know what it is to have a reprieve brought to

them upon the ladder, or to be rescued from thieves just going to murder them, or who have been in such like extremities, may guess what my present surprise of joy was, and how gladly I put my boat into the stream of this eddy; and the wind also freshening, how gladly I spread my sail to it, running cheerfully before the wind, and with a strong tide or eddy under foot.

This eddy carried me about a league in my way back again, directly towards the island, but about two leagues more to the northward than the current which carried me away at first; so that when I came near the island, I found myself open to the northern shore of it, that is to say, the other end of the island, opposite to that which I went out from.

When I had made something more than a league of way by the help of this current or eddy, I found it was spent, and served me no farther. However, I found that being between the two great currents, viz., that on the south side, which had hurried me away, and that on the north, which lay about a league on the other side; I say, between these two, in the wake of the island, I found the water at least still, and running no way; and having still a breeze of wind fair for me, I kept on steering directly for the island, though not making such fresh way as I did before.

About four o'clock in the evening, being then within about a league of the island, I found the point of the rocks which occasioned this disaster stretching out, as is described before, to the southward, and casting off the current more southwardly had, of course, made another eddy to the north, and this I found very strong, but not directly setting the way my course lay, which was due west, but almost full north. However, having a fresh gale, I stretched across this eddy, slanting north-west; and in about an hour came within about a mile of the shore, where, it being smooth water, I soon got to land.

When I was on shore, I fell on my knees, and gave God thanks for my deliverance, resolving to lay aside all thoughts of my deliverance by my boat; and refreshing myself with such things as I had, I brought my boat close to the shore, in a little cove that I had spied under some trees, and laid me down to sleep, being quite spent with the labour and fatigue of the voyage.

I was now at a great loss which way to get home with my boat. I had run so much hazard, and knew too much the case, to think of attempting it by the way I went out; and what might be at the other side (I mean the west side) I knew not, nor had I any mind to run any more ventures. So I only resolved in the morning to make my way westward along the shore, and to see if there was no creek where I might lay up my frigate in safety, so as to have her again if I wanted her. In about three miles, or thereabouts, coasting the shore, I came to a very good inlet or bay, about a mile over, which narrowed till it came to a very little rivulet or brook, where I found a very convenient harbour for my boat, and where she lay as if she had been in a little dock made on purpose for her. Here I put in, and having stowed my boat very safe, I went on shore to look about me, and see where I was.

I soon found I had but a little passed by the place where I had been before, when I travelled on foot to that shore; so taking nothing out of my boat but my gun and my umbrella, for it was exceedingly hot, I began my march. The way it was comfortable enough after such a voyage as I had been upon, and I reached my old bower in the evening, where I found everything standing as I left it; for I always kept it in good order, being, as I said before, my country house.

I got over the fence, and laid me down in the shade to rest my limbs, for I was very weary, and fell asleep. But judge you, if you can, that read my story, what a surprise I must be in, when I was waked out of my sleep by a voice calling me by my name several times, "Robin, Robin, Robin Crusoe, poor Robin Crusoe! Where are you, Robin Crusoe? Where are you? Where have you been?"

I was so dead asleep at first, being fatigued with rowing, or paddling, as it is called, the first part of the day, and with walking the latter part, that I did not wake thoroughly; but dozing between sleeping and waking, thought I dreamed that somebody spoke to me. But as the voice continued to repeat, "Robin Crusoe, Robin Crusoe," at last I began to wake more perfectly, and was at first dreadfully frighted, and started up in the utmost consternation. But no sooner were my eyes open, but I saw my Poll sitting on the top of the hedge, and immediately knew that it was he that spoke to me; for just in such bemoaning language I had used to talk to him, and teach him; and he had learned it so perfectly, that he would sit upon my finger, and lay his bill close to my face, and cry, "Poor Robin Crusoe! Where are you? Where have you been? How come you here?" and such things as I had taught him.

However, even though I knew it was the parrot, and that indeed it could be nobody else, it was a good while before I could compose myself. First, I was amazed how the creature got thither, and then, how he should just keep about the place, and nowhere else. But as I was well satisfied it could be nobody but honest Poll, I got it over; and holding out my hand, and calling him by name, Poll, the sociable creature came to me, and sat upon my thumb, as he used to do, and continued talking to me, "Poor Robin Crusoe! and how did I come here? and where had I been?" just as if he had been overjoyed to see me again; and so I carried him home along with me.

I now had enough of rambling to sea for some time, and had enough to do for many days to sit still and reflect upon the danger I had been in. I would have been very glad to have had my boat again on my side of the island; but I knew not how it was practicable to get it about. As to the east side of the island, which I had gone round, I knew well enough there was no venturing that way; my very heart would shrink, and my very blood run chill, but to think of it. And as to the other side of the island, I did not know how it might be there; but supposing the current ran with the same force against the shore at the east as it passed by it on the other, I might run the same risks of being driven down the stream, and carried by the island, as I had been before of being carried away from it. So, with these thoughts, I contented myself to be without any boat, though it had been the product of so many months' labour to make it, and of so many more to get it into the sea.

In this government of my temper I remained near a year, lived a very sedate, retired life, as you may well suppose; and my thoughts being very much composed as to my condition, and fully comforted in resigning myself to the dispositions of Providence, I thought I lived really very happily in all things, except that of society.

I improved myself in this time in all the mechanic exercises which my necessities put me upon applying myself to, and I believe could, upon occasion, make a very good carpenter, especially considering how few tools I had. Besides this, I arrived at an unexpected perfection in my earthenware, and contrived well enough to make them with a wheel, which I found infinitely easier and better, because I made things round and shapable which before were filthy things indeed to look on. But I think I was never more vain of my own performance, or more joyful for anything I found out, than for my being able to make a tobacco-pipe. And though it was a very ugly, clumsy thing when it was done, and only burnt red, like other earthenware, yet as it was hard and firm, and would draw the smoke, I was exceedingly comforted with it; for I had been always used to smoke, and there were pipes in the ship, but I forgot them at first, not knowing that there was tobacco in the island; and afterwards, when I searched the ship again, I could not come at any pipes at all.

In my wicker-ware also I improved much, and made abundance of necessary baskets, as well as my invention showed me; though not very handsome, yet they were such as were very handy and convenient for my laying things up in, or fetching things home in. For example, if I killed a goat abroad, I could hang it up on a tree, flay it, and dress it, and cut it in pieces, and bring it home in a basket; and the like by a turtle; I could cut it up, take out the eggs, and a piece or two of the flesh, which was enough for me, and bring them home in a basket, and leave the rest behind me. Also, large deep baskets were my receivers for my corn, which I always rubbed out as soon as it was dry, and cured, and kept it in great baskets.

I began now to perceive my powder abated considerably, and this was a want which it was impossible for me to supply, and I began seriously to consider what I must do when I should have no more powder; that is to say, how I should do to kill any goats. I had, as it observed, in the third year of my being here, kept a young kid, and bred her up tame, and I was in hope of getting a he-goat. But I could not by any means bring it to pass, till my kid grew an old goat; and I could never find it in my heart to kill her, till she dies at last of mere age.

But being now in the eleventh year of my residence, and, as I have said, my ammunition growing low, I set myself to study some art to trap and snare the goats, to see whether I could not catch some of them alive; and particularly, I wanted a she-goat great with young.

To this purpose, I made snares to hamper them, and I do believe they were more than once taken in them: but my tackle was not good, for I had no wire, and I always found them broken, and my bait devoured. At length I resolved to try a pitfall; so I dug several large pits in the earth, in places where I had observed the goats used to feed, and over these pits I placed hurdles, of my own making too, with a great weight upon them; and several times I put ears of barley and dry rice, without setting the trap, and I could easily perceive that the goats had gone in and eaten up the corn, for I could see the mark of their feet. At length I set three traps in one night, and going the next morning, I found them all standing, and yet the bait eaten and gone; this was very discouraging. However, I altered my trap; and, not to trouble you with particulars, going one morning to see my trap, I found in one of them a large old he-goat, and in one of the other three kids, a male and two females.

As to the old one, I knew not what to do with him, he was so fierce I durst not go into the pit to him; that is to say, to go about to bring him away alive, which was what I wanted. I could have killed him, but that was not my business, nor would it answer my end; so I even let him out, and he ran away, as if he had been frighted out of his wits. But I had forgot then what I learned afterwards, that hunger will tame a lion. If I had let him stay there three or four days without food, and then have carried him some water to drink, and then a little corn, he would have been as tame as one of the kids, for they are mighty sagacious, tractable creatures where they are well used.

However, for the present I let him go, knowing no better at that time. Then I went to the three kids, and taking them one by one, I tied them with strings together, and with some difficulty brought them all home.

It was a good while before they would feed, but throwing them some sweet corn, it tempted them, and they began to be tame. And now I found that if I expected to supply myself with goat-flesh when I had no powder or shot left, breeding some up tame was my only way, when perhaps I might have them about my house like a flock of sheep.

But then it presently occurred to me that I must keep the tame from the wild, or else they would always run wild when they grew up; and the only way for this was to have some enclosed piece of ground, well fenced either with hedge or pale, to keep them in so effectually, that those within might not break out, or those without break in.

This was a great undertaking for one pair of hands; yet as I saw there was an absolute necessity of doing it, my first piece of work was to find out a proper piece of ground, viz., where there was likely to be herbage for them to eat, water for them to drink, and cover to keep them from the sun.

Those who understand such enclosures will think I had very little contrivance when I pitched upon a place very proper for all these, being a plain open piece of meadow land, or savanna (as our people call it in the western colonies), which had two or three little drills of fresh water in it, and at one end was very woody. I say, they will smile at my forecast, when I shall tell them I began my enclosing of this piece of ground in such a manner, that my hedge or pale must have been at least two miles about. Nor was the madness of it so great as to the compass, for if it was often miles about, I was likely to have time enough to do it in. But I did not consider that my goats would be as wild in so much compass as if they had had the whole island and I should have so much room to chase them in that I should never catch them.

My hedge was begun and carried on, I believe, about fifty yards, when this thought occurred to me, so I presently stopped short, and, for the first beginning, I resolved to enclose a piece of about 150 yards in length, and 100 yards in breadth; which, as it would maintain as many as should have in any reasonable time, so, as my flock increased, I could add more ground to my enclosure.

This was acting with some prudence, and I went to work with courage. I was about three months hedging in the first piece, and, till I had done it, I tethered the three kids in the best part of it, and used them to feed as near me as possible, to make them familiar; and very often I would go and carry them some ears of barley, or a handful of rice, and feed them out of my hand; so that after my enclosure was finished, and I let them loose, they would follow me up and down, bleating after me for a handful of corn.

This answered my end, and in about a year and a half I had a flock of about twelve goats, kids and all; and in two years more I had three and forty, besides several that I took and killed for my food. And after that I enclosed five several pieces of ground to feed them in, and with little pens to drive them into, to take them as I wanted, and gates out of one piece of ground into another.

But this was not all, for now I not only had goat's flesh to feed on when I pleased, but milk too, a thing which, indeed, in my beginning, I did not so much as think of, and which, when it came into my thoughts, was really an agreeable surprise. For now I set up my dairy, and had sometimes a gallon or two of milk in a day; and as Nature, who gives supplies of food to every creature, dictates even naturally how to make use of it, so I, that had never milked a cow, much less a goat, or seen butter or cheese made, very readily and handily, though after a great many essays and miscarriages, made me both butter and cheese last, and never wanted it afterwards.

How mercifully can our great Creator treat His creatures, even in those conditions in which they seemed to be overwhelmed in destruction! How can He sweeten the bitterest providences, and give us cause to praise Him for dungeons and prisons! What a table was here spread for me in a wilderness, where I saw nothing at first but to perish for hunger!

It would have made a stoic smile, to have seen me and my little family sit down to dinner. There was my majesty, the prince and lord of the whole island; I had the lives of all my subjects at my absolute command. I could hang, draw, give liberty, and take it away; and no rebels among all my subjects.

Then to see how like a king I dined, too, all alone, attended by my servants. Poll, as if he had been my favourite, was the only person permitted to talk to me. My dog, who was now grown very old and crazy, and had found no species to multiply his kind upon, sat always at my right hand, and two cats, one on one side of the table, and one on the other, expecting now and then a bit from my hand, as a mark of special favour.

But these were not the two cats which I brought on shore at first, for they were both of them dead, and had been interred near my habitation, by my own hand. But one of them having multiplied by I know not what kind of creature, these were two which I had preserved tame, whereas the rest run wild in the woods, and became indeed troublesome to me at last; for they would often come into my house, and plunder me too, till at last I was obliged to shoot them, and did kill a great many; at length they left me. With this attendance, and in this plentiful manner, I lived; neither could I be said to want anything but society; and of that in some time after this, I was like to have too much.

I was something impatient, as I have observed, to have the use of my boat, though very loth to run any more hazards; and therefore sometimes I sat contriving ways to get her about the island, and at other times I sat myself down contented enough without her. But I had a strange uneasiness in my mind to go down to the point of the island, where, as I have said, in my last ramble, I went up the hill to see how the shore lay, and how the current set, that I might see what I had to do. This inclination increased upon me every day, and at length I resolved to travel thither by land, following the edge of the shore. I did so; but had anyone in England been to meet such a man as I was, it must either have frighted them, or raised a great deal of laughter; and as I frequently stood still to look at myself, I could not but smile at the notion of my travelling through Yorkshire, with such an equipage, and in such a dress. Be pleased to take a sketch of my figure, as follows.

I had a great high shapeless cap, made of a goat's skin, with a flap hanging down behind, as well to keep the sun from me, as to shoot the rain off from running into my neck; nothing being so hurtful in these climates as the rain upon the flesh, under the clothes.

I had a short jacket of goat-skin, the skirts coming down to about the middle of my thighs; and a pair of open-kneed breeches of the same. The breeches were made of the skin of an old he-goat, whose hair hung down such a length on either side, that, like pantaloons, it reached to the middle of my legs. Stockings and shoes I had none, but had made me a pair of somethings, I scarce know what to call them, like buskins, to flap over my legs, and lace on either side like spatterdashes; but of a most barbarous shape, as indeed were all the rest of my clothes.

I had on a broad belt of goat's skin dried, which I drew together with two thongs of the same, instead of buckles; and in a kind of a frog on either side of this, instead of a sword and a dagger, hung a little saw and a hatchet, one on one side, and one on the other. I had another belt, not so broad, and fastened in the same manner, which hung over my shoulder; and at the end of it, under my left arm, hung two pouches, both made of goat's skin too; in one of which hung my powder, in the other my shot. At my back I carried my basket, on my shoulder my gun, and over my head a great clumsy ugly goat-skin umbrella, but which, after all, was the most necessary thing I had about me, next to my gun. As for my face, the colour of it was really not so mulatto-like as one might expect from a man not at all careful of it, and living within nineteen degrees of the equinox. My beard I had once suffered to grow till it was about a quarter of a yard long; but as I had both scissors and razors sufficient, I had cut it pretty short, except what grew on my upper lip, which I had trimmed into a large pair of Mahometan whiskers, such as I had seen worn by some Turks whom I saw at Sallee; for the Moors did not wear such, though the Turks did. Of these mustachios or whiskers, I will not say they were long enough to hang my hat upon them, but they were of a length and shape monstrous enough, and such as, in England, would have passed for frightful.

But all this is by the bye; for, as to my figure, I had so few to observe me, that it was of no manner of consequence; so I say no more to that part. In this kind of figure I went my new journey, and was out five or six days. I travelled first along the sea-shore, directly to the place where I first brought my boat to an anchor, to get upon the rocks. And having no boat now to take care of, I went over the land, a nearer way, to the same height that I was upon before; when, looking forward to the point of the rocks which lay out, and which I was obliged to double with my boat, as is said above, I was surprised to see the sea all smooth and quiet, no rippling, no motion, no current, any more there than in any other places.

I was at a strange loss to understand this, and resolved to spend some time in the observing it, to see if nothing from the sets of the tide had occasioned it. But I was presently convinced how it was, viz., that the tide of ebb setting from the west, and joining with the current of waters from some great river on the shore, must be the occasion of this current; and that according as the wind blew more forcibly from the west, or from the north, this current came near, or went farther from the shore; for waiting thereabouts till evening, I went up to the rock again, and then the tide of ebb being made, I plainly saw the current again as before, only that it run farther off, being near half a league from the shore; whereas in my case it set close upon the shore, and hurried me and my canoe along with it, which, at another time, it would not have done.

This observation convinced me that I had nothing to do but to observe the ebbing and the flowing of the tide, and I might very easily bring my boat about the island again. But when I began to think of putting it in practice, I had such a terror upon my spirits at the remembrance of the danger I had been in, that I could not think of it again with any patience; but, on the contrary, I took up another resolution, which was more safe, though more laborious; and this was, that I would build, or rather make me another *periegua* or canoe; and so have one for one side of the island, and one for the other.

You are to understand that now I had, as I may call it, two plantations in the island; one, my little fortification or tent, with the wall about it, under the rock, with the cave behind me, which, by this time, I had enlarged into several apartments or caves, one within another. One of these, which was the driest and largest, and had a door out beyond my wall or fortification, that is to say, beyond where my wall joined to the rock, was all filled up with the large earthen pots, of which I have given an account, and with fourteen or fifteen great baskets, which would hold five or six bushels each, where I laid up my stores of provision, especially my corn, some in the ear, cut off short from the straw, and the other rubbed out with my hand.

As for my wall, made, as before, with long stakes or piles, those piles grew all like trees, and were by this time grown so big, and spread so very much, that there was not the least appearance, to anyone's view, of any habitation behind them.

Near this dwelling of mine, but a little farther within the land, and upon lower ground, lay my two pieces of corn ground, which I kept duly cultivated and sowed, and which duly yielded me their harvest in its season; and whenever I had occasion for more corn, I had more land adjoining as fit as that.

Besides this, I had my country seat, and I had now a tolerable plantation there also; for, first, I had my little bower, as I called it, which I kept in repair; that is to say, I kept the hedge which circled it in constantly fitted up to its usual height, the ladder standing always in the inside. I kept the trees, which at first were no more than my stakes, but were now grown very firm and tall, I kept them always so cut, that they might spread and grow thick and wild, and make the more agreeable shade, which they did effectually to my mind. In the middle of this, I had my tent always standing, being a piece of a sail spread over poles, set up for that purpose, and which never wanted any repair or renewing; and under this I had made me a squab or couch, with the skins of the creatures I had killed, and with other soft things, and a blanket laid on them, such as belonged to our sea-bedding, which I had saved, and a great watch-coat to cover me; and here, whenever I had occasion to be absent from my chief seat, I took up my country habitation.

Adjoining to this I had my enclosure for my cattle, that is to say, my goats. And as I had taken an inconceivable deal of pains to fence and enclose this ground, so I was uneasy to see it kept entire, less the goats should break through, that I never left off till, with infinite labour, I had struck the outside of the hedge so full of small stakes, and so near to one another, that it was rather a pale than a hedge, and there was scarce room to put a hand through them; which afterwards, when those stakes grew, as they all did in the next rainy season, made the enclosure strong like a wall, indeed, stronger than any wall.

This will testify for me that I was not idle, and that I spared no pains to bring to pass whatever appeared necessary for my comfortable support; for I considered the keeping up a breed of tame creatures thus at my hand would be a living magazine of flesh, milk, butter, and cheese for me as long as I lived in the place, if it were to be forty years; and that keeping them in my reach depended entirely upon my perfecting my enclosures to such a degree, that I might be sure of keeping them together; which, by this method, indeed, I so effectually secured, that when these little stakes began to grow, I had planted them so very thick I was forced to pull some of them up again.

In this place also I had my grapes growing, which I principally depended on for my winter store of raisins, and which I never failed to preserve very carefully, as the best and most agreeable dainty of my whole diet. And indeed they were not agreeable only, but physical, wholesome, nourishing, and refreshing to the last degree.

As this was also about half-way between my other habitation and the place where I had laid up my boat, I generally stayed and lay here on my way thither; for I used frequently to visit my boat, and I kept all things about, or belonging to her, in very good order. Sometimes I went out in her to divert myself, but no more hazardous voyages would I go, nor scarce ever above a stone's cast or two from the shore, I was so apprehensive of being hurried out of my knowledge again by the currents or winds, or any other accident. But now I come to a new scene of my life.

It happened one day, about noon, going towards my boat, I was exceedingly surprised with the print of a man's naked foot on the shore, which was very plain to be seen in the sand. I stood like one thunderstruck, or as if I had seen an apparition. I listened, I looked round me, I could hear nothing, nor see anything. I went up to a rising ground, to look farther. I went up the shore, and down the shore, but it was all one; I could see no other impression but that one, I went to it again to see if there were any more, and to observe if it might not be my fancy; but there was no room for that, for there was exactly the very print of a foot – toes, heel, and every part of a foot. How it came thither I knew not, nor could in the least imagine. But after innumerable fluttering thoughts, like a man perfectly confused and out of myself, I came home to my fortification, not feeling, as we say, the ground I went on, but terrified to the last degree, looking behind me at every two or three steps, mistaking every bush and tree, and fancying every stump at a distance to be a man; nor is it possible to describe how many various shapes affrighted imagination represented things to me in, how many wild ideas were found every moment in my fancy, and what strange unaccountable whimsies came into my thoughts by the way.

When I came to my castle, for so I think I called it ever after this, I fled into it like one pursued. Whether I went over by the ladder, as first contrived, or went in at the hole in the rock, which I called a door, I cannot remember; no, nor could I remember the next morning, for never frighted hare fled to cover, or fox to earth, with more terror of mind than I to this retreat.

I slept none that night. The farther I was from the occasion of my fright, the greater my apprehensions were; which is something contrary to the nature of such things, and especially to the usual practice of all creatures in fear. But I was so embarrassed with my own frightful ideas of the thing, that I formed nothing but dismal imaginations to myself, even though I was now a great way off it. Sometimes I fancied it must be the devil, and reason joined in with me upon this supposition; for how should any other thing in human shape come into the place? Where was the vessel that brought them? What marks were there of any other footsteps? And how was it possible a man should come there? But then to think that Satan should take human shape upon him in such a place, where there could be no manner of occasion for it, but to leave the print of his foot behind him, that even for no purpose too, for he could not be sure I should see it; this was an amusement the other way. I considered that the devil might have found out abundance of other ways to have terrified me than this of the single print of a foot; that as I lived quite on the other side of the island, he would never have been so simple to leave a mark in a place where it was ten thousand to one whether I should ever see it or not, and in the sand too, which the first surge of the sea, upon a high wind, would have defaced entirely. All this seemed inconsistent with the thing itself, and with all the notions we usually entertain of the subtilty of the devil.

Abundance of such things as these assisted to argue me out of all apprehensions of its being the devil; and I presently concluded then, that it must be some more dangerous creature, viz., that it must be some of the savages of the mainland over against me, who had wandered out to sea in their canoes, and, either driven by the currents or by contrary winds, had made the island, and had been on shore, but were gone away again to sea, being as loth, perhaps, to have stayed in this desolate island as I would have been to have had them.

While these reflections were rolling upon my mind, I was very thankful in my thoughts that I was so happy as not to be thereabouts at that time, or that they did not see my boat, by which they would have concluded that some inhabitants had been in the place, and perhaps have searched farther for me. Then terrible thoughts racked my imagination about their having found my boat, and that there were people here; and that if so, I should certainly have them come again in greater numbers, and devour me; that if it should happen so that they should not find me, yet they would find my enclosure, destroy all my corn, carry away all my flock of tame goats, and I should perish at last for mere want.

Thus my fear banished all my religious hope. All that former confidence in God, which was founded upon such wonderful experience as I had had of His goodness, now vanished, as if He that had fed me by miracle hitherto could not preserve, by His power, the provision which He had made for me by His goodness. I reproached myself with my easiness, that would not sow any more corn one year than would just serve me till the next season, as if no accident could intervene to prevent my enjoying the crop that was upon the ground. And this I thought so just a reproof that I resolved for the future to have two or three years' corn beforehand, so that, whatever might come, I might not perish for want of bread.

How strange a chequer-work of Providence is the life of man! and by what secret differing springs are the affections hurried about as differing circumstances present! Today we love what tomorrow we hate; today we seek what tomorrow we shun; today we desire what tomorrow we fear; nay, even tremble at the apprehensions of. This was exemplified in me, at this time, in the most lively manner imaginable; for I, whose only affliction was that I seemed banished from human society, that I was alone, circumscribed by the boundless ocean, cut off from mankind, and condemned to what I called silent life; that I was as one whom Heaven thought not worthy to be numbered among the living, or to appear among the rest of His creatures; that to have seen one of my own species would have seemed to me a raising me from death to life, and the greatest blessing that Heaven itself, next to the supreme blessing of salvation, could bestow; I say, that I should now tremble at the very apprehensions of seeing a man, and was ready to sink into the ground at but the shadow or silent appearance of a man's having set his foot on the island!

Such is the uneven state of human life; and it afforded me a great many curious speculations afterwards, when I had a little recovered my first surprise. I considered that this was the station of life the infinitely wise and good providence of God had determined for me; that, as I could not forsee what the ends of Divine wisdom might be in all this, so I was not to dispute His sovereignty, who, as I was His creature, had an undoubted right, by creation, to govern and dispose of me absolutely as He thought fit, and who, as I was a creature who had offended Him, had likewise a judicial right to condemn me to what punishment He thought fit; and that it was my part to submit to bear His indignation, because I had sinned against Him.

I then reflected that God, who was not only righteous, but omnipotent, as He had thought fit thus to punish and afflict me, so He was able to deliver me; that if He did not think fit to do it, 'twas my unquestioned duty to resign myself absolutely and entirely to His will; and, on the other hand, it was my duty also to hope in Him, pray to Him, and quietly to attend the dictates and directions of His daily providence.

These thoughts took me up many hours, days, nay, I may say, weeks and months; and one particular effect of my cogitations on this occasion I cannot omit, viz., one morning early, lying in my bed, and filled with thought about my danger from the appearance of savages, I found it discomposed me very much; upon which those words of the Scripture came into my thoughts, "Call upon Me in the day of trouble, and I will deliver, and thou shalt glorify Me."

Upon this, rising cheerfully out of my bed, my heart was not only comforted, but I was guided and encouraged to pray earnestly to God for deliverance. When I had done praying, I took up my Bible, and opening it to read, the first words that presented to me were, "Wait on the Lord, and be of good cheer, and He shall strengthen thy heart; wait, I say, on the Lord." It is impossible to express the comfort this gave me. In answer, I thankfully laid down the book, and was no more sad, at least, not on that occasion.

In the middle of these cogitations, apprehensions, and reflections, it came into my thought one day, that all this might be a mere chimera of my own; and that this foot might be the print of my own foot, when I came on shore from my boat. This cheered me up a little too, and I began to persuade myself it was all a delusion, that it was nothing else but my own foot; and why might not I come that way from the boat, as well as I was going that way to the boat? Again, I considered also, that I could by no means tell, for certain, where I had trod, and where I had not; and that if, at last, this was only the print of my own foot, I had played the part of those fools who strive to make stories of spectre and apparitions, and then are frighted at them more than anybody.

Now I began to take courage, and to peep abroad again, for I had not stirred out of my castle for three days and nights, so that I began to starve for provision; for I had little or nothing within doors but some barley-cakes and water. Then I knew that my goats wanted to be milked too, which usually was my evening diversion; and the poor creatures were in great pain and inconvenience for want of it; and, indeed, it almost spoiled some of them, and almost dried up their milk.

Heartening myself, therefore, with the belief that this was nothing but the print of one of my own feet, and so I might be truly said to start at my own shadow, I began to go abroad again, and went to my country house to milk my flock. But to see with what fear I went forward, how often I looked behind me, how I was ready, every now and then, to lay down my basket, and run for my life, it would have made anyone have thought I was haunted with an evil conscience, or that I had been lately most terribly frighted; and so, indeed, I had.

However, as I went down thus two or three days, and having

seen nothing, I began to be a little bolder, and to think there was really nothing in it but my own imagination. But I could not persuade myself fully of this till I should go down to the shore again, and see this print of a foot, and measure it by my own, and see if there was any similitude or fitness, that I might be assured it was my own foot. But when I came to the place, first, it appeared evidently to me, that when I laid up my boat, I could not possibly be on shore anywhere thereabout; secondly, when I came to measure the mark with my own foot, I found my foot not so large by a great deal. Both these things filled my head with new imaginations, and gave me the vapours again to the highest degree; so that I shook with cold, like one in an ague; and I went home again, filled with the belief that some man or men had been on shore there; for, in short, that the island was inhabited, and I might be surprised before I was aware. And what course to take for my security, I knew not.

Oh, what ridiculous resolution men take when possessed with fear! It deprives them of the use of those means which reason offers for their relief. The first thing I proposed to myself was to throw down my enclosures, and turn all my tame cattle wild into the woods, that the enemy might not find them, and then frequent the island in prospect of the same or the like booty; then to the simple thing of digging up my two corn-fields, that they might not find such a grain there, and still be prompted to frequent the island; then to demolish my bower and tent, that they might not see any vestiges of habitation, and be prompted to look farther, in order to find out the persons inhabiting.

These were the subject of the first night's cogitation, after I had come home again, while the apprehensions which had so overrun my mind were fresh upon me, and my head was full of vapours, as above. Thus fear of danger is ten thousand times more terrifying than danger itself when apparent to the eyes; and we find the burthen of anxiety greater, by much, than the evil which we are anxious about; and, which was worse than all this,

I had not that relief in this trouble from the resignation I used to practice, that I hoped to have. I looked, I thought, like Saul, who complained not only that the Philistines were upon him, but that God had forsaken him; for I did not now take due ways to compose my mind, by crying to God in my distress, and resting upon His providence, as I had done before, for my defence and deliverance; which, if I had done, I had at least been more cheerfully supported under this new surprise, and perhaps carried through it with more resolution.

This confusion of my thoughts kept me waking all night, but in the morning I fell asleep; and having, by the amusement of my mind, been, as it were, tired, and my spirits exhausted, I slept very soundly, and woke much better composed than I had ever been before. And now I began to think sedately; and upon the utmost debate with myself, I concluded that this island, which was so exceeding pleasant, fruitful, and no farther from the mainland than as I had seen, was not so entirely abandoned as I might imagine; that although there were no stated inhabitants who lived on the spot, yet that there might sometimes come boats off from the shore, who, either with design, or perhaps never but when they were driven by cross winds, might come to this place; that I had lived here fifteen years now, and had not met with the least shadow or figure of any people yet; and that if at any time they should be driven here, it was probable they went away again as soon as ever they could, seeing they had never thought fit to fix there upon any occasion to this time; that the most I could suggest any danger from, was from any such casual accidental landing of straggling people from the main, who, as it was likely, if they were driven hither, were here against their wills; so they made no stay here, but went off again with all possible speed, seldom staying one night on shore, lest they should not have the help of the tides and daylight back again; and that, therefore, I had nothing to do but to consider of some safe retreat, in case I should see any savages land upon the spot.

Now I began sorely to repent that I had dug my cave so large as to bring a door through again, which door, as I said, came out beyond where my fortification joined to the rock. Upon maturely considering this, therefore, I resolved to draw me a second fortification, in the same manner of a semicircle, at a distance from my wall, just where I had planted a double row of trees about twelve years before, of which I made mention. These trees having been planted so thick before, they wanted but a few piles to be driven between them, that they should be thicker and stronger, and my wall would be soon finished.

So that I had now a double wall; and my outer wall was thickened with pieces of timber, old cables, and everything I could think of, to make it strong, having in it seven little holes, about as big as I might put my arm out at. In the inside of this I thickened my wall to above ten feet thick, with continual bringing earth out of my cave, and laying it at the foot of the wall, and walking upon it; and through the seven holes I contrived to plant the muskets, of which I took notice that I got seven on shore out of the ship. These, I say, I planted like my cannon, and fitted them into frames that held them like a carriage, that so I could fire all the seven guns in two minutes' time. This wall I was many a weary month a-finishing, and yet never thought myself safe till it was done.

When this was done, I stuck all the ground without my wall, for a great way every way, as full with stakes, or sticks, of the osier-like wood, which I found so apt to grow, as they could well stand; insomuch, that I believe I might set in near twenty thousand of them, leaving a pretty large space between them and my wall, that I might have room to see an enemy, and they might have no shelter from the young trees, if they attempted to approach my outer wall.

Thus in two years' time I had a thick grove; and in five or six years' time I had a wood before my dwelling, growing so monstrous thick and strong, that it was indeed perfectly impassable; and no men, of what kind soever, would ever imagine that there was anything beyond it, much less a habitation. As for the way which I proposed to myself to go in and out, for I left no avenue, it was by setting two ladders, one to a part of the rock which was low, and then broke in, and left room to place another ladder upon that; so when the two ladders were taken down, no man living could come down to me without mischieving himself; and if they had come down, they were still on the outside of my outer wall.

Thus I took all the measures human prudence could suggest for my own preservation; and it will be seen, at length, that they were not altogether without just reason; though I foresaw nothing at that time more than my mere fear suggzested to me.

While doing this, I was not altogether careless of my other affairs; for I had a great concern upon me for my little herd of goats. They were not only a present supply to me upon every occasion, and began to be sufficient for me, without the expense of powder and shot, but also without the fatigue of hunting after the wild ones; and I was loth to lose the advantage of them, and to have them all to nurse up over again.

To this purpose, after long consideration, I could think of but two ways to preserve them. One was, to find another convenient place to dig a cave under ground, and to drive them into it every night; and the other was, to enclose two or three little bits of land, remote from one another, and as much concealed as I could, where I might keep about half a dozen young goats in each place; so that if any disaster happened to the flock in general, I might be able to raise them again with little trouble and time. And this, though it would require a great deal of time and labour, I thought was the most rational design.

Accordingly I spent some time to find out the most retired parts of the island; and I pitched upon one which was as private indeed as my heart could wish for. It was a little damp piece of ground, in the middle of the hollow and thick woods, where, as is observed, I almost lost myself once before, endeavouring to come back that way from the eastern part of the island. Here I found a clear piece of land, nearly three acres, so surrounded with woods that it was almost an enclosure by Nature; at least, it did not want near so much labour to make it as the other pieces of ground I had worked so hard at.

I immediately went to work with this piece of ground, and in less than a month's time I had so fenced it round, that my flock, or herd, call it which you please, who were not so wild now as at first they might be supposed to be, were well enough secured in it. So, without any farther delay, I removed ten young she-goats and two he-goats to this piece. And when they were there, I continued to perfect the fence, till I had made it as secure as the other, which, however, I did at more leisure, and it took me up more time by a great deal.

All this labour I was at the expense of, purely from my apprehensions on the account of the print of a man's foot which I had seen; for, as yet, I never saw any human creature come near the island. And I had now lived two years under these uneasinesses, which, indeed, made my life much less comfortable than it was before, as may well be imagined by any who know what it is to live in the constant snare of the fear of man. And this I must observe, with grief too, that the discomposure of my mind had too great impressions also upon the religious part of my thoughts; for the dread and terror of falling into the hands of savages and cannibals lay so upon my spirits, that I seldom found myself in a due temper for application to my Maker, at least not with the sedate calmness and resignation of soul which I was wont to do. I rather prayed to God as under great affliction and pressure of mind, surrounded with danger, and in expectation every night of being murdered and devoured before morning; and I must testify from my experience, that a temper of peace, thankfulness, love, and affection, is much more the proper frame for prayer than that of terror and discomposure; and that under the dread of mischief impending, a man is no more fit for a comforting performance of the duty of praying to God than he is for repentance on a sick-bed. For these discomposures affect the mind, as the others do the body; and the discomposure of the mind must necessarily be as great a disability as that of the body, and much greater, praying to God being properly an act of the mind, not of the body.

But to go on. After I had thus secured one part of my little living stock, I went about the whole island, searching for another private place to make such another deposit; when, wandering more the the west point of the island than I had ever done yet, and looking out to sea, I thought I saw a boat upon the sea, at a great distance. I had found a prospective glass or two in one of the seamen's chests, which I saved out of our ship, but I had it not about me; and this was so remote that I could not tell what to make of it, though I looked at it till my eyes were not able to hold to look any longer. Whether it was a boat or not, I do not know; but as I descended from the hill, I could see no more of it, so I gave it over; only I resolved to go no more out without a prospective glass in my pocket.

When I had come down the hill to the end of the island, where, indeed, I had never been before, I was presently convinced that the seeing the print of a man's foot was not such a strange thing in the island as I imagined. And, but that it was a special providence that I was cast upon the side of the island where the savages never came, I should easily have known that nothing was more frequent than for the canoes from the main, when they happened to be a little too far out at sea, to shoot over to that side of the island for harbour; likewise, as they often met and fought in their canoes, the victors having taken any prisoners would bring them over to this shore, where, according to their dreadful customs, being all cannibals, they would kill and eat them; of which hereafter.

When I was come down the hill to the shore, as I said above, being the S.W. point of the island, I was perfectly confounded and amazed; nor is it possible for me to express the horror of my mind at seeing the shore spread with skulls, hands, feet, and other bones of human bodies; and particularly, I observed a place where there had been a fire made, and a circle dug in the earth, like a cockpit, where it is supposed the savage wretches sat down to their inhuman feastings upon the bodies of their fellow-creatures.

I was so astonished with the sight of these things, that I entertained no notion of any danger to myself from it for a long while. All my apprehensions were buried in the thoughts of such a pitch of inhuman, hellish brutality, and the horror of the degeneracy of human nature, which, though I had heard of often, yet I never had so near a view of before. In short, I turned away my face from the horrid spectacle. My stomach grew sick, and I was just at the point of fainting, when Nature discharged the disorder from my stomach. And having vomited with an uncommon violence, I was a little relieved, but could not bear to stay in the place a moment; so I got up the hill again with all the speed I could, and walked on towards my own habitation.

When I came a little out of that part of the island, I stood still a while, as amazed; and then recovering myself, I looked up with the utmost affection of my soul, and with a flood of tears in my eyes, gave God thanks, that had cast my first lot in a part of the world where I was distinguished from such dreadful creatures as these; and that, though I had esteemed my present condition very miserable, had yet given me so many comforts in it, that I had still more to give thanks for than to complain of; and this is above all, that I had, even in this miserable condition, been comforted with the knowledge of Himself, and the hope of His blessing; which was a felicity more than sufficiently equivalent to all the misery which I had suffered, or could suffer.

In this frame of thankfulness I went home to my castle, and began to be much easier now, as to the safety of my circumstances, than ever I was before; for I observed that these wretches never came to this island in search of what they could get; perhaps not seeking, not wanting, or not expecting, anything here; and having often, no doubt, been up in the covered, woody part of it, without finding anything to their purpose. I knew I had been here now almost eighteen years, and never saw the least footsteps of human creature there before; and I might be here eighteen more as entirely concealed as I was now, if I did not discovered myself to them, which I had no manner of occasion to do; it being my only business to keep myself entirely concealed where I was, unless I found a better sort of creatures than cannibals to make myself known to.

Yet I entertained such an abhorrence of the savage wretches that I have been speaking of, and of the wretched, inhuman custom of their devouring and eating one another up, that I continued pensive and sad, and kept close within my own circle for almost two years after this. When I say my own circle, I mean by it my three plantations, viz., my castle, my country seat, which I called my bower, and my enclosure in the woods. Nor did I look after this for any other use than as an enclosure for my goats; for the aversion which Nature gave me to these hellish wretches was such, that I was fearful of seeing them as of seeing the devil himself. Nor did I so much as go to look after my boat in all this time, but began rather to think of making me another; for I could not think of ever making any more attempts to bring the other boat round the island to me, lest I should meet with some of these creatures at sea, in which, if I had happened to have fallen into their hands, I knew what would have been my lot.

Time, however, and the satisfaction I had that I was in no danger of being discovered by these people, began to wear off my uneasiness about them; and I began to live just in the same composed manner as before; only with this difference, that I used more caution, and kept my eyes more about me, than I did before, lest I should happen to be seen by any of them; and particularly, I was more cautious of firing my gun, lest any of them being on the island should happen to hear of it. And it was, therefore, a very good providence to me that I had furnished myself with a tame breed of goats, that needed not hunt any more about the woods, or shoot at them. And if I did catch any of them after this, it was by traps and snares, as I had done before; so that for two years after this I believe I never fired my gun once off, though I never went out without it; and, which was more, as I had saved three pistols out of the ship, I always carried them out with me, or at least two of them, sticking them in my goat-skin belt. Also I furbished up one of the great cutlasses that I had out of the ship, and made me a belt to put it on also; so that I was now a most formidable fellow to look at when I went abroad, if you add to the former description of myself the particular of two pistols and a great broadsword hanging at my side in a belt, but without a scabbard.

Things going on thus, as I have said, for some time, I seemed, excepting these cautions, to be reduced to my former calm, sedate way of living. All these things tended to showing me, more and more, how far my condition was from being miserable, compared to some others; nay, to many other particulars of life, which it might have pleased God to have made my lot. It put me upon reflecting how little repining there would be among mankind at any condition of life, if people would rather compare their condition with those that are worse, in order to be thankful, than be always comparing them with those which are better, to assist their murmurings and complainings.

As in my present condition there were not really many things which I wanted, so indeed I thought that the frights I had been in about these savage wretches, and the concern I had been in for my own preservation, had taken off the edge of my invention for my own conveniences. And I had dropped a good design, which I had once bent my thoughts too much upon; and that was, to try if I could not make some of my barley into malt, and then try to brew myself some beer. This was really a whimsical thought, and I reproved myself often for the simplicity of it; for I presently saw there would be the want of several things necessary to the making my beer, that it would be impossible for me to supply. As, first, casks to preserve it in, which was a thing that, as I have observed already, I could never compass; no, though I spent not many days, but weeks, nay, months, in attempting it, but to no purpose. In the next place, I had no hops to make it keep, no yeast to make it work, no copper or kettle to make it boil; and yet all these things notwithstanding, I verily believe, had not these things intervened, I mean the frights and terrors I was in about the savages, I had undertaken it, and perhaps brought it to pass, too; for I seldom gave anything over without accomplishing it when I once had it in my head enough to begin it.

But my invention now run quite another way; for, night and day, I could think of nothing but how I might destroy some of these monsters in their cruel, bloody entertainment, and, if possible, save the victim they should bring hither to destroy. It would take up a larger volume than this whole work is intended to be, to set down all the contrivances I hatched, or rather brooded upon, in my thought, for destroying these creatures, or at least frighting them so as to prevent their coming hither any more. But all was abortive; nothing could be possible to take effect, unless I was to be there to do it myself. And what could one man do among them, when perhaps there might be twenty or thirty of them together, with their darts, or their bows and arrows, with which they could shoot as true to a mark as I could with my gun?

Sometimes I contrived to dig a hole under the place where they made their fire, and put in five or six pound of gunpowder, which, when they kindled their fire, would consequently take fire, and blow up all that was near it. But as, in the first place, I should be very loth to waste so much powder upon them, my store being now within the quantity of one barrel, so neither I be sure of its going off at any certain time, when it might surprise them; and, at best, that it would do little more than just blow the fire about their ears, and fright them, but not sufficient to make them forsake the place. So I laid it aside, and then proposed that I would place myself in ambush in some convenient place, with my three guns all double-loaded, and, in the middle of their bloody ceremony, let fly at them, when I should be sure to kill or wound perhaps two or three at every shot; and then falling in upon them with my three pistols and my sword, I made no doubt but that if there was twenty I should kill them all. This fancy pleased my thoughts for some weeks; and I was so full of it, that I often dreamed of it, and sometimes that I was just going to let fly at them in my sleep.

I went so far with it in my imagination, that I employed myself several days to find out proper places to put myself in ambuscade, as I said, to watch for them; and I went frequently to the place itself, which was now grown more familiar to me; and especially while my mind was thus filled with thoughts of revenge, and of a bloody putting twenty or thirty of them to the sword, as I may call it, the horror I had at the place, and at the signals of the barbarous wretches devouring one another, abated my malice.

Well, at length I found a place in the side of the hill, where I was satisfied I might securely wait till I saw any of their boats coming; and might then, even before they would be ready to come on shore, convey myself, unseen, into thickets of trees, in one of which there was a hollow large enough to conceal me entirely; and where I might sit and observe all their bloody doings, and take my full aim at their heads, when they were so close together, as that it would be next to impossible that I should miss my shot, or that I could fail wounding three of four of them at first shot.

In this place, then, I resolved to fix my design; and, accordingly, I prepared two muskets and my ordinary fowling-piece. The two muskets I loaded with a brace of slugs each, and four or five smaller bullets, about the size of pistol-bullets; and the fowling-piece I loaded with near a handful of swan-shot, of the largest size. I also loaded my pistols with about four bullets each; and in this posture, well provided with ammunition for a second and third charge, I prepared myself for my expedition.

After I had thus laid the scheme of my design, and in my imagination put it in practice, I continually made my tour every morning up to the top of the hill, which was from my castle, as I called it, about three miles, or more, to see if I could observe any boats upon the sea coming near the island, or standing over towards it. But I began to tire of this hard duty, after I had, for two or three months, constantly kept my watch, but came always back without any discovery; there having not, in all that time, been the least appearance, not only on or near the shore, but not on the whole ocean, so far as my eyes or glasses could reach every way.

As long as I kept up my daily tour to the hill to look out, so long also I kept up the vigor of my design, and my spirits seemed to be all the while in a suitable form for so outrageous an execution as the killing twenty or thirty naked savages for an offence which I had not at all entered into a discussion of in my thoughts, any farther than my passions were at first fired by the horror I conceived at the unnatural custom of that people of the country; who, it seems, had been suffered by Providence, in His wise disposition of the world, to have no other guide than that of their own abominable and vitiated passions; and consequently were left, and perhaps had been so for some ages, to act such horrid things, and receive such dreadful customs, as nothing but nature entirely abandoned of Heaven, and acted by some hellish degeneracy, could have run them into. But now when, as I have said, I began to be weary of the fruitless excursion which I had made so long and so far every morning in vain, so my opinion of the action itself began to alter; and I began, with cooler and calmer thoughts, to consider what it was I was going to engage in. What authority or call I had to pretend to be judge and executioner upon these men as criminals, whom Heaven had thought fit, for so many ages, to suffer, unpunished, to go on, and to be, as it were, the executioners of His judgments one upon another. How far these people were offenders against me, and what right I had to engage in the quarrel of that blood which they shed promiscuously one upon another. I debated this very often with myself, thus: How do I know what God Himself judges in this particular case? It is certain these people either do not commit this as a crime; it is not against their own consciences' reproving, or their light reproaching them. They do not know it to be an offence and then commit it in defiance of Divine justice, as we do in almost all the sins we commit. They think it no more a crime to kill a captive taken in war, than we do to kill an ox; nor to eat human flesh, than we do to eat mutton.

When I had considered this a little, it followed necessarily that I was certainly in the wrong in it; that these people were not murderers in the sense that I had before condemned them in my thoughts, any more than those Christians were murderers who often put to death the prisoners taken in battle; or more frequently, upon many occasions, put whole troops of men to the sword, without giving quarter, though they threw down their arms and submitted.

In the next place it occurred to me, that albeit the usage they thus give one another was thus brutish and inhuman, yet it was really nothing to me; these people had done me no injury. That if they attempted me, or I saw it necessary for my immediate preservation to fall upon them, something might be said for it; but that as I was yet out of their power, and they had really no knowledge of me, and consequently no design upon me, and therefore it could not be just for me to fall upon them. That this would justify the conduct of the Spaniards in all their barbarities practised in America, and where they destroyed millions of these people; who, however they were idolaters and barbarians, and had several bloody and barbarous rites in their customs, such as sacrificing human bodies to their idols, were yet, as to the Spaniards, very innocent people; and that the rooting them out of the country is spoken of with the utmost abhorrence and detestation by even the Spaniards themselves at this time, and by all other Christian nations of Europe, as a mere butchery, a bloody and unnatural piece of cruelty, unjustifiable either to God or man; and such, as for which the very name of a Spaniard is reckoned to be frightful and terrible to all people of humanity, or of Christian compassion; as if the kingdom of Spain were particularly eminent for the product of a race of men who were without principles of tenderness, or the common bowels of pity to the miserable, which is reckoned to be a mark of generous temper in the mind.

These considerations really put me to a pause, and to a kind of a full stop; and I began, by little and little, to be off of my design, and to conclude I had taken wrong measures in my resolutions to attack the savages; that it was not my business to meddle with them, unless they first attacked me; and this it was my business, if possible, to prevent; but that if I were discovered and attacked, then I knew my duty.

On the other hand, I argued with myself that this really was not the way to deliver myself, but entirely to ruin and destroy myself; for unless I was sure to kill every one that not only should be on shore at that time, but that should ever come on shore afterwards, if but one of them escaped to tell their country people what had happened, they would come over again by thousands to revenge the death of their fellows, and I should only bring upon myself a certain destruction, which, at present, I had no manner of occasion for.

Upon the whole, I concluded that neither in principles nor in policy I ought, one way or other, to concern myself in this affair. That my business was, by all possible means, to conceal myself from them, and not to leave the last signal to them to guess by that there were any living creatures upon the island; I mean of human shape.

Religion joined in with this prudential, and I was convinced now, many ways, that I was perfectly out of my duty when I was laying all my bloody schemes for the destruction of innocent creatures; I mean innocent as to me. As to the crimes they were guilty of towards one another, I had nothing to do with them. They were national, and I ought to leave them to the justice of God, who is the Governor of nations, and knows how, by national punishments, to make a just retribution for national offences and to bring public judgments upon those who offend in a public manner by such ways as best pleases Him.

This appeared so clear to me now, that nothing was a greater satisfaction to me than that I had not been suffered to do a thing which I now saw so much reason to believe would have been no less a sin than that of wilful murder, if I had committed it. And I gave most humble thanks on my knees to God, that had thus delivered me from blood-guiltiness; beseeching Him to grant me the protection of His providence, that I might not fall into the hands of the barbarians, or that I might not lay my hands upon them, unless I had a more clear call from Heaven to do it, in defence of my own life.

In this disposition I continued for near a year after this; and so far was I from desiring an occasion for falling upon these wretches, that in all that time I never once went up the hill to see whether there were any of them in sight, or to know whether any of them had been on shore there or not, that I might not be tempted to renew any of my contrivances against them, or be provoked, by any advantage which might present itself, to fall upon them. Only this I did, I went and removed my boat, which I had on the other side the island, and carried it down to the east end of the whole island, where I ran it into a little cove, which I found under some high rocks, and where I knew, by reason of the currents, the savages durst not, at least would not come, with their boats, upon any account whatsoever.

With my boat I carried away everything that I had left there belonging to her, though not necessary for the bare going thither, viz., a mast and sail which I had made for her, and a thing like an anchor, but indeed which could not be called either anchor or grappling; however, it was the best I could make of its kind. All these I removed, that there might not be the least shadow of any discovery, or any appearance of any boat, or of any human habitation, upon the island.

Besides this, I kept myself, as I said, more retired than ever, and seldom went from my cell, other than upon my constant employment, viz., to milk my she-goats, and manage my little flock in the wood, which, as it was quite on the other part of the island, was quite out of danger; for certain it is, that these savage people, who sometimes haunted this island, never came with any thoughts of finding anything here, and consequently never wandered off from the coast; and I doubt not but they might have been several times on shore after my apprehensions of them had made me cautious, as well as before; and indeed, I looked back with some horror upon the thoughts of what my condition would have been if I had chopped upon them and been discovered before that, when, naked and unarmed, except with one gun, and that loaded often only with small shot, I walked everywhere, peeping and peeping about the island to see what I could get. What a surprise should I have been in if, when I discovered the print of a man's foot, I had, instead of that, seen fifteen or twenty savages, and found them pursuing me, and by the swiftness of their running, no possibility of my escaping them!

The thoughts of this sometimes sunk my very soul within me, and distressed my mind so much that I could not soon recover it, to think what I should have done, and how I not only should not have been able to resist them, but even should not have had presence of mind enough to do what I might have done, much less what now, after so much consideration and preparation, I might be able to do. Indeed, after serious thinking of these things,

I should be very melancholy, and sometimes it would last a great while; but I resolved it, at last, all into thankfulness to that Providence which had delivered me from so many unseen dangers, and had kept me from those mischiefs which I could no way have been the agent in delivering myself from, because I had not the least notion of any such thing depending, or the least supposition of it being possible.

This renewed a contemplation which often had come to my thoughts in former time, when first I began to see the merciful dispositions of Heaven, in the dangers we run through in this life. How wonderfully we are delivered when we know nothing of it. How, when we are in a quandary, as we call it, a doubt or hesitation, whether to go this way, or that way, a secret hint shall direct us this way, when we intended to go that way; nay, when sense, our own inclination, and perhaps business, has called to go the other way, yet a strange impression upon the mind, from we know not what springs, and by we know not what power, shall overrule us to go this way; and it shall afterwards appear, that had we gone that way which we should have gone, and even to our imagination ought to have gone, we should have been ruined and lost. Upon these and many like reflections I afterwards made it a certain rule with me, that whenever I found those secret hints or pressings of my mind to doing, or not doing, anything that presented, or to going this way or that way, I never failed to obey the secret dictate, though I knew no other reason for it than that such a pressure, or such a hint, hung upon my mind. I could give many examples of the success of this conduct in the course of my life, but more especially in the latter part of my inhabiting this unhappy island; besides many occasions which it is very likely I might have taken notice of, if I had seen with the same eyes that I saw with now. But 'tis never too late to be wise; and I cannot but advise all considering men, whose lives are attended with such extraordinary incidents as mine, or even though not so extraordinary, not to slight such secret intimations of Providence, let them come from what invisible intelligence they will. That I shall not discuss, and perhaps cannot account for; but certainly they are a proof of the converse of spirits, and the secret communication between those embodied and those unembodied, and such a proof as can never be withstood, of which I shall have occasion to give some very remarkable instances in the remainder of my solitary residence in this dismal place.

I believe the reader of this will not think strange if I confess that these anxieties, these constant dangers I lived in, and the concern that was now upon me, put an end to all invention, and to all the contrivances that I had laid for my future accommodations and conveniences. I had the care of my safety more now upon my hands than that of my food. I cared not to drive a nail, or chop a stick of wood now, for fear the noise I should make should be heard; much less would I fire a gun, for the same reason; and, above all, I was intolerably uneasy at making any fire, lest the smoke, which is visible at a great distance in the day, should betray me; and for this reason I removed that part of my business which required fire, such as burning of pots and pipes, etc., into my new apartment in the woods; where, after I had been some time, I found, to my unspeakable consolation, a more natural cave in the earth, which went in a vast way, and where, I dare say, no savage, had he been at the mouth of it, would be so hardy as to venture in; nor, indeed, would any man else, but one who, like me, wanted nothing so much as a safe retreat.

The mouth of this hollow was at the bottom of a great rock, where, mere accident I would say (if I did not see abundant reason to ascribe all such things now to Providence), I was cutting down some thick branches of trees to make charcoal; and before I go on, I must observe the reason of my making this charcoal, which was thus.

I was afraid of making a smoke about my habitation, as I said before; and yet I could not live there without baking my bread, cooking my meat, etc. So I contrived to burn some wood here, as I had seen done in England under turf, till it became chark, or dry coal; and then putting the fire out, I preserved the coal to carry home, and perform the other services which fire was wanting for at home, without danger of smoke.

But this is by the bye. While I was cutting down some wood here, I perceived that behind a very thick branch of low brushwood, or underwood, there was a kind of hollow place. I was curious to look into it; and getting with difficulty into the mouth of it, I found it was pretty large; that is to say, sufficient for me to stand upright in it, and perhaps another with me. But I must confess to you I made more haste out than I did in when, looking farther into the place, and which was perfectly dark, I saw two broad shining eyes of some creature, whether devil or man I knew not, which twinkled like two stars, the dim light from the cave's mouth shining directly in, and making the reflection.

However, after some pause I recovered myself, and began to call myself a thousand fools, and tell myself that he that was afraid to see the devil was not fit to live twenty years in an island all alone, and that I dare to believe there was nothing in this cave that was more frightful than myself. Upon this, plucking up my courage, I took up a great firebrand, and in I rushed again, with the stick flaming in my hand. I had not gone three steps in, but I was almost as much frighted as I was before; for I heard a very loud sigh like that of a man in some pain, and it was followed by a broken noise, as if of words half expressed, and then a deep sigh again. I stepped back, and was indeed struck with such a surprise that it put me into a cold sweat; and if I had had a hat on my head, I will not answer for it, that my hair might not have lifted it off. But still plucking up my spirits as well as I could, and encouraging myself a little with considering that the power and presence of God was everywhere, and was able to protect me, upon this I stepped forward again, and by the light of the firebrand, holding it up a little over my head, I saw lying on the ground a most monstrous, frightful, old he-goat, just making his will, as we say, and gasping for life; and dying, indeed, of mere old age.

I stirred him a little to see if I could get him out, and he essayed to get up, but was not able to raise himself; and I thought with myself he might even lie there; for if he had frighted me so, he would certainly fright any of the savages, if any of them should be so hardy as to come in there while he had any life in him.

I was now recovered from my surprise, and began to look around me, when I found the cave was but very small; that is to say, it might be about twelve feet over, but in no manner of shape, either round or square, no hands having every been employed in making it but those of mere Nature. I observed also that there was a place at the farther side of it that went in farther, but was so low that it required me to creep upon my hands and knees to go into it, and whither I went I knew not; so having no candle, I gave it over for some time, but resolved to come again the next day, provided with candles and a tinder-box, which I had made of the lock of one of the muskets, with some wild-fire in the pan.

Accordingly, the next day I came provided with six large candles of my own making, for I made very good candles now of goat's tallow; and going into this low place, I was obliged to creep upon all fours, as I have said, almost ten yards; which, by the way, I thought was a venture bold enough, considering that I knew not how far it might go, nor what was beyond it. When I was got through the strait, I found the roof rose higher up, I believe nearly twenty feet. But never was such a glorious sight seen in the island, I dare say, as it was, to look round the sides and roof of this vault or cave; the walls reflected a hundred thousand lights to me from my two candles. What it was in the rock, whether diamonds, or any other precious stones, or gold, which I rather supposed it to be, I knew not.

The place I was in was a most delightful cavity or grotto of its kind, as could be expected, though perfectly dark. The floor was dry and level, and had a sort of small loose gravel upon it, so that there was no nauseous or venomous creature to be seen; neither was there any damp or wet on the sides or roof. The only difficulty in it was the entrance, which, however, as it was a place of security, and such a retreat as I wanted, I thought that was a convenience; so that I was really rejoiced at the discovery, and resolved, without any delay, to bring some of those things which I was most anxious about to this place; particularly, I resolved to bring hither my magazine of powder, and my spare arms, viz., two fowling-pieces, for I had three in all, and three muskets, for of them I had eight in all. So I kept at my castle only five, which stood ready mounted, like pieces of cannon, on my outmost fence; and were ready also to take out upon any expedition.

Upon this occasion of removing my ammunition, I took occasion to open the barrel of powder, which I took up out of the sea, and which had been wet; and I found that the water had penetrated about three of four inches into the powder on every side, which caking, and growing hard, had preserved the inside like a kernel in a shell; so that I had near sixty pounds of very good powder in the centre of the cask. And this was an agreeable discovery to me at that time; so I carried all away thither, never keeping above two or three pounds of powder with me in my castle, for fear of a surprise of any kind. I also carried thither all the lead I had left for bullets.

I fancied myself now like one of the ancient giants, which were said to live in caves and holes in the rocks, where none could come at them; for I persuaded myself, while I was here, if five hundred savages were to hunt me, they could never find me out; or, if they did, they would not venture to attack me here.

The old goat, whom I found expiring, died in the mouth of the cave the next day after I made this discovery; and I found it much easier to dig a great hole there, and throw him in and cover him with earth, than to drag him out; so I interred him there, to prevent the offence to my nose.

I was now in my twenty-third year of residence in this island; and was so naturalised to the place, and to the manner of living, that could I have but enjoyed the certainty that no savages would come to the place to disturb me, I could have been content to have capitulated for spending the rest of my time there, even to the last moment, till I had laid me down and died, like the old goat in the cave. I had also arrived to some little diversions and amusements, which made the time pass more pleasantly with me a great deal than it did before. As, first, I had taught my Poll, as I noted before, to speak; and he did it so familiarly, and talked so articulately and plain, that it was very pleasant to me; and he lived with me no less than six and twenty years. How long he might live afterwards I know not, though I know they have a notion in the Brazils that they live a hundred years. Perhaps poor Poll may be alive there still, calling after poor Robin Crusoe to this day. I wish no Englishman the ill luck to come there and hear him; but if he did, he would certainly believe it was the devil. My dog was a very pleasant and loving companion to me for no less than sixteen years of my time, and then died of mere old age. As for my cats, they multiplied, as I had observed, to that degree that I was obliged to shoot several of them at first to keep them from devouring me and all I had; but at length, when the two old ones I brought with me were gone, and after some time continually driving them from me, and letting them have no provision with me, they all ran wild into the woods, except two or three favourites, which I kept tame, and whose young, when they had any, I always drowned; and these were part of my family. Besides these, I always kept two or three household kids about me, whom I taught to feed out of my hand. And I had two more parrots, which talked pretty well, and would all call "Robin Crusoe," but none like my first; nor, indeed, did I take the pains with any of them that I had done with him. I had also several tame seafowls, whose names I know not, whom I caught upon the shore, and cut their wings; and the little stakes which I had planted before my castle wall being now grown up to a good thick grove, these fowls all lived among these low trees, and bred there, which was very agreeable to me; so that, as I said above, I began to be very well contented with the life I led, if it might but have been secured from the dread of the savages.

But it is otherwise directed; and it may not be amiss for all people who shall meet with my story, to make this just observation from it, viz., how frequently, in the course of our lives, the evil which in itself we seek most to shun, and which, when we are fallen into it, is the most dreadful to us, is oftentimes the very means or door of our deliverance, by which alone we can be raised again from the afflictions we are fallen into. I could give many examples of this in the course of my unaccountable life; but in nothing was it more particularly remarkable than in the circumstances of my last years of solitary residence in this island.

It was now the month of December, as I said above, in my twenty-third year; and this, being the southern solstice (for winter I cannot call it), was the particular time of my harvest, and required my being pretty much abroad in the fields, when, going out pretty early in the morning, even before it was thorough daylight, I was surprised with seeing a light of some fire upon the shore, at a distance from me of about two miles, towards the end of the island, where I had observed some savages had been, as before. But not on the other side; but, to my great affliction, it was on my side of the island.

I was indeed terribly surprised at the sight, and stepped short within my grove, not daring to go out lest I might be surprised; and yet I had no more peace within, from the apprehensions I had that if these savages, in rambling over the island, should find my corn standing or cut, or any of works and improvements, they would immediately conclude that there were people in the place, and would then never give over till they had found me out. In this extremity I went back directly to my castle, pulled up the ladder after me, and made all things without look as wild and natural as I could.

Then I prepared myself within, putting myself in a posture of defence. I loaded all my cannon, as I called them, that is to say, my muskets, which were mounted upon my new fortification, and all my pistols, and resolved to defend myself to the last gasp; not forgetting seriously to commend myself to the Divine protection, and earnestly to pray to God to deliver me out of the hands of the barbarians. And in this posture I continued about two hours; but began to be mighty impatient for intelligence abroad, for I had no spies to send out.

After sitting a while longer, and musing what I should do in this case, I was not able to bear sitting in ignorance any longer; so setting up my ladder to the side of the hill where there was a flat place, as I observed before, and then pulling the ladder up after me, I set it up again, and mounted to the top of the hill; and pulling out my perspective-glass, which I had taken on purpose, I laid me down flat on my belly on the ground, and began to look for the place. I presently found there was no less than nine naked savages sitting round a small fire they had made, not to warm them, for they had no need of that, the weather being extreme hot, but, as I supposed, to dress some of their barbarous diet of human flesh which they had brought with them, whether alive or dead, I could not know.

They had two canoes with them, which they had hauled up upon the shore; and as it was then tide of ebb, they seemed to me to wait for the return of the flood to go away again. It is not easy to imagine what confusion this sight put me into, especially seeing them come on my side of the island, and so near me too. But when I observed their coming must be always with the current of the ebb, I began afterwards to more sedate in my mind, being satisfied that I might go abroad with safety all the time of the tide of flood, if they were not on shore before; and having made this observation, I went abroad about my harvest-work with the more composure.

As I expected, so it proved; for as soon as the tide made to the westward, I saw them all take boat, and row (or paddle, as we call it) all away. I should have observed, that for an hour and more before they went off, they went to dancing; and I could easily discern their postures and gestures by my glasses. I could not perceive, by my nicest observation, but that they were stark naked, and had not the least covering upon them; but whether they were men or women, that I could not distinguish.

As soon as I saw them shipped and gone, I took two guns upon my shoulders, and two pistols at my girdle, and my great sword by my side, without a scabbard, and with all the speed I was able to make I went away to the hill where I had discovered the first appearance of all. And as soon as I gat thither, which was not less than two hours (for I could not go apace, being so loaden with arms as I was), I perceived there had been three canoes more of savages on that place; and looking out farther, I saw they were all at sea together, making over for the main.

This was a dreadful sight to me, especially when, going down to the shore, I could see the marks of horror which the dismal work they had been about had left behind it, viz., the blood, the bones, and part of the flesh of human bodies, eaten and devoured by those wretches with merriment and sport. I was so filled with indignation at the sight, that I began now to premeditate the destruction of the next that I saw there, let them be who or how many soever.

It seemed evident to me that the visits which they thus made to this island are not very frequent, for it was above fifteen months before any more of them came on shore there again; that is to say, I neither saw them, or any footsteps or signals of them, in all that time; for, as to the rainy seasons, then they are sure not to come abroad, at least not so far. Yet all this while I lived uncomfortably by reason of the constant apprehensions I was in of their coming upon me by surprise; from whence I observe, that the expectation of evil is more bitter than the suffering, especially if there is no room to shake off that expectation, or those apprehensions.

During all this time I was in the murdering humor, and took up most of my hours, which should have been better employed, in contriving how to circumvent and fall upon them the very next time I should see them; especially if they should be divided, as they were the last time, into two parties. Nor did I consider at all that if I killed one party, suppose ten or a dozen, I was still the next day, or week, or month, to kill another, and so another, even *ad infinitum,* till I should be at length no less a murderer than they were in being man-eaters, and perhaps more so.

I spent my days now in great perplexity and anxiety of mind, expecting that I should, one day or other, fall into the hands of these merciless creatures; and if I did at any time venture abroad, it was not without looking around me with the greatest care and caution imaginable. And now I found, to my great comfort, how happy it was that I provided for a tame flock or herd of goats; for I durst not, upon any account, fire my gun, especially near that side of the island where they usually came, lest I should alarm the savages. And if they had fled from me now, I was sure to have them come back again, with perhaps two or three hundred canoes with them, in a few days, and then I knew what to expect.

However, I wore out a year and three months more before I ever saw any more of the savages, and then I found them again, as I shall soon observe. It is true they might have been there once or twice, but either they made no stay, or at least I did not hear them; but in the month of May, as near as I could calculate, and in my four and twentieth year, I had a very strange encounter with them; of which in its place.

The perturbation of my mind, during this fifteen or sixteen months' interval, was very great. I slept unquiet, dreamed always frightful dreams, and often started out of my sleep in the night. In the day great troubles overwhelmed my mind, and in the night I dreamed often of killing the savages, and of the reasons why I might justify the doing of it. But, to waive all this for a while, it was the middle of May, on the sixteenth day, I think, as well as my poor wooden calendar would reckon, for I marked all upon the post still; I say, it was the sixteenth of May that it blew a very great storm of wind all day, with a great deal of lightning and thunder, and a very foul night it was after it. I know not what was the particular occasion of it, but as I was reading in the Bible, and taken up with very serious thoughts about my present condition, I was surprised with a noise of a gun, as I thought, fired at sea.

This was, to be sure, a surprise of a quite different nature from any I had met with before; for the notions this put into my thoughts were quite of another kind. I started up in the greatest haste imaginable and, in a trice, clapped my ladder to the middle place of the rock, and pulled it after me; and mounting it the second time, got to the top of the hill the very moment that a flash of fire bid me listen for a second gun, which accordingly, in about half a minute, I heard; and, by the sound, knew that it was from the part of the sea where I was driven down the current in my boat.

I immediately considered that this must be some ship in distress, and that they had some comrade, or some other ship in company, and fired these gun for signals of distress, and to obtain help. I had this presence of mind, at that minute, as to think that though I could not help them, it might be that they might help me; so I brought together all the dry wood I could get at hand, and, making a good handsome pile, I set it on fire upon the hill. The wood was dry, and blazed freely; and though the wind blew very hard, yet it burnt fairly out; so that I was certain, if there was any such thing as a ship, they must needs to see it, and no doubt they did; for as soon as ever my fire blazed up I heard another gun, and after that several others, all from the same quarter. I plied my fire all night long till day broke; and when it was broad day, and the air cleared up, I saw something at a great distance at sea, full east of the island, whether a sail or a hull I could not distinguish, no, not with my glasses, the distance was so great, and the weather still something hazy also; at least it was so out at sea.

I looked at it all that day, and soon perceived that it did not move; so I presently concluded that it was a ship at an anchor. And being eager, you may be sure, to be satisfied, I took my gun in hand and ran toward the south side of the island, to the rocks where I had formerly been carried away with the current; and getting up there, the weather by this time being perfectly clear, I could plainly see, to my great sorrow, the wreck of a ship, cast away in the night upon those concealed rocks which I found when I was out in my boat; and which rocks, as they checked the violence of the stream, and made a kind of counter stream or eddy, were the occasion of my recovering from the most desperate, hopeless condition that ever I had been in in all my life.

Thus, what is one man's safety is another man's destruction; for it seems these men, whoever they were, being out of their knowledge, and the rocks being wholly under water, had been driven upon them in the night, the wind blowing hard at E. and E.N.E. Had they seen the island, as I must necessarily suppose they did not, they must, as I thought, have endeavoured to have saved themselves on shore by the help of their boat; but their firing of guns for help, especially when they saw, as I imagined, my fire, filled me with many thoughts. First, I imagined that upon seeing my light, they might have put themselves into their boat, and have endeavoured to make the shore; but that the sea going very high, they might have been cast away. Other times I imagined that they might have lost their boat before, as might be the case many ways; as, particularly, by the breaking of the sea upon their ship, which many times obliges men to stave, or take in pieces of their boat, and sometimes to throw it overboard with their own hands. Other times I imagined they had some other ship or ships in company, who, upon the signals of distress they had made, had taken them up and carried them off. Other whiles I fancied they were all gone off to sea in their boat, and being hurried away by the current that I had been formerly in, were carried out into the great ocean, where there was nothing but misery and perishing and that, perhaps, they might by this time think of starving, and of being in a condition to eat one another.

All these were but conjectures at best, so, in the condition I was in, I could no more than look on upon the misery of the poor men, and pity them; which had still this good effect on my side, that it gave me more and more cause to give thanks to God, who had so happily and comfortably provided for me in my desolate condition; and that of two ships' companies who were now cast away upon this part of the world, not one life should be spared but mine. I learned here again to observe, that it is very rare that the providence of God casts us into any condition of life so low, or any misery so great, but we may see something or other to be thankful for, and may see other in worse circumstances than our own.

Such certainly was the case of these men, of whom I could not so much as see room to suppose any of them were saved. Nothing could make it rational so much as to wish or expect that they did not all perish there, except the possibility only of their being taken up by another ship in company; and this was but mere possibility indeed, for I saw not the least signal or appearance of any such thing.

I cannot explain, by any possible energy of words, what a strange longing or hankering of desires. I felt in my soul upon this sight, breaking out sometimes thus: "Oh that there had been but one or two, nay, or but one soul, saved out of this ship, to have escaped to me, that I might but have had one companion, one fellow-creature, to have spoken to me, and to have conversed with!" In all the time of my solitary life I never felt so earnest, so strong a desire after the society of my fellow-creatures, or so deep a regret at the want of it.

There are some secret moving springs in the affections which, when they are set agoing by some object in view, or be it some object, though not in view, yet rendered present to the mind by the power of imagination, that motion carries out the soul by its impetuosity to such violent, eager embracings of the object, that the absence of it is insupportable.

Such were these earnest wishings that but one man had been saved! "Oh that it had been but one!" I believe I repeated the words, "Oh that it had been one!" a thousand times; and the desires were so moved by it, that when I spoke the words my hands would clinch together, and my fingers press the palms of my hands, that if I had had any soft thing in my hand, it would have crushed it involuntarily; and my teeth in my head would strike together, and set against one another so strong that for some time I could not part them again.

Let the naturalists explain these things and the reason and manner of them. All I can say to them is to describe the fact, which was even surprising to me when I found it, though I knew not from what it should proceed. It was doubtless the effect of ardent wishes, and of strong ideas formed in my mind, realising the comfort which the conversation of one of my fellow-Christians would have been to me.

But it was not to be. Either their fate or mine, or both, forbid it; for, till the last year of my being on this island, I never knew whether any were saved out of that ship or no; and had only the affliction, some days after, to see the corpse of a drowned boy come on shore at the end of the island which was next to the shipwreck. He had on no clothes but a seaman's waistcoat, a pair of open kneed-linen drawers, and a blue linen shirt; but nothing to direct me so much as to guess what nation he was of. He had nothing in his pocket but two pieces of eight and a tobacco-pipe. The last was to me of often times more value than the first.

It was now calm, and I had a great mind to venture out in my boat to this wreck, not doubting but I might find something on board that might be useful to me. But that did not altogether press me so much as the possibility that there might be yet some living creature on board, whose life I might not only save, but might, by saving that life, comfort my own to the last degree. And this thought clung so to my heart that I could not be quiet night or day, but I must venture out in my boat on board this wreck; and committing the rest to God's providence I thought, the impression was so strong upon my mind that it could not be resisted, that it must come from some invisible direction, and that I should be wanting to myself if I did not go.

Under the power of this impression, I hastened back to my castle, prepared everything for my voyage, took a quantity of bread, a great pot for fresh water, a compass to steer by, a bottle of rum (for I had still a great deal of that left), a basket full of raisins. And thus, loading myself with everything necessary, I went down to my boat, got the water out of her, and got her afloat, loaded all my cargo in her, and then went home again for more. My second cargo was a great bag full of rice, the umbrella to set up over my head for shade, another large pot full of fresh water, and about two dozen of my small loaves, or barley-cakes, more than before, with a bottle of goat's milk and a cheese; all which, with great labour and sweat, I brought to my boat. And praying to God to direct my voyage, I put out; and rowing, or paddling, the canoe along the shore, I came at last to the utmost point of the island on that side, viz., N.E. And now I was to launch out into the ocean, and either to venture or not to venture. I looked on the rapid currents which ran constantly on both sides of the island at a distance, and which were very terrible to me, from the remembrance of the hazard I had been in before, and my heart began to fail me; for I foresaw that if I was driven into either of those currents, I should be carried a vast way out to sea, and perhaps out of my reach, or sight of the island again; and that then, as my boat was but small, if any little gale of wind should rise, I should be inevitably lost.

These thoughts so oppressed my mind that I began to give over my enterprise; and having hauled my boat into a little creek on the shore, I stepped out, and sat me down a little rising bit of ground, very pensive and anxious, between fear and desire, about my voyage; when, as I was musing, I could perceive that the tide was turned, and the flood come on; upon which my going was for so many hours impracticable. Upon this, presently it occurred to me that I should go up to the highest piece of ground I could find and observe, if I could, how the sets of the tide, or currents, lay when the flood came in, that I might judge whether, if I was driven one way out, I might not expect to be driven another way home, with the same rapidness of the currents. This thought was no sooner in my head but I cast my eye upon a little hill, which sufficiently overlooked the sea both ways, and from whence I had a clear view of the currents, or sets of the tide, and which way I was to guide myself in my return. Here I found, that as the current of the ebb set out close by the south point of the island, so the current of the flood set in close by the shore of the north side; and that I had nothing to do but to keep to the north of the island on my return, and I should do well enough.

Encouraged with this observation, I resolved the next morning to set out with the first of the tide, and reposing myself for the night in the canoe, under the great watch-coat I mentioned, I launched out. I made first a little out to sea, full north, till I began to feel the benefit of the current which set eastward, and which carried me at a great rate; and yet did not so hurry me as the southern side current had done before, and so as to take from me all government of the boat; but having a strong steerage with my paddle, I went at a great rate directly for the wreck, and less than two hours I came up to it.

It was a dismal sight to look at. The ship, which, by its building, was Spanish, stuck fast, jammed in between two rocks. All the stern and quarter of her was beaten to pieces with the sea; and as her forecastle, which stuck in the rocks, had run on with violence, her mainmast and foremast were brought by the board; that is to say broken short off; but her bowsprit was sound, and the head and bow appeared firmer. When I came close to her a dog appeared upon her, who, seeing me coming, yelped and cried; and as soon as I called him, jumped into the sea to come to me, and I took him into the boat, but found him almost dead for hunger and thirst. I gave him a cake of my bread, and he eat it like a ravenous wolf that had been starving a fortnight in the snow. I then gave the poor creature some fresh water, with which, if I would have let him, he would have burst himself.

After this I went on board; but the first sight I met with was two men drowned in the cook-room, or forecastle of the ship, with their arms fast about one another. I concluded, as is indeed probable, that when the ship struck, it being in a storm, the sea broke so high, and so continually over her, that the men were not able to bear it, and were strangled with the constant rushing in of the water, as much as if they had been under water. Besides the dog, there was nothing left in the ship that had life, nor any goods that I could see but what were spoiled by the water. There were some casks of liquor, whether wine or brandy I knew not, which lay lower in the hold, and which, the water being ebbed out, I could see; but they were too big to meddle with. I saw several chests, which I believed belonged to some of the seamen; and I got two of them into the boat, without examining what was in them.

Had the stern of the ship been fixed, and the fore part broken off, I am persuaded I might have made a good voyage; for by what I found in these two chests, I had room to suppose the ship had a great deal of wealth on board; and if I may guess by the course she steered, she must have been bound from the Buenos Ayres, or the Rio de la Plata, in the south part of America, beyond the Brazils, to the Havana, in the Gulf of Mexico, and so perhaps to Spain. She had, no doubt, a great treasure in her, but of no use, at that time, to anybody; and what became of the rest of her people, I then knew not.

I found, besides these chests, a little cask full of liquor, of about twenty gallons, which I got into my boat with much difficulty. There were several muskets in a cabin, and a great powder horn, with about four pounds of powder in it. As for the muskets, I had no occasion for them, so I left them, but took the powder horn. I took a fire hovel and tongs, which I wanted extremely; as also two little brass kettles, a copper pot to make chocolate, and a gridiron. And with this cargo, and the dog, I came away, the tide beginning to make home again; and the same evening, about an hour within night, I reached the island again, weary and fatigued to the last degree.

I reposed that night in the boat; and in the morning I resolved to harbour what I had gotten in my new cave, not to carry it home to my castle. After refreshing myself, I got all my cargo on shore, and began to examine the particulars. The cask of liquor I found to be a kind of rum, but not such as we had at the Brazils, and, in a word, not at all good. But when I came to open the chests, I found several things of great use to me. For example, I found in one a fine case of bottles, of an extraordinary kind, and filled with cordial waters, fine, and very good; the bottles held about three pints each, and were tipped with silver. I found two pots of very good succades, or sweetmeats, so fastened also on top, that the salt water had not hurt them; and two more of the same, which the water had spoiled. I found some very good shirts, which were very welcome to me; and about a dozen and half of linen white handkerchiefs and coloured neckcloths. The former were also very welcome, being exceeding refreshing to wipe my face in a hot day. Besides this, when I came to the till in the chest, I found there three great bags of pieces of eight, which held out about eleven hundred pieces in all; and in one of them, wrapped up in a paper, six doubloons of gold, and some small bars or wedges of gold. I suppose they might all weigh near a pound.

The other chest I found had some clothes in it, but of little value; but by the circumstances, it must have belonged to the gunner's mate; though there was no powder in it, but about two pounds of fine glazed powder, in three small flasks, kept, I suppose, for charging their fowling-pieces on occasion. Upon the whole, I got very little by this voyage that was of any use to me; for as to the money, I had no manner of occasion for it; It was to me as the dirt under my feet; and I would have given it all for three or four pair of English shoes and stockings, which were things I greatly wanted, but had not had on my feet now for many years. I had indeed gotten two pair of shoes now, which I took off of the feet of the two drowned men whom I saw in the wreck, and I found two pair more in one of the chests, which were very welcome to me; but they were not like our English shoes, either for ease or service, being rather what we call pumps than shoes. I found in the seaman's chest about fifty pieces of eight in royals, but no gold. I suppose this belonged to a poorer man than the other, which seemed to belong to some officer.

Well, however, I lugged this money home to my cave, and laid it up, as I had done that before which I brought from our own ship; but it was a great pity, as I said, that the other part of this ship had not come to my share, for I am satisfied I might have loaded my canoe several times over with money, which, if I had ever escaped to England, would have lain here safe enough till I might have come again and fetched it.

Having now brought all my things on shore, and secured them, I went back to my boat, and rowed or paddled her along the shore to her old harbour, where I laid her up, and made the best of my way to my old habitation, where I found everything safe and quiet. So I began to repose myself, live after my old fashion, and take care of my family affairs; and, for a while, I lived easy enough, only that I was more vigilant than I used to be, looked out oftener, and did not go abroad so much; and if at any time I did stir with any freedom, it was always to the east part of the island, where I was pretty well satisfied the savages never came, and where I could go without so many precautions, and such a load of arms and ammunition as I always carried with me if I went the other way.

I lived in this condition nearly two years more; but my unlucky head, that was always to let me know if it was born to make my body miserable, was all of this two years filled with projects and designs, how, if it were possible, I might get away from this island; for sometimes I was for making another voyage to the wreck, though my reason told me that there was nothing left there worth the hazard of my voyage; sometimes for a ramble one way, sometimes another; and I believe verily, if I had had the boat that I went from Sallee in, I should have ventured to sea, bound anywhere, I knew not whither.

I have been, in all my circumstances, a memento to those who are touched with the general plague of mankind, whence, for aught I know, one-half of their miseries flow; I mean, that of not being satisfied with the station wherein God and Nature had placed them; for not to look back upon my primitive condition, and the excellent advice of my father, the opposition to which was, as I may call it, my *original sin,* my subsequent mistakes of the same kind had been the means of my coming into this miserable condition; for had that Providence, which so happily had seated me at the Brazils as a planter, blessed me with confined desires, and I could have been contented to have gone on gradually, I might have been, by this time, I mean in the time of my being in this island, one of the most considerable planters in the Brazils; nay, I am persuaded that by the improvements I had made in that little time I lived there, and the increase I should probably have made if I had stayed, I might have been worth a hundred thousand moidores. And what business had I to leave a settled fortune, a well-stocked plantation, improving and increasing, to turn supercargo to Guinea to fetch negroes, when patience and time would so have increased our stock at home, that we could have bought them at our own door from those whose business it was to fetch them; and though it had cost us something more, yet the difference of that price was by no means worth saving at so great a hazard.

But as this is ordinarily the fate of your heads, so reflection upon the folly of it is as ordinarily the exercise of more years, or the dear-bought experience of time; and so it was with me now. And yet, so deep had the mistake taken root in my temper, that I could not satisfy myself in my station, but was continually poring upon the means and possibility of my escape from this place. And that I may, with the greater pleasure to the reader, bring on the remaining part of my story, it may not be improper to give some account of my first conceptions on the subject of this foolish scheme for my escape, and how and upon what foundation I acted.

I am now to be supposed retired into my castle, after my late voyage to the wreck, my frigate laid up and secured under water, as usual, and my condition restored to what it was before. I had more wealth, indeed, that I had before, but was not at all the richer; for I had no more use for it than the Indians of Peru had before the Spaniards came there.

It was one of the nights in the rainy season in March, the four and twentieth year of my first setting foot in this island of solitariness. I was lying in my bed, or hammock, awake, very well in health, had no pain, no distemper, no uneasiness of body, no, nor any uneasiness of mind, more than ordinary, but could by no means close my eyes, that is, so as to sleep; no, not a wink all night long, otherwise than as follows.

It is as impossible, as needless, to set down the innumerable crowd of thoughts that whirled through that great thoroughfare of the brain, the memory, in this night's time. I ran over the whole history of my life in miniature, or by abridgment, as I may call it, to my coming to this island, and also of the part of my life since I came to this island. In my reflections upon the state of my case since I came on shore on this island, I was comparing the happy posture of my affairs in the first years of my habitation here compared to the life of anxiety, fear, and care which I had lived ever since I had seen the print of a foot in the sand; nor that I did not believe the savages had frequented the island even all the while, and might have been several hundreds of them at times on shore there; but I had never known it, and was incapable of any apprehensions about it. My satisfaction was perfect, though my danger was the same; and I was as happy in not knowing my danger, as if I had never really been exposed to it. This furnished my thoughts with many very profitable reflections, and particularly this one: how infinitely good that Providence is which has provided, in its government of mankind, such narrow bounds to his sight and knowledge of things; and though he walks in the midst of so many thousand dangers, the sight of which, if discovered to him, would distract his mind and sink his spirits, he is kept serene and calm, by having the events of things hid from his eyes, and knowing nothing of the dangers which surround him.

After these thoughts had for some time entertained me, I came to reflect seriously upon the real danger I had been in for so many years in this very island, and how I had walked about in the greatest security, and with all possible tranquillity, even when perhaps nothing but a brow of a hill, a great tree, or the casual approach of night had been between me and the worst kind of destruction, viz., that of failing into the hands of cannibals and savages, who would have seized on me with the same view as I did of a goat or a turtle, and have thought it no more a crime to kill and devour me, than I did of a pigeon or a curlew. I would unjustly slander myself if I should say I was not sincerely thankful to my great Preserver, to whose singular protection I acknowledged, with great humility, that all these unknown deliverances were due, and without which I must inevitably have fallen into their merciless hands.

When these thoughts were over, my head was for some time taken up in considering the nature of these wretched creatures, I mean the savages, and how it came to pass in the world that the wise Governor of all things should give up any of His creatures to such inhumanity; nay, to something so much below even brutality itself, as to devour its own kind. But as this ended in some (at that time fruitless) speculations, it occurred to me to inquire what part of the world these wretches lived in? how far off the coast was from whence they came? what they ventured over so far from home for? what kind of boats they had? and why I might not order myself and my business so, that I might be able to go over thither as they were to come to me.

I never so much as troubled myself to consider what I should do with myself when I came thither; what would become of me, if I fell into the hands of the savages; or how I should escape from them, if they attempted me; no, nor so much as how it was possible for me to reach the coast, and not be attempted by some or other of them, without any possibility of delivering myself; and if I should not fall into their hands, what I should do for provision, or whither I should bend my course. None of these thoughts, I say, so much as came in my way; but my mind was wholly bent upon the notion of my passing over in my boat to the mainland. I looked back upon my present condition as the most miserable that could possibly be; that I was not able to throw myself into anything, but death, that could be called worse; that if I reached the shore of the main, I might perhaps meet with relief, or I might coast along, as I did on the shore of Africa, till I came to some inhabited country, and where I might find some Christian ship that might take me in; and if the worse came to the worst, I could but die, which would put an end to all these miseries at once. Pray note, all this was the fruit of a disturbed mind, an impatient temper, made as it were, desperate by the long continuance of my troubles, and the disappointments I had met in the work I had been on board of, and where I had been so near the obtaining of what I so earnestly longed for, viz., somebody to speak to, and to learn some knowledge from the place where I was, and of the probable means of my deliverance. I say, I was agitated wholly by these thoughts. All my calm of mind, in my resignation to Providence, and waiting the issue of the dispositions of Heaven, seemed to be suspended; and I had, as it were, no power to turn my thoughts to anything but to the project of a voyage to the main, which came upon me with such force, and such an impetuosity of desire, that it was not to be resisted.

When this had agitated my thoughts for two hours, or more, with such violence that it set my very blood into a ferment, and my pulse beat as high as if I had been in a fever, merely with the extraordinary fervour of my mind about it, Nature, as if I had been fatigued and exhausted with the very thought of it, threw me into a sound sleep. One would have thought I should have dreamed of it, but I did not, nor of anything relating to it; but I dreamed that as I was going out in the morning, as usual, from my castle, I saw upon the shore two canoes and eleven savages coming to land, and that they brought with them another savage, whom they were going to kill in order to eat him; when, on a sudden, the savage that they were going to kill jumped away, and ran for his life. And I thought, in my sleep, that he came running into my little thick grove before my fortification to hide himself; and that I, seeing him alone, and not perceiving that the other sought him that way, showed myself to him, and smiling upon him, encouraged him; that he kneeled down to me, seeming to pray me to assist him; upon which I showed my ladder, made him go up, and carried him into my cave, and he became my servant; and that as soon as I had gotten this man, I said to myself, "Now I may certainly venture to the mainland; for this fellow will serve me as a pilot, and will tell me what to do, and whither to go for provisions, and whither not to go for fear of being devoured; what places to venture into, and what to escape." I waked with this thought, and was under such inexpressible impressions of joy at the prospect of my escape in my dream, that the disappointments which I felt upon coming to myself and finding it was no more than a dream were equally extravagant the other way, and threw me into a very great dejection of spirit.

Upon this, however, I made this conclusion: that my only way to go about an attempt for an escape was, if possible, to get a savage into my possession; and, if possible, it should be one of their prisoners whom they had condemned to be eaten, and should bring thither to kill. But these thoughts were attended with this difficulty, that it was impossible to effect this without attacking a whole caravan of them, and killing them all; and this was not only a very desperate attempt, and might miscarry; but, on the other hand, I had greatly scrupled the lawfulness of it to me; and my heart trembled at the thoughts of shedding so much blood, though it was for my deliverance. I need not repeat the arguments which occurred to me against this, they being the same mentioned before. But though I had other reasons to offer now, viz., that those men were enemies to my life, and would devour me if they could; that it was self-preservation, in the highest degree, to deliver myself from this death of a life, and was acting in my own defence as much as if they were actually assaulting me, and the like; I say, though these things argued for it, yet the thoughts of shedding human blood for my deliverance were very terrible to me, and such as I could by no means reconcile myself to a great while.

However, at last, after many secret disputes with myself, and after great perplexities about it, for all these arguments, one way and another, struggled in my head a long time, the eager prevailing desire of deliverance at length mastered all the rest, and I resolved, if possible, to get one of those savages into my hands, cost what it would. My next thing then was to contrive how to do it, and this indeed was very difficult to resolve on. But as I could pitch upon no probable means for it, so I resolved to put myself upon the watch, to see them when they came on shore, and leave the rest to the event, taking such measures as the opportunity should present, let be what would be.

With these resolutions in my thoughts, I set myself upon the scout as often as possible, and indeed so often, till I was heartily tired of it; for it was above a year and half that I waited; and for great part of that time went out to the west end, and to the south-west corner of the island, almost every day, to see for canoes, but none appeared. This was very discouraging, and began to trouble me much; though I cannot say that it did in this case, as it had done some time before that, viz., wear off the edge of my desire to the thing. But the longer it seemed to be delayed, the more eager I was for it. In a word, I was not at first so careful to shun the sight of these savages, and avoid being seen by them, as I was now eager to be upon them.

Besides, I fancied myself able to manage one, nay, two or three savages, if I had them, so as to make them entirely slaves to me, to do whatever I should direct them, and to prevent their being able at any time to do me any hurt. It was a great while that I pleased myself with this affair; but nothing still presented. All my fancies and schemes came to nothing, for no savages came near me for a great while.

About a year and half after I had entertained these notions, and by long musing had, as it were, resolved them all into nothing, for want of an occasion to put them in execution, I was surprised, one morning early, with seeing no less than five canoes all on shore together on my side the island, and the people who belonged to them all landed, and out of my sight. The number of them broke all my measures; for seeing so many, and knowing that they always came four, or six, or sometimes more in a boat, I could not tell what to think of it, or how to take my measures to attack twenty or thirty men single-handed; so I lay still in my castle, perplexed and discomforted. However, I put myself into all the same postures for an attack that I had formerly provided, and was just ready for action if anything had presented. Having waited a good while, listening to hear if they made any noise, at length, began very impatient, I set my guns at the foot of my ladder, and clambered up to the top of the hill, by my two stages, as usual; standing so, however, that my head did not appear above the hill, so that they could not perceive me by any means. Here I observed, by the help of my perspective glass, that they were no less than thirty in number, that they had a fire kindled, that they had had meat dressed. How they had cooked it, that I knew not, or what it was; but they were all dancing, in I know not how many barbarous gestures and figures, their own way, round the fire.

While I was thus looking on them, I perceived by my perspective two miserable wretches dragged from the boats, where, it seems, they were laid by, and were now brought out for the slaughter. I perceived one of them immediately fell, being knocked down, I suppose, with a club or wooden sword, for that was their way, and two or three others were at work immediately, cutting him open for their cookery, while the other victim was left standing by himself, till they should be ready for him. In that very moment this poor wretch seeing himself a little at liberty, Nature inspired him with hopes of life, and he started away from them, and ran with incredible swiftness along the sands directly towards me, I mean towards that part of the coast where my habitation was.

I was dreadfully frighted (that I must acknowledge) when I perceived him to run my way, and especially when, as I thought, I saw him pursued by the whole body; and now I expected that part of my dream was coming to pass, and that he would certainly take shelter in my grove; but I could not depend, by any means, upon my dream for the rest of it, viz., that the other savages would not pursue him thither, and find him there. However, I kept my station, and my spirits began to recover when I found that there was not above three men that followed him; and still more was I encouraged when I found that he outstripped them exceedingly in running, and gained ground of them; so that if he could but hold it for half an hour, I saw easily he would fairly get away from them all.

There was between them and my castle the creek, which I

mentioned often at the first part of my story, when I landed my cargoes out of the ship; and this I saw plainly he must necessarily swim over, or the poor wretch would be taken there. But when the savage escaping came thither he made nothing of it, though the tide was then up; but plunging in, swam through in about thirty strokes or thereabouts, landed, and ran on with exceeding strength and swiftness. When the three persons came to the creek, I found that two of them could swim, but the third could not, and that, standing on the other side, he looked at the other, but went no further, and soon after went softly back, which, as it happened, was very well for him in the main.

I observed that the two who swam were yet more than twice as long swimming over the creek as the fellow was that fled from them. It came now very warmly upon my thoughts, and indeed, irresistibly, that now was my time to get me a servant, and perhaps a companion assistant, and that I was called plainly by Providence to save this poor creature's life. I immediately run down the ladders with all possible expedition, fetches my two guns, for they were both but at the foot of the ladders, as I observed above, and getting up again, with the same haste, to the top of the hill, I crossed towards the sea, and having a very short cut, and all down hill, clapped myself in the way between the pursuers and the pursued, hallooing aloud to him that fled, who, looking back, was at first perhaps as much frighted at me as at them; but I beckoned with my hands to him to come back; and, in the meantime, I slowly advanced toward the two that followed; then rushing at once upon the foremost, I knocked him down with the stock of my piece. I was loth to fire, because I would not have the rest hear; though, at that distance, it would not have been easily heard, and being out of sight of the smoke too, they would not have easily known what to make of it. Having knocked this fellow down, the other who pursued with him stopped, as if he had been frighted, and I advanced apace towards him; but as I came nearer, I perceived presently he had a bow and arrow, and was fitting it to shoot at me; so I was then necessitated to shoot at him first, which I did, and killed him at the first shot.

The poor savage who fled, but had stopped, though he saw both his enemies fallen and killed, as he thought, yet was so frighted with the fire and noise of my piece, that he stood stock-still, and neither came forward nor went backward, though he seemed rather inclined to fly still than to come on. I hallooed again to him, and made signs to come forward, which he easily understood, and came a little way, then stopped again, and then a little further; and stopped again; and I could then perceive that he stood trembling, as if he had been taken prisoner, and had just been to be killed, as his two enemies were. I beckoned him again to come to me, and gave him all the signs of encouragement that I could think of; and he came nearer and nearer, kneeling down every often or twelve steps, in token of acknowledgment for my saving his life. I smiled at him, and looked pleasantly, and beckoned to him to come still nearer. At length he came close to me, and then he kneeled down again, kissed the ground, and laid his head upon the ground, and taking me by the foot, set my foot upon his head. This, it seems, was in token of swearing to be my slave forever. I took him up, and made much of him, and encouraged him all I could. But there was more work to do yet; for I perceived the savage whom I knocked down was not killed, but stunned with the blow, and began to come to himself; so I pointed to him, and showing him the savage, that he was not dead, upon this he spoke some words to me; and though I could not understand them, yet I thought they were pleasant to hear; for they were the first sound of a man's voice that I had heard, my own excepted, for above twenty-five years. But there was no time for such reflections now. The savage who was knocked down recovered himself so far as to sit up upon the ground, and I perceived that my savage began to be afraid; but when I was that, I presented my other piece at the man, as if I would shoot him. Upon this my savage, for so I call him now, made a motion to me to lend him my sword, which hung naked in a belt by my side; so I did. He no sooner had it but he runs to his enemy, and, at one blow, cut off his head as cleverly, no executioner in Germany could have done it sooner or better; which I thought very strange for one who, I had reason to believe, never saw a sword in his life before, except their own wooden swords. However, it seems, as I learned afterwards, they make their wooden swords so sharp, so heavy, and the wood is so hard, that they will cut off heads even with them, ay, and arms, and that at one blow too. When he had done this, he comes laughing to me in sign of triumph, and brought me the sword again, and with abundance of gestures, which I did not understand, laid it down, with the head of the savage that he had killed, just before me.

But that which astonished him most, was to know how I had killed the other Indian so far off; so pointing to him, he made signs to me to let him go to him; so I bade him go, as well as I could. When he came to him, he stood like one amazed, looking at him, turned him first on one side, then t'other, looked at the wound the bullet had made, which, it seems, was just in his breast, where it had made a hole, and no great quantity of blood had followed; but he had bled inwardly, for he was quite dead. He took up his bow and arrows, and came back; so I turned away, and beckoned to him to follow me, making signs to him that more might come after them.

Upon this he signed to me that he should bury them with sand, that they might not be seen by the rest if they followed; and so I made signs again to him to do so. He fell to work, and in an instant he had scraped a hole in the sand with his hands big enough to bury the first in, and then dragged him into it, and covered him, and did so also by the other. I believe he had buried them both in a quarter of an hour. Then calling him away, I carried him, not to my castle, but quite away to my cave, on the farther part of the island; so I did not let my dream come to pass in that part, viz., that he came into my grove for shelter.

Here I gave him bread and a bunch of raisins to eat, and a draught of water, which I found he was indeed in great distress for, by his running; and having refreshed him, I made signs for him to go lie down and sleep, pointing to a place where I had laid a great parcel of rice-straw, and a blanket upon it, which I used to sleep upon myself sometimes; so the poor creature laid down, and went to sleep.

He was a comely, handsome fellow, perfectly well made, with straight, strong limbs, not too large, tall, and well-shaped, and, as I reckoned, about twenty-six years of age. He had a very good countenance, not a fierce and surly aspect, but seemed to have something very manly in his face; and yet he had all the sweetness and softness of an European in his countenance too, especially when he smiled. His hair was long and black, not curled like wool; his forehead very high and large; and a great vivacity and sparkling sharpness in his eyes. The colour of his skin was not quite black, but very tawny; and yet not of an ugly, yellow, nauseous tawny, as the Brazilians and Virginians, and other natives of America are, but of a bright kind of a dun olive colour, that had in it something very agreeable, though not very easy to describe. His face was round and plump; his nose small, not flat like the negroes; a very good mouth, thin lips, and his fine teeth well set, and white as ivory.

After he had slumbered, rather than slept, about half an hour, he waked again, and came out of the cave to me, for I had been milking my goats, which I had in the enclosure just by. When he espied me, he came running to me, laying himself down again upon the ground, with all the possible signs of an humble, thankful disposition, making as many antic gestures to show it. At last he lays his head flat upon the ground, close to my foot, and sets my other foot upon his head, as he had done before, and after this made all the signs to me of subjection, servitude, and submission imaginable, to let me know how he would serve me as long as he lived. I understood him in many things, and let him know I was very well pleased with him. In a little time I began to speak to him, and teach him to speak to me; and, first, I made him know his name should be Friday, which was the day I saved his life. I called him so for the memory of the time. I likewise taught him to say master, and then let him know that was to be my name. I likewise taught him to say Yes and No, and to know the meaning of them. I gave him some milk in an earthen pot, and let him see me drink it before him, and sop my bread in it; and I gave him a cake of bread to do the like, which he quickly complied with, and made signs that it was very good for him.

I kept there with him all that night; but as soon as it was day, I beckoned to him to come with me, and let him know I would give him some clothes; at which he seemed very glad, for he was stark naked. As we went by the place where he had buried the two men, he pointed exactly to the place, and showed me the marks that he had made to find them again, making signs to me that we should dig them up again, and eat them. At this I appeared very angry, expressed my abhorrence of it, made as if I would vomit at the thoughts of it, and beckoned with my hand to him to come away; which he did immediately, with great submission. I then led him up to the top of the hill, to see if his enemies were gone; and pulling out my glass, I looked, and saw plainly the place where they had been, but no appearance of them or of their canoes; so that it was plain that they were gone, and had left their two comrades behind them, without any search after them.

But I was not content with this discovery; but having now more courage, and consequently more curiosity, I takes my man Friday with me, giving him the sword in his hand, with the bow and arrows at his back, which I found he could use very dexterously, making him carry one gun for me, and I two for myself, and away we marched to the place where these creatures had been; for I had a mind now to get some fuller intelligence of them. When I came to the place, my very blood ran chill in my veins, and my heart sunk within me, at the horror of the spectacle.

Indeed, it was a dreadful sight, at least it was so to me, though Friday made nothing of it. The place was covered with human bones, the ground dyed with their blood, great pieces of flesh left here and there, half-eaten, mangled and scorched; and, in short, all the tokens of the triumphant feast they had been making there, after a victory of their enemies. I saw three skulls, five hands, and the bones of three or four legs and feet, and abundance of other parts of the bodies; and Friday, by his signs, made me understand that they brought over four prisoners to feast upon; that three of them were eaten up, and that he, pointing to himself, was the fourth; that there had been a great battle between them and their next king, whose subjects it seems he had been one of, and that they had taken a great number of prisoners; all which were carried to several places, by those who had taken them in the fight, in order to feast upon them, as was done here by these wretches upon those they brought hither.

I caused Friday to gather all the skulls, bones, flesh, and whatever remained, and lay them together on a heap, and make a great fire upon it, and burn them all to ashes. I found Friday had still a hankering stomach after some of the flesh, and was still a cannibal in his nature; but I discovered so much abhorrence at the very thoughts of it, and at the least appearance of it, that he durst not discover it; for I had, by some means, let him know that I would kill him if he offered it.

When we had done this we came back to our castle, and there I fell to work for my man Friday; and, first of all, I gave him a pair of linen drawers, which I had out of the poor gunner's chest I mentioned, and which I found in the wreck; and which, with a little alteration, fitted him very well. Then I made him a jerkin of goat's-skin, as well as my skill would allow, and I was now grown a tolerable good tailor; and I gave him a cap, which I had made of a hare-skin, very convenient and fashionable enough; and thus he was clothed for the present tolerably well, and was mighty well pleased to see himself almost as well clothed as his master. It is true he went awkwardly in these things at first; wearing the drawers was very awkward to him, and the sleeves of the waistcoat galled his shoulders, and the inside of his arms; but a little easing them where he complained they hurt him, using himself to them, at length he took to them very well.

The next day after I came home to my hutch with him, I began to consider where I should lodge him. And that I might do well for him, and yet be perfectly easy myself, I made a little tent for him in the vacant place between my two fortifications, in the inside of the last and in the outside of the first; and as there was a door or entrance there into my cave, I made a formal framed door-case, and a door to it of boards, and set it up in the passage, a little within the entrance; and causing the door to open on the inside, I barred it up in the night, taking in my ladders, too; so that Friday could no way come at me in the inside of my innermost wall without making so much noise in getting over that it must need waken me; for my first wall had now a complete roof over it of long poles, covering all my tent, and leaning up to the side of the hill, which was again laid across with smaller sticks instead of laths, and then thatched over a great thickness with the rice-straw, which was strong, like reeds; and at the hole or place which was left to go in or out by the ladder, I had placed a kind of trap-door, which, if it had been attempted on the outside, would not have open at all, but would have fallen down, and made a great noise; and as to weapons, I took them all in to my side every night.

But I needed none of all this precaution; for never man had a more faithful, loving, sincere servant than Friday was to me; without passions, sullenness, or designs, perfectly obliged and engaged; his very affections were tied to me like those of a child to a father; and I dare say he would have sacrificed his life for saving mine, upon any occasion whatsoever. The many testimonies he gave me of this put it out of doubt, and soon convinced me that I needed to use no precautions as to my safety on his account.

This frequently gave me occasion to observe, and that with wonder, that however it had pleased God, in His providence, and in the government of the works of His hands, to take from so great a part of the world of His creatures the best uses to which their faculties and the powers of their soul are adapted, yet that He has bestowed upon them the same powers, the same reason, the same affections, the same sentiments of kindness and obligation, the same passions and resentments of wrongs, the same sense of gratitude, sincerity, fidelity, and all the capacities of doing good, and receiving good, that He has given to us; and that when He pleases to offer to them occasions of exerting these, they are as ready, nay, more ready, to apply them to the right uses for which they were bestowed that we are. And this made me very melancholy sometimes, in reflecting, as the several occasions presented, how mean a use we make of all these, even though we have these powers enlightened by the great lamp of instruction, the Spirit of God, and by the knowledge of His Word added to our understanding; and why it has pleased God to hide the like saving knowledge from so many millions of souls, who, if I might judge by this poor savage, would make a much better use of it than we did.

From hence, I sometimes was led too far to invade the sovereignity of Providence, and as it were, arraign the justice of so arbitrary a disposition of things that should hide that light from some, and reveal it to others, and yet expect a like duty from both. But I shut it up, and checked my thoughts with this conclusion: first, that we did not know by what light and law these should be condemned; but that God was necessarily, and, by the nature of His being, infinitely holy and just, so it could not be but that if these creatures were all sentenced to absence from Himself, it was on account of sinning against that light, which, as the Scripture says, was a law to themselves, and by such rules as their consciences would acknowledge to be just, though the foundation was not discovered to us; and, second, that still, as we are all the clay in the hand of the potter, no vessel could say to Him, "Why hast Thou formed me thus?"

But to return to my new companion. I was greatly delighted with him, and made it my business to teach him everything that was proper to make him useful, handy, and helpful; but especially to make him speak, and understand me when I spoke. And he was the aptest scholar that ever was; and particularly was so merry, so constantly diligent, and so pleased when he could but understand me, or make me understand him, that it was very pleasant to me to talk to him. And now my life began to be so easy that I began to say to myself, that could I but have been safe from more savages, I cared not if I was never to remove from the place while I lived.

After I had been two or three days returned to my castle, I thought that, in order to bring Friday off from his horrid way of feeding, and from the relish of a cannibal's stomach, I ought to let him taste other flesh; so I took him out with me one morning to the woods. I went, indeed, intending to kill a kid out of my own flock, and bring him home and dress it; but as I was going, I saw a she-goat lying down in the shade, and two young kids sitting by her. I caught hold of Friday. "Hold," says I, "stand still," and made signs to him not to stir. Immediately I presented my piece, shot and killed one of the kids. The poor creature, who had, at a distance indeed, seen me kill the savage, his enemy, but did not know, or could imagine, how it was done, was sensibly surprised, trembled and shook, and looked so amazed, that I thought he would have sunk down. He did not see the kid I had shot at, or perceive I had killed it, but ripped up his waistcoat to feel if he was not wounded; and, as I found presently, thought I was resolved to kill him; for he came and kneeled down to me, and embracing my knees, said a great many things I did not understand; but I could easily see that the meaning was to pray me not to kill him.

I soon found a way to convince him that I would do him no harm; and taking him up by the hand, laughed at him, and pointing to the kid which I had killed, beckoned to him to run and fetch it, which he did; and while he was wondering, and looking to see how the creature was killed, I loaded my gun again; and by and bye I saw a great fowl, like a hawk, sit upon a tree, within shot; so, to let Friday understand a little what I would do, I called him to me again, pointing at the fowl, which was indeed a parrot, though I thought it had been a hawk; I say, pointing to the parrot, and to my gun, and to the ground under the parrot, to let him see I would make it fall, I made him understand that I would shoot and kill that bird. Accordingly I fired, and bade him look, and immediately he saw the parrot fall. He stood like one frighted again, notwithstanding all I had said to him; and I found he was the more amazed, because he did not see me put anything into the gun, but thought that there must be some wonderful fund of death and destruction in that thing, able to kill man, beast, bird, or anything near or far off and the astonishment this created in him was such as could not wear off for a long time; and I believe, if I would have let him, he would have worshipped me and my gun. As for the gun itself, he would not so much as touch it for several days after; but would speak to it, and talk to it, as if it had answered him, when he was by himself; which, as I afterwards learned of him, was to desire it not to kill him.

Well, after his astonishment was a little over at this, I pointed to him to run and fetch the bird I had shot, which he did, but stayed some time; for the parrot, not being quite dead, had fluttered a good way off from where she fell. However, he found her, took her up, and brought her to me; and as I had perceived his ignorance about the gun before, I took this advantage to charge the gun again, and not let him see me do it, that I might be ready for any other mark that might present. But nothing more offered at that time; so I brought home the kid, and the same evening I took the skin off, and cut it out as well as I could; and having a pot for that purpose, I boiled or stewed some of the flesh, and made some very good broth; and after I had begun to eat some, I gave some to my man, who seemed very glad of it, and liked it very well; but that which was strangest to him, was to see me eat salt with it. He made a sign to me that the salt was not good to eat, and putting a little into his own mouth, he seemed to nauseate it, and would spit and sputter at it, washing his mouth with fresh water after it. On the other hand, I took some meat in my mouth without salt, and I pretended to spit and sputter for want of salt, as fast as he had done at the salt. But it would not do; he would never care for salt with his meat or in his broth; at least, not a great while, and then but very little.

Having thus fed him with boiled meat and broth, I was resolved to feast him the next day with roasting a piece of the kid. This I did by hanging it before the fire on a string, as I had seen many people do in England, setting two poles up, one on each side of the fire, and one across on the top, and tying the string to the cross stick, letting the meat turn continually. This Friday admired very much. But when he came to taste the flesh, he took so many ways to tell me how well he liked it, that I could not but understand him; and at last he told me he would never eat man's flesh any more, which I was very glad to hear.

The next day I set him to work to beating some corn out, and sifting it in the manner I used to do, as I observed before; and he soon understood how to do it as well as I, especially after he had seen what the meaning of it was, and that it was to make bread of; for after that I let him see me make my bread, and bake it too; and in a little time Friday was able to do all the work for me, as well as I could do it myself.

I began now to consider that, having two mouths to feed instead of one, I must provide more ground for my harvest, and plant a larger quantity of corn than I used to do; so I marked out a larger piece of land, and began to fence in the same manner before, in which Friday not only worked very willingly and very hard, but did it very cheerfully; and I told him what it was for; that it was for corn to make more bread, because he was now with me, and that I might have enough for him and myself too. He appeared very sensible of that part, and let me know that he thought I had much more labour upon me on his account than I had for myself; and that he would work the harder for me, if I would tell him what to do.

This was the pleasantest year of all the life I led in this place. Friday began to talk pretty well, and understand the names of almost everything I had occasion to call for, and of every place I had to send him to, and talk a great deal to me; so that, in short, I began now to have some use for my tongue again, which, indeed, I had very little occasion for before, that is to say, about speech. Besides the pleasure of talking to him, I had a singular satisfaction in the fellow himself. His simple, unfeigned honesty appeared to me more and more every day, and I began really to love the creature; and, on his side, I believe he loved me more than it was possible for him ever to love anything before.

I had a mind once to try if he had any hankering inclination to his own country again; and having learned English so well that he could answer me almost any questions, I asked him whether the nation that he belonged to never conquered in battle? At which he smiled, and said, "Yes, yes, we always fight the better;" that is, he meant, always get the better in fight; and so we began the following discourse: "You always fight the better," said I. "How came you to be taken prisoner then, Friday?"

FRIDAY. My nation beat much for all that.

MASTER. How beat? If your nation beat them, how came you to be taken?

FRIDAY. They more many than my nation in the place where me was; they take one, two, three, and me. My nation overbeat them in the yonder place, where me no was; there my nation take one, two, great thousand.

MASTER. But why did not your side recover you from the hands of your enemies, then?

FRIDAY. They run one, two, three, and me, and make go in the canoe; my nation have no canoe that time.

MASTER. Well, Friday, and what does your nation do with the men they take? Do they carry them away and eat them, as these did?

FRIDAY. Yes, my nation eat mans too; eat all up.

MASTER. Where do they carry them?

FRIDAY. Go to other place, where they think.

MASTER. Do they come hither?

FRIDAY. Yes, yes, they come hither; come other else place.

MASTER. Have you been here with them?

FRIDAY. Yes, I been here. (*Points to the N.W. side of the island, which, it seems, was their side.*)

By this I understood that my man Friday had formerly been among the savages who used to come on shore on the farther part of the island, on the same man-eating occasions that he was now brought for; and, some time after, when I took the courage to carry him to that side, being the same I formerly mentioned, he presently knew the place, and told me he was there once when they eat up twenty men, two women, and one child. He could not tell twenty in English, but he numbered them by laying so many stones on a row, and pointing to me to tell them over.

I have told this passage, because it introduces what follows; that after I had had this discourse with him, I asked him how far it was from our island to the shore, and whether the canoes were not often lost. He told me there was no danger, no canoes ever lost; but that, after a little way out to the sea, there was a current and a wind, always one way in the morning, the other in the afternoon.

This I understood to be no more than the sets of the tide, as going out or coming in; but I afterwards understood it was occasioned by the great draught and reflux of the mighty river Oroonoko, in the mouth or the gulf of which river, as I found afterwards, our island lay; and this land which I perceived to the W. and N.W. was the great island Trinidad, on the north point of the mouth of the river. I asked Friday a thousand questions about the country, the inhabitants, the sea, the coast, and what nations were near. He told me all he knew, with the greatest openness imaginable. I asked him the names of the several nations of his sort of people, but could get no other name than Caribs; from whence I easily understood that these were the Caribbees, which our maps place on the part of America which reaches from the mouth of the River Oroonoko to Guiana, and onwards to St. Martha. He told me that up a great way beyond the moon, that was, beyond the setting of the moon, which must be W. from their country, there dwelt white-bearded men, like me, and pointed to my great whiskers, which I mentioned before; and they had killed much mans, that was his word; by all which I understood he meant the Spaniards, whose cruelties in America had been spread over the whole countries, and was remembered by all the nations father to son.

I inquired if he could tell me how I might come from this island and get among those white men. He told me, "Yes, yes, I might go in two canoe." I could riot understand what he meant, or make him describe to me what he meant by two canoe; till at last, with great difficulty, I found he meant it must be in a large great boat, as big as two canoes.

This part of Friday's discourse began to relish with me very well; and from this time I entertained some hopes that, one time or other, I might find an opportunity to make my escape from this place, and that this poor savage might be a means to help me to do it.

During the long time that Friday had now been with me, and that he began to speak to me, and understand me, I was not wanting to lay a foundation of religious knowledge in his mind; particularly I asked him one time, Who made him? The poor creature did not understand me at all, but thought I had asked who was his father. But I took it by another handle, and asked him who made the sea, the ground we walked on, and the hills and woods? He told me it was one old Benamuckee, that lived beyond all. He could describe nothing of this great person, but that he was very old, much older, he said, than the sea or the land, than the moon or the stars, I asked him then, if this old person had made all things, why did not all things worship him? He looked very grave, and with a perfect look of innocence said, "All things do say O to him." I asked him if the people who die in his country went away anywhere? He said, "Yes, they all went to Benamuckee." Then I asked him whether these they eat up went thither too? He said "Yes."

From these things I began to instruct him in the knowledge of the true God. I told him that the great Maker of all things lived up there, pointing up towards heaven; that He governs the world by the same power and providence by which he made it; that he was omnipotent, could do everything for us, give everything to us, take everything from us; and thus, by degrees, I opened his eyes. He listened with great attention, and received with pleasure the notion of Jesus Christ being sent to redeem us, and of the manner of making our prayers to God, and His being able to hear us, even into heaven. He told me one day that if our God could hear us up beyond the sun, He must needs be a greater God than their Benamuckee, who lived but a little way off, and yet could not hear till they went up to the great mountains where he dwelt to speak to him. I asked him if he ever went thither to speak to him? He said, "No;" they never went that were young men; none went but the old men, whom he called their Oowokakee, that is, as I made him explain it to me, their religious or clergy; and that they went to say O (so he called saying prayers), and then came back, and told them what Benamuckee said. By this I observed that there is priestcraft even amongst the most blinded, ignorant pagans in the world; and the policy of making a secret religion in order to preserve the veneration of the people to the clergy is not only to be found in the Roman, but perhaps among all religions in the world, even among the most brutish and barbarous savages.

I endeavoured to clear up this fraud to my man Friday, and told him that the pretence of their old men going up to the mountains to say O to their god Benamuckee was a cheat, and their bringing word from thence what he said was much more so; that if they met with any answer, or spoke with anyone there, it must be with an evil spirit; and then I entered into a long discourse with him about the devil, the original of him, his rebellion against God, his enmity to man, the reason of it, his setting himself up in the dark parts of the world to be worshipped instead of God, and as God, and the many stratagems he made use of to delude mankind to their ruin; how he had a secret access to our passions and to our affections, to adapt his snares so to our inclinations, as to cause us even to be our own tempters, and to run upon our destruction by our own choice.

I found it was not so easy to imprint right notions in his mind about the devil, as it was about the being of a God. Nature assisted all my arguments to evidence to him even the necessity of a great First Cause and overruling, governing Power, a secret directing Providence, and of the equity and justice of paying homage to Him that made us, and the like. But there appeared nothing of all this in the notion of an evil spirit; of his original, his being, his nature, and above all, of his inclination to do evil, and to draw us in to do so too; and the poor creature puzzled me once in such a manner by a question merely natural and innocent, that I scarce knew what to say to him. I had been talking a great deal to him of the power of God, His omnipotence, His dreadful aversion to sin, His being a consuming fire to the workers of iniquity; how, as He had made us all, He could destroy us and all the world in a moment; and he listened with great seriousness to me all the while.

After this I had been telling him how the devil was God's enemy in the hearts of men, and used all his malice and skill to defeat the good designs of Providence, and to ruin the kingdom of Christ in the world, and the like. "Well," says Friday, "but you say God is so strong, so great; is He not much strong, much might as the devil?" "Yes, yes," says I, "Friday, God is stronger than the devil; God is above the devil, and therefore we pray to God to tread him down under our feet, and enable us to resist his temptations, and quench his fiery darts." "But," says he again, "if God much strong, much might as the devil, why God no kill the devil, so make him no more do wicked?"

I was strangely surprised at his question; and after all, though I was now an old man, yet I was but a young doctor, and ill enough qualified for a causist, or a solver of difficulties; and at first I could not tell what to say; so I pretended not to hear him, and asked him what he said. But he was too earnest for an answer to forget his question, so that he repeated it in the very same broken words as above. By this time I had recovered myself a little, and I said, "God will punish him severely; he is reserved for the judgment, and is to be cast into the bottomless pit, to dwell with everlasting fire." This did not satisfy Friday; but he returns upon me, repeating my words, "Reserve at last! me no understand; but why not kill the devil now? not kill great ago?" "You may as well ask me," said I, "why God does not kill you and I, when we do wicked things here that offend Him; we are preserved to repent and be pardoned." He muses awhile at this. "Well, well," says he, mighty affectionately, "that well; so you, I, devil, all wicked, all preserve, repent, God pardon all." Here I was run down again by him to the last degree, and it was a testimony to me how the mere notions of nature, though they will guide reasonable creatures to the knowledge of a God, and of a worship or homage due to the supreme being of God, as the consequence of our nature, yet nothing by Divine revelation can from the knowledge of Jesus

Christ, and of a redemption purchased for us, of a Mediator of the new covenant, and of an Intercessor at the footstool of God's throne; I say, nothing but a revelation from heaven can form these in the soul, and that therefore the Gospel of our Lord and Saviour Jesus Christ, I mean the Word of God, and the Spirit of God, promised for the guide and sanctifier of His people, are the absolutely necessary instructors of the souls of men in the saving knowledge of God, and the means of salvation.

I therefore diverted the present discourse between me and my man, rising up hastily, as upon some sudden occasion of going out; then sending him for something a good way off, I seriously prayed to God that He would enable me to instruct savingly this poor savage, assisting, by His Spirit, the heart of the poor ignorant creature to receive the light of the knowledge of God in Christ, reconciling him to Himself, and would guide me to speak so to him from the Word of God as his conscience might be convinced, his eyes opened, and his soul saved. When he came again to me, I entered into a long discourse with him upon the subject of redemption of man by the Saviour of the world, and of the doctrine of the Gospel preached from heaven, viz., of repentance towards God, and faith in our blessed Lord Jesus. I then explained to him as well as I could why our blessed Redeemer took not on Him the nature of angels, but the seed of Abraham; and how, for that reason, the fallen angels had no share in the redemption; that He came only to the lost sheep of the house of Israel, and the like.

I had, God knows, more sincerity than knowledge in all the methods I took for this poor creature's instruction, and must acknowledge, what I believe all that act upon the same principle will find, that in laying things open to him, I really informed and instructed myself in many things that either I did not know, or had not fully considered before, but which occurred naturally to my mind upon searching into them for the information of this poor savage. And I had more affection in my inquiry after things upon this occasion than ever I felt before; so that whether this poor wild wretch was the better for me or no, I had great reason to be thankful that ever he came to me. My grief set lighter upon me, my habitation grew comfortable to me beyond measure; and when I reflected that in this solitary life which I had been confined to, I had not only been moved myself to look up to heaven, and to seek to the Hand that had brought me there, but was now to be made an instrument, under Providence, to save the life, and, for aught I know, the soul of a poor savage, and bring him to the true knowledge of religion, and of the Christian doctrine, that he might know Christ Jesus, to know whom is life eternal; I say, when I reflected upon all these things, a secret joy ran through every part of my soul, and I frequently rejoiced that ever I was brought to this place, which I had so often thought the most dreadful of all afflictions that could possibly have befallen me.

In this thankful frame I continued all the remainder of my time, and the conversation which employed the hours between Friday and I was such as made the three years which we lived there together perfectly and completely happy, if any such thing as complete happiness can be formed in a sublunary state. The savage was now a good Christian, much better than I; though I have reason to hope, and bless God for it, that we were equally penitent, and comforted, restored penitents. We had here the Word of God to read, and no farther off from His Spirit to instruct than if we had been in England.

I always applied myself to reading the Scripture, to let him know, as well as I could, the meaning of what I read; and he again, by his serious inquiries and questions, made me, as I said before, a much better scholar in the Scripture knowledge than I should ever have been by my own private mere reading. Another thing I cannot refrain from observing here also, from the experience in this retired part of my life, viz., how infinite and inexpressible a blessing it is that the knowledge of God, and the doctrine of salvation of Christ Jesus, is so plainly laid down in the

Word of God, so easy to be received and understood; that as the bare reading the Scripture made me capable of understanding enough of my duty to carry me directly on to the great work of sincere repentance for my sins, and laying hold of a Saviour for life and salvation, to a stated reformation in practice, and obedience to all God's commands, and this without any teacher or instructor (I mean human); so the same plain instruction sufficiently served to the enlightening this savage creature, and bringing him to be such a Christian, as I have known few equal to him in my life.

As to all the disputes, wranglings, strife, and contention which has happened in the world about religion, whether niceties in doctrines or schemes of Church government, they were all perfectly useless to us; as, for aught I can yet see, they have been to all the rest in the world. We had the sure guide to heaven, viz., the Word of God; and we had, blessed by God, comfortable views of the Spirit of God teaching and instructing us by His Word, leading us into all truth, and making us both willing and obedient to the instruction of His Word; and I cannot see the least use that the greatest knowledge of the disputed points in religion, which have made such confusions in the world, would have been to us if we could have obtained it. But I must go on with the historical part of things, and take every part in its order.

After Friday and I became more intimately acquainted, and that he could understand almost all I said to him, and speak fluently, though in broken English, to me, I acquainted him with my own story, or at least so much of it as related to my coming into the place; how I had lived there, and how long. I let him into the mystery, for such it was to him, of gunpowder and bullet, and taught him how to shoot; I gave him a knife, which he was wonderfully delighted with, and I made him a belt, with a frog hanging to it, such as in England we wear hangers in; and in the frog, instead of a hanger, I gave him a hatchet, which was not only as good a weapon, in some cases, but much more useful upon other occasions.

I described to him the country of Europe, and particularly England, which I came from; how we lived, how we worshipped God, how we behaved to one another, and how we traded in ships to all parts of the world. I gave him an account of the wreck which I had been on board of, and showed him, as near as I could, the place where she lay; but she was all beaten in pieces before, and gone.

I showed him the ruins of our boat, which we lost when we escaped, and which I could not stir with my whole strength then, but was now fallen almost all to pieces. Upon seeing this boat, Friday stood musing a great while, and said nothing. I asked him what it was he studied upon. At last says he, "Me see such boat like come to place at my nation."

I did not understand him a good while; but at last, when I had examined further into it, I understood by him that a boat such as that had been, came on shore upon the country where he lived; that is, as he explained it, was driven thither by stress of weather. I presently imagined that some European ship must have been cast away upon their coast, and the boat might get loose and drive ashore; but was so dull that I never once thought of men making escape from a wreck thither, much less whence they might come; so I only inquired after a description of the boat.

Friday described the boat to me well enough; but brought me better to understand him when he added with some warmth, "We save the white mans from drown." Then I presently asked him if there was any white mans, as he called them, in the boat. "Yes," he said, "the boat full of white mans." I asked him how many. He told upon his fingers seventeen. I asked him then what became of them. He told me, "They live, they dwell at my nation."

This put new thoughts into my head; for I presently imagined that these might be the men belonging to the ship that was cast away in sight of my island, as I now call it; and who, after the ship was struck on the rock, and they saw her inevitably lost, had saved themselves in their boat, and were landed upon that wild shore among the savages.

Upon this I inquired of him more critically what was become of them. He assured me they lived still there; that they had been there about four years; that the savages let them alone, and gave them victuals to live. I asked him how it came to pass they did not kill them, and eat them. He said, "No, they make brother with them;" that is, as I understood him, a truce; and then he added, "They no eat mans but when make the war fight;" that is to say, they never eat any men but such as come to fight with them and are taken in battle.

It was after this some considerable time that being on the top of the hill, at the east side of the island (from whence, as I have said, I had in a clear day discovered the main or continent of America), Friday, the weather being very serene, looks very earnestly towards the mainland, and, in a kind of surprise, falls a-jumping and dancing, and calls out to me, for I was at some distance from him. I asked him what was the matter. "O joy!" says he, "O glad! there see my country, there my nation."

I observed an extraordinary sense of pleasure appeared in his face, and his eyes sparkled, and his countenance discovered a strange eagerness, as if he had a mind to be in his own country again; and this observation of mine put a great many thoughts into me, which made me at first not so easy about my new man Friday as I was before; and I made no doubt but that if Friday could get back to his own nation again, he would not only forget all his religion, but all his obligation to me; and woud be forward enough to give his countrymen an account of me, and come back perhaps with a hundred or two of them, and make a feast upon me, at which he might be as merry as he used to be with those of his enemies, when they were taken in war.

But I wronged the poor honest creature very much, for which I was very sorry afterwards. However, as my jealousy increased, and held me some weeks, I was a little more circumspect, and not so familiar and kind to him as before; in which I was certainly in the wrong too, the honest, grateful creature having no thought about it but what consisted with the best principles, both as a religious Christian and as a grateful friend, as appeared afterwards to my full satisfaction.

While my jealousy of him lasted, you may be sure I was every day pumping him, to see if he would discover any of the new thoughts which I suspected were in him; but I found everything he said was so honest and so innocent that I could find nothing to nourish my suspicion; and, in spite of all my uneasiness, he made me at last entirely his own again, nor did he in the least perceive that I was uneasy, and therefore I could not suspect him of deceit.

One day, walking up the same hill, but the weather being hazy at sea, so that we could not see the continent, I called to him, and said, "Friday, do not you wish yourself in your own country, your own nation?" "Yes," he said, "I be much O glad to be at my own nation." What would you do there?" said I. "Would you turn wild again, eat men's flesh again, and be a savage as you were before?" He looked full of concern, and shaking his head said, "No, no; Friday tell them to live good; tell them to pray God; tell them to eat corn-bread, cattle flesh, milk, no eat man again." "Why then," said I to him, "they will kill you." He looked grave at that, and then said, "No, they no kill me, they willing love learn." He meant by this they would be willing to learn. He added, they learned much of the bearded mans that come in the boat. Then I asked him if he would go back to them? He smiled at that, and told me he could not swim so far. I told him I would make a canoe for him. He told me he would go, if I would go with him. "I go!" says I; "why, they will eat me if I come there." "No, no," says he, "me make they no eat you; me make they much love you." He meant, he would tell them how I killed his enemies, and saved his life, and so he would make them love me. Then he told me, as well as he could, how kind they were to seventeen white men, or bearded men, as he called them, who came on shore there in distress.

From this time I confess I had a mind to venture over, and see if I could possibly join with these bearded men, who, I made on doubt, were Spanish or Portuguese; not doubting but, if I could, we might find some method to escape from thence, being upon the continent, and a good company together, better than I could from an island forty miles off the shore, and alone, without help. So, after some days, I took Friday to work again, by way of discourse, and told him I would give him a boat to go back to his own nation; and accordingly I carried him to my frigate, which lay on the other side of the island, and having cleared it of water, for I always kept it sunk in the water, I brought it out, showed it to him, and we both went into it.

I found he was a most dexterous fellow at managing it, would make it go almost as swift and fast again as I could. So when he was in I said to him, "Well now, Friday, shall we go to your nation?" He looked very dull at my saying so, which, it seems, was because he thought the boat too small to go so far. I told him then I had a bigger; so the next day I went to the place where the first boat lay which I had made, but which I could not get into water. He said that was big enough; but then, as I had taken no care of it, and it had lain two or three and twenty years there, the sun had split and dried it, that it was in a manner rotten. Friday told me such a boat would do very well, and would carry "much enough victual, drink, bread;" that was his way of talking.

Upon the whole, I was by this time so fixed upon my design of going over with him to the continent that I told him we would go and make one as big as that, and he should go home in it. He answered not one word, but looked very grave and sad. I asked him what was the matter with him. He asked me again thus: "Why you angry mad with Friday? what me done?" I asked him what he meant. I told him I was not angry with him at all. "No angry! no angry!" says he, repeated the words several times. "Why send Friday home away to my nation?" "Why," says I,

"Friday, did you not say you wished you were there?" "Yes, yes," says he, "wish be both there, no wish Friday there, no master there." In a word, he would not think of going there without me. "I go there, Friday!" says I; "what shall I do there?" He turned very quick upon me at this. "You do great deal much good," says he; "you teach wild mans to be good, sober, tame mans; you tell them know God, pray God, and live new life." "Alas! Friday," says I, "thou knowest not what thou sayest. I am but an ignorant man myself." "Yes, yes," says he, "you teachee me good, you teachee them good." "No, no, Friday," says I, "you shall go without me; leave me here to live by myself, as I did before." He looked confused again at that word, and running to one of the hatchets which he used to wear, he takes it up hastily, comes and gives it to me. "What must I do with this?" says I to him. "You take kill Friday," says he. "What must I kill you for?" said I again. He returns very quick, "What you send Friday away for? Take kill Friday, no send Friday away." This he spoke so earnestly that I saw tears stand in his eyes. In a word, I so plainly discovered the utmost affection in him to me, and a firm resolution in him, that I told him then, and often after, that I would never send him away from me if he was willing to stay with me.

Upon the whole, as I found by all his discourse a settled affection to me, and that nothing should part him from me, so I found all the foundation of his desire to go to his own country was laid in his ardent affection to the people, and his hopes of my doing them good; a thing which, as I had no notion of myself, so I had not the least thought or intention or desire of undertaking it. But still I found a strong inclination to my attempting an escape, as above, founded on the supposition gathered from the discourse, viz., that there were seventeen bearded men there; and, therefore, without any more delay I went to work with Friday, to find out a great tree proper to fell, and make a large *periegua,* or canoe, to undertake the voyage. There were trees enough in the island to have built a little fleet, not of *perieguas* and canoes, but even of good large vessels. But the main thing I looked at was, to get one so near the water that we might launch it when it was made, to avoid the mistake I committed at first.

At last Friday pitched upon a tree, for I found he knew much better than I what kind of wood was fittest for it; nor can I tell, to this day, what wood to call the tree we cut down, except that it was very like the tree we call fustic, or between that and the Nicaragua wood, for it was much of the same colour and smell. Friday was for burning the hollow or cavity of this tree out, to make it for a boat, but I showed him how rather to cut it out with tools; which, after I had showed him how to use, he did very handily; and in about a month's hard labour we finished it, and made it very handsome; especially when, with our axes, which I showed him how to handle, we cut and hewed the outside into the true shape of a boat. After this, however, it cost us near a fortnight's time to get her along, as it were, inch by inch, upon great rollers into the water; but when she was in, she would have carried twenty men with great ease.

When she was in the water, and though she was so big, it amazed me to see with what dexterity, and how swift my man Friday would manage her, turn her, and paddle her along. So I asked him if he would, and if we might venture over in her. "Yes," he said, "he venture over in her very well, though great blow wind." However, I had a farther design that he knew nothing of, and that was to make a mast and sail, and to fit her with an anchor and cable. As to a mast, that was easy enough to get; so I pitched upon a straight young cedar tree, which I found near the place, and which there was great plenty of in the island; and I set Friday to work to cut it down, and gave him directions how to shape and order it. But as to the sail, that was my particular care. I knew I had old sails, or rather pieces of old sails enough; but as I had had them now twenty-six years by me, and had not been very careful to preserve them, not imagining that I should ever have this kind of use for them, I did not doubt but they were all rotten, and, indeed, most of them were so. However, I found two pieces which appeared pretty good, and with these I went to work, and with a great deal of pains, and awkward tedious stitching (you may be sure) for want of needles, I, at length, made a three-cornered ugly thing, like what we call in England a shoulder-of-mutton sail, to go with a boom at bottom, and a little short sprit at the top, such as usually our ships' longboats sail with, and such as best knew how to manage; because it was such a one as I had to the boat in which I made my escape from Barbary, as related in the first part of my story.

I was nearly two months performing this last work, viz., rigging and fitting my masts and sails; for I finished them very complete, making a small stay, and a sail, or foresail, to it, to assist, if we should turn to windward; and, which was more than all, I fixed a rudder to the stern of her to steer with; and though I was but a bungling shipwright, yet as I knew the usefulness, and even necessity, of such a thing, I applied myself with so much pains to do it, that at last I brought it to pass; though, considering the many dull contrivances I had for it that failed, I think it cost me almost as much labour as making the boat.

After all this was done, too, I had my man Friday to teach as to what belonged to the navigation of my boat; for though he knew very well how to paddle a canoe, he knew nothing what belonged to a sail and a rudder; and was the most amazed when he saw me work the boat to and again in the sea by the rudder, and how the sail jibbed, and filled this way, or that way, as the course we sailed changed; I say, when he saw this, he stood like one astonished and amazed. However, with a little use I made all these things familiar to him, and he became an expert sailor, except that as to the compass I could make him understand very little of that. On the other hand, as there was very little cloudy weather, and seldom or never any fogs in those parts, there was the less occasion for a compass, seeing the stars were always to be seen by night, and the shore by day, except in the rainy season, and then nobody cared to stir abroad, either by land or sea.

I had now entered on the seven and twentieth year of my captivity in this place; though the three last years that I had this creature with me ought rather to be left out of the account, my habitation being quite of another kind than in all the rest of the time. I kept the anniversary of my landing here with the same thankfulness to God for His mercies as at first; and if I had such cause of acknowledgment at first, I had much more so now, having such additional testimonies of the care of Providence over me, and the great hopes I had of being effectually and speedily delivered; for I had an invincible impression upon my thoughts that my deliverance was at hand, and that I should not be another year in this place. However, I went on with my husbandry, digging, planting, fencing, as usual. I gathered and cured my grapes, and did every necessary thing as before.

The rainy season was, in the meantime, upon me, when I kept more within doors than at any other times; so I had stowed our new vessel as secure as we could, bringing her up into the creek, where, as I said in the beginning, I landed my rafts from the ship; and hauling her up to the shore at high-water mark, I made my man Friday dig a little dock, just big enough to hold her, and just deep enough to give her water enough to float in, and then, when the tide was out, we made a strong dam across the end of it, to keep the water out; and so she lay dry, as to the tide, from the sea; and to keep the rain off, we laid a great many boughs of trees, so thick, that she was well thatched as a house; and thus we waited for the month of November and December, in which I designed to make my adventure.

When the settled season began to come in, as the thought of my designed returned with the fair weather, I was preparing daily for the voyage; and the first thing I did was to lay by a certain quantity of provisions, being the stores for our voyage; and intended, in a week or a fortnight's time, to open the dock, and launch out our boat. I was busy one morning upon something of this kind, when I called to Friday, and bid him go to the sea-shore and see if he could find a turtle, or tortoise, a thing which we generally got once a week, for the sake of the eggs as well as the flesh. Friday had not been long gone when he came running back, and flew over my outer wall, or fence, like one that felt not the ground, or the steps he set his feet on; and before I had time to speak to him, he cries out to me, "O master! O master! O sorrow! O bad!" "What's the matter, Friday?" says I. "O yonder, there," says he, "one, two, three canoe! one, two, three!" By his way of speaking, I concluded there were six; but on inquiry, I found it was but three. "Well, Friday," says I, "do not be frighted." So I heartened him up as well as I could. However, I saw the poor fellow was most terribly scared; for nothing ran in his head but that they were come to look for him, and would cut him in pieces, and eat him; and the poor fellow trembled so, that I scarce knew what to do with him. I comforted him as well as I could, and told him I was in as much danger as he, and that they would eat me as well as him. "But," says I, "Friday, we must resolve to fight them. Can you fight, Friday?" "Me shoot," say he; "but there come many great number." No matter for that," said I again; "our guns will fright them that we do not kill." So I asked him whether, if I resolved to defend him, he would defend me, and stand by me, and do just as I bid him. He said, "Me die when you bid die, master." So I went and fetched a good dram of rum, and gave him; for I had been so good a husband of my rum that I had a great deal left. When he had drank it, I made him take the two fowling-pieces, which we always carried, and load them with large swan-shot, as big as small pistol-bullets. Then I took four muskets, and loaded them with two slugs and five small bullets each; and my two pistols I loaded with a brace of bullets each. I hung my great sword, as usual, naked, by my side, and gave Friday his hatchet.

When I had thus prepared myself, I took my perspective-glass and went up to the side of the hill to see what I could discover; and I found quickly, by my glass, that there were one and twenty savages, three prisoners, and three canoes, and that their whole business seemed to be the triumphant banquet upon these three human bodies; a barbarous feast indeed, but nothing more than, as I had observed, was usual with them.

I observed also that they had landed, not where they had done when Friday made his escape, but nearer to my creek, where the shore was low, and where a thick wood came close almost down to the sea. This, with the abhorrence of the inhuman errand these wretches came about, filled me with such indignation that I came down again to Friday, and told him I was resolved to go down to them, and kill them all, and asked him if he would stand by me. He was now gotten over his fright, and his spirits being a little raised with the dram I had given him, he was very cheerful, and told me, as before, he would die when I bid die.

In this fit of fury, I took first and divided the arms which I had charge, as before, between us. I gave Friday one pistol to stick in his girdle, and three guns upon his shoulder; and I took one pistol, and the other three myself, and in this posture we marched out. I took a small bottle of rum in my pocket, and gave Friday a large bag with more powder and bullet; and as to orders, I charged him to keep close behind me, and not to stir, or shoot, or do anything, till I bid him, and in the meantime not to speak a word. In this posture I fetched a compass to my right hand of near a mile, as well to got over the creek as to get into the wood, so that I might come within shot of them before I should be discovered, which I had seen, by my glass, it was easy to do.

While I was making this march, my former thoughts returning, I began to abate my resolution. I do not mean that I entertained any fear of their number; for as they were naked, unarmed wretches, 'tis certain I was superior to them; nay, though I had been alone. But it occurred to my thoughts what call, what occasion, much less what necessity, I was in to go and dip my hands in blood, to attack people who had neither done or intended me any wrong; who, as to me, were innocent, and whose barbarous customs were their own disaster; being in them a token, indeed, of God's having left them, with the other nations of that part of the world, to such stupidity, and to such inhuman courses; but did not call me to take upon me to be a judge of their actions, much less an executioner of His justice; that whenever He thought fit, He would take the cause into His own hands, and by national vengeance, punish them, as a people, for national crimes; but that, in the meantime, it was none of my business; that, it was true, Friday might justify it, because he was a declared enemy, and in a state of war with those very particular people, and it was lawful for him to attack them; but I could not say the same with respect to me. These things were so warmly pressed upon my thoughts all the way as I went, that I resolved I would only go and place myself near them, that I might observe their barbarous feast, and that I would act then as God should direct; but that, unless something offered that was more a call to me than yet I knew of, I would not meddle with them.

With this resolution I entered the wood, and with all possible wariness and silence, Friday following close at my heels, I marched till I came to the skirt of the wood, on the side which was next to them; only that one corner of the wood lay between me and them. Here I called softly to Friday, and showing him a great tree, which was just at the corner of the wood, I bade him go to the tree and bring me word if he could see there plainly what they were doing. He did so, and came immediately back to me, and told me they might be plainly viewed there; that they were all about their fire, eating the flesh of one of their prisoners, and that another lay bound upon the sand, a little from them, which, he said, they would kill next, and, which fired all the very soul within me, he told me it was not one of their nation, but one of the bearded men, whom he had told me of, that came to their country in the boat. I was filled with horror at the very naming the white, bearded man; and, going to the tree, I saw plainly, by my glass, a white man, who lay upon the beach of the sea, with his hands and feet tied with flags, or things like rushes, and that he was a European, and had clothes on.

There was another tree, and a little thicket beyond it, about fifty yards nearer to them than the place where I was, which, by going a little way about, I saw I might come at undiscovered, and that then I should be within half shot of them; so I withheld my passion, though I was indeed enraged to the highest degree; and going back about twenty paces, I got behind some bushes, which held all the way till I came to the other tree; and then I came to a little rising ground, which gave me a full view of them, at the distance of about eighty yards.

I had now not a moment to lose, for nineteen of the dreadful wretches sat upon the ground, all close huddled together, and had just sent the other two to butcher the poor Christian, and bring him, perhaps limb by limb, to their fire; and they were stooped down to untie the bands at this feet. I turned to Friday. "Now, Friday," said I, "do as I bid thee." Friday said he would. "Then, Friday," says I, "do exactly as you see me do; fail in nothing." So I set down one of the muskets and the fowling-piece upon the ground, and Friday did the like by his; and with the other musket took my aim at the savages, bidding him do the like. Then asking him if he was ready, he said, "Yes." "Then fire at them," said I; and the same moment I fired also.

Friday took his aim so much better than I, that on the side that he shot, he killed two of them, and wounded three more; and on my side I killed one and wounded two. They were, you may be sure, in a dreadful consternation; and all of them who were not hurt jumped up upon their feet, but did not immediately know which way to run, or which way to look, for they knew not from whence their destruction came. Friday kept his eyes close upon me, that, as I had bid him, he might observe what I did; so as soon as the first shot was made I threw down the piece, and took up the fowling-piece, and Friday did the like. He sees me cock and present; he did the same again. "Are you ready, Friday?" said I. "Yes," says he. "Let fly, then," says I, "in the name of God!" and with that I fired again among the amazed wretches, and so did Friday; and as our pieces were now loaded with what I called swan-shot, or small pistol-bullets, we found only two drop, but so many were wounded that they ran about yelling and screaming like mad creatures, all bloody, and miserably wounded most of them; whereof three more fell quickly after, though not quite dead.

"Now, Friday," says I, laying down the discharged pieces, and taking up the musket which was yet loaded, "follow me," says I, which he did with a great deal of courage; upon which I rushed out of the wood, and showed myself, and Friday close at my foot. As soon as I perceived they saw me, I shouted as loud as I could, and bade Friday to do so too; and running as fast as I could, which, by the way, was not very fast, being loaden with arms as I was, I made directly towards the poor victim, who was, as I said, lying upon the beach, or shore, between the place where they sat and the sea. The two butchers, who were just going to work with him, had left him at the surprise of our first fire, and fled in a terrible fright to the seaside, and had jumped into a canoe, and three more of the rest made the same way. I turned to Friday, and bid him step forwards and fire at them. He understood me immediately, and running about forty yards, to be near them, he shot at them, and I thought he had killed them all, for I saw them all fall of a heap into the boat; though I saw two of them up again quickly. However, he killed two of them and wounded the third, so that he lay down in the bottom of the boat as if he had been dead.

While my man Friday fired at them, I pulled out my knife and cut the flags that bound the poor victim; and loosing his hands and feet, I lifted him up, and asked him in the Portuguese tongue what he was. He answered in Latin, Christianus; but was so weak and faint that he could scarcely stand or speak. I took my bottle out of my pocket and gave it to him, making signs that he should drink, which he did; and I gave him a piece of bread, which he ate. Then I asked him what countryman he was; and he said, Espagniole; and being a little recovered, let me know, by all the signs he could possibly make, how much he was in my debt for his deliverance. "Seignior," said I, with as much Spanish as I could make up, "we will talk afterwards, but we must fight now. If you have any strength left, take this pistol and sword, and lay about you." He took them very thankfully, and no sooner had he the arms in his hands but, as if they had put new vigor into him, he flew upon his murderers like a fury, and had cut two of them in pieces in an instant; for the truth is, as the whole was a surprise to them, so the poor creatures were so much frighted with the noise of our pieces that they fell down for mere amazement and fear, and had no power to attempt their own escape than their flesh had to resist our shot; and that was the case of those five that Friday shot at in the boat; for as three of them fell with the hurt they received, so the other two fell with the fright.

I kept my piece in my hand still without firing, being willing to keep my charge ready, because I had given the Spaniard my pistol and sword. So I called to Friday, and bade him run up to the tree from whence we first fired, and fetch the arms which lay there that had been discharged, which he did with great swiftness; and then giving him my musket, I sat down myself to load all the rest again, and bade them come to me when they wanted. While I was loading these pieces, there happened a fierce engagement between the Spaniard and one of the savages, who made at him with one of their great wooden swords, the same weapon that was to have killed him before if I had not prevented it. The Spaniard, who was as bold and brave as could be imagined, though weak, had fought this Indian a good while, and had cut him two great wounds on his head; but the savage being a stout, lusty fellow, closing in with him, had thrown him down, being faint, and was wringing my sword out of his hand, when the Spaniard, though undermost, wisely quitting the sword, drew the pistol from his girdle, shot the savage through the body, and killed him upon the spot, before I, who was running to help him, could come near him.

Friday being now left to his liberty, pursued the flying wretches with no weapon in his hand but his hatchet; and with that he despatched those three who, as I said before, were wounded at first, and fallen, and all the rest he could come up with; and the Spaniard coming to me for a gun, I gave him one of the fowling-pieces, with which he pursued two of the savages, and wounded them both; but as he was not able to run, they both got from him into the wood, where Friday pursued them, and killed one of them; but the other was too nimble for him, and though he was wounded, yet had plunged himself into the sea, and swam with all his might off to those two who were left in the canoe; which three in the canoe, with one wounded, who we know not whether he died or no, were all that escaped our hands of one and twenty. The account of the rest is as follows:

3 killed at our first shot from the tree
2 killed at the next shot
2 killed by Friday in the boat
2 killed by ditto, of those at first wounded
1 killed by ditto in the wood
3 killed by the Spaniard
4 killed, being found dropped here and there of their wounds, or killed by Friday in his chase of them
4 escaped in the boat, whereof one wounded, if not dead

—

21 in all.

Those that were in the canoe worked hard to get out of gun-shot; and though Friday made two or three shots at them, I did not find that he hit any of them. Friday would fain have had me take one of their canoes, and pursue them; and, indeed, I was very anxious about their escape, lest carrying the news home to their people they should come back perhaps with two or three hundred of their canoes, and devour us by mere multitude. So I consented to pursue them by sea, and running to one of their canoes I jumped in, and bade Friday to follow me. But when I was in the canoe, I was surprised to find another poor creature lie there alive, bound hand and foot, as the Spaniard was, for the slaughter, and almost dead with fear, not knowing what the matter was; for he had not been able to look up over the side of the boat, he was tied so hard, neck and heels, and had been tied so long, that he had really but little life in him.

I immediately cut the twisted flags or rushes, which they had bound him with, and would have helped him up; but he could not stand or speak, but groaned most piteously, believing, it seems, still that he was only unbound in order to be killed.

When Friday came to him, I bade him speak to him, and tell him of his deliverance; and pulling out my bottle, made him give the poor wretch a dram; which, with the news of his being delivered, revived him, and he sat up in the boat. But when Friday came to hear him speak, and look in his face, it would have moved any one to tears to have seen how Friday kissed him, embraced him, hugged him, cried, laughed, hallooed, jumped about, danced, sung; then cried again, wrung his hands, beat his own face and head, and then sung and jumped about again, like a distracted creature. It was a good while before I could make him speak to me, or tell me what was the matter; but when he came a little to himself, he told me that it was his father.

It was not easy for me to express how it moved me to see what ecstasy and filial affection had worked in this poor savage at the sight of his father, and of his being delivered from death; nor, indeed, can I describe half the extravagances of his affection after this; for he went into the boat, and out of the boat, a great many times. When he went in to him, he would sit down by him, open his breast, and hold his father's head close to his bosom, half an hour together, to nourish it; then he took his arms and ankles, which were numbed and stiff with the binding, and chafed and rubbed them with his hands; and I, perceiving what the case was, gave him some rum out of my bottle to rub them with, which did them a great deal of good.

This action put an end to our pursuit of the canoe with the other savages who were now gotten almost out of sight; and it was happy for us that we did not, for it blew so hard within two hours after, and before they could be gotten a quarter of their way, and continued blowing so hard all night, and that from the north-west, which was against them, that I could not suppose their boat could live, or that they ever reached to their own coast.

But to return to Friday. He was so busy about his father that I could not find in my heart to take him off for some time; but after I thought he could leave him a little, I called him to me, ands he came jumping and laughing, and pleased to the highest extreme. Then I asked him if he had given his father any bread. He shook his head, and said, "None; ugly dog eat all up self." So I gave him a cake of bread out of a little pouch I carried on purpose. I also gave him a dram for himself, but he would not taste it, but carried it to his father. I had in my pocket also two or three bunches of my raisins, so I gave him a handful of them for his father. He had no sooner given his father these raisins, but I saw him come out of the boat and run away, as if he had been bewitched, he ran as such a rate; for he was the swiftest fellow of his foot that ever I saw. I say, he ran at such a rate that he was out of sight, as it were, in an instant; and though I called, and hallooed, too, after him, it was all one, away he went; and in a quarter of an hour saw him come back again, though not so fast as he went; and as he came nearer, I found his pace was slacker, because he had something in his hand.

When he came up to me, I found he had been quite home for an earthen jug, or pot, to bring his father some fresh water, and that he had got two more cakes or loaves of bread. The bread he gave me, but the water he carried to his father. However, as I was very thirsty too, I took a little sip of it. This water revived his father more than all the rum or spirits I had given him, for he was just fainting with thirst.

When his father had drank, I called to him to know if there was any water left. He said, "Yes;" and I bade him give it to the poor Spaniard, who was in as much want of it as his father; and I sent one of the cakes, that Friday brought, to the Spaniard, too, who was indeed very weak, and was reposing himself upon a green place under the shade of a tree; and whose limbs were also very stiff, and very much swelled with the rude bandage he had been tied with. When I saw that upon Friday's coming to him with the water he sat up and drank, and took the bread, and began to eat. I went to him, and gave him a handful of raisins. He looked up in my face with all the tokens of gratitude and thankfulness that could appear in any countenance; but was so weak, notwithstanding he had so exerted himself in the fight, that he could not stand up upon his feet. He tried to do it two or three times, but was really not able, his ankles were so swelled and so painful to him; so I bade him sit still, and caused Friday to rub his ankles, and bathe them with rum, as he had done his father's.

I observed the poor affectionate creature, every two minutes, or perhaps less, all the while he was here, turn his head about to see if his father was in the same place and posture as he left him sitting; and at last he found he was not to be seen; at which he started up, and without speaking a word, flew with that swiftness to him, that one could scarcely perceive his feet to touch the ground as he went. But when he came, he only found he had laid himself down to ease his limbs; so Friday came back to me presently, and I then spoke to the Spaniard to let Friday help him up, if he could, and lead him to the boat, and then he should carry him to our dwelling, where I would take care of him. But Friday, a lusty strong fellow, took the Spaniard quite up upon his back, and carried him away to the boat, and set him down softly upon the side of gunnel of the canoe, with his feet in the inside of it, and then lifted him quite in, and set him close to his father; and presently stepping out again, launched the boat off, and paddled it along the shore faster than I could walk, though the wind blew pretty hard, too. So he brought them both safe into our creek, and leaving them in the boat, runs away to fetch the other canoe. As he passed me, I spoke to him, and asked him whither he went. He told me, "Go fetch more boat." So away he went like the wind, for sure never man or horse ran like him; and he had the other canoe in the creek almost as soon as I got to it by land; so he wafted me over, and then went to help our new guests out of the boat, which he did; but they were neither of them able to walk, so that poor Friday knew not what to do.

To remedy this I went to work in my thought, and calling to Friday to bid them sit down on the bank while he came to me, I soon made a kind of hand-barrow to lay them on, and Friday and I carried them up both together upon it between us. But when we got them to the outside of our wall, or fortification, we were at a worse loss than before, for it was impossible to get them over, and I was resolved not to break it down. So I set to work again; and Friday and I, in about two hours' time, made a very handsome tent, covered with old sails, and above that with boughs of trees, being in the space without our outward fence, and between that and the grove of young wood which I had planted; and here we made them two beds of such things as I had, viz., of good rice straw, with blankets laid upon it to lie on, and another to cover them, on each bed.

My island was now peopled, and I thought myself very rich in subjects; and it was a merry reflection, which I frequently made, how like a king I looked. First of all, the whole country was my own mere property, so that I had an undoubted right of dominion. Secondly, my people were perfectly subjected. I was absolute lord and lawgiver; they all owned their lives to me, and were ready to lay down their lives, if there had been occasion of it, for me. It was remarkable, too, we had but three subjects, and they were of three different religions. My man Friday was a Protestant, his father was a pagan and a cannibal, and the Spaniard was a Papist. However, I allowed liberty of conscience throughout my dominions. But this is by the way.

As soon as I had secured my two weak rescued prisoners, and given them shelter and a place to rest them upon, I began to think of making some provision for them; and the first thing I did, I ordered Friday to take a yearling goat, betwixt a kid and a goat, out of my particular flock, to be killed; when I cut off the hinder-quarter, and chopping it into small pieces. I set Friday to work to boiling and stewing, and made them a very good dish, I assure you, of flesh and broth, having put some barley and rice also into the broth; and as I cooked it without doors, for I made no fire within my inner wall, so I carried it all into the new tent, and having set a table there for them, I sat down and ate my own dinner also with them, and as well as I could cheered them, and encouraged them; Friday being my interpreter, especially to his father, and, indeed, to the Spaniard too; for the Spaniard spoke the language of the savages pretty well.

After we had dined, or rather supped, I ordered Friday to take one of the canoes and go and fetch our muskets and other firearms, which, for want of time, we had left upon the place of battle; and the next day I ordered him to go and bury the dead bodies of the savages, which lay open to the sun, and would presently be offensive; and I also ordered him to bury the horrid remains of their barbarous feast, which I knew were pretty much, and which I could not think of doing myself; nay, I could not bear to see them, if I went that way. All which he punctually performed, and defaced the very appearance of the savages being there; so that when I went again I could scarcely know where it was, otherwise than by the corner of the wood pointing to the place.

I then began to enter into a little conversation with my two new subjects; and first, I set Friday to inquire of his father what he thought of the escape of the savages in that canoe, and whether we might expect a return of them, with a power too great for us to resist. His first opinion was, that the savages in the boat never could live out the storm which blew that night they went off, but must, of necessity, be drowned, or driven south to those other shores, where they were as sure to be devoured as they were to be drowned if they were cast away. But as to what they would do if they came safe on shore, he said he knew not; but it was his opinion that they were so dreadfully frighted with the manner of their being attacked, the noise, and the fire, that he believed they would tell their people they were all killed by thunder and lightning, not by the hand of man; and that the two which appeared, viz., Friday and me, were two heavenly spirits, or furies, come down to destroy them, and not men with weapons. This, he said, he knew, because he heard them all cry out so in their language to one another; for it was impossible to them to conceive that a man could dart fire, and speak thunder, and kill at a distance without lifting up the hand, as was done now. And this old savage was in the right; for, as I understood since by other hands, the savages never attempted to go over to the island afterwards. They were so terrified with the accounts given by those four men (for, it seems, they did escape the sea), that they believed whoever went to that enchanted island would be destroyed with fire from the gods.

This however, I knew not, and therefore was under continual apprehensions for a good while, and kept always upon my guard, me and all my army; for as we were now four of us, I would have ventured upon a hundred of them, fairly in the open field, at any time.

In a little time, however, no more canoes appearing, the fear of their coming wore off, and I began to take my former thoughts of a voyage to the main into consideration; being likewise assured by Friday's father that I might depend upon good usage from their nation, on his account, if I would go.

But my thoughts were a little suspended when I had a serious discourse with the Spaniard, and when I understood that there were sixteen more of his countrymen and Portuguese, who, having been cast away, and made their escape to that side, lived there at peace, indeed, with the savages, but were very sore put to it for necessaries, and indeed for life. I asked him all the particulars of their voyage, and found they were a Spanish ship bound from the Rio de la Plata to the Havana, being directed to leave their loading there, which was chiefly hides and silver, and to bring back what European goods they could meet with there; that they had five Portuguese seamen on board, whom they took out of another wreck; that five of their own men were drowned when the first ship was lost, and that these escaped, through infinite dangers and hazards, and arrived, almost starved, on the cannibal coast, where they expected to have been devoured every moment.

He told me they had some arms with them, but they were perfectly useless, for that they had neither powder nor ball, the washing of the sea having spoiled all their powder but a little, which they used, at their first landing, to provide themselves some food.

I asked him what he thought would become of them there, and if they had formed no design of making any escape? He said they had many consultations about it; but that having neither vessel, or tools to build one, or provisions of any kind, their councils always ended in tears and despair.

I asked him how he thought they would receive a proposal from me, which might tend towards an escape; and whether, if they were all here, it might not be done. I told him with freedom, I feared mostly their treachery and ill usage of me if I put my life in their hands; for that gratitude was no inherent virtue in the nature of man, nor did men always square their dealings by the obligations they had received, so much as they did by the advantages they expected. I told him it would be very hard that I should be the instrument of their deliverance, and that they should afterwards make me their prisoner in New Spain, where an Englishman was certain to be made a sacrifice, what necessity or what accident soever brought him thither; and that I had rather be delivered up to the savages, and be devoured alive, than fall into the merciless claws of the priests, and be carried into the Inquisition. I added, that otherwise I was persuaded, if they were all here, we might, with so many hands, build a bark large enough to carry us all away, either to the Brazils, southward, or to the islands, or Spanish coast, northward; but that if, in requital, they should when I had put weapons into their hands, carry me by force among their own people, I might be ill used for my kindness to them, and make my case worse than it was before.

He answered, with a great deal of candor and ingenuity, that their condition was so miserable, and they were so sensible of it, that he believed they would abhor the thought of using any man unkindly that should contribute to their deliverance; and that, if pleased, he would go to them with the old man, and discourse with them about it, and return again, and bring me their answer; that he would make conditions with them upon their solemn oath that they should be absolutely under my leading, as their commander and captain; and that they should swear upon the holy sacraments and the gospel to be true to me, and to go to such Christian country as that I should agree to, and no other, and to be directed wholly and absolutely by my orders till they were landed safely in such country as I intended; and that he would bring a contract from them, under their hands, for that purpose.

Then he told me he would first swear to me himself that he would never stir from me as long as he lived till I gave him orders; and that he would take my side to the last drop of his blood, if there should happen the least breach of faith among his countrymen.

He told me they were all of them very civil, honest men, and they were under the greatest distress imaginable, having neither weapons nor clothes, nor any food, but at the mercy and discretion of the savages; out of all hopes of ever returning to their own country; and that he was sure, if I would undertake their relief, they would live and die by me.

Upon these assurances, I resolved to venture to relieve them, if possible, and to send the old savage and this Spaniard over to them to treat. But when we had gotten all things in a readiness to go, the Spaniard himself started an objection, which had so much prudence in it on one hand, and so much sincerity on the other hand, that I could not but be very well satisfied in it, and by his advice put off the deliverance of his comrades for at least half a year. The case was thus:

He had been with us now about a month, during which time I had let him see in what manner I had provided, with the assistance of Providence, for my support; and he saw evidently what stock of corn and rice I had laid up; which, as it was more than sufficient for myself, so it was not sufficient, at least without good husbandry, for my family, now it was increased to number four; but much less would it be sufficient if his countrymen, who were, as he said, fourteen, still alive, should come over; and least of all would it be sufficient to victual our vessel, if we should build one for a voyage to any of the Christian colonies of America. So he told me he thought it would be more advisable to let him and the two others dig and cultivate some more land, as much as I could spare seed to sow; and that we should wait another harvest, that we might have a supply of corn for his countrymen when they should come; for want might be a temptation to them to disagree, or not to think themselves delivered, otherwise than out of one difficulty into another. "You know," says he, "the children of Israel, though they rejoiced at first for their being delivered out of Egypt, yet rebelled even against God Himself, that delivered them, when they came to want bread in the wilderness."

His caution was so reasonable, and his advice so good, that I could not but be very well pleased with his proposal, as well as I was satisfied with his fidelity. So we fell to digging all four of us, as well as the wooden tools we were furnished with permitted; and in about a month's time, by the end of which it was seed-time, we had gotten as much land cured and trimmed up as we sowed twenty-two bushels of barley on, and sixteen jars of rice; which was, in short, all the seed we had to spare; nor, indeed, did we leave ourselves barley sufficient for our own food for the six months that we had to expect our crop; that is to say, reckoning from the time we set our seed aside for sowing; for it is not to be supposed it is six months in the ground in that country.

Having now society enough, and our numbers being sufficient to put us out of fear of the savages, if they had come, unless their number had been very great, we went freely all over the island, wherever we found occasion; and as here we had our escape or deliverance upon our thoughts, it was impossible, at least for me, to have the means of it out of mine. To this purpose I marked out several trees which I thought fit for our work, and I set Friday and his father to cutting them down; and then I caused the Spaniard, to whom I imparted my thought on that affair, to oversee and direct their work. I showed them with what indefatigable pains I had hewed a large tree into single planks, and I caused them to do the like, till they had made about a dozen large planks of good oak, near two feet broad, thirty-five feet long, and from two inches to four inches thick. What prodigious labour it took up, anyone may imagine.

At the same time I contrived to increase my little flock of tame goats as much as I could; and to this purpose I made Friday and the Spaniard go out one day, and myself with Friday the next day, for we took our turns, and by this means we got above twenty young kids to breed up with the rest; for whenever we shot the dam, we saved the kids, and added them to our flock. But above all, the season for curing the grapes coming on, I caused such a prodigious quantity to be hung up in the sun, that I believe had we been at Alicant, where the raisins of the sun are cured, we could have filled sixty or eighty barrels; and these, with our bread, was a great part of our food, and very good living too, I assure you; for it is an exceedinly nourishing food.

It was now harvest, and our crop in good order. It was not the most plentiful increase I had seen in the island, but however, it was enough to answer our end; for from our twenty-two bushels of barley we brought in and thrashed out above two hundred and twenty bushels, and the like in proportion of the rice; which was store enough for our food to the next harvest, though all the sixteen Spaniards had been on shore with me; or if we had been ready for a voyage, it would very plentifully have victualled our ship to have carried us to any part of the world, that is to say, of America.

When we had thus housed and secured our magazine of corn, we fell to work to make more wicker-work, viz., great baskets, in which we kept it; and the Spaniard was very handy and dextrous at this part, and often blamed me that I did not make some things for defence of this kind of work; but I saw no need of it.

And now having a full supply of food for all the guests I expected, I gave the Spaniard leave to go over to the main, to see what he could do with those he had left behind him there. I gave him strict charge in writing not to bring any man with him who would not first swear, in the presence of himself and of the old savage, that he would no way injure, fight with, or attack the person he should find in the island, who was so kind to send for them in order to their deliverance; but that they would stand by and defend him against all such attempts, and they would be entirely under and subjected to his commands; and that this should be put in writing, and signed with their hands. How we were to have this done, when I knew they had neither pen nor ink, that indeed was a question which we never asked.

Under these instructions, the Spaniard and the old savage, the father of Friday, went away in one of the canoes which they might be said to come in, or rather were brought in, when they came as prisoners to be devoured by the savages.

I gave each of them a musket, with a firelock on it, and about eight charges of powder and ball, charging them to be very good husbands of both, and not to use either of them but upon urgent occasion.

This was a cheerful work, being the first measures used by me, in view of my deliverance, for now twenty-seven years and some days. I gave them provisions of bread and of dried grapes sufficient for themselves for many days, and sufficient for all their countrymen for about eight days' time; and wishing them a good voyage, I saw them go, agreeing with them about a signal they should hang out at their return, by which I should know them again, when they came back, at a distance, before they came on shore.

They went away with a fair gale on the day that the moon was at full, by my account in the month of October, but as for an exact reckoning of days, after I had once lost it, I could never recover it again; nor had I kept even the number of years so punctually as to be sure that I was right, though as it proved, when I afterwards examined my account, I found I had kept a true reckoning of years.

It was no less than eight days I had waited for them, when a strange and unforeseen accident intervened, of which the like has not perhaps been heard of in history. I was fast asleep in my hutch one morning, when my man Friday came running in to me, and called aloud, "Master, master, they are come, they are come!"

I jumped up, and, regardless of danger, I went out as soon as I could get my clothes on, through my little grove, which, by the way, was by this time grown to be a very thick wood; I say, regardless of danger, I went without my arms, which was not my custom to do; but I was surprised when, turning my eyes to the sea, I presently saw a boat at about a league and half's distance standing in for the shore, with a shoulder-of-mutton sail, as they call it, and the wind blowing pretty fair to bring them in; also I observed presently that they did not come from that side which the shore lay on, but from the southernmost end of the island. Upon this I called Friday in, and bid him lie close, for these were not the people we looked for, and that we might not know yet whether they were friends or enemies.

In the next place, I went in to fetch my perspective-glass, to see what I could make of them; and having taken the ladder out, I climbed up to the top of the hill, as I used to do when I was apprehensive of anything, and to take my view the plainer, without being discovered.

I had scarce set my foot on the hill, when my eye plainly discovered a ship lying at an anchor at about two leagues and a half's distance from me, south-south-east, but not above a league and a half from the shore. By my observation, it appeared plainly to be an English ship, and the boat appeared to be an English longboat.

I cannot express confusion I was in; though the joy of seeing a ship, and one who I had reason to believe was manned by my own countrymen, and consequently friends, was such as I cannot describe. But yet I had some secret doubts hung about me, I cannot tell from whence they came, bidding me keep upon my guard. In the first place, it occurred to me to consider what business an English ship could have in that part of the world, since it was not the way to or from any part of the world where the English had any traffic; I knew there had been no storms to drive them in there, as in distress; and that if they were English really, it was most probable that they were here upon no good design; and that I had better continue as I was than fall into the hands of thieves and murderers.

Let no man despise he secret hints and notices of danger which sometimes are given him when he may think there is no possibility of its being real. That such hints and notices are given us, I believe few that have made any observations of things can deny; that there are certain discoveries of an invisible world, and a converse of spirits, we cannot doubt; and if the tendency of them seems to warn us of danger, why should we not suppose they are from some friendly agent, whether supreme, or inferior and subordinate, is not the question, and that they are given for our good?

The present question abundantly confirms me in the justice of this reasoning; for had I not been made cautious by this secret admonition, come it from whence it will, I had been undone inevitably, and in a far worse condition than before, as you will see presently.

I had not kept myself long in this posture, but I saw the boat draw near the shore, as if they looked for a creek to thrust in at, for the convenience of landing. However, as they did not come quite far enough, they did not see the little inlet where I formerly landed my rafts; but ran their boat on shore upon the beach, at about half a mile from me, which was very happy for me; for otherwise they would have landed just, as I may say, at my door, and would soon have beaten me out of my castle, and perhaps have plundered me of all I had.

When they were on shore, I was fully satisfied that they were Englishmen, at least most of them; one or two I thought were Dutch, but it did not prove so. There were in all eleven men, whereof three of them I found were unarmed, and, as I thought, bound; and when the first four or five of them had jumped on shore, they took those three out of the boat, as prisoners. One of the three I could perceive using the most passionate gestures of entreaty, affliction, and despair, even to a kind of extravagance; the other two, I could perceive, lifted up their hands sometimes, and appeared concerned indeed, but not to such a degree as the first.

I was perfectly confounded at the sight, and knew not what the meaning of it should be. Friday called out to me in English as well as he could, "O master! you see English mans eat prisoner as well as savage mans." "Why," says I, "Friday, do you think they are agoing to eat them then?" "Yes," says Friday, "they will eat them." "No, no," says I, "Friday, I am afraid they will murder them indeed, but you may be sure they will not eat them."

All this while I had no thought of what the matter really was, but stood trembling with the horror of the sight, expecting every moment when the three prisoners should be killed; nay, once I saw one of the villains lift up his arm with a great cutlass, as the seamen call it, or sword, to strike one of the poor men; and I expected to see him fall every moment, at which all the blood in my body seemed to run chill in my veins.

I wished heartily now for my Spaniard, and the savage that was gone with him; or that I had any way to have come undiscovered within shot of them, that I might have rescued the three men, for I saw no fire arms they had among them; but it fell out to my mind another way.

After I had observed the outrageous usage of the three men by the insolent seamen, I observed the fellows run scattering about the land, as if they wanted to see the country. I observed that the three other men had liberty to go also where they pleased; but they sat down all three upon the ground, very pensive, and looked like men in despair.

This put me in mind of the first time when I came on shore, and began to look about me; how I gave myself over for lost; how wildly I looked round me; what dreadful apprehensions I had; and how I lodged in the tree all night, for fear of being devoured by wild beasts.

As I knew nothing that night of the supply I was to receive by the providential driving of the ship nearer the land by the storms and tide, by which I have since been so long nourished and supported; so these three poor desolate men knew nothing how certain of deliverance and supply they were, how near it was to them, and how effectually and really they were in a condition of safety, at the same time that they thought themselves lost, and their case desperate.

So little do we see before us in the world, and so much reason have we to depend cheerfully upon the great Maker of the world, that He does not leave His creatures so absolutely destitute, but that, in the worst circumstances, they have always something to be thankful for, and sometimes are nearer their deliverance than they imagine; nay, are even brought to their deliverance by the means by which they seem to be brought to their destruction.

It was just at the top of high-water when these people came on shore; and while partly they stood parleying with the prisoners they brought, and partly while they rambled about to see what kind of a place they were in, they had carelessly stayed till the tide was spent, and the water was ebbed considerably away, leaving their boat aground.

They had left two men in the boat, who, as I found afterwards, having drank a little too much brandy, fell asleep. However, one of them waking sooner than the other, and finding the boat too fast aground for him to stir it, hallooed for the rest, who were straggling about, upon which they all soon came to the boat; but it was past all their strength to launch her, the boat being very heavy, and the shore on that side being a soft oozy sand, almost like a quicksand.

In this condition, like true seamen, who are perhaps the least of all mankind given to forethought, they gave it over, and away they strolled about the country again; and I heard one of them say aloud to another, calling them off from the boat, "Why, let her alone, Jack, can't ye? she will float next tide;" by which I was fully confirmed in the main inquiry of what countrymen they were.

All this while I kept myself very close, not once daring to

stir out of my castle, any farther than to my place of observation near the top of the hill; and very glad I was to think how well it was fortified. I knew it was no less than ten hours before the boat could be on float again, and by that time it would be dark, and I might be at more liberty to see their motions, and to hear their discourse, if they had any.

In the meantime, I fitted myself up for a battle, as before, though with more caution, knowing I had to do with another kind of enemy than I had at first. I ordered Friday also, whom I had an excellent marksman with his gun, to load himself with arms. I took myself two fowling-pieces, and I gave him three muskets. My figure, indeed, was very fierce. I had my formidable goat-skin coat on, with the great cap I have mentioned, a naked sword by my side, two pistols in my belt, and a gun upon each shoulder.

It was my design, as I said above, not to have made any attempt till it was dark; but about two o'clock, being the heat of the day, I found that, in short, they were all gone straggling into the woods, and, as I thought, were laid down to sleep. The three poor distressed men, too anxious for their condition to get any sleep, were, however, set down under the shelter of a great tree, at about a quarter of a mile from me, and, as I thought, out of sight of any of the rest.

Upon this I resolved to discover myself to them, and learn something of their condition. Immediately I marched in the figure as above, my man Friday at a good distance behind me, as formidable for his arms as I, but not making quite so staring a spectre-like figure as I did.

I came as near them undiscovered as I could, and then, before any of them saw me, I called aloud to them in Spanish, "What are ye, gentlemen?"

They started up at the noise, but were ten times more confounded when they saw me, and the uncouth figure that I made. They made no answer at all, but I thought I perceived them just going to fly from me, when I spoke to them in English. "Gentlemen," said I, "do not be surprised at me; perhaps you may have a friend near you, when you did not expect it." "He must be sent directly from heaven then," said one of them very gravely to me, and pulling off his hat at the same time to me, "for our condition is past the help of man." "All help is from heaven, sir," said I. "But can you put a stranger in the way how to help you, for you seem to me to be in some great distress? I saw you when you landed; and when you seemed to make applications to the brutes that came with you, I saw one of them lift up his sword to kill you."

The poor man, with tears running down his face, and trembling, looking like one astonished, returned, "Am I talking to God, or man? Is it a real man, or an angel?" "Be in no fear about that, sir," said I. "If God had sent an angel to relieve you, he would have come better clothed, and armed after another manner than you see me in. Pray lay aside your fears; I am a man, an Englishman, and disposed to assist you, you see. I have one servant only; we have arms and ammunition; tell us freely, can we serve you? What is your case?"

"Our case," said he, "sir, is too long to tell you while our murderers are so near; but in short, sir, I was commander of that ship; my men have mutinied against me, they have been hardly prevailed on not to murder me; and at last have set me on shore in this desolate place, with these two men with me, one my mate, the other a passenger, where we expected to perish, believing the place to be uninhabited, and know not yet what to think of it."

"Where are those brutes, your enemies?" said I. "Do you know where they are gone?" "There they lie, sir," said he, pointing to a thicket of trees. "My heart trembles for fear they have seen us, and heard you speak. If they have, they will certainly murder us all."

"Have they any firearms?" said I. He answered they had only two pieces, and one which they left in the boat. "Well then," said I, "leave the rest to me, I see they are all asleep; it is an easy thing to kill them all; but shall we rather take them prisoners?" He told me there were two desperate villains among them that it was scarcely safe to show any mercy to; but if they were secured, he believed all the rest would return to their duty. I asked him which they were. He told me he could not at that distance describe them, but he would obey my order in anything I would direct. "Well," says I, "let us retreat out of their view or hearing, lest they awake, and we will resolve further." So they willingly went back with me, till the woods covered us from them.

"Look you, sir," said I, "if I venture upon your deliverance, are you willing to make two conditions with me?" He anticipated my proposals by telling me that both he and the ship, if recovered, should be wholly directed and commanded by me in everything; and if the ship was not recovered he would live and die with me in what part of the world soever I would send him; and the two other men said the same.

"Well," says I, "my conditions are but two.

1. That while you stay on this island with me, you will not pretend to any authority here; and if I put arms into your hands, you will, upon all occasions, give them up to me, and do no prejudice to me or mine upon this island; and in the meantime, be governed by my orders.

2. That if the ship is, or may be, recovered, you will carry me and my man to England, passage free."

He gave me all the assurances that the invention and faith of man could devise that he would comply with these most reasonable demands; and, besides, would owe his life to me, and acknowledge it upon all occasions, as long as he lived.

"Well then," said I, "here are three muskets for you, with powder and ball; tell me next what you think is proper to be done." He showed all the testimony of his gratitude that he was able, but offered to be wholly guided by me. I told him I thought it was hard venturing anything; but the best method I could think of was to fire upon them at once, as they lay; and if any was not killed at the first volley, and offered to submit, we might save them, and so put it wholly upon God's providence to direct the shot.

He said very modestly that he was loth to kill them if he could help it, but that those two were incorrigible villains, and had been the authors of all the mutiny in the ship, and if they escaped, we should be undone still; for they would go on board and bring the whole ship's company, and destroy us all. "Well then," says I, "necessity legitimates my advice, for it is the only way to save our lives." However, seeing him still cautious of shedding blood, I told him they should go themselves, and manage as they found convenient.

In the middle of this discourse we heard some of them awake, and soon after we saw two of them on their feet. I asked him if either of them were of the men who he had said were the heads of the mutiny. He said, "No." "Well then," said I, "you may let them escape; and Providence seems to have wakened them on purpose to save themselves. Now," says I, "if the rest escape you, it is your fault."

Animated with this, he took the musket I had given him in his hand, and a pistol in his belt, and his two comrades with him, with each man a piece in his hand. The two men who were with him going first made some noise, at which one of the seamen who was awake turned about, and seeing them coming cried out to the rest; but it was too late then, for the moment he cried out they fired, I mean the two men, the captain wisely reserving his own piece. They had so well aimed their shot at the men they knew, that one of them was killed on the spot, and the other very much wounded; but not being dead, he started up upon his feet, and called eagerly for help to the other. But the captain stepping to him, told him it was too late to cry for help, he should call upon God to forgive his villainy; and with that word knocked him down with the stock of his musket, so that he never spoke more. There were three more in the company, and one of them was also slightly wounded. By this time I was come; and when they saw their danger, and that it was in vain to resist, they begged for mercy. The captain told them he would spare their lives if they would give him any assurance of their abhorrence of the treachery they had been guilty of, and would swear to be faithful to him in recovering the ship, and afterwards in carrying her back to Jamaica, from whence they came. They gave him all the protestations of their sincerity that could be desired, and he was willing to believe them, and spare their lives, which I was not against, only I obliged him to keep them bound hand and foot while they were upon the island.

While this was done, I sent Friday with the captain's mate to the boat, with orders to secure her, and bring away the oars and sail, which they did; and by and by three straggling men that were (happily for them) parted from the rest, came back upon hearing the guns fired; and seeing their captain, who before was their prisoner, now their conqueror, they submitted to be bound also, and so our victory was complete.

It now remained that the captain and I should inquire into one another's circumstances. I began first, and told him my whole history, which he heard with an attention even to amazement; and particularly at the wonderful manner of my being furnished with provisions and ammunition; and, indeed, as my story is a whole collection of wonders, it affected him deeply. But when he reflected from thence upon himself, and how I seemed to have been preserved there on purpose to save his life, the tears ran down his face, and he could not speak a word more.

After this communication was at an end, I carried him and his two men into my apartment, leading them in just where I came out, viz., at the top of the house, where I refreshed them with such provisions as I had, and showed them all the contrivances I had made during my long, long inhabiting that place.

All I showed them, all I said to them, was perfectly amazing; but above all, the captain admired my fortification, and how perfectly I had concealed my retreat with a grove of trees, which, having been now planted nearly twenty years, and the trees growing much faster than in England, was become a little wood, and so thick, that it was unpassable in any part of it but at that one side where I had reserved my little winding passage into it. I told him this was my castle and my residence, but that I had a seat in the country, as most princes have, whither I could retreat upon occasion, and I would show him that, too, another time; but at present our business was to consider how to recover the ship. He agreed with me as to that, but told me he was perfectly at a loss what measures to take, for that there were still six and twenty hands on board, who having entered into a cursed conspiracy, by which they had all forfeited their lives to the law, would be hardened in it now by desperation, and would carry it on, knowing that if they were reduced they should be brought to the gallows as soon as they came to England, or to any of the English colonies; and that therefore there would be no attacking them with so small a number as we were.

I mused for some time upon what he said, and found it was a very rational conclusion, and that therefore something was to be resolved on very speedily, as well to draw the men on board into some snare for their surprise as to prevent their landing upon us, and destroying us. Upon this it presently occurred to me that in a while the ship's crew, wondering what was become of their comrades and of the boat, would certainly come on shore in their other boat to see for them; and that then, perhaps, they might come armed, and be too strong for us. This he allowed was rational.

Upon this, I told him the first thing we had to do was to stave the boat, which lay upon the beach, so that they might not carry her off; and taking everything out of her, leave her so far useless as not to be fit to swim. Accordingly we went on board, took the arms which were left on board out of her, and whatever else we found there, which was a bottle of brandy, and another of rum, a few biscuit-cakes, a horn of powder, and a great lump of sugar in a piece of canvas – the sugar was five or six pounds; all which was very welcome to me, especially the brandy and sugar, of which I had had none left for many years.

When we had carried all these things on shore (the oars, mast, sail, and rudder of the boat were carried away before, as above), we knocked a great hole in her bottom, that if they had come strong enough to master us, yet they could not carry off the boat.

Indeed, it was not much in my thoughts that we could be able to recover the ship; but my view was, that if they went away without the boat I did not much question to make her fit again to carry us away to the Leeward Islands, and call upon our friends the Spaniards on my way; for I had them still in my thoughts.

While we were thus preparing our designs, and had first, by main strength, heaved the boat upon the beach so high that the tide would not fleet her off at high-water mark; and besides, had broke a hole in her bottom too big to be quickly stopped, and were sat down musing what we should do, we heard the ship fire a gun, and saw her make a waft with her ancient as a signal for the boat to come on board. But no boat stirred; and they fired several times, making other signals for the boat.

At last, when all their signals and firings proved fruitless, and they found the boat did not stir, we saw them, by the help of my glasses, hoist another boat out, and row towards the shore; and we found, as they approached, that there was no less than ten men in her, and that they had firearms with them.

As the ship lay almost two leagues from the shore, we had a full view of them as they came, and a plain sight of the men, even of their faces; because the tide having set them a little to the easts of the other boat, they rowed up under shore, to come to the same place where the other had landed, and where the boat lay.

By this means, I say, we had a full view of them, and the captain knew the persons and characters of all the men in the boat, of whom he said that there were three very honest fellows, who, he was sure, were led into this conspiracy by the rest, being overpowered and frighted; but that was for the boatswain, who, it seems, was the chief officer among them, and all the rest, they were as outrageous as any of the ship's crew, and were no doubt made desperate in their new enterprise; and terribly apprehensive he was that they would be too powerful for us.

I smiled at him, and told him that men in our circumstances were past the operation of fear; that seeing almost every condition that could be was better than that which we were supposed to be in, we ought to expect that the consequence, whether death or life, would be sure to be a deliverance. I asked him what he thought of the circumstances of my life, and whether a deliverance were not worth venturing for. "And where, sir," said I, "is your belief of my being preserved here on purpose to save your life, which elevated you a little while ago? For my part," said I, "there seems to be but one thing amiss in all the prospect of it." "What's that?" says he. "Why," said I, it is that, as you say, there are three or four honest fellows among them which should be spared; had they been all of the wicked part of the crew I should have thought God's providence had singled them out to deliver them into your hands; for depend upon it, every man of them that comes ashore are our own, and shall die or live as they behave to us."

As I spoke this with a raised voice and cheerful countenance, I found it greatly encouraged him; so we set vigorously to our business. We had, upon the first appearance of the boat's coming from the ship, considered of separating our prisoners, and had, indeed, secured them effectually.

Two of them, of whom the captain was less assured than ordinary, I sent with Friday and one of the three delivered men to my cave, where they were remote enough, and out of danger of being heard or discovered, or of finding their way out of the woods, if they could have delivered themselves. Here they left them bound, but gave them provisions, and promised them, if they continued there quietly, to give them their liberty in a day or two; but that if they attempted their escape, they should be put to death without mercy. They promised faithfully to bear their confinement with patience, and were very thankful that they had such good usage as to have provisions and a light left for them; for Friday gave them candles (such as we made ourselves) for their comfort; and they did not know but that he stood sentinel over them at the entrance.

The other prisoners had better usage. Two of them were kept pinioned, indeed, because the captain was not free to trust them; but the other two were taken into my service, upon the captain's recommendation, and upon their solemnly engaging to live and die with us; so with them and the three honest men we were seven men well armed; and I made no doubt we should be able to deal well enough with the ten that were a-coming, considering that the Captain had said there were three or four honest men among them also.

As soon as they got to the place where their other boat lay, they ran their boat into the beach, and came all on shore, hauling the boat up after them, which I was glad to see; for I was afraid they would rather have left the boat at an anchor some distance from the shore, with some hands in her to guard her, and so we should not be able to seize the boat.

Being on shore, the first thing they did they ran all to their other boat; and it was easy to see that they were under a great surprise to find her, stripped, as above, of all that was in her, and a great hole in her bottom.

After they had mused a while upon this, they set up two or three great shouts, hallooing with all their might, to try if they could make their companions hear; but all was to no purpose. Then they came all close in a ring, and fired a volley of their small arms, which, indeed, we heard, and the echoes made the woods ring. But it was all one; those in the cave we were sure could not hear, and those in our keeping, though they heard it well enough, yet dare not give no answer them.

They were so astonished at the surprise of this, that, as they told us afterwards, they resolved to go all on board again, to their ship, and let them know there that the men were all murdered, and the longboat staved. Accordingly, they immediately launched their boat again, and got all of them on board.

The captain was terribly amazed, and even confounded at this, believing they would go on board the ship again, and set sail, giving their comrades for lost, and so he should still lose the ship, which he was in hopes we should have recovered; but he was quickly as much frighted the other way.

They had not been long put off with the boat but we perceived them all coming on shore again; but with this new measure in their conduct, which it seems they consulted together upon, viz., to leave three men in the boat, and the rest to go on shore, and go up into the country to look for their fellows.

This was a great disappointment to us, for now we were at a loss what to do; for our seizing those seven men on shore would be no advantage to us if we let the boat escape, because they would then row away to the ship, and then the rest of them would be sure to weigh and set sail, and so our recovering the ship would be lost. However, we had no remedy but to wait and see what the issue of things might present. The seven men came on shore, and the three who remained in the boat put her off to a good distance from the shore, and came to an anchor to wait for them; so that it was impossible for us to come at them in the boat.

Those that came on shore kept close together, marching towards the top of the little hill under which my habitation lay; and we could see them plainly, though they could not perceive us. We could have been very glad they would have come nearer to us, so that we might have fired at them, or that they would have gone farther off, that we might have come abroad.

But when they had come to the brow of the hill, where they could see a great way into the valleys and woods which lay towards the north-east part, and where the island lay lowest, they shouted and hallooed till they were weary; and not caring, it seems, to venture far from the shore, nor far from one another, they sat down together under a tree, to consider of it. Had they thought fit to have gone to sleep there, as the other party of them had done, they had done the job for us; but they were too full of apprehensions of danger to venture to go to sleep, though they could not tell what the danger was they had to fear neither.

The captain made a very just proposal to me upon this consultation of theirs, viz., that perhaps they would all fire a volley again, to endeavour to make their fellows hear, and that we should all sally upon them, just at the juncture when their pieces were all discharged, and they would certainly yield, and we should have them without bloodshed. I liked the proposal, provided it was done while we were near enough to come up to them before they could load their pieces again.

But this event did not happen, and we lay still a long time, very irresolute what course to take. At length I told them there would be nothing to be done, in my opinion, till night; and then, if they did not return to the boat, perhaps we might find a way to get between them and the shore, and so might use some stratagem with them in the boat to get them on shore.

We waited a great while, though very impatient for their removing; and were very uneasy when, after long consultations, we saw them start all up, and march down towards the sea. It seems they had such dreadful apprehensions upon them of the danger of the place that they resolved to go on board the ship again, give their companions over for lost, and so go on with their intended voyage with the ship.

As soon as I perceived them go towards the shore, I imagined it to be, as it really was, that they had given over their search, and were for going back again; and the captain, as soon as I told him my thoughts, was ready to sink at the apprehensions of it; but I presently thought of a stratagem to fetch them back again, and which answered my end to a tittle.

I ordered Friday and the captain's mate to go over the little creek westward, towards the place where the savages came on shore when Friday was rescued, and as soon as they came to a little rising ground, at about half a mile distance. I bade them halloo as loud as they could, and wait till they found the seamen heard them; that as soon as ever they heard the seamen answer them, they should return it again; and then keeping out of sight, take a round, always answering when the other hallooed, to draw them as far into the island, and among the woods, as possible, and then wheel about again to me by such ways as I directed them.

They were just going into the boat when Friday and the mate hallooed; and they presently heard them, and answering, ran along the shore westward, towards the voice they heard, when they were presently stopped by the creek, where the water being up, they could not get over, and called for the boat to come up and set them over, as, indeed, I expected.

When they had set themselves over, I observed that the boat being gone up a good way into the creek, and, as it were, in a harbour within the land, they took one of the three men out of her to go along with them, and left only two in the boat, having fastened her to the stump of a little tree on the shore.

This was what I wished for; and immediately leaving Friday and the captain's mate to their business, I took the rest with me, and crossing the creek out of their sight, we surprised the two men before they were aware; one of them lying on shore, and the other being in the boat. The fellow on shore was between sleeping and waking, and going to start up. The captain, who was foremost, ran in upon him, and knocked him down, and then called out to him in the boat to yield, or he was a dead man.

There needed very few arguments to persuade a single man

to yield when he saw five men upon him, and his comrade knocked down; besides, this was, it seems, one of the three who were not so hearty in the mutiny as the rest of the crew, and therefore was easily persuaded, not only to yield, but afterwards to join very sincerely with us.

In the meantime, Friday and the captain's mate so well managed their business with the rest, that they drew them, by hallooing and answering, from one hill to another, and from one wood to another, till they not only heartily tired them, but left them where they were very sure they could not reach back to the boat before it was dark; and, indeed, they were heartily tired themselves also by the time they came back to us.

We had nothing now to do but to watch for them in the dark, and to fall upon them, so as to make sure work with them.

It was several hours after Friday came back to me before they came back to their boat; and we could hear the foremost of them, long before they came quite up, calling to those behind to come along, and could also hear them answer and complain how lame and tired they were, and not able to come any faster; which was very welcome to us.

At length they came up to the boat; but 'tis impossible to express their confusion when they found the boat fast aground in the creek, the tide ebbed out, and their two men gone. We could hear them call to one another in a most lamentable manner, telling one another they were gotten into an enchanted island; that either there were inhabitants in it, and they should all be murdered, or else there were devils and spirits in it, and they should all be carried away and devoured.

They hallooed again, and called their two comrades by their names a great many times; but no answer. After some time we could see them, by the little light there was, run about, wringing their hands like men in despair, and that sometimes they would go and sit down in the boat to rest themselves; then come ashore again and walk about again, and do the same thing over again.

My men would fain have me give them leave to fall upon them at once in the dark; but I was willing to take them at some advantage, so to spare them, and kill as few of them as I could; and especially I was unwilling to hazard the killing any of our own men, knowing the other were very well armed. I resolved to wait, to see if they did not separate; and, therefore, to make sure of them, I drew my ambuscade nearer, and ordered Friday and the captain to creep upon their hands and feet, as close to the ground as they could, that they might not be discovered, and get as near them as they could possibly, before they offered to fire.

They had not been long in that posture but that the boatswain, who was the principal ringleader of the mutiny, and had now shown himself the most dejected and dispirited of all the rest, came walking towards them, with two more of their crew. The captain was so eager, as having this principal rogue so much in his power that he could hardly have patience to let him come so near as to be sure of him, for they only heard his tongue before, but when they came nearer, the captain and Friday, starting up on their feet, let fly at them.

The boatswain was killed upon the spot; the next man was shot into the body, and fell just by him, though he did not die till an hour or two after; and the third ran for it.

At the noise of the fire I immediately advanced with my whole army, which was now eight men, viz., myself, generalissimo, Friday, my lieutenant-general; the captain and his two men, and the three prisoners of war, whom we had trusted with arms.

We came upon them, indeed, in the dark, so that they could not see our number; and I made the man we had left in the boat, who was now one of us, call to them by name, to try if I could bring them to a parley, and so might perhaps reduce them to terms, which fell out just as we desired; for indeed it was easy to think, as their condition then was, they would be very willing to capitulate. So he called out as loud as he could to one of them.

"Tom Smith! Tom Smith!" Tom Smith answered immediately "Who's that? Robinson?" For it seems he knew his voice. The other answered, "Ay, ay; for God's sake, Tom Smith, throw down your arms and yield, or you are all dead men this moment."

"Who must we yield to? Where are they?" says Smith again. "Here they are," says he; "here's our captain, and fifty men with him, have been hunting you this two hours; the boatswain is killed, Will Frye is wounded, and I am a prisoner; and if you do not yield, you are all lost."

"Will they give us quarter, then," says Tom Smith, "and we will yield?" "I'll go and ask, if you promise to yield," says Robinson. So he asked the captain, and the captain then calls himself out, "You, Smith, you know my voice, if you lay down your arms immediately and submit, you shall have your lives, all but Will Atkins."

Upon this Will Atkins cried out, "For God's sake, captain, give me quarter; what have I done? They have been all as bad as I;" which, by the way, was not true neither; for it seems, this Will Atkins was the first man that laid hold of the captain when they first mutinied, and used him barbarously, in tying his hands, and giving him injurious language. However, the captain told him he must lay down his arms at discretion, and trust to the governor's mercy; by which he meant me, for they all called me governor.

In a word, they all laid down their arms, and begged their lives; and I sent the man that had parleyed with them and two more, who bound them all; and then my great army of fifty men, which, particularly with those three, were all but eight, came up and seized upon them all, and upon their boat; only that I kept myself and one more out of sight for reasons of state.

Our next work was to repair the boat, and think of seizing the ship; and as for the captain, now he had leisure to parley with them, he expostulated with them upon the villainy of their practices with him, and at length upon the farther wickedness of their design, and how certainly it must bring them to misery and distress in the end, and perhaps to the gallows.

They all appeared very penitent, and begged hard for their lives. As for that, he told them they were none of his prisoners, but the commander of the island; that they thought they had set him on shore in a barren, uninhabited island; but it had pleased God so to direct them that the island was inhabited, and that the governor was an Englishman; that he might hang them all there, if he pleased; but as he had given them all quarter, he supposed he would send them to England, to be dealt with there as justice required, except Atkins, whom he was commanded by the governor to advise to prepare for death, for that he would be hanged in the morning.

Though this was all a fiction of his own, yet it had its desired effect. Atkins fell upon his knees, to beg the captain to intercede with the governor for his life; and all the rest begged of him, for God's sake, that they might not be sent to England.

It now occurred to me that the time of our deliverance had come, and that it would be a most easy thing to bring these fellows in to be hearty in getting possession of the ship; so I retired in the dark from them, that they might not see what kind of a governor they had, and called the captain to me. When I called, as at a good distance, one of the men was ordered to speak again, and say to the captain, "Captain, the commander calls for you." And presently the captain replied, "Tell his excellency I am just a-coming." This more perfectly amused them, and they all believed that the commander was just by with his fifty men.

Upon the captain's coming to me, I told him my project for seizing the ship, which he liked wonderfully well, and resolved to put it in execution the next morning. But in order to execute it with more art, and secure of success, I told him we must divide the prisoners, and that they should go and take Atkins and two more of the worst of them, and send them pinioned to the cave where the others lay. This was committed to Friday and the two men who came on shore with the captain.

They conveyed them to the cave, as to a prison. And it was, indeed, a dismal place, especially to men in their condition. The others I ordered to my bower, as I called it, of which I have given a full description; and as it was fenced in, and they pinioned, the place was secure enough, considering they were upon their behaviour.

To these in the morning I sent the captain, who was to enter into a parley with them; in a word, to try them, and tell me whether he thought they might be trusted or not to go on board and surprise the ship. He talked to them of the injury done to him, of the condition they were brought to; and that though the governor had given them quarter for their lives as to the present action, yet that if they were sent to England they would also he hanged in chains, to be sure; but that if they would join so just an attempt as to recover the ship, he would have the governor's engagement for their pardon.

Anyone may guess how readily such a proposal would be accepted by men in their condition. They fell down on their knees to the captain, and promised, with the deepest imprecations, that they would be faithful to him to the last drop, and that they should owe their lives to him, and would go with him all over the world; that they would own him for a father to them as long as they lived.

"Well," says the captain, "I must go and tell the governor what you say, and see what I can do to bring him to consent to it." So he brought me an account of the temper he found them in, and that he verily believed they would be faithful.

However, that we might be very secure, I told him he should go back again and choose out five of them, and tell them they might see that he did not want men, that he would take out those five to be his assistants, and that the governor would keep the other two and the three that were sent prisoners to the castle, my cave, as hostages for the fidelity of those five; and that *if* they proved unfaithful in the execution, the five hostages should be hanged in chains alive upon the shore.

This looked severe, and convinced them that the governor was in earnest. However, they had no way left them but to accept it; and it was now the business of the prisoners, as much as of the captain, to persuade the other five to do their duty.

Our strength was now thus ordered for the expedition.

1. The captain, his mate, and passenger.
2. Then the two prisoners of the first gang, to whom, having their characters from the captain, I had given their liberty, and trusted them with arms.
3. The other two whom I had kept till now in my bower, pinioned, but upon the captain's motion had now released.
4. These five released at last; so that they were twelve in all, besides five we kept prisoners in the cave as hostages.

I asked the captain if he was willing to venture with these hands on board the ship; for as for me and my man Friday, I did not think it was proper for us to stir, having seven men left behind, and it was employment enough for us to keep them asunder and supply them with victuals. As to the five in the cave, I resolved to keep them fast; but Friday went in twice a day to them, to supply them with necessaries, and I made the other two carry provisions to a certain distance, where Friday was to take it.

When I showed myself to the two hostages, it was with the captain, who told them I was the person the governor had ordered to look after them, and that it was the governor's pleasure they should not stir anywhere but by my direction; that if they did, they should be fetched into the castle, and be laid in irons; so that as we never suffered them to see me as governor, so I now appeared as another person, and spoke of the governor, the garrison, the castle, and the like, upon all occasions.

The captain now had no difficulty before him but to furnish his two boats, stop the breach of one, and man them. He made his passenger captain of one, with four other men; and himself, and his mate, and five more went in the other; and they contrived their business very well, for they came up to the ship about midnight. As soon as they came within call of the ship, he made Robinson hail them, and told them they had brought off the men and the boat, but that it was a long time before they had found them, and the like, holding them in a chat till they came to the ship's side; when the captain and the mate entering first, with their arms, immediately knocked down the second mate and carpenter with the butt-end of their muskets, being very faithfully secured by their men. They secured all the rest that were upon the main and quarter-decks, and began to fasten the hatches to keep them down who were below; when the other boat and their men entering at the fore chains, secured the forecastle of the ship, and the scuttle which went down into the cook-room, making three men they found there prisoners.

When this was done, and all safe upon deck, the captain ordered the mate, with three men, to break into the round-house, where the new rebel captain lay, and having taken the alarm was gotten up, and with two men and a boy had gotten firearms in their hands; and when the mate with a crow split open the door, the new captain and his men fired boldly among them, and wounded the mate with a musket ball, which broke his arm, and wounded two more of the men, but killed nobody.

The mate calling for help, rushed, however, into the round-house wounded as he was, and with his pistol shot the new captain through the head, the bullet entering at his mouth and came out again behind one of his ears, so that he never spoke a word; upon which the rest yielded, and the ship was taken effectually, without any more lives lost.

As soon as the ship was thus secured, the captain ordered seven guns to be fired, which was the signal agreed upon with me to give me notice of his success, which you may be sure I was very glad to hear, having sat watching upon the shore for it till near two of the clock in the morning.

Having thus heard the signal plainly, I laid me down; and it having been a day of great fatigue to me I slept very sound, till I was something surprised with the noise of a gun; and presently starting up, I heard a man call me by the name of "Governor," "Governor," and presently I knew the captain's voice; when climbing up to the top of the hill, there he stood, and pointing to the ship he embraced me in his arms. "My dear friend and deliverer," says he, "there's your ship, for she is all yours, and so are we, and all that belong to her." I cast my eyes to the ship, and there she rode within little more than half a mile of the shore; for they had weighed her anchor as soon as they were masters of her, and the weather being fair had brought her to an anchor just against the mouth of the little creek, and the tide being up, the captain had brought the pinnace in near the place where I at first landed my rafts, and so landed just at my door.

I was at first ready to sink down with the surprise; for I saw my deliverance, indeed, visibly put into my hands, all things easy, and a large ship just ready to carry me away whither I pleased to go. At first, for some time, I was not able to answer him one word; but as he had taken me in his arms, I held fast by him, or I should have fallen to the ground.

He perceived the surprise, and immediately pulls a bottle out of his pocket, and gave me a dram of cordial, which he had brought on purpose for me. After I had drank it, I sat down upon the ground; and though it brought me to myself, yet it was a good while before I could speak a word to him.

All this while the poor man was in as great an ecstasy as I, only not under any surprise, as I was; and he said a thousand kind tender things to me, to compose me and bring me to myself. But such was the flood of joy in my breast that it put all my spirits into confusion. At last it broke out into tears, and in a little while after I recovered my speech.

Then I took my turn, and embraced him as my deliverer, and we rejoiced together. I told him I looked upon him as a man sent from heaven to deliver me, and that the whole transaction seemed to be a chain of wonders; that such things as these were the testimonies we had of a secret hand of Providence governing the world, and an evidence that the eyes of an infinite Power could search into the remotest corner of the world, and send help to the miserable whenever He pleased.

I forgot not to lift up my heart in thankfulness to heaven; and what heart could forbear to bless Him, who had not only in a miraculous power provided for one in such a wilderness, and in such a desolate condition, but from whom every deliverance must always be acknowledged to proceed?

When we had talked a while, the captain told me he had brought me some little refreshment, such as the ship afforded, and such as the wretches that had been so long his masters had not plundered him of. Upon this he called aloud to the boat, and bid his men bring the things ashore that were for the governor; and, indeed, it was a present as if I had been one, not that was to be carried away along with them, but as if I had been to dwell upon the island still, and they were to go without me.

First, he had brought me a case of bottles full of excellent cordial waters, six large bottles of Madeira wine (the bottles held two quarts a piece), two pounds of excellent good tobacco, twelve good pieces of the ship's beef, and six pieces of pork, with a bag of peas, and about a hundredweight of biscuits.

He brought me also a box of sugar, a box of flour, a bag full of lemons, and two bottles of lime-juice, and abundance of other things; but besides these, and what was a thousand times more useful to me, he brought me six clean new shirts, six very good neck-cloths, two pair of gloves, one pair of shoes, a hat, and one pair of stockings, and a very good suit of clothes of his own, which had been worn but very little; in a word, he clothed me from head to foot.

It was a very kind and agreeable present, as any one may imagine, to one in my circumstances; but never was anything in the world of that kind so unpleasant, awkward, and uneasy, as it was to me to wear such clothes at their first putting on.

After these ceremonies passed, and after all his good things were brought into my little apartment, we began to consult what was to be done with the prisoners we had; for it was worth considering whether we might venture to take them away with us or no, especially two of them, whom we knew to be incorrigible and refractory to the last degree; and the captain said he knew they were such rogues that there was no obliging them; and if he did carry them away, it must be in irons, as malefactors, to be delivered over to justice at the first English colony he could come at; and I found that the captain himself was very anxious about it.

Upon this I told him that, if he desired it, I dare undertake to bring the two men he spoke of to make it their own request that he should leave them upon the island. "I should be very glad of that," says the captain, "with all my heart."

"Well," says I, "I will send for them up, and talk with them for you." So I caused Friday and the two hostages, for they were now discharged, their comrades having performed their promise; I say, I caused them to go to the cave and bring up the five men, pinioned as they were, to the bower, and keep them there till I came.

After some time I came thither, dressed in my new habit; and now I was called governor again. Being all met, and the captain with me, I caused the men to be brought before me, and I told them I had had a full account of their villainous behaviour to the captain, and how they had run away with the ship, and were preparing to commit farther robberies, but that Providence had ensnared them in their own ways, and that they were fallen into the pit which they had digged for others.

I let them know that by my direction the ship had been seized, that she lay now in the road, and they might see, by and bye, that their new captain had received the reward of his villainy, for that they might see him hanging at the yard arm; that as to them, I wanted to know what they had to say why I should not execute them as pirates, taken in the fact, as by my commission they could not doubt I had authority to do.

One of them answered in the name of the rest that they had nothing to say but this, that when they were taken the captain promised them their lives, and they humbly implored my mercy. But I told them I knew not what mercy to show them; for as for myself, I had resolved to quit the island with all my men, and had taken passage with the captain to go for England. And as for the captain, he could not carry them to England other than as prisoners in irons, to be tried for mutiny, and running away with the ship; the consequence of which, they must need know, would be the gallows; so that I could not tell which was best for them, unless they had a mind to take their fate in the island. If they desired that, I did not care, as I had liberty to leave it. I had some inclination to give them their lives, if they thought they could shift on shore.

They seemed very thankful for it, said they would much rather venture to stay there than to be carried to England to be hanged; so I left it on that issue.

However, the captain seemed to make some difficulty of it, as if he dare not leave them there. Upon this I seemed a little angry with the captain, and told him that they were my prisoners, not his; and that seeing I had offered them so much favour, I would be as good as my word; and that if he did not think fit to consent to it, I would set them at liberty, as I found them; and if he did not like it, he might take them again if he could catch them.

Upon this they appeared very thankful, and I accordingly set them at liberty, and bade them retire into the woods to the place whence they came, and I would leave them some fire arms, some ammunition, and some directions how they should live very well, if they thought fit.

Upon this I prepared to go on board the ship, but told the captain that I would stay that night to prepare my things, and desired him to go on board in the meantime, and keep all right in the ship, and send the boat on shore the next day for me; ordering him, in the meantime, to cause the new captain, who was killed, to be hanged at the yard-arm, that these men might see him.

When the captain was gone, I sent for the men up to me to my apartment, and entered seriously into discourse with them of their circumstances. I told them I thought they had made a right choice; that if the captain carried them away, they would certainly be hanged. I showed them the new captain hanging at the yard-arm of the ship, and told them they had nothing less to expect.

When they had all declared their willingness to stay, I then told them I would let them into the story of my living there, and put them into the way of making it easy to them. Accordingly I gave them the whole history of the place, and of my coming to it, showed them my fortifications, the way I made my bread, planted my corn, cured my grapes; and in a word, all that was necessary to make them easy. I told them the story also of the sixteen Spaniards that were to be expected, for whom I left a letter, and made them promise to treat them in common with themselves.

I left them my firearms, viz., five muskets, three fowling-pieces, and three swords. I had above a barrel and half of powder left; for after the first year or two I used but little, and wasted none. I gave them a description of the way I managed the goats, and directions to milk and fatten them, and to make both butter and cheese.

In a word, I gave them every part of my own story, and I told them I would prevail with the captain to leave them two barrels of gunpowder more, and some garden seeds, which I told them I would have been very glad of. Also I gave them the bag of peas which the captain had brought me to eat, and bade them be sure to sow and increase them.

Having done all this, I left them the next day, and went on board the ship. We prepared immediately to sail, but did not weigh that night. The next morning early two of the five men came swimming to the ship's side, and making a most lamentable complaint of the other three, begged to be taken into the ship for God's sake, for they should be murdered, and begged the captain to take them on board, though he hanged them immediately.

Upon this the captain pretended to have no power without me; but after some difficulty, and after their solemn promises of amendment, they were taken on board, and were some time after soundly whipped and pickled, after which they proved very honest and quiet fellows.

Some time after this the boat was ordered on shore, the tide being up, with the things promised to the men, to which the captain, at my intercession, caused their chests and clothes to be added, which they took, and were very thankful for. I also encouraged them by telling them that if it lay in my way to send any vessel to take them in, I would not forget them.

When I took leave of this island, I carried on board, for relics, the great goat-skin cap I had made, my umbrella, and my parrot; also I forgot not to take the money I formerly mentioned, which had lain me so long useless that it was grown rusty or tarnished, as also the money I found in the wreck of the Spanish ship.

And thus I left the island, the 19th of December, as I found by the ship's account, in the year 1686, after I had been upon it eight and twenty years, two months, and nineteen days, being delivered from this second captivity the same day of the month that I first made my escape in the *barco-longo,* from among the Moors of Sallee.

In this vessel, after a long voyage, I arrived in England, the 11th of June, in the year 1687, having been thirty and five years absent.

When I came to England I was a perfect a stranger to all the world as if I had never been known there. My benefactor and faithful steward, whom I had left in trust with my money, was alive, but had had great misfortunes in the world, was become a widow the second time, and very low in the world. I made her easy as to what she owed me, assuring her that I would give her no trouble; but on the contrary, in gratitude to her former care and faithfulness to me, I relieved her as my little stock would afford; which, at that time, would indeed allow me to do but little for her; but I assured her I would never forget her former kindness to me, nor did I forget her when I had sufficient to help her, as shall be observed in its place.

I went down afterwards into Yorkshire; but my father was dead, and my mother and all the family extinct, except that I found two sisters, and two of the children of one of my brothers; and as I had been long ago given over for dead, there had been no provision made for me; so that, in a word, I found nothing to relieve or assist me; and that little money I had would not do much for me as to settling in the world.

I met with one piece of gratitude, indeed, which I did not expect; and this was, that the master of the ship whom I had so happily delivered, and by the same means saved the ship and cargo, having given a very handsome account to the owners of the manner how I had saved the lives of the men, and the ship, they invited me to meet them, and some other merchants concerned, and all together made me a very handsome compliment upon the subject, and a present of almost £200 sterling.

But after making several reflections upon the circumstances of my life, and how little way this would go towards settling me in the world, I resolved to go to Lisbon, and see if I might not come by some information of the state of my plantation in the Brazils, and of what was become of my partner, who I had reason to suppose had some years now given me over for dead.

With this view I took shipping for Lisbon, where I arrived in April following; my man Friday accompanying me very honestly in all these ramblings, and proving a most faithful servant upon all occasions.

When I came to Lisbon, I found out, by inquiry, and to my particular satisfaction, my old friend, the captain of the ship who first took me up at sea off the shore of Africa. He was now grown old, and had left off the sea, having put his son, who was far from a young man, into his ship, and who still used the Brazil trade. The old man did not know me; and, indeed, I hardly knew him; but I soon brought him to my remembrance, and as soon brought myself to his remembrance when I told him who I was.

After some passionate expressions of the old acquaintance, I inquired, you may be sure, after my plantation and my partner. The old man told me he had not been in the Brazils for about nine years; but that he could assure me that, when he came away, my partner was living; but the trustees, whom I had joined with him to take cognizance of my part, were both dead. That, however, he believed that I would have a very good account of the improvement of the plantation; for that upon the general belief of my being cast away and drowned, my trustees had given in the account of the produce of my part of the plantation to the procurator-fiscal, who had appropriated it, in case I never came to claim it, one third to the king, and two thirds to the monastery of St. Augustine, to be expended for the benefit of the poor, and for the conversion of the Indians to the Catholic faith; but that if I appeared, or any one for me, to claim the inheritance, it should be restored; only that the improvement or annual production, being distributed to charitable uses, could not be restored. But he assured me that the steward of the king's revenue from lands, and the *provididore,* or steward of the monastery, had taken great care all along that the incumbent, that is to say, my partner, gave every year a faithful account of the produce, of which they received duly my moiety.

I asked him if he knew to what height of improvement he had brought the plantation, and whether he thought it might be worth looking after; or whether, on my going thither, I should meet with no obstruction to my possessing my just right in the moiety.

He told me he could not tell exactly to what degree the plantation was improved; but this he knew, that my partner was grown exceeding rich upon the enjoying but one-half of it; and that, to the best of his remembrance, he had heard that the king's third of my part, which was, it seems, granted away to some other monastery or religious hòuse, amounted to above two hundred moidores a year. That as to my being restored to a quiet possession of it, there was no question to be made of that, my partner being alive to witness my title, and my name being also enrolled in the register of the country. Also he told me that the survivors of my two trustees were very fair, honest people, and very wealthy; and he believed I would not only have their assistance for putting me in possession, but would find a very considerable sum of money in their hands for my account, being the produce of the farm while their father held the trust, and before it was given up, as above; which, as he remember, was for about twelve years.

I showed myself a little concerned and uneasy at this account, and inquired of the old captain how it came to pass that the trustees should thus dispose my effects, when he knew that I had made my will, and had made him, the Portuguese captain, my universal heir, etc.

He told me, that was true; but that as there was no proof of my being dead, he could not act as executor until some certain account should come of my death; and that besides, he was not willing to intermeddle with a thing so remote; that it was true he had registered my will, and put in his claim; and could he have given any account of my being dead or alive, he would have acted by procuration, and taken possession of the *ingenio,* so they called the sugar-house, and had given his son, who was now at the Brazils, order to do it.

"But," says the old man, "I have one piece of news to tell you, which perhaps may not be so acceptable to you as the rest; and that is, that believing you were lost, and all the world believing so also, your partner and trustees did offer to account to me, in your name, for six or eight of the first years of profits, which I received; but there being at that time," says he, "great disbursements for increasing the works, building an *ingenio,* and buying slaves, it did not amount to near so much as afterwards it produced. However," says the old man, "I shall give you a true account of what I have received in all, and how I have disposed of it."

After a few days' farther conference with this ancient friend, he brought me an account of the six first years' income of my plantation, signed by my partner and the merchant-trustees, being always delivered in goods, viz., tobacco in roll, and sugar in chests, besides rum, molasses, etc. which is the consequence of a sugar work; and I found, by this account, that every year the income considerably increased; but, as above, the disbursement being large, the sum at first was small. However, the old man let me see that he was debtor to me 470 moidores of gold, besides 60 chests of sugar, and 15 double rolls of tobacco, which were lost in his ship, he having been shipwrecked coming home to Lisbon, about eleven years after my leaving the place.

The good man then began to complain of his misfortunes, and how he had been obliged to make use of my money to recover his losses, and buy him a share in a new ship. "However, my old friend," says he, "you shall not want a supply in your necessity; and as soon as my son returns, you shall be fully satisfied."

Upon this he pulls out an old pouch, and gives me 160 Portugal moidores in gold; and giving me the writing of his title to the ship, which his son was gone to the Brazils in, of which he was a quarter part owner, and his son another, he puts them both into my hands for security of the rest.

I was too much moved with the honesty and kindness of the poor man to be able to bear this; and remembering what he had done for me, how he had taken me up at sea, and how generously he had used me on all occasions, and particularly how sincere a friend he was now to me, I could hardly refrain weeping at what he said to me; therefore first I asked him in his circumstances admitted him to spare so much money at that time, and if it would not straiten him? He told me he could not say but it might straiten him a little; but, however, it was my money, and I might want it more than he.

Everything the good man said was full of affection, and I could hardly refrain from tears while he spoke; in short, I took 100 of the moidores, and called for a pen and ink to give him a receipt for them. Then I returned him the rest, and told him if ever I had possession of the plantation, I would return the other to him also, as, indeed, I afterwards did; and that as to the bill of sale of his part in his son's ship, I would not take it by any means; but that if I wanted the money, I found he was honest enough to pay me; and if I did not, but came to receive what he gave me reason to expect, I would never have a penny more from him.

When this was passed, the old man began to ask me if he should put me into a method to make my claim to my plantation? I told him I thought to go over it myself. He said I might do so if I pleased; but that if I did not, there were ways enough to secure my right, and immediately to appropriate the profits to my use; and as there were ships in the river of Lisbon just ready to go away to Brazil, he made me enter my name in a public register, with his affidavit, affirming, upon oath, that I was alive, and that I was the same person who took up the land for planting the said plantation at first.

This being regularly attested by a notary, and a procuration affixed, he directed me to send it, with a letter of his writing, to a merchant of his acquaintance at the place, and then proposed my staying with him till an account came of the return.

Never anything was more honourable than the proceedings upon this procuration; for in less than seven months I received a large packet from the survivors of my trustees, the merchants, for whose account I went to sea, in which were the following particular letters and papers enclosed.

First, there was the account-current of the produce of my farm or plantation from the year when their fathers had balanced with my old Portugal captain, being for six years; the balance appeared to be 1174 moidores in my favour.

Secondly, there was the account of four years more, while they kept the effects in their hands, before the government claimed the administration, as being the effects of a person not to be found, which they called civil death; and the balance of this, the value of the plantation increasing, amounted to 38,892 crusadoes, which made 3241 moidores.

Thirdly, there was the prior of the Augustines' account, who had received the profits for above fourteen years; but not being able to account for what was disposed to the hospital, very honestly declared he had 872 moidores not distributed, which he acknowledged to my account; as to the king's part, that refunded nothing.

There was a letter of my partner's, congratulating me very affectionately upon my being alive, giving me an account how the estate was improved, and what it produced a year, with a particular of the number of squares or acres that it contained; how planted, how many slaves there were upon it, and making two and twenty crosses for blessings, told me he had said so many *Ave Marias* to thank the blessed Virgin that I was alive; inviting me very passionately to come over and take possession of my own; and in the meantime, to give him orders to whom he should deliver my effects, if I did not come myself; concluding with a hearty tender of his friendship, and that of his family; and sent me as a present seven fine leopards' skins, which he had, it seems, received from Africa by some other ship which he had sent thither, and who, it seems, had made a better voyage than I. He sent me also five chests of excellent sweetmeats, and a hundred pieces of gold uncoined, not quite so large as moidores. By the same fleet, my two merchant trustees shipped me 1200 chests of sugar, 800 rolls of tobacco, and the rest of the whole account in gold.

I might well say now, indeed, that the latter end of Job was better than the beginning. It is impossible to express the flutterings of my very heart when I looked over these letters, and especially when I found all my wealth about me; for as the Brazil ship come all in fleets, the same ships which brought my letters brought my goods, and the effects were safe in the river before the letters came to my hand. In a word, I turned pale, and grew sick; and had not the old man run and fetched me a cordial, I believe the sudden surprise of joy had overset Nature, and I had died upon the spot.

Nay, after that I continued very ill, and was so some hours, till a physician being sent for, and something of the real cause of my illness being known, he ordered me to be let blood, after which I had relief, and grew well; but I verily believe, if it had not been eased by a vent given in the manner to the spirits, I should have died.

I was now master, all on a sudden, of above £5000 sterling in money, and had an estate, as I might well call it, in the Brazils, of above a thousand pounds a year, as sure as an estate of lands in England; and in a word, I was in a condition which I scarce knew how to understand, or how to compose myself for the enjoyment of it.

The first thing I did was to recompense my original benefactor, my good old captain, who had been first charitable to me in my distress, kind to me in my beginning, and honest to me at the end. I showed him all that was sent to me. I told him that, next to the providence of Heaven, which disposes all things, it was owing to him; and that it now lay on me to reward him, which I would do a hundredfold. So I first returned to him the hundred moidores I had received of him; then I sent for a notary, and caused him to draw up a general release or discharge for the 470 moidores which he had acknowledged he owed me in the fullest and firmest manner possible; after which I cause a procuration to be drawn, empowering him to be my receiver of the annual profits of my plantation, and appointing my partner to account to him, and make the returns by the usual fleets to him in my name; and a clause in the end, being a grant of 100 moidores a year to him, during his life, out of the effects, and 50 moidores a year to his son after him, for his life; and thus I requited my old man.

I was now to consider which way to steer my course next, and what to do with the estate that Providence has thus put into my hands; and, indeed, I had more care upon my head now than had in my silent state of life in the island, where I wanted nothing but what I had, and had nothing but what I wanted; where as I had now a great charge upon me, and my business was how to secure it. I had never a cave now to hide my money in, or a place where it might lie without lock or key till it grew mouldy and tarnished before anybody would meddle with it. On the contrary, I knew not where to put it, or whom to trust with it. My old patron, the captain, indeed, was honest, and that was the only refuge I had.

In the next place, my interest in the Brazils seemed to summon me thither; but now I could not tell how to think of going thither till I had settled my affairs, and left my affects in some safe hands behind me. At first I thought of my old friend the widow, who I knew was honest, and would be just to me; but then she was in years, and but poor, and for aught I knew might be in debt; so that, in a word, I had no way but to go back to England myself, and take my effects with me.

It was some months, however, before I resolved upon this; and therefore, as I had rewarded the old captain fully, and to his satisfaction, who had been my former benefactor, so I began to think of my poor widow, whose husband had been my first benefactor, and she, while it was in her power, my faithful steward and instructor. So the first thing I did, I got a merchant in Lisbon to write his correspondent in London, not only to pay a bill, but to go find her out, and carry her in money a hundred pounds from me, and to talk with her, and comfort her in her poverty, by telling her she should, if I lived, have a further supply. At the same time I sent my two sisters in the country each of them hundred pounds, they being, though not in want, yet not in very good circumstances; one having been married, and left a widow; and the other having a husband not so kind to her as he should be.

But among all my relations or acquaintances, I could not yet pitch upon one to whom I durst commit the gross of my stock, that I might go away to the Brazils, and leave things safe behind me; and this greatly perplexed me.

I had once a mind to have gone to the Brazils and have settled myself there, for I was, as it were, naturalised to the place. But I had some little scruple in my mind about religion, which insensibly drew me back, of which I shall say more presently. However, it was not religion that kept me from going there for the present; and as I had made no scruple of being openly of the religion of the country all the while I was among them, so neither did I yet; only that, now and then, having the late thought more of than formerly, when I began to think of living and dying among them, I began to regret my having professed myself a papist, and thought it might not be the best religion to die with.

But, as I have said, this was not the main thing that kept me from going to the Brazils, but that really I did not know with whom to leave my effects beind me; so I resolved, at last, to go to England with it, where, if arrived, I concluded I should make some acquaintance, or find some relations, that would be faithful to me; and accordingly I prepared to go for England, with all my wealth.

In order to prepare things for my going home, I first, the Brazil fleet being just going away, resolved to give answers suitable to the just and faithful account of things I had from thence. And first, to the prior of St. Augustine I wrote a letter full of thanks for their just dealings, and the offer of the 872 moidores which was undisposed of, which I desired might be given, 500 to the monastery, and 372 to the poor, as the prior should direct, desiring the good padre's prayers for me, and the like.

I wrote next a letter of thanks to my two trustees, with all the acknowledgment that so much justice and honesty called for. As for sending them any present, they were far above having any occasion of it.

Lastly, I wrote to my partner, acknowledging his industry in the improving the plantation, and his integrity in increasing the stock of the works, giving him instructions for his future government of my part, according to the powers I had left with my old patron, to whom I desired him to send whatever became due to me till he should hear from me more particularly; assuring him that it was my intention not only to come to him, but to settle myself there for the remainder of my life. To this I added a very handsome present of some Italian silks for his wife and two daughters, for such the captain's son informed me he had, with two pieces of fine English broadcloth, and best I could get in Lisbon, five pieces of black baize, and some Flanders lace of a good value.

Having thus settled my affairs, sold my cargo, and turned all my effects into good bills of exchange, my next difficulty was which was to go to England. I had been accustomed enough to the sea, and yet I had a strange aversion to going to England by sea at that time; and though I could give no reason for it, yet the difficulty increased upon me so much, that though I had once shipped my baggage in order to go, yet I altered my mind, and that not once, but two or three times.

It is true that I had been very unfortunate by sea, and this might be some of the reason; but let no man slight the strong impulses of his own thoughts in cases of such moment. Two of the ships which I had singled out to go in, I mean more particularly singled out than any other, that is to say, so as in one of them to put my things on board, and in the other way to have agreed with the captain; I say, two of these ships miscarried, viz., one was taken by the Algerines, and the other was cast away on the Start, near Torbay, and all the people drowned except three; so that in either of those vessels I had been made miserable; and in which most, it was hard to say.

Having been thus harassed in my thoughts, my old pilot, to whom I communicated everything, pressed me earnestly not to go by sea, but either to go by land to the Groyne, and cross over the Bay of Biscay to Rochelle, from whence it was an easy and safe journey by land to Paris, and so to Calais and Dover; or to go up to Madrid, and so all the way by land through France.

In a word, I was so prepossessed against my going by sea at all, except from Calais to Dover, that I resolved to travel all the way by land; which as I was not in haste, and did not value the charge, was by much the pleasanter way. And to make it more so, my old captain brought an English gentleman, the son of a merchant in Lisbon, who was willing to travel with me; after which we picked up two or more English merchants also, and two young Portuguese gentlemen, the last going to Paris only; so that we were in all six of us, and five servants, besides my man Friday, who was too much a stranger to be capable of supplying the place of a servant on the road.

In this manner I set out from Lisbon; and our company being all very well mounted and armed, we made a little troop, whereof they did me the honour to call me captain, as well because

I was the oldest man, as because I had two servants, and indeed was the original of the whole journey.

As I have troubled you with none of my sea journals, so I shall trouble you now with none of my land journal; but some adventures that happened to us in this tedious and difficult journey I must not omit.

When we came to Madrid, we being all of us strangers to Spain, were willing to stay some time to the court of Spain, and to see what was worth observing; but it being the latter part of the summer we hastened away, and set out from Madrid about the middle of October; but when we came to the edge of Navarre, we were alarmed at several towns on the way with an account that so much snow was fallen on the French side of the mountains that several travellers were obliged to come back to Pampeluna, after having attempted, at an extreme hazard, to pass on.

When we came to Pampeluna itself, we found it so indeed; and to me, that had been always used to a hot climate, and indeed to countries where we could scarcely bear any clothes on, the cold was insufferable; nor indeed was it more painful than it was surprising to come but often days before out of the old Castile, where the weather was not only warm, but very hot, and immediately to feel a wind from the Pyrenean mountains so very keen, so severely cold, as to be intolerable, and to endanger benumbing and perishing of our fingers and toes.

Poor Friday was really frightened when he saw the mountains all covered with snow, and felt cold weather, which he had never seen or felt before in his life.

To mend the matter, when we came to Pampeluna it continued snowing with so much violence, and so long, that the people said winter was come before its time; and the roads, which were difficult before, were now quite impassable; for, in a word, the snow lay in some places too thick for us to travel, and being not hard frozen, as is the case in northern countries, there was no going without being in danger of being buried alive every step.

We stayed no less than twenty days at Pampeluna; when seeing the winter coming on, and no likelihood of its being better, for it was the severest winter all over Europe that had been known in the memory of man, I proposed that we should all go away to Fontarabia, and there take shipping for which was a very little voyage.

But while we were considering this, there came in four French gentlemen, who having been stopped on the French side of the passes, as we were on the Spanish, had found out a guide, who, traversing the country near the head of Languedoc, had brought them over the mountains by such ways that they were not much incommoded by the snow; and were they met with snow in any quantity, they said it was frozen hard enough to bear them and their horses.

We sent for this guide, who told us he would undertake to carry us the same way with no hazard from the snow, provided we were armed sufficiently to protect us from wild beasts; for he said, upon these great snows it was frequent for some wolves to show themselves at the foot of the mountains, being made ravenous for want of food, the ground being covered with snow. We told him we were well enough prepared for such creatures as they were, if he would ensure us from a kind of two-legged wolves, which, we were told, we were in the most danger from, especially on the French side of the mountains.

He satisfied us there was no danger of that kind in the way that we were to go; so we readily agreed to follow him, as did also twelve other gentlemen, with their servants, some French, some Spanish, who, as I said, had attempted to go, and were obliged to come back again.

Accordingly, we all set out from Pampeluna, with our guide, on the 15th of November; and, indeed, I was surprised when, instead of going forward, he came directly back with us on the same road that we came from Madrid, above twenty miles; when being passed two rivers, and come into the plain country, we found ourselves in a warm climate again, where the country was pleasant, and no snow to be seen; but on a sudden, turning to his left, he approached the mountains another way; and though it is true the hills and precipices looked dreadful, yet he made so many tours, such meanders, and led us by such winding ways, that we were insensibly passed the height of the mountains without being much encumbered with the snow; and all on a sudden he showed us the pleasant fruitful provinces of Languedoc and Gascoign, all green and flourishing, though, indeed, it was at a great distance, and we had some rough way to pass yet.

We were a little uneasy, however, when we found it snowed one whole day and a night so fast that we could not travel; but he bid us to be easy, we should soon be past it all. We found, indeed, that we began to descend every day, and to come more north than before; and so, depending upon our guide, we went on.

It was about two hours before night when, our guide being something before us, and not just in sight, out rushed three monstrous wolves, and after them a bear, out of a hollow way adjoining to a thick wood. Two of the wolves flew upon the guide, and had he been half a mile before us he had been devoured, indeed, before we could have helped him. One of them fastened upon his horse, and the other attacked the man with that violence that he had not time, or not presence of mind enough, to draw his pistol, but hallooed and cried out to us most lustily. My man Friday being next to me, I bid him to ride up, and see what was the matter. As soon as Friday came in sight of the man, he hallooed as loud as t' other, "O master! O master!" but, like a bold fellow, rode directly up to the poor man, and with his pistol shot the wolf that attacked him into the head.

It was happy for the poor man that it was my man Friday, for he having been used to that kind of creature in his country, had no fear upon him, but went close up to him and shot him, as above; whereas any of us would have fired at a farther distance, and have perhaps either missed the wolf, or endangered shooting the man.

But it was enough to have terrified a bolder man than I; and, indeed, it alarmed all our company, when, with the noise of Friday's pistol, we heard on both sides the dismallest howling of wolves; and the noise, redoubled by the echo of the mountains, that it was to us as if there had been a prodigious multitude of them; and perhaps indeed there was not such a few as that we had no cause of apprehensions.

However, as Friday had killed this wolf, the other that had fastened upon the horse left him immediately and fled, having happily fastened upon his head, where the bosses of the bridle had stuck in his teeth, so that he had not done him much hurt. The man indeed was most hurt; for the raging creature had bit him twice, once on the arm, and the other time a little above his knee; and he was just, as it were, tumbling down by the disorder of his horse, when Friday came up and shot the wolf.

It is easy to suppose that at the noise of Friday's pistol we all mended our pace, and rid up as fast as the way, which was very difficult, should give us leave, to see what was the matter. As soon as we came clear of the trees, which blinded us before, we saw clearly what had been the case, and how Friday had disengaged the poor guide, though we did not presently discern what kind of creature it was he had killed.

But never was a fight managed so hardily, and in such a surprising manner, as that which followed between Friday and the bear, which gave us all, though at first we were surprised and afraid for him, the greatest diversion imaginable. As the bear is a heavy, clumsy creature, and does not gallop as the wolf does, who is swift and light, as he has two particular qualities, which generally are the rule of his actions; first, as to men, who are not his proper prey; I say, not his proper prey, because, though I cannot say what excessive hunger might do, which was now their case, the ground being all covered with snow; but as to men, he does not usually attempt them, unless they first attack him. On the contrary, if you meet him in the woods, if you don't meddle with him, he won't meddle with you; but then you must take care to be very civil to him, and give him the road, for he is a very nice gentleman. He won't go a step out of his way for a prince; nay, if you are really afraid, your best way is to look another way, and keep going on; for sometimes if you stop, and stand still, and look steadily at him, he takes it for an affront; but if you throw or toss anything at him, and it hits him, though it were but a bit of a stick as big as your finger, he takes it for an affront, and sets all his other business aside to pursue his revenge; for he will have satisfaction in point of honour. That is his first quality; the next is, that if he be once affronted, he will never leave you, night or day, till he has his revenge, but follows, at a good round rate, till he overtakes you.

My man Friday had delivered our guide, and when we came up to him he was helping him off from his horse; for the man was both hurt and frighted, and indeed the last more than the first; when, on the sudden, we spied the bear come out of the wood, and a vast monstrous one it was, the biggest by far that ever I saw. We were all a little surprised when we saw him; but when Friday saw him, it was easy to see joy and courage in the fellow's countenance. "O! O! O!" says Friday, three times pointing to him. "O master! you give me te leave; me shakee the hand with him; me make you good laugh."

I was surprised to see the fellow so pleased. "You fool you," says I, "he will eat you up." "Eatee me up! eatee me up!" says Friday, twice over again; "me eatee him up; me make you good laugh; you all stay here, me show you good laugh." So down he sits, and gets his boots off in a moment, and put on a pair of pumps, as we call the flat shoes they wear, and which he had in his pocket, gives my other servant his horse, and with his gun away he flew, swift like the wind.

The bear was walking softly on, and offered to meddle with nobody till Friday, coming pretty near, calls to him, as if the bear could understand him, "Hark ye, hark ye," says Friday, "me speakee wit you." We followed at a distance; for now being come down on the Gascogn side of the mountains, we were entered a vast great forest, where the country was plain and pretty open, though many trees in it scattered here and there.

Friday, who had, as we say, the heels of the bear, came up with him quickly, and takes up a great stone and throws at him, and hit him just on the head, but did him no harm than if he had thrown it against a wall. But it answered Friday's end, for the rogue was so void of fear, that he did it purely to make the bear follow him, and show us some laugh, as he called it.

As soon as the bear felt the stone, and saw him, he turns about, and comes after him, taking devilish long strides, and shuffling along at a strange rate, so as would have put a horse to a middling gallop. Away runs Friday, and takes his course as if he run towards us for help; so we all resolved to fire at once upon the bear, and deliver my man; though I was angry at him heartily for bringing the bear back upon us, when he was going about his own business another way; and especially I was angry that he had turned the bear upon us, and then ran away; and I called out, "You dog," said I, "is this your making us laugh? Come away, and take your horse, that we may shoot the creature." He hears me, and cries out, "No shoot, no shoot; stand still, you get much laugh." And as the nimble creature run two feet for the beast's one, he turned on a sudden, on one side of us, and seeing a great oak tree fit for his purpose, he beckoned to us to follow; and doubling his pace, he got nimbly up the tree, laying his gun down upon the ground, at about five or six yards from the bottom of the tree.

The bear soon came to the tree, and we followed at a distance. The first thing he did, he stopped at the gun, smelt to it, but let it lie, and up he scrambles into the tree, climbing like a cat, though so monstrously heavy. I was amazed at the folly, as I though it, of my man, and could not for my life see anything to laugh at yet, till seeing the bear get up the tree, we all rode nearer to him.

When we came to the tree, there was Friday got out to the small end of a large limb of the tree, and the bear got about half way to him. As soon as the bear got out to that part where the limb of the tree was weaker, "Ha!" says he to us, "now you see me teachee the bear dance." So he falls a-jumping and shaking the bough, at which the bear began to totter, but stood still, and began to look behind him, to see how he should get back. Then, indeed, we did laugh heartily. But Friday had not done with him again, as if he had supposed the bear could speak English, "What, you no come farther? pray you come farther;" so he left jumping and shaking the tree; and the bear, just as if he had understood what he said, did come a little farther; then he fell a jumping again, and the bear stopped again.

We thought now was a good time to knock him on the head, and I called to Friday to stand still, and we would shoot the bear; but he cried out earnestly, "O pray! O pray! no shoot, me shoot by and then;" he would have said by and bye. However, to shorten the story, Friday danced so much, and the bear stood so ticklish, that we had laughing enough indeed, but still could not imagine what the fellow would do; for first we thought he depended upon shaking the bear off; and we found the bear was too cunning for that too; for he would not go out far enough to be thrown down, but clings fast with his great broad claws and feet, so that we could not imagine what would be the end of it, and where the jest would be at last.

But Friday put us out of doubt quickly; for seeing the bear cling fast to the bough, and that he would not be persuaded to come any farther, "Well, well," says Friday, "you no come farther, me go, me go; you no come to me, me no come to you;" and upon this he goes out to the smallest end of the bough, where it would bend with his weight, and gently lets himself down by it, sliding down the bough till he came near enough to jump down on his feet, and away he ran to his gun, takes it up, and stands still.

"Well," said I to him, "Friday, what will you do now? Why don't you shoot him?" "No shoot," says Friday, "no yet; me shoot now, me no kill; me stay, give you one more laugh." And, indeed, so he did, as you will see presently; for when the bear sees his enemy gone, he comes back from the bough where he stood, but did it mighty leisurely, looking behind him every step, and coming backward till he got into the body of the tree; then with the same hinder end foremost he comes down the tree, grasping it with his claws, and moving one foot at a time, very leisurely. At this juncture, and just before he could set his hind feet upon the ground, Friday stepped up close to him, clapped the muzzle of his piece into his ear, and shot him dead as a stone.

Then the rogue turned about to see if we did not laugh; and when he saw we were pleased by our looks, he falls a laughing himself very loud. "So we kill bear in my country," says Friday. "So you kill them?" says I; "why, you have no guns." "No," says he, "no gun, but shoot great much long arrow."

This was indeed a good diversion to us; but we were still in a wild place, and our guide very much hurt, and what to do we hardly knew. The howling of the wolves ran much in my head; and indeed, except the noise I once heard on the shore of Africa, of which I have said something already, I never heard anything that filled me with so much horror.

These things, and the approach of night, called us off, or else, as Friday would have had us, we should certainly have taken the skin of this monstrous creature off, which was worth saving; but we had three leagues to go, and our guide hastened us; so we left him, and went forward on our journey.

The ground was still covered with snow, though not so deep and dangerous as on the mountains; and the ravenous creatures, as we heard afterwards, had come down into the forest and plain country, pressed by hunger, to seek for food, and had done a great deal of mischief in the villages, where they surprised the country people, killed a great many of their sheep and horses, and some people, too.

We had one dangerous place to pass, which our guide told us if there were any more wolves in the country we should find them there; and this was in a small plain, surrounded with woods on every side, and a long narrow defile, or lane, which we were to pass to get through the wood, and then we should come to the village where we were to lodge.

It was within half an hour of sunset when we entered the first wood, and a little after sunset when we came into the plain. We met with nothing in the first wood, except that, in a little plain within the wood, which was not above two furlongs over, we saw five great wolves cross the road, full speed, one after another, as if they had been in chase of some prey, and had it in view; they took no notice of us, and were gone and out of our sight in a few moments. Upon this our guide, who, by the way, was a wretched faint-hearted fellow, bid us to keep in a ready posture, for he believed there were more wolves a-coming.

We kept our arms ready, and our eyes about us; but we saw no more wolves till we came through that wood, which was near half a league, and entered the plain. As soon as we came into the plain, we had occasion enough to look about us. The first object we met with was a dead horse, that is to say, a poor horse which the wolves had killed, and at least a dozen of them at work; we could not say eating of him, but picking of his bones rather, for they had eaten up all the flesh before.

We did not think fit to disturb them at their feast, neither did they take much notice of us. Friday would have let fly at them, but I would not suffer him by any means, for I found we were likely to have more business upon our hands than we were aware of. We were not gone half over the plain, but we began to hear the wolves howl in the wood on our left in a frightful manner, and presently after we saw about a hundred coming on directly towards us, all in a body, and most of them in a line, as regularly as an army drawn up by experienced officers. I scarcely knew in what manner to receive them, but found to draw ourselves in a close line was the only way; so we formed in moment; but that we might not have too much interval, I ordered that only every other man should fire, and that the others who had not fired should stand ready to give them a second volley immediately, if they continued to advance upon us; and that then those who had fired at first should not pretend to load their fuses again, but stand ready with every one a pistol, for we were all armed with a fusee and a pair of pistols each man; so we were, by this method, able to fire six volleys, half of us at a time. However, at present we had no necessity; for upon firing the first volley the enemy made a full stop, being terrified as well with the noise as with the fire. Four of them being shot into the head, dropped; several others were wounded, and went bleeding off, as we could see by the snow. I found they stopped, but did not immediately retreat; whereupon, remembering that I had been told that the fiercest creatures were terrified at the voice of a man, I cause all our company to halloo as loud as we could, and I found the notion not altogether mistaken, for upon our shout they began to retire and turn about. Then I ordered a second volley to be fired in their rear, which put them to the gallop, and away they went to the woods.

This gave us leisure to charge our pieces again; and that we might lose no time we kept going. But we had but little more than loaded our fusees, and put ourselves into a readiness, when we heard a terrible noise in the same wood, on our left, only, that it was farther onward, the same way we were to go.

The night was coming on, and the light began to be dusky, which made it worse on our side; but the noise increasing, we could easily perceive that it was the howling and yelling of those hellish creatures; and on a sudden, we perceived two or three troops of wolves, one on our left, one behind us, and one on our front, so that we seemed to be surrounded with them. However, as they did not fall upon us we kept our way forward as fast as we could make our horses go, which, the way being very rough, was only a good large trot, and in this manner we came in view of the of a wood, though which we were to pass, at the farther side of the plain; but we were greatly surprised when, coming nearer the lane, or pass, we saw a confused number of wolves standing just at the entrance.

On a sudden, at another opening of the wood, we heard the noise of a gun, and looking that way, out rushed a horse, with a saddle and a bridle on him, flying like the wind, and sixteen or seventeen wolves after him, full speed; indeed, the horse had the heels of them; but as we supposed that he could not hold it at that rate, we doubted not but they would get up with him at last, and no question but they did.

But here we had a most horrible sight; for riding up to the entrance where the horse came out, we found the carcass of another horse and of two men, devoured by the ravenous creatures; and one of the men was no doubt that same whom we heard fire the gun, for there lay a gun just by him fired off; but as to the man, his head and the upper part of his body was eaten up.

This filled us with horror, and we knew not what course to take; but the creatures resolved us soon, for they gathered about us presently in hopes of prey, and I verily believe there were three hundred of them. It happened very much to our advantage that, at the entrance into the wood, but a little was from it, there lay some large timber-trees, which had been cut down the summer before, and I suppose lay there for carriage. I drew my little troop in among those trees, and placing ourselves in a line behind one long tree, I advised them all to light, and keeping that tree before us for a breastwork, to stand in a triangle or three fronts, enclosing our horses in the centre.

We did so, and it was well we did; for never was a more furious charge than the creatures made upon us in the place.

They came on us with a growling kind of a noise, and mounted the piece of timber, which, as I said, was our breastwork, as if they were only rushing upon their prey; and this fury of theirs, it seems, was principally occasioned by their seeing our horses behind us, which was the prey they aimed at. I ordered our men to fire as before, every other man; and they took their aim so sure that indeed they killed several of the wolves at the first volley; but there was a necessity to keep a continual firing, for they came on like devils, those behind pushing on those before.

When we had fired our second volley of our fusees, we thought they stopped a little, and I hoped they would have gone off but it was but a moment, for others came forward again; so we fired two volleys of our pistols; and I believe in these four firings we had killed seventeen or eighteen of them, and lamed twice as many, yet they came on again.

I was loth to spend our last shot too hastily; so I called my servant, not my man Friday, for he was better employed, for with the greatest dexterity imaginable he had charged my fusee and his own while we were engaged; but as I said, I called my other man, and giving him a horn of powder, I bade him lay a train all along the piece of timber, and let it be a large train. He did so, and had but just time to get away when the wolves came up to it, and some were got up upon it, when I, snapping an uncharged pistol close to the powder, set it on fire. Those that were upon the timber were scorched with it, and six or seven of them fell, or rather jumped, in among us with the force and fright of the fire. We despatched these in an instant, and the rest were so frightened with the light, which the night, for it was now very near dark, made them terrible, that they drew back a little; upon which I ordered our last pistol to be fired off in one volley, and after that we gave a shout. Upon this the wolves turned tail, and we sallied immediately upon near twenty lame ones, whom we found struggling on the ground, and fell a-cutting them with our swords, which answered our expectation; for the crying and howling they made was better understood by their fellows, so that they all fled and left us.

We had, first and last, killed about threescore of them, and had it been daylight we had killed many more. The field of battle being thus cleared, we made forward again, for we had still near a league to go. We heard the ravenous creatures howl and yell in the woods as we went several times, and sometimes we fancied we saw some of them, but the snow dazzling our eyes, we were not certain. So in about an hour more we came to the town where we were to lodge, which we found in a terrible fright, and all in arms; for it seems that the night before the wolves and some bears had broke into the village in the night, and put them into a terrible fright; and they were obliged to keep guard night and day, but especially in the night, to preserve their cattle, and, indeed, their people.

The next morning our guide was so ill, and his limbs swelled with the rankling of his two wounds, that he could go no farther; so we were obliged to take a new guide there, and go to Toulouse, where we found a warm climate, a fruitful, pleasant country, and no snow, no wolves, or anything like them. But when we told our story at Toulouse, they told us it was nothing but what was ordinary in the great forest at the foot of the mountains, especially when the snow lay on the ground; but they inquired much what kind of a guide we had gotten that would venture to bring us that way in such a severe season, and told us it was very much we were not all devoured. When we told them how we placed ourselves, and the horses in the middle, they blamed us exceedingly, and told us it was a fifty to one but we had been all destroyed; for it was the sight of the horses which made the wolves so furious, seeing their prey; and that, at other times, they are really afraid of a gun; but the being excessive hungry, and raging on that account, the eagerness to come at the horses had made them senseless of danger and that if we had not, by the continued fire, and at last by the stratagem of the train of powder, mastered them, it had been great odds but that we had been torn to pieces; whereas had we been content to have sat still on horseback, and fired as horsemen, they would not have taken the horses for so much their own, when men were on their backs, as otherwise; and withal they told us, that at last, if we had stood all together, and left our horses, they would have been so eager to have devoured them, that we might have come off safe, especially having our firearms in our hands, and being so many in number.

For my part, I was never so sensible of danger in my life; for seeing above three hundred devils come roaring and open-mouthed to devour us, and having nothing to shelter us or retreat to, I gave myself over for lost; and as it was, I believe I shall never care to cross those mountains again. I think I would much rather go a thousand leagues by sea, though I were sure to meet with a storm once a week.

I have nothing uncommon to take notice of in my passage through France; nothing but what other travellers have given an account of with much more advantage than I can. I travelled from Toulouse to Paris, and without any considerable stay came to Calais, and landed safe at Dover, the 14 of January, after having had a severe cold season to travel in.

I was now come to the centre of my travels, and had in a little time all my new discovered estate safe about me, the bills of exchange which I brought with me having been very currently paid.

My principal guide and privy councillor was my good ancient widow; who, in gratitude for the money I had sent her, thought no pains too much, or care too great, to employ for her; and I trusted her so entirely with everything that I was perfectly easy as to the security of my effects; and indeed I was very happy from my beginning, and now to the end, in the unspotted integrity of this good gentlewoman.

And now I began to think of leaving my effects with this woman and setting out for Lisbon, and so to the Brazils. But now another scruple came in my way, and that was religion; for I had entertained some doubts about the Roman religion even while I was abroad, especially in my state of solitude, so I knew there was no going to the Brazils for me, much less going to settle there, unless I resolved to embrace the Roman Catholic religion without any reserve; unless on the other hand I resolved to be a sacrifice to my principles, be a martyr for religion, and die in the Inquisition. So I resolved to stay at home, and if I could find means for it, to dispose of my plantation.

To this purpose I wrote to my old friend at Lisbon, who in return gave me notice that he could easily dispose of it there; but that if I thought fit to give him leave to offer it in my name to the two merchants, the survivors of my trustees, who lived in the Brazils, who most fully understand the value of it, who lived just upon the spot, and whom I knew were very rich, so that he believed they would be fond of buying it, he did not doubt but I should make 4000 or 5000 pieces of eight the more of it.

Accordingly I agreed, gave him order to offer it to them, and he did so; and in about eight months more, the ship being then returned, he sent me an account that they had accepted the offer, and had remitted 33,000 pieces of eight to a correspondent of theirs at Lisbon to pay for it.

In return, I signed the instrument of sale in the form which they sent from Lisbon, and sent it to my old man, who sent me bills of exchange for 32,800 pieces of eight to me, for the estate; reserving the payment of 100 moidores a year to him, the old man, during his life, and 50 moidores afterwards to his son for this life, which I had promised them, which the plantation was to make good as a rent-charge. And thus I have given the first part of a life of fortune and adventure, a life of Providence's chequer-work, and of a variety the world will seldom be able to show the like of; beginning foolishly, but closing much more happily than any part of it ever gave me leave so much as to hope for.

Anyone would think that in this state of complicated good fortune I was past running any more hazards; and so indeed I had been, if other circumstances had concurred. But I was inured to a wandering life, had no family, not many relations, nor, however rich, had I contracted much acquaintance; and though I had sold my estate in the Brazils, yet I could not keep the country out of my head, and had a great mind to be upon the wing again; especially I could not resist the strong inclination I had to see my island, and to know if the poor Spaniards were in being there, and how the rogues I left there had used them.

My true friend, the widow, earnestly dissuaded me from it, and so far prevailed with me, that for almost seven years she prevented my running abroad, during which time I took my two nephews, the children of one of my brothers, into my care. The eldest having something of his own, I bred up as a gentleman, and gave him a settlement of some addition to his estate after my decease. The other I put out to a captain of a ship, and after five years, finding him a sensible, bold, enterprising young fellow, I put him into a good ship, and sent him to sea; and this young fellow afterwards drew me in, as old as I was, to farther adventures myself.

In the meantime, I in part settled myself here; for, first of all, I married, and that not either to my disadvantage or dissatisfaction, and had three children, two sons and one daughter; but my wife dying, and my nephew coming home with good success from a voyage to Spain, my inclination to go abroad, and his importunity, prevailed, and engaged me to go in his ship as a private trader to the East Indies. This was in the year 1694.

In this voyage I visited my new colony in the island, saw my successors the Spaniards, had the whole story of lives, and of the villains I left there; how at first they insulted the poor Spaniards, how they afterwards agreed, disagreed, united, separated, and how at last the Spaniards were obliged to use violence with them;

how they were subjected to the Spaniards; how honestly the Spaniards used them; a history, if it were entered into, as full of variety and wonderful accidents as my own part; particularly also as to their battles with the Caribbeans, who landed several times upon the island, and as to the improvement they made upon the island itself; and how five of them made an attempt upon the mainland, and brought away eleven men and five women prisoners, by which, at my coming, I found about twenty young children on the island.

Here I stayed about twenty days, left them supplies of all necessary things, and particularly of arms, powder, shot, clothes, tools, and two workmen, which I brought from England with me, viz., a carpenter and a smith.

Besides this, I shared the island into parts with them, reserved to myself the property of the whole, but gave them such parts respectively as they agreed on; and having settled all things with them, and engaged them not to leave the place, I left them there.

From thence I touched at the Brazils, from whence I sent a bark, which I bought there, with more people, to the island; and in it, besides other supplies, I sent seven women, being such as I found proper for service, or for wives to such as would take them. As to the Englishmen, I promised them to send them some women from England, with a good cargo of necessaries, if they would apply themselves to planting; which I afterwards performed; and the fellows proved very honest and diligent after they were mastered, and had their properties set apart for them. I sent them also from the Brazils five cows, three of them being big with calf, some sheep, and some hogs, which, when I came again, were considerably increased.

But all these things, with an account how three hundred Caribbees came and invaded them, and ruined their plantations, and how they fought with that whole number twice, and were at first defeated and three of them killed; but at last a storm destroying their enemies' canoes, they famished or destroyed almost all the rest, and renewed and recovered the possession of their plantation, and still lived upon the island; – all these things, with some very surprising incidents, in some new adventures of my own, for ten years more, I may perhaps give a farther account of hereafter.

THE END